Understanding Nonprofit Organizations

Understanding Nonprofit Organizations

Governance, Leadership, and Management

J. STEVEN OTT, EDITOR

Westview
PRESS

Westview Press
A Member of the Perseus Books Group

Copyright © 2001 by Westview Press, A Member of the Perseus Books Group

Published in 2001 in the United States of America by Westview Press, 5500 Central Avenue, Boulder, Colorado 80301-2877, and in the United Kingdom by Westview Press, 12 Hid's Copse Road, Cumnor Hill, Oxford OX2 9JJ

Find us on the World Wide Web at www.westviewpress.com

Library of Congress Cataloging-in-Publication Data
Nonprofit organizations : governance, leadership, and management / edited by J. Steven Ott
    p.   cm.
  Includes bibliographical references and index.
  ISBN 0-8133-6787-5 (pbk. : alk. paper)
  1. Nonprofit organizations—United States.   2. Voluntarism—United States.   I. Ott, J. Steven.

HD2769.2.U6 N65   2000
658'.048—dc21   00-043998

The paper used in this publication meets the requirements of the American National Standard for Permanence of Paper for Printed Library Materials Z39.48-1984.

10   9   8   7   6   5   4   3   2

Contents

Figures and Tables

Figures

Tables

Preface

Understanding Nonprofit Organizations is a collection of thirty-seven of the most important and informative articles, chapters, and essays written about the workings of nonprofit organizations in the United States. It speaks to the governance, leadership, and management functions of the thousands of organizations in the nonprofit sector that engage in a surprisingly wide array of activities and provide an enormous range of services mostly for the purpose of improving aspects of the quality of life in the United States—or preventing their deterioration. In my opinion, this volume includes much of the most insightful and interesting literature that can be found about nonprofit organizations. I hope you agree.

Understanding Nonprofit Organizations does not just tell the reader what these authors have written; it presents their works in their own words. It is designed for individuals who are hoping and planning to move into paid or voluntary leadership and management positions in nonprofit organizations—as well as for those who are already involved with nonprofits and want to learn more about their workings. The book provides a cohesive set of readings for a course on nonprofit organizations and management. Probably it will be used most often as a supplement to other texts in courses at the upper-division undergraduate or graduate level, but it also could stand on its own.

All the introductory essays and the reprinted readings attempt to answer two defining questions:

- What is "distinctive" about governance, leadership, and management of nonprofit organizations? and
- What has caused it to be distinctive?

In an attempt to provide rich answers to the book's two defining questions, each part addresses an important set of long-standing, historic functions and issues from a variety of contemporary perspectives. Thus the book addresses standard nonprofit organization leadership and management topics, but in the context of the turn of the millennium. The essays that open each of the eleven parts introduce the important issues and concepts, place them in the context of their environment, and explain what students should be looking for as they read the reprinted articles.

Understanding Nonprofit Organizations focuses on internal organizational issues and the environmental forces that affect them directly. Theories and concepts of the nonprofit sector are the topics of a companion book, *The Nature of the Nonprofit Sector*,[1] that I also edited with Westview Press.

A listing of the part titles and the authors and dates of the chapters reveals the scope, depth, and currency of the book's coverage—and its usefulness for graduate and upper-division undergraduate courses in nonprofit organizations and management. (See Contents for a complete listing of authors and titles.)

Contents by Part

Strategic Planning and Management. John M. Bryson (1998), Philip Kotler and Alan R. Andreasen (1996), Henry Mintzberg (1987)

Fund-Raising: Generating Revenues. Elizabeth T. Boris (1998), Karen A. Froelich (1999), Erna Gelles (1998), Adrian Sargeant and Jürgen Kähler (1999)

Entrepreneurship and Commercialism. Alan R. Andreasen (1996), Burton A. Weisbrod (1998), Dennis R. Young (1998)

Managing Under Government Contracts. Jennifer Alexander, Renee Nank, and Camilla Stivers (1999), Susan R. Bernstein (1991), Nigel Gann (1996), Steven R. Smith and Michael Lipsky (1993)

Budgets, Financial Reports, and Management Control. Regina E. Herzlinger and Denise Nitterhouse (1994), Jerry L. McCaffery (1998), Thomas Wolf (1999)

Managing Volunteers. Jeffrey L. Brudney (1998), Jone L. Pearce (1993), Ivan H. Scheier (1993)

Accountability and Evaluation. Robert D. Herman and David O. Renz (1997), Kevin P. Kearns (1996), Susan Paddock (1998)

Nonprofit Organizations Internationally. Helmut K. Anheier and Kusuma Cunningham (1994), Thomas W. Dichter (1999), Brian H. Smith (1998)

Although I fully expect to be criticized for excluding other excellent articles and writers, it will be more difficult to criticize my inclusions. The readings are the best readings or the best "fits" that I could find for the parts. The authors are among the most thoughtful and perceptive who have written in this field in recent years. My tasks as the book editor were to

- create a clear vision of what this collection of readings would accomplish;
- select previously published articles and chapters that tell the story well;
- edit-down reprinted readings to make them more readable and to help students focus-in on the central ideas that make the reading worth including;
- write introductory essays that provide frameworks for the topic that is the focus of each part; and
- let the authors speak for themselves.

The nonprofit sector as we know it is a unique democratic phenomenon, and the governance, management, and leadership of its organizations have differed from the other two sectors. In the past two decades, however, there has been a blurring of the lines between organizations in the nonprofit, government, and business sectors that has eroded some of the distinctiveness of nonprofit organizations and thus also aspects of governing, leading, and managing nonprofits. Most nonprofit organizations are becoming more business-like and/or more government-like in important ways. These changes, however, are beneficial and necessary because the nonprofit sector is facing an array of challenges that may collectively be of a magnitude beyond any in the sector's history.[2] The governance, leadership, and management of nonprofit organizations must rise to the challenges.

Criteria for Selection

Several criteria were used to make final selections about readings to include in this book. The first "test" that any reading had to pass was "yes" answers to two questions: Should the serious student of the nonprofit sector be expected to identify the authors and their basic themes—the crux of their arguments? Does the reading provide a reason or reasons why the governance, leadership or management of nonprofit organizations is "distinctive"?

The second criterion is related to the first: Each reading had to make a statement. This criterion does not eliminate controversial readings—quite the contrary; it simply requires that a reading not be ignored. Third, the article had to be readable. Students who have already had reason to peruse the literature of nonprofit organizations will appreciate the importance of this criterion.

Last, the reading had to fit in this volume. It had to address issues or ideas that are important to the governance, leadership, and/or management of nonprofit organizations. Because this book is about internal structures and workings of nonprofit organizations—not macro issues and macro theories—many interesting readings about the nonprofit sector can be found in the companion book, *The Nature of the Nonprofit Sector*.[3] Most of the readings that I reviewed fit cleanly into either *Understanding Nonprofit Organizations* or *The Nature of the Nonprofit Sector*. Decisions as to where they belong were easy to make; decisions about readings on intersectoral relations and international nonprofit organizations were the most difficult.

Notes

1. J. Steven Ott, ed., *The Nature of the Nonprofit Sector* (Boulder: Westview Press, 2001).

2. Lester M. Salamon, "The Current Crisis," in L. Salamon, *Holding the Center: America's Nonprofit Sector at a Crossroads,* 11–47 (New York: Nathan Cummings Foundation, 1997).

3. J. Steven Ott, ed., *The Nature of the Nonprofit Sector* (Boulder: Westview Press, 2001).

Acknowledgments

I wish that I could acknowledge everyone who contributed ideas, insights, support, challenges, and constructive criticisms during the creation and development of this volume. Space and propriety, however, require that I limit my statements of appreciation to those who played central roles in shaping my early vision and preliminary ideas into a cohesive anthology. Among those whose intellectual contributions absolutely must be acknowledged are: Stephen Block, Denver Options; William Boise, New York University; Kirsten Grønbjerg, Indiana University-Bloomington; Kevin Kearns, University of Pittsburgh; Naomi Wish, Seton Hall University; Jacquelyn Thayer Scott, University College of Cape Breton; and Albert Hyde, The Brookings Institution. Peter C. Nelson, John M. Bradley, and Jared C. Bennett provided invaluable assistance with the chapters on leadership, strategic planning, volunteer management, and the legal framework. Frederick Lane, City University of New York, graciously took the time several years ago to offer suggestions about how to improve the organization of a book to fit better with a graduate course on nonprofit organizations. Pitima Boonyarak and Jamie Momberger helped with the editing.

Finally, I owe a special debt of gratitude to David Gies, Animal Assistance Foundation, Denver, Colorado, and Jay Shafritz, University of Pittsburgh, my co-collaborators in editing the 1990 book, *The Nonprofit Organization: Essential Readings.*[1] Their ahead-of-the-time ideas and insights helped shape my thinking about the nonprofit sector and its organizations, and thus also the concept of this book.

Note

1. David L. Gies, J. Steven Ott, and Jay M. Shafritz, eds., *The Nonprofit Organization: Essential Readings* (Ft. Worth, TX: Harcourt Brace, 1990). Brooks/Cole, Pacific Grove, California, published this book originally. It is now out of print.

Permissions

Chapters 1, 2, 7, 10, 13, 16, 17, 25, 27, 29, 32 are from *The International Encyclopedia of Public Policy and Administration*, by Jay Shafritz. Copyright © 1998 by Jay Shafritz. Reprinted by permission of Westview Press, a member of Perscus Books, L.L.C.

Chapter 3 is from *Boards That Make A Difference : A New Design For Leadership In Nonprofit And Public Organizations*, second edition, by John Carver, Copyright © 1997 Jossey-Bass. Reprinted by permission of Jossey-Bass, Inc., a subsidiary of John Wiley & Sons, Inc.

Chapter 4 is from Ronald G. Shaiko's *Nonprofit & Voluntary Sector Quarterly* (23/3) pp. 302–320, copyright © 1996 by Sage Publications. Reprinted by permission of Sage Publications.

Chapter 5 is from the Harvard Law Review, (1992). "Developments in the Law: Nonprofit Corporations," in *Harvard Law Review*, *105* (7) (pp. 1578–1699), MA: Harvard Law Review Association.

Chapter 6 is from *The Law of Tax-Exempt Organizations*, seventh edition, Bruce R. Hopkins, Copyright © 1998 John Wiley & Sons. Reprinted by permission of John Wiley & Sons.

Chapter 8 is from "Ethics in Nonprofit Management: Creating a Culture of Integrity," by Thomas H. Jeavons, in Robert D. Herman, ed., *The Jossey-Bass Handbook of Nonprofit Leadership and Management*, Copyright © 1994 Jossey-Bass. Reprinted by permission of Jossey-Bass, Inc., a subsidiary of John Wiley & Sons, Inc.

Chapter 9 is from Mary Tschirhart's *Artful Leadership: Managing Stakeholder Problems in Nonprofit Arts*, (Bloomington: Indiana University Press, 1996)

Chapter 11 is from Kotler, Philip, and Alan R. Andreason. (1996). "The Strategic Planning Marketing Process,"in P. Kotler and A. Andreason, *Strategic Planning for Nonprofit Organizations*. Englewood Cliffs, NJ: Prentice-Hall.

Chapter 12 is adapted and reprinted by permission of *Harvard Business Review*. From "Crafting Strategy" by Henry Mintzberg July-August 1987. Copyright ©1987 by the President and Fellows of Harvard College, all rights reserved.

Chapter 14 is from Karen A. Froelich, *Nonprofit & Voluntary Sector Quarterly* (28/3) pp. 246–268, copyright © 1999 by Sage Publications. Reprinted by permission of Sage Publications.

Chapter 15 is from "Returns on Fundraising Expenditures in the Voluntary Sector," by Adrian Sargeant and Jürgen Kähler, *Nonprofit Management & Leadership* 10(1), Fall 1999, pp. 5–19. Copyright ©1999.Reprinted by permission of Josey-Bass, Inc. a subsidiary of John Wiley & Sons, Inc.

Chapter 18 is reprinted by permission of *Harvard Business Review*. From "Profits for Nonprofits: Finding a Corporate Partner" by Alan R. Andreasen November-December 1996. Copyright ©1996 by the President and Fellows of Harvard College, all rights reserved.

Chapter 19 is from Burton A. Weisbrod, (ed.), *To Profit or Not to Profit: The Commercial Transformation of The Non-Profit Sector*, ©1998, Burton A. Weisbrod. Reprinted with the permission of Cambridge University Press.

Chapter 20 is the edited version of Chapter 2 "Towards a Contract Culture" from *Managing Change in Voluntary Organizations* by Nigel Gann, Open University Press, 1996.

Chapter 21 is reprinted by permission of the publisher from *Nonprofits For Hire: The Welfare State in the Age of Contracting*, by Steven Smith and Michael Lipsky, Cambridge, Mass: Harvard University Press, Copyright © 1993 by the President and Fellows of Harvard College.

Chapter 22 is from *Managing Contracted Services in the Nonprofit Agency: Administrative, Ethical, and Political Issues* by Susan R. Bernstein. Reprinted by per-mission of Temple University Press. ©1991 by Temple University. All Rights Reserved.

Chapter 23 is from Jennifer Alexander, Renee Nank and Camilla Stivers, *Nonprofit and Voluntary Sector Quarterly*, (28/4) pp. 452–475, copyright ©1999 Sage Publications. Reprinted by Permission of Sage Publications.

Chapter 24 is from *Financial Accounting and Managerial Control for Nonprofit Organizations, 1st edition*, by R. Herzlinger and D. Nitterhouse. ©1994. Reprinted with permission of South-Western College Publishing, a division of Thomson Learning. Fax 800 730–2215.

Chapter 26 is reprinted by permission of Simon & Schuster from *Managing a Nonprofit Organization in the Twenty-First Century*, by Thomas Wolf. Copyright© 1984, 1990 by Prentice Hall Press. Copyright ©1999 by Simon & Schuster Inc.

Chapter 28 is from *Volunteers: The Organizational Behaviour of Unpaid Workers*, Jone L. Pearce, 1993, Routledge (Allen & Unwin).

Chapter 30 is from Scheier, Ivan H., "Building Staff/Volunteer Relations: Setting the Stage." In I.H. Scheier, *Building Staff/Volunteer Relations*, (pp. 3–11). Philadelphia: Energize, Inc. 1993. www.energizeinc.com.

Chapter 31 is from *Managing for Accountability* by Kevin D. Kearns. Copyright © 1996 by Jossey-Bass. Reprinted by permission of Josey-Bass, Inc. a subsidiary of John Wiley & Sons, Inc.

Chapter 33 is from Robert D. Herman and David O. Renz, *Nonprofit & Voluntary Sector Quarterly* (26/2) pp. 185–206, copyright © 1997 by Sage Publications. Reprinted by permission of Sage Publications.

Chapter 34 is from "Internationalization of the Nonprofit Sector," by Helmut K. Anheier and Kusuma Cunningham, in Robert D. Herman, ed., *The Jossey-Bass Handbook of Nonprofit Leadership and Management*, Copyright © 1994 Jossey-Bass. Reprinted by permission of Jossey-Bass, Inc., a subsidiary of John Wiley & Sons, Inc.

Chapter 35 is from Thomas W. Dichter, *Nonprofit & Voluntary Sector Quarterly* (28/4) pp. 38–58, copyright © 1999 by Sage Publications. Reprinted by permission of Sage Publications.

Chapter 36 is from Walter W. Powell and Elisabeth S. Clemens, eds., *Private Action and the Public Good* (Yale University Press, 1998). © 1998 Yale University Press.

PART 1

GOVERNANCE OF NONPROFIT ORGANIZATIONS*

Governance is an umbrella term that includes the ultimate authority, accountability, and responsibility for an organization. Nonprofit organizations are governed through complex sets of functional roles and procedures that are defined in laws and tax codes, influenced by numerous external constituencies,[1] and shaped to fit their own missions, structures, activities, personalities, policies, and procedures. Governance of a nonprofit organization is a product of its purposes, people, resources, contracts, clients, boundaries, community coalitions and networks, and actions as prescribed (or prohibited) in its articles of incorporation[2] and bylaws, state laws and codes, and the U.S. Internal Revenue Service (IRS) codes and rules.

A nonprofit organization that incorporates becomes a *corporation* and therefore is similar in many ways "in the eyes of the law" to a for-profit business.[3] Corporations are *artificial persons*, groups of individuals who obtain legal identities and legal standing through the act of incorporation or, in some cases, through the act of legally associating—forming and filing with a state as *associations*.

The statutes of nonprofit incorporation in all states specify that the board of trustees** is the ultimate point of responsibility and accountability for a nonprofit

---

*This essay is adapted and updated from David L. Gies, J. Steven Ott, and Jay M. Shafritz, "Governance: The Roles and Functions of Boards of Directors," in D. L. Gies, J. S. Ott, and J. M. Shafritz, eds., *The Non-profit Organization: Essential Readings* (Fort Worth, TX: Harcourt Brace, 1990), 177–181.

**The terms *board of trustees* (or simply *board*) and *trustees* (or *board members*) are used here instead of *board of directors* and *directors*. Because the chief executive officers (CEOs) of most nonprofit organizations are called "executive directors" (or "directors"), the use of the term *trustees* should prevent confusion between board and staff roles.

organization.[4] In some states, the laws are even more detailed—the statutes define specific responsibilities of boards. The courts have also been active in defining the basic responsibilities of boards. In the landmark 1974 *Sibley Hospital*[5] case, for example, the Federal District Court for the District of Columbia held (among other things) that the trustees are responsible for active supervision of a nonprofit corporation's managers and for overseeing its financial management.

By statute, a nonprofit organization's articles of incorporation and bylaws must specify the composition of the board, its responsibilities, and the rules and procedures under which the board will govern. The legal objective is to ensure that the board of trustees abides by applicable laws, makes certain that the organization's activities are directed toward the purposes stated in the articles of incorporation, and protects the organization and its assets through oversight activities.

Most statutes of nonprofit incorporation deal with boards of trustees as legal entities (as "artificial persons"), not as individual persons. When directors are acting in their capacities as members of a board, for the most part they are not "persons" in the eyes of the law; they are parts of a corporation board—unless they individually violate provisions of law, bylaws, or articles. The "corporate veil" is the legal assumption that actions of a corporation are not the actions of its owners and directors, and thus its owners and directors usually cannot be held responsible for corporate actions; also, a nonprofit board of trustees and its members are protected from undue personal liability when it is incorporated under the laws of a state.[6] In the past two decades, however, the courts have been more inclined to hold individual board members co-responsible for the collective actions of a board; thus, service on a board of trustees involves a degree of exposure to legal liability.

Governance Defined

Merriam Webster's Dictionary defines *govern* as:

> 1. to direct and control; rule 2. To regulate; restrain. 3. To be a rule of law for; to determine. Syn. Govern, rule means to exercise power or authority in controlling others. Govern connotes as its end a keeping in a straight course or smooth operation for the good of the individual and the whole.

> The word *govern* comes from the Greek noun *Kybernatas* (Latin—*gubernator*), a helmsman. Plato gave us the apt metaphor of the "ship of state" in his *Republic*. Both Plato and Aristotle were concerned with such fundamental questions as: "Who should govern?"; "What happens when one group governs rather than another?"; and "What qualities are essential in those who govern?"[7]

Governance is the function of oversight that a group of people assume when they incorporate under the laws of a state for an organizational purpose that qualifies for nonprofit status. For most observers of nonprofit organizations, governance is "a general term referring to the collective actions of a board of directors or board of trustees in its governing of a tax-exempt organization."[8] Governance includes serving on a board of trustees and exercising and expressing one's attitudes, beliefs, and value systems on matters pertaining to the organization. Some writers disagree with this narrow construction of governance and believe the definition should be broader:

> The term *governance* is defined to mean the strategic leadership of nonprofit organizations. . . . In current parlance, the term has taken on a more specific meaning as a process for making certain types of management decisions. These are commonly referred to as strategic decisions.[9]

Who Governs?

Virtually everyone agrees that a nonprofit organization's board of trustees is—and should be—the final authority on governance decisions.[10]

> When referring to the term "board of directors [or trustees]," the reference is to a governing board. A governing board is a group of individuals who has assumed a legal responsibility for an organization's existence. They make policy and are responsible for how money is generated and spent toward the accomplishment of a mission which can be beneficial to the general public or to a segment of the population.[11]

Most discussions of governance in nonprofit organizations, however, emphasize the executive director's roles and functions as well as the board's.[12] "In the voluntary sector context, *governance* generally refers to the arena of action in which boards of directors *and* executive staff are key players. . . . In most nonprofit organizations supported in part by public funds, . . . the governance challenge is met by both executive staff and board members."[13]

Why Governance Is Needed

Nonprofit governance may sound like an unnecessary complication. Why is governance even needed in nonprofit organizations—types of organizations that provide services or engage in other activities that are not for the personal gain of the people who volunteer with, are employed by, or serve on their boards? Only in modern times have legal structures and formal rules seriously affected the intent of people to help their neighbors. The complexities of our society, the force of law (notably laws that involve licensure and tax-exempt status), and citizens' growing concerns about potential abuses, fraud, and violations of expectations (implied social contracts) among nonprofit organizations, government, small businesses, and communities have collectively changed the environment for nonprofits and with it the "ground rules."[14]

A well-functioning, mission-focused, informed, and perhaps influential board of trustees is essential for long-term organizational effectiveness and survival. Networks of information, interorganizational linkages, and knowledge come together through the connections between executive directors and boards of trustees.[15]

Nonprofit organizations also need the benefit of free (or nearly free) advice. Executive directors must be able to turn to board members for counsel and support. The day-to-day time and energy needed to manage the dynamics of a given nonprofit's mission, goals, programs, personnel, volunteers, board officers, and external constituencies do not permit an executive director to stay current on all important laws, court rulings, and regulations. Without rapid access to accurate information from experts who are sympathetic board members and, therefore, who also know the organization and its programs, a nonprofit organization may sometimes be at considerable risk.

This "advice and counsel" function of trustees is only one vital piece of their larger set of responsibilities and accountabilities, however. Not only do board members have responsibilities as parts of the organization's formal internal control and oversight mechanism but they also fill important boundary-spanning roles that connect the organization with segments of its environment.[16] Board members are the primary links between a nonprofit organization and its community. Trustees thus function as information channels, interorganizational intermediaries, and sources of legitimacy who buffer an organization from pressures in its environment;[17] they also seek and attract external resources and information through their established networks of relationships.

Thus governance is both the "steering" and the overseeing of organizational activities, assets, and relationships by boards of trustees and executives, within a framework of law and ethics. From this perspective, governing is a form of philanthropy: "voluntary giving, voluntary serving, and voluntary association to achieve some vision of the public good."[18] Governing is a form of philanthropy because it represents individuals giving their time, effort, and influence to help improve an aspect of the quality of life, or to prevent it from deteriorating.[19]

Readings Reprinted in Part One

In *"Governance of Nonprofit Organizations,"* Vic Murray[20] defines the term *governance* as "the strategic leadership of nonprofit organizations. . . . as a process for making certain types of management decisions." Because governance is a process, two questions define it: "Who plays, or should play, which roles in the process, or, in practical terms, who is in charge of the organization and to whom is it accountable? The other issue is *how* governance decisions are, or should be, made." Murray analyzes the normative approach to governance (the "should" questions) and the analytic approach (the "who plays" and "how decisions actually are made" questions). The relationship between decisionmaking, strategic planning, and organizational effectiveness receive considerable attention from Murray. "When one looks at the very limited research attempting to examine the link between governance decisionmaking processes and the actual performance of the nonprofit organization in achieving its mission, the picture is indistinct at best. . . . The available evidence suggests that . . . there is no one pattern of decisionmaking that is more effective than the others." And, "the field will remain dominated by successive fads offering 'the answers' to the problems of governance" until there is much more understanding of the decisionmaking processes and the factors that influence them.

Stephen Block views governance somewhat differently from Murray. In *"Board of Directors,"*[21] Block emphasizes the unequivocal governance responsibilities of boards.

> Accountability for any nonprofit organization ultimately rests with its board of directors (sometimes called board of trustees). Although the board may delegate management authority to a paid staff person, . . . the board can never be relieved of its legal and fiduciary responsibilities. Governing board members are stewards of the public interest.

Block addresses many board-related issues, including board purposes, relationships between a board and an executive director, important board responsibilities, functions of specific board officers, the board's role in development, board diversity, the desirable size of a board, board liability, dismissing board members who are not performing, and fundamental differences between governing, advisory, and honorary boards.

John Carver has been one of the most widely cited writers about effective nonprofit boards in the past decade. In *"Setting Limits: Standards of Ethics and Prudence,"*[22] from his 1997 book, *Boards That Make a Difference,* Carver explains that the only way a board can have the *"control over* the complexity and details of staff operations" that it needs to be accountable is for it also "to be *free from* the complexity and details of staff operations." His solution approach is for boards to set limits and then allow staff wide freedom to act within the limits. Although Carver's "control by freedom through limits" approach may appear to be reasonable and practical, it is difficult to use in practice for a host of reasons. "Boards study, invest meeting and committee time in, and worry and argue about that complex, never-ending intriguing body of staff activities" to the detriment of both the staff and the board.

Specifically, "the board has neither the time nor the expertise to state everything that should be done." Instead, *"with regard to executive means [activities] the board should remain silent except to state clearly what it will not put up with. . . .* The total message the board sends to staff, then, consists of what outputs are to be achieved (Ends) and what may not be done in the process of achievement (Executive Limitations)." Board statements of policy limitations should be created proactively from board members' worries—before problems occur. Statements of policy always should start with the broadest, most generally applicable limitations. Narrower policy limitations should be stated only with caution. The most typical topics addressed in executive limitation policies include vendor relations, asset protection, indebtedness, financial condition, budgeting, funded depreciation, growth, and compensation and benefits. "Board and staff need as much freedom as possible to perform. . . . The staff needs freedom from the board's friendly intrusions to do its work. The board cheats the mission by constraining too much; it risks cheating standards of acceptable conduct by constraining too little."

"Female Participation in Public Interest Nonprofit Governance: Yet Another Glass Ceiling?" by Ronald Shaiko[23] uses information collected from more than 200 public interest nonprofit organizations to provide "insights into the organizational biases and candidate attributes that inhibit women in their efforts at attaining governing positions in the nonprofit sector." Although the nonprofit sector workforce is "disproportionately composed of women . . . getting to the top [executive directors and boards], however, is another matter." Shaiko examined four organizational attributes in an attempt to learn why some public interest nonprofits are more likely than others to employ women in executive roles. His study found that nonprofit organizations with small budgets (less than $1 million per year), that are young (in existence less than twenty years), located in Washington, D.C., and/or have at least one woman on their boards are more likely to have female executive directors.[24]

Public interest nonprofit organizations "have far greater female representation" on their boards than Fortune 1000 companies. "Balance is achieved by implicitly designating various board seats for certain governing roles." Shaiko observes two patterns: First, women who are executives in major public interest nonprofit organizations often fill board leadership roles in other public interest organizations. They are recruited to boards because of their policy-influencing and executive experience. Second, a high percentage of other women on boards of these nonprofits are significant financial contributors.

Notes

1. See Robert D. Herman and David O. Renz, "Multiple Constituencies and the Social Construction of Nonprofit Organization Effectiveness" (reprinted in Part 10).

2. In some states, the term *charter* or *articles of association* is used instead of *articles of incorporation.*

3. Although nonprofit organizations and for-profit corporations share many similarities, they also have important differences. From a legal perspective, however, both are corporations.

4. For a more detailed discussion, see Part 2, "The Legal Framework."

5. "The *Sibley Hospital* Case" is the popular name for *Stern v. Lucy Webb Hayes National Training School* (381 F. Supp. 1003 [D. DC, 1974]).

6. Statutes vary widely among states, however, and court interpretations of liability statutes have changed considerably in recent decades. See Part 2, "The Legal Framework."

7. Gary L. Wamsley, Charles T. Goodsell, John A. Rohr, Orion White, and James Wolf, "A Legitimate Role for Bureaucracy in Democratic Governance," in L. B. Hill, ed., *The State of Public Bureaucracy* (Armonk, NY: M. E. Sharpe, 1992), 59–86.

8. J. Steven Ott and Jay M. Shafritz, "Governance," in J. S. Ott and J. M. Shafritz, *The Facts on File Dictionary of Nonprofit Organization Management* (New York: Facts on File, 1986), 172.

9. Vic Murray, "Governance of Nonprofit Organizations," in J. M. Shafritz, ed., *International Encyclopedia of Public Policy and Administratio* (Boulder: Westview Press, 1998), 9934.

10. See, for example, John Carver, *Boards That Make a Difference,* 2d ed. (San Francisco: Jossey-Bass, 1997); and Cyril O. Houle, *Governing Boards,* 2d ed. (San Francisco: Jossey-Bass, 1997).

11. Stephen R. Block, *Perfect Nonprofit Boards: Myths, Paradoxes and Paradigms* (Needham Heights, MA: Simon & Schuster Custom Publishing, 1998), 30.

12. See Murray, "Governance of Nonprofit Organizations," 993–997 (reprinted in this part), and Judith R. Saidel, "Expanding the Governance Construct: Functions and Contributions of Nonprofit Advisory Groups," *Nonprofit and Voluntary Sector Quarterly* 27, no. 4 (December, 1998): 421, 422.

13. Saidel, "Expanding the Governance Construct," 421, 422. Saidel argues that advisory groups and committees also fill important governance in many nonprofit organizations with government grants or contracts. Also see Part 7, "Managing under Government Contracts."

14. See Parts 10 and 11 in J. Steven Ott, ed., *The Nature of the Nonprofit Sector* (Boulder: Westview Press, 2001).

15. Melissa Middleton-Stone, "Nonprofit Boards of Directors: Beyond the Governance Function," in W. W. Powell, ed., *The Nonprofit Sector: A Research Handbook* (New Haven: Yale University Press, 1987), 141–153.

16. See Part 7, "Social and Community Theories of the Nonprofit Sector," in J. Steven Ott, ed., *The Nature of the Nonprofit Sector* (Boulder: Westview Press, 2001).

17. Pamela A. Popielarz and J. Miller McPherson, "On the Edge or In Between: Niche Position, Niche Overlap, and the Duration of Voluntary Association Memberships," *American Journal of Sociology* 101, no. 3 (November 1995): 698–720.

18. Warren F. Ilchman, "Philanthropy," in J. M. Shafritz, ed., *International Encyclopedia of Public Policy and Administration* (Boulder: Westview Press, 1998), 1654–1661.

19. See Part 9, "Giving Theories of the Nonprofit Sector," in J. Steven Ott, ed., *The Nature of the Nonprofit Sector* (Boulder: Westview Press, 2001).

20. Murray, "Governance of Nonprofit Organizations," 993–997.

21. Stephen R. Block, "Board of Directors," in J. M. Shafritz, ed., *International Encyclopedia of Public Policy and Administration* (Boulder: Westview Press, 1998), 201–209.

22. Carver, *Boards That Make a Difference,* 74–100.

23. Ronald G. Shaiko, "Female Participation in Public Interest Nonprofit Governance: Yet Another Glass Ceiling?" *Nonprofit and Voluntary Sector Quarterly* 25, no. 3 (September 1996): 302–320.

24. Also see Teresa Odendahl and Sabrina Youmans, "Women on Nonprofit Boards," in T. Odendahl and M. O'Neill, eds., *Women and Power in the Nonprofit Sector* (San Francisco: Jossey-Bass, 1994), 183–221.

CHAPTER 1

Governance of Nonprofit Organizations

Vic Murray

The term "*governance*" is defined to mean the strategic leadership of nonprofit organizations. It is therefore important to understand how this use of the term differs from the way it is used in the context of traditional public administration. In the latter context governance usually refers to the process of government policy making, which is intimately related to the political activities of elected officials.

Outside the realm of government, the concept of governance refers to an aspect of the management of a given organization. Indeed, in most dictionaries, the synonyms of governance are words such as management and administration. In current parlance, the term has taken on a more specific meaning as a process for making certain types of management decisions. These are commonly referred to as strategic decisions, which have to do with such matters as setting the organization's mission, establishing the values it wishes to embody, deciding the broad strategy for achieving the mission, and evaluating its effectiveness in meeting its goals.

This concept of governance is rooted in the positivist tradition of social science, which assumes that individuals can rationally choose among alternative actions based on information that is consciously gathered and assessed. These

decisions are believed to then determine actual behavior, and the outcomes of such behavior, are thought to modify the subsequent decisions (Burrell and Morgan 1979). As we shall see, so-called postmodern critical theory takes issue with this concept of governance as an intendedly rational process, preferring instead to see the behavior of organizational members emerging from a much more complex, less-deterministic process.

This brief explication of the governance of nonprofit organizations focuses on problematic issues in the process of making governance decisions and their relationship to organizational effectiveness.

Problematic Issues in Nonprofit Governance

Considering governance as a decisionmaking process, there are two dominant issues of concern to scholars. One issue is who plays, or should play, which roles in the process, or, in practical terms, who is in charge of the organization and to whom is it accountable? The other issue is *how* governance decisions are, or should be, made.

Who Governs?

The literature on the question of roles in governance decisionmaking tends to be of two distinct types: normative and analytic.

The Normative Approach

The normative literature takes the position that the final authority on governance decisions ought to be the nonprofit organization's board of directors, governors, or trustees (e.g., Carver 1990; Houle 1989). It is the body to whom the rest of the organization is accountable and that, in turn, is accountable for the organization to the community, for which it acts as "trustee." It follows that the board must be both legally and morally responsible for establishing the organization's mission and ensuring that it is carried out.

The most common theme in this literature is to suggest that there are too many organizations in which the boards fail to govern properly. They are perceived as committing one of two cardinal sins. On one hand are those boards that allow the organization's paid top executives to make the governance decisions, which they then "rubber-stamp." On the other hand are those that do not have a clear understanding of how governance issues differ from detailed operational issues and, hence, get too involved in the day-to-day micromanagement of the organization, leaving no one to focus on the big picture of setting the strategic direction.

At this point, the normative literature launches into prescriptive recommendations on how the nonprofit board should be reformed so as to ensure that it effectively plays its governance role (and *only* this role). A brief summary of some of the most common recommendations is as follows:

- Since the role of the board is to act as trustee for the "owners" of the organization, it therefore ought to represent such owners and be fully aware of what the owners want from the organization. The problem, unfortunately, is that, except for nonprofit organizations created only to serve members who pay a membership fee, it is rarely clear who a nonprofit's owners actually are. The same dilemma arises when the term "*community*" is used in place of owners. This point is discussed further.
- The board must be the primary body to define the organization's mission and to articulate the values for which it stands.
- The board must obtain *independent* information on the threats and opportunities facing the organization and the organization's internal strengths and weaknesses in confronting its changing environment. To have this information selected and interpreted solely by the top management is to run the risk of becoming a rubber-stamp board.
- Board members must be carefully selected and thoroughly trained in how to make governance decisions, otherwise they can be lured into becoming either "rubber-stampers" or meddling micromanagers. Furthermore, this selection and training should not be the responsibility of the paid chief executive officer but of the organization's "owners" and the board itself.

Many other general recommendations are also offered on how to create better boards, involving such matters as optimal size, number and type of committees, meeting leadership techniques, and so forth. These are not discussed here, however, since they do not explicitly relate to the governance function per se.

In sum, the normative position on the governance of nonprofit organizations is quite clear and remarkably homogenous across a large number of writers on the subject: It ought to be the sole purview of the board of directors, and it ought to follow the classic principles of rational strategic planning.

The Analytic Approach

The alternative approach to nonprofit governance is to be found in the rather small body of literature that is concerned primarily with describing how governance decisions are actually made and with trying to discover why they emerge as they do. A subset of this literature takes on an implicitly normative cast in that it looks for what connections exist between the processes followed in making strategic decisions and the effectiveness of the organization. (See, for example, Herman and Heimovics 1990; Middleton 1987; Bradshaw, Murray, and Wolpin 1992, for surveys of this literature).

One of the primary concerns of the analytic approach to governance is who actually plays what role in governance decisionmaking. To address this question, a taxonomy of roles must be identified and the concept of the stakeholder must be evoked. As Jay Galbraith (1983), among others, has pointed out, there are three distinct roles in administrative decisionmaking. There are those who *make* the decisions de facto; there are those that *influence* those decisionmakers by providing information or recommendation; and there are those that *ratify* decisions. The latter role involves having little involvement in the choice of a preferred course of action but, in the last stage, having the authority to accept it or veto it. For example, in many nonprofit organizations, the chief executive officers (CEOs) are the primary decisionmakers, but some of their decisions are put to the board for ratification. The great majority of the time, the board routinely approves these motions, though occasionally one may be vetoed and returned to the CEO to be reconsidered.

The concept of stakeholder refers to any party that sees its interests being affected by the actions of a given organization. The potential stakeholders involved in governance decision for most nonprofits include some combination of the board as a whole, individual board members, board committees, the chief executive officer, other senior management staff, other paid staff and volunteers, users of the organization's services, members, funders, and government regulators.

Empirical studies of actual governance decisions in nonprofit organizations reveal several patterns to be quite common (e.g., Middleton-Stone 1991; Herman and Heimovics 1990; Bradshaw, Murray, and Wolpin 1992). The most common design in larger, more-established nonprofits is the "CEO-dominant" pattern, in which the CEO gathers information and advice from many stakeholders, formulates a decision, and has it ratified (rubber-stamped) by the board as a whole.

The next most common pattern is the "board-dominant pattern," often found in smaller, younger, more volunteer-driven nonprofit organizations, in which a small core group in the board plays a very influential role in recommending a course of action on governance issues. These are then debated and decided upon by the whole board. The CEO role in this situation is primarily one of several providers of information and advice.

Another common pattern is that of the "staff-dominant" situation, often found in "professional bureaucracies" such as universities and hospitals. As described by Henry Mintzberg (1979), these are organizations in which a core of senior professional staff (such as doctors or faculty members) have the power to make strategic decisions, which both the CEO and the board usually feel constrained to ratify.

Finally, there is the "collective governance" pattern, which operates according to an ideology of consensus among all key stakeholder groups. This design often turns out to be an active coalition of board members, staff of all levels, volunteers, and service users. Every effort is made to avoid giving any one of them more power than another. This pattern is commonly found in nonprofits with strong self-help or advocacy missions.

The Relationship Between Patterns of Governance and Outcomes

When one looks at the very limited research attempting to examine the link between governance decisionmaking processes and the actual performance of the nonprofit organization in achieving its mission, the picture is indistinct at best. The available evidence suggests that, contrary to the assertions of the writers of the normative literature on nonprofit governance, there is no one pattern of decisionmaking that is more effective than the others. Thus, even though it may be legally and morally desirable for the board of directors to play the dominant role in setting the strategic direction and assessing the effectiveness of the organization, there is no guarantee that, if they do so, the organization will be better off than one dominated by its CEO or a group of professional staff or an all-stake-holder collective. It would seem that the decision pattern for governance issues that is most effective depends on the unique configuration of history, organization culture, key personalities, and contextual conditions in which the organization finds itself at any given point in time.

How Governance Decisions Are Made

As noted, nonprofit governance refers to the strategic leadership of the organization. The two most important aspects of this leadership are setting the strategic direction for the organization and assessing its past performance. Like the question of who governs, the literature on how these decisions are made divides into normative and analytic schools.

The Normative Approach to Strategic Planning

There is a vast body of literature on how organizational strategies ought to be arrived at (e.g., Bryson 1988; Nutt and Backoff 1992; Byers 1984). Although it is not possible to go into any detail here, it is fair to say that all processes for deriving these strategies share certain common characteristics. For example,

- It is a rational process, which involves setting clear objectives and priorities based on careful analysis of the organization's present, and likely future, its environment, and its internal strengths and weaknesses.
- It is based on the fullest and best possible information gathered and synthesized specifically for strategy-setting purposes. This information not only considers present conditions but also attempts to forecast likely futures.
- The process culminates in a planning document (the strategic plan), which is to be used as the basis for all subsequent policy decisions for a given period of time (though most suggest that the plan be reviewed at least annually and changed as needed if the environmental conditions have changed significantly).

The Normative Approach to Evaluating Effectiveness

The process of assessing how well an organization is performing in its efforts to reach its goals is similarly viewed as a rational process (e.g., Wholey et al., 1994; Love 1991; Murray and Tassie 1994). Though normative writers admit that it is difficult to reach in practice, most have in mind an ideal evaluation process to which evaluators should at least aspire. It involves (1) having clear objectives and criteria to be applied in judging the degree of success in attaining them; and (2) devising objective measures of progress that yield results that can be compared to the criteria, thereby producing an accurate evaluation.

The Analytic Approach to Strategic Planning

Perhaps the best, and most recent, work summarizing the empirical literature on what actually goes on when organizations develop strategies is that of Henry Mintzberg (1994). Several key points are made in this work and in others.

- Most documents that emerge labeled "strategic plan" have little influence on the strategic (board direction-setting) decisions actually made after the planning document is created.
- Organizations could be said to have "strategies" in the form of general guiding ideas that influence how problems are perceived and solved, but they "emerge" rather than appear as formal plans from a special planning group or process. Various stakeholders have varying amounts and kinds of power, and those with the greatest influence shape a strategy from a number of specific decisions.
- Major changes in strategy can and do occur but do so at disjointed intervals rather than evolving gradually over time; that is, the organization adheres to a given strategic position without changing it until eventually a "revolution" occurs that brings about a new strategy, which similarly lasts unchanged for a period, until the next revolution (Miller and Friesen 1984).
- The activity of engaging in a formal strategic planning process may, however, prove to be

beneficial for reasons other than the limited value of the planning document it creates. It is valuable insofar as the process involves consulting with various external and internal stakeholders who do not have a regular influence on decisionmaking and requires gathering information on the organization's environment. Such activity can have the effect of improving the support of the external groups consulted, enhancing staff commitment to the mission, and resolving intraorganizational conflicts (Bradshaw, Murray, and Wolpin 1992).

The Analytic Approach to Evaluating Effectiveness

Despite the vociferous rhetoric from all sides calling for more and better evaluation of organizational performance, rigorous evaluation is not common in the nonprofit sector. Furthermore, what is done deviates substantially from the "ideal" model (Osborne, 1992; Murray and Tassie 1994). Other key points from the empirical literature are as follows:

- Evaluation tends to be carried out primarily at the program level, rather than at the organizational level. This means that comparisons of the relative costs and benefits of the range of programs are rare.
- The focus of evaluations tends to be on processes and inputs rather than on outcomes. Process-based evaluation checks the policies, practices, and procedures followed by organizations, under the assumption that certain actions will lead to certain outcomes; for example, that "participative decisionmaking" will eventually result in a reduction in substance abuse by low-income youth in an agency set up for that purpose; or that an increase in donations (inputs) will produce a corresponding increase improving the environment in an environmental protection agency.
- The "ideal" methods of evaluation are rarely followed because goals are unclear, criteria are not defined or prioritized, and measurement instruments yield ambiguous results. In addition, behind the formal evaluation procedures there are often nonformal methods at work.

These methods may involve making judgments of effectiveness based on the organization's unofficial reputation in the eyes of key stakeholders (called "isomorphism" by Di Maggio and Powell 1983). Judgments are also based on the degree to which those in the organization being evaluated appear to hold values and beliefs that are congruent with unspoken values and beliefs held by the evaluator (Tassie and Murray 1995).

- When all is said and done, many evaluations only marginally affect major policy decisions, such as funding allocations or downsizing plans; this is because of the strength of other variables such as pressures from other, more powerful, stakeholders.

Conclusion

The study of the process of nonprofit governance is of great importance but suffers at present from the wishful thinking of normative writers and the general lack of knowledge about what really goes on. The possibility of improving governance depends on acquiring a better understanding of the actual processes and the factors that influence them. Until that time, the field will remain dominated by successive fads offering "the answer" to the problems of governance.

References

Bradshaw, Pat, Vic Murray, and Jacob Wolpin, 1992. "Do Nonprofit Boards Make a Difference?" *Nonprofit and Voluntary Sector Quarterly,* vol., 21, no. 3 (Fall): 227–250.

Bryson, John, 1988. *Strategic Planning for Public and Nonprofit Organizations.* San Francisco: Jossey-Bass.

Burrell, Gibson, and Gareth Morgan, 1979. *Sociological Paradigms of Organizational Analysis.* London: Heinemann.

Byers, Lloyd, 1984. *Strategic Management.* New York: Harper & Row.

Carver, John, 1990. *Boards That Make a Difference.* San Francisco: Jossey-Bass.

Di Maggio, P. J., and W. W. Powell, 1983. "The Iron Cage Revisited: Institutional Isomorphism and Collective Rationality in Organizational Fields," *American Sociological Review* 48: 147–160.

Galbraith, Jay, 1983. *Designing Complex Organizations.* Reading, MA: Addison-Wesley.

Hardy, Cynthia, ed., 1994. *Managing Strategic Action.* London: Sage.

Herman, R. D., and R. D. Heimovics, 1990. "An Investigation of Leadership Skills in Chief Executives of Nonprofit Organizations," *American Review of Public Administration,* vol. 20, no. 2: 107–124.

_____, 1991. *Executive Leadership in Nonprofit Organizations.* San Francisco: Jossey-Bass.

Houle, Cyril, 1989. *Governing Boards.* San Francisco: Jossey-Bass.

Knauft, E. B., R. A. Berger, and S. T. Gray, 1991. *Profiles of Excellence: Achieving Success in the Nonprofit Sector.* San Francisco: Jossey-Bass.

Love, Arnold, 1991. Internal Evaluation: *Building Organizations from Within.* Newbury Park, CA: Sage.

Middleton, M., 1987. "Nonprofit Boards of Directors: Beyond the Governance Function." In W. W. Powell, ed., *The Nonprofit Sector: A Research Handbook.* New Haven, CT: Yale University Press.

Middleton-Stone, M. 1991. "The Propensity of Governing Boards to Plan," *Nonprofit Management and Leadership,* vol. 1, no. 3 (Spring): 203–216.

Miller, D., and P. H. Friesen, 1984. *Organizations: A Quantum View.* Englewood Cliffs, NJ: Prentice-Hall.

Mintzberg, Henry, 1979. *The Structuring of Organizations.* Englewood Cliffs, NJ: Prentice-Hall.

_____, 1994. *The Rise and Fall of Strategic Planning.* New York: Free Press.

Murray, Vic, and Bill Tassie, 1994. "Evaluating the Effectiveness of Nonprofit Organizations." In R. D. Herman, ed., *The Jossey-Bass Handbook of Nonprofit Leadership and Management,* San Francisco: Jossey-Bass.

Nutt, Paul, and Robert Backoff, 1992. *Strategic Management of Public and Third Sector Organizations.* San Francisco: Jossey-Bass.

Osborne, David, 1992. *Reinventing Government.* Reading, MA: Addison-Wesley.

Tassie, William, and Vic Murray, forthcoming. "Rationality and Politics: What Really Goes on When Funders Evaluate the Performance of Fundees." *Nonprofit and Voluntary Sector Quarterly.*

Wholely, Joseph, H. P. Hatry, and K. E. Newcomer, eds., 1994. *Handbook of Practical Program Evaluation.* San Francisco: Jossey-Bass.

► CHAPTER 2

Board of Directors

STEPHEN R. BLOCK

People vested with the legal responsibility to govern and control the affairs of organizations. Accountability for any nonprofit organization ultimately rests with its board of directors (sometimes called board of trustees). Although the board may delegate management authority to a paid staff person, known as the executive director, the board can never be relieved of its legal and fiduciary responsibilities. Governing board members are stewards of the public interest and have a burden of responsibility to use and preserve the organization's assets for advancing a beneficial mission.

Board membership is an admirable act of citizenship for those who are willing to accept a significant amount of volunteering. These special people are generally not compensated for their board service, and they must balance their board obligations with personal demands of work, family responsibilities, and other community activities. This commitment to community service is tied to a long history of voluntary action, with roots that precede the founding of the United States. The innate desire to help is said to be a unique quality in America, a democratic attribute that influences the modern nonprofit board of directors.

Because of the board's legal responsibilities, personal limitations on directors' time, and the

daily involvement of the executive director, there is often confusion between the board and staff over roles, responsibilities, turf, and expectations for performance. The board and executive director must clearly understand their mutual expectations if they are to develop a healthy governing body.

Why Have a Board?

Of the many reasons for having a board of directors, legal necessity is primary. In some states, only one board member is required for incorporating an organization, but most states require at least three or more individuals to serve as directors of a governing board. The Internal Revenue Service also requires nonprofit organizations seeking or maintaining recognition for tax-exempt purposes to have governing boards of directors. Members of governing boards are expected to engage willingly in board activities, without receiving any benefit of the organization's assets or earnings.

Aside from the legal necessities, the most practical reasons for having a board of directors are to ensure that the organization is effectively managed and is working toward the achievement of a mission that has a public purpose. Few nonprofit organizations have the resources to employ the personnel with the expertise that is necessary to accomplish their organizational activities. The collective wisdom of the board of directors can serve as a bank of skilled and knowledgeable resources to provide support, advice, and counsel. It has been widely proposed that board members should comprise the three Ws; individuals who are willing to "work," some with "wisdom," and others with "wealth."

Why Would Someone Want to Serve on a Board?

Each person has his or her own reason for voluntary board service; however, one of the most often-stated is to serve one's community. Volunteering as a board member is an honor and a fundamental privilege of a free people.

There are many reasons for joining or for staying on a board. For example, board participation may be an expectation of one's employer. It may provide an opportunity for gaining or maintaining social status in the community, satisfy socializing needs, lead to new knowledge and skills, and enhance one's résumé. For some people, voluntary board service satisfies religious convictions based on a belief in the organization's cause or mission; or is based on personal experience of a problem (such as a disease or tragedy) that is addressed by the work and mission of the organization.

The Board's Relationship with Its Executive Director

Various authors have described their ideas about the ideal working relationship between the board and executive director. Two governance models prevail. One model builds on the traditional view that the executive director is employed as a subordinate to the board. The working relationship is characterized by distinct and separate roles for the board and executive director, with the board directing, supervising, and limiting the director's activities as the board sees fit.

The other governance model builds on ideas of partnership and collegiality between the exec-

utive director and board of directors. This model acknowledges that the board of directors has clearly defined legal responsibilities. However, the model differs from traditional approaches in a fundamental way: The executive director takes an active role in assisting with or coordinating the participation of board members in fulfilling their governance commitment. This form of board management makes full use of the executive director's distinctive management and leadership skills. Consequently, the quality of the board's performance is a direct result of the executive director's ability to steer and promote productive interaction among board members. The executive director can call upon board managers to intervene when necessary in either the internal or external environment of the organization.

Who Is in Charge of Making Policy?

Prescriptions for effective board practice often state that the board is legally responsible for making policy and the staff is responsible for carrying it out. Though this division of labor is technically correct, it is inaccurate in its practice. The staffs of nonprofit organizations have a significant level of influence on the creation of policy. Since they are closest to the operations and programs of the agency, they may know when a new policy would provide the guidance needed to get the job done. Thus, staff input is almost always required to create new policies. In addition, the staff often shapes the policy by drafting proposed policy statements.

In effective nonprofit organizations, the staff's point of view on matters of policy development is considered an integral part of governance. Often, effective organizations are those in which the board adopts policy with input of the staff, and the staff implement policy with the advice, counsel, and support of the board.

What Are the Major Areas of Board Responsibility?

There are at least nine major areas of board responsibility; namely, to

1. determine the organization's mission;
2. set policies and adopt plans for the organization's operations;
3. approve the budget, establish fiscal policies and financial controls, and monitor financial position of the organization;
4. provide adequate resources for the organization through establishment of resource-development goals and commitment to fund-raising through giving and soliciting;
5. develop organizational visibility through networking and linkage to the community;
6. ensure that the organization's corporate and governance documents are updated and secured, and all reports are filed as required;
7. recruit and select new board members and provide them with an orientation to the board's business;
8. recruit, hire, evaluate, reward, or terminate, if necessary, the executive director of the organization; and
9. protect and preserve the organization's nonprofit tax-exempt status.

The Role of Board Officers

The officers of the board of directors have a responsibility to set the tone for organizational leadership. The duties of the president (chairperson), vice-president, treasurer, and secretary are described in the organization's bylaws.

President

In most nonprofit organizations the title and position of president refers to the highest level volunteer who also serves as chairperson of the organization. However, in some nonprofit organizations a corporate model of governance is followed, therefore, the title of "president" replaces the more commonly used title of "executive director." If the president is also the paid chief executive, the position usually allows for participation as a board member. In this instance, the role of chairperson is handled by the chief volunteer.

The volunteer president or chairperson is responsible for the activities of the board and for assigning board committee chairs, unless assignments are automatically spelled out in the bylaws. The chair is responsible for monitoring the work of the board and evaluating the board's performance. The chair presides at and calls special meetings of the board and sets the direction for organizational goal setting. This volunteer position requires a great deal of time commitment and responsibility.

Vice-President

In the absence of the volunteer president, the vice-president usually assumes the duties of president and the responsibility for chairing board meetings. Often, the role of vice-president entails chairing a major committee of the board. In some organizations, the vice-president automatically becomes president-elect, a succession plan that may not be effective in all organizations.

Secretary

The board secretary has the obligation to protect the organization's corporate documents, such as the bylaws, the articles of incorporation, board and committee minutes, and important correspondence.

Many individuals try to avoid election to the office of secretary because of the myth that the board secretary must take the minutes of the board and executive committee meetings. The board secretary does not have to write the minutes, but he or she is responsible for ensuring that the minutes are taken and accurately reflect the business meetings of the board and executive committee. Upon becoming official annals of the organization, the board minutes should be signed and dated by the board secretary. In organizations that rely on parliamentary rules and procedures (such as *Robert's Rules of Order, Newly Revised*), the board secretary is required to become familiar with the meeting procedures and may have to make procedural rulings.

Treasurer

The treasurer should not be expected to do the bookkeeping and accounting for the organization. Instead, the treasurer is responsible for making sure that the organization's finances are properly accounted for and excess revenues are wisely invested. If a finance committee exists, the treasurer often serves as its chairperson. On behalf of the board, the treasurer ensures that financial controls are in place and tested on a periodic basis. The treasurer also participates in the selection and recommendation of an auditing firm. The treasurer reports on the financial statements at board meetings, executive committee meetings, and, if applicable, at annual meetings of the organization.

The Board's Role in Fund-Raising

The board must play a fundamental role in raising money and resources. Board members also have the personal responsibility of making financial contributions in addition to giving their voluntary time to the organization. Instituting a policy that requires board members to contribute is sometimes employed.

Unanimous giving among the board sets the right tone for fund-raising. It enhances the credibility of the organization when it seeks contributions from others. Unanimous-board-giving practices have even become an expectation among many funders.

Giving is only one part of the board member's obligation; the other part is to assist in planning and solicitation activities. Collectively, the board can identify a pool of potential contributors. Friends, business associates, relatives, and vendors are among likely prospects. Some board members shy away from verbally asking for money, but they may be able to write letters or at least sign letters that have been drafted for them by staff.

Board Composition

Determining the composition of a board of directors is claimed by some to be a blend of science and art.

Board composition should not be the result of opening the door to just anyone who is willing to serve but should result from purposeful recruitment strategies. Prospective board mem-

bers, for example, should be familiarized with the organization's purpose, mission, vision, goals, and objectives, as well as board duties, responsibilities, and the organization's expectations.

The task of filling vacancies on the board should be approached carefully and should result in a board composition that is able to advance the organization's mission. There are two preparatory steps to actively recruiting the right person. The initial step is to acknowledge that organizations go through different stages of development similar to the various life cycles experienced by individuals. Various maturational stages lead to differing organizational issues and needs. Assessing which phase an organization is in is useful not only to prepare the organization for change but also to determine the leadership qualities required of potential board members. Matching an organization's life cycle to the requisite skills of a board member could lead to more effective and purposeful organizational outcomes.

A second step is to conduct a thorough demographic inventory of board composition, which will reveal the board's weakest representational areas. Inventory results will show a compositional balance or imbalance in such variables as gender, age range, ethnicity, socioeconomic status, political party affiliation, educational level, professional or vocational interests, knowledge of consumer issues, and location of primary residence. Information of this type can be valuable to organizations especially seeking to create a diverse board.

As suggested, the composition of a board can contribute to the level of ease or difficulty with which an organization is governed and managed. A board composed of individuals with similar socioeconomic backgrounds or other familiar traits may reach consensus more often, but it is less likely to formulate challenging ideas or seek out policy reforms. Compared to homogeneous boards, those that reflect diversity among their members are likely to experience greater participatory challenges. Even though diversity is an enriching quality in a board, its members must contend with differing values, mores, and interpretations of community information and beliefs.

The Executive Director as Board Member

Some nonprofit organizations use a corporate model of governance structure in which the position of executive director is transformed from staff to member of the board as its president-chief executive officer (CEO).

The model of corporate governance may not be an appropriate structure for all nonprofit organizations. It is used by larger and more complex institutions that rely on a strong CEO. Regardless of size, the CEO as staff and board member must be wary of conflicts of interest and must avoid participating in discussions or decisionmaking that will lead to personal benefits. Critics of nonprofit organizations using corporate models suggest that the CEOs have no choice but to use the knowledge they have acquired in managing the day-to-day operations. This knowledge is often used to influence the direction of the board and organization.

There is a dearth of comparative research on the benefits and disadvantages of corporate models as compared to traditional models in use by nonprofit organizations. Consequently, it is impossible to suggest that any one model will lead to success.

Board Recruitment and Orientation

Preconditions of board recruitment include identifying the governance needs of organizations in (life cycle) transition and discovering the characteristics and qualities to be found in new board members. There are many variables to consider in sizing up a board prospect, including:

1. an individual's ability to create a vision, problem-solve, and facilitate conflict resolution;
2. an individual's commitment of time to participate fully;
3. enthusiasm for the organization's mission, vision, goals, and values;
4. a person's skills and experience in such areas as public policy analysis and fund-raising, or expertise in program service delivery; and
5. diversity factors.

Once a profile is developed that describes the ideal board member, the recruitment task can formally begin. On the basis of expediency, many nonprofit organizations make the mistake of ignoring the profile and recruiting the friends of board members. Sometimes, individuals are invited to become prospective board members for the simple reason that they are alive and seem agreeable to serving! Serious problems may occur when attempts have not been made to match the needs of the organization with the ideal board member. Locating someone who matches the profile and agrees to serve, however, is not a guarantee of board success. In fact, most governance problems seem to stem from the recruitment process. Though using a profile can increase the likelihood of finding the right person, a perfect match does not guarantee that problems will not arise, such as, nonattendance at board meetings, lack of participation in board committees, an unwillingness to contribute financially, or interfering or trying to micromanage the day-to-day operations of the organization.

Finding a board prospect who fits the profile is, indeed, a critical part of the assignment, as is fully informing the prospect about specific board duties. The lack of knowledge about the expectations for board member role and governance responsibilities will directly contribute to organizational confusion, ineffectiveness, and a breach in a board member's commitment. Since each organization's board of directors has a different mission and focus for its work, even the seasoned board member who joins a new board should receive a briefing on the organization, its expectations of board members, and board responsibilities. It is imperative to seek an agreement to serve only after the board prospect understands the parameters of board service.

Organizations sometimes give prospects a board-prospecting packet, which may contain some or all of the following: a history of the organization; board job-descriptions; a copy of the articles of incorporation and bylaws; a copy of the organization's purpose or mission statement; an organizational chart; and a description of program services, with a list of committees and duties of each. This packet may also include a roster of the current board, with work affiliations, addresses, and phone numbers; dates of future meetings and special events; an annual report and organization brochures, newsletters, or related materials; and a copy of a recent auditor's financial report, annual budget, and financial statements.

It may also be helpful for the organization's board to assign a veteran member to assist the prospect in "learning the ropes." The availability of a support person may encourage the board prospect to join a concerned board of directors. The veteran could serve as a resource person during the recruitment phase and then as a mentor or helper during the transition period following induction.

How Many Board Members?

There is no formula for determining the appropriate size of an organization's board of directors. The size of the board must be tailored to suit the needs of the organization.

One helpful way to determine board size is an organizational life-cycle analysis, referred to previously as a pre-requisite to board recruitment. Organizations and their boards experience various developmental stages, all of which can influence the number and type of skilled board members that are needed.

Large- and small-sized boards have both advantages and disadvantages. The number of people on a board can be a factor that influences how board members comport themselves. Large boards are generally unwieldy because it is difficult to pay attention to so many people. Because the larger group will find it more difficult to become cohesive and familiar with the cohort, it may tend to be more formal in its board conduct and meetings. Organizations that are just starting out, or those in need of a boost in financial resources, may be better served by a larger board of 20 to 25 individuals. In this case, the larger the number of board members the greater the chances of reaching out to potential donors.

On one hand, smaller boards are limited in accomplishing supportive activities such as fund-raising. On the other hand, a smaller group may have to rely on its creativity, such as developing a fund-raising plan for implementation by a committee of staff, board members, and other community volunteers. Organizations that do not rely heavily on the board alone for fund-raising or other supportive activities might be better served by a board of no more than ten members. The smaller group would have more of an opportunity to become cohesive; learn experientially how to mesh effectively their collective wisdom, advice, and counsel; reach decisions through consensus; and it would have no need to use controlling, parliamentary procedures for conducting board meetings.

Board Liability

Though nonprofit boards of directors are infrequently sued, the risk of liability is nevertheless a legitimate concern for volunteer board members. Financial losses associated with a lawsuit can be devastating to an organization and its board members. The quality and manner in which boards make decisions or fail to make decisions can result in a legal challenge that tests whether they have met or failed in their responsibilities as stewards of public interest.

Board members and prospective members are often comforted by the knowledge that the nonprofit organization has purchased a director's and officers' (D&O) liability insurance policy. Concerns about lawsuits have caused a rising demand for this type of insurance, and consequently, premium costs vary widely.

A factor that affects the cost of D&O insurance is the nature of the organization's work, whether it is, for example, a direct service health care agency or an organization that promotes the arts. Features and exclusions may also differ greatly from one policy to another and affect the price and value of the policy.

Indemnification refers to the organization ensuring that it will pay the reasonable costs associated with liability suits, such as judgments and settlements against its board members. This practice is sometimes compelled by state law. In other situations it may be an optional practice of the board. In either event, the organization's bylaws outline the extent of indemnification. Indemnification cannot, however, be exercised when the organization brings a suit against its own board members. In practice, indemnification is a form of self-insurance and assumes that the organization has the funds to pay legal costs. Given the resources of some nonprofit organizations, this assumption may not be valid.

In addition to indemnification and D&O liability insurance coverage, a board of directors can purchase various liability insurance policies, including, but not limited to, the following specialty policies: general liability, employees' liability, malpractice, automobile, and fiduciary.

To encourage board and other voluntary service in community organizations, all 50 states have passed volunteer protection laws. The extent of protection varies among the states, and this form of legislation has largely been untested in the courts.

Volunteer protection laws and the varieties of liability insurance premiums are not the only ways boards can protect themselves. The most effective form of protection is limiting risk by adhering to effective governance practices. There are three standards of conduct that should guide the board member, as follows:

- *Duty of care:* imposes an obligation that all board members discharge their duties with the care that an ordinarily prudent person would exercise under similar circumstances. This includes being diligent, attending meetings, and becoming acquainted with issues before reaching a decision.
- *Duty of loyalty:* requires that each board member act primarily in the best interest of the organization and not in his or her own personal best interest or in the interest of individuals at the expense of the organization.
- *Duty of obedience:* imposes an obligation that board members will act in conformity with all laws in addition to acting in accordance with the organization's mission.

For the voluntary members of boards of directors, acting prudently, lawfully, and in the best interests of the organization can, in part, be achieved by adhering to the following six responsible board practices:

1. *Becoming an active board member.* Board members who are familiar with the organization's mission and purpose are generally able to make better decisions for the organization. Members may wish to review the mission annually to serve as a reminder that the board uses the mission statement as its guide in decisionmaking.

2. *Attending all meetings.* Being absent from meetings will not necessarily excuse a board member from responsibilities for decisions reached by those in attendance. In fact, a member's absence from meetings increases potential risks for the entire board because it is making decisions without the benefit of the views of all of its members.

3. *Insisting on having sound financial management tools and control systems.* Board members need to learn how to read and use financial statements and audit reports to understand and monitor the organization's fiscal health. They also need to understand that their decisions have a financial impact on the organization.

4. *Speaking up.* Members should not remain silent when they disagree with a decision or an opinion expressed by others. Additionally, board members should ask questions when the organization's goals and objectives are not being met.

5. *Identifying conflicts of interest.* Board members need to avoid participating in discussions or decisionmaking when they have conflicts of interest. Even the perception of a conflict of interest must be avoided, if possible. If they are faced with an actual conflict or even the perception of one, board members must inform the other directors of the situation and excuse themselves from participation in related areas of decisionmaking or transactions.

6. *Staffing.* In addition to its having personnel policy guidelines for the executive director, the board must be certain that these personnel policies are adequate and updated to reflect all applicable mandates of law.

In summary, minimizing the risk of board liability requires an active and involved board of directors.

Dismissal of Board Members

Terminating a member from the board of directors for nonattendance at board meetings or lack of follow through on assignments that are required for the board's decisionmaking purposes, for example, is a delicate procedure. Unfortunately, there are times when it becomes necessary to discharge board members because their actions create liability risks.

The chairperson of the board has the responsibility to request resignations from board members. The executive director plays a supportive role to the board chair and board member in what for all can be emotionally trying and embarrassing.

Confidence and sensitivity should be used when approaching the board member with the idea of resignation. A board member should be given every consideration to effect a smooth departure. Ultimately, the member's "saving face" is important for maintaining relationships at this level of community involvement.

To prevent the need for board dismissals or to support the actions of the board chair when a dismissal is called for, the board should adopt a principle stating that its work and organizational mission are too important to allow for unnecessary liability risks associated with uncommitted board members. The board can do some prevention work by adopting a bylaw passage and job description that reflect standards for board member conduct and participation. Of course, some organizations have rules of this type but choose not to enforce them. For a member to violate or ignore such bylaw provisions suggests poor judgment and raises the liability risks of the board.

How Often Should the Board Meet?

A board is generally required to meet at least once a year. In practice, some hold meetings once a month, every other month, or once each calendar quarter. Frequency of board meetings and the duration of each meeting should reflect the culture of the organization and the type of strategic issues requiring board attention. Dealing with planning and policy issues, threats of litigation or bad publicity, and concerns of financial obligations are reasons for a board to meet more frequently. Organizations that are new in their development, or in process of managing significant changes, as compared with an organization in a steady state, would also benefit from meeting more frequently.

Effective meetings are focused, to the point, and stick to the agenda. Meetings can be effective when board members come prepared, having studied the agenda and the issues prior to the meeting. The agenda should be mailed out at least a week to ten days in advance. Agenda items should be allocated realistic time frames for discussion and taking action, in addition to time designated for the routine review of minutes, financial reports, and progress reports on the implementation of the organization's strategic plans.

Newly identified obstacles are not always solved during board meetings. Instead of reacting to unfinished issues and business with more board meetings, attempts should first be made to streamline the review of issues by assigning the task to an appropriate standing or ad hoc committee. In this way, the committees can try to remedy issues or bring their findings and recommendations back to the board or executive committee without monopolizing the board's time and agenda.

How Long Should a Board Member Serve?

The solution to a member's length of service that is practiced by many organizations is to stagger the expiring terms of office. Rotations of three-year terms, for example, would mean that each member serves for three years, but, at the end of each year, obligations would end for one-third of the members. This system gives the board ample time to evaluate the performance of board members, to determine whether they should be invited back for another term. Additionally, the experience base accumulated by outgoing board members is information these members use to decide whether they would like to be reelected for another three-year term.

Some organizations also place a limit on the number of consecutive terms a person may serve. After reaching the maximum number of consecutive terms of service, the board member would automatically leave the board. A board member who rotated off could be elected again after a year or more, when consecutive service would not be an issue. After reaching the allowable service limit, an individual could also continue to support the organization's cause in some other capacity, such as on a committee or advisory board.

It is important that all board member terms do not expire at the same time. Without some overlapping representation from members of the board, the organization would lose its important history and continuity of policy development and strategic direction. Veteran board members bring a maturity and depth of understanding about the issues the organization faces, and when the board adds a group of newer members it brings enthusiasm and fresh ideas to the board's governing role.

How Are Governing Boards, Advisory Boards, and Honorary Boards Different?

When one is referring to the term "board of directors" or "board of trustees," the reference is to a *governing board*, a grouping of individuals who have assumed a legal responsibility for an organization's existence. These people make policy and are responsible for how money is generated and spent, toward the accomplishment of a mission that can be beneficial to the general public or to a segment of the population.

Advisory boards, however, do not bear the legal burdens of governing boards. An advisory board exists to assist the governing board or the executive director in examining issues and recommendations. Recommendations that result from the work of an advisory board do not have to be accepted or followed by the governing board.

Honorary boards are usually composed of individuals who are well-known because of some measure of celebrity or prominence in the community. Honorary boards do not necessarily meet. In fact, some individuals agree to serve as honorary members because they do not have the time or inclination to attend meetings. Individu-

als serving in this honorary capacity lend credibility to an organization by allowing the use of their prominent names in brochures and on letterheads.

Sometimes, members of honorary boards and advisory boards are enlisted to assist in organizational fund-raising activities. The visibility and credibility of the honorary or advisory member sends a signal to the community that the organization is worthy of financial support.

Types of Committees

Committees are categorized as either standing committees or ad hoc committees. Ad hoc (or special) committees, on one hand, have a lifespan equal to the completion of the committee's assignment. Standing committees, on the other hand, are part of the permanent governance structure of an organization with duties and responsibilities described in bylaws. Standing committees may include executive, finance, bylaws, fund-raising, public relations, nominating, personnel, planning, and policy committees, or any other committee that the organization believes should exist indefinitely to aid in governance. Seven of the most common standing committees are described as follows:

1. The *executive committee* functions in place of the full board and handles routine and crisis matters between full board meetings. Empowered to make decisions for the organization, the executive committee is usually composed of the organization's officers. Depending on the size of the organization's board of directors, composition of the executive committee could include committee chairs or other selected leaders among the board. The executive committee is usually chaired by the board's volunteer president or chairperson.

2. The *finance committee* is responsible for monitoring the organization's finances and financial controls and attending to audit requirements. Typical functions for the finance committee are to oversee organizational investments and to work with the executive director to develop an annual budget.

3. The *nominations committee* is responsible for identifying and recruiting appropriate candidates for board positions and bringing forward its recommendations to the full board. This committee sometimes has the responsibility for planning board development activities and board retreats.

4. The *personnel committee* is usually responsible for recommending policies to guide the supervision of staff. In some organizations, this committee may have the responsibility for overseeing the search for an executive director and then for her or his performance evaluation. Members of this committee may need to acquaint themselves with personnel laws and regulations that regulate labor practices.

5. The *program committee* is responsible for monitoring the organization's service delivery system and may assist in evaluating client services. This committee is often responsible for keeping track of community trends that might affect the organization's short-term and long-term objectives. In complex organizations with multiple services, there may be subcommittees that are responsible for monitoring each of the organization's program services.

6. The *resource development committee* is responsible for examining alternate methods of fund-raising and for establishing annual fund-raising goals. This committee often is active in the solicitation of gifts or participation in special events. In addition to raising money, it may solicit in-kind contributions.

7. The *public relations* or *community relations committee* has the responsibility for developing good relations with the larger community and with important community groups. The committee examines opportunities to participate in community events that will bring visibility to the organization. It may oversee the writing of press releases and may develop relationships with media professionals.

Participants appointed to standing or ad hoc committees do not need to be members of the board of directors. Committee members may include staff, volunteers, representatives from community agencies, and consumers of service. Committee chairs are usually appointed by the board's chairperson.

References

Block, Stephen R., and Jeffrey W. Pryor, 1991. *Improving Nonprofit Management Practice: A Handbook for Community-Based Organizations.* Rockville, MD: OSAP/Public Health Service, U.S. Dept. of Health and Human Services.

Carver, John, 1990. *Boards That Make a Difference.* San Francisco:Jossey-Bass.

Chait, Richard P., and Barbara E. Taylor, 1989. "Charting the Territory of Nonprofit Boards." *Harvard Business Review* (Jan.–Feb.): 44–54.

Conrad, William, and William E. Glenn, 1976. *The Effective Voluntary Board of Directors.* Chicago: Swallow Press.

Drucker, Peter F., 1989. "What Business Can Learn from Nonprofits." *Harvard Business Review* (Sept.–Oct.): 88–93.

_____, 1990. "Lessons for Successful Nonprofit Governance." *Nonprofit Management and Leadership,* vol. 1, no. 1 (Fall): 7–14.

Hadden, Elaine M., and Blaire A. French, 1987. *Nonprofit Organizations: Rights and Liabilities for Members, Directors and Officers.* Wilmette, IL: Callaghan & Co.

Herman, Robert Dean, and Stephen R. Block, 1990. "The Board's Crucial Role in Fund Raising": 222–241. In Jon Van Til, et al., *Critical Issues in American Philanthropy.* San Francisco: Jossey-Bass.

Herman, Robert Dean, and Richard D. Heimovics, 1991. *Executive Leadership in Nonprofit Organizations.* San Francisco: Jossey-Bass.

Herman, Robert Dean, and Jon Van Til, eds., 1989. *Nonprofit Boards of Directors: Analyses and Applications,* New Brunswick, NJ: Transaction Publishers.

Kurtz, Daniel L., 1988. *Board Liability* New York: Moyer Bell.

Middleton, Melissa, 1987. "Nonprofit Boards of Directors: Beyond the Governance Function":141–153. In Walter W. Powell, ed., *The Nonprofit Sector: A Research Handbook,* New Haven: Yale University Press.

O'Connell, Brian, 1985. *The Board Members Book.* New York: The Foundation Center.

O'Houle, Cyril, 1989. *Governing Boards.* San Francisco: Jossey-Bass.

Saidel, Judith R., 1993. "The Board Role in Relation to Government: Alternative Models": 32–51. In Dennis R. Young, Robert M. Hollister, and Virginia A. Hodgkinson, eds., *Governing, Leading, and Managing Nonprofit Organizations.* San Francisco: Jossey-Bass.

CHAPTER 3

Setting Limits

Standards of Ethics and Prudence

JOHN CARVER

The board must have *control over* the complexity and details of staff operations. It is also important for a board to be *free from* the complexity and details of staff operations. The board needs control because it is accountable for all organizational activity, however obscure or far removed. Yet the board needs to be free from operational matters because it is a part-time body with little time to get its own job done.

It is common to sacrifice one need for the other. Some boards relinquish control to be free from details or to grant the CEO freedom from board intrusion; such boards may be guilty of rubber-stamping. Others forgo freedom in order to control many details; such boards may be guilty of meddling.

The responsible board cannot escape its obligation to prescribe at least the broad sweep of Ends and perhaps a few levels below. In other words, with a broad brush the board determines where the organization is going. In this chapter, however, I am concerned not with where the organization is going, but with what staff members do to get it there. I deal with the myriad of "how to" questions facing the CEO and his or her staff. Or, more accurately, I deal with how the board might best relate to the staff's "how to" issues. The board's challenge is to be reasonably certain

nothing goes awry and at the same time to grant as much unimpeded latitude as possible to those with the skill and talent to get the work done.

The Enticing Complexity of Operations

For most boards, the greatest source of complexity is not the Ends but staff operations. Boards struggle with budgets, personnel procedures and issues, purchasing, staffing patterns, compensation, and staff plans. Self-perpetuating cycles are in effect wherein staff members bring their issues to the board because they think the board wants to hear them. Board members request information and attend to staff-level issues because they believe that the staff will feel abandoned if they do otherwise. Sometimes, staff members bring matters to the board to avoid making choices: "This item is a hot one; we'd better get the board to decide." Often, no prior board guidance has been given; consequently, there are no parameters within which the board protects the staff's right to make such choices.

On the other hand, boards delve into staff matters because a particular board member has either the relevant expertise or mere curiosity about some aspect of operations. It is not uncommon for an entire board to be drawn into an issue only because of the minority concern. The board's job is thus defined, not by a carefully constructed design of the task, but by the laundry list of individual interests.

Boards study, invest meeting and committee time in, and worry and argue about that complex, never-ending, intriguing body of staff activities. To the detriment both of carefully deliberated results and of effective board process, boards are entangled in and seduced by the means of their subordinates. The following staff issues draw in board members.

Personnel: Job design, hiring, firing, promotion, discipline, training, grievances up through the CEO, deployment, evaluation

Compensation (except that of the CEO): Salary ranges, grades, adjustments, incentives, benefits, pensions

Supply: Purchasing, bidding, authorization, storage, inventories, distribution, salvage

Accounting: Forecasting, budgeting, depositories, controls, investments, retrenchment, growth, cost center designation

Facilities: Space allocation and requirements, rentals, purchases, sales, upkeep, refurbishing

Risk management: Insurance, exposures, protective maintenance, disclaimers

Consumer record keeping: Forms, waivers, consents, service tracking, actions taken or services rendered

Reporting: Grant reports, tax reporting, law and regulation compliance

Communications: Memoranda, telephone systems, meetings, postings, mail distribution

Management methods: Objective setting, staffing patterns, team definitions, feedback loops, planning techniques, control methods, participation levels

The foregoing list is not exhaustive. Means issues with which staff members contend are endless. There are always far more issues than any board can keep up with, even if the board totally neglects its own job in order to do so. Keeping up with all these issues—much less providing leadership for them—is utterly impossible. The ideal of reviewing and approving everything is illusory. Yet the board must attend to its legitimate

interest in these matters, an interest that can be overlooked only with severe damage to the organization's concept of board accountability.

The board's challenge is to exercise oversight with respect to staff operations without obscuring role differences and without taking the staff off the hook for making decisions. The appropriate expression of the board's legitimate interest is not to make a staff issue into a board issue, but to curtail or confine the available staff choices to an acceptable range.

The Board's Stake in Staff Practices

The preceding partial list of executive means includes important aspects of corporate life. Such material in board mailings and meetings may be so impressive that it seems to capture the essence of the enterprise. No matter how important, how technically sophisticated, how impressively carried out, or how great the professional training of experts in the various areas, these items are means, not ends. They are not what organization is all about; they serve what organization is all about. And, for the most part, the degree to which they serve Ends well is the source of their value.

For the most part, but not totally. Boards have more than one interest in staff practices.

Effectiveness

By far, executive means are of importance to a board because of their effectiveness. Do they work? That is the primary test and the only justification for having means. The major measure of means is to look not at the means but at what they were intended to produce. Means are assessed best by focusing on Ends. In fact, the greatest impediment to measuring the effectiveness of means is to look at the means themselves.

In this area, nonprofit and public administrative practice is prone to a monumental flaw. People inspect means through site visits, certifications, and agency evaluations, but there is very little inspection of results. Rewards are handed out on the basis of the means' purported excellence rather than attainment of results. Organizational means come to have a life and momentum of their own, driven by the overpowering tendency to assess them apart from their ability to produce results. Perhaps this source of managerial perversity should not surprise us. Individuals and particularly disciplines or professions are heavily invested in—and, in large part, formed around—distinctive methods or practices.

So if a board is willing to make judgments about means based primarily on attainment of ends ("effectiveness"), then this largest single concern about executive means can be laid aside. I dealt with it in Chapter Four, and the board deals with it by measuring how well the organization performs with respect to the board's Ends policies.

Approvability

Granting that the board discharges its central legitimate interest in executive means by assessing Ends, we must now deal with the fuzzy concept of approvability. Most boards would be unwilling to rest with mere effectiveness as the only test, but would require that, apart from effectiveness, executive means be carried out in an *approvable manner*.

What is meant by an approvable staff activity or plan? By observing boards proceeding through a traditional approval process, we note three phenomena. First, as a body the board is not quite sure what *"approvability"* means. Consequently, boards tend to go through the motions. Different board members question different items, usually against idiosyncratic criteria. Sometimes, they question effectiveness, but are likely to fall back into the trap of trying to judge effectiveness by closely inspecting the means. A telling test is for a board to ask itself what it would *disapprove*. If a board does not know what it would disapprove, its approval is a process without direction and, at worst, a sham.

Second, board members may equate "approvability" with the question "Would I do it this way?" When an approval is rendered from this point of view, the real chief executive finds that there are a number of would-be executives to

contend with. Board members sometimes see it as their prerogative to play part-time CEO. This phenomenon leads a politically inclined CEO to manipulate documents so as to satisfy the various board member interests. Such maneuvering is not without cost. Ends suffer a loss of primacy, and the staff's selection of means is less true to its own best judgment.

Third, board members want to ensure that staff means—however effective in reaching prescribed ends—are prudent and ethical. And to the extent that inspection and approval of executive means fulfill this board interest, they are justifiable.

Legitimate Control of Means

To summarize the foregoing points: (1) effectiveness requires no inspection of means and, in fact, is best measured by intentionally not looking at means; (2) a simple preference that means be arranged or selected in a certain way is an indulgence the board may want to allow itself, but one that reduces the integrity of management; and (3) boards cannot ensure prudence and ethics by measuring the attainment of Ends—but unlike mere preference, the board has a moral obligation to ensure the prudence and ethics of operations.

Consequently, the only legitimate, direct interest a governing board need have in how the staff conducts its business is that all is prudent and ethical. Stated more pointedly, *apart from being prudent and ethical, the activities that go on at and below the level of chief executive are completely immaterial*. The board need only involve itself in executive means to determine that acceptable standards of prudence and ethics are being met. This can save much board time, as well as a great deal of executive frustration. And it becomes clear what the board, in its best moments, was approving or disapproving.

Control Through Proactive Constraint

Most means are justified by the ends because producing results is what justifies means. Some means, however, are not justifiable regardless of how effective they are. If this were not so, a board would not need to test anything about executive means except their effectiveness. Focusing on which means are *not* approvable, rather than on those that are, simplifies the task and makes it less onerous on management as well.

A board that wishes to ensure that the organization's actions are prudent and ethical must delineate *ahead of time* exactly what is imprudent and unethical. Any staff action that does not violate the board's standards, then, is automatically approvable. Note that the board's standards are negative or limiting rather than positive or prescriptive. The board has neither the time nor the expertise to state everything that should be done. It does have the sense of values necessary to recognize what should not be done. The principle is simple and, perhaps more than any other principle, enables excellence in governing.

Although the board speaks to Ends prescriptively, with *regard to executive means the board should remain silent except to state clearly what it will not put up with.*

A small number of policies can enunciate the board's values with respect to minimum levels of prudence and ethics. The board can govern the vast array of executive means through policy, not through direct involvement in staff activities. The category of policies that limits or constrains executive authority is called Executive Limitations.

The total message the board sends to staff, then, consists of what outputs are to be achieved (Ends) and what may not be done in the process of achievement (Executive Limitations). Board thought is proactive and general rather than reactive and specific. Such a policy saves the board from making countless separate decisions in the future.

Despite the breakthrough in board effectiveness that this approach makes possible, some board members find it difficult to place limits on staff means. As persons and as governors, they desire to be positive rather than negative. Such a motivation is commendable, but it overlooks an irony of downward communication in an organization.

The most positive approach a board can take toward its subordinates' means is verbally nega-

tive. Conversely, the most negative approach is prescriptive and positive. Telling a subordinate how to do a task automatically eliminates all other methods. Telling a subordinate how not to do it leaves open all other possible methods. Better supervision leaves as much freedom as possible.

No one can presume to know ahead of time all the innovative combinations of means. No one can divine all the possible ways to improve tasks, systems, structures, and relationships. In the best of enterprises, leaders "define the boundaries, and their people figure out the best way to do the job within those boundaries" (Waterman, 1988, p. 7).

Board prescription of means is a stultifying and anti-innovative process of control. This would be true even if a board were available full-time and were fully versed in all organizational areas of expertise. But boards are available to render decisions only a few hours per year and do not have knowledge of every part of organizational life. The common, albeit incomplete, prescription of means not only produces an untenable amount of work for the board but unduly hampers staff effectiveness. Such board positiveness is a serious cause of lost staff potential. Given the availability of a more effective alternative, it is completely unnecessary as well.

There is a subtler way in which a board does the same damage without directly prescribing executive means: it retains approval authority over staff plans. When staff must bring specific decisions to the board for approval (for example, of annual budgets and compensation changes), the board implies that only the staff actions it approves are legitimate. Although staff members generate the board-approved actions, the board empowers them. For staff, means that have board approval, regardless of their origin, are frozen in place until the board has time and sees fit to approve changes. The effect on management is only a little better than if the board had generated the means prescription itself. Consequently, board approvals, even of staff-submitted documents, constitute unnecessary interference with the CEO's staff delegation system and decision flow.

Consider the alternative of being minimal but "negative" in dealing with staff means. *Ignoring* staff means, except to prohibit them with explicit policies, frees both board and staff. The board is free of the endless details of staff work and can do its own job. As long as the board-stated Ends are accomplished and the board-stated Executive Limitations are not violated, staff action is by definition supported by the board.

Using this approach, the board is proactive. Approval of staff documents is reactive. Further, approval is a practice in which the board is always "one down"; it can never know quite as much about the details of staff action and planning as the staff itself. Moreover, by being proactive, the board can be more confident that it has dealt with the issues of prudence and ethics. As painstaking as many approval processes might be, they ordinarily focus on the acceptability of *specific* actions or documents rather than on the underlying values that form the basis for board decisions on those actions and documents. Consequently, after the board approves specific actions or documents, its *policy* remains unstated. Another payoff, more important than it seems, is reducing the board's burden of paperwork. The board can then invest the bulk of its leadership in determining expected results rather than in helping staff be staff.

Policies to Limit Staff Action

The task, then, with respect to board oversight of staff means is to create a workable set of policies that constrain or limit executive latitude. In this section, I first review the necessity of saying what seems unnecessary to say, even at the broadest and most obvious level, in a negative or limiting fashion. Second, I argue that broad policies should grow out of the *board's*, not the staff's, values and perspectives. Last, I consider the board's worry areas as a natural origin of these Executive Limitations policies.

As with all policy control, proper governance lies an uncomfortable arm's length from the action for some board members. "Being relegated to a position of *simply* setting policies," comments the Rev. Lyon, "seems like a less important job to them." There may be discomfort, but not

difficulty, because it is not hard to write policies that safely allow board withdrawal from the prescriptive details of staff means. Doing so does require close attention to the few simple rules proposed here for policy development. For example, we must start with the largest, most inclusive level before moving on to lesser levels.

Remember that the intent of the Executive Limitations category of policies is to prohibit staff practices that the board regards as imprudent or unethical. Note that preventing imprudent and unethical behavior is the board's *sole* aim in setting these policies. Note further that the wording here is negative. We could as easily say positively that the board is trying to ensure that behavior is prudent and ethical. The meaning is the same; however, because boards face the almost irresistible temptation to slip back into prescribing staff means, they are wise to maintain a proscriptive demeanor throughout, even when it seems pedantic to do so. Establishing the limiting approach at this basic level ensures a board's ability to maintain that discipline in more complex issues.

The board's first and broadest staff means policy position is a simple constraint on executive authority: "The chief executive may neither cause nor allow any organizational practice that is imprudent or unethical." This sentiment is so obvious. Why should the board have to dignify it as policy? There are two reasons for beginning at such a simple level. First, this position is the source from which all further constraints spring. It is the beginning. As further policies are built on this foundation, it becomes increasingly important to maintain simplicity or, at least, clear connections with simplicity. In addition, as we must learn again and again, organizations attain excellence by doing the simple things well.

Second, approaching constraints from the broadest perspective, regardless of how simplistic this appears, ensures that the board can never, through oversight, leave a policy vacuum. Although the "backup" policy may be broader than the board would like (allowing more room for interpretation), it is impossible for an issue not to be covered by board policy at some level. If the extent of reasonable latitude under a constraint of "imprudence" is greater than the board desires, then it needs to create further policy. But at no time will there be a lack of policy. In organizations where this principle of logical containment is not followed, executives or boards continually find issues not covered by board policy. Consequently, forceful staff action can be bottlenecked or staff members may take an unnecessary risk or miss an opportunity while the policy hole is being plugged.

Optimal policymaking produces neither a long list of disjointed pieces nor a mere restatement of approved staff documents. It produces a *fabric of values* that, no matter how thin, effectively blankets all possibilities. Creating this fabric with respect to executive means must begin with the broadest proscription. Without this broad statement there is no all-inclusive point of departure for further, more detailed explicit board constraints.

The most effective move a CEO can make is to inform the board of the unspoken constraint he or she is assuming and to ask for confirmation. If the CEO asks about the broadest level instead of a specific application, the board creates policy by answering the question. It is simpler to begin from that point, rather than to have the process depend on the CEO's motivation and integrity, not to mention luck.

Making Board Policies the Board's Policies

For integrity of governance, the board must generate policies from board values, not parrot them from staff wishes. A side effect of traditional patchwork policymaking is that the staff members repeatedly ask the board for approvals. As the staff members obviously know what they need, boards ordinarily issue approvals after a cursory review. Even a detailed review would not change the fact that the board is passing policy without the board's needing it. In the governance design presented here, the board adopts only policies for which its values dictate a need. Board policies are not passed to please staff, even the CEO. The CEO is already empowered to adopt policies, as long as they are consistent with the board's policies. The CEO is unlikely to request that the board restrict executive latitude

further. As he or she is already empowered to make such choices, it would be clear that the CEO is merely using the board to avoid making a decision.

Despite the churning commotion of implementation, a board's ethics and prudence standards remain constant. The board's standards written into policy serve as an anchor for all staff action. There is room for staff to move around when tossed about in stormy weather, but there is not so much room that staff loses its bearings or strays from what the organization holds itself to be. Like an anchor, good policymaking is not complicated; its simplicity is why it works. Staff must be given a free hand to do what they know how to do, but should not be stranded by the board's failure to define boundaries.

Boards can provide this leadership only if they are not subjected to the same short-term pressures. If the board is tossed in the same stormy seas as the staff, it will have difficulty seeing past the next wave, much less to the horizon. The stability of a relaxed governance arena allows the board to ride above the fray fairly unperturbed. The board saves its energy for the more contemplative struggle about underlying values. A board that is more hurried than contemplative has probably fallen into staff-level issues and ceased to govern.

Having prohibited only "unethical and imprudent" behavior, the board may worry that its brush has been a little too broad. Any staff practice that fits within a reasonable interpretation of this range must be considered acceptable. A "reasonable" range is that determined by the board to be a prudent person's reading of the policy. If the majority of board members feel that practices that pass the "reasonable person" test are not acceptable, then the constraint on staff activity must be further defined and narrowed. As might be surmised, I have never found a board that did not wish to constrict the acceptable latitude further.

Transforming Worries into Policies

The broadest constraint (no imprudent and unethical behavior) applies without differentiation to all areas of organizational activity. When building policy beyond this general proscription, the board will doubtless apply its caution more to some subjects than to others. That is why moving to the next lower level takes the form of addressing specific aspects of the organization. Thus, policy not only drops to a lower level, but begins to differentiate among organizational topics.

Subjects differentiated for further constraint could be seen as specific "worry areas." The most common worry areas in which policy is then written, to define unethical and imprudent behavior further, involve financial condition, personnel, compensation, asset protection, and budgeting. Addressing each of these subjects (1) affords board members the opportunity to agree on what is unacceptable; (2) sends the executive a clear message about what must be avoided, an explicitness that most executives find refreshing albeit less manipulable; (3) enables the board to streamline future monitoring because it has established criteria against which to measure performance; and (4) enables the board to codify its anxieties and, consequently, to relax.

In conceiving these policies, the board should not constrain its thinking with *current* worries. A board should create Executive Limitations policies that cover the entire range of unpalatable circumstances. What a board would find unpalatable is not a function of recent agency problems, even though heightened sensitivity to one or another condition might be.

Listening to worries voiced by board members helps the board establish Executive Limitations policies specific to the organization. One member of an Arizona board wondered aloud how disruptive it would be if the CEO were to be unexpectedly lost. The others were persuaded that this was a legitimate board worry. Converting that worry into an Executive Limitations policy resulted in immediate relaxation about the problem. The board adopted a policy requiring that the CEO never have fewer than two senior staff substantially familiar with board and executive officer activities. The majority of the board members felt that this policy provided all the emergency preparedness needed. The policy fit their values, precluded further worry, and was stated in two sentences.

It is important that policies represent the values of the board that establishes them. Policies are not chosen from a catalogue, issued by an agency of government, enunciated by staff, derived by consultants, or taken from books. Policies are personal for the board.

Typical Executive Limitations Topics

Because Executive Limitations policies spring from a board's sense of prudence and ethics, they are more likely than other categories of policy to resemble the policies of other boards using this model. Prudence and ethics are relatively common across boards, more so than Ends. Note these few, common Executive Limitations policy titles.

Vendor relations	A "floor" for their fair treatment
Treatment of parents	Minimum standards for interactions with parents of students
Asset protection	Unacceptable risk and treatment of fixed and liquid assets
Indebtedness	Limits on circumstances in which the executive could allow the organization to incur debt
Financial condition	Conditions of fiscal jeopardy to be avoided
Budgeting	Characteristics unacceptable in any budget
Funded depreciation	Limits on amounts and conditions under which the executive can spend money from the funded depreciation reserve
Growth	Limit on the amount of growth that can occur from one fiscal year to the next, regardless of the availability of funds
Compensation and benefits	Characteristics not tolerated in any wage and salary plan

All Executive Limitations policies are messages from the board to its CEO. They are *not* messages from the board to staff, for the CEO is the only staff member to whom the board gives directions. Further, the policies do not give the CEO power to do this or that. They take power or latitude away ("You may not . . ."). The CEO has whatever power the board does not withhold: "Go till we say stop" rather than "Stop till we say go."

To illustrate three Executive Limitations areas, let us look at board concerns with respect to financial management and personnel administration. The financial concern is traditionally expressed in two ways: monthly reports on the actual financial condition and annual inspection of budget. The personnel concern traditionally manifests as approval of personnel "policies."

Financial Condition Policy

Boards put great stock in monthly or quarterly financial reports. Yet a substantial number of board members do not understand these reports. Even in boards comprising persons competent at analyzing financial statements, it is uncommon for the board to know *as a body* what it finds unacceptable (Carver, 1991c, 1993b, 1996). This gives the approval process questionable importance and repeatedly invites discussion about financial details. Actually, even if the standards were clear to everyone, "approval" of a financial report is simply an acknowledgment that the data exist, that the preceding month or quarter actually took place.

In converting to control by Executive Limitations policies, boards are usually unwilling to let the standard rest simply on avoiding imprudence. Some practices or conditions might not be imprudent in the general sense, but are outside what a given board is willing to countenance. To adopt a policy that further defines the acceptable boundaries of ongoing financial conditions, the board must discuss and debate those circumstances it finds unacceptable. Financial condition is a wavering phenomenon; most of its squiggles are of no consequence. Some aspects, however, are worrisome or even frightening.

Ordinarily, the top level within this policy is that the financial condition never result in fiscal jeopardy or disruption of programmatic integrity. Beneath this broad proscription, foremost among the several considerations is usually that spending never exceed revenues. If the agency has the ability to borrow funds or has reserves, the prohibition might be to limit the

amount of indebtedness or withdrawals from reserves. Or it might be to prohibit indebtedness or withdrawal except under specified conditions. Moreover, that an executive has not yet spent more than has been received might be a rather hollow datum if expenses have been put off and revenues rushed into the reporting period. Further, shifts of wealth hidden within the overall numbers may obscure important fiscal jeopardies such as a decreasing ratio of current assets to current liabilities. Fine-tuning the policy language can address these points and, at the same time, enhance the board's appreciation of the issues of fiscal jeopardy.

The board must discuss and understand these and related issues to create a financial condition policy. In the short run, as much value is derived from the new level of understanding as from the policy itself. A board can use expert counsel in producing such a policy, as long as the expert does not create the policy. The expert should help board members attain a more complete understanding. The understanding supplies data on which board members' values about risk, safety, conservatism, brinkmanship, and so forth can operate. The aggregated and debated board values create the policy. For most boards, the list of unacceptable conditions thus derived is more complete and more systematic than the items it would have routinely inspected using the standard approval method. Though more complete, the subsequent monitoring of financial statements (Carver, 1994b) requires far less time than many boards and finance committees traditionally spend.

Voyageur Outward Bound's policy limited its executive director (Figure 3.1) on criteria that the board felt to be conditions of jeopardy. The board felt it could accept any reasonable definition of "timely manner" in Criterion 7, though another board might need to restrict the range by using words such as "within the discount period or thirty days, whichever is earliest." Figures in Criterion 9 would be periodically amended.

Of course, an additional Executive Limitations policy specifically focused on investments per se would be needed by organizations dealing with a sizable endowment. A simple form useful even for boards with more modest reserves

---

FIGURE 3.1   Voyageur Outward Bound School Policy: "Financial Condition."

With respect to operating the School in a sound and prudent fiscal manner, the Executive Director may not jeopardize the long-term financial strength of the School. Accordingly, he or she may not:

1. Cause the School to incur indebtedness other than trade payables incurred in the ordinary course of doing business.
2. Use advances from the Cash Reserve Fund or the Building Fund other than for ordinary operating expenses.
3. Allow advances from the Building Fund to remain outstanding for more than 90 days.
4. Allow advances from the Cash Reserve Fund or the Building Fund to remain outstanding on the August 1 next following the advance.
5. Use earnings on the Scholarship Endowment Fund for any purpose other than scholarships.
6. Use restricted contributions for any purpose other than that required by the contribution.
7. Settle payroll and debts in other than a timely manner.
8. Allow expenditures to deviate materially from Board-stated priorities.
9. Allow the Cash Reserve Fund to fall below $90,000 in 1988, 6 percent of operating expenses in 1989, 7 percent in 1990, 8 percent in 1991, and 10 percent in 1992 and beyond.

SOURCE: Voyageur Outward Bound School.

---

might merely instruct that the CEO shall not "invest or hold operating capital in insecure investments, including uninsured checking accounts and bonds of less than AA rating, or in non-interest-bearing accounts except where necessary to facilitate ease in operational transactions." Having policy control over investments is normally better than having board members on an investment committee make investment decisions (Guy, 1992, 1995).

Budget Policy

A financial condition policy establishes the boundaries of an acceptable monthly or quarterly financial status. Boards can go further and establish those characteristics of financial *intentions* that would not be acceptable. Financial intentions or financial planning takes the form of a budget and often numerous budget adjustments during a year.

Most nonprofit and public boards consider the budget approval process sacrosanct. To suggest that board budget approval might not be a necessary element of fiscal stewardship runs against a firmly held belief, one so firm that some board members contend that no regularly occurring board activity is as important as budget approval. The reason given is that the board

must have control over the budget because of the board's fiduciary responsibility. In addition, some say that the budget is the most important "policy document" the board passes.

Both contentions are correct. The board must have control over that for which it is accountable. And the budget does, usually implicitly, represent much of what is important to an organization—its aims, its risks, its conservatism. Neither argument, however, dictates *how* a board should control a budget and the budget's policy implications. The starting questions for any board are: "What is it about the budget that we wish to control?" and "If we were never to see a budget, what specific conditions would we worry about?"

A budget concerns events that have not yet occurred. It is a plan. Like all plans, it makes suppositions, conveys intentions, and designs process or flow. It is a rather special plan inasmuch as it is denominated in money. Most budgets, moreover, are line-item budgets rather than program budgets or result-package budgets, so they illustrate some of the less salient aspects of creating the future. What is it that the board wishes to control?

To fine-tune its fiduciary responsibility, a board must decide which aspects of the budget to control. If the board has been checking these budgetary characteristics all along, jotting them down will take but a few moments. If the board finds it cannot do this readily, there is reason to question what the detailed budget approvals have been seeking.

Enlightenment is nearly inescapable when a board sets out to codify its worries about financial planning. What would worry board members about a budget? What would cause them not to approve a budget? The important features begin to stand out and the less important ones recede. The vast array of figures becomes less intimidating for nonfinancial people. Financial people are afforded the opportunity to connect their technical expertise with their wisdom. It is on the wisdom level that they meet the other board members; they are no longer strangers divided by a language barrier.

On this journey, the board gets serious about the meaning of fiduciary responsibility. This responsibility does not mean controlling the number of phone lines, but it does mean controlling the ability to pay the bills. It does not mean controlling out-of-state travel, but it does mean controlling the conservatism with which revenues are projected. Or are those issues the wrong ones? Debate ensues. Values about risk, brinkmanship, judiciousness, proportions of effort, and so forth begin to receive more attention than the mundane factors. And throughout, the process is disciplined by a progression from big questions to small ones, as it should be in all policy creation.

As in all other Executive Limitations policies, the message is directed to the CEO and is one of limitation, not empowerment. The CEO is already empowered by the "Go till we say stop" system of delegation. What he or she needs to know are the limits to power, the acceptable latitude in exercising it. The CEO must ponder these questions: "How liberal may I be in counting chickens prior to their hatching (projecting revenues)? How low may I let the current ratio slip to save programs? How much may I dip into reserves when pinched for cash? To what extent may I meet cash flow necessities by shifting money temporarily among special-purpose funds?" These and other value questions arise during financial planning, whether for next month or next year. Agile, empowered management can address these choices within board values far more effectively than a board can.

An additional bonus to the Executive Limitations approach is the policy's applicability to all financial planning, that is, the plans for next month and next year and all the replanning that occurs in the real world of constant change. An organization rarely has one budget for a year. As conditions shift and assumptions fail to pan out, it may have many. Every budget alteration made by the CEO, no matter how many, must meet the test of the board's budget policy. CEOs can respect the stability of this type of board leadership. The only fixed aspects of budgets, then, are the policies on which they are based and the certainty that specifics will be endlessly amended.

Most boards that I have helped through this process have had a hard time coming up with more than half a page of budgeting constraints. What message does this send? All those years of painstaking board budget approvals, not to mention finance committee time, resulted in half a page of unacceptable conditions. The approval process had always gone far beyond checking for unacceptable conditions. Having no policy that delineated the unacceptable conditions, the board foraged about wherever individual interests and fears directed them. Moreover, this painstaking scrutiny seldom resulted in material change to the submitted budgets and not infrequently overlooked dangerous conditions until it was almost too late.

Boards are accountable for budgets, but not more accountable than they are for what the organization accomplishes in actual results for people per dollar. Budgets are simply not the board's most important job. Determining what good is done for which people and at what cost is its most important job. Missing the mark with respect to Ends even by a small percentage costs the world far more than most budgetary errors. Gwendolyn Calvert Baker, executive director for the National Board of the YWCA, found that when you deal with financial planning this way, "The program drives your budget, your budget doesn't drive your program" (personal communication).

Personnel Policy

When boards are asked to show their policies, they invariably produce their personnel "policies." It is ironic that the one document in which the word *policy* is almost always misused is the most frequent example of board policy that comes to mind. The question for boards, beyond the broader ethics-prudence proscription, is: "What is it about dealings with personnel that we need to control?" The answer is anything that a reasonable person might consider ethical or prudent but that the board does not want to have happen.

The board of the Orchard Country Day School decided that secretive decision processes, which it found unacceptable, constituted mistreatment that might slip by as acceptable under the "Don't be unethical" rule. Another board decided the same about any prejudice toward an employee who had filed a grievance. Most boards have decided to omit references to sex, race, and age discrimination insofar as the law now covers these items. Violation of the law is so patently a case of imprudent behavior that no additional words need be wasted. But a board that believes that the law does not go far enough could increase the constraint beyond the law's protection.

The board does have a personnel policy under this model, but it is unlikely to be more than a page long. The previous board personnel manual becomes the property of the CEO, to change within the board constraints as he or she sees fit.

"Staff Treatment" is the title that the board of the Tennessee Managed Care Network chose to address the personnel issue (Figure 3.2). Because they were just dealing with the "don't" list, their only concern about personnel was that they not be subjected to "inhumane, unfair or undignified" situations, as further defined by Points 1 through 4.

Range of Executive Limitation Policies

In Executive Limitation policies, different boards have varying things to say, both in volume and in restrictiveness. One board may find another's policies too restrictive or irresponsibly loose. It is critical only that the CEO and board always know precisely what the marching orders are at any point in time.

Although most boards will face a number of policy topics, such as the three just discussed, the full list of policies will differ from board to board within the same type of organization and will certainly differ from one type of organization to another. An international development agency will have policies different from those of a family planning agency. Boards of county commissioners, library boards, chambers of commerce, and trade or professional associations will all differ, though they are subject to the same principles.

The Executive Limitations policies of People Services to the Developmentally Disabled (Figure 3.3) and the College of Medical Laboratory Technologists of Ontario (Figure 3.4) illustrate two very different types of constraints a board might impose. The first ensures that the board is sufficiently informed and supported to do its

---

FIGURE 3.2   Tennessee Managed Care Network Policy: "Staff Treatment."

With respect to treatment of paid and volunteer staff, the chief executive may not cause or allow conditions which are inhumane, unfair or undignified. Accordingly, he or she may not:

1. Discriminate among employees on other than clearly job-related, individual performance or qualifications.
2. Fail to take reasonable steps to protect staff from unsafe or unhealthy conditions.
3. Withhold from staff a due-process grievance procedure, able to be used without bias.
4. Fail to acquaint staff with their rights under this policy.

SOURCE: Tennessee Managed Care Network.

FIGURE 3.3   People Services to the Developmentally Disabled Policy: "Communication and Support to the Board."

With respect to providing information and counsel to the board, the CEO may not permit the board to be uninformed. Accordingly, he or she may not:

1. Neglect to submit monitoring data required by the board (see policy on Monitoring Executive Performance) in a timely, accurate and understandable fashion, directly addressing provisions of the board policies being monitored.
2. Let the board be unaware of relevant trends, anticipated negative media coverage, and material external and internal changes, particularly changes in assumptions upon which any board policy has previously been established.
3. Fail to advise the board if, in the CEO's opinion, the board is not in compliance with its own policies on Governance Process and Board-Staff Relationship, particularly in the case of board behavior which is detrimental to the work relationship between the board and the CEO.
4. Fail to marshal for the board as many staff and external points of view, issues and options as needed for fully informed board choices.
5. Present information in unnecessarily complex or lengthy form.
6. Fail to provide a mechanism for official board, officer, or committee communications.
7. Fail to deal with the board as a whole except when (a) fulfilling individual requests for information or (b) responding to officers or committees duly charged by the board.
8. Fail to report in a timely manner an actual or anticipated noncompliance with any policy of the board.

SOURCE: People Services to the Developmentally Disabled.

FIGURE 3.4   College of Medical Laboratory Technologists of Ontario Policy: "Asset Protection."

The Registrar shall not allow assets to be unprotected, inadequately maintained or unnecessarily risked. Accordingly, the Registrar shall not:

1. Fail to insure against theft and casualty losses to at least 80 percent replacement value and against liability losses to Council members, staff, or the organization itself in an amount greater than the average for comparable organizations.
2. Allow uninsured personnel to handle funds or College property or pledge credit of the College.
3. Subject plant and equipment to improper wear and tear or insufficient maintenance.
4. Unnecessarily expose the organization, its Council or staff to claims of liability.
5. Make any purchase or commit the organization to any expenditure of greater than $10,000. Make any purchase: (a) wherein normally prudent protection has not been given against conflict of interest; (b) of over $1,500 without having obtained comparative prices and quality; (c) of over $10,000 without an adequate review of ongoing costs, value and durability.
6. Fail to protect intellectual property, information and files from loss or significant damage or unauthorized duplication.
7. Receive, process or disburse funds under controls which are insufficient to meet the Council-appointed auditor's standards.
8. Invest or hold operating capital in insecure instruments, including uninsured checking accounts and bonds of less than AA rating, or in non-interest bearing accounts except where necessary to facilitate ease in operational transactions.
9. Acquire, encumber or dispose of real property. Endanger the organization's public image or credibility, particularly in ways that would hinder its accomplishment of mission.

SOURCE: College of Medical Laboratory Technologists of Ontario.

job. The second limits the asset risk that the board finds palatable.

In practice, most boards get by with fewer than ten Executive Limitations policies. These tend to average less than a page in length. But the vessel is adjustable to have as much restriction or freedom that a board feels is right. In the final analysis, however, boards must realize that no matter how narrow a policy is intended to be, there is still room for interpretation. The CEO's job is largely one of making those interpretations as he or she delegates to others. Unless the board itself wishes to do the organization's work, this will *always* be the case. Interpretation is so integral to the nature of management that one could describe managers' jobs as translation from one level of abstraction to another.

Consequently, it is never legitimate to complain that board policy with respect to the CEO and staff is fuzzy, open to interpretation, or too general. It is on that *degree of fuzziness*, interpretive range, and generality that board debate must turn. A board member who feels that certain policy language allows too great a range of interpretation is obligated to argue for language that narrows the range. The member only detracts from his or her good argument to complain, in effect, that policy should not allow any range. It is in studious management of the generalities that a board enhances both its contributions and those of staff.

Board and staff need as much freedom as possible to perform. The board is responsible for creating the future, not minding the shop. Chait and Taylor (1989) bemoaned boards' time being "frittered away on operations" (p. 45), mired in minutiae, and thus unavailable for policy and strategy. "Rather than do more, boards would be better advised to demand more" (p. 52). The staff needs freedom from the board's friendly intrusions to do its work. The board cheats the mission by constraining too much; it risks cheating standards of acceptable conduct by constraining too little. Proactively setting relatively few limits for the CEO increases the freedom of both the board and the CEO (Barth, 1992).

References

Barth, N. "Clear Policy Statements Can Free You to Act Creatively." *Board Leadership,* 1992, no. 1, p. 8.

Carver, J. "Redefining the Board's Role in Fiscal Planning." *Nonprofit Management and Leadership,* 1991c, 2(2), 177–192.

Carver, J. *Board Leadership: A Bimonthly Workshop with John Carver.* Special fiduciary issue, no. 6, 1993b.

Carver, J. "One Board Fails to Follow Its Own Monitoring Policy and Courts Fiscal Disaster." *Board Leadership,* 1994b, no. 14, pp. 3–5.

Carver, J. *Three Steps to Fiduciary Responsibility.* The CarverGuide Series on Effective Board Governance, no. 3. San Francisco: Jossey-Bass, 1996.

Chait, R. P., and Taylor, B. E. "Charting the Territory of Nonprofit Boards." *Harvard Business Review,* 1989, 129, 44–54.

Guy, J. "Good Investment Decisions Are Policy Driven." *Board Leadership,* 1992, no. 4, p. 8.

Waterman, R. H., Jr. *The Renewal Factor: How the Best Get and Keep the Competitive Edge.* New York: Bantam Books, 1988.

CHAPTER 4

Female Participation in Public Interest Nonprofit Governance

Yet Another Glass Ceiling?

RONALD G. SHAIKO

The recent publication of *Women and Power in the Nonprofit Sector* sheds new and important light on the increasingly controversial topic of women's roles in the nonprofit sector by providing new evidence of the changing roles of women and by raising important research questions yet to be addressed in the literature (Odendahl & O'Neill, 1994). One research controversy lies in the explanation of the disjunction between levels of female representation in the staffing and governance of nonprofit organizations.

On the one hand, the nonprofit sector workforce is disproportionately composed of women. Currently 75% of the nonprofit labor force is female compared to 50% of the total workforce (Preston, 1990, 1994). Further, 50% of the women in the nonprofit sector occupy professional/managerial positions compared to 21% in the government public sector and less than 10% in the for-profit sector (Shackett & Trapani, 1987). And, although nonprofit salaries lag behind those provided in the for-profit sector, women's salaries in the nonprofit sector have improved vis-à-vis men's salaries and are comparatively more equal, even if absolute pay equity has not been attained (Preston, 1994; Steinberg & Jacobs, 1994). On the other hand, the few empirical studies focused on the governance of nonprofit entities present consistent evidence of male domination of nonprofit leadership positions such as executive directorships and board memberships (see, e.g., Odendahl & Youmans, 1994, and Middleton, 1987).[1] The empirical analysis presented in this article seeks to address the disparity in the roles of women in the staffing and governance of nonprofit organizations by focusing on the more politically attentive component of the nonprofit sector: public interest nonprofit organizations.

Much of the empirical research on the roles of women in nonprofit governance has focused on the composition of boards of foundations (Gittell, 1990), hospitals, art museums, and federated charities and libraries (see Abzug, DiMaggio, Gray, Kang, & Useem, 1992; Baughman, 1987, also analyzes university boards, as does Capek, 1988). In addition, there are numerous studies that focus on local volunteer civic associations (see, e.g., Daniels, 1988; Jenner, 1982; Loeser & Falon, 1978) and other community-based social agencies (Babchuk, Marsey, & Gordon, 1960; Ostrander, 1987; Widmer, 1991). What sets this analysis apart from much of the earlier research on women in nonprofit governance is that it focuses on 501(c)(3) and 501(c)(4) nonprofits that attempt to influence the governmental policymaking process, largely at the national level in Washington, DC. Political scientists identify such organizations as "public interest groups" (see Berry, 1977, and McFarland, 1976, for classic treatments). Berry (1977) defines a public interest group as an organization "that seeks a collective good, the achievement of which will not selectively or materially benefit the membership or activists of the organization" (p. 7).

Many of the organizations included in this analysis will be familiar to readers of this journal. Some of the prominent public interest nonprofit organizations to be analyzed are the American Civil Liberties Union, American Conservative Union, American Jewish Congress, Children's Defense Fund, Common Cause, Eagle Forum, Environmental Defense Fund, Handgun Control, Inc., Mothers Against Drunk Driving, National Association for the Advancement of Colored People, National Council of Senior Citizens, National Rifle Association, Public Citizen, Urban Institute, and Women's Legal Defense Fund.

Organizational data for these groups and more than 200 additional public interest nonprofit organizations are made available by the Foundation for Public Affairs in a published compendium, *Public Interest Profiles* (Bergner, 1986). The organizational data for each group is based on characteristics and attributes present in 1985. From its files of more than 2,500 public interest nonprofit organizations, the foundation selected 250 organizations for inclusion in *Public Interest Profiles* based on the following criteria: (a) the extent of the group's influence on national policy, (b) the number of requests received for information on the group, (c) the range and quantity of news coverage generated

by the group, and (d) the representative nature of the group in its field of interest (p. iii).

The organizations selected by the Foundation for Public Affairs provide a representative sampling of nonprofit organizations active in public interest advocacy in 1985.

The analysis that follows is divided into two substantive sections, focusing on women's roles as executive directors of public interest organizations and as organizational board members. In the first section, four organizational characteristics are analyzed to discern any structural biases in the selection of executive directors. In addition, individual-level characteristics and attributes of executive directors are presented and discussed. In the second section, the characteristics and attributes of board members of public interest nonprofits are analyzed. The representation and roles of women as board members are presented and analyzed, followed by a concluding discussion of the findings.

Women at the Helm: Female Executive Directors in the Public Interest Nonprofit Sector

Organizations in the public interest nonprofit sector are disproportionately staffed by women (Shaiko, 1989). Consequently, women in the public interest sector face somewhat better prospects for advancement than they do in government entities or in private industry for several reasons. First, the public interest sector is a relatively new nonprofit industry. With the rapid growth of the early to mid-1970s and the continued growth today, opportunities for employment in positions of significant policy importance are comparatively broad (Berry, 1989; Walker, 1991). Second, as with other political industries (e.g., congressional staffing), turnover rates are fairly high, thereby allowing for significant advancements in relatively short time periods (Fox & Hammond, 1977; Malbin, 1980). Third, given the relative lack of organizational wealth among the majority of public interest organizations, men and women in search of entry into the public interest sector are paid equally low wages (Steinberg & Jacobs, 1994). Women in such organizations may be more likely to persevere, have greater commitment, and hence remain involved long enough to climb the organizational ladder.

Getting to the top, however, is another matter. Effective executive leadership in the public interest sector and, more generally, in the nonprofit sector requires that individuals holding such positions possess a number of specialized attributes (Herman & Heimovics, 1991). Analyzing executive leadership in nonprofit organizations, Young (1987) concludes that "the appropriate model for the non-profit executive is not the political wheeler-dealer, the capitalist venturer and marketer, the disciplined technical manager, or the master of interpersonal relations—but a special mix of all these things" (p. 177).

Finding individuals with this "special mix" of political entrepreneurialism and management ability is a difficult task. Most often, the task of hiring executive directors involves casting out one's search net as widely as possible. As is the practice in the larger nonprofit sector, the hiring of a new executive director often involves going outside of the organization. Search committees of public interest organizations, in particular, find previous (high-level) federal government experience related to their policy concerns to be an important attribute (Shaiko, 1989). This qualification presents a serious barrier for women. There is ample evidence to demonstrate the significant disparity between the number of men and women who occupy political appointive positions in the federal executive branch (Campbell, 1986; Heclo, 1977; Macey, Adams, & Walter, 1983; Martin, 1989; Pfiffner, 1994) and among employees in the federal civil service (Lewis, 1987; Naff, 1994). Therefore, if membership in the administrative elite is one of the important requisites for attainment of a public interest leadership position, then the existing talent pools skew the potential candidate lists significantly in favor of male candidates.

Women, however, are able to circumvent the government experience barrier by building strong credentials in the area of public interest advocacy. Although there are a few instances in

which women have emerged from previous public interest and high-level government service to direct large public interest organizations (e.g., Joan Claybrook, former administrator of the National Highway Traffic Safety Administration under President Carter, now heads Public Citizen), most female directors have developed their expertise through exclusive experience within the public interest sector. Of the 240 groups analyzed, approximately 20% are directed by women. Not surprisingly, a far greater percentage of male directors come to their jobs with significant federal government experience. Conversely, three quarters of the female directors have previous public interest nonprofit experience, whereas only half of their male counterparts have any training in public interest advocacy.

Another possible avenue leading to executive directorship in the public interest sector is through the private sector. As executive directors are normally the chief administrators of the organizations, management skills learned in the private sector are becoming increasingly useful in professionalized public interest organizations. Accordingly, approximately one quarter of the male directors have neither federal government nor public interest experience but rather are trained in corporate management. Approximately one fifth of the female directors are included in this category.

As mentioned earlier, approximately 20% of the public interest organizations in the sample are directed by women. There is some variation, however, within the public interest nonprofit sector regarding the selection of female directors. Table 4.1 offers evidence of this variation by organizational mission. Obviously, certain types of organizations are less receptive to women as leaders than are others. Think tanks and business/economic-related public interest organizations in the sample have no female directors. Conversely, almost half of the consumer/health groups are directed by women.

The organizational types presented in Table 4.1 offer some insight into the differences in receptiveness of women as executive directors. It is necessary to identify the similarities and differences between the organizations in these classifi-

TABLE 4.1 Female Directorships, by Organizational Type (percentage)

Type of Public Interest Organization	Percentage of Female Directors
Business/economic	0.0 (13)
Think tanks	0.0 (22)
Environmental	7.1 (28)[a]
International affairs	13.6 (22)
Public interest law	18.8 (16)
Media	22.2 (9)
Religious	22.2 (9)[a]
Community/grassroots	22.7 (20)[a]
Civil/constitutional rights	27.3 (33)
Corporate accountability/ responsibility	27.8 (18)
Political/governmental process	28.1 (32)
Consumer/health	44.4 (18)
Mean	19.2 ($N = 240$)

NOTE: *ns* are in parentheses.

[a] Category includes one organization with male and female codirectors.

cations. What characteristics, for example, do the business/economic groups, think tanks, environmental groups, international affairs organizations, and public interest law firms have in common that would lead them to shy away from hiring women as their organization leaders? Conversely, what characteristics do the other organizations exhibit that make them more receptive to women as directors?

There are at least four organizational/structural attributes that may help explain some of the variation in these relationships: (a) size of the organization budget, (b) age of the organization, (c) geographic location of the organization, and (d) percentage of female board members in the organization. First, if there exists a male bias in the governance of public interest organizations, then one might manifest itself in the form of differential access to the most powerful positions in each of the substantive public interest arenas. Women may be given (have earned) positions of leadership power in the less visible, less powerful organizations, whereas their male counterparts direct the showcase organizations (McPherson & Smith-Lovin, 1982, 1986).

Proposition 1: The wealthier the organization, the greater the likelihood of the organization being managed by a male executive director.

Table 4.2 provides some evidence in support of this proposition. Organizations with annual budgets of less than $1 million are much more likely to have female directors than are the larger organizations with multimillion-dollar budgets.

Related to the possible male bias in the more wealthy public interest organizations, there may also exist a bias regarding the longevity of these groups.

Proposition 2: The older the organization, the more likely the executive director is to be male.

This will be particularly evident in organizations formed prior to the massive mobilizations of the late 1960s and early 1970s. Location as well may have some impact on the probability of women holding executive directorships. The public interest nonprofit sector has been drawn disproportionately toward our nation's capital. Almost two thirds of the sample organizations have headquarters in Washington, with more than 85% located in the Northeast Corridor between Boston and the nation's capital. Given this concentration, one might plausibly argue that there are more opportunities for women in Washington than there are elsewhere. This may be true; however, the competition for these positions is

TABLE 4.2 Directorships, by Annual Budgets (percentages except *ns*)

Annual Budgets (1985)	Executive Directors		
	Female	Male	n
Under $500,000	26.9	73.1	52
$500,000–$999,999	38.1	61.9	42
$1,000,000–$1,999,999	14.6	85.4	41
$2,000,000–$4,999,999	7.5	92.5	40
$5,000,000 or over	6.3	93.7	48
N			223
Chi-square	21.13*		
	(4 *df*)		

*Significant at .001 level.

much greater than it is outside of the Washington area.

> Proposition 3: Organizations with headquarters in Washington are more likely to be directed by males than are organizations located outside of Washington.

Finally, boards of directors usually play an important role in the selection of executive directors. If the earlier male bias infiltrates the governing boards as well, then the chances of selecting female directors are equally diminished.

> Proposition 4: The smaller the percentage of women serving on governing boards, the more likely males will serve as executive directors.

Table 4.3 offers evidence of the influence of female board members on the selection of female leaders. One fifth of the sample organizations have no female board members; not coincidentally, all of these organizations are directed by men. In looking at the organizations with overwhelming majorities of women board members (listed in Table 4.3), one finds that these groups have significant female membership bases. When one removes from the analysis the seven organizations identified in Table 4.3, the mean percent-

age of female board members falls below 20%, almost exactly the percentage of female executive directors in the sample of organizations.

To test the four propositions outlined in the preceding, logistic regression analysis is used.

Given the findings presented in Tables 4.2 and 4.3, one should not be surprised by the significant relationships between the dependent variable and the Budget and Board variables. Organizations with budgets greater than $1 million are more likely to have male directors. Similarly, as the percentage of women sitting on governing boards increases, the likelihood of appointing a female leader increases as well. Age of organization also affects the likelihood of having a female executive director. Organizations established more than 20 years ago are more likely to have male directors than are those formed more recently. Finally, the location of organizations in Washington tends to bias the choice of an executive director toward men.[2]

Overall, each of these four organizational attributes has a significant effect on the selection of executive directors of public interest organizations, with each providing evidence of a male bias. Obviously, other factors affect the selection of an executive director, including those candidate qualifications mentioned earlier: federal government experience, public interest experience, and management skills. Federal govern-

TABLE 4.3   Board Positions Occupied by Women Executive Directors

Female Board Members	Percentage of Organizations	Percentage of Executive Directors	
		Female	Male
0%	21.1 (38)	0.0	100.0
1%–20%	32.2 (58)	15.6	84.4
21%–40%	30.6 (55)	21.8	78.2
41%–60%	9.4 (17)	35.3	64.7
61%–80%	2.8 (5)	60.0	40.0
81%–100%[a]	3.9 (7)	85.7	14.3
Mean	22.7 (N = 180)		
Chi-square		36.72*	
		(5 df)	

NOTE: *ns* are in parentheses.

*Significant at .001 level.

[a] Organizations with more than 80% female representation on boards include the Gray Panthers, National Abortion Rights Action League, Women's Equity Action League, Women's Legal Defense Fund, Eagle Forum, League of Women Voters, and National Women's Political Caucus.

TABLE 4.4   Logistic Regression Analysis

	Dependent Variable = Director (1 = male, 0 = female)
Intercept	−0.827
	(0.551)
Budget	2.357**
	(0.580)
Age	1.225*
	(0.534)
Location	1.229*
	(0.502)
Board	2.169**
	(0.515)
Gamma	.773
Chi-square	44.52**
R^2	.261 (N = 160)

NOTE: Standard errors are in parentheses. Budget = 1985 organizational budget (1 = budget ≥ $1 million, 0 = budget < $1 million); Age = age of organization (1 = organizational in existence for more than 20 years, 0 = organization in existence for 20 years or less); Location = headquarters of organizations outside the Washington, D.C. area; Board = percentage of female board members (1 = board with less than 25% female representation, 0 = board with 25% or greater female representation).

*Significant at .05 level.
**Significant at .001 level.

ment experience and management skills attributes tend to support a consistent male bias. Nonetheless, from an organizational perspective, the four structural attributes identified in Table 4.4 provide significant indications of the institutional barriers women face in rising to the top in the public interest sector.

Women on Board: Female Board Members in the Public Interest Nonprofit Sector

Governing boards of public interest organizations are vital linkages between rank-and-file memberships and the leadership staffs. Whether selected directly by memberships or solicited through an appointive selection process, governing boards act as representative checks on the wills of potentially dominating staffs. William Turnage, past president of the Wilderness Soci-

ety, accurately articulates the duties and responsibilities of governing boards:

> The [governing board's] role is in some ways ambidextrous. On the one hand they need to be the conscience, the repository of the history and traditions, the guardians of the long-term philosophical integrity of the organization, and on the other hand their role is to be supportive in every sense of the word, to help the active full-time staff in a myriad of ways without, at the same time, taking over the organization. (quoted in Watkins & Turnage, 1985, p. 46)

As both guardians of the public interest and supporters of staff endeavors, boards of directors must be particularly suited to represent both the wishes of members and the needs of staff. To do so, the boards should themselves be at least somewhat representative of the particular sector of society they are "acting for" (Pitkin, 1967). In an effort to formulate "representative" boards, virtually all nonprofit organizations adhere to some set of rules, whether informal and unwritten or through strict guidelines and recruitment criteria, regarding the balance maintained on boards.

There is much variation in the composition of governing boards (Fletcher, 1992; Hall & Abzug, 1995; Houle, 1989). Some organization boards are tenured for life (or for as long as each particular member wishes to serve). These boards, therefore, have much lower annual turnover rates. Other groups allow board members to serve for fixed terms. Accordingly, the replacement of board membership in these organizations is an ongoing process. Through extensive interviewing of public interest nonprofit board members, the author has discerned a set of criteria that influence the recruitment efforts of public interest governing boards.[3]

Those organizations that "elect" their boards by offering a slate of candidates to their memberships maintain qualitatively different boards as a result. Candidates, in some instances, are rewarded for time well served by being placed on the ballot. Consequently, boards comprise members who have worked their way up the organizational ladder, beginning at the local level and

TABLE 4.5 Percentages of Female Board Members,
by Organizational Type

Type of Public Interest Organization	Percentage of Female Board Members
Business/economic	5.5 (11)
Public interest law	14.2 (15)
Think tanks	15.4 (21)
International affairs	16.2 (13)
Religious	19.2 (5)
Environmental	19.9 (20)
Corporate accountability	20.4 (14)
Media	22.0 (9)
Political/governmental process	22.0 (25)
Consumer/health	30.2 (13)
Community/grassroots	36.1 (17)
Civil/constitutional rights	47.4 (17)
Mean	22.7 ($N = 180$)

NOTE: *ns* are in parentheses.

ending with election to the national boards. Not surprisingly, public interest nonprofit organizations that elect their boards have organizational infrastructures that reach beyond the national headquarters. Table 4.5 provides some indication of the variation in female board membership, by organizational mission.

In comparison to female board membership among Fortune 1000 companies, public interest nonprofits have far greater female representation. As shown in Table 4.3, 79.9% of the public interest organizations have at least one woman on their boards; conversely, only 52.6% of Fortune 1000 companies have any female board membership, according to a 1993 census of female board members conducted by Catalyst, Inc. The study also found that on many of the Fortune 1000 boards with female representation, only one female board member was identified. As a result, only 6% of the more than 11,000 board positions are occupied by women compared to 22.7% of the public interest board positions, as identified in Table 4.5 (Tifft & Bamford, 1994).

Despite the disparities in the representation of women of corporate boards and public interest boards, the recruitment efforts of appointed boards in each sector are not totally dissimilar. The priorities set forth in establishing potential candidate pools, however, are often quite differ-

ent. Nonetheless, it is clear that concerted efforts are made to achieve a certain "balance" on these panels. Balance is achieved by implicitly designating various board seats for certain governing roles. Potential candidates for governing boards are judged on their abilities to offer one or more of the following skills or attributes to enhance the strength and balance of the boards: (a) managerial skills, (b) policy/issue expertise, (c) constituency representation, (d) financial input, (e) political connections, and (f) celebrity status (Drucker, 1990; Fletcher, 1992; Houle, 1989; Middleton, 1987; Stone, 1991).

As organizational budgets have grown tighter in the nonprofit sector in recent years, many organizations are explicitly including financial input as a necessary condition for board service. According to Elizabeth Dole, president of the American Red Cross: "In this new day of board responsibility, the board is called upon to give both the time and the money. No longer is it 'either-or.' Today, it's 'and.' They must do both" (Dole, 1992, p. 30).

In addition to the aforementioned substantive criteria, boards look for demographic representation as well—a much tougher task. In many instances, there is a built-in inertia in the recruitment efforts of boards of public interest organizations. Although a growing number of boards have resorted to hiring "head-hunting" firms to acquire new board members, the most prevalent means of filling vacancies on appointed boards is to have existing board members attempt to cajole social acquaintances, business associates, and various others with whom members come in contact in their daily lives. As a result, one finds significant social inbreeding on these boards (Middleton, 1987, p. 148; for efforts to overcome this problem, see Whitt & Moore, 1995).

David Challinor, assistant secretary for science at the Smithsonian Institution and board member on several of the public interest organizations analyzed in the preceding, argues that boards do seek demographic representation but often succumb to just this problem.

It's nice to have a mix—a racial, age mix, sex mix, and everything else. And all the boards I'm on are doing pretty well of getting more women on. I'd say that women represent somewhere between one-quarter and one-third of most of these boards. . . . Younger people don't have the time or energy or don't fit that criterion of expertise or the money sources. . . . There is a tendency to look for people within your age or social peer group, so even when you are looking at minorities, those are people serving on boards elsewhere or that you've met on social or business occasions. (interview with author)

Given Challinor's observation, one would expect that women (and minorities) who are recruited onto one board quickly become valuable resources sought out by other organizations. The data presented here support this assertion. The complete list of female board members includes 798 women.[4] Of the board positions occupied by women, less than 10% of the nearly 800 occupy approximately one quarter of the female board seats. Due to the often fierce competition for members between organizations and the resultant recruitment strategies employed by the competing groups and other internal strategic decisions that must be affirmed by the board members, the problem of overlapping boards, a general malady in the public interest sector, is particularly acute among this small group of women.

For the most part, the busiest women are the ones most often asked to serve on yet another board. Not surprisingly, the 20% of executive directors who are women show up regularly on related (and sometimes totally unrelated) organization boards. In this sample, for instance, Joan Claybrook of Public Citizen, mentioned earlier, serves on numerous boards; Maggie Kuhn, Louise Dunlap, Gale Cincotta, and Sarah Brady, all executive directors of public interest organizations, serve on several governing boards as well. Perhaps one of the most overworked women in the public interest nonprofit sector is Marian Wright Edelman, head of the Children's Defense Fund. As an African American woman with extensive expertise in the public interest sector, Edelman is constantly being solicited by board recruiting committees. Many times, she has accepted these added responsibilities. Al-

though the burdens on male executive directors may not be as great, one does also find the names of male organization leaders appearing on the boards of several groups as well.

Both male and female executive directors satisfy at least two of the criteria presented earlier: policy expertise and managerial skills. Some may, by their leadership styles and general notoriety, also qualify as celebrities. As political entrepreneurs, public interest leaders develop personal followings that related groups attempt to transfer to their causes (Salisbury, 1969). However, the celebrity criterion most often is attributed to stars of stage, screen, and television. From this pool, women are more likely to be drawn. Although male stars are identified among the ranks of board members (e.g., Warren Beatty, Steve Allen, Robert Redford, Hal Holbrook, Neil Simon, Hugh Downs, Andy Williams, Paul Newman), as a percentage of males serving on boards, they represent a much smaller minority. Female celebrities represent a larger segment of women board members; female stars include Ellen Burstyn, Ann Landers, Marsha Mason, Helen Hayes, Rita Moreno, Anne Bancroft, Nancy Walker, Joanne Woodward, and Julia Child. Celebrities with wide name recognition have become increasingly important to public interest organizations. Membership recruitment efforts, based largely on direct mail and, more recently, direct video, rely heavily on celebrities as signatories of direct mail solicitations or as narrators in direct video efforts (Godwin, 1988).

In addition to the female executive directors, there is an additional small core of women who provide significant policy expertise. In this group are those women with public service/political backgrounds such as Elizabeth Dole, Diane Feinstein, Anne Wexler, Alice Rivlin, and Susan Estrich (Michael Dukakis's 1988 presidential campaign adviser and member of the national board of directors of the American Civil Liberties Union). In the area of public service, however, men are more abundant and, hence, have a larger presence of public interest boards. One finds broad political representation from male current and former elected officials such as Jack Kemp, Barry Goldwater, Orrin Hatch, Tom

Bradley, George McGovern, Jesse Helms, Andrew Young, Henry Cisneros, Ron Dellums, Ted Weiss, and William Proxmire. Appointed high-ranking administration officials, past and present, are also represented and are almost entirely male (e.g., Stuart Eizenstat, Robert McNamara, Allan Greenspan, Henry Kissinger, Drew Lewis).

If women are underrepresented in the areas of managerial skills and policy expertise, then where is the influence of women felt? Interestingly, there are at least two discernible patterns of female board membership involvement. First, it would appear that women are significant financial contributors to the public interest nonprofit sector. Challinor, again, stresses the necessity of financial support on the boards.

> I think there is at least a subconscious, if not a conscious effort made to divide the board or to have a representative board. So that some people that you know will not necessarily be active on the board, but will give you a $10,000 or $5,000 check every year and lend their name. . . . Those are consciously weighed by the nominating committee when people come up. We realize that you can't have a whole board like that—you have to weight it. (interview with author)

Consistently, board members (male and female) offer anecdotal evidence in their chronicles of board meetings that document the appearance of wealthy women of boards who provide little or no policy input or direction. The list of 798 female board members includes many well-known women in the Washington and New York City social and political circles (e.g., Sloan, Hames, Mountcastle, Determan, Ball, Hurst, Ware). Robert Blake, a retired career diplomat in the foreign service and member of more than a half-dozen boards of the organizations analyzed in the preceding, discusses his qualifications as a board member. Many women, by virtue of their wealth or their marriage, play similar roles.

> Every organization is looking for people that have money, which I don't have a lot of, but I have a little of, people with contacts who know a town like Washington. And I am very much in-

volved in the politics of the town—I know well 15 senators and 40 or 50 members of the House, mostly because they were guests at my table when I was in the diplomatic service. You get to know them; you get to be pals. They're looking for people like that, they can be friendly with them, they're not going to pin them to the wall. (Challinor, interview with author)

Although some of the women who serve as board members may not know a dozen senators or 50 House members, there are some who do by virtue of being the wives of men with either past government service or ongoing political/social ties to Congress or the administration. Often public interest nonprofit service is a family affair. Although it is rare to find both husband and wife on the same board, it is common to find both among the ranks of board members. Whether it is Mrs. former attorney general or Mrs. former secretary of state, political wives are significantly represented in the pool of female public interest board members.

Discussion

What is the overall impact of women on the governance of public interest organizations? In the public interest nonprofit sector, women occupy approximately 20% of the leadership positions including memberships on governing boards and executive directorships. Similar patterns of female participation are found throughout the nonprofit sector. Women occupy approximately 20% of positions on foundation boards (Gittell, 1990; Nason, 1977) but occupy only 15% of college and university board positions (Baughman, 1987; Capek, 1988; Kohn & Mortimer, 1983). Finally, Kramer (1981), in his study of institutions for the mentally and physically handicapped, finds the governing boards to be composed predominantly of White male professionals. Between one quarter and one third of the board positions were occupied by women.

Beyond board-level participation in the public interest nonprofit sector, women fare comparatively worse in executive leadership participation in foundations, colleges/universities, and mental/physical rehabilitation institutions, although significant progress during the past 2 years has been made in attaining college and university presidencies, including the University of Pennsylvania's selection of Judith Rodin as the first female president of an Ivy League institution and the choice of Nannerl Keohane to preside over Duke University (Dembner, 1994). In none of these arenas does female participation approach the 20% mark attained in the public interest nonprofit sector.

This is not to say that the level of participation of women as executive directors in public interest organizations is acceptable. With women comprising less than one quarter of the organizational leaders in the public interest sector, it is apparent that a glass ceiling exists at the governance level. More importantly, the barriers to breaking through are organizationally based and are linked to the individual attributes and qualifications of potential candidates.

To expand the ranks of women, more women are needed who meet the criteria established by the nominating committees of the various boards. Meeting the criteria, particularly the managerial and policy expertise attributes, requires that women develop such skills. Dole (1992) foresees that the disproportionate female staff representation in the nonprofit sector will eventually yield dividends in the form of nonprofit executive leadership.

> I believe that the skills learned in the independent sector—communicating, organizing, long-range planning—are skills necessary to be a Chief Executive Officer or manager of any organization. We can break the glass ceiling by ensuring that our ranks are open to all Americans and by taking steps to remove the disparity in pay between male and female employees. (p. 32)

As public interest nonprofit organizations grow and continue to professionalize, one would hope that those women who joined the public interest sector during its formative years will rise to occupy more and more positions of leadership. Compared to women in other sectors of the national workforce, women in the public interest nonprofit sector are better positioned to

move into leadership positions. The representation of women in trade union leadership, for example, lags well behind that demonstrated in the public interest nonprofit sector. Women now account for more than one third of all trade union members in the United States, yet only 2 of the 95 unions of the AFL-CIO are led by women. Similarly, only 10% of union governing board positions are held by women (Swoboda, 1993).

As for the current state of the influence of women in nonprofit sector governance, it seems an interesting turn of events when women are mobilized for service based on their financial wherewithal. However, the relative scarcity of women with federal government experience remains a serious problem. It is not clear whether this barrier will be overcome in the near future. As for female (and male) celebrities, lending one's name to a particular cause has significant value for organizations, perhaps not in directly influencing policy outcomes but more indirectly in maintaining the organizations through membership recruitment.

Overcoming the structural/organizational barriers identified in Table 4.4 is a more daunting task. The old guard, wealthy, Washington-based public interest nonprofits remain disproportionately male-dominated institutions at the leadership level. Nonetheless, it is important to note that the most significant variable in the model, Board, is fortuitously the most open to proactive change. It is impossible to transform older organizations into younger ones; it is similarly impractical to divest wealthy organizations of their financial resources or to move the organizations outside of Washington. It is feasible, however, to organize and facilitate a public interest sector-wide movement toward redressing the inadequacies of female representation at the board level.

Overall, the findings presented here mirror the conclusions reached by Guy (1993) in her analysis of women in the public sector: "Vertical representation is currently missing. Women occupy the lower rungs on the . . . ladders and men occupy the upper rungs" (p. 291; see also Kleiman, 1994). Nevertheless, women have established a foothold in the public interest nonprofit sector. Nominating committees are attempting to seek out more and different women as executive directors and board members. Whether they are not looking hard enough or whether qualified women simply do not exist is open to speculation. More rigorous recruiting efforts must uncover more qualified women or else existing female board members and executive directors will quickly be spread too thin. At the same time, the female talent pool is, in fact, much smaller than the male talent pool, due in no small part to the biases that exist in the larger nonprofit, corporate, and political communities. Women, like African Americans, Hispanics, and younger adults, provide vital representation in the governance of public interest organizations. As nonprofit organizations strive to become" value based and market driven" (Young, 1993, p. 11), the potential for change exists, but barriers to entry remain as well.

Notes

1. The Odendahl and Youmans chapter, "Women on Nonprofit Boards," in Odendahl and O'Neill (1994), contains a bibliography of more than 80 books and articles on the topic. One may also wish to explore the vast collection of more than 200 papers available through Yale University's Program on Non-Profit Organizations. Many of these papers address issues relating to the roles of women in the nonprofit sector.

2. The Age and Budget variables are moderately correlated at .376; the remaining correlations in the matrix of independent variables are no greater than .102.

3. As a part of a larger project on public interest nonprofit organizations, the author interviewed 42 board members from public interest groups in the foundation sample of 240 organizations. These interviewees represented more than 100 of the organizations as board members. Each interview followed a semistructured interview format that consisted of six broad themes: personal history of board member, description of job on board, composition/selection of board members, board policymaking, legitimization of organization through board, and view of organization and membership. Each interview lasted between 1 and $1^{1}/_{2}$ hours. The conclusions reached regarding the internal board decision-making practices were derived from these interviews.

4. The entire list of female board members identified in the Catalyst study of all Fortune 1000 companies includes only 721 women. See Tifft and Bamford (1994).

References

Abzug, R., DiMaggio, P. J., Gray, B. H., Kang, C. H., & Useem, M. (1992). *Change in the structure and composition of non-profit boards of trustees: Cases from Boston and Cleveland, 1925–1985* (Working Paper No. 173). New Haven, CT: Yale University, Institution for Social and Policy Studies, Program on Non-Profit Organizations.

Babchuk, N., Marsey, R., & Gordon, C. W. (1960). Men and women in community agencies: A note on power and prestige. *American Sociological Review, 44,* 399–404.

Baughman, J. C. (1987). *Trustees, trusteeship, and the public good: Issues of accountability for hospitals, museums, universities, and libraries.* New York: Quorum.

Bergner, D. J. (Ed.). (1986). *Public interest profiles: 1986–1987* (5th ed.). Washington, DC: Foundation for Public Affairs.

Berry, J. M. (1977). *Lobbying for the people: The political behavior of public interest groups.* Princeton, NJ: Princeton University Press.

_____. (1989). *The interest group society.* Glenview, IL: Scott, Foresman/Little, Brown.

Campbell, C. (1986). *Managing the presidency: Carter, Reagan, and the search for executive harmony.* Pittsburgh, PA: University of Pittsburgh Press.

Capek, M.E.S. (1988). Women as trustees. In M. K. Chamberlain (Ed.), *Women in academe: Progress and prospects.* New York: Russell Sage.

Daniels, A. K. (1988). *Invisible careers: Women civic leaders from the volunteer world.* Chicago: University of Chicago Press.

Dembner, A. (1994, July 31). In academia, women taking hold at the top. *Boston Globe,* p. 1 (Metro/Region).

Dole, E. (1992, December). [Speech to Independent Sector national convention on October 26]. *Leadership IS,* 23–34, .pp

Drucker, P. F. (1990). *Managing the nonprofit organization.* New York: HarperCollins.

Fletcher, K. B. (1992). On defining and developing effective boards. *Nonprofit Management and Leadership, 2,* 283–293.

Fox, H. J., Jr., & Hammond, S. W. (1977). *Congressional staffs: The invisible force in American lawmaking.* New York: Free Press.

Gittell, M. (1990). The mysterious 7:3: The token representation of women on foundation boards. In *Far from done: The challenge of diversifying philanthropic leadership.* New York: Women and Foundations/Corporate Philanthropy.

Godwin, R. K. (1988). *One billion dollars of influence: The direct marketing of politics.* Chatham, NJ: Chatham House.

Guy, M. E. (1993). Three steps forward, two steps backward: The status of women's integration into public management. *Public Administration Review,* 53, 285–291.

Hall, P. D., & Abzug, R. (1995, November). *No one best way: A summary of findings from Yale's project on the changing dimensions of trusteeship.* Paper presented at the annual meeting of the Association for Research on Nonprofit Organizations and Voluntary Action, Cleveland, Ohio.

Harrell, F. E., Jr. (1983). The LOGIST procedure. In *SUGI supplemental library user's guide.* Cary, NC: SAS Institute.

Heclo, H. (1977). *A government of strangers: Executive politics in Washington.* Washington, DC: Brookings Institution.

Herman, R. D., & Heimovics, R. D. (1991). *Executive leadership in nonprofit organizations.* San Francisco: Jossey-Bass.

Houle, C. O. (1989). *Governing boards.* San Francisco: Jossey-Bass.

Jenner, J. R. (1982). Participation, leadership, and the role of volunteerism among selected women volunteers. *Journal of Voluntary Action Research,* 11(4), 27–38.

Kleiman, C. (1994, April 21). Power eludes women in non-profit sector. *Chicago Tribune,* p. 3 (Business).

Kohn, P. F., & Mortimer, K. P. (1983). Selecting effective trustees. *Change,* 15(5), 30–37.

Kramer, R. (1981). *Voluntary agencies in the welfare state.* Berkeley: University of California Press.

Lewis, G. B. (1987). Changing patterns of sexual discrimination in federal employment. *Review of Public Personnel Administration,* 7(2), 1–13.

Loeser, H., & Falon, J. (1978). Women board members and voluntary agencies. *Volunteer Administration,* 10(4), 7–11.

Macey, J. W., Adams, B., & Walter, J. J. (1983). *America's unelected government: Appointing the president's team.* Cambridge, MA: Ballinger.

Malbin, M. J. (1980). *Unelected representatives: Congressional staff and the future of representative government.* New York: Basic Books.

Martin, J. M. (1989). The recruitment of women to cabinet and subcabinet posts. *Western Political Quarterly,* 42(1), 161–172.

McFarland, A. S. (1976). *Public interest lobbies: Decision making on energy.* Washington, DC: American Enterprise Institute.

McPherson, J. M., & Smith-Lovin, L. (1982). Women and weak ties: Differences by sex in voluntary associations. *American Journal of Sociology,* 87, 883–903.

_____. (1986). Sex segregation in voluntary associations. *American Sociological Review,* 51, 61–79.

Middleton, M. (1987). Nonprofit boards of directors: Beyond the governance function. In W. W. Powell (Ed.), *The nonprofit sector: A research handbook* (pp. 141–153). New Haven, CT: Yale University Press.

Mirvis, P. H. (1992). The quality of employment in the nonprofit sector: An update on employee attitudes in nonprofits versus business and government. *Nonprofit Management and Leadership,* 3(1), 23–41.

Mirvis, P. H., & Hackett, E. J. (1983). Work and workforce characteristics in the nonprofit sector. *Monthly Labor Review* (April), pp. 3–12.

Naff, K. C. (1994). Through the glass ceiling: Prospects for advancement of women in the federal civil service. *Public Administration Review,* 54, 507–514.

Nason, J. (1977). *Trustees and the future of foundations.* New York: Council on Foundations.

Odendahl, T., & O'Neill, M. (Eds.). (1994). *Women and power in the nonprofit sector.* San Francisco: Jossey-Bass.

Odendahl, T., & S. Youmans. (1994). Women on nonprofit boards. In T. Odendahl & M. O'Neill (Eds.) *Women and power in the nonprofit sector,* 183–221. San Francisco: Jossey-Bass.

Ostrander, S. A. (1987). Elite domination in private social agencies: How it happens and how it is challenged. In G. W. Domhoff & T. R. Dye (Eds.), *Power elites and organizations.* Newbury Park, CA: Sage.

Pfiffner, J. P. (1994). *The modern presidency.* New York: St. Martin's.

Pitkin, H. F. (1967). *The concept of representation.* Berkeley: University of California Press.

Preston, A. E. (1990). Women in the white collar nonprofit sector: The best option or the only option. *Review of Economics and Statistics,* 72, 560–568.

_____. (1994). Women in the nonprofit labor market. In T. Odendahl & M. O'Neill (Eds.). *Women and power in the nonprofit sector*, 39–77. San Francisco: Jossey-Bass.

Salisbury, R. H. (1969). An exchange theory of interest groups. *Midwest Journal of Political Science*, 13(1), 1–32.

Shackett, J. P., & Trapani, J. M. (1987). Earnings differentials and market structure. *Journal of Human Resources*, 12, 518–531.

Shaiko, R. G. (1989). *The public interest dilemma: Organizational maintenance and political representation in the public interest sector*. Unpublished doctoral dissertation, Maxwell School of Citizenship and Public Affairs, Syracuse University.

_____. (1991). More bang for the buck: The new era of full-service public interest organizations. In A. J. Cigler & B. A. Loomis (Eds.). *Interest group politics*, 109–129. (3rd ed., pp. 109–129). Washington, DC: Congressional Quarterly Press.

_____. (In press). *Voices and echoes for the environment: Public interest representation in the 1990s*. Philadelphia: Temple University Press.

Steinberg, R. J., & Jacobs, J. A. (1994). Pay equity in nonprofit organizations: Making women's work visible. In T. Odendahl & M. O'Neill (Eds.). *Women and power in the nonprofit sector*, 79–120. San Francisco: Jossey-Bass.

Stone, M. M. (1991). The propensity of governing boards to plan. *Nonprofit Management and Leadership*, 1, 203–215.

Swoboda, F. (1993). Women aspiring to union leadership roles find limits there too. *Washington Post*, February 13) p. H2.

Tifft, S. E., & Bamford, J. (1994.) Board gains. *Working Woman* (April)), pp. 36–40.

Walker, J. L., Jr. (1991). *Mobilizing interest groups in America: Patrons, professionals and social movements*. Ann Arbor: University of Michigan Press.

Watkins, T. H., & Turnage, W. A. (1985, Summer). We still want no straddlers. *Wilderness* pp. 34–37.

Weisbrod, B. A. (1988). *The nonprofit economy*. Cambridge: Harvard University Press.

Whitt, J. A., G. & Moore. (1995). Using community networks to diversify the board. In M. M. Wood (Ed.), *Nonprofit boards and leadership: Cases on governance, change, and board-staff dynamics*. San Francisco: Jossey-Bass.

Widmer, C. (1991). Board members' perceptions of their roles and responsibilities. In *Association for Research on Nonprofit Organizations and Voluntary Action (ARNOVA) conference proceedings*, 145–160, October 17–19, in Cleveland, Ohio. Indianapolis: ARNOVA, Indiana University Center on Philanthropy.

Young, D. R. (1987). Executive leadership in nonprofit organizations. In W. W. Powell (Ed.), *The nonprofit sector: A research handbook*, 167–179. New Haven, CT: Yale University Press.

_____. (1993). Emerging themes in nonprofit leadership and management. In D. R. Young, R. M. Hollister, V. A. Hodgkinson, and associates (Eds.), *Governing, leading, and managing nonprofit organizations: New insights from research and practice*, 1–13. San Francisco: Jossey-Bass.

PART 2

THE LEGAL FRAMEWORK

JARED C. BENNETT

Why should the government regulate organizations that provide shelter and a warm meal for the homeless, help abused children cope with their physical and psychological wounds, and protect endangered animals from malicious treatment by unscrupulous humans? The most obvious purpose for regulation is to protect the public from fraud; however, the laws governing nonprofit organizations regulate far more than fraud. Such legislation serves two main purposes: to protect the public from fraud, and encourage nonprofits to provide needed services that lighten the government's burden. The "encouragement/regulation dichotomy" of nonprofit law encourages the growth of nonprofit organizations and at the same time attempts to ensure that they do not take advantage of the favorable treatment they are accorded under the law, become too powerful, or participate too actively in politics.

Several lawmaking bodies regulate and influence the activities of nonprofit corporations. The federal government and most states have enacted statutes that broadly outline how a nonprofit corporation must be organized and the type of activities a nonprofit can participate in but still remain tax exempt. For example, in the Internal Revenue Code §501(c)(3), Congress declared that the following types of organizations are exempt from federal taxation:

> Corporations and any community chest, fund, or foundation, organized and operated exclusively for religious, charitable, scientific, testing for public safety, literary, or educational purposes, or to foster national or international amateur sports competitions (but only if no part of its activities involve the provision of athletic facilities and equipment), or for the prevention of cruelty to children or animals, no part of the net earnings of which inures to the benefit of any private shareholder

or individual, no substantial part of the activities of which is carrying on propaganda, or otherwise attempting, to influence legislation (except as otherwise provided in subsection(h)), and which does not participate in, or intervene in (including publishing or distributing of statements), any political campaign on behalf of (or in opposition to) any candidate for public office.

Congress has not provided a definition within the law that allows us to know precisely what a charitable organization is. Instead, Congress has delegated regulatory authority over nonprofit organizations to the Department of Treasury, and Treasury is empowered to make rules that further define the term *charitable organization*.[1] Congress also has empowered the Internal Revenue Service (a subdivision of Treasury) to conduct adjudicatory proceedings to decide whether organizations that claim to be charitable are in actuality charitable organizations for tax-exempt purposes. When the IRS decides that an organization is not charitable within the IRS's meaning of the word, it may appeal to the federal courts. The federal courts will look under the standards of the Internal Revenue Code, the Treasury regulations, or the Administrative Procedure Act to determine whether the IRS has applied the law appropriately. Although laws from state to state are different, each state has rather similar legislative, administrative and judicial processes that nonprofits are required to follow. Thus, the leader of a nonprofit organization needs to know about laws and regulations that govern nonprofit organizations at the federal level and in the states where the nonprofit corporation conducts its business.

In addition to tax law, several other bodies of law govern nonprofit organizations. Board members and executives in nonprofits need to be aware of the liabilities they may incur under tort law, contract law, securities law, antitrust law, property law, labor law, and bankruptcy law. When directors act without first thinking through the potential consequences that an action may have under the several bodies of law that govern nonprofits, damage may result. A nonprofit organization may lose its tax-exempt status or risk financial ruin through litigation and adverse jury awards for damages.

Although many nonprofits hire lawyers to handle complex questions and sometimes ask their lawyers to (in effect) make decisions for the organization, dependence on lawyers is neither wise nor practical. Having a basic understanding of the laws that govern nonprofits could save trustees and directors time, money, and possibly even the survival of the organization and the personal assets of its leaders.

This chapter provides an overview of the most important laws governing nonprofit corporations. Each state, however, has its own variations from general law, and thus a single chapter cannot provide exhaustive coverage of the innumerable legal situations that a nonprofit may encounter. Trustees and directors have an obligation—to the nonprofit and to themselves—to become familiar with the basic issues involved in nonprofit law and to learn about the laws specific to the jurisdictions in which the nonprofit operates.

The Organizational Test

In order to qualify for tax-exempt status and for donors to be able to "write off" their contributions (tax deductions), a nonprofit must meet the requirements of the organizational test;[2] this test demonstrates to the government that the primary purpose of the organization is an exempt purpose listed in §501(c)(3). The question is not whether the organization is engaged in exempt activities, but whether the incorporating documents state that the organization's primary purpose is to pursue one of the exempt purposes listed in §501(c)(3). The organizational test has two parts. First, a nonprofit must provide a statement of purpose. Second, a nonprofit must show that upon dissolution all of its assets will continue to be used for a tax-exempt purpose as defined in §501(c)(3). If either part of the organizational test is not met, the organization will not be granted tax-exemption and will be treated as a for-profit corporation under the law.

Statement of Purpose

The primary purpose of the organization must be limited to the categories listed in §501(c)(3). This statement of purpose may be as broad as the language in §501(c)(3): "This organization is formed for charitable purposes," or it may be more specific, such as: "This organization has been created for the purpose of engaging in scientific and educational activities, namely an earth science museum for children."[3]

Dissolution

The dissolution requirement is intended to ensure that an organization's assets would be used to fulfill a §501(c)(3) exempt purpose if it were to be dissolved. For example, the articles of incorporation may state that if the nonprofit should be dissolved, all of its assets would be distributed to the federal, state or local government agencies for a public purpose, or to another organization with an exempt primary purpose through a court order.[4]

The Operational Test

Treasury Regulation §1.501(c)(3)-1(a)(1) states:

> In order to be exempt as an organization described in section 501(c)(3), an organization must be both organized and operated exclusively for one or more of the purposes specified in this section. If an organization fails to meet either the organizational test or the operational test, it is not exempt.

Thus, once a nonprofit organization has satisfied the organizational test, it also must satisfy the operational test. The operational test examines whether the activities of the organization further the primary exempt purpose of the organization. The operational test contains three main parts: primary activities, distribution of earnings, and action organizations.

Primary Activities

The primary activities test requires a nonprofit organization to demonstrate that a substantial portion of its activities accomplish an exempt purpose. Recall that §501(c)(3) grants tax-exempt status only to organizations "operated exclusively" for enumerated exempt purposes. If this phrase was interpreted literally, no organization could engage in unrelated business activities—a prohibition that would severely hamper the entrepreneurial endeavors that so many nonprofits have turned to for new revenue sources in recent decades. Thus, the IRS has interpreted "exclusively" to mean "primarily." Treasury Regulation §1.501(c)(3)-1(c)(1) states:

> An organization will be regarded as operated exclusively for one or more exempt purposes only if it engages primarily in activities which accomplish one or more such exempt purposes specified in section 501(c)(3). An organization will not be so regarded if *more than an insubstantial part* of its activities is not in furtherance of an exempt purpose. (emphasis added)

The United States Supreme Court upheld the IRS's interpretation of "exclusively." Writing for the majority of the Supreme Court, Justice Murphy stated:

> [Exclusively] plainly means that the presence of a single [nonexempt] purpose, if *substantial in nature,* will destroy the exemption regardless of the number or importance of truly [exempt] purposes. It thus becomes unnecessary to determine the correctness of the [exempt] characterization of petitioner's operations, it being apparent beyond dispute that an important, if not the *primary,* pursuit of petitioner's organization is to promote not only [exempt but mostly profit making activities].[5] (emphasis added)

A nonprofit organization can engage in profit-making enterprises as long as it can show that the most substantial part of its operations fulfill a §501(c)(3) exempt purpose. If, however, an organization's profit-making enterprises are the most substantial part of its activities, the nonprofit will not be tax-exempt, no matter how many important exempt activities it conducts.

Unfortunately, neither the Supreme Court nor the Treasury Department has defined *substantial* or *insubstantial.* There is no answer to the question, "What percentage of nonprofit activities can be nonexempt purposes without disqualifying it for tax exemption?" Tax courts in various jurisdictions have used different percentages, but there is no standard rule.[6] This determination is a fact-intensive inquiry decided case by case. Because courts in various jurisdictions disagree about how much nonexempt activity justifies revoking tax-exempt status, the officers and executives of the nonprofit must be familiar with court rulings in the jurisdiction where the nonprofit operates.

Distribution of Earnings

To avoid being taxed like for-profit businesses, nonprofits must not distribute earnings for the personal benefit of the trustees, directors, or other individuals. Treasury Regulation §1.501(c)(3)-1(c)(2) states unequivocally: "An organization is not operated exclusively for one or more exempt purposes if its net earnings inure in whole or in part to the benefit of private shareholders or individuals."

Action Organizations

A substantial portion of an action organization's activities involve contacting or urging the public or members of a legislative body for the purpose of proposing, supporting, or opposing certain specific legislation. If an organization participates or intervenes directly or indirectly in a political campaign on behalf of or in opposition to a candidate for public office, it is considered an action organization—whether or not the intervention in a political candidate's campaign represents a substantial part of the organization's activities.[7] Action organizations are not tax exempt under 501(c)(3).

Nonprofits must be careful about how often and how extensively they fight for specific legislation. U.S. Treasury Regulations define the term *legislation* as "an action by Congress, by any State legislature, by any local council or similar governing body."[8] If, for example, a nonprofit organization lobbies for or against local school board ordinances too frequently or with too much energy, the nonprofit's tax exemption may be revoked because it will fail this element of the operational test.

Nonprofits that spend time and money lobbying for legislation—and thus do not qualify as §501(c)(3) charitable organizations—may still qualify as §501(c)(4) tax-exempt social welfare organizations. A social welfare organization is "primarily engaged in promoting in some way the common good and general welfare of the people of the community."[9] Treasury Regulation §1.501(c)(4)-1(a) permits social welfare organizations to be tax exempt if they are not organized or operated for a profit and if they are operated exclusively for the promotion of social welfare purposes; however, contributors to organizations organized under §501(c)(4) may not deduct their donations from their taxes.

Nonprofit organizations and their leaders may not campaign for or against candidates for political office; if they do, they almost assuredly will lose their tax-exempt status; however, a tax-exempt nonprofit may engage in such educational activities as distributing a booklet to its members that states the policy positions of candidates running for office. Disseminating pamphlets about political candidates and policies candidates support is not considered "campaigning" if the pamphlet provides information only and does not ask or tell people who to vote for.

Tax Exemption and Public Policy

A nonprofit organization that satisfies both the organizational and operational tests still may not receive tax exempt status if its primary purpose is contrary to public policy. For example, a nonprofit organization that would otherwise qualify as a §501(c)(3) organization would still be denied tax-exempt status if it were to discriminate against individuals because of race, gender, color, or religion. In 1967, the Internal Revenue Service began denying tax-exemption to racially discriminatory private schools that received state aid.[10] This IRS ruling was appealed to the Federal District Court in Washington, D.C., where a three-judge panel held in 1971 that racially discriminatory schools did not qualify for exempt status because they violated well-defined federal policy against discrimination in education.[11]

In the landmark 1974 decision, *Bob Jones University v. United States,* the Supreme Court upheld the public policy doctrine despite the religious university's argument that this IRS policy violated the Free Exercise and Establishment Clauses of the U.S. Constitution. The Court reasoned that

> When the Government grants exemptions or allows deductions all taxpayers are affected. . . . Charitable exemptions are justified on the basis that the exempt entity confers a public benefit . . . [an institution] must demonstrably serve and be in harmony with the public interest. The institution's purpose must not be so at odds with the common community conscience as to undermine any public benefit that might be otherwise conferred.[12]

Since these 1971 and 1974 rulings, the IRS has rigorously enforced a nondiscriminatory policy with all schools, including religious schools that have discriminatory policies inspired by sincere religious beliefs. Tax-exempt status is a symbol of public support for what a nonprofit organization does. The U.S. government will not grant tax-exempt status to an organization whose conduct is repugnant to commonly held values of society.

Many questions surround the public policy doctrine. How does the IRS or a court determine what the "common community conscience" is? How broad is "the community" that the Court uses to determine what "common community conscience" is? If, for example, a charitable nonprofit organization provides condoms and other informational materials on safe sex for teens in a small rural town, and the vast majority of voters would like to "run it out of town," is this nonprofit sufficiently "at odds with the common community conscience" to warrant revoking its tax-exempt status? Questions such as these do not have clear-cut answers.

Boards of Directors and Trustees

The laws governing nonprofit organizations' boards of trustees are as diverse as the fifty state legislatures that have passed them. Some states include nonprofit organizations in laws governing for-profit corporations; other states have separate laws governing each sector. The American Bar Association has adopted the Revised Model Nonprofit Corporation Act to guide states in passing sensible laws governing nonprofits. The Model Nonprofit Act contains several sections governing boards. For example, the Model Act requires a nonprofit to have a board of trustees (or directors) consisting of at least three elected members (if the organization has members), and trustees may not serve terms longer than five years.[13] Board members must serve as individuals, not represent the interests of corporations.

The Model Act imposes a duty of loyalty and a duty of care on directors and officers. "Directors and officers of a nonprofit must discharge their office under a duty of good faith, exercising the care an ordinarily *prudent person* in a *like position* would exercise under *similar circumstances,* and in a manner the director or other officers *reasonably believe* to be in the best interests of the corporation."[14] The standard of good faith also is known as the duty of loyalty.

The duty to act "with the care an ordinarily prudent person in a like position would exercise under similar circumstances, in a manner the director [or other officers] believe to be in the best interests of the corporation," is known as the duty of care. Consider two hypothetical examples:

> *Example 1:* A nonprofit corporation needs a loan to construct a new building. The executive director has a niece who works in a lending institution who offers a loan at a high interest rate. A second lending institution offers the nonprofit a much lower interest rate. The executive director wants to help her niece's career and dishonestly recommends to the board of directors that they accept a loan from the niece because her lending institution "offered the best deal." Without first verifying the executive director's information, the board accepts the loan from the niece's bank. A year later, a board member accidentally discovers that the other bank had offered a lower interest rate. What should the directors do, as a board and individually? What parts of the standard of care did the executive director violate, if any? Did the board of directors violate their duties as well?

Example 2: While looking for a loan for a new building, the executive director receives a written report from the organization's accountant asserting that Bank X has the best loan available in the area. The accountant prepares a report for the executive director demonstrating how the nonprofit will save thousands of dollars by borrowing from Bank X. The executive director recommends Bank X, and the board of directors approves the recommendation. The nonprofit pays $50,000 in advance costs and other fees as required by Bank X. When the executive director goes to Bank X to sign the note, however, she is shocked to discover that Bank X has closed and left town, and no one knows how to reach the bank executives. The board of directors seeks to hold the executive director liable for breaching her duty of care. On what grounds, if any, will the board seek to recover its loss from the executive director? What is the likelihood that the board will recover from the executive director?[15]

Although these standards may sound ambiguous, they are the tests that directors will be judged against if sued for breaching their fiduciary duty to the nonprofit corporation. The ABA's Model Act states, "A director [or other officer] is not liable to the corporation, any member, or any other person for any action taken or not taken as a director, if the director acted in compliance with [the duties of care]."[16]

Directors may be sued for breaching either the duty of care or the duty of loyalty. They may be prosecuted criminally by the state attorney general or sued civilly by the board of trustees of the nonprofit, its members, donors, and those with a "special relationship" to the corporation, for instance, beneficiaries.[17] Some states do not allow members to sue the nonprofit, but other states allow all individuals with a "special relationship" to sue. Taking into account the interests of potential litigants and the consequences of breaching the duty of care or the duty of loyalty may save a nonprofit and its directors time and money and may save the executive director's job.

General Tort Liability

In addition to favorable treatment under tax law, nonprofit organizations historically have received favorable treatment in other areas of the law; for example, the laws governing unemployment insurance, bankruptcy, Social Security, labor relations, securities regulation, copyrights, antitrust, custom duties, and postal rates.[18] General tort liability arguably is the most salient other branch of the law that affects nonprofits directly. Under common law, courts developed the doctrine of charitable immunity that barred all suits against nonprofit corporations.[19] Contemporary laws impose more liability on nonprofit corporations and their directors than in earlier years, but they are still treated favorably.

The public policy reasons for favorable treatment under the charitable immunity doctrine are evident. Nonprofit organizations provide benefits to the public and often rely heavily on volunteers. If the courts should impose too much liability on nonprofit organizations, volunteers might not participate for fear of being sued. The burden of providing these benefits to the public would shift to the government, thereby increasing the costs and size of government or denying needed services to individuals. Therefore, the legislatures and courts have concluded that nonprofits deserve some protection from lawsuits so that they may continue to provide public benefit services independent from the government.

Many scholars question whether this long-standing rationale for protecting nonprofits remains valid in the twenty-first century. Does a multi-million-dollar nonprofit corporation such as the National Football League or the United Way deserve the same protection as a local soup kitchen? If a nonprofit corporation has liability insurance, does this change the need for legal protection for trustees and volunteers? Some states think so. In a few states, for example, volunteers who are associated with nonprofits are protected by law from tort liability, but only if the nonprofit carries liability insurance. Several other states have laws that specify the maximum amount a plaintiff can recover from a nonprofit, and the amount is the maximum that the organization's liability insurance policy will pay. Other states have statutorily established maximum damages limits, the maximum amount which a nonprofit may be required to pay in the event of a lawsuit.[20]

Conclusion

This essay presents a few fundamentals of law that nonprofit organization trustees and executives should know about. Because every state is different in how it governs organizations in the nonprofit sector, however, this chapter can only introduce the basic legal issues to look for when researching a state's laws. Be aware that the laws governing nonprofits cannot be found by looking at a single source. Nonprofits are affected by law-making bodies and regulatory agencies at all levels of government.

Readings Reprinted in Part Two

In *"Developments in the Law: Nonprofit Corporations,"*[21] the *Harvard Law Review* staff provides a far-ranging overview of nonprofit law. Federal and state issues pertaining to the fiduciary duties of directors are discussed, and many problems associated with current laws governing director responsibility are identified. The article recommends ways to increase the accountability of trustees and argues that local municipalities, and possibly also states, should decide whether nonprofits should be tax-exempt—not the Internal Revenue Service. It also presents an overview of legal and constitutional issues associated with fund-raising, potential pitfalls of political activity by nonprofit corporations, tort law, and administrative law. Thus the authors propose reform policy for the special treatment of nonprofits under tort law.

In *"The Law of Tax-Exempt Organizations: Organizational, Operational, and Similar Tests,"*[22] Bruce R. Hopkins outlines the legal framework and the public policy reasons behind the tests governing the formation of nonprofit corporations. Hopkins describes the organizational and operational tests and their constituent parts in considerable detail, and provides examples of how these tests can be met. The chapter describes the current state of the law and identifies questions that the courts have not yet answered.

Notes

1. *See* Treasury Regulations §1.501(c)(3)-1(d)(2).
2. *See* Treasury Regulations §1.501(c)(3)-1(a)(1).
3. *See* Treasury Regulations §1.501(c)(3)-1(b)(1)(b)(ii).
4. *See* Treasury Regulations §1.501(c)(3)-1(b)(4).
5. *Better Business Bureau of Washington, D.C. v. United States,* 326 U.S. 279, 283 (1945).
6. *See Orange County Agric. Soc'y, Inc. v. Commissioner,* 55 T.C.M. 1602 (1988); *Kentucky Bar Found v. Commissioner,* 78 T.C. 921 (1982).
7. *See* Treasury Regulations §1.501(c)(3)-1(c)(3).
8. *See* Treasury Regulations §1.501(c)(3)-1(c)(3)(b).
9. *See* Treasury Regulations §1.501(c)(4)-1(a)(2).
10. *See Bob Jones University v. United States,* 461 U.S. 574 (1974).
11. *See Green v. Connally,* 330 F.Supp. 1150 (D.D.C. 1971).
12. *Bob Jones Univ. v. United States,* 461 U.S. at 591.
13. *See* Revised Model Nonprofit Corporation Act §8.01, 8.02, 8.03.
14. *See* Revised Model Nonprofit Corporation Act §8.30, 8.42.
15. Revised Model Nonprofit Corporation Act §8.30(b) states: (b) In discharging his or her duties, a director is entitled to rely on information, opinions, reports, or statements including financial statements and other financial data, if prepared and presented by: (1) one or more officers or employees of the corporation whom the director reasonably believes to be reliable and competent in the matters presented. . . .
16. *See* Revised Model Nonprofit Corporation Act §8.30, 8.42.
17. *See* 105 *Harvard Law Review* 1595 (1992).
18. *See* 105 *Harvard Law Review* 1677–1678 (1992).
19. *See* 105 *Harvard Law Review* 1677–1678 (1992); *see also* 100 *Harvard Law Review* 1382, 1383–1384 (1987).
20. *See* 105 *Harvard Law Review* 1683–1684 (1992).
21. *See* 105 *Harvard Law Review* 1578 (1992).
22. Bruce R. Hopkins, "The Law of Tax-Exempt Organizations: Organizational, Operational, and Similar Tests," in Bruce R. Hopkins, *The Law of Tax-Exempt Organizations* (NY: John Wiley & Sons, 1998).

► CHAPTER 5

Developments in the Law
Nonprofit Corporations

HARVARD LAW REVIEW

Introduction

Nonprofit corporations encompass more than charitable organizations such as the American Red Cross and the Salvation Army. Nonprofit corporations are America's churches, soup kitchens, political associations, its business leagues, social clubs, sports leagues and some of its most important schools and hospitals. Indeed, a roster of nonprofit corporations would include such household names as the National Football League, the Sierra Club, the Girl Scouts of America, the National Geographic Society, the AFL-CIO, and even the *Harvard Law Review.* The nonprofit sector includes not only organizations commanding wide public support, but also a number of controversial organizations and special interest groups such as the Ku Klux Klan, People for Ethical Treatment of Animals (PETA), the Federalist Society, and the Star Trek Fan Club.

Whether the entity is large or small, charitable or not, two categories of law govern all nonprofit corporations. The first sets forth the structure of nonprofit corporate governance. In some states, the same incorporation statute governs both for-profit and nonprofit corporations; however, most states have enacted a separate nonprofit corporation statute. Nonprofit corporate gover-

nance provisions typically parallel the provisions that govern for-profit corporations, and, in most states, a nonprofit corporation can conduct the same activities as a for-profit corporation. However, one crucial feature distinguishes nonprofit corporate governance from that of for-profit corporations: nonprofit corporations are subject to the non-distribution constraint. The nondistribution constraint prevents the organization from distributing its net earnings to those in control of the corporation; it does not, however, prevent a nonprofit from accumulating earnings. Therefore, the "common stock holder" of a for-profit corporation has no strict analogue in the nonprofit context.

Once a nonprofit is incorporated under state law, a second legal regime governs its relations with parties external to the corporate structure. This regime is nothing more than the body of laws under which all organizations operate—for example, the tort, contract, tax, bankruptcy, labor, securities, and antitrust laws. Many of these laws differentiate between for-profit and nonprofit corporations, and either treat nonprofits more leniently or completely exempt them from the regulations governing their for-profit counterparts.

The special regulatory regimes for nonprofits subsidize nonprofits' activities. Although the most commonly recognized subsidy is exemption from federal income taxation, exemption from other regulatory regimes is also important. For example, the federal securities laws favor nonprofit corporations that issue debentures by relieving them of burdensome and costly registration requirements.

This Development surveys several areas of nonprofit corporation law. Each Part sets forth the law in its particular field, discusses and critiques recent developments, and then suggests how the law should evolve.

The nonprofit corporate form is merely a private organizational structure selected from a menu of business forms that includes partnerships, for-profit corporations, mutual corporations, cooperatives and unincorporated nonprofit associations. Parties select the nonprofit corporate form when they believe that coupling the nondistribution constraint with the corporate structure allows for the production of a superior good or service. The nondistribution constraint prevents a nonprofit from distributing funds to shareholders and other third parties, thereby increasing the likelihood that the funds will be used solely to produce a quality product or service. Ordinarily, a purchaser will not care about how a firm uses its receipts because the purchaser can directly compare the price and quality of goods offered by for-profit and nonprofit firms, thereby determining which firm offers the best deal. However, in some instances, the consumer cannot tell if the delivered product conforms to his expectations either because he will not receive the product (e.g.,, food that is shipped to Africa) or because he cannot evaluate the good's quality ex ante (e.g., surgery). A consumer in this position may prefer to purchase services from a nonprofit because he believes that the nonprofit is more likely to commit a greater percentage of its funds to delivering a quality product than is a for-profit, which may exploit this informational gap to earn more profits for its shareholders.

Although the nonprofit corporation is a type of private business form, the nonprofit corporate sector produces both public and private goods. Consumers might organize a nonprofit primarily to produce a private benefit (such as a country club) when they view the non-distribution constraint as important. Citizens might also organize a nonprofit corporation to purchase a public benefit (such as the Sierra Club). Occasionally, the government will subsidize these organizations by giving them direct grants, tax-exempt status, and the ability to receive tax deductible donations. In this manner, the government increases the public provision of goods by leveraging its resources with private resources. Finally, in many instances, the good will possess both public and private characteristics. For example, a private university may be viewed as privately oriented insofar as students exchange their tuition dollars for an education that enhances their employment opportunities. The university is publicly oriented to the extent that society benefits from an educated citizenry.

Many statutes recognize that nonprofits serve both public and private purposes. Consequently, these statutes explicitly distinguish among different types of organizations. The specific criteria for distinguishing among nonprofits differs from statute to statute. For example, the Internal Revenue Code has long contained a very elaborate classification scheme within section 501(c) that distinguishes between organizations that primarily provide public goods and those that provide private benefits. The Model Nonprofit Corporation Act separates nonprofit corporations into three categories: those that primarily provide public benefits; those that primarily provide private benefits (called mutual organizations); and those that provide religious services. The Securities Act of 1933 uses language similar to section 501(c)(3) in describing which organizations should be exempt from the Act's registration requirements, but the Act does not look to an organization's actual section 501(c)(3) status. Other statutes have developed their own classification systems.

Even when statutes facially apply to "any corporation" or to "all organizations engaged in commerce," judges frequently establish their own scheme for differentiating among nonprofits. In interpreting these statutes, judges often conclude that the strict application of the statutes' terms would work an injustice. Consequently, judges often develop criteria to ascertain whether a particular nonprofit corporation falls within a statute's reach.

Both the statutory and judicial methods for differentiating among nonprofits are overly dependent upon judicial discretion. When legislation neglects to specify how nonprofits should be treated, courts frequently look to the purpose of the statute and then examine the particular characteristics of the individual nonprofit to determine its treatment. At best, ad hoc judicial inquiry is subjective and imprecise, and, at worst it can operate as a facade for judicial bias. Although courts may justify their decisions by invoking a large number of factors, little comfort is provided because any one particular criterion is rarely dispositive. Judicial recourse to a large number of criteria prevents nonprofit corporations from predicting their status under a particular statute, and frustrates effective appellate review.

Even when statutes categorize nonprofits by setting forth a number of broad classes, judges still retain a large measure of discretion. Categorization may appear to reduce the need for judicial discretion because the scheme typically directs judges to treat certain classes of nonprofits in a specified manner. However, an exercise of discretion is still required to determine into which category a particular organization falls. Courts must deploy a number of criteria to make these determinations, and therefore, many of the same weaknesses appear that arise in situations when the status of the organization in question is not explicitly covered by legislation.

The Fiduciary Duties of Directors

Introduction

Over one million nonprofit organizations in the United States—operating in fields as important as health care, education, and research and development—spend a total of nearly $300 billion each year. The directors of these organizations, like directors of for-profit corporations, wield significant power. This power, however, often goes unchecked because nonprofit corporations lack the controls on director behavior present in the business sector. Indeed, many nonprofit directors have abused their positions in order to reap personal benefits at the corporation's expense or have ignored their duty to promote actively the purposes of the organization.

Recent examples of abuse have prompted efforts to clarify the standards of conduct for nonprofit directors and, in particular, the fiduciary duties of care and loyalty. The fiduciary duties are especially important in the nonprofit sector because the nondistribution constraint on nonprofit corporations specifically ensures the use of corporate assets for corporate purposes. For example, consumers who cannot determine how much of the purchase price goes to production of a service may prefer to deal with nonprofit entities because these entities, which lack an incentive to generate profit, are likely to direct more resources toward actual production. Similarly, donors to a charity who cannot determine precisely how their funds will be spent may prefer to donate to a nonprofit charity because the nonprofit will use their donations for a charitable end rather than for shareholder enrichment. By prohibiting distributions to shareholders, the structure of a nonprofit entity ensures that any funds raised are used to serve corporate purposes. Thus, enforcement of the fiduciary duties serves the same goal as does the nonprofit corporate structure.

The Fiduciary Duties and Their Enforcement

The fiduciary duties of nonprofit directors stem from at least two sources—state corporate statutes specifically applicable to nonprofit corporations and federal income tax law. Each of these sources defines the substantive fiduciary standards applicable to nonprofits and establishes a mechanism by which to enforce those standards.

Fiduciary Duties Under State Corporate Law

Under state statutory and common law, directors of business corporations must satisfy two fiduciary duties—the duty of care and the duty of loyalty. These fiduciary standards recognize that directors cannot be subjected to liability for every business decision. As such, the duty of care typically requires directors to discharge their duties "with the care an ordinarily prudent person in a like position would exercise under similar circumstances." To satisfy the duty of loyalty, the corporate director must act in "good faith" and "in a manner he reasonably believes to be in the best interests of the corporation." In satisfying these duties, corporate directors may rely on the opinions of assistants, such as other directors, corporate officers, and legal counsel. The directors need not individually investigate every decision to act (or to refrain from acting) in order to insulate themselves from liability to the corporation or its shareholders.

The Standards as Applied to Nonprofit Directors

Courts have held the directors of nonprofit corporations to a variety of fiduciary standards. Some courts have indicated that nonprofit directors should be held to the high standards typically associated with trustees. Other courts have been unwilling to scrutinize the actions of nonprofit directors closely, lest stringent standards discourage volunteers from assuming the responsibilities of a directorship. Finally, many courts have simply applied the standards applicable to for-profit directors, and thus have recognized the similarities between the corporate structure (and activities) of for-profits and nonprofits.

The third option, for the most part, has prevailed. The Revised Model Nonprofit Corporation Act ("Model Act"), adopted by the ABA in 1987, includes a standard of care nearly identical to the standard applicable in the for-profit sector. The Model Act states that "[a]director shall not be deemed to be a trustee with respect to the corporation," and makes no exception for volunteer directors. The Model Act similarly adopts the generally accepted for-profit standard for the duty of loyalty. Unlike the higher standard for trustees, the Model Act does not strictly forbid transactions that implicate the interests of cor-

porate directors if the transactions are fair to the corporation or are approved in accordance with statutory provisions.

Limitations of the Current System

Neither state nonprofit corporation statutes nor existing federal tax provisions sufficiently deter directors from violating their fiduciary duties. Although both bodies of law attempt to establish significant controls on director behavior, the two approaches lack sufficient enforcement mechanisms to discourage directors from breaching their fiduciary duties.

Problems with Enforcement Under Nonprofit Corporation Statutes

The enforcement of fiduciary duties under state corporate law depends largely on private actions. In the business sector, "entrepreneurial attorneys" enforce fiduciary duties by seeking out profitable causes of action on behalf of corporations' shareholders. The plaintiff's attorney has an incentive to file an action only if the attorney's fees award is likely to be greater than the costs of investigating and preparing for litigation. In these suits, the named party in a derivative action is only nominally a plaintiff; the case really belongs to the attorney, and the attorney benefits the most from a court award or a negotiated settlement. In the business context, then, an entrepreneurial attorney presumably discovers many fiduciary duty violations and seeks out an appropriate plaintiff.

Attorney-driven litigation cannot be as effective in the nonprofit sector. In the business sector, the public has relatively easy access to information about corporations, and attorneys are able to seek out profitable derivative actions. Indeed, attorneys typically bring private derivative actions after a citation for a securities violation is issued or the price of a corporation's stock falls dramatically. By contrast, nonprofit corporations neither issue publicly traded stock nor are subject to securities reporting provisions. Consequently, the lack of available information often deters attorneys from taking action against nonprofit directors because of potentially high discovery costs.

The lack of information concerning nonprofit corporations increases the plaintiff's role in litigation because the plaintiff, rather than a profit-seeking attorney, must come forward to initiate an action in the name of the corporation. However, because damages are paid to the corporation (and to the plaintiff's attorney), individual plaintiffs may have little incentive to bring a suit. The result is fewer actions against nonprofit directors who breach their fiduciary duties.

Problems with Enforcement Under the Internal Revenue Code

The fiduciary duties embodied in the Internal Revenue Code are similarly insufficient to deter improper nonprofit director conduct. First, like any other government organization, the IRS has limited resources to seek out violations. As a result, many fiduciary duty breaches are unchallenged or unnoticed. Second, the remedies available to the IRS are often inadequate. For example, the IRS may fine only the directors of private foundations. Private foundations are only a subset of tax-exempt corporations, which are, in turn, only a subset of all nonprofit entities. The only other remedy available to the IRS, the denial of nonprofit status based on s 501(c)(3) violations, punishes the corporation as a whole and not the individual director who violates a fiduciary duty. For a penalty to be most effective, a director must internalize the full cost of his violation. Penalizing the entire corporation for the improper activities of a director is not the most desirable, nor most effective, means by which to encourage compliance with the fiduciary duties; the penalty must focus on the individual director.

Analyzing the Fiduciary Duties: How to Ensure Careful and Loyal Directors

In general, three methods exist for encouraging directors to comply with their fiduciary duties: (1) revising the substantive fiduciary standards upwards, (2) expanding the class of plaintiffs given standing to enforce the duties, and (3) increasing the liability of directors who violate their duties.

Determining the Appropriate Fiduciary Standards

The central purpose of fiduciary duties is to ensure that a corporation's resources are used to achieve the corporation's purposes and not to enrich the directors. Fiduciary standards must be set with this goal in mind.

The Duty of Care and the Business Judgment Rule

The Model Act expressly adopts the lenient for-profit duty of care for application to nonprofit directors. In the business sector, the business judgment rule, which requires gross negligence or willful misconduct to support a holding adverse to a director, typically complements this permissive standard of care. Although the Model Act does not mandate use of the business judgment rule, it certainly does not prohibit application of the rule to directors of nonprofits. In fact, several courts have used the business judgment rule to review the acts of nonprofit directors.

A stricter standard of care has two other potential advantages. First, more directors will be held liable after suits are initiated because they will be held to the higher standard. Second, a stricter standard will encourage the initiation of additional actions against corporate directors because it increases the likelihood of a successful plaintiff's action.

A stricter standard of care, however, imposes severe costs. First, many nonprofit directors also serve on the boards of for-profit corporations. Holding these directors to two different sets of standards might result in confusion. Second, an increase in the standard of care would discourage nonprofit directors from supporting risky or innovative projects that, if successful, might produce worthy and unique results. Directors would not involve their corporations in risky projects if there was a significant chance that they would erroneously be found negligent. Finally, an increase in the standard of care would make service as a director more burdensome and might discourage qualified individuals from accepting directorships on the boards of nonprofit corporations.

The Duty of Loyalty

The trustee standard for the duty of loyalty, which prohibits any self-dealing on the part of a trustee, is both demanding and inflexible. This approach has its advantages. First, if nonprofit directors were held to the trustee standard of loyalty, breaches of fiduciary duty would be easy to spot because any transaction involving the director's personal interests could automatically be set aside. The standard would be easier to administer than a more permissive one. Professor Hansmann argues that "[s]uch a straightforward prohibition of self-dealing could have an enormously salutary effect." According to Hansmann, most cases of self-dealing are easily discoverable and could be prevented by adoption of the stricter standard. Second, provisions in the federal tax code hold private foundations to the strict trustee standard and suggest that Congress approved of using the stricter standard in contexts that are subject to an especially serious risk of self-dealing.

However, imposing such a strict duty of loyalty may cause a nonprofit corporate director to forego opportunities that would benefit the corporation. As the Model Act notes, "many individuals are elected to nonprofit boards because of their ability to enter into or cause an affiliate to enter into a transaction with and for the benefit of the corporation." For example, a banker on the board of a nonprofit corporation may be able to obtain an attractive loan for the corporation. Under the strict trustee standard, the director would violate his duty of loyalty if he arranged such a loan because he would stand to gain if the arrangement generates a profit for the bank. Under the strict standard, the director would be held liable regardless of any benefit accrued by the corporation. Recognizing the potential losses that stem from a blanket prohibition on all self-dealing transactions, the Model Act has adopted the

typical business standard for use in the nonprofit context. Although the standards applicable to the public benefit and mutual benefit corporations differ somewhat, both standards give directors the opportunity to engage in transactions that involve their own interests.

Proposal: Imposing Penalties on Directors Who Violate Their Fiduciary Duties

Increased penalties for breaches of fiduciary duties can be achieved most easily through the imposition of fines on breaching directors. Such fines have long been used to enforce fiduciary duties—for example, the IRS fines directors of private foundations for improper self-dealing. Those fines can be quite steep—up to 200% of the amount involved in the prohibited transactions.

The value of a system of fines can be illustrated through a simple hypothetical. Assume that D, a director of a public benefit nonprofit corporation and sole owner of a bank, arranges for the corporation to obtain a loan from his bank. Interest on the loan has a present value equal to $100 more than loans available at other banks. In other words, D is willing to sacrifice $100 of the corporation's assets to increase his bank's profits by $100. This maneuver would constitute a clear case of impermissible self-dealing regardless of the substantive standard applied because the transaction is patently unfair to the nonprofit corporation. Furthermore, assume that the entire $100 involved in the prohibited transaction accrues to D's benefit.

Theoretically, either an increase in the probability of getting caught or an increase in the fine will deter D sufficiently. Imposing a fine, however, costs far less than increasing the probability of an enforcement action. First, increased fines reduce the number of necessary lawsuits. Second, increased levels of enforcement through the adoption of permissive standing rules open the door to frivolous suits that impose additional costs with little gain. The goal of efficient deterrence is to deter breaches of duty as long as the cost of deterrence is lower than the cost of director breaches as measured by corporate losses. Because it is less expensive to increase a fine than to increase the level of enforcement, the optimal level of undeterred breaches will be lower when fines are levied on breaching directors.

Corporations would not be able to undermine the effectiveness of this system of fines by indemnifying their directors or by purchasing director liability insurance. If directors are fined exclusively for violations of the duty of loyalty, state corporation statutes prohibit the corporation from indemnifying the directors. Furthermore, although states would not prohibit corporations from purchasing insurance to cover such fines, corporations would be unable to purchase insurance that covers duty of loyalty violations. Finally, states will not permit corporations to eliminate director liability for breaches of the duty of loyalty merely by including a liability limitation provision in its certificate of incorporation.

Even if fines could be increased with minimal cost, the imposition of overly burdensome fines would be undesirable in both the mutual and public benefit corporate contexts. If the fine is too high, risk-averse corporate directors may avoid engaging in all self-dealing transactions, even those transactions that would benefit the corporation, for fear that their acts will be found impermissible and that they will be subject to the fine. The determination of the level of fines to be imposed is thus a significant issue.

In addition to determining the level of fines, a penalty system must address the question of who receives the payment. If the penalty system awarded damages directly to the plaintiff instead of to the state or to the corporation, the system might encourage private actions and partially remedy the underenforcement problem discussed above. On the other hand, direct payments to the plaintiffs might encourage additional frivolous actions.

Tax Exemption

Introduction

Many nonprofit organizations are exempt from various forms of taxation under federal and state law. In a debate that has largely focused on the commercial activity of nonprofits, many academics and tax analysts have openly questioned the merits of these exemptions. The central question posed is whether organizations with the ability to generate profits merit public subsidy.

Framing the debate is a lack of consensus regarding the rationale for tax exemption. Some commentators have observed that both the Treasury Department and the courts have administered the tax exemption for nonprofits in a haphazard and inconsistent manner. In response to this apparent disarray, some have sought to develop a rationale that both explains the current system and offers guidance for reform. Unfortunately, much of the academic commentary on tax exemption has understated the significance of local government action to revoke the property tax exemption for certain types of nonprofits.

Because of the significant and tangible value of the local property tax exemption, local authorities have begun to challenge the exempt status of nonprofit organizations. Most of the litigation over the property tax exemption has revolved around interpreting the elusive term "*charitable,*" upon which much of tax exemption law hinges. An examination of this conflict at the state level offers more guidance than exclusively focusing upon the positions of the IRS and the holdings of federal courts.

Overview of Basic Exemption Schemes

Charitable nonprofit organizations are exempt from federal income taxation under provisions of the Internal Revenue Code. In addition, the Code entitles qualifying charitable entities to receive tax deductible contributions from donors, and to issue bonds for which the interest accrued is excluded from the investor's taxable income. Furthermore, organizations that qualify as charitable under state constitutional or statutory provisions are exempt from state income and local property tax.

Federal Income Tax Exemption

Not all nonprofit organizations are exempt from the federal income tax. Section 501(a) limits the exemption to specifically prescribed entities. Organizations described in section 501(c)(3), including those organized for "religious, charitable, scientific . . . or educational purposes," constitute the majority of the organizations that benefit from the exemption. Because most organizations receiving the exemption qualify under the section 501(c)(3) charitable exemption, the reach of that section is the focus of this analysis.

To qualify for tax exemption under section 501(c)(3) an organization must satisfy both the organizational and operational tests described in treasury regulation section 1.501(c)(3)–1. Thus, the organization must be "both organized and operated exclusively for the furtherance of one or more of the purposes" enumerated in section 501(c)(3).

Organizational Test

To satisfy the organizational test, the articles of organization (for example, trust instruments, corporate charters, or articles of association) must limit an organization's purposes to one or more of the listed exempt purposes, and must not expressly empower the organization (except to an insubstantial degree) to engage in any activities that are not in furtherance of an exempt purpose. Further, the articles of organization must provide for the distribution of assets for a public or charitable purpose upon dissolution of the organization.

Operational Test

Even if its articles of organization conform to the requirements of the organizational test, the organization must also satisfy the operational test. The regulations state that "[a]n organization will be regarded as 'operated exclusively' for one or more exempt purposes only if it engages primarily in activities which accomplish one or more of such exempt purposes specified in section 501(c)(3)." Activities other than those that further an exempt purpose are permissible. However, an organization will not be regarded as operating exclusively for exempt purposes "if more than an insubstantial part of its activities is not in furtherance of an exempt purpose."

Exempt Purpose

Specified Exempt Purposes

Although section 501(c)(3) authorizes a variety of qualifying exempt purposes, the most common include educational, religious and charitable. Defining the scope of activities deemed to further such purposes is the most contested aspect of tax exemption law. As defined in the regulations, education relates to "[t]he instruction or training of the individual for the purpose of improving or developing his capabilities [and the] instruction of the public on subjects useful and beneficial to the community." The regulations specify that an educational organization may advocate a particular position as long as it "presents a sufficiently full and fair exposition of the pertinent facts." An organization, however, is not considered educational "if its principal function is the mere presentation of unsupported opinion." Attempting to distinguish educational material from mere propaganda has embroiled the IRS in constitutional controversy.

Religion is specifically designated an exempt purpose by section 501(c)(3). Because of the constitutional separation of church and state, it may be difficult to advance a direct challenge to an organization's claim to be organized and operated for religious purposes. Thus, the IRS must be careful not to discriminate against any religious group in the administration of tax exemptions. However, the IRS has revoked the exempt status of religious organizations when the organization conferred private benefits on its members, or when the organization did not serve an exclusively religious purpose.

The law of tax exemption cannot be understood without interpreting the term *charitable.* The term implies both a statutory definition of a category of exempt activities, and a common law requirement that the organization must advance charitable ends. The first meaning of charitable is, as previously noted, reflected in the Code's enumeration of certain specific categories of activities that presumably justify exemption. The term *"charitable,"* as used in section 501(c)(3), is a catch-all phrase encompassing all activities that, although not specified in the subsection, can reasonably be claimed to serve a charitable purpose. Unfortunately, neither the statute nor the regulations explicitly define *"charitable."* According to the treasury regulations, the term *"charitable"* is used "in its generally accepted legal sense . . . [and includes] [r]elief of the poor . . . ; advancement of religion; advancement of education or science; erection or maintenance of public buildings, monuments, or works; lessening of the burdens of Government; and promotion of social welfare." This list, however, does not purport to be exhaustive.

Concerning the second use of *"charitable,"* the Supreme Court has held that all organizations exempt from taxation under section 501(c)(3) must be charitable in practice, regardless of their specifically enumerated purpose. In *Bob Jones University v. United States,* the Court held that, "underlying all relevant parts of the Code, is the intent that entitlement to tax exemption depends on meeting certain common-law standards of charity—namely, that an institution seeking tax-exempt status must serve a public purpose and not be contrary to established public policy." For example, discrimination on the basis of race violates public policy, and will deprive an otherwise charitable educational organization of exempt status. Similarly, evidence of engaging in illegal activity jeopardizes an organization's exempt status.

Commercial Activity

Engaging in commercial activity does not preclude an organization from being deemed to serve an exempt purpose. However, the commercial activity cannot constitute the organization's primary purpose. Income generated from commercial activity that is unrelated to the organization's exempt purpose may be subject to the unrelated business income tax.

Unrelated Business Income Tax

A nonprofit's exemption from federal income tax is limited to income derived from activity substantially related to the organization's exempt purpose. Income derived from unrelated activities is subject to the unrelated business income tax. The rationale underlying the unre-

lated business income tax is to limit unfair competition between for-profit businesses and tax-exempt nonprofits.

Unrelated business taxable income (UBTI) is the "gross income derived by any organization from any unrelated trade or business . . . regularly carried on by it, less the deductions . . . directly connected with the carrying on of such trade or business." Unrelated trade or business means "any trade or business the conduct of which is not substantially related . . . to the exercise or performance by such organization of its charitable, educational, or other purpose or function constituting the basis for its exemption." Exceptions to this general provision cover work performed by volunteers, revenue from business conducted for the convenience of the nonprofit's members or employees, sale of donated goods, certain hospital services, and certain activities of conventions and trade shows.

The law has not yet clearly resolved when income received by exempt organizations should be considered UBTI. The regulations set out the three factors to be considered in determining whether income should be taxed as UBTI. Revenue is includable in UBTI if, "1) it is income from a trade or business; 2) such trade or business is regularly carried on by the organization; and 3) the conduct of such trade or business is not substantially related . . . to the organization's performance of its exempt functions."

The term *trade* or *business,* as used in section 513, means any activity carried on to produce income from the sale of goods or the performance of services. Regularly carried on activities are those that "manifest a frequency and continuity, and are pursued in a manner, generally similar to comparable commercial activities of nonexempt organizations." To constitute a substantially related activity, the commercial activity from which the income is derived must "contribute importantly" to accomplishing the exempt charitable purpose.

General Prohibitions

In addition to meeting the specific criteria enumerated above, an organization must abide by two additional general prohibitions in order to qualify for tax exemption. Regardless of its particular purpose, no organization can be granted tax-exempt status if part of its earnings inure to the benefit of private shareholders. This prohibition of private inurement is not limited to the distribution of dividends, but also applies to the conferral of any direct or indirect benefit to a private interest.

The Code specifically provides that a section 501(c)(3) organization must not carry on propaganda, attempt to influence legislation, or participate or intervene in political campaigns. The regulations define any organization that violates this provision as an "action organization" that is not exempt from income taxation.

Tax Exemption and State Law

All states with a corporate tax provide an exemption for nonprofit charitable organizations. In administering the corporate income tax exemption, most states simply follow federal practice either by granting a statutory exemption to any organization exempt under section 501(c)(3), or by using statutory language similar to that used in the Code without specific reference to it.

Real and personal property that is owned by nonprofit charitable organizations and is used for a charitable purpose is also exempt from taxation under state constitutional and statutory provisions. To qualify for property tax exemption under most state schemes, an organization must, at a minimum, meet two organizational requirements. First, the entity must be organized as a nonprofit that pays out no dividends or income other than wages. Second, its assets must be irrevocably committed to serving charitable purposes. In addition, the property in question must be used primarily for an exempt purpose that benefits an indefinite, non-exclusive class of people.

The property tax exemption differs from income tax exemption in that it is granted by the state, yet the impact from lost revenues falls upon local governmental entities. If a state legislature authorizes an exemption broader than one deemed appropriate by municipal officials, courts must frequently mediate the conflict.

Charitable Solicitation

Nonprofit charitable organizations raise the bulk of their working capital through telephone, mail, and in-person solicitation of prospective individual donors. Of the $122.57 billion given to charity in 1990, some 83% came from individuals. Federal and state tax codes promote charitable solicitation by providing numerous incentives to both donors and controllers of nonprofit organizations; furthermore, common law contract rules accord charities certain special advantages in fundraising.

The preferred legal status of charities and charitable fundraising, however, has come under mounting attack in recent decades. The increased technological and organizational sophistication of modern charities, coupled with the appearance of extremely profitable professional solicitation firms, has created opportunities for sharp practice beyond the traditional evils of solicitation fraud and small-scale confidence games. One practice—contingent-fee fundraising—tends to provoke special outrage from the donating public. The contingent-fee solicitor typically contracts to raise funds through direct mail or telemarketing campaigns in return for a percentage of the donated receipts. Because of the high start-up costs of such campaigns, charities sometimes receive only 5%–10% of the gross donated amount.

As state agencies have realized that traditional anti-fraud laws do not apply to contingent-fee solicitation, states have attempted either to establish upper limits on the percentages that solicitors can charge charities or to require disclosure of fundraising contract terms to potential donors. However, a growing body of federal decisional law in the 1980s found these new legal controls on charitable solicitation to be unconstitutional invasions of charities' and solicitors' First Amendment rights. The end result is a system that maintains state and federal incentives for charitable solicitation, but in which countervailing legal restrictions have disappeared. In an attempt to reassert control, states have imposed a crazy-quilt of burdensome registration and auditing requirements.

The Regulatory Framework

Legal rules affecting charitable solicitation can generally be classified as either codified contribution incentives or as regulations designed to minimize opportunities for deceptive fundraising. These categories are complementary; conditions on the availability of incentives extend government control over charities seeking benefits, while direct regulatory schemes often enhance public willingness to contribute by establishing classes of 'safe' charities. Both state and federal law provide incentives, but direct regulation is almost exclusively the province of state law.

Restrictions on Charitable Solicitation

At present, mandatory restrictions upon charitable solicitors—rules that prescribe disclosure and recordkeeping, as well as controls on the time, place and manner of solicitation—derive from state statutory law. Although, in practice, restrictions on eligibility for federal tax incentives secure compliance from nonprofit firms, nonprofits retain a legal option to refuse the federal subsidy and continue the disfavored behavior.

Reporting and accounting requirements intended to curtail solicitation abuse constitute the most common form of state regulation. Most states require charities to register before commencing a solicitation campaign. In addition, charities often must file an annual financial statement with the state. However, because many states have idiosyncratic statutory specifications and are reluctant to penalize technical violations of registration and reporting guidelines, increasing state regulation has led to substantial non-compliance by impecunious charities.

Some states' regulatory schemes distinguish "fundraising counsel" from "professional solicitors." Fundraising counsel are typically companies that work for a flat fee, have established charities as clients, and perform little or no in-person or telephone solicitation. Professional solicitors are contingent-fee fundraisers who, in the view of state officials, are more likely to exploit charities by demanding "unreasonable" fees

or misappropriating solicited funds. In many states, solicitors must post a substantial bond before initiating campaigns, especially if the solicitor will take custody of funds before passing on the charity's share.

Restrictions on contingent-fee fundraising contracts are the most controversial category of direct state regulation of solicitation. Contingent-fee contracts typically provide that the solicitor's fundraising expenses will be reimbursed from gross receipts and that the solicitor will receive a fixed percentage of receipts as a fee. High percentage fundraising contracts are used by new, small, or unpopular charities trying to establish a solid presence in the charitable solicitation market. By contrast, large and established charities more frequently rely upon in-house fundraisers, employ a substantial number of volunteers, or pay flat fees to fundraising counsel.

Contingent-fee agreements tend to incite substantial outcry among donors, for donors who learn that the lion's share of their contribution has gone to pay fundraising fees often feel that they have been victims of fraud, regardless of the financial necessity of the charity in question to use such methods. The tendency for small, local charities to pay high contingent fees, and to be the vehicles or victims of actual solicitation fraud, only exacerbates these perceptions. As a result, state legislatures and attorneys general have historically displayed substantial hostility towards contingent-fee fundraising; established charities that resent competing for donor dollars with new organizations have also discouraged this type of fundraising. Many states have tried to regulate contingent-fee arrangements by enacting percentage ceilings on the contingent fee or by providing for mandatory disclosure of fundraising percentages. However, these efforts have encountered insurmountable constitutional barriers.

Constitutional Restrictions on State Regulation

In the 1980s, the Supreme Court embarked on a course of broadly interpreting the First Amendment to provide constitutional protection for both charities and professional fundraisers seeking to enter into percentage-based contracts. It is now settled law that states may neither directly set upper limits on a professional fundraiser's percentage fees nor establish a statutory minimum percentage of donations that must be devoted to charitable programs. Furthermore, it is unconstitutional for states to force solicitors to make pre-solicitation disclosures of the percentage of donations that will actually be turned over to the charity.

Political Activity of Nonprofit Corporations

Nonprofit corporations play an increasingly prominent role in shaping American public opinion and in influencing public policy. Nonprofit organizations such as the Sierra Club, the American Civil Liberties Union, and the National Rifle Association are perennial high-profile participants in political discourse. Other, less overtly political groups, such as the Child Poverty Action Group and the Catholic Church, also lobby the government and mount public opinion campaigns to affect the formulation of social policy. Even many nonprofit corporations whose principal mission is the direct provision of services to their beneficiaries engage in some degree of advocacy.

The political advocacy of nonprofit corporations enhances the political influence of underrepresented groups and secures a place on the social agenda for otherwise neglected concerns. Consumer safety, the environment, and drunk driving are but three important contemporary issues that nonprofit organizations have helped to place in the forefront of public consciousness.

Federal and state governments primarily rely on the tax codes and the election laws that restrict campaign financing and expenditures to regulate nonprofit corporations' political activity. Federal and state tax codes link a nonprofit organization's tax-exempt status and its eligibility to receive deductible contributions to limitations on the organization's political speech. Election laws restrict nearly all corporations' campaign expenditures in an attempt to protect

both the political system as a whole and the organizations' individual members from the potentially negative consequences of corporate political activity.

Nonetheless, nonprofits' political expression does receive some protection under the First Amendment. In two recent cases, the Supreme Court has weighed campaign expenditure regulations against the demands of the First Amendment's guarantee of freedom of expression. In *Federal Election Commission v. Massachusetts Citizens for Life,* the Court held that election law spending restrictions violate the First Amendment when they are applied to nonprofit corporations that were established to promote political ideas, have no shareholders, and receive no funds from business corporations. According to the Court, these characteristics serve to indicate that the organization's funds and membership mirror the organization's political support. Three years later, however, in *Austin v. Michigan Chamber of Commerce,* the Court upheld the constitutionality of similar spending restrictions as applied to a different nonprofit corporation. The *Austin* Court used a three-prong test to identify those nonprofit corporations whose independent expenditures were unrepresentative of the organization's political base and therefore not constitutionally protected.

Constraints on Political Advocacy by Nonprofit Corporations

Both the tax code and the laws regulating election expenditures restrict the political speech of nonprofit corporations. The tax laws condition the tax-exempt status of a nonprofit corporation as well as its eligibility to receive deductible contributions on the extent of its lobbying activity. In addition, federal and state election laws restrict campaign expenditures by all corporations, whether operated for profit or not.

Limitations Under the Tax Code

A nonprofit corporation may qualify for federal tax exemption through one of twenty-seven provisions codified in sections 501(c)(1) through 501(c)(23), sections 501(d), (e), and (f), and section 521(a) of the Internal Revenue Code. Each of these provisions specifies permissible organizational activities. Some provisions impose particular limitations on the covered organization's political activity. Thus, the Code provision under which an organization seeks exemption defines the range of political activities in which it may engage. The Code provisions governing public charities and social welfare organizations impose much tighter restrictions on the political activities of these nonprofits than other sections of the tax code do on other types of nonprofits. In general, the political activity of other types of nonprofit organizations is not limited by the Code. The Code also imposes a number of other general structural requirements on charitable and social welfare organizations that are not imposed on other types of nonprofit organizations. For example, other types of nonprofit organizations such as homeowners' clubs and trade associations are permitted to have a variety of purposes, most of which involve the provision of economic or social benefits to the organization's members.

Public Charitable Organizations: Section 501(c)(3)

Nonprofit corporations that qualify for exemption under section 501(c)(3) must have an educational, religious, charitable, or other public purpose. In addition to granting them tax-exempt status, the Code allows these corporations to receive deductible contributions. Accordingly, their political expression is strictly controlled—they may not intervene in political campaigns and may not devote a substantial portion of their activity to legislative lobbying. They can, however, engage in activities that enhance the general political awareness of the citizenry, as long as they do so in a nonpartisan manner. For example, section 501(c)(3) organizations may conduct surveys and sponsor debates to focus public attention on candidates and on pressing social issues. The presidential debates formerly sponsored by the League of Women Voters provide a more specific example of the kind of activity permissible under section 501(c)(3). Because the

League did not use the debates to evaluate the candidates themselves, prevented the debates from becoming biased, and allowed all qualified candidates to participate, it did not lose its tax exemption under the section. Under no circumstances may a section 501(c)(3) organization criticize candidates or incumbents. An organization may, however, express an opinion about a politician's position on a given issue as long as it does not do so during a political campaign.

If a policy-related, political communication displays both specificity and subjectivity, it will be held to be an attempt to influence legislation. Specificity refers to the relationship between the communication and a concrete policy objective. The IRS does not equate efforts to alter general societal attitudes with efforts to influence legislation. Instead, an organization violates the specificity test only if its political message encourages specific legislative action or calls for a policy change that could occur only through legislative action. For example, the IRS has ruled that an organization's attempts to increase societal tolerance for homosexuality through presenting seminars and discussion groups focusing on the positive role of homosexual men and women in society did not constitute an attempt to influence legislation.

In contrast, the subjectivity test focuses on the methods of persuasion rather than the message itself. The test represents an attempt to identify communications that employ argument rather than fact in advocating particular positions. It treats factual analysis and logical reasoning as less egregious methods of influencing legislation than appeals to emotion and normative judgments. Thus, even if a communication addresses a specific legislative proposal, it may not result in the loss or denial of tax-exempt status if the organization has relied exclusively on objective evidence and not on subjective assertions in presenting its positions. For example, the IRS ruled that a legal education organization that collected and disseminated research findings on the probable efficiency of a proposal for the reform of state courts was not attempting to influence legislation.

If a court finds that a nonprofit organization is attempting to influence legislation, it must then determine whether such attempts consti- tute a "substantial" part of the organization's ac- tivities. Although courts sometimes focus on the absolute amount spent on lobbying, they gener- ally make this determination by comparing the amount the organization spent on lobbying with its total expenditures. However, neither the IRS nor the courts have determined what percentage of its income a nonprofit corporation may spend on lobbying before its efforts will be deemed substantial. For example, when an orga- nization's lobbying expenditures are large in ab- solute terms, courts may deem them substantial even though they comprise a relatively small part of the organization's overall outlay. The in- ability to predict limitations on lobbying activity has caused some organizations to avoid engag- ing in lobbying altogether.

In an effort to address the vagueness and sub- jectivity of the substantiality test, Congress in- cluded more precise lobbying expenditure limits in the 1976 Tax Reform Act. Moreover, the IRS issued additional regulations in August 1990 to help courts and organizations determine what activities should be considered attempts to in- fluence legislation under the revised standard. Sections 501(h) and 4911 of the Internal Rev- enue Code, provisions under which nonprofit organizations may choose to be regulated, now impose a numerical upper-limit for lobbying ex- penditures. This numerical limit provides a clear, more easily administered standard by which to assess the substantiality of an organiza- tion's lobbying efforts. Unfortunately, only about one percent of the organizations eligible to operate under the limit have elected to do so.

Social Welfare Organizations: Section 501(c)(4)

Section 501(c)(4), which governs the activities of "social welfare organizations," confers tax-ex- empt status on many politically active nonprofit corporations, including environmental organi- zations such as the Sierra Club, and political re- form advocates such as the Heritage Founda- tion and the League of Women Voters. To qualify for section 501(c)(4) tax exempt status, an organization must confer benefits on either a

charitable class or the community at large. These benefits may not be limited to the organi- zation's membership or particular individuals or businesses.

Both section 501(c)(3) and section 501(c)(4) regulate nonprofit corporations that serve "char- itable" goals. This term has been defined to in- clude not only traditional relief for the disad- vantaged, but also activities that benefit the community and lessen the burdens of govern- ment. These activities must demonstrably ad- vance the public interest. Examples include maintaining a volunteer fire department, beauti- fying public areas, providing consumer credit counseling to the general public, providing secu- rity patrols, and working to improve neighbor- hood housing and residential parking. Organi- zations whose activities primarily benefit their membership are not eligible for exemption un- der section 501(c)(4). For example, nonprofit organizations that purchase goods at discount prices on behalf of their members do not qual- ify, nor do those that provide their members with retirement or death benefits. The distinc- tion between a group's membership and the general public is often strictly maintained. Thus, although an organization that planned to supply closed-circuit television to its members in an area where conventional television signals were unavailable did not qualify as a social welfare or- ganization, a group in a similar community that broadcast its signal to the general public did.

Because the IRS has not recognized endorse- ments of, or opposition to, particular candidates as an activity that promotes social welfare, sec- tion 501(c)(4) organizations are limited in the amount of election-related advocacy in which they can engage. Although the IRS regards *some* level of campaign advocacy as consistent with exemption under section 501(c)(4), precisely what that level is remains unclear. Thus, social welfare organizations cannot engage in substan- tial amounts of election-related advocacy with- out fear of losing their tax-exempt status.

Although section 501(c)(4) social welfare or- ganizations and section 501(c)(3) public chari- ties are the two most similar types of nonprofit organizations, two important differences exist between them. First, section 501(c)(3) organizations are regulated with respect to both their electoral and legislative advocacy, whereas section 501(c)(4) organizations are restricted only in their attempts to intervene in elections. Second, section 501(c)(3) organizations are eligible for deductible contributions, whereas section 501(c)(4) groups are not.

Election and Campaign Finance Restrictions

Apart from the classifications of the tax code, election finance laws that restrict the ability of all corporations to make both campaign contributions and other independent political expenditures provide the major source of regulation of nonprofit corporations' political activity. These laws limit the amount of money that corporations are permitted to contribute both directly and indirectly to support candidates or causes.

Direct Contributions

The Federal Election Campaign Act (FECA) and many states' election laws forbid corporations—including nonprofit corporations—from making direct contributions to candidates. Under FECA, however, a corporation may establish a separate segregated fund, or political action committee (PAC). This segregated fund, which must be funded by independent contributions, not by the corporation's general treasury funds, may be used to make political contributions. Each PAC may contribute up to $5,000 per candidate per election, if it has qualified as a multicandidate committee; if it has not, it may contribute up to $1,000.

Most states have enacted election laws, modeled after FECA, that restrict the amount corporations may contribute to candidates. Nineteen states prohibit all direct corporate contributions, although most of these states permit the corporation to administer a PAC. Four states prohibit only certain types of corporations, such as public utilities, from making contributions. Louisiana and Missouri require a corporation's board of directors to authorize political contributions before they are made. Ten states set a statutory ceiling on the amount a corporation

may contribute; Indiana and the District of Columbia limit the amount of contributions according to the office being contested. The remaining thirteen states impose no restrictions on corporate contributions.

Independent Expenditures

Election laws also regulate nonprofit corporations' independent political expenditures—that is, expenses such as newspaper advertisements incurred by the corporation without prior approval of, or consultation with, a candidate or campaign organization. Federal law prohibits corporations from using general treasury funds to cover any such expenditures; corporations must instead use segregated PAC funds to pay for these activities. The federal government has not, however, set a ceiling on independent PAC expenditures.

On the state level, independent political expenditures are subject to much less regulation than are direct contributions. Most states require only that corporations making political expenditures follow the procedures set forth in the general campaign finance laws of the particular state. Only thirteen states prohibit independent corporate expenditures entirely, compared with the nineteen that do so in the case of direct contributions. Five states permit independent expenditures but limit their amount. Finally, Louisiana and Missouri impose the same broad authorization requirements on independent expenditures as they do on corporate contributions.

Special Treatment and Tort Law

Nonprofit organizations receive their most conspicuously favorable treatment through the tax laws. They have, however, historically received privileged treatment in many other areas of the law as well. Specifically, nonprofits have enjoyed special treatment under the laws governing unemployment insurance, bankruptcy, Social Security, collective bargaining, securities regulation, the minimum wage, copyright, antitrust, custom duties, and postal rates. Just as many commentators have debated and questioned the favorable tax treatment that non-profit organizations enjoy, many have also questioned the advantages afforded nonprofits in other areas. Commentators have argued that the policies underlying many of these regulatory regimes do not support privileged treatment for all nonprofits. In some fields, the law has responded by eliminating or curtailing the special treatment provided to nonprofit organizations.

The Evolution of Special Tort Treatment

Advantageous tort treatment of nonprofit organizations has assumed several forms over the past hundred years. Near the turn of the century, courts developed the doctrine of charitable immunity that barred virtually all suits against nonprofit organizations. The doctrine emerged from dicta in two early English cases and, over time, charitable immunity has been grounded on four questionable justifications. Despite its weak theoretical basis, the doctrine had been accepted in forty states by 1938. The tide turned during the 1940s and 1950s when the broad movement to eliminate restraints on tort recovery caused charitable immunity to fall into disfavor. By 1985, almost every American jurisdiction had at least partially renounced the doctrine.

Recent developments affecting nonprofit liability have rekindled the debate over favorable tort treatment for nonprofit organizations. First, the general expansion of tort liability has exposed nonprofit and charitable organizations to a larger amount of potential liability. A number of recent, high-profile tort cases against nonprofits and charities have revealed their vulnerability to suit. The large judgments and settlements obtained by plaintiffs in these cases have saddled the defendant charities with staggering financial burdens.

Second, the hard insurance market of the 1980s revealed that nonprofits cannot always readily obtain liability insurance. The development of an advanced insurance industry had led many judges and commentators to argue for the abrogation of charitable immunity, claiming that charities could alleviate their liability problems simply by purchasing insurance. However, the mid–1980s brought a period of rising rates and shrinking coverage, and many nonprofit and charitable organizations reported severe difficulties in procuring affordable liability insurance.

Third, individuals working in the nonprofit sector have faced an increase in personal liability. Historically, the number of lawsuits filed against nonprofit directors and officers or direct service volunteers in their individual capacity has been very small. During the past decade, however, there has been a marked increase in the number of suits filed against individuals acting for nonprofit organizations. Because for-profit organizations typically have far greater resources than individuals to pay tort judgments, victims ordinarily prefer to sue parent organizations. In the nonprofit sector, however, the situation is often reversed. Plaintiffs frequently bring suit against individuals serving in the nonprofit sector because those individuals have "deeper pockets" than the organizations they serve. Because of the prohibitive cost of merely defending against even the weakest of tort claims, the threat of liability strongly deters many individuals from working or volunteering for nonprofit organizations. Because many nonprofits rely heavily on volunteers, these organizations are less able to fulfill their mission when the specter of liability frightens individuals from service.

The State of the Law

Driven largely by these developments, favorable tort treatment for nonprofit and charitable organizations has persisted and reemerged in a wide variety of modified forms. Some states have addressed liability issues at the organizational level by retaining old charitable immunity rules or by ratifying new statutes that establish partial immunity or limited liability for nonprofit and charitable organizations. Other states have directed their efforts at the individual level and have passed new laws designed to shield specific sets of actors in the nonprofit sector from liability.

In creating new forms of charitable and individual immunity, most state legislatures have tried to balance competing public policies. On the one hand, states are concerned that unlimited liability will deter organizations and individuals from engaging in beneficial activity. On the other hand, states fear that blanket immunity will systematically deny compensation to a class of victims and will fail to deter certain organizations from engaging in too much risky and harmful behavior. As a result, legislators have struck a variety of compromises and enacted liability arrangements that fall somewhere between the extremes of full liability and complete immunity. Yet no consensus has developed among states on exactly how or where to strike the balance between the extremes of full liability and complete immunity. Thus, nonprofit tort law across the United States is currently an erratic patchwork of rules.

The Organizational Level

Case Law

Because traditional charitable immunity was a judicially-created doctrine, some states have preserved organizational immunity through case law. By never fully abrogating the common law doctrine, the courts of six states have retained some form of immunity for charitable organizations. Complete immunity has been retained by one state. Two jurisdictions shield charities from suits brought by the beneficiaries of its activities. Organizations that render services without charge remain fully immune from suit in one state. In another state, organizations that derive their funds from charitable donations retain full immunity, and another state grants immunity to organizations whose assets are in trust and who have no liability insurance.

A similar montage of rules exists in the four states in which limited liability for charitable organizations has evolved through case law. In two states, charitable assets and property are exempt from tort judgments. In another state, liability is limited to the amount of an organization's liability insurance coverage. One state protects trust funds from liability.

Statutory Law

A total of nine state legislatures have provided either partial immunity or limited liability for nonprofit or charitable organizations. Four states have placed absolute dollar limits on the recovery allowed in suits against certain organizations. The level of these limits varies significantly among these jurisdictions. Two states limit recovery to the extent of an organization's insurance coverage. One state provides blanket immunity to organizations providing free services, and another grants immunity against suits brought by beneficiaries. Finally, one state shields organizations from suits based on a volunteer's criminal activity.

The Individual Level

State Activity

Because the common law doctrine of charitable immunity shielded only organizations, protection of individuals affiliated with nonprofits has come solely through state statutory developments. Almost every state has passed legislation that affects the liability of individuals involved with nonprofit or charitable organizations. Again, both the type and extent of immunity vary greatly from state to state.

The state statutes differ regarding the type of organization an individual must be serving in order to qualify for tort immunity. Many of the statutes define qualified organizations in terms of tax-exempt status under the Internal Revenue Code. Other states use their own definitions of charities, nonprofit organizations, and nonprofit corporations to identify qualified institutions. Still other jurisdictions employ a combination of definitions and often include in their statutes specific provisions that are designed to include or exclude particular types of organizations. In some states, volunteers working for a nonprofit or charitable organization are shielded from tort suits only if the organization has liability insurance.

The statutes also vary regarding which individuals are entitled to protection. The majority of statutes cover the directors, officers, and board members of nonprofit or charitable organizations. Most of these laws protect only unpaid board members; however, some statutes shield even the paid directors and officers of nonprofit or charitable organizations. Only about half of the states have statutes that protect all uncompensated volunteers regardless of their position within a qualified organization. Thus, in many instances, those individuals who govern and manage nonprofit and charitable organizations receive more protection from liability than those who donate their services. Many states, however, do have specific statutes that immunize volunteers involved with sports programs or particular sporting events.

Every statute that shields individuals from liability has exceptions. Willful, wanton, or intentional harmful behavior by an individual is not protected under the vast majority of statutes. Similarly, most statutes deny immunity if an individual's behavior is reckless or grossly negligent. Another common provision strips liability protection if an individual was not acting in good faith. Some laws also provide that liability protection does not extend to harms caused during the operation of a motor vehicle. A variety of more particularized exceptions also appear in a number of statutes.

Special Treatment Across Regulatory Regimes

The previous section's tort analysis provides broad insights into various other regulatory privileges that nonprofit organizations have traditionally received. As with tort law, there are theoretical reasons why standard regulatory rules should not be applied generally to nonprofit organizations. Nevertheless, the special treatment given to nonprofits in other regulatory regimes engenders problems akin to those associated with forms of tort immunity.

As with standard tort law, most other regulatory rules were developed under the assumption that they would be applied to for-profit actors with standard economic motivations. Thus, given the distinctly non-economic motivations of nonprofit organizations, standard regulatory rules appear inappropriate, if not unnecessary,

in the nonprofit context. For example, securities regulations or unfair competition rules might seem superfluous because nonprofit organizations, lacking a profit motive, are presumably less apt to violate these regulations than for-profit organizations. Similarly, because certain nonprofits intentionally do not capture the full monetary value of what they produce, forcing them to pay full postal rates or to contribute fully to Social Security seems inappropriate. Furthermore, complete regulatory compliance necessarily entails certain costs. Therefore, even if it is suitable to apply certain regulations to nonprofits, enforcing standard regulatory rules will tax nonprofits' resources and thus operate to diminish or deter at least some nonprofit activity. Regulatory exemption might thus seem justified as one way to subsidize the work of nonprofit organizations.

Yet even though full application of standard regulatory rules may be inappropriate for nonprofits, complete regulatory exemptions or large regulatory advantages are worse alternatives. First, the benefits provided by regulatory exemptions or advantages are usually correlated not to an organization's overall level of good works, but rather to some unsound factor. Indeed, the amount of benefits received by a nonprofit often depends on the extent to which the nonprofit can exploit its regulatory advantages. For example, exemptions from collective bargaining rules and special postal rates benefit a nonprofit to the extent that it strikes hard labor bargains and uses the mail. Even more troubling, the advantages nonprofits receive from favorable regulatory treatment often come either directly or indirectly at the expense of the very parties that the regulations are designed to protect. For example, exemptions from securities regulations and antitrust laws allow nonprofit organizations to take advantage of investors and engage in monopolistic behavior to the detriment of consumers.

The current structure of many of the regulatory advantages presents a further concern. The primary rationales justifying special treatment of nonprofit organizations are that they work in the public interest and that they produce significant external benefits. Appropriately, special treatment in tort law has traditionally been confined to pure charities—organizations that as a class generally engage in public works and seek to externalize benefits. Yet in many other regulatory regimes, special treatment is afforded to most if not all nonprofits, many of which neither work in the public interest nor seek to produce significant external benefits.

Finally, beyond the problems stemming from individual regulatory advantages, there is a "double-counting" problem that arises from special treatment across regulatory regimes. Reaping extensive benefits under one regulatory advantage does not preclude a nonprofit from obtaining further benefits under another regulatory scheme. Because there is no mechanism to limit nonprofits' benefits, the amorphic notion that nonprofits do "good work" has resulted in an array of regulatory advantages that allows nonprofits to garner repeated indirect subsidies. These regulatory subsidies, moreover, come in addition to the favorable tax treatment nonprofits traditionally receive.

Unfortunately, because of the absence of any systematic empirical data, it is again difficult to determine the precise practical consequences of nonprofit regulatory privileges. Nevertheless, anecdotal accounts of the Harvard Law School exploiting its postal advantages and hospitals taking advantage of their collective bargaining exemption suggest that regulatory privileges create more than merely theoretical problems. Though many general arguments can be made for subsidizing certain types of nonprofits, administering indirect benefits through the vast regulatory system is clearly not a sound means of doing so. Consequently, legislators should no longer reflexively provide privileged treatment, but rather should generally apply standard regulatory rules to nonprofits. Only when special treatment can be specifically justified should regulatory advantages even be considered. Furthermore, even when a sufficient rationale exists for the special treatment of nonprofits, legislators must look for more sophisticated and efficient solutions than simple regulatory exemptions. As the discussion of tort law illustrates, there are often alternatives to complete exemption that pro-

vide better solutions to the problems created by the full application of regulatory regimes to nonprofits. Thus, the law should continue to eliminate or curtail broad regulatory advantages for nonprofits, and retain at most narrow provisions designed to remedy the specific problems that standard regulatory rules create.

Conclusion

The pendulum has swung back and forth with regard to the tort treatment of nonprofit and charitable organizations. At one extreme, the common law historically immunized these organizations from suit. Swinging to the other extreme, almost all states, responding to modern tort principles, eliminated tort advantages and imposed full liability. However, when the economic consequences of full liability began to threaten the operations of nonprofit and charitable organizations, many state legislatures propelled the law toward a middle course by creating liability arrangements for nonprofit and charitable organizations between the extremes of complete immunity and full liability.

Unfortunately, state laws steer a middle course that is unsound both practically and theoretically. Although recognizing the problems that need to be addressed, state legislators fail to adopt the best solutions to these problems. Instead of creating new liability standards, states should directly help nonprofit organizations that externalize benefits to cover their accident costs. Only by devising government-supported comprehensive tort schemes can legislators properly respond to the special tort problems in the nonprofit sector.

Finally, legislators cannot operate myopically when granting any form of privileged treatment to nonprofits. When providing tort subsidies, states must be cognizant of the advantages different nonprofits are able to glean in other areas of the law. To create optimal legislation, lawmakers must observe the entire regulatory landscape and coordinate all subsidies and preferential treatment granted to nonprofit and charitable organizations.

CHAPTER 6

The Law of Tax-Exempt Organizations
Organizational, Operational, and Similar Tests

BRUCE R. HOPKINS

§ 4.1 Considerations of Form

Generally, the Internal Revenue Code does not prescribe a specific organizational form for entities to qualify for tax exemption. Basically, the choices are nonprofit corporation, trust, or unincorporated association.[1] However, some provisions of the Code expressly mandate, in whole or in part, the corporate form,[2] and other Code provisions mandate the trust form.[3] Throughout the categories of tax-exempt organizations are additional terms such as *clubs, associations, societies, leagues, companies, boards, orders, posts,* and *units,* which are not terms referencing legal forms. For tax purposes, an organization may be deemed a corporation even though it is not formally incorporated.[4]

The federal tax provision which describes charitable organizations[5] provides that an organization described in that provision must be a corporation, community chest, fund, or foundation. An unincorporated association or trust can qualify under this provision, presumably as a fund or foundation or perhaps, as noted, as a corporation.[6] However, a partnership cannot be tax-exempt as a charitable organization.[7]

An organization already exempt from federal taxation may establish a separate fund or like entity that is itself an exempt organization.[8] The attributes of this type of a fund include a separate category of tax exemption (for example, an educational research and scholarship fund established by a bar association[9]), a separate governing body, and separate books and accounts.[10] However, a mere bank deposit cannot amount to a requisite fund; thus, a contribution to it would be considered a nondeductible gift to an individual rather than a possibly deductible gift to a qualified organization.[11]

The formalities of organization of an entity may have a bearing on the tax exemption. This is the case not only in connection with the sufficiency of the governing instruments,[12] but also, and more fundamentally, with regard to whether there is a separate organization in the first instance. An individual may perform worthwhile activities, such as providing financial assistance to needy students, but will receive no tax benefits from his or her beneficence, unless he or she establishes and funds a qualified organization that in turn renders the charitable works, such as scholarship grants. One court observed, in the process of denying a charitable contribution deduction, that the federal tax law makes no provision for a charitable deduction in the context of personal ventures, however praiseworthy in character. The court noted that "[t]here is no evidence of such enterprise being a corporation, community chest, fund, or foundation and little information, if any, as to its organization or activities.[13] However, assuming the organization is not operated to benefit private interests, its tax exemption will not be endangered because its creator serves as the sole trustee and exercises complete control,[14] although state law may limit or preclude close control.

It is the position of the IRS that a "formless aggregation of individuals" cannot be tax-exempt as a charitable entity.[15] At a minimum, the entity—to be exempt—must have an organizing instrument, some governing rules, and regularly chosen officers.[16] These rules have been amply illustrated in the cases concerning so-called personal churches.[17]

As of January 1, 1997, a tax-exempt organization generally is treated for tax purposes as a corporation. This is a consequence of adoption by the IRS of entity classification regulations largely pertaining to business corporations, by which they elect to be regarded for tax purposes as corporations or partnerships. Under these regulations, an exempt organization is treated as having made an election to be classified as an *association*.[18] This classification, in turn, causes the entity to be regarded as a corporation.[19]

Among the nontax factors to be considered in selecting an organizational form are legal liabilities in relation to the individuals involved (the corporate form can limit certain personal liabilities), local law requirements, necessities of governing instruments, local annual reporting requirements, organizational expenses, and any membership requirements.[20] Federal law, other than the tax laws, may also have a bearing on the choice, such as the organization's comparable status under the postal laws.[21]

A change in form may require a tax-exempt organization to reapply for recognition of tax-exempt status. For example, an unincorporated organization that has been recognized by the IRS as a tax-exempt charitable entity must commence the application anew if it incorporates.[22]

§ 4.2 Governing Instruments

An organization must have governing instruments to qualify for tax exemption, if only to satisfy the appropriate organizational test. This is particularly the case for charitable organizations, as to which the federal tax law imposes specific organizational requirements.[23] These rules are more stringent if the charitable organization is a private foundation.[24]

If the corporate form is used, the governing instruments will be articles of incorporation and bylaws. An unincorporated organization will have articles of organization, perhaps in the form of a constitution, and, undoubtedly, also bylaws. If a trust, the basic document will be a declaration of trust or trust agreement.

The articles of organization should contain provisions stating the organization's purposes; whether there will be members and, if so, their qualifications and classes; the initial board of directors or trustee(s); the registered agent and incorporators (if a corporation); the dissolution or liquidation procedure; and the required language referencing the appropriate tax law (federal and state) requirements and prohibitions. If the organization is a corporation, particular attention should be given to the appropriate state nonprofit corporation statute, which will contain requirements that may supersede the provisions of the articles of incorporation and bylaws or may apply where the governing instruments are silent.

The bylaws may also contain the provisions of the articles of organization and, in addition, should contain provisions amplifying or stating the purposes of the organization; the terms and conditions of membership (if any); the manner of selection and duties of the directors or trustees, and officers; the voting requirements; the procedure for forming committees; the accounting period; any indemnification provisions; the appropriate tax provisions; and the procedure for amendment of the bylaws.[25]

§ 4.3 Organizational Test

An organization, to be exempt as a charitable entity, must be both organized and operated exclusively for one or more of the permissible exempt purposes. This requirement has given rise to an organizational test and an operational test for charitable organizations. If an organization fails to meet either the organizational test or the operational test, it cannot qualify for exemption from federal income taxation as a charitable entity.[26]

The income tax regulations contemplate two types of governing instruments for a charitable organization: the instrument by which the organization is created (articles of organization) and the instrument stating the rules pursuant to which the organization is operated (bylaws).[27] For the incorporated organization, the articles of organization are articles of incorporation. For the unincorporated entity, the articles of organization may be so termed or may be termed otherwise, such as a *constitution, agreement of trust,* or *declaration of trust.* Occasionally, an unincorporated organization will combine these two types of instruments in one document; while this is technically inappropriate, the IRS is unlikely to find the practice a violation of the organizational test.

An organization is organized exclusively for one or more tax-exempt, charitable purposes only if its articles of organization limit its purposes to one or more exempt purposes[28] and do not expressly empower it to engage, otherwise than as an insubstantial part of its activities, in activities that in themselves are not in furtherance of one or more exempt purposes.[29]

(a) Statement of Purposes

In meeting the organizational test, the charitable organization's purposes, as stated in its articles of organization, may be as broad as, or more specific than, the particular exempt purposes, such as religious, charitable, or educational ends. Therefore, an organization that, by the terms of its articles of organization, is formed "for literary and scientific purposes within the meaning of section 501(c)(3) of the Internal Revenue Code" shall, if it otherwise meets the requirements of the organizational test, be considered to have met the test. If the articles of organization state that the organization is formed for "charitable purposes," the articles ordinarily will be adequate for purposes of the organizational test.[30]

Articles of organization of charitable entities may not authorize the carrying on of nonexempt activities (unless they are insubstantial), even though the organization is, by the terms of its articles, created for a purpose that is no broader than the specified charitable purposes.[31] Thus, an organization that is empowered by its articles "to engage in a manufacturing business" or "to engage in the operation of a social club" does not meet the organizational test, regardless of the fact that its articles of organization may state that the organization is created "for charitable purposes within the meaning of section 501(c)(3) of the Internal Revenue Code."[32]

In no case will an organization be considered to be organized exclusively for one or more exempt charitable purposes if, by the terms of its articles of organization, the purposes for which the organization is created are broader than the specified charitable purposes. The fact that the actual operations of the organization have been exclusively in furtherance of one or more exempt purposes is not sufficient to permit the organization to meet the organizational test. An organization wishing to qualify as a charitable entity should not provide in its articles of organization that it has all of the powers accorded under the particular state's nonprofit corporation act, since those powers are likely to be broader than those allowable under federal tax law.[33] Similarly, an organization will not meet the organizational test as a result of statements or other evidence that its members intend to operate only in furtherance of one or more exempt purposes.[34]

An organization is not considered organized exclusively for one or more exempt charitable purposes if its articles of organization expressly authorize it to (1) devote more than an insubstantial part of its activities to attempting to influence legislation by propaganda or otherwise;[35] (2) directly or indirectly participate in, or intervene in (including the publishing or distributing of statements), any political campaign on behalf of or in opposition to any candidate for public office;[36] or (3) have objectives and engage in activities that characterize it as an action organization.[37] However, the organizational test is not violated where an organization's articles empower it to make the expenditure test election (relating to expenditures for legislative activities)[38] and, only if it so elects, to make direct lobbying or grass roots lobbying expenditures that are not in excess of the ceiling amounts prescribed by that test.[39]

It is the position of the IRS that only a creating document may be looked to in meeting the organizational test.[40]

(b) Dissolution Requirements

An organization is not organized exclusively for one or more exempt charitable purposes unless its assets are dedicated to an exempt purpose. An organization's assets will be considered dedicated to an exempt purpose, for example, if, upon dissolution, the assets would, by reason of a provision in the organization's articles of organization or by operation of law, be distributed for one or more exempt purposes, or to the federal government, or to a state or local government, for a public purpose or would be distributed by a court to another organization to be used in a manner as in the judgment of the court will best accomplish the general purposes for which the dissolved organization was organized. However, a charitable organization does not meet the organizational test if its articles of organization or the law of the state in which it was created provide that its assets would, upon dissolution, be distributed to its members or shareholders.[41] Consequently, federal income tax exemption as a charitable organization will be denied where, upon dissolution of the organization, its assets would revert to the individual founders rather than to one or more qualifying charities.[42] However, a charitable organization's assets may, upon dissolution, be transferred for charitable purposes without necessarily being transferred to a charitable organization.[43]

The dedication-of-assets requirement contemplates that, notwithstanding the dissolution of a charitable entity, the assets will continue to be devoted to a charitable purpose (albeit a substituted one).

§ 4.4 Primary Purpose Test

Section 501(c)(3) of the Internal Revenue Code provides that an organization must, to qualify as a tax-exempt organization by reason of that provision, be organized and operated exclusively for an exempt purpose. It is clear that the term *exclusively* as employed in this context does not mean solely but rather primarily.[44]

Although the term *exclusively* is not used with respect to categories of tax-exempt organizations other than charitable ones, its presence may be presumed. That is, as a general precept, any type of tax-exempt organization must operate primarily for its exempt purpose to remain exempt.[45] This is the primary purpose test.

The general rule, as stated by the U.S. Supreme Court, is that the "presence of a single . . . [nonexempt] purpose, if substantial in nature, will destroy the exemption regardless of the number or importance of truly . . . [exempt] purposes."[46] In the words of the IRS, the rules applicable to charitable organizations in general have "been construed as requiring all the resources of the organization [other than an insubstantial part] to be applied to the pursuit of one or more of the exempt purposes therein specified."[47] So, the existence of one or more truly exempt purposes of an organization will not be productive of tax exemption as a charitable entity if there is present in its operations a substantial nonexempt purpose.[48]

There is no definition of the term *insubstantial* in this context. Thus, application of these rules is an issue of fact to be determined under the facts and circumstances of each case.[49] However, a court opinion in one case suggested that, where a function represents less than 10 percent of total efforts, the primary purpose test will not be contravened.[50] By contrast, another court opinion stated that an organization that received approximately one third of its revenue from an unrelated business could not qualify for tax-exempt status.[51]

It is essential to observe at the outset that the primary purpose test looks to an organization's purposes rather than its activities.[52] The focus should not be on an organization's primary activities as the test of tax exemption but on whether the activities accomplish one or more tax-exempt purposes.[53] This is why, for example, an organization may engage in nonexempt or profit-making activities and nonetheless qualify for tax exemption.[54]

The Operational Test

(a) In General

An organization, to qualify as a charitable entity, is regarded as operated exclusively for one or more tax-exempt purposes only if it engages primarily in activities that accomplish one or more of its exempt purposes.[55] The IRS observed that, to satisfy this operational test, the "organization's resources must be devoted to purposes that qualify as exclusively charitable within the meaning of section 501(c)(3) of the Code and the applicable regulations."[56] An organization will not be so regarded if more than an insubstantial part of its activities is not in furtherance of an exempt purpose.[57] An organization is not considered as operated exclusively for one or more exempt purposes if its net earnings inure in whole or in part to the benefit of private shareholders or individuals.[58] An organization can be substantially dominated by its founder without, for that reason alone, failing to satisfy the operational test.[59] However, one court concluded that an organization cannot qualify for tax exemption where one individual controls all aspects of the organization's operations and "is not checked" by any governing body.[60]

An organization may meet the federal tax law requirements for charitable entities even though it operates a trade or business as a substantial part of its activities.[61] However, if the organization has as its primary purpose the carrying on of a trade or business, it may not be tax-exempt.[62] Even though the operation of a business does not deprive an organization of classification as a charitable entity, there may be unrelated trade or business tax consequences.[63]

In one instance, the operational test was said to look more toward an organization's purposes rather than its activities, in recognition of the fact that an organization may conduct a business in furtherance of a tax-exempt purpose and qualify as a charitable entity:

> Under the operational test, the purpose towards which an organization's activities are directed, and not the nature of the activities themselves, is ultimately dispositive of the organization's right to be classified as a section 501(c)(3) organization exempt from tax under section 501(a).. . . [I]t is possible for . . . an activity to be carried on for more than one purpose. . . . The fact that . . . [an] activity may constitute a trade or business does not, of course, disqualify it from classification under section 501(c)(3), provided the activity furthers or accomplishes an exempt purpose. . . . Rather, the critical inquiry is whether . . . [an organization's] primary purpose for engaging in its . . . activity is an exempt purpose, or whether its primary purpose is the nonexempt one of operating a commercial business producing net profits for . . . [the organization] . . . Factors such as the particular manner in which an organization's activities are conducted, the commercial hue of those activities and the existence and amount of annual or accumulated profits are relevant evidence of a forbidden predominant purpose.[64]

(b) Action Organizations

An organization is not operated exclusively for one or more exempt purposes if it is an action organization.[65]

An organization is an action organization if a substantial part of its activities is attempting to influence legislation by propaganda or otherwise. For this purpose, an organization is regarded as attempting to influence legislation if the organization contacts, or urges the public to contact, members of a legislative body for the purpose of proposing, supporting, or opposing legislation or if it advocates the adoption or rejection of legislation. The term *legislation* includes action by the

U.S. Congress, a state legislature, a local council or similar governing body, or the public in a referendum, initiative, constitutional amendment, or similar procedure. An organization will not fail to meet the operational test merely because it advocates, as an insubstantial part of its activities, the adoption or rejection of legislation.[66]

An organization is an action organization if it participates or intervenes, directly or indirectly, in any political campaign on behalf of or in opposition to any candidate for public office. The phrase *candidate for public office* means an individual who offers himself or herself, or is proposed by others, as a contestant for an elective public office, whether the office is national, state, or local. Activities that constitute participation or intervention in a political campaign on behalf of or in opposition to a candidate include, but are not limited to, the publication or distribution of written or printed statements or the making of oral statements on behalf of or in opposition to the candidate.[67]

An organization is an action organization if it has the following two characteristics: (1) Its main or primary objective or objectives (as distinguished from its incidental or secondary objectives) may be attained only by legislation or a defeat of proposed legislation, and (2) it advocates or campaigns for the attainment of this main or primary objective or objectives as distinguished from engaging in nonpartisan analysis, study, or research, and making the results thereof available to the public. In determining whether an organization has these characteristics, all the surrounding facts and circumstances, including the articles of organization (see above) and all activities of the organization, are considered.[68]

The IRS is aware that the regulations' terms *exclusively, primarily,* and *insubstantial* present "difficult conceptual problems."[69] The IRS concluded that "[q]uestions involving the application of these terms can more readily be resolved on the basis of the facts of a particular case."[70]

§ 4.6 The Exclusively Standard

To be tax-exempt as a charitable organization, an entity must be organized and operated *exclu-*sively for exempt purposes. As noted,[71] this rule is reflected in the primary purpose test. However, there is additional law pertaining to the exclusively rule.

One of the more controversial opinions in this regard was authored by a federal court of appeals, which accorded tax exemption to a public parking facility as a charitable organization.[72] The organization was formed by several private businesses and professional persons to construct and operate the facility, utilizing a validation stamp system in an effort to attract shoppers to a center city. The government contended that the operation of a commercial parking facility is not an exempt activity[73] and that a substantial objective of the organization was to encourage the general public to patronize the businesses that participate in the validation stamp system, which constituted private inurement and only incidental public benefit.[74] Concluding that the city involved was the primary beneficiary of the organization's activities, the district court had held that the "business activity itself is similar to that which others engage in for profit, but it is not carried on in the same manner; it is carried on only because it is necessary for the attainment of an undeniably public end."[75] On appeal, the appellate court observed that the lower court "made a quantitative comparison of the private versus the public benefits derived from the organization and operation of the plaintiff corporation" and determined that the requirements for exemption were "adequately fulfilled."[76] The opinion is not illustrative of blind adherence to the exclusively doctrine.

The IRS does not subscribe to the principles of the public parking corporation case and announced that it does not follow the decision.[77] The IRS asserts that this type of a public parking corporation does not operate exclusively for charitable purposes and carries on a business with the general public in a manner similar to organizations that are operated for profit. This position was made clear earlier when the IRS ruled that an organization formed to revive retail sales in an area suffering from continued economic decline by constructing a shopping center that would complement the area's existing retail facilities could not qualify for tax exemption as a charitable entity. The IRS, then taking no notice of the appellate court decision, said that the activities of the organization "result in major benefits accruing to the stores that will locate within the shopping center," thereby precluding the exemption.[78] (However, an organization that provided free parking to persons visiting a downtown area can qualify as a social welfare organization.[79])

Application of the concept of exclusively may require even more flexibility than has been previously displayed. This may be particularly unavoidable as respects organizations performing services that are considered necessary in today's society, even where the services are parallel with those rendered in commercial settings. For example, the provision of medical services can obviously be an enterprise for profit, yet the IRS was able to rule that an organization formed to attract a physician to a medically underserved rural area, by providing the doctor with a building and facilities at a reasonable rent, qualified as a charitable organization.[80] "In these circumstances," said the IRS, "any personal benefit derived by the physician (the use of the building in which to practice medicine) does not detract from the public purpose of the organization nor lessen the public benefit flowing from its activities."[81] Similarly, an organization formed to provide legal services for residents of economically depressed communities was ruled to be engaged in charitable activities.[82] Even though those providing the services were subsidized by the organization, the IRS minimized this personal gain by the rationale that they were merely the instruments by which the charitable purposes were accomplished.[83]

§ 4.7 The Commensurate Test

Somewhat related to the operational test is another test that the IRS has developed but, until recently, had rarely used. This test is termed the *commensurate test,* which was first articulated in 1964.[84] Under this test, the IRS is empowered to assess whether a charitable organization is maintaining program activities that are commensurate in scope with its financial resources.

In the particular facts underlying the 1964 ruling, the organization derived most of its income from rents, yet was successful in preserving its tax-exempt status because it satisfied the test, in that it was engaging in an adequate amount of charitable functions notwithstanding the extent of its rental activities.

The commensurate test lay dormant for years, then surfaced again in 1990, when the IRS began a close review of the fund-raising practices of charitable organizations. In that connection, the IRS developed an 82-question "checksheet" for use by its auditing agents; its full title is "Exempt Organizations Charitable Solicitations Compliance Improvement Program Study Checksheet." One question asks the reviewing agent to determine whether the charitable organization being examined is meeting the commensurate test.[85] In this context, the agent is to ascertain whether the charitable organization is engaging in sufficient charitable activity in relation to its available resources, including gifts received through fund-raising campaigns, as measured against the time and expense of fund-raising.

Later in 1990, the IRS revoked the tax-exempt status of a charitable organization on a variety of rationales, including the ground that its fund-raising costs were too high and thus violated the commensurate test. In a technical advice memorandum, unpublished by the IRS,[86] the IRS concluded that the test was transgressed because of its finding that the charity involved expended, during the two years examined, only about 4 percent of its revenue for charitable purposes; the rest was allegedly spent for fund-raising and administration. (The matter of the organization's tax-exempt status was ultimately resolved in court, albeit without application of the commensurate test; the case turned out to be one involving private inurement.[87])

The commensurate test and the primary purpose test have an awkward co-existence; the former may, at least in some contexts, be replacing the latter. For example, a charitable organization was allowed to retain its tax-exempt status while receiving 98 percent of its support from unrelated business income, since 41 percent of the organization's activities were charitable programs.[88]

§ 4.8 Boards of Directors

There is nothing in the federal statutory law, the federal tax regulations, or the rulings from the IRS that, as a general rule, dictates the composition of the board of directors (or other governing body) of a tax-exempt organization.[89]

Nonetheless, the courts are building up some presumptions in this area. For example, it is the view of the U.S. Tax Court that "where the creators [of an organization] control the affairs of the organization, there is an obvious opportunity for abuse, which necessitates an open and candid disclosure of all facts bearing upon the organization, operation, and finances so that the Court can be assured that by granting the claimed exemption it is not sanctioning an abuse of the revenue laws."[90] The court added that, where this disclosure is not made, "the logical inference is that the facts, if disclosed, would show that the taxpayer [organization] fails to meet the requirements" for tax-exempt status.[91]

Thus, while there is nothing specific in the operational test concerning the size or composition of the governing board of a charitable organization, the courts are engrafting onto the test greater burdens of proof when the organization has a small board of directors, dominated by an individual.

§ 4.9 Operations for Profit

The IRS, when alleging that an organization is not operated exclusively for an exempt purpose, frequently bases its contention on a finding that the organization's operation is similar to a commercial enterprise operated for profit. However, as one court observed, "the presence of profit-making activities is not *per se* a bar to qualification of an organization as exempt if the activities further or accomplish an exempt purpose."[92] Similarly, the IRS expressly acknowledged that a charitable organization can have a qualified[93] profit-sharing plan for its employees without endangering its tax exemption.[94]

In one instance, a plan was designed by a hospital as an employee incentive plan, with "prof-

its" defined in the general accounting sense of excess of receipts over expenses.[95] Plan distributions must be reasonable; the distributions were held to not be "dividends" and to not constitute private inurement.[96]

The question as to whether, and if so to what extent, a tax-exempt organization (particularly one that is classified as a charitable entity) can earn a profit is at once difficult and easy to answer. The question is easy to answer in the sense that it is clear that the mere showing of a profit (excess of revenue over expenses) for one or more tax years will not bar tax exemption. However, if the profit is from what is perceived as a business activity and the fact of a profit is used to show the commercial hue of the activity, the answer to the question will depend upon the facts and circumstances of the particular case. That is, the decisive factor is likely to be the nature of the activities that give rise to the profits.[97]

An illustrative body of law is that concerning organizations that prepare and sell publications at a profit.[98] In one case, an organization sold religious publications to students attending classes it sponsored and to members of its religious following, for a relatively small profit.[99] In rejecting the government's argument that the receipt of the income indicated that the organization was not operated exclusively for religious purposes, a court held that the sale of religious literature was an activity "closely associated with, and incidental to" the organization's tax-exempt purposes and bore "an intimate relationship to the proper functioning" of it, and thus that the receipt of the income did not prevent the organization from being an organization organized and operated exclusively for religious purposes.[100]

By contrast, a court denied status as a charitable entity to an organization that prepared and sold religious literature on a nondenominational basis. Because the organization's materials were competitively priced and the sales over a seven-year period yielded substantial accumulated profits that greatly exceeded the amount expended for its activities, the court concluded that the sales activities were the organization's primary concern and that it was engaging in the conduct of a trade or business for profit.[101] Another organization was denied tax exemption for publishing on a for-profit basis, with the court observing that, were the law otherwise, "every publishing house would be entitled to an exemption on the ground that it furthers the education of the public."[102] Likewise, an organization could not achieve tax exemption because its primary activity—the publication and sale of books that are religiously inspired and oriented and written by its founder—was conducted in a commercial manner, at a profit.[103]

Each case on this point, therefore, must reflect one of these two analyses. In one case, a court accepted the contention by an organization that its publishing activities furthered its religious purpose of improving the preaching skills and sermons of the clergy of the Protestant, Roman Catholic, and Jewish faiths. Subscriptions for the publications were obtained by advertising and direct mail solicitation, and the publications were sold at a modest profit. The court found that the organization was not in competition with any commercial enterprise and that the sale of religious literature was an integral part of the organization's religious purposes. Said the court: "The fact that . . . [the organization] intended to make a profit, alone, does not negate [the fact] that . . . [it] was operated exclusively for charitable purposes."[104]

By contrast, an organization was denied tax exemption as a charitable entity because it was directly engaged in the conduct of a commercial leasing enterprise for the principal purpose of realizing profits. The enterprise was regarded as its principal activity (measured by total gross income), in which it was an active participant, and not related to an exempt purpose. Further, its charitable activities were deemed to be of relatively minimal consequence.[105] Similarly, a court reflected upon a nonprofit organization's accumulated profits and decided that this was evidence that the primary function of the organization was commercial in nature.[106]

Yet, given an appropriate set of circumstances, the greater the extent of profits, the greater the likelihood that the revenue-producing activity may be considered to be in furtherance of tax-exempt purposes. In one case, an activity—which the organization regarded as fund-raising and the IRS considered a business—was held to

not be a business because the activity generated a "staggering amount of money" and "astounding profitability" in a manner that could not be replicated in a commercial context.[107] Also, the organization was much more candid with its supporters than would be the case in a commercial setting, leading the court to note that, "[b]y any standard, an enterprise that depends on the consent of its customers for its profits is not operating in a commercial manner and is not a trade or business."[108]

Thus, the mere fact of profit-making activities should not, as a matter of law, adversely affect an organization's tax-exempt status. As another federal court of appeals has noted, the "pertinent inquiry" is "whether the [organization's] exempt purpose transcends the profit motive rather than the other way around."[109] However, the IRS may use the existence of a profit to characterize the activity as being commercial in nature, thus placing at issue the question as to whether the organization's activities are devoted exclusively to tax-exempt purposes. This approach is sometimes also taken by the courts, such as in a case where the publications of an organization were held to produce an unwarranted profit, thereby depriving it of qualification as an educational organization.[110]

Notes

1. Rev. Proc. 82–2, 1982–1 C.B 367.
2. IRC § 501(c)(1), 501(c)(2), 501(c)(3), 501(c)(14), 501(c)(16).
3. IRC § 501(c)(17), 501(c)(18), 501(c)(19), 501(c)(20), 401(a).
4. IRC § 7701(a)(3).
5. IRC § 501(c)(3).
6. *Fifth-Third Union Trust Co. v. Comm'r*, 56 F.2d 767 (6th Cir. 1932).
7. IRS Exempt Organizations Handbook (IRM 7751) § 315.1. Also *Emerson Inst. v. United States*, 356 F.2d 824 (D.C. Cir. 1966), *cert. den.*, 385 U.S. 822 (1966). In one opinion, a court, in deciding that an organization could not quality for tax-exempt status because of its role as a general partner in a limited partnership (see § 32.2), placed emphasis on the fact that the partnerships involved "are admittedly for-profit entities" and that none of these partnerships is

"intended to be nonprofit" (*Housing Pioneers, Inc. v. Comm'r*, 65 T.C.M. 2191, 2195 [1993]); however, the law does not make provision for an entity such as a nonprofit partnership.

8. E.g., IRC § 509(a), last sentence.

9. *American Bar Ass'n v. United States*, 84–1 U.S.T.C. ¶ 9179 (N.D. Ill. 1984); Rev. Rul. 58–293, 1958–1 C.B. 146.

10. Rev. Rul. 54–243, 1954–1 C.B. 92.

11. E.g., *Pusch v. Comm'r*, 39 T.C.M. 838 (1980).

12. *Cone v. McGinnes*, 63–2 U.S.T.C. ¶ 9551 (E.D. Pa. 1963). Also *infra* § 2.

13. *Hewitt v. Comm'r*, 16 T.C.M. 468, 471 (1957). Also *Doty, Jr. v. Comm'r*, 6 T.C. 587 (1974); *Walker v. Comm'r*, 37 T.C.M. 1851 (1978).

14. Rev. Rul. 66–219, 1966–2 C.B. 208.

15. IRS Exempt Organizations Handbook (IRM 7751) § 315.1, 315.2(3), 315.4(2).

16. *Kessler v. Comm'r*, 87 T.C. 1285 (1986); *Trippe v. Comm'r*, 9 T.C.M. 622 (1950). Cf. *Morey v. Riddell*, 205 F. Supp. 918 (S.D. Cal. 1962).

17. E.g., *United States v. Jeffries*, 88–2 U.S.T.C. ¶ 9,459 (7th Cir. 1988). In general, Chapter 8, text accompanying notes 96–99.

18. Reg. § 301.7701–3(c)(1)(v)(A).

19. Reg. § 301.7701–2(b)(2), 301.7701–3(a).

20. However, a separate form (even the corporate form) is not always respected. For example, courts find charitable organizations to be the "alter ego" of their founders or others in close control and operating proximity, so that IRS levies against the organizations for their income and assets to satisfy the individuals' tax obligations are upheld (e.g., *Towe Antique Ford Found. v. Internal Revenue Serv.*, 999 F.2d 1387 (9th Cir. 1993); *United States v. Kitsos*, 770 F. Supp. 1230 (N.D. Ill. 1991), *aff'd*, 968 F.2d 1219 (7th Cir. 1992); *Zahra Spiritual Trust v. United States*, 910.F.2d 240 (5th Cir. 1990); *Loving Savior Church v. United States*, 556 F. Supp. 688 (D.S.D. 1983), *aff'd*, 728 F.2d 1085 (8th Cir. 1984); *Faith Missionary Baptist Church v. Internal Revenue Serv.*, 174 ¶ 454 (U.S. Bankr. Ct. E.D. Tex. 1994); *Church of Hakeem v. United States*, 79–2 U.S.T.C. ¶ 9651 (N.D. Cal. 1979)). In general, Henn & Pfeifer, "Nonprofit Groups: Factors Influencing Choice of Form," 11 *Wake Forest L. Rev.* 181 (1975).

21. 39 C.F.R. Part 132 (second class), Part 134 (third class).

22. See § 24.1(6).

23. See *infra* s 4.

24. See § 11.1(g).

25. In general, see Oleck, *Non-Profit Corporations, Organizations, and Associations* (6th ed. 1996); Web-

ster, *The Law of Associations* (Matthew Bender); Chaffe, "The Internal Affairs of Associations Not For Profit," 43 *Harv. L. Rev.* 993 (1930).

26. Reg. § 1.501(c)(3)–1(a); *Levy Family Tribe Found. v. Comm'r*, 69 T.C. 615, 618 (1978).

27. Reg. § 1.501(c)(3)–1(b)(2).

28. See Reg. § 1.501(c)(3)–1(d).

29. Reg. § 1.501(c)(3)–1(b)(1)(i).

30. Reg. § 1.501(c)(3)–1(b)(1)(ii).

31. Rev. Rul. 69–279, 1969–1 C. B. 152; Rev. Rul. 69–256, 1969–1 C.B. 151.

32. Reg. § 1.501(c)(3)–1(b)(iii). Also *Interneighborhood Housing Corp. v. Comm'r.*, 45 T.C.M. 115 (1982); *Santa Cruz Bldg. Ass'n v. United States*, 411 F. Supp. 871 (E. D. Mo. 1976).

33. E.g., Gen. Couns. Mem. 39633.

34. Reg. § 1.501(c)(3)–1(b)(1)(iv).

35. See Chapter 20.

36. See Chapter 21.

37. Reg. § 1.501(c)(3)–1(b)(3). See *infra* § 4.5(b).

38. See § 20.5(a).

39. Reg. § 1.501(c)(3)–1(b)(3).

40. IRS Exempt Organizations Handbook (IRM 7751) § 332(2).

41. Reg. § 1.501(c)(3)–1(b)(4). E.g., *Chief Steward of the Ecumenical Temples and the Worldwide Peace Movement and His Successors v. Comm'r*, 49 T.C.M. 640 (1985). Cf. *Bethel Conservative Mennonite Church v. Comm'r*, 746 F.2d 388 (7th Cir. 1984).

42. *Church of Nature in Man v. Comm'r*, 49 T.C.M. 1393 (1985); *Stephenson v. Comm'r*, 79 T.C. 995 (1982); *Truth Tabernacle v. Comm'r*, 41 T.C.M. 1405 (1981); *Calvin K. of Oakknoll v. Comm'r*, 69 T.C. 770 (1978), *aff'd*, 603 F.2d 211 (2d Cir. 1979); *General Conference of the Free Church of Am. v. Comm'r*, 71 T.C. 920 (1979).

43. Gen. Couns. Mem. 37126, clarifying Gen. Couns. Mem. 33207. Moreover, the absence of a dissolution clause has been held to not be fatal to IRC § 501(c)(3) status, in *Universal Church of Scientific Truth, Inc. v. United States*, 74–1 U.S.T.C. ¶ 9360 (N.D. Ala. 1973).

44. Reg. § 1.501(c)(3)–1(c)(1). Also Reg. § 1.501(c)(3)–1(a)(1).

45. E.g., *Orange County Agric. Soc'y, Inc. v. Comm'r*, 55 T.C.M. 1602 (1988), *aff'd*, 893 F.2d 647 (2d Cir. 1990).

46. *Better Business Bureau of Washington, D.C. v. United States*, 326 U.S. 279, 283 (1945). E.g., *Universal Church of Jesus Christ, Inc. v. Comm'r*, 55 T.C.M. 143 (1988).

47. Rev. Rul. 77–366, 1977–2 C.B. 192.

48. *Stevens Bros. Found. v. Comm'r*, 324 F.2d 633 (8th Cir. 1963), *cert. den.*, 376 U.S. 969 (1964); *Scrip-*

ture Press Found. v. United States, 285 F.2d 800, 806 (Ct. Cl. 1961), *cert. den.,* 368 U.S. 985 (1962); *Fides Publishers Ass'n v. United States,* 263 F. Supp. 924, 935 (N.D. Ind. 1967); *Edgar v. Comm'r,* 56 T.C. 717, 755 (1971); *The Media Sports League, Inc. v. Comm'r,* 52 T.C.M. 1093 (1986).

49. E.g., *Kentucky Bar Found. v. Comm'r,* 78 T.C. 921 (1982).

50. *World Family Corp. v. Comm'r,* 81 T.C. 958 (1983).

51. *Orange County Agric. Soc'y, Inc. v. Comm'r, supra* note 76 (where the unrelated business was held to have "exceeded the benchmark of insubstantiality" (55 T.C.M., at 1604)). This view of the law may be changing, in the aftermath of increasing emphasis on the *commensurate test* (see *infra* § 7).

52. Reg. § 1.501(c)(3)–1(c)(1).

53. *Aid to Artisans, Inc. v. Comm'r,* 71 T.C. 202 (1978).

54. Nonetheless, the courts occasionally stretch this criterion, as illustrated by the decision denying tax-exempt status to a scholarship fund, for violation of the primary purpose test, because its fund-raising activities were conducted in a cocktail lounge and attracted customers to the lounge (*P.L.L. Scholarship Fund v. Comm'r,* 82 T.C. 196 (1984); also *KJ's Fund Raisers, Inc. v. Comm'r.,* 74 T.C.M. 669 (1997)). Cf. *Hope Charitable Found. v. Ridell,* 61–1 U.S.T.C. ¶ 9437 (S.D. Cal. 1961).

55. Reg. § 1.501(c)(3)–1(a)(1).

56. Rev. Rul. 72–369, 1972–2 C.B. 245.

57. Reg. § 1.501(c)(3)–1(c)(1). In one instance, the operational test was found to be unmet because the organization involved, which was organized for the study and promotion of the philately of the Central American republics, operated a mail bid stamps sales service for its members as a substantial activity (*Society of Costa Rica Collectors v. Comm'r,* 49 T.C.M. 304 (1984)).

58. Reg. § 1.501(c)(3)–1(c)(2), 1.501(a)–1(c). Also *Wildt's Motorsport Advancement Crusade, Bill v. Comm'r,* 56 T.C.M. 1401 (1989); *Athenagoras I Christian Union of the World, Inc. v. Comm'r,* 55 T.C.M. 781 (1988); *Levy Family Tribe Found. v. Comm'r, supra* note 31. See Chapter 19.

59. E.g., *The Church of the Visible Intelligence That Governs the Universe v. United States,* 83–2 U.S.T.C. ¶ 9726 (Cl. Ct. 1983).

60. *Chief Steward of the Ecumenical Temples and the Worldwide Peace Movement and His Successors v. Comm'r, supra* note 55, at 643.

61. E.g., Rev. Rul. 64–182, 1964–1 (Part 1) C.B. 186.

62. Reg. § 1.501(c)(3)–1(e)(1).

63. See Part Five.

64. *B.S.W. Group, Inc. v. Comm'r,* 70 T.C. 352, 356–357 (1978). Also *Ohio Teamsters Educ. & Safety Training Fund v. Comm'r,* 77 T.C. 189 (1981), *aff'd,* 692 F.2d 432 (6th Cir. 1982).

65. Reg. § 1.501(c)(3)–1(c)(i).

66. Reg. § 1.501(c)(3)-(c)(3)(ii).

67. Reg. § 1.501(c)(3)–1(c)(3)(iii).

68. Reg. § 1.501(c)(3)–1(c)(3)(iv).

69. IRS Exempt Organizations Handbook (IRM 7751) § 341.1(2).

70. *Id.*

71. See § 4.4.

72. *Monterey Pub. Parking Corp. v. United States,* 481 F.2d 175 (9th Cir. 1973), *aff'd.* 321 F. Supp. 972 (N.D. Cal. 1970).

73. See Chapter 25.

74. See Chapter 19.

75. *Monterey Pub. Parking Corp. v. United States, supra* note 150, 321 F. Supp., at 977.

76. *Monterey Public Parking Corp. v. United States, supra* note 150, 481 F. 2d at 177. Cf. Rev. Rul. 73–411, 1973–2 C.B. 180.

77. Rev. Rul. 78–86, 1978–1 C.B. 151.

78. Rev. Rul. 77–111, 1977–1 C.B. 144. Also Rev. Rul. 64–108, 1964–1 (Part I) C.B. 189.

79. Rev. Rul. 81–116, 1981–1 C.B. 333. Social welfare organizations are the subject of Chapter 12.

80. Rev. Rul. 73–313, 1973–2 C.B. 174.

81. *Id.* at 176 citing In re Estate of Carlson, 358 P.2d 669 (Kan. 1961). Cf. Rev. Rul. 69–266, 1969–1 C.B. 151.

82. Rev. Rul. 72–559, 1972–2 C.B. 247. Also Rev. Rul. 70–640, 1970–2 C.B. 117; *Golf Life World Entertainment Golf Championship, Inc. v. United States,* 65–1 U.S.T.C. ¶ 9174 (S. D. Cal. 1964). Cf. Rev. Rul. 72–369, 1972–2 C.B. 245.

83. See § 5.5(d).

84. Rev. Rul. 64–182, 1964–1 C.B. (Part I) 186.

85. This checksheet is discussed in detail in Hopkins, *The Law of Fund-Raising, Second Edition* (New York: John Wiley & Sons, Inc., 1996), Chapter 6 § 1.

86. This technical advice memorandum is reproduced at 4 *Exempt Org. Tax Rev.* (No. 5) 726 (July 1991), and is discussed in detail in Hopkins, *supra* note 173, at Chapter 6 § 15, text accompanied by notes 564–576.

87. *United Cancer Council, Inc. v. Comm'r,* 109 T.C. No. 17 (1997). (U.S. Tax Ct., Docket No. 2008–91X.) This case is discussed in § 19.3, 19.4, and in Hopkins, note 173, at Chapter 6 § 15 text accompanied by notes 577–584, and at Chapter 8 § 12.

88. IRS Tech. Adv. Mem. 9711003.

89. A charitable organization that wishes to avoid private foundation status as a donative publicly supported organization by means of the *facts-and-circumstances test* (see § 11.3(6)(ii)) may have to meet certain criteria as to the composition of its governing board.

90. *United Libertarian Fellowship, Inc. v. Comm'r,* 65 T.C.M. 2175, 2181 (1993).

91. *Id.* Identical language was used by the court in a prior opinion (*Bubbling Well Church of Universal Love, Inc. v. Comm'r,* 74 T.C. 531, 535 (1980), *aff'd,* 670 F.2d 104 (9th Cir. 1981)).

92. *Aid to Artisans, Inc. v. Comm'r, supra* note 86, at 211.

93. IRC § 401(a).

94. See § 19.4(i)

95. Gen. Couns. Mem. 38283.

96. Priv. Ltr. Rul. 8442064. In general, Note, "The Semantic Anomaly: Maintenance of Qualified Profit-Sharing Plans by Non-Profit Organizations—A Concept Whose Time Has Come," 59 *Notre Dame L. Rev.* (No. 3) 754 (1984).

97. See the discussion of the *commerciality doctrine* in Chapter 25.

98. See Chapter 8 § 4.

99. Saint Germain Found. v. Comm'r, 26 T.C. 648 (1956).

100. *Id.* at 658. Also *Elisian Guild, Inc. v. United States,* 412 F.2d 121 (1st Cir. 1969), *rev'g* 292 F. Supp. 219 (D. Mass. 1968).

101. *Scripture Press Found. v. United States, supra* note 81.

102. *Fides Publishers Ass'n v. United States, supra* note 81, at 936.

103. *Christian Manner Int'l, Inc. v. Comm'r,* 71 T.C. 661 (1979).

104. *Pulpit Resource v. Comm'r, supra* note 88, at 611. Also *Junaluska Assembly Housing, Inc. v. Comm'r, supra* note 100; Industrial Aid for the Blind v. Comm'r, 73 T.C. 96 (1979).

105. *Greater United Navajo Dev. Enters., Inc v. Comm'r,* 74 T.C. 69 (1980).

106. Elisian Guild, Inc. v. United States, *supra* note 193, at 412 F.2d 124.

107. *American Bar Endowment v. United States,* 84–1 U.S.T.C. ¶ 9204 (Cl. Ct. 1984).

108. *Id.* at 83, 353.

109. *The Incorporated Trustees of the Gospel Worker Soc'y v. United States,* 510 F. Supp. 374 (D.D.C. 1981), *aff'd,* 672 F.2d 894 (D.C. Cir. 1981), *cert. den.,* 456 U.S. 944 (1982).

110. *American Institute for Economic Research v. United States,* 302 F.2d 934 (Ct. Cl. 1962). See § 7.6.

PART 3

EFFECTIVE, ETHICAL LEADERSHIP[*]

All organizations require leadership and management.[1] But are leading and managing in the nonprofit sector sufficiently different from leading and managing private businesses or government agencies to warrant separate attention? I believe they are, but the question raises interesting questions. Although many aspects of nonprofit organization leadership and management are unique, others are similar to leadership in government agencies and businesses.

All organizations—including nonprofit organizations—are affected by their contexts, philosophies, governance structures, value systems, and the legal ground rules under which they operate.[2] These same forces and factors also influence their leadership and management needs; for example, nonprofit organizations must satisfy numerous constituencies who often have objectives that compete or conflict with those of other constituencies.[3] Thus, nonprofit leaders need to be accountable to many varied constituencies beyond the board of trustees.

> "Responsibility" exists in all forms of management, . . . this responsibility has both technical and moral aspects, and . . . nonprofit management may well include more complex forms of moral responsibility than do other types of management.[4]

Nonprofit organizations also vary in structure and culture according to their functions, and they vary by their primary sources of income. Some nonprofit organizations derive most of their financial support from private sources; others from the general public; others from member individuals or organizations; others from public sector contracts or grants; and yet others from combinations of these sources. The

---

[*]Peter M. Nelson contributed to this essay.

leadership needs of a nonprofit organization that "lives" a grants economy-based existence differ from the needs of an exchange economy-based private business.[5] Often, executives in nonprofit organizations are responsible for resources that do not directly yield tangible results or measurable outcomes. All these political, structural, cultural, and economic influences affect the nature of a nonprofit organization and thus its leadership and management needs and the leadership styles of directors and board officers who will perform effectively in it.

Leadership and Management

Over the years, the importance attributed to the roles, functions, and traits of leaders and, more specifically, to leaders of nonprofit organizations, has led innumerable practitioners and theorists to ask the seemingly unanswerable question: "What is an effective leader and why?" Almost as many social and behavioral scientists have tried to offer answers. The readings reprinted in this part address this question directly. Leadership, however, is a surprisingly complex and elusive concept that requires explanation.

Although we need to understand what leadership is so that we can recruit leaders onto boards and into executive direction positions, for example, it is important to warn the reader in advance: There are no clear-cut, universally-accepted views on leadership. "'Leadership' is one of the most magnetic words in the English language. Mention it, and a perceptible aura of excitement, almost mystical in nature, appears. . . . [Yet] if leadership is bright orange, leadership research is slate gray."[6] In addition, it is important to distinguish between *leadership* (or leader) and *management* (or manager or director). Although these two functions and roles overlap substantially, the term *manager* connotes that authority has been formally granted to an individual by an organization. Management involves power—legitimate formal authority—that is granted to the occupant of a position by a higher organizational authority. Responsibility and accountability for the use of organizational resources accompany the power accorded to a manager or director. Thus, this introductory essay explores fundamental questions about what leadership is, offers several perspectives on leadership, and explains how leadership differs from management.

In contrast, the term *leader* implies effective use of influence that is somewhat independent of the formal authority granted to an individual because of position. Leadership cannot be granted to a person by a higher authority; rather, those who decide to follow bestow it on an individual. Whereas managers and directors have formal authority, leaders have the informal ability to get things done by attracting and influencing followers. Effective managers in nonprofit organizations must be leaders also, and many leaders become managers, leaders, and directors. The two sets of roles and functions, however, differ.

Leadership raises many complex issues that have plagued behavioral scientists for generations; for example, what gives a manager or leader legitimacy? Shafritz[7] describes legitimacy as a "characteristic of a social institution, such as a government or a family [or an organization], whereby it has both a legal and a perceived right to make binding decisions." Thus, managers presumably have legitimacy because of the legal and perceived rights that accompany their organizational positions.

In contrast, however, the legitimacy of the leader—which is separate and distinct from the legitimacy of a manager—cannot be addressed without introducing the concept of charisma. Charisma is a type of "leadership based on the compelling personality of the leader rather than on formal position."[8] This concept was first articulated by the German sociologist Max Weber, who distinguished *charismatic authority* from the *traditional authority* of a monarch and the *legal authority* one receives by virtue of the law—such as the authority that legitimizes nonprofit organization directors and executives.

Is the job of a leader to ask—or tell—others what to do? Probably not. Chester Barnard[9] was one of the first to conclude that the ability to give directives is not among the important skills needed for leadership effectiveness. Barnard identified the three most essential functions of leaders, and these remain salient today: (1) provide a system of communication, (2) promote the securing of essential efforts, and (3) formulate and define the purposes and goals of the organization. Barnard argued that the most essential function a chief executive performs is to establish and communicate a system of organizational values among organizational members. If the value system is clear and strong, he argued, day-to-day concerns will take care of themselves.

Although many unanswered questions remain about leadership, two important practical points stand virtually uncontested: (1) Leadership involves a relationship between people in which influence and power are unevenly distributed on a legitimate basis; and (2), a leader cannot function in isolation. For there to be a leader, there must be followers.[10]

Who Leads a Nonprofit Organization?

Historically, the nonprofit organization literature had placed responsibility for leadership squarely on the board officers, usually the president. Stern,[11] for example, argued that the elected board chair (president) is literally responsible for the organization. When Stern chaired a hospital board, he occupied an office in the organization's building. For him, it was important for the board chair to be able to communicate regularly with all levels of staff and participate in decisionmaking. In

this leadership model, the executive director (or CEO) was portrayed as the imple-
menter of board policies—a leadership role that relegated the executive director to
garnering and mobilizing support needed to accomplish the board's plans.

This "traditional model" (or myth) of nonprofit organization leadership began to
fade in the decades of the 1970s and the 1980s. Fenn, for example, "asked executive volunteers what they would like to do as board members. . . . They did not want
to initiate projects on behalf of the organization but enjoyed implementing tasks
given to them by staff."[12] McAdam and Gies[13] were among the first writers who argued for "leadership partnerships" between board officers and executive directors
with explicit understandings about mutual expectations. Ostrowski[14] explained that
leadership needs and relationships between a board of trustees and staff are dynamic. They shift with the life cycle stages of a nonprofit organization.

Others took this argument further, contending that true leadership in most nonprofits lies with the executive director. Forget that the traditional model of nonprofit leadership argued that leadership should reside with the board; reality showed otherwise.
"Which leader are you talking about—our volunteer board chair or our executive director? Our focus . . . is primarily on the executive director. In the groups we examined, when true leadership emerged, it was usually the executive director."[15]

The strongest and most convincing evidence to date on the leadership primacy of
executive directors emerged from Herman and Heimovic's study of nonprofit organizations in the Kansas City area:

> We believe that in most established, staffed nonprofit organizations chief execu-
> tives come to be expected by board members, other staff, and themselves to be fi-
> nally responsible for the successes and failures of the organization. . . . We dis-
> covered that . . . effective executives provided substantially more leadership for
> their boards than those in the comparison group; that is, they took responsibility
> for providing board-centered leadership. We consider this a most significant find-
> ing to support our alternative model [alternative to the "traditional model"] of
> leadership in nonprofit organizations.[16]

Summary

Executive directors are appointed by the board. Board members and officers are
elected. In contrast, a person emerges as a leader when others willingly agree to follow—the employees, trustees, and/or volunteers. A manager who is also a leader
can guide a nonprofit organization responsibly, engage the organization in activities
that advance its mission, ensure the organization's survival in an uncertain environment, and create an organizational culture centered on ethical values. According to
Michael O'Neill,

Any serious attempt to understand the nature of managerial responsibility in the nonprofit sector must consider not only what the manager owes the organization but also what the organization—and the sector and the society—owe the manager. To go back to the etymology of responsibility, we are talking about a pledge, a promise, a moral pact; and the pact goes both ways.[17]

Readings Reprinted in Part Three

Stephen Block's essay, *"Executive Director,"*[18] examines the differences between leaders and managers in for-profit and nonprofit organizations. Block also asks: "How does a person become an executive director?" He explores different career paths and development options, as well as the kind of competencies that are required for an effective executive director. Using Mintzberg's[19] model, the ten roles of an executive director are explored within the framework of three sets of behavior: *informational* (monitor, disseminator, spokesperson), *interpersonal* (figurehead, leader, liaison), and *decisional* (entrepreneur, disturbance handler, resource allocator, negotiator).

In *"Ethics in Nonprofit Management: Creating a Culture of Integrity,"*[20] Thomas Jeavons explores the importance of an ethical organizational culture; responsibility for creating an ethical culture is laid at the feet of organizational leaders. Lack of an ethical base ultimately destroys a nonprofit organization—and other organizations around it. When one nonprofit organization is discovered to be dishonest, other nonprofits suffer: The belief that the nonprofit sector is somehow immune to scandal is outmoded. Never before have nonprofit organizations been subject to the level of public and regulatory scrutiny they are today. Ethical leadership of nonprofit organizations has moved onto the front pages of newspapers, trade magazines, and professional journals. Not only is it desirable for an ethical organizational culture to avoid legal problems, it also is good business strategy. The study of leadership ethics thus is of high practical importance for nonprofit executives and trustees.

Jeavons examines some of the scandals and incidents that have marred the nonprofit sector in recent years. He includes some well-known scandals, such as Jimmy Bakker's PTL and the United Way scandals, and looks at the lines that were crossed and the social contracts that were violated. But he does not ignore other difficult but less blatantly ethical situations that all nonprofit leaders face sooner or later. For example, is it acceptable—ethical—for a nonprofit organization that serves victims of hunger and poverty to create a news story using a composite victim?* Do the photographs used in a news story or brochure need to show the real victims or recipients

---

*Depicting a variety of victims' experiences as the experience of a single victim.

of services? Should a leader in a nonprofit accept large donations for the organization from a polluter if the organization's mission is environmental protection? Most nonprofit organization leaders must deal with and ultimately resolve this type of ethical problem—eventually.

Mary Tschirhart identifies and discusses the ins-and-outs and the organizational implications of stakeholder management in *"Artful Leadership."*[21] Tschirhart argues that organizational leaders, working with other staff and board members, are responsible for identifying and resolving stakeholder problems. "Artful Leadership" is the result of an extensive study she conducted into the aspects, components, and dimensions that effective leaders use to lead and manage their organizations.

Notes

1. For a more comprehensive review of leadership theory, see J. Steven Ott, "Leadership," in J. S. Ott, ed., *Classic Readings in Organizational Behavior,* 2d ed. (Fort Worth, TX: Harcourt Brace, 1996), 163–174.

2. See Parts 1 and 2; also see J. Steven Ott, ed., *The Nature of the Nonprofit Sector:* (Boulder: Westview Press, 2001).

3. See Robert D. Herman and David O. Renz, "Multiple Constituencies and the Social Construction, of Nonprofit Organization Effectiveness," *Nonprofit and Voluntary Sector Quarterly* 26, no. 2 (June, 1997):185–206; and J. Steven Ott, "Organization Theories of the Nonprofit Sector," Part 8 in J. S. Ott, ed., *The Nature of the Nonprofit Sector* (Boulder: Westview Press, 2001).

4. Michael O'Neill, "Responsible Management in the Nonprofit Sector," in V. A. Hodgkinson and R. W. Lyman, eds., *The Future of the Nonprofit Sector* (San Francisco: Jossey-Bass, 1989):262.

5. Steven J. Ott, "Economic and Political Theories of the Nonprofit Sector," Part 6 in J. S. Ott, ed., *The Nature of the Nonprofit Sector* (Westview Press, 2001).

6. Michael M. Lombardo and Morgan W. McCall, Jr., "Leadership," in M. W. McCall, Jr., and M. M. Lombardo, eds., *Leadership: Where Else Can We Go?* (Durham, NC: Duke University Press, 1978): 3–34.

7. Shafritz, Jay M. 1988. *The Dorsey Dictionary of Politics and Government.* Chicago: Dorsey.

8. Ibid.

9. Chester I. Barnard, *The Functions of the Executive* (Cambridge: Harvard University Press, 1938/1968).

10. Fred E. Fiedler and Martin M. Chemers, *Leadership Styles and Effective Management* (Glenview, IL: Scott, Foresman, 1974).

11. Alfred R. Stern, "Instilling Activism in Trustees," *Harvard Business Review* (January–February 1980): 24–32.

12. Melissa Middleton-Stone, "Nonprofit Boards of Directors: Beyond the Governance Function," in W. W. Powell, ed., *The Nonprofit Sector: A Research Handbook* (New Haven: Yale University Press, 1987), 143; citing Dan H. Fenn, Jr., "Executives and Community Volunteers," *Harvard Business Review* 49, no. 2 (1971): 4ff.

13. Terry W. McAdam and David L. Gies, "Managing Expectations: What Effective Board Members Ought to Expect from Nonprofit Organizations," *Journal of Voluntary Action Research* 14, no. 4 (October–December 1985): 77–88.

14. Michael Ostrowski, "Nonprofit Boards of Directors," in D. L. Gies, J. S. Ott, and J. M. Shafritz, eds., *The Nonprofit Organization: Essential Readings* (Fort Worth, TX: Harcourt Brace, 1990), 182–189.

15. E. G. Knauft, Renee A. Berger, and Sandra T. Gray, *Profiles of Excellence: Achieving Success in the Nonprofit Sector* (San Francisco: Jossey-Bass, 1991), 9.

16. Robert D. Herman and Richard D. Heimovics, *Executive Leadership in Nonprofit Organizations* (San Francisco: Jossey-Bass, 1991), 55, 57; also see Robert D. Herman and Richard D. Heimovics, "Critical Events in the Management of Nonprofit Organizations: Initial Evidence," *Nonprofit and Voluntary Sector Quarterly* 18, no. 2 (summer 1989):119–131.

17. Michael O'Neill, "Responsible Management in the Nonprofit Sector," in V. A. Hodgkinson and R. W. Lyman, eds., *The Future of the Nonprofit Sector* (San Francisco: Jossey-Bass, 1989), 272.

18. Stephen R. Block, "Executive Director," in J. M. Shafritz, ed., *The International Encyclopedia of Public Policy and Administration* (Boulder: Westview Press, 1998), 832–837.

19. Henry Mintzberg, *The Nature of Managerial Work* (New York: Harper & Row, 1973).

20. Thomas H. Jeavons, "Ethics in Nonprofit Management: Creating a Culture of Integrity," in Robert D. Herman, ed., *The Jossey Bass, Handbook of Nonprofit Leadership and Management* (San Francisco: Jossey-Bass, 1994), 184–207.

21. Mary Tschirhart, *Artful Leadership* (Indianapolis: Indiana University Press, 1996).

CHAPTER 7

Executive Director

STEPHEN R. BLOCK

A title that accompanies the management role for the highest-ranking staff position in a private nonprofit organization. In some states, the heads of public agencies are also referred to as executive directors.

Early developments in commerce, followed by improved manufacturing technologies during the Industrial Revolution, led to stronger interests in management techniques during the late 1800s and into the twentieth century. During the same time period that scientific management principles were being advanced, Congress in 1894 created public policy that formally supported tax exemptions for charitable organizations. The development of management as a field of professional practice began to flourish during the first 20 years of the twentieth century. As attention to university programs developed and societies concerned with management practices formed, the importance of senior management positions became significant, not only in business but also in public administration and organizations of the private nonprofit sector.

The title and position of executive director is equivalent to chief executive officer (CEO) or president, both of which are executive management titles generally used in for-profit organizations to designate the foremost decisionmaker who is in charge of operations.

Among private nonprofit organizations, the title of president is often reserved for the highest-ranking volunteer (sometimes called the chief volunteer officer or otherwise known as chairperson of the board of directors). In some nonprofit organizations, however, the corporate title of president is substituted for the title of executive director. In such situations, the highest-ranking volunteer will be referred to as the chairperson of the board of directors.

The relationship between the chairperson, the board of directors, and the executive director position is initially forged through the process of hiring the executive director. In fact, the board of directors has ultimate responsibility for hiring and establishing the compensation of the executive director. The board is also responsible for evaluating the performance of the executive director and rewarding (or terminating, if required) him or her.

Once hired, the executive director may assume many governance and management roles and responsibilities. Though boards of directors can never truly delegate their legal obligations and fiduciary responsibilities, they are known to assign (or expect) their executive directors to help them fulfill their roles as effective board members. In some organizations, the role of the executive director is not shaped through the board's articulation of expectations, but rather the position is shaped by the executive director's experiences and know-how. In public sector organizations, the executive director has a responsibility to manage a department. Above all, the focus of the position is to support the policies and direction of the elected official who appointed the executive director.

How Does a Person Become an Executive Director?

How a person becomes an executive director of a private nonprofit organization may not always follow a clear and logical career path. There is much anecdotal evidence to suggest that many executive directors have been hired on the basis of their programmatic skills and not on their qualifications as executive managers. Laurence J. Peter coined the phrase "the Peter Principle," to identify this type of organizational ascendency into positions beyond one's competency. For example, competent social workers known for outstanding family counseling skills can find themselves hired into executive director positions on the basis of their proven clinical activities. In this example, the social worker may have no training or education in management, no experience with policy implementation, or no other competencies usually required of the executive director position. Consequently, the person is promoted into the highest of management level positions and removed from the one position in which he or she excelled.

More recently, hiring pools of executive director applicants comprise candidates with varied backgrounds. Some include individuals with program expertise along with a mix of individuals who have been trained or educated in nonprofit management. Many management oriented candidates seek management expertise through nonprofit management workshops, conferences, and continuing education opportunities, some of which lead to a certificate in nonprofit management from a host college or university. In more recent years, executive director position applicants may include individuals who have earned graduate degrees in nonprofit management or degrees from other disciplines that offer a concentration in nonprofit management, such as those degrees or areas of academic concentration available in the fields of human services, business, or public administration.

Whether individuals have backgrounds emphasizing program capabilities, management skills, or a combination of the two, there does not appear to be a shortage of candidates who willingly express their interest in vacant executive director positions, for a variety of reasons. The size of a nonprofit organization's budget and the complexity of the operations can be factors in attracting an executive director. Salary range and fringe benefits for the executive director position may influence both the size of an applicant pool and the characteristics and competencies of the candidates. For example, one would expect an executive director hired at US $20,000 a year to have competencies different from those of an individual who is paid US $100,000 a year. One might also expect that the larger, more-established nonprofit organization will be able to attract the most experienced and seasoned of executive directors, but the smaller-budgeted organization might be a valuable training ground for the newer and emerging executive manager.

Other important factors that have a bearing on the interest level of qualified applicants include the organization's mission, beliefs, and values; the geographical location of the organization; the reputation of the organization; the status of the board members in the community; the extent of (under-, over-, or balanced) involvement of board members in the organization; and the clarity of the board's expectations of the executive director.

When an organization is searching for a new executive director, it is important to identify clearly the skills and characteristics necessary for leading the organization toward the achievement of its mission and vision. When the board is clear about its organization's direction and purpose, the board has a higher probability of selecting the right person. The most critical factors are a candidate's knowledge about the role of executive director, proven management and human resource skills, and solid (and candid) references.

What Are Required Competencies for an Executive Director?

The executive director position comprises many multifaceted roles and responsibilities. The effective executive director possesses a range of qualifications that take into account personal characteristics, skills, knowledge, and abilities. Management expert Henry Mintzberg (1973) suggested that the position of an executive manager is organized around ten roles within three sets of behaviors: (1) four decisional roles (entrepreneur, disturbance handler, resource allocator, negotiator); (2) three informational roles (monitor, disseminator, spokesperson); and (3) three interpersonal roles (figurehead, leader, liaison). Mintzberg's concepts have also been applied to managing nonprofit organizations.

Daily work experiences of the nonprofit executive director illustrate the continuum of skills and abilities that are required of the position. Since executive directors tend to be involved in many activities simultaneously, their management focus must continually shift. This shifting can cause a blurring of the boundaries among the various roles categorized as either informational, decisional, or interpersonal, as illustrated in the following scenarios.

Informational. The executive director monitors the opinions of local stakeholders to determine if there will be any impact on the organization's reputation and its ability to raise private funds. This information is shared (as disseminator) in different formats with key staff and board members in order to plan appropriate responses and fund-raising activities. The executive director speaks (spokesperson) before civic groups and corporate funders to explain the mission and direction of the organization.

Interpersonal. The executive director represents the organization and its board of directors (as figurehead) at important community meetings. At a monthly meeting the executive director (as leader) encourages the staff to work on improving its skills and offers guidance for exploring individual beliefs in comparison with the organization's mission and purpose. The executive director (as liaison) meets with the staff of the mayor's office to determine (as entrepreneur) if local community development funds exist to help finance a volunteer youth program.

Decisional. In response to a negative article in the local newspaper, the executive director (as disturbance handler) reacts to the external pressures to fend off a public relations crisis. In preparation for drafting the coming year's budget for the board's consideration, the executive director studies the agency's finances (as resource allocator) to shift the revenues among the key priorities and programs of the organization. The executive director also plays a negotiating role among department managers and board members with regard to establishing funding priorities and eliminating some favorite but underfunded projects.

Demands of the executive director position will vary among nonprofit organizations. Regardless of the organizational complexity of the position, the job generally requires some functional ability to shift attention back and forth between internal and external issues. Executive directors are expected to have the skill to assess their organizations' strengths and weaknesses and to analyze the results of the information. The results can be used to develop a purposeful and strategic course of action, such as designing activities to improve or maintain the capability of staff or to protect or enhance the quality of the organization's service delivery system.

The ability to project how current events or emerging trends in the community will positively or adversely impact the nonprofit organization is another critical management trait that is necessary for controlling or influencing outcomes and for planning thoughtful strategic reactions. The executive director is also expected to respond to the pressures of the external environment by developing a network of community supports and collaborative working relationships.

Paying attention to the organization's internal and external environments is just one of many important components of the executive director's job. In fact, there are several essential management tasks in which the results-oriented executive director will participate, lead, or carry out explicitly or implicitly.

The tasks are as follows: *mission development, visioning, goal setting*. The executive director will have an opportunity to assist the board, staff, and other community members in the creation of an organizational mission statement or to annually review and, if necessary, revise the organization's mission statement. The mission statement is a reflection of the needs of the community and represents a collective vision of what the community could strive to become as a result of the efforts of the organization. By exerting leadership, the executive director is in a position to interpret the significance of the mission statements for establishing operational goals and objectives, recommending policy changes, and for motivating staff, volunteers and others to believe in the importance of the mission.

Planning

The executive director plays an instrumental role in working with the board and staff to use the mission statement as a guide for establishing short-term and long-term goals and objectives of the organization and for developing action steps for implementation. The executive director is positioned to communicate to staff the purpose, time lines, and strategies of the plan. Managing the resources of money and people to accomplish the organization's plan and monitoring and developing strategies when obstacles impede progress are also major responsibilities of the executive director. The executive director assists the board of directors with its duties by assuring an evaluation of the plan's progress and reporting its results and, likewise, communicating the need to revise aspects of the plan on an ongoing basis.

Organizing

In practice, the executive director is responsible for determining what monetary resources and people are needed to accomplish an organization's plan, projects, and program services. Structuring the staffing patterns of the organiza-

tion and establishing performance standards are other management responsibilities of the executive director.

Motivating

It is sometimes said that an effective manager is one who is able to get things accomplished through the work of the other people. The complexity of motivating individuals either through intrinsic or extrinsic rewards requires an understanding of basic human nature. The effective executive director is one who understands the varying needs of individuals and responds by providing enriching opportunities, which build a sense of spirit and belief in the organization. If the director stimulated an interest in the work of the organization, the staff, board members, and other volunteers will use their energies, knowledge, and skills to achieve accomplishments for the organization and to enhance its service capacity.

Decisionmaking

Herbert A. Simon once suggested that decisionmaking is synonymous with managing. Decisionmaking is a pervasive management task of the executive director and includes making a choice among varying alternatives and weighing the likely consequences and risks of choosing one alternative over another. The effective executive director is one who uses a model or framework for approaching complex and far-reaching organizational decisions. Of particular importance is the recurring task of seeking and analyzing information through informal and formal communication channels that are internal and external to the organ. Information is a necessary ingredient for recognizing the need to make a decision and for serving as a pertinent database for developing a decision. Savvy executive directors also monitor reactions to their decisions and use the feedback as additional critical bits of data for ongoing decisionmaking.

Delegating

To be efficient and effective, the executive director must be able to recognize which aspects of his or her work can be scheduled or reorganized for attention during another time period. Also, it is important to identify which portions of the job can be accomplished by assigning responsibility to others within the organization or by making temporary assignments to outside consultants. Appropriate delegation of the executive director's work assignments to staff requires an understanding of staff's skills and abilities; a sensitivity to its workload demands; a level of trust in staff's ability and willingness to accomplish tasks at a level that will meet or exceed the executive director's own standards; and the capacity to thank staff for helping out, either on temporary or permanently assigned tasks. Even though executive directors can never truly delegate away their organizational management responsibilities, their uses of delegation can help to alleviate the stresses of work overload, which can adversely impact outcomes.

Coordinating

Executive directors of moderate to large organizations have a management challenge of coordinating the variety of tasks and activities that take place among different specialized departments within an organization. In addition, they need to assure the coordination of work activities that occur up and down the organizational hierarchy. Almost thirty years ago, the term *"integration"* was introduced, referring to the process of managing the linkages across the formal structures of the organization. Without attending to the function of coordination, departments and staff may work at cross purposes and thereby waste resources and adversely impact the opportunity for organizational success. The coordination of tasks and activities is also at play in smaller nonprofit organizations, due to smaller size and fewer staff, the executive director may have a greater level of participation in the different activities, thus minimizing the coordination challenges.

Reporting

The accountability concept of reporting is tied to the idea of lines of responsibilities and a chain of command. Different individuals in the orga-

nization are responsible for a variety of outcomes and are responsible to their supervisor for reporting on the progress of achieving assignments, goals, and objectives. The aggregate of all of this information is eventually reported by senior management staff to the executive director, who similarly must report on the organization's progress to the board of directors. The executive director's responsibility is to assure that there is no confusion in the lines of reporting, and that staff have available to them the proper supports and supervision that enable them to do their work and report their outcomes.

Supervising

The executive director must rely heavily on the capabilities of staff to accomplish the organization's plans; therefore, human resource management is central to an effective organization. In addition to the ability to motivate staff, coordinate activities, and delegate to other personnel, the executive director must have a mechanism of identifying performance outcomes and an acceptable process of supporting or promoting change among staff. The process of supervision is an interactive approach that is centered on developing the abilities of the employee by reflecting on work performance, jointly searching for solutions to work problems, clarifying expectations of the position, clarifying the direction of the organization, assessing the employee's progress in achieving performance objectives, and by modeling the values and beliefs of the organization. Supervisors will typically style their supervision of staff based on how executive directors comport themselves in supervisory conferences with senior management staff.

Managing Finances

All management decisions have some level of impact on an organization's allocation of resources, expenditure of funds, or the need for securing additional money. Technically, a board of directors has a fiduciary responsibility as representatives of the public to assure that there is an annual budget and a plan to acquire an adequate amount of financial resources for stabilizing the organization and implementing its services. Practically speaking, the management of the daily operations requires that the executive director be the one to provide the oversight for carefully monitoring the level of available cash, the organization's current debt, and its outstanding liabilities and receivables.

Complex or simple managerial decisions require that the executive director be fully aware of the organization's fiscal health. Most responsible executive directors rely on the use of financial management tools and the information they produce for making decisions. The tools include: financial statements, functional expense reports, and cash flow statements. An effective executive director knows how to interpret the financial reports and understands the implications of analysis on the stewardship of the organization's budget and resources. In addition, the executive director analyzes the organization's fiscal health by paying close attention to the effects of rising costs, increased or decreased activities, and the variable impacts from planned or unplanned changes in the organization's internal or external environment—including the organization's available working capital, current ratio, and debt-to-equity ratio.

The executive director also plays an important role in the organization's investment strategies. The executive director advises and supports the board after seeking expert advice on the development investment policy and its execution by locating reasonable investment risks. The executive director can also help the board to be prudent in its decisionmaking by watching the returns on investments and forecasting both the current and future needs of the organization.

Fund-Raising

Although many fund-raising experts claim that a primary leadership role of the board of directors is to raise sufficient capital for the operations and program, in reality, fund-raising becomes a management responsibility. The executive director should be as concerned, if not more so, for the organization to be financially sound and have the necessary funding to operate programs and pay staff wages and salary.

The executive director may take on a varying level of direct involvement for raising funds or see to it that the fund-raising activities are shared or carried out by specific staff, consultants, or volunteers. An executive director, for example, might secure appointments with community funders and solicit funding, but be accompanied by board members who bring credibility with their volunteer concerns and as examples for other volunteers like themselves who commit unpaid time and energy to the organization's cause.

Though the support and participation of board members is undeniably a critical factor to fund-raising success, the board's ability to be successful is often dependent on the management expertise and involvement of the executive director. The basis for successful fund-raising, for example, is to build off the needs, achievements and plans of the organization. The short-term or long-term capability of an organization's fund-raising program requires that the organization be in good working order, operating productively and efficiently, both of which are results of effective management. The executive director assures the soundness of the organization's operations and programs through the controls, processes, and systems that he or she manages, making certain they are supported by skillful and knowledgeable staff and, if applicable, a cadre of committed and dedicated volunteers, all of whom are knowledgeable about the organization's mission, vision, and direction.

The basic characteristics of volunteer support requires the involvement of the executive director, providing oversight and assurances that the tools of fund-raising are in place. Necessary fund-raising tools include a well-crafted "case statement," a donor or prospect list, an annual report or other significant brochures that illustrate the achievements of the organization, and a plan that has realistic goals with a time frame that is also reasonable. With regard to the implementation of a fund-raising plan, the executive director must also be up-to-date about the efforts of the staff, volunteers, or resource development committee members so that people are working together and not inadvertently at cross-purposes.

Volunteers are very important to fund-raising success; however, if volunteers do not follow through on important assignments or find that their personal lives and occupational demands are interfering with their volunteer commitment, the executive director must be ready to step in. More than one executive director has found him- or herself "jumping-in" to salvage a fund-raising project, while publicly giving the credit for the project's success to the volunteers, board, and staff.

Executive Director's Leadership Role in Relation to the Board's Governance Role

Clarifying the differences between the responsibilities of the board and those of the executive director, Kenneth Dayton stated simply that governance is governance, and not management. It is largely an indisputable custom that the executive director's role is to oversee the day-to-day operations of the organization, as well as to share jointly with the board in matters critical to the strategic direction and survival of the organization. Because the organizational stakes are high, there is good reason to have concern over the ambiguity that sometimes exists between what board members should actually do and what executive directors are expected to do on behalf of the board.

Some authors have suggested that the board-executive director relationship would be more productive if it were conceptualized as a partnership. Research investigations into what constitutes effective governance and executive leadership have led some researchers to suggest that an especially effective executive director is one who takes active responsibility for the accomplishment of the organizational mission and its stewardship by providing substantial "board-centered" leadership for steering the efforts of the board of directors.

This view also asserts that there are several flaws in the traditional governance model. In the traditional model, the executive director is ranked in a subordinate position to the board.

The hierarchical relationship would suggest that the executive director's daily work activities are being directed and supervised by the board of directors. Robert Herman and Richard Heimovics (1991) affirm through their research findings what many executive directors have come to believe through practical experience: that the board may legally be in charge, but the work of the organization is accomplished by the leadership demonstrated by the executive director. In this alternative "board-centered" model of governance, the executive director's distinctive leadership skills, information base, and management expertise is used for leading the organization toward the accomplishment of its mission. Furthermore, this model acknowledges that board performance is reliant on the leadership and management skills of the executive director. In this way, the executive director works to promote board participation and to facilitate decisionmaking. In addition, the executive director uses his or her interpersonal skills to craft respectful and productive interaction among the board members. With this approach, the executive director is (justifiably) credited with successful or unsuccessful organizational outcomes.

References

Bennis, Warren, and Burt Nanus, 1985. *Leaders: The Strategies for Taking Charge.* New York: Harper & Row.

Block, Peter, 1989. *The Empowered Manager: Positive Political Skills at Work.* San Francisco: Jossey-Bass.

Boyatzis, Richard E., 1982. *The Competent Manager: A Model for Effective Performance.* New York: John Wiley & Sons.

Drucker, Peter F., 1990. *Managing the Non-Profit Organization.* Oxford, England: Butterworth-Heinemann.

Heimovics, Richard D., and Robert D. Herman, 1989. "The Salient Management Skills: A Conceptual Framework for a Curriculum for Managers in Nonprofit Organizations." *American Review of Public Administration,* vol. 18, no. 2:119–132.

———, 1991. *Executive Leadership in Nonprofit Organizations.* San Francisco: Jossey-Bass.

McCauley, Cynthia D., and Martha W. Hughes, 1993. In Dennis R. Young, Robert M. Hollister, and Virginia A. Hodgkinson, eds., *Governing, Leading, and Managing Nonprofit Organizations.* San Francisco: Jossey-Bass, 155–169.

Mintzberg, Henry, 1973. *The Nature of Managerial Work.* New York: Harper & Row.

Young, Dennis R., 1987. "Executive Leadership in Nonprofit Organizations." In Walter W. Powell, ed., *The Nonprofit Sector: A Research Handbook.* New Haven: Yale University Press, 167–179.

CHAPTER 8

Ethics in Nonprofit Management
Creating a Culture of Integrity

THOMAS H. JEAVONS

In the mid-1970s in the aftermath of the Watergate scandal there was a surge of interest in "professional ethics." This was particularly true for lawyers, but it involved other professionals as well. (It should be recalled that almost all those convicted of crimes in the Watergate scandal were lawyers, some from the most prestigious law schools.) There was also some skepticism in the larger public at the time, however, about how sincere this new interest in ethics was.

In a pointed way this highlights two key assumptions about ethics and the consideration of ethical matters that are unfortunately too often operative among professionals of all types. The first is the belief that careful, skilled thinking about these matters, ethical matters, is more the business of philosophers and academics than practitioners.

The second assumption is found among many who believe, even while they admit the importance of ethical questions and issues, that these questions and issues may be isolated and dealt with as discrete concerns in professional practice, apart from others. This perspective may be exemplified in the tendency to have one course on ethics in a professional program, or to have one or two sessions in courses on other subjects take up ethical issues—rather than work to en-sure that the ethical implications of all subjects and of every aspect of professional practice are dealt with wherever they might arise in a professional education.

I lift up these two assumptions because they are both, I believe, false; and they both certainly undermine the maintenance of appropriate ethical standards and behavior in the management and operation of nonprofit organizations.

The analysis that follows begins, in fact, with two quite opposite assumptions. The first is that reflecting critically and actively on ethical issues is an obligation of every "professional," including nonprofit managers. The capacity for and inclination to socially responsive, historically grounded, critical, ethical judgment should be one of the outcomes of any sound professional education program, and one of the capacities of a "professional" as "reflective practitioner" (Schön, 1983, 1987). The second is that a concern for the ethical content or implications of one's decisions and actions is salient in every aspect of professional practice and in relation to every facet of the life of nonprofit organizations.

Indeed, I will argue here, as the title for this chapter implies, that we are most likely to see consistently ethical behavior among nonprofit managers and organizations only where an emphasis on ethical values and behavior is deeply embedded in the cultures of these organizations. So, building and reinforcing that kind of organizational culture becomes a primary responsibility for those concerned that ethical practice be a hallmark of all the functions, including the management, of their organization.

An Overview of This Chapter

The argument that will be proffered and supported in this chapter claims first that ethical behavior in and by nonprofit organizations cannot be assured simply by employing encouraging rhetoric about ethics, nor just be establishing specific rules for ethical behavior. Most people with any significant experience in organizational life know there is often a marked disparity between rhetoric and practice in organizational behavior. They also know that rules (about ethics and other matters) can be, and frequently are, followed "in the letter" while being totally ignored or even violated "in the spirit."

Thus, the claim to be argued here is that ethical behavior will be assured only by creating an organizational culture where key ethical ideals and expectations are incorporated in the "core values" (Schein, 1985) of an organization and thus permeate its operations.

Additionally, I will argue that because of the unique historical and societal dimensions of their character and function, expectations about what constitutes ethical behavior in and by nonprofit, and especially by philanthropic, organizations differ from expectations placed on other organizations. Specifically, the question of trustworthiness goes to the core of the reason for the existence of these organizations and their ability to satisfy public expectations. The very existence of most nonprofit organizations, their capacity to garner resources—and so to survive and carry out their missions—depends on their moral standing and integrity (see Hansmann, 1987; Douglas, 1987; Ostrander and Schervish, 1990; and Jeavons, 1992a).

There exists in this context, I would contend, an *implicit social contract* undergirding the presence and function of private nonprofit, especially philanthropic, organizations in our society. These organizations are given a special standing, and even certain legal advantages over other private organizations, on the basis of the promise that they will serve the public good. The public expects these organizations to be motivated by and adhere to such a commitment in their performance. The public also expects that these organizations will honor a set of widely accepted moral and humanitarian values—deriving from these organization's historical and philosophical roots—and that they will (virtually) never act in a self-serving manner.

Accordingly, if the managers of nonprofit, especially philanthropic, organizations wish to ensure the ethical behavior of their organizations, staffs, and themselves, they need to work at creating and maintaining organizational cultures that accept and honor in practice (as fundamental) a set of "core values" that are in continuity with the historic philosophical and religious roots of the voluntary sector and that meet the public's current expectations. In this context we need to see that trust is the essential lifeblood of the nonprofit sector—trust that nonprofits will fulfill this implicit social contract. And to ensure that this trust is sustained, five core values must permeate these organizations, shaping their ethics. These values are integrity, openness, accountability, service, and charity (in the original sense of that term).

What Are "Ethics"?

As a field of study or discipline, "ethics" refers to "the study of moral topics, including moral issues, moral responsibilities, and moral ideals of character." In a normative sense, "ethics" may be seen simply to refer to "justified moral standards"—which is to say, not just what people *do* believe about how they should act, but what they *should* believe.

Webster's New World Dictionary of the American Language (2nd College Edition, 1970) defines ethics as "the system or code of morals of a particular person, religion, group, profession, etc." The *Oxford English Dictionary* (Compact Edition, 1971) notes the derivation of the word *ethics* from the Greek term *ethos,* meaning "custom, usage, manner or habit," and goes on to offer the following definitions (for *ethics*): "the moral principles by which a person is guided" and "the rules of conduct recognized in certain associations or departments of human life." The derivation of the term and the differences we see in these common definitions highlight two facets of the origins and purposes of ethics that we might examine.

The etymology and definitions of *ethics* also remind us that much of what we typically think about as ethical principles or judgments, especially when our concern is application and practice, are not derived in any case from philosophical absolutes, but rather from the reference point of social or community standards. To play with the words, *ethics* (as we commonly use the term) may be as much a matter of "ethos"—what is expected or socially acceptable, what is customary—as a matter of indisputable moral vision. Of course, these two aspects of ethics are often intertwined; what a particular community views as ethically acceptable will often be determined by what its members believe that some source of absolute moral authority (God, perhaps) requires.

Understanding this about the origins and meaning of "ethics" makes it clear that when we raise and examine questions about ethics— ethics generally, professional ethics, the ethics of nonprofit managers, or the ethics of the behavior of nonprofit organizations—there are two reference points we need always to bear in mind in our considerations: one a point of moral absolutes, and another of community standard and expectations. I believe we should be asking two kinds of questions: First, What are we morally obligated to do and not do? Second, What does society require or expect of us? Moreover, ethical questions should be considered in that order, giving preference to moral obligations over customary ones.

Professional Ethics

If ethics are, as one volume observes, "a set of rules that apply to human beings over the totality of their interrelationships with one another, and that take precedence over all other rules" (Gellerman, Frankel, and Ladenson, 1990, p. 41),

then we need to ask, How are such rules more specifically defined by and applied to particular spheres of professional activity?

One commentator on "professional values" argues that in our culture "professionals are viewed as morally committed to pursuing the dominant value that defines the goals of their professional practice. . . . They are expected to pursue such goals on a social as well as individual level. . . . And they are expected to do so even when self-interest may have to be sacrificed in that pursuit" (Alan Goldman, cited in Gellerman, Frankel, Ladenson, 1990, p. 5).

In sum, the claim being made here is that professional ethics for nonprofit management and in the operation of nonprofit agencies require the articulation and internalization of standards for behavior and ways of being for those agencies and their managers that adequately reflect the sector's origins in the moral, often religious, spheres of our culture, and meet the current, morally justifiable expectations of our society.

One advantage nonprofit, especially philanthropic, organizations have in this sphere is that they can—and should—root their judgments about and commitments to ethical behavior in the moral traditions from which the non-profit sector sprang.

Understanding, then, that ethical judgments must be based on firmer moral and social considerations, let us look more closely at the particular ethical values that can and should shape the ethical perspectives of nonprofit managers, whatever the practical advantages (or disadvantages) of ethical behavior may be.

Core Values and Their Origins in the Voluntary Sector

Many explanations have been offered for the origins and use of the non-profit organizational form. The one of these explanations that rings truest to many people's experience, however, revolves around what economists and some organizational theorists call "contract failure" and an "agency problem." Simply put, this suggests that private nonprofits are created or exist to provide services, first, where governments cannot or will not provide the service for some reason, and then, where those who want a service provided either (a) will not be in a position to see that what they want to have done or to have happen will occur, or (b), because of the nature of the service to be provided, are unable to judge the quality of that service. In such circumstances, it is argued, people create or use private nonprofit— rather than for-profit—organizations because they feel nonprofit organizations will have less incentive to cheat consumers and supporters.

It is also important to recognize that in these cases the people paying for the services provided are often *not* the consumers of the services. Rather they may be donors. This being the case, they want to work through an organization that, as an "agent," they can expect to provide a service for someone else as they, the donors, would themselves provide it if they could. Consequently, they seek an agent they believe to be highly committed to providing that service for others. Crassly put, they want an agent that is involved "for the cause," not "for the money."

A quick analysis of both these situations tells us what is likely to be the most important and desirable ethical quality of nonprofit organizations. In these circumstances trust is a key consideration. That being so, we can project what kinds of operational ethical values will need to be evident in organizations that have earned and deserve the public's trust. Among the most central are integrity, openness, accountability, and service.

Also on that earlier list, though, is "charity," in the original sense of the term—from the Latin *caritas.* Obviously there are some nonprofit organizations that would not be expected to be "charitable" as that word is usually used—"generous" or "eleemosynary." Most people do not expect these to be characteristics of trade associations, for example. Still, the majority of those organizations that populate the nonprofit or voluntary sector are service providers dependent in some way on the philanthropic traditions and practices of our society. They are expected in that context to be "caring" organizations, willing to put the public good and the welfare of others above their own gain and comfort.

It is important to understand how this last expectation is a *moral* quality—ascribed to such

organizations and assumed by them as a result of their historical and sociological functions in our society. The fact is nonprofit philanthropic and service organizations occupy a distinctive place in American society because of their origins—largely in religious or other idealistic voluntary associations—and because they have traditionally been vehicles for preserving, transmitting, or promoting social values. As a result of both their historical development and their contemporary roles, these organizations carry much of the burden of mediating civic, moral, and spiritual values in the public realm and from one generation to the next (Curti, 1958; Parsons, 1960). In this light they are objects of special moral expectations that they will be charitable, caring organizations.

There are, thus, ethical qualities or values that are essential in the character and behavior of nonprofit, especially philanthropic, organizations. They are expected to be—and should be—organizations that demonstrate integrity, openness, accountability, service, and a caring demeanor. And what is required of managers of these organizations is that they give special attention to seeing that these ethical values are reflected in every aspect of these organizations. This requires that the managers model ethical qualities in their own behavior as well as articulate and foster them as ideals for others.

Ethical Management in Ethical Organizations

It will be useful at this point to consider each of the key ethical attributes of nonprofit managers and their organizations more fully. In this process we should undertake an analysis at two levels—the individual and the organizational— asking, for example, What does it mean for a manager to do his or her work with integrity, and for an organization to operate with integrity?

Integrity

It may be most useful to describe integrity as "honesty writ large." That is to say, integrity has to do with continuity between appearance and reality, between intention and action, between promise and performance, in every aspect of a person's or an organization's existence. If trust is the most crucial quality in the operation of nonprofit organizations, then "integrity" in this sense becomes a fundamental ethical characteristic they need to possess.

At the organizational level, integrity is most obviously demonstrated to be present or absent by comparing an organization's own literature—fundraising materials, reports, statements of missions and values—with its actual program priorities and performance. For instance, an organization that claims to be in existence to serve the poor, but regularly spends large amounts of resources on enlarging itself, enhancing its own image before the public, or improving the comfort or security levels of its staff must be suspect.

This is not to say that staff in such organizations should not have reasonable salaries and benefits; that being in the public eye for fundraising purposes is not important to support the work to be done; or that an organization might not be able to improve its service delivery by growing. But it is to say that a careful examination of budgets, allocations of staff time, and the application of other resources too often show that nonprofit and philanthropic organizations that were created and claim to be serving the public good are giving more attention to caring for and improving themselves than others. Moreover, the public is sensitive to these issues. If we need proof of this, we would do well to recall the controversies involving United Way of America or some television ministries in the late 1980s and early 1990s.

In an event injurious to the credibility of charities in the spring of 1992 it was revealed that the head of the United Way of America was receiving a salary of almost $500,000, traveling about the world first-class, and setting up subsidiary organizations run by his friends and relatives. When the millions of small donors to local United Ways found out that a portion of their gifts were going to support a lavish life-style for an executive of a charitable organization, most were again outraged. Despite the massive efforts of local United Ways to explain that only a tiny portion of income went to the national organi-

zation, which was a legally separate entity, the giving to local United Ways (and hence to their member agencies) in the following year fell significantly. Once more a great many ethical and efficient charitable organizations found themselves tarnished with guilt by association.

Dramatic disparities between the ethical or practical promise (implicit or explicit) and the performance of one charitable organization may precipitate difficulties for the entire nonprofit sector. As one economist studying the nonprofit sector has observed, "Whenever any nonprofit is found to have abused its trusted position, the reputation of trustworthy nonprofits also suffers. . . . Nonprofits that do not act opportunistically, as well as those who do, will find it increasingly difficult to obtain resources" (Weisbrod, 1988, p. 13).

"*Integrity*" may have different meanings for different individuals, but in the context of professional ethics it must mean doing one's job as honestly and as fully in adherence to one's professed principles as possible. Careful observers of organizational behavior have noted that managers and leaders in organizations tend to have a significant effect in setting behavioral standards, either as a matter of personal influence, or because of their control of reward systems, or for both reasons. The manager who wants her or his employees to deal honestly with others had better deal honestly with them, and, further, had better reward honesty and discourage any dishonesty. If the manager is willing to cut corners, tell "little" lies, or act in self-serving ways, it becomes more likely the employees too will see this as acceptable behavior, at least within the work setting. So the manager who wants the organization she or he oversees to be known for its integrity, and to be trustworthy, must begin by being completely trustworthy in her or his dealings with all those who are part of the organization, and make it clear that similar behavior is expected of all those people.

Put more simply, integrity must be one of the hallmarks of nonprofit management. It is an ethical obligation, both as a matter of morality, because it is right, and as a matter of societal necessity, because the public expects nonprofit organizations to do these things. Failing to embody and uphold the highest standards for personal and organizational integrity can have enormous consequences for nonprofit managers and their agencies or institutions.

Openness

It would be inaccurate to call the quality of openness a "moral" value, at least within the context of the most common value systems of American culture. So the claim to be made about openness as an ethical value is not based so much on moral absolutes—as may be the case for integrity—as on social values and expectations. In this context, we might think of openness as a "derivative virtue."

In any case, for an organization or individual to try to hide their philanthropic endeavors from public view has almost always been to raise profound skepticism about the motivation for and character of those endeavors. In colloquial terms, the public's attitude here has been, "If they are really doing good, why would they be reluctant (or embarrassed) to have us see what they are doing?"

This is especially true for organizations. It is possible to put forth a reasonable argument, even one based on religious grounds (see Matthew 6:2–4 or the Mishneh Torah), for individuals "doing good works" anonymously or in secret. However, for organizations that operate in the public sphere, especially in areas of service or advocacy that can have an impact on public policy or community life, it is hard to argue convincingly for secrecy. Indeed, it may be crucial for these organizations to conduct their business in a way that is open to public scrutiny. One reason for this is that, if nothing else, openness undergirds other ethical behavior. The organization that does operate openly cannot afford to cut other ethical corners.

Another reason for this is historical. There have long been critical questions raised about the roles philanthropic and service organizations play in shaping people's and communities' lives. (See, for instance, Griffin, 1957, or Nielsen, 1985.) This is, in part, because some of these organizations appear to have had ulterior motives—for example, intentions of "social con-

trol" or protection of the interests of the privileged, embedded in their work.

In addition, from the point of view of those who are concerned about the continuing vitality of nonprofit organizations and who recognize that maintaining a climate of trust is essential to that vitality, we should see that operating openly is one of the best ways to build trust. Organizations that wish to engage people's support and good faith can find no better way to do so than to do good works well, and then welcome the inquiries and inspection of anyone interested in their methods.

What is more, the same kind of logic applies to those who would lead these organizations, in terms of their leadership and management style. In the effort to build the support and commitment of staff, volunteers, and donors, a manager's willingness to talk openly and honestly about rationales for programs, the reasons for and ways in which decisions are made, and approaches to problem solving can be invaluable.

All this is finally to say that openness in the business of decision making, in matters of raising and allocating resources, and, more generally, in the manner of their operation should be seen as a key ethical value for nonprofit organizations and their managers. Moreover, openness is, of course, a necessary prerequisite to accountability.

Accountability

Not only is it important for nonprofit organizations, especially philanthropic ones, to be open about the things they do, and how and why they do them, it is also important that they be ready to explain and generally be accountable for their choices. This is an extension of the implicit social contract of privilege and trust these organizations enjoy in our society.

In accepting the privilege of tax exemption and the right to solicit tax-deductible contributions, the public benefit agencies and philanthropic organizations also accept an obligation to be ready to answer not only to their membership but to the broader public as well, for the way they use resources that would otherwise have gone into the public treasury. And while the level of public support is not nearly as great for "mutual benefit" organizations—which are exempt but cannot receive deductible contributions—their exempt status is based in part on the expectation that they will also, at the least, be answerable to their membership in pursuing the articulated mission of their organizations.

All of this is to say that in social and contractual terms, all nonprofit organizations have an ethical responsibility to be accountable to their supporters, their members, and their donors; and some, the public benefit organizations, have an even larger responsibility to be accountable to the broader public for the ways in which they undertake to fulfill their philanthropic purposes. We would do well to note here that a confirmation of the growing public expectations in this regard (and some organizations' recognition of those expectations) can be found in the growth in recent years of "watch-dog" groups like the National Charities Information Bureau, the Better Business Bureau's section on nonprofit organizations, and the Evangelical Council for Financial Accountability. In addition, more and more states are passing laws to mandate financial disclosure and regulate fundraising practices of nonprofits.

How does this obligation of accountability extend to nonprofit managers? In much the same way as the obligations of integrity and openness do. First, if this is a quality managers and leaders want to see reflected in their organization, it is one they had better model in their own behavior. It then becomes an expectation that they can articulate credibly to others.

Second, managers can establish this commitment most firmly by making sure they hold themselves accountable to their organization's board, and work to build a board that will hold them accountable for their performance. Much of the most useful recent literature on board/executive relationships has pointed out that a full and vital partnership between executives and managers is essential for there to be effective leadership in nonprofit organizations (Drucker, 1990; Herman and Heimovics, 1991; Middleton, 1987).

Service

The grounds for the ethical obligation here are virtually identical with those for accountability. Nonprofit organizations, especially public benefit organizations, exist and are granted specific privileges with the explicit understanding that they are committed in some way to *serve* the public good.

The social contract extended to these organizations assumes that they will primarily devote themselves to service. In operating under the privileges they have been granted, these organizations acknowledge their ethical obligation to be service oriented. Moreover, in accepting the support—membership dues, donations, volunteers' time—of people who sustain them, these organizations reinforce their ethical obligations in this regard.

This ethical obligation to service should be manifest in the conduct of managers in a number of ways. Many people now make a career of work in the nonprofit sector. We could not have a meaningful discussion of nonprofit management as a "profession" if people did not commit themselves to and build careers in this area. But while this creates the ground for our discussion of professional ethics, it also creates a context in which managers can easily work with as much concern for their own advancement as for the people or cause their organization is supposed to serve.

To say that nonprofit managers should make the ethical obligation of service a primary concern is to say that they must give precedence to fulfilling the mission of their organization over possibilities for advancing their own status and careers. This is *not* to say that managers are required to sacrifice themselves—their health, their basic financial security, or their personal well being—for the benefit of their organization. Nonprofit organizations, especially cause-oriented ones, are notorious for exploiting and burning out their staff in the name of noble ideals (see Greene, 1991). Rather it is to say that the undergirding values of the nonprofit sector are altruistic, and while it is fine to be concerned for one's own career and fulfillment in one's work in nonprofit organizations, it is never acceptable for managers to advance themselves at the expense of the people and causes they have promised to serve.

In addition, observation suggests that the willingness of managers and leaders to see themselves as servants of others may be crucial to focusing others in an organization on that organization's commitment to service. Here the notion of "servant leadership" (Greenleaf, 1977) takes on both profound significance and immediate salience.

"Charity"

Finally, the last, but certainly not least important ethical obligation of nonprofit, especially philanthropic, organizations is to charity, in the original sense of the term. The word "*charity*" comes from the Latin *caritas*. This means more than giving to those in need. It originally was translated as "love"; not romantic love, but the love of neighbor and committed concern for the welfare of others illustrated in the parable of the Good Samaritan. It meant caring, putting the welfare of others on a par with one's own, being generous with one's own resources, not out of a sense of pity but out of a sense of relationship with and concern for others.

It can surely be argued that for nonprofit organizations an ethical obligation to "charity" in this sense derives from reciprocity. That is, many of these organizations depend on the generosity of their supporters for their existence, and ought to display such generosity themselves. Furthermore, at least in the case of the philanthropic organizations, the motivation of most of their supporters rests in no small way on a belief that these organizations are committed to caring for others. As I noted in earlier discussion of the origins of nonprofit organizations and the voluntary sector, the basis of much of these organizations' support is the expectation that they will be vehicles for building a more caring, more just society.

This expectation is manifest in an interesting range of phenomena. For instance, the preference of many clients and supporters of social service agencies for private nonprofit groups appears to be based on an assumption that they will provide services in a more personal, more caring way than a government agency. In industries where potential employees—for example, teachers, nurses, or social workers—might work for either government or private organizations, the preference of some for private nonprofits is often explained in terms of their expectation (or experience) of these organizations as more caring work environments. And this expectation is certainly confirmed by the public indignation that is often evident when an organization that is itself the beneficiary of charity turns around and acts in uncaring ways.

Once more, the way in which this expectation applies to the ethics of management seems obvious. An uncaring or mean-spirited manager can undermine the caring quality of an organization as fast as any negative influence imaginable. Managers and leaders help set the tone of an organization's life—whether they intend to or not—and that tone is almost certainly going to be reflected in the way that organization—and all its staff—interacts at every level with its various constituencies.

Finally, we should see again, as we noted before, that the organizations of the nonprofit sector have been seen as having a special role in transmitting civic, social, and ethical values in our society from one generation to the next. If that is true, then we have yet another reason to be concerned that these organizations reflect the highest ideals for a caring society.

From Ideals to Operative Values

If we can agree, then, that these five concepts or ideals—integrity, openness, accountability, service, and charity—may describe key ethical qualities and obligations of nonprofit organizations and their managers, we are still left to ask how these ideals get translated into behavior.

At the individual level this may be easy. If one assumes that people can choose what to value and choose to embody those values in their actions, then for individuals, ethical behavior is a matter of choice and will. If this is the case, then the managers of nonprofit organizations simply need to choose to act with integrity, to be open and accountable in their work, to make commitment to service and charity a cornerstone for their decision making and interaction with others. However, this still leaves open the question of how these ethical ideals become the operational values of an organization as a whole.

At this point we need to turn to the work that has been done over the last several years on "organizational culture." This field offers some valuable insights to our discussion. In particular, I want to draw heavily on the careful research and analysis of Edgar Schein in his book, *Organizational Culture and Leadership* (1985).

Much of the thinking about organizational culture has tended to focus, often somewhat shallowly, on "rites and rituals" of organizational life (see Deal and Kennedy, 1982; Peters and Waterman, 1982). Schein takes a different tack, arguing that an excessive focus on what he calls "the manifestations of culture" will obscure the fact that very similar rituals, conventions, or regular practices in various companies are undertaken for very different reasons. Thus, he claims, to understand organizational culture one must focus on the essential values these visible practices are meant to express. These values are "the substance of culture," in Schein's view.

There are in fact, Schein suggests, some values that represent the basic assumptions of a group of people—as, for instance, the membership of an organization—about the way the world is and how they, as a group, can function most successfully in it. These "core values" will shape the organization's behavior, not only by dictating what are right or acceptable responses to different kinds of situations but also by shaping the way those situations are perceived, by influencing what people see as important or unimportant information.

In this vein, Schein argues that leaders or managers can shape the direction, character, and operations of an organization most fundamentally and effectively by shaping the core values of the participants within it, or selecting new participants who share those values. Indeed, he

claims that "there is a possibility—underemphasized in leadership research—that the only things of real importance that leaders do is to create and manage culture" (1985, p. 2). The implications of this for people who are concerned about creating and maintaining organizations that behave ethically is obvious.

The connection between the ethical behavior of managers and the maintenance of the highest ethical standards of behavior by nonprofit organizations is manifest in those managers' capability to create a culture of integrity. Such a culture is one wherein the ethical ideals we have been discussing come to be accepted as "givens," and where the expectation that these ideals will be honored in the life and work of the organization permeates every participant's thinking. This can only occur where these ethical values are both articulated and modeled by those in positions of responsibility and leadership. In this way leaders and managers can shape the core values of an organization as a whole—and the individuals within it—around these ethical ideals.

Creating and Maintaining a Culture of Integrity

Finally we must see that clear, strong commitments to ethical ideals and behavior on the part of managers is a prerequisite to creating organizational cultures of integrity in nonprofits that will enable the organizations themselves to behave ethically. The importance of the example of leadership in this process cannot be overemphasized. As one commentator has observed, "CEOs . . . are ultimately accountable for [their] organization's ethical posture. . . . No organization can rise above the ethical level of its manager" (Mason, 1992b, p. 30).

Still, even where the management of an organization is consistent in both preaching and practicing the right values, more will probably be needed to create and sustain a culture of integrity. Organizational structures and reward systems must also support and encourage ethical behavior among all employees and volunteers. People's best intentions can be undermined or confused by organizational structures and processes that lead them to make choices that have negative ethical consequences.

As in many organizations that are hierarchically ordered, some nonprofits have a tendency to punish the bearers of bad news—and even reward the bearers of false news, so long as it is good. That tends to leave the organization less able to perform its mission and encourages employees to be less than honest about policies and programs that are failing. The leadership and management of nonprofit organizations must put in place systems that reward participants for honesty in every form, even forms that lead to the revelation of difficulties and deficiencies of the organization.

Similarly, one has to wonder about organizations that constantly emphasize short-term goals and focus solely on raw numbers (of dollars raised) in evaluating and rewarding development efforts, rather than asking questions about the quality of relationships with donors and other potentially positive effects of fundraising—such as its educational impact. Where these kinds of emphases and reward systems dominate, what is the impact on fundraisers' approaches to donors? Are they as honest and caring as they should be? What is the effect on individual and organizational reporting? Is the information about fundraising costs and results as complete and fully revealing as it should be?

These kinds of questions about the relationship between reward systems and structures and ethical behavior become even more complex, but no less important, when the behaviors at issue are not so simple—whether the truth is being told, for example—and when more subtle matters are involved—such as whether an organization is exploiting its employees or whether it is being true to the values it claims to represent.

Summary

This chapter has demonstrated that ethical questions and issues must be primary concerns of all nonprofit managers, and that these issues and questions are salient in all aspects of the operation of nonprofit organizations. It has been argued that the ethical values most important for

nonprofit managers and organizations to honor and exhibit center on the qualities of integrity, openness, accountability, service, and charity. We have seen how these particular ethical ideals are prescribed for nonprofit organizations by virtue of the distinctive history of the voluntary and nonprofit sector and the roles that these organizations play in American society. It is crucial that nonprofit organizations embody these ethical ideals in practice, both because ethical conduct and character is what moral duty requires—it is right—and because the public expects this of nonprofit organizations that say they are serving the public good. Only in this way can nonprofits fulfill the implicit social contract that supports their existence in our society.

It is important to note the educational implications of this. The last decade has seen the emergence of a number of programs around the country to educate people specifically for the work of managing nonprofit organizations. How much attention do these programs give to helping those people understand the special history and unique roles and expectations that should shape the way these organizations function and are managed? Some would say not enough. Those being educated to take on the responsibilities of management and leadership in nonprofit organizations must be taught sound approaches to, as well as the profound importance of, careful, responsible reflection on the ethical issues embedded in the various facets of the life of these organizations.

Managing an organization so that key ethical values will be consistently embodied in the organization's life requires more than rhetoric. It requires that managers demonstrate these values through their own conduct in their professional lives and service. It also requires that they create and maintain organizational structures and dynamics by which ethical conduct is rewarded and unethical conduct, in any manifestation, is discouraged. This has to involve an examination of all organizational systems and structures, from fundraising strategies to human resources policies to accounting systems, to ensure that those structures and systems do not generate pressures on personnel to ignore or violate the standards and assumptions for ethical behavior espoused in broader contexts. The chapters that follow will offer more illustrations of how ethical questions arise and come into play in specific facets of the work of nonprofit organizations and their managers.

The vital significance of these matters cannot be overemphasized. The lifeblood of the nonprofit sector is trust. Without trust on the part of donors, clients, and the larger public, nonprofit organizations will not be able to do the important work, to fulfill the crucial roles, which are theirs in our society. And nothing will erode this foundation of trust—for the good nonprofits as well as the bad—as quickly as new (or continuing) scandals involving unethical behavior by nonprofit organizations and their managers.

When the temptation to cut an ethical corner, tell a little lie, not bother with full disclosure, or let the ends justify the means arises, it is essential that the leadership and management of nonprofit organizations understand the implications of such actions and refuse to compromise on upholding rigorous ethical standards. We have to remember that, ultimately, noble ends are never served by ignoble means. We have to understand that inevitably our "ethical chickens will come home to roost."

Nonprofit, especially philanthropic, organizations have special responsibilities to serve the public good in our society; to do the right thing—for those in need and for important causes and those who care about them—because it is right. This represents the ethical and essential foundation of the nonprofit sector. Without this foundation intact, it is quite likely the sector will—and probably should—disappear from our society. Attention to ethical concerns must therefore continue to be a primary concern of every nonprofit manager.

References

Bellah, R. N., and others. *Habits of the Heart: Individualism and Commitment in American Life*. Berkeley, Calif.: University of California Press, 1985.

Curti, M. "American Philanthropy and the National Character." *American Quarterly*, 1958, 10, 420–437.

Deal, T. E., and Kennedy, A. A. *Corporate Cultures: The Rites and Rituals of Corporate Life*. Reading, Mass.: Addison-Wesley, 1982.

Douglas, J. "Political Theories of Nonprofit Organization." In W. Powell (ed.), *The Nonprofit Sector: A Research Handbook*. New Haven, Conn.: Yale University Press, 1987.

Drucker, P. F. *Managing the Nonprofit Organization*. New York: HarperCollins, 1990.

Gellerman, W., Frankel, M. S., and Ladenson, R. (eds.). *Values and Ethics in Organization and Human Systems Development*. San Francisco, Calif.: Jossey-Bass, 1990.

Goldman, A. H. "Professional Values and the Problem of Regulation." *Business and Professional Ethics Journal*, n.d., 5(2), 47–59.

Greene, S. G. "Poor Pay Threatens Leadership." *Chronicle of Philanthropy*, Mar. 26, 1991, pp. 28–31.

Greenleaf, R. K. *Servant Leadership*. Ramsey, N.J.: Paulist Press, 1977.

Griffin, C. S. "Religious Benevolence as Social Control, 1815–1860." *Mississippi Historical Review*, 1957, 44(3), 423–444.

Herman, R. D., and Heimovics, R. D. *Executive Leadership in Nonprofit Organizations: New Strategies for Shaping Executive-Board Dynamics*. San Francisco, Calif.: Jossey-Bass, 1991.

INDEPENDENT SECTOR. *Ethics and the Nation's Voluntary and Philanthropic Community*. Washington, D.C.: INDEPENDENT SECTOR, 1991.

Jeavons, T. H. "When Management Is the Message: Relating Values to Management Practice in Nonprofit Organizations." *Nonprofit Management & Leadership*, 1992a, 2(4), 403–421.

Larson, M. S. *The Rise of Professionalism: A Sociological Analysis*. Berkeley, Calif.: University of California Press, 1977.

Mason, D. E. "Ethics and the Nonprofit Leader." *Nonprofit World*, 1992b, 10(4), 30–32.

Middleton, M. "Nonprofit Boards of Directors: Beyond the Governance Function." In W. Powell (ed.), *The Nonprofit Sector: A Research Handbook*. New Haven, Conn.: Yale University Press, 1987.

Nielsen, W. *The Golden Donors: A New Anatomy of the Great Foundations*. New York: Dutton, 1985.

Ostrander, S. A., and Schervish, P. G. "Giving and Getting: Philanthropy as a Social Relation." In J. Van Til and Associates, *Critical Issues in American Philanthropy: Strengthening Theory and Practice*. San Francisco, Calif.: Jossey-Bass, 1990.

Parsons, T. *Structures and Process in Modern Societies*. Glencoe, Ill.: Free Press, 1960.

Peters, T. J., and Waterman, R. *In Search of Excellence.* New York: HarperCollins, 1982.

Schein, E. *Organizational Culture and Leadership.* (2nd ed.) San Francisco, Calif.: Jossey-Bass, 1985.

Schön, D. A. *The Reflective Practitioner.* San Francisco, Calif.: Jossey-Bass, 1983.

_____. *Educating the Reflective Practitioner: Toward a New Design for Teaching and Learning in the Professions.* San Francisco, Calif.: Jossey-Bass, 1987.

Weisbrod, B. *The Nonprofit Economy.* Cambridge, Mass.: Harvard University Press, 1988.

► **CHAPTER 9**

Artful Leadership

Mary Tschirhart

This chapter presents aspects and implications of stakeholder management that were not fully elaborated in the previous chapters' analyses of predictors of responses and key stakeholder groups. First, I discuss the nature of the process of managing problems. Then, I explore goals and responsibilities guiding the process. Next, I explain how leaders use a network perspective in their problem management. The chapter ends with a brief discussion of the applicability of the frameworks and findings to other settings.

The Deliberate and Emergent Nature of Problem Management

I have described the process of problem management as involving scanning for problems in relationships with stakeholders, interpreting the problems, evaluating options, and responding to the problems. Feedback from this process influences future problem-management cycles. Leaders may approach this process with more or less deliberateness and consistency. Common interests, constraints, preferences, and understandings, along with other internal and external pressures, may lead to patterns in problem re-

sponses, no matter how conscious and planned the actual decision-making process.

Primarily, I have treated stakeholder management as a boundedly rational process (Simon, 1960) in which leaders or their representatives consider a variety of factors in choosing responses. Leaders do not know all there is to know about a problem situation, but given information limitations, they choose a strategy that they think will lead to satisfactory consequences. For example, when leaders thought it was in their organization's interests, they compromised. When they wanted to gain legitimacy with a stakeholder, they often adapted their organization to be more congruent with the stakeholder.

Not all responses to problems with stakeholders are the outcomes of a deliberate decision-making process. Some responses to stakeholders may be routinized or scripted. Over time, positive consequences of the use of a response may reinforce the response's perceived value and encourage its automatic adoption when new problems arise. Leaders may be unaware of this patterned behavior and their consistent assumptions. For example, leaders may assume that "the customer is always right" and consistently adjust their organization in response to complaints by patrons. The resulting positive feedback from the complainers (or negative feedback if no apparent change is made in response to the complaint) may reinforce the leaders' sense that adaptation was appropriate and encourage a customer-satisfaction script. As another example, leaders may have a long history of contract battles with unions. Because of this history, they may consistently approach unions as adversaries and fail to see collaborative potential.

Some response options may be prescribed. For example, agreements with a union may prevent leaders from cutting ties to an employee if predetermined conditions are not met. Bylaws may state the requirements and procedures for electing board members and revoking their board positions. Directors may be required by law to reveal information to external stakeholders.

Leaders may plan responses that are not implemented as desired, or that do not lead to expected outcomes. Incorrect assumptions about causes and effects, unforeseen circumstances, chance, and other constraints may undermine plans. For example, a board may dictate that volunteers be treated a certain way, but it is up to the staff to see that the plans are implemented.

Statements of Values and Goals for Stakeholder Relationships

Much has been written about how to improve decision-making processes. Brainstorming techniques, procedures for avoiding groupthink (Janis, 1982), ranking of an option's capability to satisfy multiple goals, and other decision tools are available to help solve specific problems. It is unreasonable to believe that leaders will spend the time and effort to use these tools every time they face a problem with a stakeholder. Some problems receive little if any attention if the benefits of considering the problem do not outweigh perceived costs. Leaders also may not have the time or resources to employ the tools.

Leaders can find value in discussing stakeholder management more generally. Explicit discussion of goals for their organization, and how these goals may be reflected in the quality of their relationships with key stakeholders, can

lead to standard criteria for evaluating response options. A formal mission statement serves as an orienting and accountability device for programs. Similarly, a statement of values and goals for relationships with stakeholders can help ensure that responses to stakeholders are cohesive and serve the organization's interests. For example, to maintain some level of organizational independence and financial stability, leaders may set a maximum percentage of total income that one stakeholder can contribute to their organization's income. The board and staff's acceptance of this goal reduces the possibility that such a contribution would be pursued and that conflicts would result if the contribution were offered.

Analysis of History of Problems with Stakeholders and Relevant Trends

Grouping past problems with stakeholders according to shared themes may be helpful in building awareness about systematic pressures and organizational weaknesses. Two recurring problems experienced by more than one organization in the study involved poor performance of volunteers and inability to honor promises to contributors. By seeing how often the same types of problems occurred, leaders have the beginnings of a priority list for designing new structures and policies to avoid problems in the future. For example, leaders of organizations who have a disproportionate number of performance problems with volunteers may decide to hire a volunteer coordinator or prepare an orientation manual for volunteers. If leaders do not regularly review their history of stakeholder problems, they may fail to see the patterns and the need for changes.

By searching for patterns in experiences with stakeholders, leaders may uncover the assumptions, values, and norms guiding organizational and stakeholder actions. Assumptions can be challenged and changed if appropriate. Understanding the values and norms that are consistently in conflict can help in the prediction of future problems with stakeholders. This understanding can guide the resolution of problems if leaders can find ways to improve the congruence of the values and norms without compromising their organizations' or stakeholders' integrity.

If congruence is not possible, leaders may proactively search for stakeholders who hold more compatible values and norms. By switching from a resource provider who holds incongruent values and norms to one more compatible, leaders may remove a source of potential problems. Of course, it is not always possible for leaders to dictate who will and will not be their stakeholders. For example, government regulatory agencies cannot be removed from a stakeholder map. However, leaders can reduce regulators' power to influence their organization by adding other external watchdogs to their stakeholder map. Leaders may get endorsements of their practices from an association within their industry that shares their values and norms. Accreditations or certifications may help bolster an organization's legitimacy with other stakeholders and make it less vulnerable to scrutiny or criticism.

No organization has complete control over its environment. Recognizing the diverse pressures affecting relationships with stakeholders may help leaders see what forces they can and cannot control. Monitoring changes in these pressures may help leaders appropriately adjust the dynamics of their relationships with stakeholders. For example, recent well-publicized scandals involving nonprofit organizations appear to have encouraged greater accountability demands from external stakeholders. Some leaders in this study addressed changes in the public's cynicism by proactively making potential and current donors more aware of their organization's accounting practices and financial standing. Expectations of economic pressures from cutbacks in state arts funding prompted many leaders to seek more foundation and corporate support to alter their resource dependencies. Without looking ahead to identify future pressures, these leaders may not have been as prepared to face external demands for accountability and internal needs for new funding sources.

Goals and Responsibilities Guiding Problem Management

This study revealed that arts leaders operate with some common goals. The leaders share a strong focus on preserving their mission. Most are greatly concerned with resource flows and adjust their relationships with stakeholders to help maintain their financial viability. Many leaders also have a missionary zeal in expanding their audience, improving public awareness, and maintaining a good reputation. Leaders not only act to achieve these goals, they simultaneously try to honor their responsibilities to their stakeholders. Leaders' varying commitments to satisfying stakeholders' interests, legal rights, and moral rights led to many of their problem-management challenges.

Mission Delivery over Resource Needs

Maintaining mission integrity is the premier motivation for nonprofit leaders. The leaders in my study clearly have a "mission-centered focus. As one director put it, "If you judge the success of an event by the dollars that come in, we feel that's looking at it from the wrong way."

Those worried that the financial stability and survival of arts organizations may be in danger because of a strict mission focus also may be reassured. Despite Brinkerhoff's (1994) admonition that nonprofits must not sacrifice the goal of "doing well" to "do good," most of the leaders studied are able to remain focused on their mission while pursuing needed resources. When mission is not threatened, the leaders actively seek to maintain or increase resource flows from problematic stakeholders. They are more willing to invest their organization's efforts to satisfy a stakeholder when the stakeholder controls important resources than when the stakeholder's resources are less critical to their organization.

Still, there is some cause for concern. Under conditions of continuous financial stress and uncertainty, some leaders operate with faith that needed resources will emerge. Instead of considering adapting to reduce financial strains, they endure the strains with the expectation that in time their financial woes will somehow end. Their confidence in their mission's value to their community and an eventual increase in support lead them to a strategy of trying to maintain the status quo with stakeholders. Given this optimism, they did little to establish new sources of support and were reluctant to end relationships with stakeholders that were draining resources from their organization. A few of the leaders also felt justified in deceiving stakeholders when their honesty might result in reduced financial support and, consequently, more difficulty in delivering their missions.

Strong commitment to a mission is generally desirable. However, if it creates stagnation and resistance to innovation in response to environmental changes, it may be dangerous for the organization's long-term viability and service to patrons. Patrons' interests may shift over time as do organizational capabilities and constraints. Willingness to adjust or add to a mission to capture new patron demands and funding interests may save an organization from death. Only if an organization survives can it continue to serve its traditional patrons without engaging in deceit.

Missionary Work: Improving Public Awareness and Perceptions of Legitimacy

My interviews revealed that many directors and board members were not satisfied with the level of public awareness and support of their organizations. Their desire to change these impressions influenced their interactions with stakeholders. Although the directors rarely used the word *"legitimacy,"* they stressed the importance of maintaining their organization's image, reputation, and prestige, and keeping the public's or other stakeholders' trust, respect, approval, and goodwill. When stakeholders disapproved of their organization's activities or outcomes, leaders often adapted their organizations. When they discovered that a stakeholder had acted illegitimately, they generally cut or weakened their ties to the stakeholder, particularly when

the stakeholder had a position of authority in their organization.

Many leaders talked about the education, or in one director's words, the "missionary work," needed to raise community awareness, acceptance, and involvement. Younger and smaller organizations in particular faced this challenge. So did those that did not have a facility and that had a history as a "women's organization." Leaders of two such organizations hoped that moving into a new facility, and drawing in more male patrons and service providers, would bring greater respect to their organizations. One board member explained why legitimacy was a problem for her organization:

> . . . mostly because it's been a women's organization, and I feel a number of people discount that: 'Oh yes, the ladies are doing this or that.' It isn't given enough credit because it's women doing it. As more men are brought into the organization and become part of it, then the community will give it more credit.

Even some leaders of larger, more established organizations felt that they weren't reaching everyone who could benefit from their programs. One leader of an arts museum stated, "I think there is this perception on the part of people that arts organizations like ours are always struggling, which is true, never get enough people to come in, which is true, and are always dismal failures, which is not true." Convincing the public that their organization is going to survive, and that it offers something of value to their community, are two campaigns that most leaders waged at least once during their organization's history.

Legitimacy judgements are applied to specific acts, not just to organizational entities (Rawls, 1971). The legitimacy of particular purposes, activities, or outcomes involved in problems with stakeholders predicted responses to the problems. Directors never discussed their view of a stakeholder's overall legitimacy. The directors' focus was on the legitimacy of something the stakeholder had done or was planning to do. They reacted to the legitimacy of the act. An organization's and stakeholder's consistent perfor mance of legitimate acts may have as much to do with their survival and ability to attract resources as their overall legitimacy.

In his manual for board members, O'Connell (1985) argues that the most essential quality of a leader is the ability to determine what is right. Boards members who can decide what is right, and act based on that decision, best protect their organization's public image. Selecting board members with demonstrated integrity can help ensure that the right decisions are made. Encouraging boards to discuss their organization's image and how best it can be promoted and protected also can help.

Satisfying Stakeholders' Interests and Claims

The success of leaders in delivering their mission and attracting needed resources may be related to the configuration of "stakes" in their organization. A stake is an interest or a claim (Carroll, 1996) held by a stakeholder. According to Carroll, a stakeholder has an interest in an organization when the organization's decisions can affect the stakeholder. A stakeholder has a claim in an organization when the stakeholder has a legal or moral right to be treated a certain way by the organization.

Another example involves the "decency standard" of the National Endowment for the Arts. The Endowment required arts organizations receiving funds to sign a statement that they would not present "obscenity." Many leaders of arts organizations refused to accept Endowment grants because the attached legal requirement might compromise their missions, and the artists' right to freedom of speech. But the leader of one theater in the study with a grant intentionally presented plays that could be interpreted as violating the standard. The leader hoped to challenge the law through any resulting media attention. Despite the difficulty in enforcing the standard, the legal right changed some funding relationships and, for some organizations accepting Endowment grants, led to modifications of arts programs.

Moral rights are beliefs that one should be treated a certain way, not that one is legally required to be treated a certain way. Stakeholders who claim moral rights argue that certain treatment is appropriate or normatively correct. For example, the church group that wanted the exhibit of nude male statues removed had no legal basis for their demand, but felt they were morally justified in requesting this action. Parents who demanded that their children be exposed to art in the schoolroom, and insisted that a school's contracts with professional artists be honored despite budget cuts, called upon their children's moral right to receive cultural education.

Stakeholders may vary in their interests in an organization. For example, arts patrons may attend performances to satisfy a variety of interests: to enjoy the art, network socially, gain status as an art lover, etc. Depending on the nature of their interests, changes in organizational purposes or activities may not affect them. A transformation of a theater from one that welcomes amateur actors to one that only uses actors with Equity cards may not be of much consequence to a stakeholder who attends performances to talk to his friends during intermission. It would more deeply affect a stakeholder who enjoys the amateur quality of the theater.

Understanding the basis for stakeholders' concerns may help leaders develop appropriate responses. Knowledge of legal rights may help leaders avoid legal actions pursued by stakeholders. Use of formal ethical codes and standards may help leaders identify stakeholders' moral rights and evaluate the importance of the rights. A variety of ethical codes are available to guide interactions with stakeholders (see for example, the National Charities Information Bureau, 1995, and INDEPENDENT SECTOR, 1991.) Identifying the conflicting interests in a problem situation may lead to more effective solutions. Persuading stakeholders of the benefits of an organization's activities, or adapting to provide more benefits, may increase stakeholders' perceptions of their interests in the organization and lead to greater stakeholder support.

Leaders may implicitly or explicitly prioritize their responsibilities as part of problem management. Business leaders rely on the common judgement that their first priority is to satisfy owners' interests in profits. Nonprofit leaders' priorities are less clear. There are no owners of nonprofit organizations claiming its profits as a return on their investments. Is nonprofit leaders' first priority to satisfy donors, patrons, board members or some other stakeholders? Guidelines from INDEPENDENT SECTOR (1991) argue that nonprofit leaders' first responsibility is to obey the law. Then they should consider their ethical responsibilities, and only then consider responsibilities to satisfy specific stakeholders' interests. This pyramid of responsibilities is similar to those proposed for the for-profit sector, except that at the base of the for-profit pyramid is the responsibility to make owner's profits, and at the top is the responsibility to be philanthropic and act as a good corporate citizen (see Carroll, 1991).

Leaders' Network Perspective

Leaders shared the perspective that problems with particular stakeholders should not be treated as isolated incidents. Many leaders explicitly noted that poor management of a problem with one stakeholder might lead to new problems with other stakeholders. Even when this assumption was not explicitly stated, the leaders' actions generally reflected a strategic decision-making process that considered how responses to one stakeholder might affect other stakeholders. For example, directors knew that to satisfy some stakeholders' rights and interests, other stakeholders' rights and interests had to be sacrificed. Also, directors considered how satisfying some stakeholders could create new concerns and demands from the same or other stakeholders. Examination of only the rights and interests of the stakeholders directly involved in a problem situation fails to capture the broader context addressed by the problem-management strategies.

The directors' treatment of resource dependencies also reflect a network perspective. Leaders look beyond the resources they can attract from a specific stakeholder to judge how their relationship with that stakeholder might influence resource exchanges with other stakeholders. A dissatisfied stakeholder might publicly complain and convince other stakeholders to withdraw support. Calculations of resource dependencies that look only at the resources directly controlled by a stakeholder fail to capture the real power of stakeholders to influence organizational responses through a threat of lost resources from other stakeholders. The threat of losing a single source of resources may fail to motivate leaders to act to preserve that source. Leaders may believe that other sources of support can be found or expanded. Constructs capturing the larger context of resource dependencies better predict organizational actions than measures of resource importance attached to particular stakeholders without regard to their network character.

Stakeholder maps that address all the stakeholders and issues related to a problem can help leaders sort through the complexities of problem management. The maps can be designed to reflect stakeholders' rights and interests related to the problem, stakeholders' influence mechanisms, and communication and other links among the stakeholders. The maps may help leaders identify the current boundaries of a problem (which stakeholders are involved and what are their concerns) and how the problem might escalate (who may become involved and with what concerns.)

Applicability of the Problem Management Model to Other Fields and Sectors

Organizations are not just marketplaces in which stakeholders' interests and desires for control are pursued. They also are embodiments of values and norms fostered in their network of stakeholder relationships. Organizational leaders attempt to shape their external and internal environments to improve the environments' congruence with organizational interests, values, and norms. At the same time, a variety of institutional, economic, political, and technological forces push organizations to conform with stakeholders' interests, expectations, values, and norms.

It is important to compare the management of problems with stakeholders across nonprofit fields. Leaders of social service, environmental advocacy, religious, and other types of nonprofit organizations may vary in the problem-management patterns they exhibit. Responsibilities and goals may differ across fields.

The details of the applications may differ among nonprofit, government, and for-profit sectors. For example, business leaders may not be as willing to adapt in response to organizational legitimacy problems as leaders of nonprofit organizations. The proportion of legitimacy problems experienced by organizations in the nonprofit sector may be greater than in the for-profit sector because of the generally more values-based character of their work.

The Practice of Artful Leadership

There are no simple formulas to adopt. The leaders' patterned behaviors and the recurring issues they face may be found in other leaders' experiences. By using the frameworks provided in the book to interpret problems and understand their responses, leaders may find previously unrecognized assumptions, values, norms, and interests guiding their actions. A search for links among the problems may reveal common issues and management challenges. Thoughtful debate and consensus about the issues may offer guidance for resolving and preventing future problems related to the issues. Once common challenges are identified, leaders can build coherent sets of responses and evaluate their long-term benefit.

It is in the process of unlearning unsuccessful problem-management patterns and reinforcing successful ones that frameworks may be most helpful. Mission statements alone cannot provide adequate guidance for leaders. Leaders may find benefit in a shared understanding of the nature of relationships they desire with stakeholders and the behavioral options for managing those relationships.

References

Brinckerhoff, P.C. *Mission-Based Management.* Dillon, Colorado: Alpine Guild, Inc., 1994.

Carroll, A.B. *Business and Society: Ethics and Stakeholder Management.* Cincinnati: Southwestern College Publishing, 1996.

_____. "The pyramid of corporate social responsibility: Toward the moral management of organizational stakeholders." *Business Horizons,* July-August, 1991.

Homans, G. *The Human Group.* New York: Harcourt Brace, 1950.

INDEPENDENT SECTOR. *Ethics and the Nation's Voluntary and Philanthropic Community: Obedience to the Unenforceable.* Washington, D.C. 1991.

Janis, I.L. *Groupthink: Psychological Studies of Policy Decisions and Fiascoes,* 2nd Ed. Boston: Houghton Mifflin.

Mueller, C. *The Politics of Communication.* London: Oxford University Press, 1973.

National Charities Information Bureau. "NCIB standards in philanthropy." *Wise Giving Guide.* June 1995.

O'Connell, B. *The Board Member's Book,* 2nd Ed. New York: The Foundation Center, 1993.

Rawls, J. *A Theory of Justice.* Cambridge: Harvard University Press, 1971.

PART 4

STRATEGIC PLANNING*‡

Strategic planning is a process of assessment that employs a "disciplined effort to produce fundamental decisions and actions that shape and guide what an organization is, what it does and why it does it."[1] It assesses the internal and external strengths, weaknesses, opportunities, and threats faced by an organization ("SWOT analysis") and devises strategies to deal effectively with the issues raised during assessment.

Strategic planning provides the means—the tools and the processes—that boards, executives, donors, contractors, clients, staff, and others use to decide and act upon fundamental issues of who and what an organization is, how it fits into and shapes its environment, how it influences and copes with changes in its environment, what it values, and the scope of its charitable mission. Strategic planning sets parameters or limits within which day-to-day decisions can be made, and is a means for helping the board of trustees, executive director, and staff bring order to a nonprofit organization's response to rapidly changing environments.

Nonprofit Sector Strategic Planning

Strategic planning has been used by private firms for several decades, but the nonprofit sector has for several reasons been slow to use strategic planning as a management tool. Perhaps the most important reason for this is that although the mission of profit-making companies is usually clear (they are in business to make a profit), the

*This essay is adapted from David L. Gies, J. Steven Ott, and Jay M. Shafritz, "Governance: The Roles and Functions of Boards of Directors," in D. L. Gies, J. S. Ott, and J. M. Shafritz, eds., The Nonprofit Organization: Essential Readings (Fort Worth, TX: Harcourt Brace, 1990), 177–181.
†Peter M. Nelson and John M. Bradley provided invaluable assistance with this part.

missions of nonprofit organizations are multiple and ambiguous, and success or fail-ure is difficult to measure. In addition, strategic planning requires a lot of valuable time, effort, and resources. Some leaders of nonprofit organizations may believe that the time and effort might be used better in performing the organizations' socially im-portant work.[2]

Peter Pekar[3] lists three reasons why nonprofit organizations have been slow to en-gage in strategic planning:

1. In the early stages of start up and growth, many nonprofit organizations are single-goal oriented. This focus results in little emphasis on the need to plan.
2. Part-time employees or volunteers often perform important functions, and staff salaries are often quite low. This may result in staff that is not able to plan or who may not even believe that planning is worthwhile.
3. It is often difficult for staff to take the initiative for planning when an organiza-tion is dependent on either a single (monopsony) or a limited number of (duop-sony and oligopsony) entities for funding and decisionmaking. For many non-profit organizations, the person or organization that holds the purse strings also dictates objectives, strategies, and activities.

The funding revolution that the nonprofit sector has experienced during the last twenty years, however, has changed the nonprofit sector's perception of the value of strategic planning.[4] Most nonprofit organizations now realize that they must make money to survive, even though they are "nonprofit" entities. They also realize that the opportunity for success is greatly enhanced by engaging in effective strategic plan-ning, and that the failure to plan can have disastrous consequences.

Unfortunately, there is no easy path to effective, useful planning. There are many methods and approaches, none of which may be appropriate for any given organi-zation. The classic model is the Harvard Policy Model, which uses the "SWOT analy-sis" as its centerpiece;[5] there are, however, as many other models as there are plan-ning experts. In the readings that follow, you will be introduced to a number of these models, and you are invited to note their similarities and their differences. None is necessarily the "right" model for your organization, but at least you will have an overview of various possibilities.

Mission Statement

An essential first step in any strategic planning process for a nonprofit organization is the development of a mission statement. Often the stakeholders of a nonprofit organi-zation do not agree about the scope of the organization's mission. Development of a clear and concise mission statement can provide the foundation to resolve these dif-ferences and make day-to-day decisions easier in an ever-changing environment.[6]

The process of creating an organizational mission and strategy enables management to understand the environment and the organization's place in it. It helps build a set of shared assumptions, understandings, and information. When an organization's identity, mission, and strategy are widely "owned" by its stakeholders, decisions usually become more consistent and are made with fewer conflicts. Working relations among stakeholders become more productive. A shared mission and strategy also establish the parameters for political and program debates within the context of a nonprofit organization's human, managerial, and fiscal resource capabilities.

Developing the Mission Statement

A mission statement is often developed at a retreat involving the most important members of the nonprofit organization's constituencies, including staff, board members, management, donors, patrons, and clients.[7] Although time-consuming, the process often strengthens an organization's identity and increases understanding and camaraderie among the stakeholders. Properly done, a mission statement can serve as a unifying force that propels a nonprofit organization to new levels of accomplishment.

Mission Statement Follow-Up

Development of a mission statement is the beginning of a long process that includes adoption of organizational goals, objectives, strategies, and a plan of action.[8] When the plan of action has been carried out, the results must be evaluated and the entire process reviewed in light of the evaluation. Thus, strategic planning is time-consuming, often mundane, and never finished, but it is essential to an organization's success or possibly even its continued existence.

Conclusion

Strategic planning is a necessity for nonprofit organizations today; the articles reprinted in this part collectively present a compelling argument for this conclusion. With growing client bases, reductions in public-sector funding and services, restrictions on unrelated businesses activities, and pressures to change or expand an organization's mission (mission creep), nonprofit organization managers and their boards will be "at sea" if they fail to chart their courses by planning strategically.

Readings Reprinted in Part Four

John Bryson's essay, *"Strategic Planning,"*[9] compares and contrasts six approaches to corporate strategic planning and discusses their applicability to the public sector. The article concludes that (1) strategic planning is becoming standard practice in the public and nonprofit sectors; and (2) not all approaches are equally useful in these two contexts.

Philip Kotler and Alan Andreason[10] approach strategic planning from a marketing perspective and incorporate private-sector marketing strategies into nonprofit-sector strategic planning. This process requires managers to identify market forces and directions for their organizations, and question how these market forces can be harnessed to meet organizational imperatives.

Henry Mintzberg's article, *"Crafting Strategy,"*[11] concludes the part. Rather than viewing strategic planning as a series of formulaic steps to be followed, Mintzberg's strategic planner is an artist who crafts strategy much as a potter molds clay. Using past experiences, current constraints, and future expectations and desires, the artist-planner molds a strategy that synthesizes the present, the future, and the past.

Notes

1. John M. Bryson, "Strategic Planning," in Jay M. Shafritz, ed., *International Encyclopedia of Public Policy and Administration* (Boulder: Westview Press, 1998), 2160–2169 (reprinted in this part); see also John M. Bryson, *Strategic Planning for Public and Nonprofit Organizations: A Guide to Strengthening and Sustaining Organizational Achievement,* rev. ed. (San Francisco: Jossey-Bass, 1995).

2. Thomas Wolf, *Managing a Nonprofit Organization in the Twenty-First Century* (New York: Simon & Schuster, 1999), 280–281.

3. Peter P. Pekar, Jr., "Setting Goals in the Non-Profit Environment," *Managerial Planning* 30, no. 5 (March–April 1982):43–46.

4. See, for example, J. Steven Ott, Part 10, "The Blending and Blurring of the Three Sectors: Nonprofit, Government, and Business," and Part 11, "Challenges Facing the Nonprofit Sector," in J. S. Ott, ed., *The Nature of the Nonprofit Sector* (Boulder: Westview Press, 2001).

5. Bryson, "Strategic Planning," 2160–2169.

6. Wolf, *Managing a Nonprofit Organization in the Twenty-First Century,* 280–281.

7. See Robert D. Herman and David O. Renz, "Multiple Constituencies and the Social Construction of Nonprofit Organization Effectiveness," 1997 (reprinted in Part 10, "Accountability and Evaluation").

8. Ibid., Note 6.

9. Ibid., Note 5.

10. Philip Kotler and Alan R. Andreason, "The Strategic Planning Marketing Process," in P. Kotler and A. Andreason, *Strategic Planning for Nonprofit Organizations* (Englewood Cliffs, NJ: Prentice-Hall, 1996).

11. Henry, Mintzberg, "Crafting Strategy," *Harvard Business Review* (July-August, 1987):66–75.

► CHAPTER 10

Strategic Planning

JOHN M. BRYSON

S trategic planning consists of a set of concepts, procedures, and tools developed primarily, but far from exclusively, in the private sector. The experience of the last fifteen years, and a growing body of literature indicate that strategic planning approaches either developed in the private sector, or else strongly influenced by them, can help public organizations, as well as communities or other entities, deal in effective ways with their dramatically changing environments.

That does not mean, however, that all approaches to what might be called corporate-style strategic planning are equally applicable to the public sector. This entry, therefore, will compare and contrast six approaches to corporate strategic planning (actually eight approaches grouped into six categories), discuss their applicability to the public sector, and identify the most important contingencies governing their use.

It should be noted that careful tests of corporate-style strategic planning in the public sector are few in number (Bryson 1983b; Boal and Bryson 1987; Boschken 1988, 1994; Bryson, Bromiley, and Jung 1990; Bryson and Bromiley 1993; Stone and Crittenden 1993; Mintzberg 1994). Nevertheless, there is enough experience with corporate strategic planning in the private sector, and increasingly in the public sector, to

reach some tentative conclusions about what works under what conditions and why.

The remainder of this entry is divided into two sections. The first discusses the six approaches and compares and contrasts them along several dimensions, including key features, assumptions, strengths, weaknesses, and contingencies governing their use in the public sector. The second section presents conclusions about the applicability of strategic planning to public organizations and purposes. The principal conclusions are (1) that public strategic planning is well on its way to becoming part of the standard repertoire of public leaders, managers, and planners and (2) that, nevertheless, public personnel must be very careful how they engage in strategic planning, since not all approaches are equally useful and since a number of conditions govern the successful use of each approach.

Approaches to Strategic Planning

This section briefly sets forth six schools of strategic planning thought developed primarily, but by no means exclusively, in the private sector. The strategic planning process includes general policy and direction setting, situation assessments, strategic issues identification, strategy development, decisionmaking, implementation, and evaluation (Bryson 1988b, 1995, 1996).

Approaches That Cover Much of the Process and Emphasize Policy and Direction Setting

The Harvard Policy Model

The Harvard policy model was developed as part of the business policy courses taught at the Harvard Business School since the 1920s (Bower et al. 1993). The approach provides the principal (though often implicit) inspiration behind the most widely cited recent models of public and nonprofit sector strategic planning, including my own (Olsen and Eadie 1982; Barry 1986; Bryson 1988b, 1995; Nutt and Backoff 1992).

The main purpose of the Harvard model is to help a firm develop the best "fit" between itself and its environment; that is, to develop the best strategy for the firm. As articulated by K. Andrews (1980), strategy is "a pattern of purposes and policies defining the company and its business." One discerns the best strategy by analyzing the internal strengths and weaknesses of the company and the values of senior management and by identifying the external threats and opportunities in the environment and the social obligations of the firm. Then one designs the appropriate organizational structure, processes, relationships, and behaviors necessary to implement the strategy and focuses on providing the leadership necessary to implement the strategy.

Effective use of the model presumes that senior management can agree on the firm's situation and the appropriate strategic response and has enough authority to enforce its decisions. A final important assumption of the model, common to all approaches to strategic planning, is that if the appropriate strategy is identified and implemented, the organization will be more effective. Attention also is paid to the need for effective implementation.

In the business world, the Harvard model appears to be best applied at the strategic business unit (SBU) level. A strategic business unit is a distinct business that has its own competitors and can be managed somewhat independently of other units within the organization (Rue and Holland 1986). The SBU, in other worlds, provides an important yet bounded and manageable focus for the model. John Montanari and Jeffrey Bracker (1986) argued that the public equivalent of the SBU is the strategic public planning unit (SPPU), which typically would be an agency or department that addresses issues fundamentally similar to one another (such as related health issues, related transportation issues, or related education issues).

The Harvard model is also applicable at the higher and broader corporate level in the private and public sectors. The model probably would have to be supplemented with other approaches, however, such as the portfolio and strategic issues management approaches, to be discussed later.

The systematic assessment of strengths, weaknesses, opportunities, and threats—known as a SWOT analysis—is a primary strength of the Harvard model. This element of the model appears to be applicable in the public sector to organizations, functions, and communities. Another strength is its emphasis on the need to link strategy formulation and implementation in effective ways. The main weaknesses of the Harvard model are that it does not draw attention to strategic issues or offer specific advice on how to develop strategies, except to note that effective strategies will build on strengths, how to take advantage of opportunities, and how to overcome or minimize weaknesses and threats.

Strategic Planning Systems

Strategic planning is often viewed as a system whereby managers go about making, implementing, and controlling important decisions across functions and levels in the firm. Peter Lorange (1980), for example, has argued that any strategic planning system must address four fundamental questions:

1. Where are we going? (mission)
2. How do we get there? (strategies)
3. What is our blueprint for action? (budgets)

4. How do we know if we are on track? (control)

Strategic planning systems vary along several dimensions: The comprehensiveness of decision areas included, the formal rationality of the decision process, and the tightness of control exercised over implementation of the decisions (Armstrong 1982; Goold, Campbell, and Luchs 1993a, 1993b), as well as how the strategy process itself will be tailored to the organization and managed (Chakravarthy and Lorange 1991). The strength of these systems is their attempt to coordinate the various elements of an organization's strategy across levels and functions. Their weakness is that excessive comprehensiveness, prescription, and control can drive out attention to mission, strategy, and organizational structure (Frederickson and Mitchell 1984; Frederickson 1984; Mintzberg 1994) and can exceed the ability of participants to comprehend the system and the information it produces (Bryson, Van de Ven, and Roering 1987).

Strategic planning systems are applicable to public organizations (and to a lesser extent communities), for regardless of the nature of the particular organization, it makes sense to coordinate decisionmaking across levels and functions and to concentrate on whether the organization is implementing its strategies and accomplishing its mission (Boschken 1988, 1992, 1994). It is important to remember, however, that a strategic planning system characterized by substantial comprehensiveness, formal rationality in decisionmaking, and tight control will work only in an organization that has a clear mission, clear goals and objectives, relatively simple tasks to perform, centralized authority, clear performance indicators, and information about actual performance available at reasonable cost. While some public organizations—such as hospitals and police and fire departments—operate under such conditions, most do not. As a result, most public sector strategic planning systems typically focus on a few areas of concern, rely on a decision process in which politics play a major role, and control something other than program outcomes (e.g., budget expenditures) (Wildavsky 1979a; Barzelay 1992;

Osborne and Gaebler 1992; Bryson 1995). That is changing, however. For example, the U.S. federal government is now moving toward performance-based strategic management as a result of the Government Performance and Results Act of 1993 (Public Law 103-62) and a number of states are following suit (National Governors Association 1993).

Stakeholder Management Approaches

R. Edward Freeman (1984) stated that corporate strategy can be understood as a corporation's mode of relating or building bridges to its stakeholders. A stakeholder for Freeman is any group or individual who is affected by or who can affect the future of the corporation; for example, customers, employees, suppliers, owners, governments, financial institutions, and critics.

Because it integrates economic, political, and social concerns, the stakeholder model is one of the approaches most applicable to the public sector. Many interest groups have stakes in public organizations, functions, and communities. John Bryson, R. E. Freeman, and William Roering (1986) argue in addition that an organization's mission and values ought to be formulated in stakeholder terms. That is, an organization should figure out what its mission ought to be in relation to each stakeholder group; otherwise, it will not be able to differentiate its responses well enough to satisfy its key stakeholders.

The strengths of the stakeholder model are its recognition of the many claims—both complementary and competing—placed on organizations by insiders and outsiders and its awareness of the need to satisfy at least the key stakeholders if the organization is to survive. The weaknesses of the model are the absence of criteria with which to judge competing claims and the need for more advice on developing strategies to deal with divergent stakeholder interests.

Freeman has applied the stakeholder concept primarily at the corporate and industry levels in the private sector, but it seems applicable to all levels in the public sectors. Researchers have not yet made rigorous tests of the model's usefulness in the private, public, or nonprofit sectors, but several public and nonprofit case studies indicate that stakeholder analyses are quite useful as part of the strategic planning effort (Bryson, 1988b, 1995; Nutt and Backoff 1992; Bryson and Crosby 1992; Kemp 1993; Boschken 1992, 1994). If the model is to be used successfully, there must be the possibility that key decisionmakers can achieve reasonable agreement about who the key stakeholders are and what the response to their claims should be.

Content Approaches

The three approaches presented so far have more to do with managing an entire strategic planning process than with identifying specific strategy content. The process approaches do not prescribe answers, although good answers are presumed to emerge from appropriate application. In contrast, the tools to be discussed next—portfolio models and competitive analysis—primarily concern content and do yield answers. In fact, the models are antithetical to process when process concerns get in the way of developing the "right" answers.

Portfolio Models

The idea of strategic planning as managing a portfolio of businesses is based on an analogy with investment practice. Just as an investor assembles a portfolio of stocks to manage risk and to realize optimum returns, a corporate manager can think of the corporation as a portfolio of businesses with diverse potentials that can be balanced to manage return and cash flow. For our purposes, it is adequate to use as an example the portfolio model developed by the Boston Consulting Group (BCG): the famous BCG matrix (Henderson 1979; Hax and Majiluf 1984).

Bruce Henderson, founder of the Boston Consulting Group, argued that all business costs followed a well-known pattern: unit costs dropped by one-third every time volume (or turnover) doubled. Hence, he postulated a relationship, known as the experience curve, between unit costs and volume. This relationship leads to some generic strategic advice: Gain market share, for then unit costs will fall and profit potential will increase.

Henderson said that any business could be categorized into one of four types, depending on how its industry was growing and how large a share of the market it had:

1. High growth/high share businesses ("stars"), which generate substantial cash but also require large investments if their market share is to be maintained or increased.
2. Low growth/high share businesses ("cash cows"), which generate large cash flows but require low investment and therefore generate profits that can be used elsewhere.
3. Low growth/low share businesses ("dogs"), which produce little cash and offer little prospect of increased share.
4. High growth/low share businesses ("question marks"), which would require substantial investment in order to become stars or cash cows. The question is whether the investment is worth it.

Although the applications of portfolio theory to the public sector may be less obvious than those of the three approaches described earlier, they are nonetheless just as powerful (MacMillan 1983; Ring 1988; Nutt and Backoff 1992). Many public organizations consist of "multiple businesses" that are only marginally related. Often resources from various sources are committed to these unrelated businesses. That means the public and managers must make portfolio decisions, although usually without the help of portfolio models that frame those decisions strategically. The BCG approach, like most private-sector portfolio models, uses only economic criteria, not political or social criteria that might be necessary for public applications. Private-sector portfolio approaches, therefore, must be modified substantially for public and nonprofit use. (Indeed, thoughtful critics argue that because private-sector portfolio approaches ignore the missions, values, cultures, and competencies of the companies that comprise the portfolios, they can do far more harm than good. Strategic management which relies only on economically based portfolio analysis can produce disastrous results and, therefore, is itself probably bankrupt; see Hurst 1986; Mintzberg 1994).

The strength of portfolio approaches is that they provide a method of measuring entities of some sort (businesses, investment options, proposals, or problems) against dimensions that are deemed to be of strategic importance (share and growth, or position and attractiveness). Weaknesses include the difficulty of knowing what the appropriate strategic dimensions are, difficulties of classifying entities against dimensions, and the lack of clarity about how to use the tool as part of larger strategic planning process.

If modified to include political and social factors, portfolio approaches can be used in the public sector to make informed strategic decisions. They can be used in conjunction with an overall strategic planning process to provide useful information on an organization, function, or community in relation to its environment. Unlike the process models, however, portfolio approaches provide an "answer;" that is, once the dimensions for comparison and the entities to be compared are specified, the portfolio models prescribe how the organization or community should relate to its environment. Such models will work only if a dominant coalition is convinced that the answers they produce are correct.

Competitive Analysis

Another important content approach that assists strategy selection has been developed by Michael Porter (1980, 1985, 1990, 1994) and his associates. Called "competitive analysis," it assumes that by analyzing the forces that shape an industry, one can predict the general level of profits throughout the industry and the likely success of any particular strategy for a strategic business unit.

Porter (1980) hypothesized that five key competitive forces shape an industry: relative power of customers, relative power of suppliers, threat of substitute products, threat of new entrants, and the amount of rivalrous activity among the players in the industry. Katherine Harrigan (1981) has argued that "exit barriers"—that is, the barriers that would prevent a company from leaving an industry—are a sixth force influencing success in some industries. Two of the main propositions in the competitive analysis school

are as follows: (1) The stronger the forces that shape an industry, the lower the general level of returns in the industry; and (2) the stronger the forces affecting a strategic business unit, the lower the profits for that unit.

Two additional concepts are crucial in Porter's view. Competitive advantage grows out of the value a firm creates for its customers that exceeds the cost of producing it. Competitive advantage grows out of the value chain, the linkage of discrete primary activities (inbound logistics, operations, outbound logistics, marketing and sales, service) and support activities (firm infrastructure, human resource management, technology development, procurement) that create value for which the customer is willing to pay. Profits are found in the margin between what things cost and what their value is to the customer. Every buyer and supplier has a value chain, which leads to an additional important proposition: The more a supplier understands a buyer's value chain, the greater the firm's ability to create value for that buyer.

For many public organizations, there are equivalents to the forces that affect private industry. For example, client or customer power is often important; suppliers of services (contractors and the organization's own labor supply) also can exercise power. There are fewer new entrants in the public sector, but recently private and nonprofit organizations have begun to compete more forcefully with public organizations.

An effective organization in the public sector, therefore, must understand the forces at work in its "industry" in order to compete effectively and must offer value to its customers that exceeds the cost of producing it. On another level, planning for a specific public function (health care, transportation, or recreation) can benefit from competitive analysis if the function can be considered an industry. In addition, economic development agencies must understand the forces at work in given industries and on specific firms if they are to understand whether and how to nurture those industries and firms. Finally, although communities do compete with one another, competitive analysis probably does not apply at this level because communities are not industries in any meaningful sense.

By contrast, Porter points out in *The Competitive Advantage of Nations* (1990) that for the foreseeable future self-reinforcing agglomerations of firms and networks are crucial aspects of successful international economic competition. Regions interested in competing on the world stage, therefore, should try to develop the infrastructure necessary for virtuous (rather than vicious) cycles of economic growth to unfold. In other words, wise investments in education, transportation and transit systems, water and sewer systems, parks and recreation, housing, and so on, can help firms reduce their costs—particularly the costs of acquiring an educated labor force—and thus improve firms' abilities to compete internationally.

The strength of competitive analysis is that it provides a systematic way of assessing industries and the strategic options facing SBUs within those industries. Public organizations can use competitive analysis to discover ways to help the private firms in their regions. When applied directly to public organizations, however, competitive analysis has two weaknesses: It is often difficult to know what the "industry" is and what forces affect it, and the key to organizational success in the public world is often collaboration instead of competition. Competitive analysis for the public organizations, therefore, must be coupled with a consideration of social and political forces and the possibilities for collaboration (Huxham 1993; Winer and Ray 1994).

Another Process Approach

We now leave content approaches to focus again on a process approach—strategic issues management—that is less encompassing than the previous process approaches and typically is less encompassing than the content approaches as well.

Strategic Issues Management

The concept of strategic issues first emerged when practitioners of corporate strategic planning realized a step was missing between the SWOT analysis of the Harvard model and the development of strategies. That step was the identification of strategic issues. Many organizations now include a strategic issue identification step as part of full-blown strategy revision exercises and also as part of less comprehensive annual strategic reviews (Chakravarthy and Lorange 1991). Full-blown annual revision has proved impractical because strategy revision takes substantial management energy and attention, and in any case most strategies take several years to implement. Instead, most firms are undertaking comprehensive strategy revisions several years apart (typically four or five) and in the interim are focusing their annual strategic planning processes on the identification and resolution of a few key strategic issues that emerge from SWOT analyses, environmental scans, and other analyses (Hambrick 1982; Pflaum and Delmont 1987; Heath 1988).

In recent years, many organizations also have developed strategic issues management processes actually separated from their annual strategic planning processes. Many important issues emerge too quickly, with too much urgency, to be handled as part of an annual process. When confronted with such issues, top managers typically appoint temporary teams or task forces to develop responses for immediate implementation.

Strategic issue management is clearly applicable to public organizations, since the agendas of these organizations consist of issues that should be managed strategically (Nutt and Backoff 1992; Bryson and Crosby 1992). In other words, they should be managed based on a sense of mission and mandates and in the context of an environmental assessment and stakeholder analysis. The strength of the approach is its ability to recognize and analyze key issues quickly. The approach also applies to functions or communities, as long as some group, organization, or coalition is able to engage in the process and to manage the issue. The main weakness is that in general the approach offers no specific advice on exactly how to frame the issues other than to precede their identification with a situational analysis of some sort. Nutt (1992, pp. 119–145), and Nutt and Backoff (1995) have gone the furthest in remedying this defect. They argued that public organizations exist within "tension fields" comprised of often conflicting or contradictory pressures for equity, preservation of the status quo, transition to a new state, and productivity improvement. Nutt and Backoff argued that exploration of the various combinations of these tensions, as they apply in specific circumstances, can lead strategic planners to the wisest formulation of strategic issues and strategies.

Process Strategies

The final two approaches to be discussed are process strategies. They are logical incrementalism and strategic planning as a framework for innovation. Process strategies are approaches to implementing a strategy that already has been developed in very broad outline and is subject to revision based on experience with its implementation.

Logical Incrementalism

In incremental approaches, strategy is a loosely linked group of decisions that are handled incrementally. Decisions are handled individually below the corporate level because such decentralization is politically expedient—organizational leaders should reserve their political clout for crucial decisions. Decentralization also is necessary since often only those closest to decisions have enough information to make good ones.

The incremental approach is identified principally with James Quinn (1980; Mintzberg and Quinn 1991), although the influence of Charles Lindblom (1959; Braybrook and Lindblom 1963; Lindblom 1965, 1977, 1980) is apparent. Quinn developed the concept of logical incrementalism—or incrementalism in the service of overall corporate purposes—and as a result transformed incrementalism into a strategic approach. Logical incrementalism is a process approach that, in effect, fuses strategy formulation and implementation. The strengths of the approach are its ability to handle complexity and change, its emphasis on minor as well as major decisions, its attention to informal as well as formal processes, and its political realism. A related strength is that incremental changes in degree can add up over time into changes in time

(Mintzberg 1987; Bryson 1988a, 1995; Bryson and Crosby 1992). The major weakness of the approach is that it does not guarantee that the various loosely linked decisions will add up to fulfillment of corporate purposes.

Logical incrementalism would appear to be very applicable to public organizations, as it is possible to establish some overarching set of strategic objectives to be served by the approach. When applied at the community level, there is a close relationship between logical incrementalism and collaboration. Indeed, collaborative purposes and arrangements typically emerge in an incremental fashion as organizations individually and collectively explore their self-interests and possible collaborative advantages, establish collaborative relationships, and manage changes incrementally within a collaborative framework (Huxham 1993; Winer and Ray 1994).

Strategic Planning as a Framework for Innovation

The earlier discussion about strategic planning systems noted that excessive comprehensiveness, prescription, and control can drive out attention to mission, strategy, and organizational structure. The systems in other words, can become ends in themselves and drive out creativity, innovation, and new product and market development, without which most businesses would die. Many businesses, therefore, have found it necessary to emphasize innovative strategies as a counterbalance to the excessive control orientation of many strategic planning systems.

The framework-for-innovation approach to corporate strategic planning relies on many elements of the approaches discussed earlier, such as SWOT analyses and portfolio methods. This approach differs from earlier ones in four emphases: (1) innovation as a strategy, (2) specific management practices to support the strategy (such as project teams; venture groups; diversification, acquisition, and divestment task forces; research and development operations; new product and market groups; and a variety of organizational development techniques), (3) development of a "vision of success" that provides the decentralized and entrepreneurial parts of the organization with a common set of superordinate goals toward which to work, and (4) nurture of an entrepreneurial company culture (Pinchot 1985).

The main strength of the approach is that it allows for innovation and entrepreneurship while maintaining central control. It also is quite compatible with other approaches, such as reinventing government, systems analysis, reengineering the organization, and total quality management. The weaknesses of the approach are that typically—and perhaps necessarily—a great many, often costly, mistakes are made as part of the innovation process and that there is a certain loss of accountability in very decentralized systems (Peters and Waterman 1982; Mintzberg 1994). Those weaknesses reduce the applicability to the public sector, in particular, in which mistakes are less acceptable and the pressures to be accountable for details (as opposed to results) are often greater (Barzelay 1992; Jackson and Palmer 1992).

Nonetheless, the innovation approach would appear to be applicable to public organizations when the management of innovation is necessary, as in the redesign of a public service. Innovation as a strategy also can and should be pursued for functions and communities. Too often a distressing equation has operated in the public sector: More money equals more service, less money equals less service. As public budgets have become increasingly strapped, there has not been enough innovation in public service redesign. The equation does not have to be destiny; it is possible that creative effort and innovation might actually result in more service for less money (Osborne and Gaebler 1992; Gore 1993). It is particularly interesting to note that private and nonprofit sector innovations may be the answer to many public-sector problems. For example, many governments rely on private and nonprofit organizations to produce essentially "public" services on a contract basis.

Conclusions

Several conclusions emerge from this review and analysis. First, it should be clear that strategic planning is not a single concept, procedure, or tool. In fact, it embraces a range of approaches that vary in their applicability to public purposes and in the conditions that govern their successful use. The approaches vary in the extent to which they encompass broad policy and direction setting, internal and external assessments, attention to key stakeholders, the identification of key issues, development of strategies to deal with each issue, decisionmaking, implementation, and monitoring and interpretation of results.

Second, a strategic planning process applicable to public organizations and communities will need to allow for the full range of strategic planning activities from policy and direction setting through monitoring of results. Such a process will contrast, therefore, with most private-sector approaches that tend to emphasize different parts of such a complete process. A further contrast would be that private-sector approaches typically are focused only on organizations and not on functions that cross governmental or organizational boundaries, or on communities or larger entities.

Third, while any generic strategic planning process may be a useful guide to thought and action, it will have to be applied with care in a given situation, as is true of any planning process (Bryson and Delbecq 1979; Christensen 1985; Chakravarthy and Lorange 1991; Nutt 1992; Sager 1994). Because every planning process should be tailored to fit specific situations, every process in practice will be a hybrid (Bryson 1988b, 1995).

Fourth, familiarity with strategic planning should be a standard part of the intellectual and skill repertoire of all public managers and planners. Given the dramatic changes in the environments of their organizations in recent years, we can expect key public decisionmakers and planners to seek effective strategies to deal with the changes. When applied appropriately, strategic planning provides a set of concepts, procedures, and tools for formulating and implementing such strategies. The most effective leaders, managers, and planners no doubt are now, and will be increasingly in the future, the ones who are best at strategic planning.

Fifth, asserting the increased importance of strategic planning raises the question of the appropriate role of the strategic planner. In many ways, this is an old debate in the planning literature. Should the planner be a technician, politician, or hybrid-both technician and politician (Howe and Kaufman 1979; Howe 1980)? Should the planner be a process facilitator (Schein 1988) or what Bolan (1971) calls an "expert on experts?" Or should the planner not be a planner at all, at least formally, but rather a policymaker or a line manager (Bryson, Van de Ven, and Roering 1987; Mintzberg 1994)? Clearly, the strategic planner can be solely a technician only when content approaches are used. When all other approaches are used, the strategic planner (or planning team) should be a hybrid so that there is some assurance that both political and technical concerns are addressed. Furthermore, since strategic planning tends to fuse planning and decisionmaking, it is helpful to think of decisionmakers as strategic planners and to think of strategic planners as facilitators of strategic decisionmaking across levels and functions in organizations or communities.

Finally, research must explore a number of theoretical and empirical issues in order to advance the knowledge and practice of public-sector strategic planning. In particular, strategic planning processes that are responsive to different situations must be developed and tested. These processes should specify key situational factors governing their use; provide specific advice on how to formulate and implement strategies in different situations; be explicitly political; indicate how to deal with plural, ambiguous, or conflicting goals or objectives; link context, content, process, and outcomes; indicate how collaboration as well as competition is to be handled; and specify roles for those involved in the process. Other topics in need of attention include the nature of strategic leadership; ways to promote and institutionalize strategic planning across organizational levels, functions that bridge organizational boundaries, and intra- and interorganizational networks; and the ways in which information technologies can help or hinder the process. Progress has been made on all of these fronts (Checkoway 1986; Bryson and Einsweiler 1988; Boschken 1988, 1994; Kemp 1993; Bryson 1995), but work clearly is necessary if we are to understand better when and how to use strategic planning to further public purposes.

NOTE: Adapted from Bryson (1988b, p. 22–45) and from a paper prepared for presentation at the workshop on "Strategic Approaches to Planning: Towards Shared Urban Policies," Politecnico die Milano, Facolta di Architettura, Milano, Italy, March 16–17, 1995.

References

Andrews, Kenneth, 1980. *The Concept of Corporate Strategy.* Homewood, IL: R. D. Irwin.

Armstrong, J. S., 1982. The Value of Formal Planning for Strategic Decisions: Review of Empirical Research. *Strategic Management Journal,* vol. 3, no. 2: 197–211.

Backoff, Robert, and Paul Nutt, 1992. *Strategic Management for Public and Third-Sector Organizations.* San Francisco, CA: Jossey-Bass.

Barry, B., 1986. *Strategic Planning Workbook for Nonprofit Organizations.* St. Paul, MN: Amherst H. Wilder Foundation.

Barzelay, M., 1992. *Breaking Through Bureaucracy.* Berkeley: University of California Press.

Boal, K. B., and J. M. Bryson, 1987. "Representation, Testing, and Policy Implications of Planning Processes." *Strategic Management Journal,* vol. 8: 211–231.

Bolan, R. S., 1971. "Generalist With a Specialty—Still Valid? Educating the Planner: An Expert on Experts." *Planning 1971: Selected Papers from the ASPO National Conference.* Chicago: American Society of Planning Officials.

Boschken, H. L., 1988. *Strategic Design and Organizational Change,* London: The University of Alabama Press.

———, 1992. "Analyzing Performance Skewness in Public Agencies: The Case of Urban Mass Transit." *Journal of Public Administration Research and Theory,* vol. 2, no. 3: 265–288.

———, 1994. "Organizational Performance and Multiple Constituencies." *Public Administration Review,* vol. 54: 308–312.

Bower, J., C. Bartlett, C. Christensen, A. Pearson and K. Andrews, 1993. *Business Policy: Text and Cases,* 7th ed. Homewood, IL: Irwin.

Braybrook, D., and C. Lindblom, 1963. *A Strategy for Decision: Policy Evaluation as a Social Process.* New York: Free Press.

Bryson, J. M., 1983. "Representing and Testing Procedural Planning Methods." In I. Masser, ed., *Evaluating Urban Planning Efforts.* Aldershot, England: Gower.

––––––, 1988a. "Strategic Planning: Big Wins and Small Wins." *Public Money and Management,* vol. 8, no. 3: 11–15.

––––––, 1988b. *Strategic Planning for Public and Nonprofit Organizations.* San Francisco, CA: Jossey-Bass.

––––––, 1995. *Strategic Planning for Public and Nonprofit Organizations,* rev. ed. San Francisco, CA: Jossey-Bass.

––––––, 1996. "Understanding Options for Strategic Planning." In J. Perry, ed., *Handbook of Public Administration,* 479–598 San Francisco, CA: Jossey-Bass.

Bryson, J. M., and P. Bromiley, 1993. "Critical Factors Affecting the Planning and Implementation of Major Projects." *Strategic Management Journal,* vol. 14: 319–337.

Bryson, J., P. Bromily, and Y. S. Jung, 1990. "Influences of Context and Process on Project Planning Success." *Journal of Planning Education and Research,* vol. 9, no. 3: 183–195.

Bryson, J. M., and B. C. Crosby, 1992. *Leadership for the Common Good.* San Francisco, CA: Jossey-Bass.

Bryson, J. M., and A. L. Delbecq, 1979. "A Contingent Approach to Strategy and Tactics in Project Planning." *Journal of the American Planning Association,* vol. 45: 167—179.

Bryson, J. M., and R. C. Einsweiler, eds., 1988. *Strategic Planning for Public Purposes—Threats and Opportunities for Planners.* Chicago, IL, and Washington, DC: Planners Press of the American Planning Association.

Bryson, J. M., R. E. Freeman, and W. D. Roering, 1986. "Strategic Planning in the Public Sector: Approaches and Directions." In B. Checkoway, ed., *Strategic Perspectives on Planning Practice,* 65–85 Lexington, MA.: Lexington Books.

Bryson, J. M., A. H. Van de Ven, and W. D. Roering, 1987. "Strategic Planning and the Revitalization of the Public Service." In R. Denhardt and E. Jennings, eds., *Toward a New Public Service,* 55–75 Columbia: Extension Publications, University Of Missouri.

Chakravarthy, B., and P. Lorange, 1991. *Managing the Strategy Process: A Framework for the Multi-business Firm.* Englewood Cliffs, NJ: Prentice-Hall.

Checkoway, B., ed., 1986. *Strategic Perspectives on Planning Practice.* Lexington, MA: Lexington Books.

Christensen, K. S., 1985. "Coping with Uncertainty in Planning". *Journal of the American Planning Association,* vol. 51, no. 1: 63–73.

Frederickson, James, 1984. "The Comprehensiveness of Strategic Decision Processes," *Academy of Management Journal.* vol. 39 (10): 445–466.

Frederickson, James, and R. R. Mitchell, 1984. "Strategic Decision Processes: Comprehensiveness and Performance in an Industry with an Unstable Environment." *Academy of Management Journal,* vol. 27, no. 2: 399–423.

Freeman, R. E., 1984. "Strategic Management: A Stakeholder Approach." Boston: Pitman.

Friend, J., and A. Hickling, 1987. *Planning Under Pressure.* Oxford: Pergamon Press.

Goold, M., A. Campbell, and K. Luchs, 1993a. "Strategies and Styles Revisited: Strategic Planning and Financial Control." *Long Range Planning,* vol. 26, no. 5: 49–60.

––––––, 1993b. "Strategies and Styles Revisited: Strategic Control Companies." *Long Range Planning,* vol. 26, no. 6: 150–162

Gore, A., 1993. *The Gore Report on Reinventing Government.* New York: Times Books.

Hambrick, D. C., 1982. "Environmental Scanning and Organizational Strategy." *Strategic Management Journal,* vol. 3, no. 2: 159–174.

Harrigan, K., 1981. "Barriers to Entry and Competitive Strategies." *Strategic Management Journal,* vol. 2: 395–412.

Hax, A. C., and N. S. Majiluf, 1984. *Strategic Management: An Integrative Approach.* Englewood Cliffs, NJ: Prentice-Hall.

Heath, R. L., 1988. *Strategic Issues Management.* San Francisco, CA: Jossey-Bass.

Henderson, B., 1979. *Henderson on Corporate Strategy.* Cambridge, MA: Abt Books.

Howe, E., 1980. "Role Choices of Urban Planners." *Journal of the American Planning Association,* vol. 46: 398–409.

Howe, E., and J. Kaufman, 1979. "The Ethics of Contemporary American Planners." *Journal of the American Planning Association,* vol. 45: 243–255.

Hurst, D. K., 1986. "Why Strategic Management Is Bankrupt." *Organizational Dynamics,* vol. 15: 4–27.

––––––, 1993. "Pursuing Collaborative Advantage." *Journal of the Operational Research Society.* vol. 44, 44: 599–611.

Jackson, P. M., and Bob Palmer, 1992. *Performance Measurement: A Management Guide.* Leicester,

England: Management Center University of Leicester.

_____, 1993. *Strategic Planning for Local Government.* Jefferson: Mcfarland and Company.

Lindblom, C. E., 1959. "The Science of Muddling Through." *Public Administration Review,* vol. 19: 79–88.

_____, 1965. *The Intelligence of Democracy.* New York: Free Press.

_____, 1977. *Politics and Markets.* New York: Free Press.

_____, 1980. *The Policy-Making Process.* 2d ed. Englewood Cliffs, NJ: Prentice-Hall.

Lorange, P., 1980. *Corporate Planning: An Executive Viewpoint.* Englewood Cliffs, NJ: Prentice-Hall.

MacMillan, I., 1983. "Competitive Strategies for Not-for-Profit Agencies." *Advances in Strategic Management,* vol. 1: 61–82.

_____, 1987. "Crafting Strategy." *Harvard Business Review,* vol. 87, no. 4: 66–75.

_____, 1994. *The Rise and Fall of Strategic Planning.* New York: Free Press.

Mintzberg, H., and James Quinn, 1991. *The Strategy Process,* 2d ed. Englewood Cliffs, NJ: Prentice-Hall.

Montanari, J. R., and J. S. Bracker, 1986. "The Strategic Management Process." *Strategic Management Journal,* vol. 7, no. 3: 251–265.

National Governors Association, 1993. An Action Agenda to Redesign State Governement. Washington, D.C.: National Governors Association.

Nutt, Paul, 1992. *Managing Planned Change.* New York: Macmillan.

Nutt, Paul, and R. W. Backoff, 1995. "Strategy for Public and Third Sector Organizations." *Journal of Public Administration Research and Theory.* vol. 5(2):189–211

Olsen, J. B., and D. C. Eadie, 1982. *The Game Plan: Governance with Foresight.* Washington, DC: Council of State Planning Agencies.

Osborne, D., and T. Gaebler, 1992. *Reinventing Government.* Reading, MA: Addison-Wesley.

Peters, T.J., and R. H. Waterman, Jr., 1982. *In Search of Excellence: Lessons from America's Best-Run Companies.* New York: Harper & Row.

Pflaum, A., and T. Delmont, 1987. "External Scanning—A Tool for Planners." *Journal of the American Planning Association,* vol. 53, no. 1: 56–67.

Pinchot, G., III, 1985. *Enterpreneuring.* New York: Harper & Row.

Porter, M., 1980. *Competitive Strategy: Techniques for Analyzing Industries and Competitors.* New York: Free Press.

_____, 1985. *Competitive Advantage: Creating and Sustaining Superior Performance.* New York: Free Press.

_____, 1990. *The Competitive Advantage of Nations.* New York: Free Press.

_____, 1994. *Competitive Strategies for Changing Industries.* Boston, MA: Harvard Business School Management Productions.

Quinn, J. B., 1980. *Strategies for Change: Logical Incrementalism.* Homewood, IL: R. D. Irwin.

Ring, Peter, 1988. "Strategic Issues and Where Do They Come From?" In John Bryson and Robert Einsweiler *Strategic Planning for Public Purposes—Threats and Opportunities for Planners:* 69–83. American Planning Association.

Rue, L. W., and P. G. Holland, 1986. *Strategic Management: Concepts and Experiences.* New York: McGraw-Hill.

Sager, T., 1994. *Communicative Planning Theory.* Aldershot, United Kingdom: Avebury.

Schein, E., 1988. *Process Consultation.* Vol. 1: *Its Role in Organization Development.* Reading, MA: Addison-Wesley.

Stone, M., and W. Crittenden, 1993. "A Guide to Journal Articles on Strategic Management in Nonprofit Organizations." *Nonprofit Management and Leadership,* vol. 4: 193–213.

Wildavsky, A., 1979a. *The Politics of the Budgetary Process.* Boston, MA: Little, Brown.

Winer, M., and K. Ray, 1994. *Collaboration Handbook.* St. Paul, MN: Amherst H. Wilder Foundation.

► **CHAPTER 11**

The Strategic Marketing Planning Process

PHILIP KOTLER AND ALAN R. ANDREASEN

Once an organization believes it has understood and internalized a customer-centered orientation up and down its ranks, the next step is to bring the organization up to the frontier of the best in current marketing practice. The approach we shall advocate to guide these detailed decisions is what we call the *Strategic Marketing Planning Process* (SMPP). Just as "customer-centeredness" is the advocated way of *thinking* about marketing, SMPP is the advocated way of *doing* marketing. It is an approach that can apply equally well to the question of what to do over the next ten years and what to do tomorrow.

The SMPP is a set of steps one must take to decide what to do in any given marketing situation. It is based on the assumption that marketing is a function that must operate within two environments. First, it operates within an organization. Therefore, what marketers do in the future must necessarily fit with what the organization as a whole wishes to do. Marketers must tell organizational planners what can and cannot be accomplished in the way of developed or changing consumer markets. At the same time, organizational planners must tell marketers where and how and what they must do to meet the organization's overall needs and plans.

Second, marketers cannot plan willy-nilly to do anything they want (say, meet an observed customer need) without taking very serious account of the organization's *abilities* to take advantage of the opportunity the external world presents. It is essential, then, that any planning process systematically consider organization strengths and weaknesses before it results in suggestions for new ventures, particularly those that take the organization far afield from its present activities.

Marketing also must operate in an external world. Marketing plans must adapt to target consumer markets as the organization finds them and as they will evolve in the future. But they must also adapt to expected competitors and to changes in the technological, economic, political, and social environments in which both the organization and its competitors function.

Management has to pay attention to market evolution and strategic fit. All markets undergo evolutionary development marked by changing customer needs, technologies, competitors, channels, and laws. The organization should be looking out of a strategic window watching these changes and assessing the requirements for continued success in each market. The fit between the requirements of a particular market and the organization's competencies is at an optimum for only a limited period. During this period, the strategic window is open, and the organization should be investing in that market. In some subsequent period the organization will find that the evolutionary path of that market is such that the organization can no longer serve it effectively and efficiently. It should then consider disinvesting and shifting its resources to areas of growing opportunity.

The distinction between external and internal environments permits us to define strategic marketing planning as follows: Strategic planning is the managerial process of developing and maintaining a strategic fit between the organization's goals and resources and its changing market opportunities.

The strategic marketing planning process includes the following steps:

1. Determine organization-wide objectives, mission, and specific goals to which marketing strategies must contribute.
2. Assess external environmental threats and opportunities that can be addressed by marketing in the interest of achieving greater organizational success.
3. Evaluate present and potential organization resources and skills to take advantage of the opportunity or repel the threat identified in the external environmental analysis.
4. Determine the marketing mission, objectives, and specific goals for the relevant planning period.
5. Formulate the core marketing strategy to achieve the specified goals.
6. Put in place the necessary organizational structure and systems within the marketing function to ensure proper implementation of the designed strategy.
7. Establish detailed programs and tactics to carry out the core strategy for the planning period, including a timetable of activities and assignment of specific responsibilities.
8. Establish benchmarks to measure interim and final achievements of the program.
9. Implement the planned program.
10. Measure performance and adjust the core strategy, tactical details, or both as needed.

The entire process is illustrated in Figure 11.1.

We shall discuss the first five steps of the strategic marketing planning process in this chapter.

Determining Organization-Level Missions, Objectives, and Goals

A marketing program is not developed in a vacuum. It must adjust to both internal and external realities. The principal internal reality is where the organization as a whole wishes to go. If the organization is mature and well managed, it should have already completed an organization-wide strategic planning process like that outlined in Figure 1. That is, before marketing planning should begin, the organization's top-level managers (including the marketing manager) and its advisory boards should ideally have:

1. Determined the organization-level long-term mission, objectives, and goals.
2. Assessed the organization's likely future external environment (of which the marketing environment is a subset).
3. Assessed the organization's present and potential strengths and weaknesses (of which marketing strengths and weaknesses are a subset).

In this sense, strategic marketing planning can be seen as a nested activity. That is, marketing strategic planning can—and should—be nested within organization-level strategic planning. Further, if the organization is large enough, the same kind of strategic planning ought to be carried out by subunits within the marketing function. In general, the further down the planning hierarchy, the more detailed the planning and the shorter the planning horizons.

Plan formulation involves the organization in determining an appropriate mission, objectives, and goals for the current or expected environment. The three terms are distinguished below:

- *Mission:* the basic purpose of an organization, that is, what it is trying to accomplish.

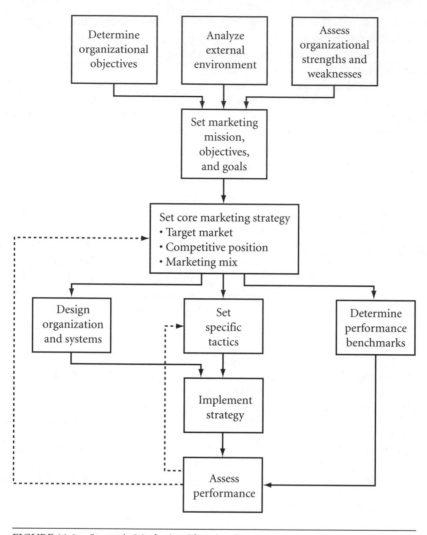

FIGURE 11.1   Strategic Marketing Planning Process

- *Objective:* a major variable that the organization will emphasize, such as market share, profitability, reputation.
- *Goal:* an objective of the organization that is made specific with respect to magnitude, time, and who is responsible.

We examine these concepts in more detail below.

Mission

Every organization starts with a mission. In fact, an organization can be defined as a *human collectivity that is structured to perform a specific mission through the use of largely rational means.* Its specific mission is usually clear at the beginning.

Each organization that wants to be responsive must answer two questions: *responsive to whom and to what?* An organization cannot serve everyone and every need. If it tried to serve everyone, it would serve no one very well. From time to time, each organization must reexamine its mission.

Years ago, Peter Drucker pointed out that organizations need to answer the following questions: *What is our business? Who is the customer?*

What is value to the customer? What will our business be? What should our business be?[1] Although the first question "What is our business?" sounds simple, it is really the most profound question an organization can ask.

Clarifying the organization's mission is a soul-searching and time-consuming process. Different members will have different views of what the organization is about and should be about. One organization held numerous meetings over a two-year period before membership consensus developed on the real mission of the organization.

A helpful approach to defining mission is to establish the organization's scope along three dimensions. The first is consumer groups, namely, who is to be served and satisfied. The second is consumer needs, namely, what is to be satisfied. The third is technologies, namely, how consumer needs are to be satisfied.

An organization should strive for a mission that is feasible, motivating, and distinctive. In terms of being feasible, the organization should avoid a "mission impossible." An institution should always reach high, but not so high as to produce incredulity in its publics.

The mission should also be motivating. Those working for the organization should feel they are worthwhile members of a worthwhile organization. The mission should be something that enriches people's lives.

A mission works better when it is distinctive. People take pride in belonging to an institution that "does it differently" or "does it better." By cultivating a distinctive mission and personality, an organization stands out more and attracts a more loyal group of members.

Objectives

The mission of an institution suggests more about where that institution is coming from than where it is going to. It describes what the institution is about rather than the specific objectives and goals it will pursue in the coming period. Each institution has to develop major objectives and goals for the coming period separate from but consistent with its mission statement.

For every type of institution, there is always a potential set of relevant objectives, and the insti-

tution's task is to make a choice among them. For example, the objectives of interest to a college are: increased national reputation, improved classroom teaching, higher enrollment, higher quality students, increased efficiency, larger endowment, improved student social life, improved physical plant, lower operating deficit, and so on. A college cannot successfully pursue all of these objectives simultaneously because of a limited budget and because some of them are incompatible, such as increased cost efficiency and improved classroom teaching. In any given year, therefore, institutions will choose to emphasize certain objectives and either ignore others or treat them as constraints. Thus, an institution's major objectives can vary from year to year depending on the administration's perception of the major problems that the institution must address at that time.

Goals

The chosen objectives must be restated in an operational and measurable form called goals. The objective "increased enrollment" must be turned into a goal, such as "a 15 percent enrollment increase in next year's fall class." A goal statement permits the institution to think about the planning, programming, and control aspects of pursuing that objective. A number of questions may arise: Is a 15 percent enrollment increase feasible? What strategy would be used? What resources would it take? What activities would have to be carried out? Who would be responsible and accountable? All of these critical questions must be answered when deciding whether to adopt a proposed goal.

Typically, the institution will be evaluating a large set of potential goals at the same time and examining their consistency. The institution may discover that it cannot simultaneously achieve "a 15 percent enrollment increase," "a 10 percent increase in student quality," and a "12 percent tuition increase" at the same time. In this case, the executive committee may make adjustments in the target levels or target dates or drop certain goals altogether in order to arrive at a meaningful and achievable set of goals. Once the set of goals are agreed upon in the goal formulation stage, the organization is ready to move on to the detailed work of strategy formulation.[2]

The issue of determining organizational goals can be broken into two distinct steps: (1) determining what the current goals are, and (2) determining what the goals should be. Sometimes the task of determining present goals is straightforward because they are written down, widely disseminated, and most importantly, understood by everyone as meaning the same thing. But frequently the image of the current goals differs from person to person and group to group in the organization. These differences reflect the fact that the organization is really a coalition of several groups, each giving and seeking different things from the organization. On the other hand, in some organizations differences in goals may signal a basic confusion that really ought to be corrected before planning proceeds much further.

Another disconcerting problem occurs when the marketing manager discovers that what the organization says its goals are and what they actually are constitute two very different things.

There are two implications of this kind of experience. First, marketing managers must be aware that many organizations will, in practice, turn out to be schizophrenic in their goal-setting, speaking and acting in different ways. Sometimes this is intentional. It is not so important to the marketing manager to know the true explanation, only that he or she be able to read the proper signals and either respond to what management really wants or, if the marketing manager believes management is misguided in what it is doing, try to bring the firm's real goals more in line with stated goals.

Analyzing External Threats and Opportunities

The external environment in which an organization operates is complex and constantly changing. The environment consists of four components:

1. *The public environment,* consisting of groups and organizations that take an interest in the activities of the focal organization. The public environment consists of local publics, activist publics, the general public, media publics, and regulatory agencies whose actions can affect the welfare of the focal organization.

2. *The competitive environment,* consisting of groups and organizations that compete for attention and loyalty from the audiences of the focal organization. The competitive environment includes desire competitors, generic competitors, form competitors, and enterprise competitors.

3. *The macroenvironment,* consisting of large-scale fundamental forces that shape opportunities and pose threats to the focal organization. The main macroenvironmental forces that have to be watched are the demographic, economic, technological, political, and social forces. These forces largely represent "uncontrollables" in the organization's situation to which it has to adapt.

4. *The market environment,* consisting of the groups and other organizations that the focal organization directly works with to accomplish its mission. The main groups in the market environment are the clients, marketing intermediaries, suppliers, and supporters. The focal organization must monitor trends and changes in the needs, perceptions, preferences, and dissatisfactions of these key groups.

We shall consider each of these environmental components in turn.

The Public Environment

When marketing managers turn to examining the external environment, they realize that it contains several publics, and the organization has to develop a strategic posture with respect to most or all of them. We define a public in the following way: A public is a distinct group of people, organizations, or both whose actual or potential needs must in some sense by served.

Not all publics are equally active or important to an organization. Publics come about because the organization's activities and policies can draw support or criticism from outside groups. A welcome public is a public that likes the organization and whose support the organization welcomes. A sought public is a public whose support the organization wants but which is currently indifferent or negative toward that organization. An unwelcome public is a public that is negatively disposed toward the organization and that is trying to impose constraints, pressures, or controls on the organization. Publics can also be classified by their functional relation to the organization. Figure 11.2 presents such a classification. An organization is viewed as a resource-conversion machine in which certain input publics supply resources that are converted by internal publics into useful goods and services that are carried by intermediary publics to designated consuming publics. Here we will look at the various publics more closely.

Input Publics. Input publics mainly supply original resources and constraints to the organization, and as such consist of donors, suppliers, and regulatory publics.

Donors

Donors are those publics who make gifts of money and other assets to the organization. Thus a university's donors consist of alumni, friends of the university, foundations, corporations, and government organizations.

Suppliers

Suppliers are those organizations that sell needed goods and services to the focal organization. Nonprofit organizations often try to obtain price concessions or even free donations of goods and services but don't often succeed. In recent times, supply shortages and the rapidly rising cost of supplies have made skillful supply planning and purchasing more important than ever.

Regulatory organizations

The third input public consists of regulatory organizations that impose rules of conduct. The regulatory publics of a university include federal, state, and local government agencies, trade unions, and various academic accreditation associations. The focal organization must keep in close contact with these regulatory organizations and be ready to argue against regulations that will harm their ability to create value for their clients.

Internal Publics. The various inputs are managed by the organization's internal publics to accomplish the organization's mission. The internal publics consist of up to four groups: management, a board of directors, staff, and volunteers. We have already considered the requirement that marketing managers be responsive to those above them in the organization hierarchy, that is, top management and the board of directors. Marketing managers must also be responsive to those below them in the organization.

Staff

The staff consists of the various employees who work on a paid basis. This would include middle management, secretaries, workmen, tele-

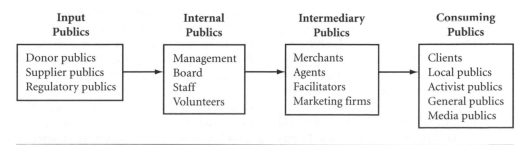

Input Publics	Internal Publics	Intermediary Publics	Consuming Publics
Donor publics Supplier publics Regulatory publics	Management Board Staff Volunteers	Merchants Agents Facilitators Marketing firms	Clients Local publics Activist publics General publics Media publics

FIGURE 11.2   The Main Publics of an Organization

phone operators, and so on. The staff would also include the skilled practitioners who deliver the organization's services to its consumers, such as the hospital's nurses, the college's professors, the police department's police officers, and the social agency's social workers.

Management faces the normal problems of building an effective staff: defining job positions and responsibilities, recruiting qualified people, training them, motivating them, compensating them, and evaluating them. Employee training is another critical task with significant marketing implications. Those employees who come in contact with consumers must be trained in a "customer service" orientation.

Motivating the staff takes careful planning. The staff wants several things from the organization: adequate salaries, fair treatment, respect and recognition, and the feeling of working for a worthwhile enterprise. Management must create these benefits if it expects to get in return solid work, high morale, and continuous support.

Volunteers

Many nonprofit organizations—churches, charities, hospitals—use volunteers as an important part of their operations. The volunteers perform work that usually requires less skill, and this helps to keep down the costs of running the organization. On the other hand, volunteers are less controllable and often less productive. They may not show up for meetings, resist doing certain tasks, and tend to be slow in getting their work done on time. Some organizations claim to be able to accomplish more by increasing the size of the paid staff and reducing the number of volunteers.

At the same time, a better answer might be for the organization to improve its skill in managing and motivating the volunteers. Volunteers are sensitive to small slights like not receiving recognition for a job well done or being pushed hard. They feel that they are giving their time free and want to be appreciated and respected.

The competent volunteer staff manager will be skilled in attracting good and reliable volunteers and in motivating and rewarding them. A

marketing approach means understanding the volunteers' needs and meeting them in a way which draws their support and hard work. The volunteer staff manager is likely to sponsor social functions for volunteers, confer awards for many years of service, and arrange a number of other benefits that will recognize their contributions.[3]

Intermediary Publics. The focal organization enlists other organizations, called marketing intermediaries, to assist in promoting and distributing its goods and services to the final consumers. They are described below.

Merchants

Merchants are organizations such as wholesalers and retailers that buy, take title to, and resell merchandise.

Agents

Agent middlemen are organizations such as manufacturer's representatives, agents, and brokers that are hired by producers to find and/or sell to buyers without ever taking possession of the merchandise.

Facilitators

Facilitators are organizations such as transportation companies, real estate firms, and media firms that assist in the distribution of products, services, and messages, but do not take title to or negotiate purchases.

Marketing firms

Marketing firms are organizations such as advertising agencies, marketing research firms, and marketing consulting firms that assist in identifying and promoting the focal organization's products and services to the right markets.

Consuming Publics. Various groups consume the output of an organization, and in varying senses have needs the marketing manager must meet. They are described below.

Clients

Customers represent the marketer's primary public, its raison d'etre. Drucker insists that the only valid purpose of a business is to create a customer. He would hold that hospitals exist to serve patients, colleges to serve students, opera companies to serve opera lovers, and social agencies to serve the needy.

Various names are used interchangeably to describe customers, such as consumers, clients, buyers, and constituents. The appropriate term is elusive in some cases. Consider a state penitentiary. The prisoners are clearly the penitentiary's consumers. A psychiatrist in the prison will have certain prisoners as clients. The prisoners are not buyers in the sense of paying money for the service; instead, the citizens are the buyers, and they are buying protection from criminal elements through their taxes. The citizens are also the prison's constituents in that the prison exists to serve their interests. We might conclude that the citizens are the prison's primary customers.

What this illustrates is that a market can have a multiple set of customers, and one of its jobs is to distinguish these customer groups and their relative importance.

Local Publics

Every organization is physically located in one or more areas and comes in contact with local publics such as neighborhood residents and community organizations. These groups may take an active or passive interest in the activities of the organization. Thus, the residents surrounding a hospital usually get concerned about ambulance sirens, parking congestion, and other things that go with living near a hospital.

Organizations usually appoint a community relations officer whose job is to keep close to the community, attend meetings, answer questions, and make contributions to worthwhile causes. Responsive organizations do not wait for local issues to erupt. They make investments in their community to help it run well and to acquire a bank of goodwill. This, too, is a marketing activity.

Activist Publics

Organizations are increasingly being petitioned by consumer groups, environmental groups, minority organizations, and other public interest groups for certain concessions or support. Hospitals, for example, have had to deal with demands by environmental groups to install more pollution control equipment and engage in better waste handling methods.

Organizations would be foolish to attack or ignore demands of activist publics. Responsive organizations can do two things. First, they can train their management to include social criteria in their decision-making to strike a better balance between the needs of the clients, citizens, and the organization itself. Second, they can assign a staff person to stay in touch with these groups and to communicate more effectively the organization's goals, activities, and intentions.

General Public

A marketer is also concerned with the attitude of the general public toward the organization's activities and policies. The general public does not act in an organized way toward the organization, as activist groups do. But the members of the general public carry around images of the organization that affect their patronage and legislative support. The marketer needs to monitor how the organization is seen by the public and to take concrete steps to improve its public image where it is weak.

Media Publics

Media publics include media companies that carry news, features, and editorial opinion: specifically, newspapers, magazines, and radio and television stations. Marketers are acutely sensitive to the role played by the press in affecting their organizations' capacity to achieve their marketing objectives. Organizations normally would like more and better press coverage than they get. Getting more and better coverage calls for understanding what the press is really interested in. The effective press relations manager knows most of the editors in the major media and systematically cultivates a mutually beneficial relation with them. The manager offers interesting news items, informational material, and quick access to top management. In return, the media editors are likely to give the organization more and better coverage.

The Competitive Environment

Today nonprofit marketers are facing increasing competition in their markets. Unfortunately, many nonprofit organizations still deny the existence of such competition, feeling that this is only characteristic of private sector markets. Thus, hospitals until recently did not like to think of other hospitals as competitors, museums tended to ignore other museums, and the Red Cross saw other blood banks as all seeking the same general public goal. They would rather think of their sister organizations as simply helping provide social services and not competing. Yet the reality of competition is driven home when one hospital starts attracting many doctors and patients from another hospital, blood banks compete for donors, or YMCAs start losing members to local racquetball clubs and gymnasiums.

By contrast, there are also nonprofits who recognize the existence of potential competitors but seem to think that competition is "not nice." They feel that since all nonprofits, in some sense, are attempting to achieve the same (obviously desirable) social goals, any attention to competition would divert energies from what each competitor should really be doing. Sometimes nonprofit marketers are rudely awakened when a competitor doesn't "play fair."

Competition may help rather than hurt the nonprofit marketers' performance in two important ways. First, the existence of two competitors in the marketplace, clamoring for attention, spending two advertising budgets, commanding even more shelf space or media interest, can stimulate increases in *the size of the total market.*

The second virtue of face-to-face competition is that it can sharpen the competitive skills of the embattled marketers. It is a serious danger in the nonprofit domain that marketers will become fat and happy by observing growing sales and pretending there is no competition. There is nothing like the effect of new competitive activity to give complaisant managers the needed slap to the side of the head. To compete, they have to rethink how their brand is positioned. They have to look to their customers more carefully to see if there are better ways to meet their needs and wants. They have to consider the possibility of changing prices, features, and advertising. This reevaluation and the continuing close attention to marketing details can only help the marketer's overall performance.

A marketer can face up to four major types of competitors in trying to serve a target market. They are:

1. *Desire competitors*—other immediate desires that the consumer might want to satisfy.
2. *Generic competitors*—other basic ways in which the consumer can satisfy a particular desire.
3. *Service form competitors*—other service forms that can satisfy the consumer's particular desire.
4. *Enterprise competitors*—other enterprises offering the same service form that can satisfy the consumer's particular desire.

We will illustrate these four types of competitors as they were faced by a New York legitimate theatre, the Barrymore, offering the play *Hurlyburly* in the spring of 1985. Consider a young professional woman in New York deciding what to do on a particular evening. She realizes that she has several desires she could satisfy—finishing a project at work, getting some exercise, meeting several household responsibilities, or being entertained. Once she determines that the desire she will satisfy is to be entertained, she has to consider various generic competitors, including TV at home, a movie, or a live performance. Choosing to be entertained by a live performance, she has to consider various forms of live entertainment—a symphony, a nightclub performance, a rock concert, or a legitimate play. Finally, after settling on a legitimate play, she has to choose the offerings of various enterprises—the Barrymore's *Hurlyburly,* the Winter Garden's

Cats, or the Promenade Theatre's *Pacific Overtures.*

If the Barrymore Theatre is experiencing poor sales, the causes may be poor marketing strategy at any or all of the four levels of competition. The Barrymore may have chosen a poor offering and so loses out to other enterprise competitors. Or the play may be terrific, but too many consumers may be choosing other form competitors such as nightclubs or rock concerts. In the latter case, the marketing manager's challenge would be to focus on those who like live entertainment and convince them that legitimate theatre is a better alternative. This could involve research into why the theatre is losing out to other forms. It may be that competitors in other forms have discovered better ways to meet consumer needs that the theatre might wish to copy (for example, reducing prices, selling popcorn or liquor). Or it might be that more people would choose the theatre except for certain disincentives ("costs") that the marketer could correct. For instance, potential customers could fear for their safety in downtown parking lots (the marketer could build a new structure, put in stronger lights, or hire a bus service to bring fearful people up to the door from a distant, safe lot). Or they could feel their friends might not want to come. In that case, the marketers could offer two-for-one ticket bargains or a "bring-a-friend-free" promotion.

At the next level of competition, if the manager found that too many promising customers were not choosing live entertainment as the preferred generic form of entertainment, the theatre manager might consider joint promotions with its generic comrades (symphony managers, rock concert promoters, nightclub owners) to get people out to "the live world of entertainment tonight." On the other hand, if the problem is at the desire level of competition, joint promotion by those in the entertainment industry (live performance promoters, movie house bookers, TV station managers) could compete with other desires by promoting the theme that "in this stressful, work-conscious world, you need more entertainment to relax, to replenish, to grow."

The important points to recognize in this extended example are:

1. Every nonprofit has competition and it is critical to recognize and accept it.
2. If one has competition, good strategic planning requires that the organization evaluate very carefully whether it is operating as an effective competitor and, if not, how its strategy should be changed to make it more competitive.
3. Competitive problems can be at any of four levels, desire, generic, form, and enterprise.
4. Evaluating one's competitive position therefore requires evaluation and potential changes of strategy at one or more of these competitive levels.

Macroenvironment

If strategic planning has its consequences in the future, it is crucial that nonprofit managers understand the broad forces creating the world in which they must operate. These broad forces can be divided into demographic, economic, technological, political-legal, and social-cultural categories. The nature of these forces varies, of course, by the country in which the nonprofit markets, and within a given country, their relative impact varies significantly by region and nonprofit sector. Demographic and political-legal trends are very important for strategic planning in social service agencies. Economic trends are important to charities, technological trends to hospitals and libraries, demographic and economic trends to the armed forces, and social-cultural trends to parks and recreation services and the performing arts.

Market Environment

Nonprofits function within markets with other "players" whom the manager must work with or attempt to influence. One of these, of course, is the set of target consumers the marketer must put at the center of the strategic planning process. Other key market groups will be discussed below.

In all cases, strategically oriented nonprofit managers must recognize that these market players are not static entities, but are themselves changing. In some sectors, change is slow and evolutionary. In others, change can be rapid, even chaotic. Three recent examples of the latter are financial services, communication, and advertising media. Nonprofit mangers who, for example, wish to plan for a future media environment must today carefully consider the challenges and threats posed by the rapid growth in cable television. VCRs and satellite dishes, the shrinkage of network TV audience shares, the consolidation of ownership of local TV stations and newspapers, the fragmentation of radio to serve narrow market segments, the willingness of public TV to carry more corporate messages more closely resembling advertising, the growth of national newspapers, and so on. Keeping up with such rapid change again can be facilitated by close observances of the trade and popular press and the use of outside experts.

Setting Marketing Mission, Objectives, and Goals

Once the marketing manager has completed the first three steps of the strategic marketing planning process, he or she must then integrate what has been learned at these earlier stages into a long-term strategy for marketing. That is, the opportunities and threats in the external environment (step 2) must be compared to the organization's strengths and weaknesses (step 3) to determine what long-term course of marketing action will best achieve what top management has communicated are its real mission and objectives (step 1).

The approach that most sophisticated for-profit marketers have adopted is to use some variation on what is known as portfolio planning. The portfolio concept assumes that most modern organizations, including nonprofits, offer multiple products or services in multiple markets and are constantly facing questions of how to treat simultaneously these sets of existing and potential products or services. They need to decide:

1. Which products or services to pour additional resources into because their future looks bright (building opportunities).

2. Which products or services to essentially maintain in their present posture as doing just fine (holding opportunities).
3. From which products or services to drain resources because they are not promising (harvesting opportunities).
4. Which products or services to drop because their future doesn't look promising or because other product or service prospects look better (divesting opportunities).
5. Which products or services to add to the portfolio over the planning period (new product opportunities).

In essence, the problem is like that of managing an investment portfolio where one must decide which stocks to buy or sell, how much to hold of each, whether to switch from stocks to bonds or real estate, whether to withdraw cash, and so on. The problem for the financial investor as well as for the marketing manager is to constantly evaluate the portfolio against changing market conditions and changing performances of individual units in the portfolio.

The first step in any portfolio analysis is to partition the organization's existing offerings into strategic business units (SBUs). These can be individual products and services or groups of similar products or services. Four criteria should be considered when deciding whether individual products and services belong together in a strategic marketing unit:

1. Do they market to essentially the same customers?
2. Are they marketed in essentially the same way? That is, do they use similar media for advertisements or common distributor channels?
3. Do they have essentially the same competitors?
4. Can they be planned for together?

Thus, in a family planning program, the sterilization marketing programs could be grouped with programs to market birth control pills and condoms for strategic planning purposes. Further analysis, however, would reveal that they more properly belong with other medical services offered by the family planning program. They have in common with the latter two important characteristics: (1) they are offered through the same distribution channel—medical clinics rather than drug stores, and (2) they face the same competitors—other clinics and other private physicians rather than other pharmaceutical manufacturers.

The next step is to assess the favorability of the market in which the SBU competes and the SBU's current performance.

General Electric (GE) has formulated an approach to portfolio evaluation that has more applicability to nonprofit organization. They call it the strategic business planning grid; it uses two basic dimensions, market attractiveness and organizational strength. The best programs to offer are those that serve attractive markets and for which the organization has high organizational strength.

Market attractiveness is a composite index made up of such factors as:

- *Market size.* Large markets are more attractive than small markets.
- *Market growth rate.* High-growth markets are more attractive than low-growth markets.
- *Profit margin.* High-profit-margin programs are more attractive than low-profit-margin programs.
- *Competitive intensity.* Markets with many strong competitors are less attractive than markets with a few weak competitors.
- *Cyclicality.* Highly cyclical markets are less attractive than cyclically stable markets.
- *Seasonality.* Highly seasonal markets are less attractive than nonseasonal markets.
- *Scale economies.* Programs where unit costs fall with large volume production and marketing are more attractive than constant cost programs.
- *Learning curve.* Programs where unit costs fall as management accumulates experience in production and distribution are more attractive than programs where management has reached the limit of its learning.

Marketing strength is a composite index made up of such factors as:

- *Program quality.* The higher the program quality relative to competitors, the greater its organizational strength.

- *Efficiency level.* The more efficient the organization is at producing the program relative to competitors, the greater its organizational strength.
- *Market knowledge.* The deeper the organization's knowledge of customers in that market and their needs and wants, the greater its organizational strength.
- *Marketing effectiveness.* The greater the organization's marketing effectiveness, the greater its organizational strength.

The factors making up each dimension are scaled and weighted so that each current SBU achieves a number indicating its market attractiveness and marketing strength.

Other portfolio approaches have been developed. As an example, consider a college administration trying to determine how much support to give to each academic department. One college developed the following criteria:

- *Centrality.* The degree to which an academic program is central to the mission of the college.
- *Quality.* The quality and reputation of the academic department relative to those in other colleges.
- *Market viability.* The degree to which the market for the academic program is sufficient in size and growth.

Each criterion is divided into high, medium, and low. (Market viability is represented by MV and its level is represented by H, M, or L, for high, medium, or low, respectively.)

Ideally, under any portfolio, the marketing manager should take one further step before taking action. This step is to forecast the future locations of the offerings under the assumption that there are no changes in the organization's own strategy.

Once the marketing manager completes the present portfolio and makes a nonchange forecast analysis, it is necessary to step back and evaluate the portfolio determining what needs to be done. Two features of the portfolio approach must be kept in mind at this point. First, portfolios require balance. The second feature of portfolios that the no-change projection should make abundantly clear is that they evolve over time.

The ultimate decision as to whether to change the portfolio may well depend on the marketing manager's or the organization's attitude toward risk. Some managers might on some occasion be quite averse to risk. A marketing manager hoping for a renewal grant from a funding agency, for example, would pursue a cautious, no-change strategy that would guarantee that the program would appear reasonably successful at the end of the period. The manager would prefer this to a riskier strategy that could look sensational but could also fail sensationally.

Developing the Core Marketing Strategy

The next step in the strategic planning process outlined in Figure 11.3 is to develop a set of core marketing strategies to achieve the desired positions.

> Core Marketing Strategy is the selection of a target market(s), the choice of a competitive position, and the development of an effective marketing mix to reach and serve the chosen customers.

Target Market Strategy. The first step in preparing a marketing strategy is to understand the market thoroughly. We define a market as follows:

> A market is the set of all people who have an actual or potential interest in an exchange and the ability to complete it.

There are many ways to segment a market. A market could be segmented by age, sex, income, geography, lifestyle, and many other variables. The market analyst tries different approaches until a useful one is found.

1. *Product/market concentration* consists of an organization concentrating on only one market segment.

2. *Product specialization* consists of the organization deciding to produce only one product for all three markets.
3. *Market specialization* consists of the organization deciding to serve only one market segment.
4. *Selective specialization* consists of the organization working in several product markets that have no relation to each other except that each constitutes an individually attractive opportunity.
5. *Full coverage* consists of an organization making the full range of products to serve all the market segments.

> **Competitive positioning is** the art of developing and communicating meaningful differences between one's offer and those of competitors serving the same target market.

The key to competitive positioning is to understand how members of the target market evaluate and choose among competitive institutions.

The next step in marketing strategy is to develop a marketing mix and a marketing expenditure level that supports the school's ability to compete in the target market.

> Marketing mix is the particular blend of controllable marketing variables that the firm uses to achieve its objective in the target market.

Although many variables make up the marketing mix, they can be classified into a few major groups. McCarthy formulated a popular classification called the "four Ps": *product, price, place,* and *promotion.*[4] The particular marketing variables under each P are shown in Figure 3. The figure emphasizes that the marketing mix must be adapted to the target market.

The organization chooses a marketing mix that will support and reinforce its chosen competitive position. In other words, the chosen competitive position dictates the elements of the marketing mix that will be emphasized.

As for the marketing expenditure level, this depends on estimating how much money is needed to accomplish the objectives.

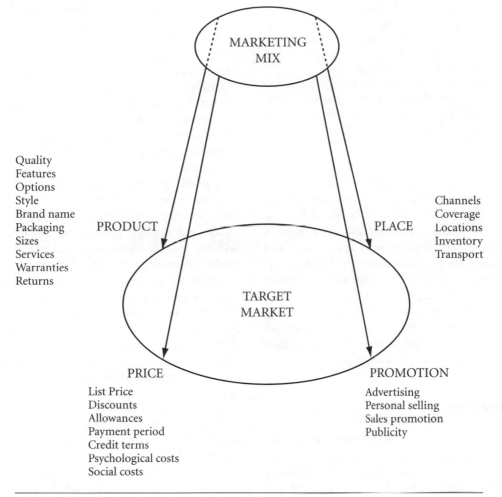

FIGURE 11.3   The Four Ps of the Marketing Mix

Remaining Steps in the SMPP Process

Developing Structure, Tactics, and Benchmarks

The next level of the strategic marketing management process outlined in Figure 11.3 is to take three steps more or less simultaneously to set the stage for implementing the core marketing strategy defined in the preceding stage. These steps are the following:

1. Developing an organizational structure and a set of management systems within the marketing group to carry out the marketing strategy. In any particular strategic planning cycle, this may involve adjusting an existing structure or set of systems or may require the development of entirely new ones. It may also involve creating bases of support from others in terms of goods, services, and/or skills or implementing specific fundraising activities.

2. At the same time, detailed tactics must be specified for carrying out each aspect of the core strategy. This will involve decisions about what

offerings to make, what channels to use and how to use them, how to manage consumer costs, and what communications tactics to use through advertising and sales promotion, personal selling, and public relations.

3. Benchmarks must be developed reflecting the core strategy's goals and objectives so that, after implementation, marketing management can learn whether its strategy, structure, and tactics are achieving what is expected of them.

Implementing and Assessing Marketing Strategy. If the strategic planning process has worked well, the task of implementation should be straightforward. The process is not complete, however, until management consciously and systematically assesses how well it is performing. Management must realize that this assessment step is crucial both to permit short-run and on-the-run fine-tuning of core strategy, marketing organization structure, and marketing tactics and to feed into subsequent cycles of this critical strategic marketing planning process.

Summary

Once the organization has developed the appropriate customer orientation and has carefully assessed its customer markets and given preliminary thought to how it might segment them, the next critical task is to develop a strategic marketing plan. Out of this plan will emerge day-to-day marketing tactics. To insure careful, consistent marketing planning, the organization should follow a Strategic Marketing Planning Process (SMPP).

The first step in the strategic planning process is to identify the organization's mission, objectives, and specific goals. The next step is to determine threats and opportunities in the external environment. This requires, first, an evaluation of the many publics the organization must consider. Organizations carry on exchanges with several publics. A public is a distinct group of people and organizations that have an actual or potential interest in or impact on an organization. Publics can be classified as input publics (donors, suppliers, and regulatory publics), internal publics (management, board, staff, and

volunteers), intermediary publics (merchants, agents, facilitators, and marketing firms), and consuming publics (clients, local publics, activist publics, general publics, media publics, and competitive publics). A public from which an organization seeks some response is called a market. A market is a distinct group of people, organizations, or both that have resources that they want to exchange, or might conceivably be willing to exchange, for distinct benefits.

The next step is to analyze the competitive environment. Here the organization must recognize that it has competitors at several levels: desire, generic, service form, and enterprise. Finally, the strategic planner must analyze the relevant macroenvironment and the specific market environment the organization faces.

The next step in the strategic planning process is to compare the opportunities and threats in the external environment to the organization's strengths and weaknesses to develop specific marketing goals, missions, and objectives that will achieve what top management has determined are real long-term objectives. One useful approach to this task is portfolio planning, in which the strategic planner assesses current and potential organizational offerings to determine which he or she should build, maintain, harvest, or terminate.

Following this analysis, the organization must develop core marketing strategies for each offer. This means selecting a target market segment or segments, choosing a competitive position, and developing an effective marketing mix to reach and serve the chosen customers. The marketing mix consists of the particular blend of offer, price, place, and promotion that the organization uses to obtain its objectives in the target market.

Once the core marketing strategy is set, the strategist must assure that the proper organizational structure and management systems are put in place, specific performance benchmarks are chosen, and detailed marketing tactics determined. The final steps then merely involve implementing the strategy and tactics and carefully assessing performance against the predetermined benchmarks. This final assessment then feeds back either immediately into on-the-run changes in core marketing strategy or more slowly into subsequent cycles of the strategic planning process itself.

Notes

1. See Peter F. Drucker, *Management: Tasks, Responsibilities, Practices* (New York: Harper & Row, 1973), Chapter 7.

2. For an advanced example of goal-setting in a university environment, see David P. Hopkins, Jean-Claude Larreche and William F. Massy, "Constrained Optimization of a University Administrator's Preference Function," *Management Science,* December 1977, pp. 365–77.

3. See David L. Sills, *The Volunteers—Means and Ends in a National Organization* (Glencoe, Ill.: Free Press, 1957). Also note that the National Center for Voluntary Action, 1785 Massachusetts Avenue, N.W., Washington, D.C., 20036, researches, runs seminars on, and disseminates up-to-date techniques on managing volunteers.

4. E. Jerome McCarthy and William D. Perreault, *Basic Marketing: A Managerial Approach,* 9th ed. (Homewood, Ill.: Richard D. Irwin, 1984).

CHAPTER 12

Crafting Strategy

HENRY MINTZBERG

I magine someone planning strategy. What likely springs to mind is an image of orderly thinking: a senior manager, or a group of them, sitting in an office formulating courses of action that everyone else will implement on schedule. The keynote is reason—rational control, the systematic analysis of competitors and markets, of company strengths and weaknesses, the combination of these analyses producing clear, explicit, full-blown strategies.

Now imagine someone *crafting* strategy. A wholly different image likely results, as different from planning as craft is from mechanization. Craft evokes traditional skill, dedication, perfection through the mastery of detail. What springs to mind is not so much thinking and reason as involvement, a feeling of intimacy and harmony with the materials at hand, developed through long experience and commitment. Formulation and implementation merge into a fluid process of learning through which creative strategies evolve.

My thesis is simple: the crafting image better captures the process by which effective strategies come to be. The planning image, long popular in the literature, distorts these processes and thereby misguides organizations that embrace it unreservedly.

In developing this thesis, I shall draw on the experiences of a single craftsman, a potter, and compare them with the results of a research project that tracked the strategies of a number of corporations across several decades. Because the two contexts are so obviously different, my metaphor, like my assertion, may seem far-fetched at first. Yet if we think of a craftsman as an organization of one, we can see that he or she must also resolve one of the great challenges the corporate strategist faces: knowing the organization's capabilities well enough to think deeply enough about its strategic direction. By considering strategy making from the perspective of one person, free of all the paraphernalia of what has been called the strategy industry, we can learn something about the formation of strategy in the corporation. For much as our potter has to manage her craft, so too managers have to craft their strategy.

At work, the potter sits before a lump of clay on the wheel. Her mind is on the clay, but she is also aware of sitting between her past experiences and her future prospects. She knows exactly what has and has not worked for her in the past. She has an intimate knowledge of her work, her capabilities, and her markets. As a craftsman, she senses rather than analyzes these things; her knowledge is "tacit." All these things are working in her mind as her hands are working the clay. The product that emerges on the wheel is likely to be in the tradition of her past work, but she may break away and embark on a new direction. Even so, the past is no less present, projecting itself into the future.

In my metaphor, managers are craftsmen and strategy is their clay. Like the potter, they sit between a past of corporate capabilities and a future of market opportunities. And if they are truly craftsmen, they bring to their work an equally intimate knowledge of the materials at hand. That is the essence of crafting strategy.

Strategies Are Both Plans for the Future and Patterns from the Past

Ask almost anyone what strategy is, and they will define it as a plan of some sort, an explicit guide to future behavior. Then ask them what strategy a competitor or a government or even they themselves haveactually pursued. Chances are they will describe consistency in past behavior—a pattern in action over time. Strategy, it turns out, is one of those words that people define in one way and often use in another, without realizing the difference.

The reason for this is simple. Strategy's formal definition and its Greek military origins notwithstanding, we need the word as much to explain past actions as to describe intended behavior. After all, if strategies can be planned and intended, they can also be pursued and realized (or not realized, as the case may be). And pattern in action, or what we call realized strategy, explains that pursuit. Moreover, just as a plan need not produce a pattern (some strategies that are intended are simply not realized), so too a pattern need not result from a plan. An organization can have a pattern (or realized strategy) without knowing it, let alone making it explicit.

Finding patterns in action organizations isn't much more difficult. Indeed, for such large companies as Volkswagenwerk and Air Canada, in our research, it proved simpler! Mapping the product mode at Volkswagenwerk from the late

1940s to the late 1970s, for example, uncovers a clear pattern of concentration on the Beetle, followed in the late 1960s by a frantic search for replacements through acquisitions and internally developed new models, to a strategic reorientation around more stylish, water-cooled, front-wheel-drive vehicles in the mid–1970s.

But what about intended strategies, those formal plans and pronouncements we think of when we use the term *strategy*? Ironically, here we run into all kinds of problems. Even with a single craftsman, how can we know what her intended strategies really were? If we could go back, would we find expressions of intention? And if we could, would we be able to trust them? We often fool ourselves, as well as others, by denying our subconscious motives. And remember that intentions are cheap, at least when compared with realizations.

Reading the Organization's Mind

If you believe all this has more to do with the Freudian recesses of a craftsman's mind than with the practical realities of producing automobiles, then think again. For who knows what the intended strategies of a Volkswagenwerk really mean, let alone what they are? Can we simply assume in this collective context that the company's intended strategies are represented by its formal plans or by other statements emanating from the executive suite? Might these be just vain hopes or rationalizations or ploys to fool the competition? And even if expressed intentions exist, to what extent do others in the organization share them? How do we read the collective mind? Who is the strategist anyway?

The traditional view of strategic management resolves these problems quite simply, by what organizational theorists call attribution. You see it all the time in the business press. When General Motors acts, it's because Roger Smith has made a strategy. Given realization, there must have been intention, and that is automatically attributed to the chief.

In a short magazine article, this assumption is understandable. Journalists don't have a lot of time to uncover the origins of strategy, and GM is a large, complicated organization. But just consider all the complexity and confusion that gets tucked under this assumption—all the meetings and debates, the man, people, the dead ends, the folding and unfolding of ideas. Now imagine trying to build a formal strategy-making system around that assumption. Is it any wonder that formal strategic planning is often such a resounding failure?

To unravel some of the confusion—and move away from the artificial complexity we have piled around the strategy-making process—we need to get back to some basic concepts. The most basic of all is the intimate connection between thought and action. That is the key to craft, and so also to the crafting of strategy.

Strategies Need Not Be Deliberate—They Can Also Emerge

Virtually everything that has been written about strategy making depicts it as a deliberate process. First we think, then we act. We formulate, then we implement. The progression seems so perfectly sensible. Why would anybody want to proceed differently?

Our potter is in the studio, rolling the clay to make a waferlike sculpture. The clay sticks to the rolling pin, and a round form appears. Why not make a cylindrical vase? One idea leads to another, until a new pattern forms. Action has driven thinking: a strategy has emerged.

In an organization of one, the implementor is the formulator, so innovations can be incorporated into strategy quickly and easily. In a large organization, the innovator may be ten levels removed from the leader who is supposed to dictate strategy and may also have to sell the idea to dozens of peers doing the same job.

Consider how the National Film Board of Canada (NFB) came to adopt a feature-film strategy. The NFB is a federal government agency, famous for its creativity and expert in the production of short documentaries. Some years back, it funded a film maker on a project that unexpectedly ran long. To distribute his film, the NFB turned to theaters and so inadvertently gained experience in marketing feature-

length films. Other filmmakers caught onto the idea, and eventually the NFB found itself pursuing a feature-film strategy—a pattern of producing such films.

My point is simple, deceptively simple: strategies can form as well as be formulated. A realized strategy can emerge in response to an evolving situation, or it can be brought about deliberately, through a process of formulation followed by implementation. But when these planned intentions do not produce the desired actions, organizations are left with unrealized strategies.

Today we hear a great deal about unrealized strategies, almost always in concert with the claim that implementation has failed. Management has been lax, controls have been loose, people haven't been committed. Excuses abound. At times, indeed, they may be valid. But often these explanations prove too easy. So some people look beyond implementation to formulation. The strategists haven't been smart enough.

While it is certainly true that many intended strategies are ill conceived, I believe that the problem often lies one step beyond, in the distinction we make between formulation and implementation, the common assumption that thought must be independent of (and precede) action. Sure, people could be smarter—but not only by conceiving more clever strategies. Sometimes they can be smarter by allowing their strategies to develop gradually, through the organization's actions and experiences. Smart strategists appreciate that they cannot always be smart enough to think through everything in advance.

Hands & Minds

No craftsman thinks some days and works others. The craftsman's mind is going constantly, in tandem with her hands. Yet large organizations try to separate the work of minds and hands. In so doing, they often sever the vital feedback link between the two. The salesperson who finds a customer with an unmet need may possess the most strategic bit of information in the entire organization. But that information is useless if he or she cannot create a strategy in response to it or else convey the information to someone who can—because the channels are blocked or because the formulators have simply finished formulating. The notion that strategy is something that should happen way up there, far removed from the details of running an organization on a daily basis, is one of the great fallacies of conventional strategic management. And it explains a good many of the most dramatic failures in business and public policy today.

We call strategies like the NFB's that appear without clear intentions—or in spite of them—emergent strategies. Actions simply converge into patterns. They may become deliberate, of course, if the pattern is recognized and then legitimated by senior management. But that's after the fact.

All this may sound rather strange, I know. Strategies that emerge? Managers who acknowledge strategies already formed? Over the years, our research group has met with a good deal of resistance from people upset by what they perceive to be our passive definition of a word so bound up with proactive behavior and free will. After all, strategy means control—the ancient Greeks used it to describe the art of the army general.

Strategic Learning

But we have persisted in this usage for one reason: learning. Purely deliberate strategy precludes learning once the strategy is formulated; emergent strategy fosters it. People take actions one by one and respond to them, so that patterns eventually form.

Our craftsman tries to make a freestanding sculptural form. It doesn't work, so she rounds it a bit here, flattens it a bit there. The result looks better, but still isn't quite right. She makes another and another and another. Eventually, after days or months or years, she finally has what she wants. She is off on a new strategy.

In practice, of course, all strategy making walks on two feet, one deliberate, the other emergent. For just as purely deliberate strategy making precludes learning, so purely emergent strategy making precludes control. Pushed to the limit, neither approach makes much sense. Learning must be coupled with control.

Likewise, there is no such thing as a purely deliberate strategy or a purely emergent one. No organization knows enough to work everything out in advance, to ignore learning en route. And no one—not even a solitary potter—can be flexible enough to leave everything to happenstance, to give up all control. Craft requires control just as it requires responsiveness to the material at hand. Thus deliberate and emergent strategy form the end points of a continuum along which the strategies that are crafted in the real world may be found. Some strategies may approach either end, but many more fall at intermediate points.

Effective Strategies Develop in all Kinds of Strange Ways

Effective strategies can show up in the strangest places and develop through the most unexpected means. There is no one best way to make strategy.

The form for a cat collapses on the wheel, and our potter sees a bull taking shape. Clay sticks to a rolling pin, and a line of cylinders results. Wafers come into being because of a shortage of clay and limited kiln space in a studio in France. Thus errors become opportunities, and limitations stimulate creativity. The natural propensity to experiment, even boredom, likewise stimulate strategic change.

Organizations that craft their strategies have similar experiences. Recall the National Film Board with its inadvertently long film. Or consider its experiences with experimental films, which made special use of animation and sound. For 20 years, the NFB produced a bare but steady trickle of such films. In fact, every film but one in that trickle was produced by a single person, Norman McLaren, the NFB's most celebrated filmmaker. McLaren pursued a personal strategy of experimentation, deliberate for him perhaps (though who can know whether he had the whole stream in mind or simply planned one film at a time?) but not for the organization. Then 20 years later, others followed his lead and the trickle widened, his personal strategy becoming more broadly organizational.

Conversely, in 1952, when television came to Canada, a consensus strategy quickly emerged at the NFB. Senior management was not keen on producing films for the new medium. But while the arguments raged, one filmmaker quietly went off and made a single series for TV. That precedent set, one by one his colleagues leapt in, and within months the NFB—and its management—found themselves committed for several years to a new strategy with an intensity unmatched before or since. This consensus strategy arose spontaneously, as a result of many independent decisions made by the filmmakers about the films they wished to make. Can we call this strategy deliberate? For the filmmakers perhaps; for senior management certainly not. But for the organization? It all depends on your perspective, on how you choose to read the organization's mind.

Grass-Roots Strategy-Making

These strategies all reflect, in whole or part, what we like to call a grass-roots approach to strategic management. Strategies grow like weeds in a garden. They take root in all kinds of places, wherever people have the capacity to learn (because they are in touch with the situation) and the resources to support that capacity. These strategies become organizational when they become collective, that is, when they proliferate to guide the behavior of the organization at large.

Of course, this view is overstated. But it is no less extreme than the conventional view of strategic management, which might be labeled the hot-house approach. Neither is right. Reality falls between the two. Some of the most effective strategies we uncovered in our research combined deliberation and control with flexibility and organizational learning.

Consider first what we call the umbrella strategy. Here senior management sets out broad guidelines and leaves the specifics to others lower down in the organization. This strategy is not only deliberate (in its guidelines) and emergent (in its specifics), but it is also deliberately emergent in that the process is consciously managed to allow strategies to emerge en route.

Deliberately emergent, too, is what we call the process strategy. Here management controls the process of strategy formation—concerning itself with the design of the structure, its staffing, procedures, and so on—while leaving the actual content to others.

Both process and umbrella strategies seem to be especially prevalent in businesses that require great expertise and creativity—a 3M, a Hewlett-Packard, a National Film Board. Such organizations can be effective only if their implementors are allowed to be formulators because it is people way down in the hierarchy who are in touch with the situation at hand and have the requisite technical expertise. In a sense, these are organizations peopled with craftsmen, all of whom must be strategists.

Strategic Reorientations Happen in Brief, Quantum Leaps

The conventional view of strategic management, especially in the planning literature, claims that change must be continuous: the organization should be adapting all the time. Yet this view proves to be ironic because the very concept of strategy is rooted in stability, not change. As this same literature makes clear, organizations pursue strategies to set direction, to lay out courses of action, and to elicit cooperation from their members around common, established guidelines. By any definition, strategy imposes stability on an organization. No stability means no strategy (no course to the future, no pattern from the past). Indeed, the very fact of having a strategy, and especially of making it explicit (as the conventional literature implores managers to do), creates resistance to strategic change!

What the conventional view fails to come to grips with, then, is how and when to promote change. A fundamental dilemma of strategy making is the need to reconcile the forces for stability and for change—to focus efforts and gain operating efficiencies on the one hand, yet adapt and maintain currency with a changing external environment on the other.

Quantum Leaps

Our own research and that of colleagues suggest that organizations resolve these opposing forces by attending first to one and then to the other. Clear periods of stability and change can usually be distinguished in any organization: while it is true that particular strategies may always be changing marginally, it seems equally true that major shifts in strategic orientation occur only rarely.

Our colleagues, Danny Miller and Peter Friesen, found this pattern of change so common in their studies of large numbers of companies that they built a theory around it, which they labeled the quantum theory of strategic change.[1] Their basic point is that organizations adopt two distinctly different modes of behavior at different times.

Most of the time they pursue a given strategic orientation. Change may seem continuous, but it occurs in the context of that orientation and usually amounts to doing more of the same, perhaps better as well. Most organizations favor these periods of stability because they achieve success not by changing strategies but by exploiting the ones they have. They, like craftsmen, seek continuous improvement by using their distinctive competencies in established courses.

While this goes on, however, the world continues to change, sometimes slowly, occasionally in dramatic shifts. Thus gradually or suddenly, the organization's strategic orientation moves out of sync with its environment. Then what Miller and Friesen call a strategic revolution must take place. That long period of evolutionary change is suddenly punctuated by a brief bout of revolutionary turmoil in which the organization quickly alters many of its established patterns. In effect, it tries to leap to a new stability quickly to reestablish an integrated posture among a new set of strategies, structures, and culture.

But what about all those emergent strategies, growing like weeds around the organization? What the quantum theory suggests is that the really novel ones are generally held in check in some corner of the organization until a strategic revolution becomes necessary. Then as an alternative to having to develop new strategies from scratch or having to import generic strategies from competitors, the organization can turn to its own emerging patterns to find its new orientation. As the old, established strategy disintegrates, the seeds of the new one begin to spread.

This quantum theory of change seems to apply particularly well to large, established, massproduction companies. Because they are especially reliant on standardized procedures, their resistance to strategic reorientation tends to be especially fierce. So we find long periods of stability broken by short disruptive periods of revolutionary change.

Cycles of Change

In more creative organizations, we see a somewhat different pattern of change and stability, one that's more balanced. Companies in the business of producing novel outputs apparently need to fly off in all directions from time to time to sustain their creativity. Yet they also need to settle down after such periods to find some order in the resulting chaos.

The National Film Board's tendency to move in and out of focus through remarkably balanced periods of convergence and divergence is a case in point. Concentrated production of films to aid the war effort in the 1940s gave way to great divergence after the war as the organization sought a new raison d'être. Then the advent of television brought back a very sharp focus in the early 1950s, as noted earlier. But in the late 1950s, this dissipated almost as quickly as it began, giving rise to another creative period of exploration. Then the social changes in the early 1960s evoked a new period of convergence around experimental films and social issues.

We use the label *"adhocracy"* for organizations, like the National Film Board, that produce individual, or custom-made, products (or designs) in an innovative way, on a project basis.[2] Our craftsman is an adhocracy of sorts too, since each of her ceramic sculptures is unique.

Whether through quantum revolutions or cycles of convergence and divergence, however, organizations seem to need to separate in time the basic forces for change and stability, reconciling them by attending to each in turn. Many strategic failures can be attributed either to mixing the two or to an obsession with one of these forces at the expense of the other.

The problems are evident in the work of many craftsmen. On the one hand, there are those who seize on the perfection of a single theme and never change. Eventually the creativity disappears from their work and the world passes them by—And then there are those who are always changing, who flit from one idea to another and never settle down. Because no theme or strategy ever emerges in their work, they cannot exploit or even develop any distinctive competence. And because their work lacks definition, identity crises are likely to develop, with neither the craftsmen nor their clientele knowing what to make of it. Miller and Friesen found this behavior in conventional business too; they label it "the impulsive firm running blind."[3]

To Manage Strategy Is to Craft Thought and Action, Control and Learning, Stability and Change

The popular view sees the strategist as a planner or as a visionary, someone sitting on a pedestal dictating brilliant strategies for everyone else to implement. While recognizing the importance of thinking ahead and especially of the need for creative vision in this pedantic world, I wish to propose an additional view of the strategist—as a pattern recognizer, a learner if you will—who manages a process in which strategies (and visions) can emerge as well as be deliberately conceived. I also wish to redefine that strategist, to extend that someone into the collective entity made up of the many actors whose interplay speaks an organization's mind. This strategist finds strategies no less than creates them, often in patterns that form inadvertently in its own behavior.

What, then, does it mean to craft strategy? Let us return to the words associated with craft: dedication, experience, involvement with the material, the personal touch, mastery of detail, a sense of harmony and integration. Managers who craft strategy do not spend much time in executive suites. They are involved, responsive to their materials, learning about their organizations through personal touch. They are also sensitive to experience, recognizing that while individual vision may be important, other factors must help determine strategy as well.

Manage Stability

Managing strategy is mostly managing stability, not change. Indeed, most of the time senior managers should not be formulating strategy at all, they should be getting on with making their organizations as effective as possible in pursuing the strategies they already have. Like distinguished craftsmen, organizations become distinguished because they master the details.

To manage strategy, then, at least in the first instance, is not so much to promote change as to know when to do so. Advocates of strategic planning often urge managers to plan for perpetual instability in the environment (for example, by rolling over five-year plans annually). But this obsession with change is dysfunctional. Organizations that reassess their strategies continuously are like individuals who reassess their jobs or their marriages continuously—in both cases, people will drive themselves crazy or else reduce themselves to inaction. The formal planning process repeats itself so often and so mechanically that it desensitizes the organization to real change, programs it more and more deeply into set patterns, and thereby encourages it to make only minor adaptations.

So-called strategic planning must be recognized for what it is: a means, not to create strategy, but to program a strategy already created—to work out its implications formally. It is essentially analytic in nature, based on decomposition, while strategy creation is essentially a process of synthesis. That is why trying to create strategies through formal planning most often leads to extrapolating existing ones or copying those of competitors.

This is not to say that planners have no role to play in strategy formation. In addition to programming strategies created by other means, they can feed ad hoc analyses into the strategy-making process at the front end to be sure that the hard data are taken into consideration. They can also stimulate others to think strategically. And of course people called planners can be strategists too, so long as they are creative thinkers who are in touch with what is relevant. But that has nothing to do with the technology of formal planning.

Detect Discontinuity

Environments do not change on any regular or orderly basis. And they seldom undergo continuous dramatic change, claims about our "age of discontinuity" and environmental "turbulence" notwithstanding. (Go tell people who lived through the Great Depression or survivors of the siege of Leningrad during World War II that ours are turbulent times.) Much of the time, change is minor and even temporary and requires no strategic response. Once in a while there is a truly significant discontinuity or, even less often, a gestalt shift in the environment, where everything important seems to change at once. But these events, while critical, are also easy to recognize.

The real challenge in crafting strategy lies in detecting the subtle discontinuities that may undermine a business in the future. And for that, there is no technique, no program, just a sharp mind in touch with the situation. Such discontinuities are unexpected and irregular, essentially unprecedented. They can be dealt with only by minds that are attuned to existing patterns yet able to perceive important breaks in them. Unfortunately, this form of strategic thinking tends to atrophy during the long periods of stability that most organizations experience. So the trick is to manage within a given strategic orientation most of the time yet be able to pick out the occasional discontinuity that really matters.

Craftsmen have to train themselves to see, to pick up things other people miss. The same holds true for managers of strategy. It is those with a kind of peripheral vision who are best able to detect and take advantage of events as they unfold.

Manage Patterns

Whether in an executive suite in Manhattan or a pottery studio in Montreal, a key to managing strategy is the ability to detect emerging patterns and help them take shape. The job of the manager is not just to preconceive specific strategies but also to recognize their emergence elsewhere in the organization and intervene when appropriate.

Like weeds that appear unexpectedly in a garden, some emergent strategies may need to be uprooted immediately. But management cannot be too quick to cut off the unexpected, for tomorrow's vision may grow out of today's aberration. (Europeans, after all, enjoy salads made from the leaves of the dandelion, America's most notorious weed.) Thus some patterns are worth watching until their effects have more clearly manifested themselves. Then those that prove useful can be made deliberate and be incorporated into the formal strategy, even if that means shifting the strategic umbrella to cover them.

To manage in this context, then, is to create the climate within which a wide variety of strategies can grow. In more complex organizations, this may mean building flexible structures, hiring creative people, defining broad umbrella strategies, and watching for the patterns that emerge.

Reconcile Change and Continuity

Finally, managers considering radical departures need to keep the quantum theory of change in mind. As Ecclesiastes reminds us, there is a time to sow and a time to reap. Some new patterns must be held in check until the organization is ready for a strategic revolution, or at least a period of divergence. Managers who are obsessed with either change or stability are bound eventually to harm their organizations. As pattern recognizer, the manager has to be able to sense when to exploit an established crop of strategies and when to encourage new strains to displace the old.

While strategy is a word that is usually associated with the future, its link to the past is no less central. As Kierkegaard once observed, life is lived forward but understood backward. Managers may have to live strategy in the future, but they must understand it through the past.

Like potters at the wheel, organizations must make sense of the past if they hope to manage the future. Only by coming to understand the patterns that form in their own behavior do they get to know their capabilities and their potential. Thus crafting strategy, like managing craft, re-

quires a natural synthesis of the future, present, and past.

Notes

1. See Danny Miller and Peter H. Friesen, *Organizations: A Quantum View* (Englewood Cliffs, N.J.: Prentice-Hall, 1984).

2. See my article "Organization Design: Fashion or Fit?" HBR January–February 1981, p. 10.3; also see my book *Structure in Fives: Designing Effective Organizations* (Englewood Cliffs, N.J.: Prentice-Hall, 1983). The term *adhocracy* was coined by Warren G. Bennis and Philip E. Slater in *The Temporary Society* (New York: Harper & Row, 1964).

3. Danny Miller and Peter H. Friesen, "Archetypes of Strategy Formulation," *Management Science,* May 1978, p. 921.

PART 5

FUND-RAISING: GENERATING REVENUES

Well-run nonprofit organizations raise funds in many ways and from a variety of sources, but most limit their fund-raising activities and sources of funds to those that "fit with" their mission and the strengths and skills of their staff and volunteers. Some nonprofit organizations raise most of their funds from private sources, for example, private and corporate foundations,[1] corporate gifts, and contracts for services; others appeal to the general public through special events, person-to-person community fund-raising drives, and direct mail campaigns; other religious, fraternal, and professional membership organizations approach their members; others turn to government agencies for grants, contracts, and subsidies; and yet others raise funds from sales of goods and services to recipients or such third-party payers as private schools and colleges, museum gift shops, client-staffed pet stores, hospitals, and home health agencies.

Types of Fund-Raising Strategies and Sources

Fund-raising strategies and sources can be grouped into the following categories.

Donations From
Individuals and families, and their trusts
Public and private foundations
Federated funding sources

Grants From
Corporations
Government agencies (for example, the National Institutes of Health)

Federated funding sources (for example, the United Way's)
Foundations (for example, community, corporate, and family)

Sales of Goods and Services from
- Contracts with government agencies
    To provide services or goods to clients of government agencies (third party
    payment arrangements)
    To provide goods or services to government agencies
- Contracts with corporations to provide services or goods
- Sales to individuals
- Sales to other nonprofit organizations

Fees, Dues, and Pledges from Members

Interest and Investment Income

Although most of these broad categories of fund-raising activities and sources are relatively self-explanatory, the category titles mask an almost infinite variety of innovative fund-raising tactics and arrangements. For example, there are many types of "sales of goods and services" to individuals, including cause-related marketing arrangements through which contractual "win-win partnerships" are formed. A business uses a nonprofit's name in promotional advertising, and the nonprofit receives a percentage of the sales or sales increase in exchange. (For more on this, see Alan R. Andreasen, "Profits for Nonprofits: Find a Corporate Partner," reprinted in Chapter 11.)

There are also many varieties of "donations." With a *charitable remainder trust,* for example, an individual or family makes a (large) gift, the gift assets are transferred to a trustee, the family receives income on the value of the assets for a specified number of years and, when the time is over, the assets and the income they generate are transferred to a preselected nonprofit. In contrast, a *charitable lead trust* allows an individual or family to transfer income-yielding assets to a trust for a specified period during which the income flows to a chosen nonprofit organization. When the period is up, the assets and the income from them are returned to the family.

Special events usually combine "donations" and "sales of goods and services." Individuals and corporations buy donated goods and services or they pay more than market value for them. In addition, corporations and sometimes government agencies may become "sponsors"—another variety of donation.

Within the category "sales of goods and services" some sales are paid for by the recipient, and others are paid for or reimbursed by a "third-party payer," such as an insurance company or a government program.

All varieties of revenue-generating activities have advantages and disadvantages for nonprofit organizations. They require different skills, time commitments, and types of efforts by board members and staff; often they involve multiple arrangements with government agencies or businesses. Different fund-raising activities also have different levels of expected pay-outs. Thus, some fund-raising strategies fit with different types of nonprofit organizations better than others. Many larger nonprofits can afford to devote considerable skilled staff effort, for example, to writing grants or organizing celebrity-studded gala events that most smaller nonprofits are not staffed to handle. Nonprofits that serve sympathy-evoking clients and causes can employ fund-raising strategies and tap sources that may not be available to nonprofits that serve unpopular causes or stigmatized populations. Nonprofits enjoying high status in the community can require members of the board of trustees to make large contributions annually and to solicit donations from their friends and associates. Many nonprofits are not as fortunate, however, and are happy when they can merely fill all the vacant board "seats"; a request for these trustees to donate or solicit funds would not be received well—and might even cause some trustees to resign.

Trustees and Fund-Raising

The trustees are at the heart of fund-raising in most nonprofits. Numerous studies have shown that most larger donations are made people to people—more so than to organizations or causes. When a respected peer who serves on a board asks for a major gift to an organization or cause, we are more likely to reach for our checkbook or credit card. "To the extent that trustees are active in the community, are givers themselves, and are not afraid to ask for money, the organization will be more successful in the fund-raising effort. Furthermore, the fiscal health of the organization depends on the extent to which the trustees feel that the income gap (the difference between what is earned and what is expended) is their responsibility."[2]

All Fund-Raising Strategies Have Advantages and Disadvantages

Almost all types of fund-raising activities place some restrictions on the nonprofit organization. Corporate partnership arrangements, for example, often prevent the nonprofit from entering arrangements with other corporations. Acceptance of United Way funding historically has required nonprofits to refrain from soliciting other funding from participating employers (for example, corporate sponsorships of special events). Government contracts to provide services may require a nonprofit to accept clients whom the nonprofit would not ordinarily serve—or to limit the quantity of services provided to some individuals. A nonprofit organization's reliance on government contracts or a corporate marketing program may cause individual donors to give to other causes in the belief that the organization doesn't need their gifts. Restricted gifts can commit a nonprofit to a long-term program or project that may decline in importance over the years, or to a project that requires a substantial amount of additional funding—thereby possibly creating organizational rigidity or draining limited resources.

The decision to pursue a certain funding source also reduces options. Once a nonprofit has committed itself to one or two major fund-raising activities in a year, it is locked in. Few nonprofits have enough staff members and volunteers to pursue multiple sources of funding simultaneously. It is important, therefore, to select carefully.

Recent Trends in Nonprofit Revenue Sources

Sources of revenue have changed markedly over the last three decades for organizations in the nonprofit sector.[3] From 1977 to 1992, for example, private contributions declined from 26.3 percent to 18.4 percent of U.S. nonprofit organizations' total annual revenues. During those same fifteen years, government payments increased from 26.6 percent to 31.3 percent, and private payments increased from 37.5 percent to 39.1 percent.[4] The percentages have continued to shift ever since.

The percent of income that nonprofit organizations receive from government varies by subsector and function, from a high of 42 percent in social and legal services, 36 percent in health services, and 17 percent in education to a low of 11 percent in the arts.[5] At the same time that many nonprofits have increased their reliance on government contracts as steady sources of revenue, the total amount of U.S. government money flowing into the human services, the arts, and environmental protection has been declining steadily—sometimes dramatically.[6] States, counties, and cities have not been anxious to replace the declining funds at a time when political pressures for tax and deficit reductions continue to enjoy public support.

Despite the cutbacks, government reliance on nonprofits—and thus government as a source of income—has continued to grow, particularly through contracts for services for persons with mental illness, disabilities (including developmental disabilities), chemical dependencies, youth (including gangs), the elderly, families, individuals who need job training, and victims of abuse (including legal services). Government funding also helps to support and coordinate the arts and to provide financial support, for example, to national parks, seashores, and rivers. Some states—Massachusetts and New Jersey, for instance—provide almost no direct human services because virtually all such services have been contracted out to nonprofits.[7] This growing reliance—or dependence—on government contracts comes at a timewhen government funding appears to be in a long-term decline. The government "downsizing, devolution, and diffusion movement" of the 1990s peaked at a time when individual and corporate donations to nonprofit organizations had been stagnant and, by many measures, declining.

Income from private and government payments now represent larger sources of nonprofit sector income than donations. Individual and corporate donations, historically the largest source of nonprofit sector revenues, remained level and even declined as a percentage of income during most of the 1990s. At least partly because of declining contributions, nonprofits have been under pressure to be more "entrepreneurial"—to pursue alternative sources of revenue if they are to survive. Nonprofit organizations have also been doing much better at meeting this "charge" than expected; they have been selling services and products aggressively and often compete for business directly with for-profit firms. (See Part 6, "Entrepreneurship and Commercialism.")

Readings Reprinted in Part Five

Erna Gelles defines "Fund Raising"[8] as "the century-old process by which nonprofit organizations formally secure the necessary capital or in-kind resources to pursue their missions." Gelles provides a concise overview of fund-raising sources and practices, the relationship between fund-raising and philanthropy, and the problems encountered in fund-raising when the environment is uncertain and changing—as has been the case for most of the past three decades in the United States. She divides funding sources into three broad categories: "(1) public, or government funding; (2) mixed funding, which includes donations from individuals, corporation and foundation grants, federated funding sources, and special event revenues as well as sales revenue; and (3) fees or service charges," and thoughtfully discusses the advantages and disadvantages of the sources.

In *"Diversification of Revenue Strategies: Evolving Resource Dependence in Nonprofit Organizations,"*[9] Karen Froelich examines the effects of three major revenue-generating strategies and the "resource dependence" that evolves when nonprofits become reliant on any of the three sources: private contributions, government funding, and commercial activities. Froelich also assesses four effects that these three strategies or sources have on nonprofit organizations: (1) revenue volatility, (2) goal displacement effects, (3) process effects, and (4) structure effects. Thus, for example, revenue volatility is high with private contributions, low with government funding, and moderate with commercial activity. The primary structural effect of private contri-butions is professionalized administration, whereas government funding leads to pro-fessionalized bureaucracy, and commercial activity to professionalized business forms.

Goal displacement "occurs when goals and activities are modified to satisfy the wishes of contributors. . . . A variation of goal displacement that is referred to as *creaming* involves shifting an organization's programs into areas that have greater appeal to donors." Also, foundation funding can cause goal displacement. Too often, rather than seek funds that "fit" them and their clients, nonprofits write grants for ac-tivities that foundations are likely to fund but are less likely to attract foundation support.

Government contracts have a formalizing "process effect" on nonprofits. Gov-ernments often require their contracted nonprofits to professionalize their staffs and bureaucratize their organizations, and they may take away some administrative autonomy.

As nonprofits increasingly strive to diversify their fund-raising strategies and avoid dependence on one or more limited sources, they need to be aware of the effects that different funding strategies will have on the organization, staff, volunteers, and clients. "Each revenue strategy has its appeal and current niches of opportunity but also carries constraints and pressures that may impinge on the autonomy of the organization. . . . Revenue diversification brings new concerns and greater complexity."

"Returns on Fundraising Expenditures in the Voluntary Sector,"[10] by Adrian Sargeant and Jürgen Kähler, reports on the comparative effectiveness of various fundraising methods. Sargeant and Kähler mailed questionnaires to the fund-raising departments of the United Kingdom's top 500 fund-raising charities. The charities were asked to identify the total amount of direct costs they had incurred for each of the fund-raising activities they had engaged in during the previous twelve months and the total revenue they had generated in each category of revenue. The cate-gories of fund-raising activities included: direct mail—recruitment; direct mail—de-velopment; telemarketing; door-to-door distribution; direct-response press advertis-ing; major gift fund-raising; local ("special events") fund-raising; corporate fund-raising; and trust fund-raising.

The overall comparative effectiveness of each fund-raising category was deter-mined by an index of the reported total revenue divided by the total cost—a measure similar to a "cost-benefit ratio." "Major gift fundraising" was far-and-away the most effective fund-raising category, followed by "trust fund-raising," "corporate fund-raising," and "direct mail—development." "Door-to-door distribution" and "direct-response press advertising" were the least effective methods, both of which cost more, on average, than they returned. The authors note, however, that some fund-raising methods serve secondary purposes and thus should not be ignored solely because of mediocre performance on this measure of effectiveness.

Sargeant and Kähler also examined several other variables; for example, the most commonly used category of fund-raising was "corporate fundraising" (used by 85.7 percent of the charities during the twelve-month period), with direct mail recruitment, direct mail development, and trust fund-raising tied for second (used by 66.7 percent). Using their index of return divided by cost, they also examined the fund-raising effectiveness of charities that serve different purposes and found that "religious—internal aid," "religious-welfare," and "animal protection" were most successful. "Charities concerned with the provision of care or support for persons with a physical disability consistently perform less well than all other categories of cause." They also determined that there "would appear to be no relationship between the returns that a charity is able to generate from each activity and its size." The sole exception is "corporate fund-raising," where larger charities have a marked advantage.

In an essay about foundations as distinctive revenue sources for nonprofit organizations (and as nonprofit organizations themselves), Elizabeth Boris defines "Foundations"[11] as "nonprofit, nongovernmental organizations that promote charitable giving and other public purposes usually by giving grants of money to nonprofit organizations, qualified individuals, and other entities. Under U.S. law, philanthropic foundations must serve the public by being organized and operated exclusively for religious, charitable, scientific, testing for public safety, literary, or educational purposes." Boris explains the differences between public foundations and private foundations, and among the three types of private foundations: independent foundations, operating foundations, and community foundations.

Foundations were not used widely until the turn of the twentieth century. Although "the foundation as an institution was an innovation, it evolved from long-standing traditions of secular and religious giving as well as popular reform movements. . . . The early foundations were formed before the adoption of a national income tax. . . . By 1917, Congress enacted a charitable tax deduction for donors, and in 1919 deductions were permitted for charitable gifts made from estates after the death of the donor."

"Foundations" also provides an overview of major achievements and common criticisms of foundations, how government regulates foundations, and patterns of governance, grant-making procedures, typical staffing patterns, and foundations worldwide.

Notes

1. For an excellent overview of the different types of foundations, see Elizabeth T. Boris, "Foundations," reprinted in this part.

2. Thomas Wolf, *Managing a Nonprofit Organization in the Twenty-first Century* (New York: Fireside, 1999), 239.

3. Sources of income vary widely across the nonprofit subsectors. See Virginia Ann Hodgkinson and Murray S. Weitzman, "Overview and Executive Summary: The State of the Independent Sector," in V. Hodgkinson and M. Weitzman, *Nonprofit Almanac 1996–1997: Dimensions of the Independent Sector* (San Francisco: Jossey-Bass, 1996), 1–21.

4. Virginia Ann Hodgkinson and Murray S. Weitzman, *Nonprofit Almanac 1996–1997: Dimensions of the Independent Sector* (San Francisco: Jossey-Bass, 1996), 5.

5. Julian Wolpert, "How Federal Cutbacks Affect the Charitable Sector," in Lynn A Staeheli, Janet E. Kodras, and Colin Flint, eds., *State Devolution in America: Implications for a Diverse Society* (Thousand Oaks, CA: Sage, 1997), 100.

6. Lester M. Salamon, "The Current Crisis," in L. Salamon, *Holding the Center: America's Nonprofit Sector at a Crossroads* (New York: Nathan Cummings Foundation, 1997), 11–47; and Virginia A. Hodgkinson, Murray Weitzman, et al, *Dimensions of the Independent Sector, 1992–93* (San Francisco: Jossey-Bass, 1996).

7. Steven R. Smith and Michael Lipsky, *Nonprofits for Hire* (Cambridge: Harvard University Press, 1993).

8. Erna Gelles, "Fund Raising," in Jay M. Shafritz, ed., *International Encyclopedia of Public Policy and Administration* (Boulder: Westview Press, 1998), 953–957.

9. Karen A. Froelich, "Diversification of Revenue Strategies: Evolving Resource Dependence in Nonprofit Organizations," *Nonprofit and Voluntary Sector Quarterly*, 28, no. 3 (September 1999):246–268.

10. Adrian Sargeant, and Jürgen Kähler, "Returns on Fundraising Expenditures in the Voluntary Sector," *Nonprofit Management & Leadership* 10, no. 1 (fall 1999): 5–19.

11. Elizabeth T. Boris, "Foundations," in Jay M. Shafritz, ed., *International Encyclopedia of Public Policy and Administration* (Boulder: Westview Press, 1998), 928–935.

► CHAPTER 13

Fund-Raising

ERNA GELLES

The century-old process by which non-profit organizations formally secure the necessary capital or in-kind resources to pursue their missions. Fundraising is often referred to as the process of development. Nevertheless, some in the nonprofit management field distinguish between fund raising and development and suggest that development is the primary task of fund-raisers (Harrah-Conforth and Borsos 1991). Despite this distinction, fund-raising executives are often referred to as development officers, without the distinction.

Fund-raising, or development, is foremost a practitioner's field, guided by the public's demand for professional standards as incalculable numbers of tax free donations move from individuals to organizations domestically and internationally every day. It is a field that is maturing; one that has begun to rely on publications and accreditation procedures in recent years. It is a field wherein processes and techniques are explored and analyzed and information is disseminated among professional fund-raisers through a growing body of literature. (See the References for organizations and some titles of their various publications.)

Various methods for fund-raising have become commonplace. Prominent among these are establishing and maintaining an annual fund

and its drive; employing computer programs to facilitate mass marketing efforts and direct mail solicitation and developing organizational-specific information campaigns about the mission, goals, achievements, and credibility of the organization seeking funds; and capital fund raising campaigns or drives for major projects. Fund-raising executives also engage in establishing and maintaining additional techniques to establish planned giving programs. Fund-raising professionalism and its trappings (specifically, certification and formalized ethical standards) result from the recognition among development personnel that the marketplace for funds is competitive and that organizational survival requires fund-raisers to be professional in their demeanor and communications as they pursue, court, and maintain major contributors.

Fund-raising professionals manage a diverse array of components, including the human resources within an organization and the organization's board of directors. In contrast, professional itinerant consultants are more often sought by small organizations unable to afford professional in-house development personnel but in need of guidance and fund-raising expertise.

Development officers rarely neglect the organization's board of trustees. This is traditionally a significant potential source of organizational sponsorship. The concept of the "power board" stems directly from the board members' capacity to provide or bring sizable donations to the organization. Development officers, as nonitinerant experts, must work to develop such boards in a way that often requires a combination of nurturing and aggressive bottomline oriented behavior.

As implied, development officers must also manage technological resources. Computer databases can be relatively simple or extremely sophisticated. Most common are those that serve the fund-raiser as he or she seeks to develop and maintain records on prior and likely donors. The more sophisticated programs incorporate coding capacity for specific interests of prior donors, from the grass roots to the corporate level. Fund-raisers who use this capacity are able to compose "personal" letters by the thousands and post them to potential contributors. More advanced systems include coding schemes by which responses to those various solicitations can be analyzed; this analysis allows the development team to refine and further personalize the next wave of requests.

The concept of strategic management in the use of resources and in the development process is common to this growing professional fund-raising field. Strategic management includes the need for managers to place resources in boundary-spanning efforts, to assure that the organization will not be caught offguard when environmental uncertainty results in heavy demands upon the organization or in a necessary change in the direction of its mission.

Nonprofit organizations serve as a link between the private corporate world, with its bottom-line economic concerns, and the public sector's inability or disinclination to provide services in (for example) the social needs realm, the arts, education, and health care. Fund-raising executives, or in-house development officers, play an integral part by providing a guided outlet for philanthropy and human need. They serve as a linkage between what John Filer (head of the Commission on Private Philanthropy and Public Needs [1975]) called the "donor" and the "donee."

Fund-Raising and Philanthropy

Fund-raising is conceptually associated with philanthropic capacity and action. The philanthropist possesses the funds that he or she chooses to donate to various or specific causes, for a variety of reasons. Such giving may result from pure magnanimous desire, independent of or (in contrast to) a direct link to the desire for public recognition. The desire to share may be a quiet anonymous act of generosity. Or, giving may have little to do with charity or recognition but may be tied to concerns about the tax liability of the donor's estate. Individual giving tends to result from a combination of these and other personal factors. Without philanthropy, large and small, fund-raising as a practitioner's field would not likely have developed. It is the institutionalized techniques of the professional fund-raiser that guide beneficence, helping organizations to serve their clients and fulfill their missions, while providing feedback to fund-raising executives, guiding them and influencing research important to their field, both practical and theoretical.

As noted in *Giving in America* (Commission 1975), philanthropic services rarely pay for themselves. Central to an understanding of philanthropic activity is that donated funds encourage the extension of benefits (charitable, educational, cultural, or social activist) to individuals regardless of their ability to pay. And since most nonprofit activities do not lend themselves to economies of scale, nonprofit organizations experience what was referred to in *Giving in America* as a costly irony; with fees rarely covering the full cost of the social, educational, or artistic service; "the more successful philanthropic 'pioneering' has been in terms of reaching more people, the greater [its] operating deficit (Commission 1975, p. 85)." In effect, as fundraising succeeds, it is even more necessary.

The 1990s have witnessed a documented increase in fund-raising activities separate from philanthropy. Through the efforts of their in-house fund-raising personnel, organizations are seeking earned revenue through setting fees, creating for-profit subsidiaries (more than in years past), and developing unrelated business income ventures through product sales, as well as responding to a growing interest in the potential of the special event fund-raiser. In addition, competition is increasing among agencies seeking donations from all sources (Gronbjerg 1993). Some of this competition among organizations stems from the early 1980s government budget cuts to social programs, which were followed by the mid-1980s economic downturn. This resulted in increased service demand on the more limited sector capacity. The traditional source of funding during the twentieth century has been government. With government funding cuts, competition for funds among service providers has increased.

Environmental Uncertainty

To understand fund-raising, it is necessary to explore what Kirsten Gronbjerg (1993) calls a world of "multiple and disparate funding sources" and "diverse organizational environments" (p. xi). Fund-raising techniques, activities, and successes hinge on diverse organizational environments and missions. At the root of all fund-raising is environmental uncertainty and the reality of organizational dependence on external funding sources.

Environmental exigencies place greater demands on the services of nonprofits but at the same time threaten their capacity to provide the services. When corporate profits decline, or questionable ethical behaviors among federated fund-raising executives are exposed (as they have been during the latter part of the twentieth century and ought to be if they occur), organizations dependent upon funding from these sources are confronted with a loss of funds. The result is organizational or program instability. This instability follows directly from public anger and uncertainty with the ethics of this mode of fund-raising.

The relationship between corporate donations through employee contributions and nonprofit organization viability is symbiotic, and the ramifications are broad. Even when nonprofit managers presume that they are independent of the corporate donors in a community, the result of corporate fiscal stress can have an indirect and powerful impact on the unwitting nonprofit manager. Frequently, when a corporate sponsor of a specific nonprofit organization faces bankruptcy, greater demands are placed on the sponsors that remain in the community. Organizations that have never directly benefited from the bankrupt organization's largess are affected. Donations suffer as the pool of philanthropic sources becomes smaller and competition for the more limited funds increases.

Professional nonprofit development officers must use creative techniques to deal with this type of environmental instability: What appears to be external to the nonprofit organization is often unanticipated by less-seasoned managers. One technique of dealing with this problem is to use managerial participation in boundary-spanning activities (Gronbjerg 1993) within the corporate or local community-activities that help organizations anticipate dramatic changes in resource availability. Such activities can serve to inform the nonprofit service provider of the probability of an increased demand for its services.

This type of corporate fiscal stress has a paradoxical quality. At the same time that philanthropic funds are ceasing to flow from the corporate sponsor to the nonprofit provider, employees of the corporation are losing their jobs, and nonprofit social service entities in the region are faced with an increased client load. This increased demand on the local nonprofit community comes from former corporate employees now seeking services, as well as from layoffs from other firms in the region, which are dependent on the corporate employees' business for their business's prior livelihood.

Development requires that fund-raisers also analyze the various demands of divergent funders. As Kirsten Gronbjerg (1993) has noted, demand complexity may be high

> if organizations receive funding from many streams of the same type. That is because nonprofit managers must give a minimum amount of attention to each discrete funding stream, to ensure that the exchange relationship meets the

expectations of both participants. The larger the number of such relationships the organization maintains . . . the less likely the organization is to know the specific interests and concerns of individual funders. Therefore, the greater is the uncertainty it encounters (p. 58).

Funding Sources

Funding sources for nonprofits fall into three broad categories: (1) Public, or government funding; (2) mixed funding, which includes donations from individuals, corporation and foundation grants, federated funding sources, and special event revenues as well as sales revenues; and (3) fees or service charges. Boundarywise organization managers seek a variety of funding sources to avoid overexposure to capricious local economies.

Public Fund-Raising

Public fund-raising has both costs and benefits for nonprofit organizations, including (in exchange for the possibility of large government contracts) the need by organizational managers to keep abreast of the budget negotiation process, as well as the political and organizational ramifications inherent in shifting governmental priorities. With grants as well as purchases of service contracts, organizations must meet reporting requirements and be willing to adhere to legislative or agency-defined rules and regulations, which often dramatically limit managerial discretion. Gronbjerg (1993, p. 197) wrote about strategies nonprofits can employ to affect control on the vagaries of the public funding process, but successful strategic behavior tends to remain in the domain of only the largest of nonprofit organizations: those with skilled, politically astute managers who have the ability to remain informed of the various contingencies as they seek out new and stable revenue sources.

When nonprofit organizations seek public funding they are giving up some organizational autonomy, and often they do so because the funds are critical to the organization's ability to fulfill its ongoing mission within a particular

program area. At times, the funds are necessary for the organization's virtual survival. Managers must accept whatever statutory or regulatory limits to funds are imposed and create organizational reserves to buffer them against the environmental uncertainty inherent in the capricious political funding environment.

Clients need to be protected. And, if not at the onset of funding, during a later funding cycle organizations often face a dramatic dilemma: to comply with new public funding guidelines that alter the organization's mission or to seek alternative, more limited, sources of revenue, with fewer strings but less to offer. One alternative is to engage in grant writing to foundations (identified later as a source of mixed-funding); this also entails complying with external demands, but these demands tend to be less politically capricious and may allow the organization to remain true to its mission and its most needy clients. Foundations often have specific programmatic objectives, and an organization's external quest for funds may threaten the organization's mission. The difference between these two types of funding sources is that although foundations tend to have a political focus that may result in an organization or program director having to confront mission issues, foundations do not change their leadership every two, four, or six years, and their goals tend to be more stable in the long term. When they are seeking foundation support, professional fund-raisers must be aware of the limits and liabilities inherent in the funding requirements.

Mixed-Funding: Donations

Even though the nondistribution constraint prohibits the distribution of profits or dividends, organizations (as a fund-raising tool) may solicit, receive, and maintain capital resources in the form of donated stocks, bonds, or physical property. One fund-raising technique that is becoming more common as the World War II baby boom generation matures and receives inheritances from its elders is the request for bequests (to be remembered in one's will) or requests from savvy development officers to potential donors for contributions of inherited securities. Usually a long-term technique, appeals for donations of this sort come with a promise to the donor of lifelong income based on the securities' earnings. The intent is to safeguard, for the organization, ownership of the stocks or bonds when the donor eventually passes away. Real estate property, too, is often sought as a donation. Real estate may not cost the organization money in property taxes and can provide a consistent base of rental income. The Catholic Church has for generations owned and maintained this type of property, and now smaller religious and nonreligious nonprofit organizations are beginning to focus their development efforts in property acquisition.

When nonprofit fund-raising includes solicitation of stocks and securities—investment capital that can, over time, provide a secure source of revenue for the organization or one of its pet programs—the "donee" (see Commission 1975) will often apply normative criteria to the types of gifts to be accepted. Tobacco stock, for example, is not readily sought by health care providers, nor is utility stock eagerly sought by groups working on environmental issues (although such groups often hold a small number of shares in such corporations to allow them access to stockholders' meetings).

Mixed-Funding: Federated Fund-Raising

Federated fund-raising drives traditionally refer to the organized efforts of United Way agencies or community chests. In this type of drive, individuals are asked to make annual contributions to an organization that serves as a clearinghouse for a large number of "worthy" organizations within a community. Traditionally, Boys' and Girls' Clubs, Big Brother and Big Sister organizations, and various quasi-religious organizations—such as the YMCA, YWCA, Jewish Community Center Association, and the Salvation Army—that provide for needy individuals of all denominations benefit from federated fund drives. In the contemporary climate wherein family planning is often linked to abortion services, some organizations such as Planned Parenthood, which have benefited historically from

federated-fund campaigns, have been dropped from the pool of recipient organizations. This action has forced them to join the large number of independent (nonfederated or creatively federated) nonprofit organizations that must seek revenues from other sources through fees, memberships, and annual, biannual, or multiannual campaigns.

One lucrative fund-raising method pioneered by federated campaigns, such as the United Way, is the workplace campaign. In this drive, employers are asked to contribute through payroll deductions. This procedure brings to the federated campaign extremely large overall contributions (small donations made by thousands of employees on a weekly or monthly basis) and carries with it a community legitimacy. Yet, it simultaneously thwarts myriad local, often very small, organizations not included on the federated-fund-raising recipient list. In the last decade of the twentieth century, complaints from smaller, independent nonprofits (those that are not federated with the community chests) have often resulted in a more inclusionary policy. Various local mechanisms have been established by the federated campaigns to include more organizations in the workplace solicitation and fund-distribution process, although the proportion of overall contributions afforded to the newer participants is significantly lower than that provided to the older, established federation recipient members. The process continues to undergo review within local communities that have active organizations seeking greater equity in fund-raising.

A new type of federated effort appeared in the early 1990s with the advent of electronic data processing methods and with the competition brought about by the breakup of the American Telephone and Telegraph monopoly. Credit card companies and telephone service providers have begun to offer various federated donation options. Customers can "join" a particular service, and when they use their credit card or phone system, they are ensured that a percentage of every dollar spent will be donated to one of a group of predetermined charities or organizations.

Environmental and social action groups from all political persuasions, often left out of the traditional federated campaigns, have found this federated route to be a lucrative supplement to their own fund-raising efforts. Unlike United Way affiliates—which distribute overall funds based on a formula defined by a local volunteer board and require that their member organizations (recipients) agree to limit their independent fund-raising efforts—these newer electronic federations each define their own system of fund distribution, often querying their contributors with annual questionnaires for philanthropic direction.

Fees and Memberships

Fees for service are a common method by which nonprofit organizations maintain their programming. Traditionally, tuition is charged at nonprofit colleges and private schools as the primary fund-raising tool. Yet, due to the nonprofit service mission of many educational institutions, such fees are often kept artificially low. This practice allows a broader range of students to enroll in the institution but requires a consistent fund-raising campaign to boost revenues to meet expenses. Schools often engage in sophisticated annual fund-raising campaigns to allow them to provide tuition or fee abatement. Sliding-scale fee reduction to needy families is also employed.

Colleges and universities with successful intercollegiate athletic departments are often able to raise large sums from alumnae seeking access to sporting events. The extent to which such fees are maintained for the benefit of the athletic program varies from institution to institution, but in recent years the needs of academic departments have seen the advent of formal demands from within the institution for a more-balanced proceeds distribution structure. Techniques for interinstitutional sharing vary but may include a required "contribution" to the university's general fund from those seeking preferred alumnae status in the purchase of season tickets to sports events, particularly when the tickets are costly and in high demand.

Membership fees to nonprofit organizations are also often provided on a sliding scale; this is common when professional organizations offer variable membership rates for students, retirees, and fully employed members. These rates are often based on a standard scale, but sometimes an additional categorical scale is defined in which members identify their level of household income and pay an annual membership fee based on this reported income status. When membership organizations do this, they often must rely on the good faith and honesty of their membership since the process necessary to confirm need is often inefficient and may offend potential members. Religious institutions frequently encounter this problem and the institution's board of directors may vote to establish a confidential procedure to confirm a parishioner or member's claim to indigence and need. In contrast, a simple procedure is sometimes employed, wherein to obtain a special membership rate or reduction based on income an individual must provide evidence of current status, enrollment, or otherwise.

Membership fees provide a stable base of income and are less capricious than funding secured from an annual special event. Yet as more and more organizations seek memberships, those with similar goals have begun to enter into a competitive marketplace to entice members. When this occurs, membership drives promise not only to provide the obvious service (such as quality programming on public radio or television, or a subscription to a professional journal or zoo magazine) but also offer to provide the member with an item of extrinsic value, such as a coffee mug, an umbrella, a calendar, or a tote bag. These items provide a dual service to the organization: The membership fee is viewed to be more competitive because a gift is included, and the gift often serves as an advertising tool. People carrying tote bags with the name of the museum act as advertising agents. Under federal law, the item received must be deducted from the tax-deductible membership fee to the organization, so such advertising is not publicly supported.

Another fund-raising technique used by nonprofit organizations with access to the airwaves is the use of the corporate challenge gift. This is the process whereby individuals or companies seek to leverage their support for a philanthropic cause or nonprofit organization during a public fund-raising campaign by requiring that a specific amount be raised from the general public prior to making a sizable donation.

Special events such as bike-a-thons, marathons, golf tournaments, concerts, and auctions are common fundraising methods employed by many organizations. School children are often involved; and recent research indicates that the demographic bump of post-World War II baby boomers, as a group, may give more readily when they can be physically involved in the process through some type of sporting event or physical competition organized to raise money for a cause.

Professional fund-raisers or development officers find that if their organization chooses to be involved in large-scale, ongoing campaigns of great significance (in health care, education, community development, or the arts, for example) they need to seek not only memberships and fees for services rendered but also additional revenues from granting agencies, corporations, or individuals, and sometimes government contracts. This desire, or the organizational need that comes from environmental uncertainty and fiscal stress, pressures the fund-raising personnel constantly and requires an ongoing attentiveness and professional focus, both intrinsic and extrinsic to the organization. Although fund-raisers may enter the field without professional training, once employed they find that other requisites of the profession (such as ethics and communication with others in the field through conferences and professional publications) are essential to their, and their organization's, success.

References

American Association of Fund-Raising Council (AAFRC), annual. *Giving USA*. New York: AAFRC.

_____, quarterly. *Giving USA Update*. New York: AAFRC.

Burlingame, Dwight F., and Lamont J. Hulse, 1991. *Taking Fund Raising Seriously: Advancing the Profession and Practice of Raising Money*. San Francisco: Jossey-Bass Nonprofit Sector Series.

Chronicle of Philanthropy, biweekly (see various issues). Washington, D.C.

Clotfelter, Charles. 1985. *Federal Tax Policy and Charitable Giving,* Chicago: University of Chicago Press.

Commission on Private Philanthropy and Public Needs, 1975. *Giving in America*. Washington, DC: Commission.

Cutlip, Scott. 1965. *Fund Raising in the United States: Its Role in American Philanthropy*. New Brunswick, NJ: Rutgers University Press.

Filer Commission. See Commission on Private Philanthropy and Public Needs.

Fund Raising Management, monthly (see various issues). Garden City, NY: Hoke Communications.

Gronbjerg, Kirsten A., 1993. *Understanding Nonprofit Funding: Managing Revenues in Social Services and Community Development Organizations*. San Francisco: Jossey-Bass Nonprofit Sector Series.

Harrah-Conforth, Jeanne, and John Borsos, 1991. "The Evolution of Professional Fund Raising: 1890–1990," 18–36. In Dwight F. Burlingame, and Lamont J. Hulse, *Taking Fund Raising Seriously: Advancing the Profession and Practice of Raising Money*. San Francisco: Jossey-Bass Nonprofit Sector Series.

National Charities Information Bureau (NCIB) (formerly National Information Bureau), quarterly publications include *Standards in Philanthropy* and *Wise Giving Guide*. New York.

National Council on Philanthropy (in 1980 merged with the Coalition of National Voluntary Organizations to create Independent Sector in Washington, D.C.). See its various publications.

National Society of Fund-Raising Executives (NSFRE) (formerly the National Society of Fund Raisers), quarterly *NSFRE Journal*. Alexandria, VA.

Seymour, H. J., 1966. *Designs for Fund-Raising*. Rockville, MD: Taft Group.

CHAPTER 14

Diversification of Revenue Strategies

Evolving Resource Dependence in Nonprofit Organizations

KAREN A. FROELICH

Nonprofit organizations must rely on a variety of activities and resource providers to support their mission-related work. The classic image is that of traditional fundraising to attract charitable donations from individuals and corporations for socially valued programs. Another common revenue strategy is the pursuit of grants and contracts from foundation and government sources. A more controversial approach involves commercial activities, such as selling products to customers or charging fees for program services. Increasing reliance on program service fees and other types of commercial activity is accompanied by anxiety and criticism as sector observers and participants anticipate its potential negative influence on organizational actions and missions (Bush, 1992; Kramer, 1985; Powell & Owen-Smith, 1998; Salamon, 1989; Tuckman, 1998; Weisbrod, 1998). However, potential negative effects associated with the more familiar revenue-generating activities and providers are seldom acknowledged. This article examines the effects of various revenue strategies in nonprofit organizations.

Evolving Resource Dependence in Nonprofit Organizations

Continual change in the environments associated with major resource providers translates into specific threats and emerging opportunities for nonprofit funding. As a result, shifting sources of funds and altered dependency relationships have been observed.

Private contributions, including individual and corporate donations and foundation grants, form a traditional cornerstone of support for nonprofit organizations. However, this source of funding has generally been declining as a percentage of total revenue.

Funding from government sources has varied over time with changes in political leadership and public policy initiatives. Increasing government funding occurred in the 1960s as the War on Poverty and related social programs were largely implemented through NPOs; the pattern was reversed throughout the 1980s as a Republican administration drastically reduced federal spending for such programs. In 1974, government funding composed a national average of approximately 46% of the income of United Way agencies (Kramer, 1986). Hodgkinson and Weitzman (1986) estimate this at 34% in the sector overall in 1980, and 27% in 1986 (Hodgkinson & Weitzman, 1988). Ten years later, apparently rebounding from the program cuts of the Reagan era, government funding increased to 32% of sector income (Boris, 1998). Much of this increase can be attributed to the growth of Medicare and Medicaid spending, as well as other entitlement programs impacted by the continually rising costs of health care (Hodgkinson & Weitzman, 1996). Thus, for many segments of the nonprofit sector outside of the health care field, the percentage of total revenue provided from government sources is still declining (Boris, 1998).

A funding approach gaining popularity as an alternative or supplement to traditional sources of nonprofit support involves various forms of commercial activity. This might include selling goods and services unrelated to the nonprofit's mission, as when a museum operates a snack bar or rents out excess space; selling goods and services related to the mission, as in museum gift stores or expert art preservation services; or directly charging fees for basic program services, such as admission fees. Commercial activities related to the mission and linked to program services appear to be far more common than unrelated activities (Hodgkinson, Weitzman, Noga, & Gorski, 1993; Young, 1998). Program service fees accounted for 25% of total revenue in 1980 (Hodgkinson & Weitzman, 1986), and grew to 38% in 1986 (Hodgkinson & Weitzman, 1988) and to 39%—the sector's largest single source of income—in 1996 (Boris, 1998). In essence, clients and customers have become the primary resource providers in the nonprofit sector, rather than donors or government entities.

That new revenue providers are being sought by nonprofit organizations is not surprising, given the growing uncertainty and resource scarcity associated with the traditional sources of income. This predictable evolution causes alarm, however, because so little is known about commercial funding strategies and their ultimate impact on the structure, behavior, philosophies, and performance of nonprofit organiza

tions. The predominant concern is clearly expressed as Weisbrod (1998) asks, "Can nonprofits simultaneously mimic private enterprise and perform their social missions?" (p. 167).

Apprehension about the possible side effects of commercial activity appears to overshadow the realities of donor and government funding criteria and their constraining influence in nonprofit organizations. Familiarity with the traditional funding sources seems to make their influence less visible or more noble. The following sections draw on the literature to review constraints associated with dependence on private contributions and government funding, and explore potential impacts of commercial strategies in nonprofit organizations.

Private Contributions

Private contributions include funds from individual donors, corporate donors, and foundations. Individual giving vastly exceeds that of the other two sources, representing 85% of private contributions in 1997, with corporate and foundation gifts comprising 6% and 9%, respectively (Boris, 1998). Private contributions are revered in NPOs as they provide not only income but indicate support for an organization's mission among constituents, thus representing legitimacy (Fogal, 1994; Gronbjerg, 1993). Similarly, Weisbrod (1998, p. 168) describes the "pure" nonprofit organization as one dependent entirely on donations, ideally without strings attached so that the organization can use the funds totally at its own discretion. This favored status and optimistic presumption may help explain why the constraints imposed by private contributions are often overlooked.

Individual Contributions

Much of the literature related to individual contributions centers on fund-raising as opposed to the funds raised. Controversies surrounding unethical practices, frequently involving outside paid solicitors rather than NPO employees, have tarnished the image of charitable giving and particular organizations (Kelly, 1998). Concerns

about excessive fund-raising costs also have negative impacts on nPO (Young, Bania, & Bailey,
1996). Aside from the fund-raising issues, two
major constraints associated with dependence
on individual contributions can be identified
from the literature: revenue volatility and goal
displacement.

Gronbjerg's (1992, 1993) case studies of NPO
revenue strategies describe the unpredictability
and instability of individual contributions. Reports of more than a 50% annual change in the
total amount received were common. Executive
directors expressed difficulties in planning for
the future or even in assuring stable operating
monies when faced with this volatility. Moreover, they perceived little control over the
amount of funds raised, as the disconnection
between donors and services provides limited
opportunity to directly influence donors via
nonprofit programming. Acquiring donations
absorbed considerable staff, board, and volunteer effort, diverted attention from other vital
functions, and steered selection of board members to those with personal networks for solicitation targets. In the end, the NPO still had to be
braced for major funding fluctuations due to the
volatility of individual donations.

A potentially more serious side effect of individual contributions is goal displacement, which
occurs when goals and activities are modified to
satisfy the wishes of contributors. Although contributed funds are typically assumed to be flexible and unencumbered, "the discretion and flexibility may be more imagined than real"
(Gronbjerg, 1993, p. 146). A survey of 296 National Society of Fund Raising Executives employed in NPOs reports that approximately 25%
of the respondents admitted altered organizational goals or priorities to acquire a particular
contribution (Kelly, 1998). Additional anecdotal
evidence abounds, describing philanthropic individuals who, through large or frequent gifts,
can steer program activities to the point of requiring recipients to hire specific people (Langley, 1998; Tuckman, 1998). It appears that funding campaigns today are increasingly anchored
by a few lead donors who typically restrict the
use of their major gifts (Kelly, 1991), which fuels
fears that small numbers of wealthy elite exert

unhealthy levels of influence over nonprofit organizations (Odendahl, 1990).

DiMaggio's (1986a, 1986b) qualitative study
of arts organizations describes the influence of
major patrons with less concern than the aggregate impact of the average donor. Whereas the
former might often defer to the expertise of respected artistic staff and be more supportive of
innovation and artistic vision, the latter was
found to mainly support established prestigious
organizations, excluding nontraditional or experimental endeavors. This observation is important, as the common assumption is that
small donors have small impact and are unable
to influence the goals and activities of organizations (Kelly, 1991).

A variation of goal displacement that is referred to as creaming involves shifting an organization's programs into areas that have greater
appeal to donors (Boris & Odendahl, 1990).
Scott's (1974) comprehensive case study of services for the blind documents a proliferation of
programs that evoke emotions of sympathy and
hope as well as dollars from the donating public.
Although employable adults and children compose less than 30% of the blind population,
roughly 90% of the organizations dedicated to
serving the blind focused primarily or exclusively on these groups. Further impacts included
the inadvertent creation of stereotypes and high
levels of competition among service providers
for the limited number of targeted clients.
Milofsky and Blades (1991) report similar findings in their case study of health charities; diseases that affect minorities, adults, or other potentially less appealing populations attracted less
support than those that arouse more sympathy
from the public. And, in cases where popular
personalities were afflicted by a particular disease, related charities grew faster than other
charities. More broadly, the shifting of priorities
to match somewhat faddish funding criteria has
been considered a key failure in the treatment
and delivery of human services (Rossi, 1978).

Corporate Contributions

Corporations contribute to nonprofit organizations in several major ways. In-kind gifts of

property and services, including use of facilities and employee time, are common. Cash contributions, however, predominate. Monetary contributions may be made directly by a corporation or by a company-sponsored foundation (Useem, 1987). Many of the constraints accompanying corporate contributions mirror the revenue volatility and goal displacement effects explained above; additional impacts on nonprofit processes and structure are also noted.

Revenue volatility can be problematic; substantial year-to-year variation in corporate contributions was found in Gronbjerg's (1993) case studies, although the volatility was less than that of individual contributions. Shifting corporate giving patterns portend even greater threat for NPOs in arts and community action, as contributions are increasingly redirected toward education (Hodgkinson & Weitzman, 1986) and international endeavors (Kelly, 1998). This can be at least partially explained by a corporation's desire to avoid controversial issues that might cause negative publicity and consumer backlash, as well as to provide support leading to more direct benefits for the corporation itself (DiMaggio, 1986a; Powell & Friedkin, 1986; Useem, 1987).

The link between a corporation's contribution patterns and its own self-interest appears to be getting tighter. Whereas top managers still play a powerful role in the allocation of corporate gifts (Useem & Kutner, 1986), major contributions are likely to be part of a broader marketing plan rather than disconnected acts of benevolence (Useem, 1987). Variously referred to as cause-related marketing or enlightened self-interest, carefully targeted giving practices can result in goal displacement in recipient organizations (Kelly, 1998).

DiMaggio (1986a) reports that, similar to individual contributions, corporate support for the arts generally goes to established mainstream organizations that will produce a highly visible program of broad appeal. Salamon (1987) found comparable trends in a broad-based survey of 3,400 NPOs. Nonprofits in pursuit of corporate funding can become strongly influenced by these corporate public relations objectives (Kelly, 1998). For example, a study of

public television programming demonstrates the impact of corporate funding on target audiences as well as on program offerings and content (Powell & Friedkin, 1986). Interviews with station employees revealed that it is easier to acquire support for programs directed toward well-educated, high-income audiences or influential male viewers; obtaining funds for programs aimed at other audiences can be considerably more challenging. Similar to this, corporate donors prefer to sponsor programs with broad national interest; funding for local programming is more difficult due to the smaller audience size. Although respondents insisted that program content was not influenced by corporate support, they demonstrated the opposite via "self-censoring" (Powell & Friedkin, 1986, p. 261) behavior that continually pressured stations to provide programming more readily salable to corporations.

Goal displacement risk appears to be higher in the increasingly popular partnerships between corporations and nonprofit organizations, where jointly sponsored programs formally and directly involve corporations in program governance. According to Useem (1987), this new form of corporate philanthropy "is probably more closely aligned to immediate corporate self-interest, more professionalized in execution, and more transforming of the recipient organizations" (p. 353) than other corporate giving practices.

Beyond revenue volatility and goal displacement, corporate contributions have also been associated with process and structure change in nonprofit organizations. The professionalization of corporate giving practices throughout the 1970s resulted in less ad hoc giving and more formalized procedures involving contribution officers and committees. Formalization is especially pronounced in the corporate foundations, which operate more independently and with less top management influence. Criteria for gift allocation, including statements of mission and measures of efficiency and effectiveness, created reciprocal pressures for more formalized procedures directed by specialized managerial staff in NPOs. The influence of corporate board members, frequently included as directors to facilitate solicitation of corporate gifts, and the impact of loaned corporate managers further reinforced the process and structure changes. Over time, a professionalized form of administration emerged, and nonprofit organizations have increasingly come to resemble for-profit corporations (Kelly, 1998; Peterson, 1986; Useem, 1987).

Foundation Grants

Independent foundations function in much the same way as corporate foundations, using professional staff and formalized procedures to allocate grant funds, and they similarly reinforce professionalization in nonprofit organizations (DiMaggio, 1986b). However, the impacts of foundation grants related to process and structure change, as well as goal displacement and income volatility, are likely greater than that of corporate philanthropy.

Ylvisaker (1987) attributes the power of foundations to their vast amounts of money and the ability to concentrate and leverage funds via highly visible selection rituals. Major foundation grants often exceed $1 million and provide multiyear support as well as the prestige associated with being a selected recipient. Venerable foundations such as Ford and Carnegie can extend their influence far beyond the selected organizations merely by announcing programmatic themes and demonstrating approval of particular organizational characteristics; hopeful applicants imitate recipients in preparation for competitive proposal review. Foundation priorities are further extended through requirements for matching funds or cosponsorships. The cumulative consequence is a potent capacity for foundation influence in nonprofit organizations.

The influence of foundation support can lead to goal displacement, as grant funds are typically restricted to purposes defined by the foundation. A pioneering study of 123 sheltered workshops demonstrates that income from grants and organizational orientation are not independent; specifically, the study found that workshops with a rehabilitation orientation were significantly more likely to have income from grants than workshops with a production orientation (Kimberly, 1975). A more recent study

finds that foundations primarily support traditional and established arts programs, most often art museums and symphony orchestras, and provide little support for innovative art forms (DiMaggio, 1986c). Additional evidence suggests that foundations seldom provide flexible support for an organization to pursue its own goals, but tend to initiate the agenda through grant priorities (Kelly, 1991). For example, much of the grant funding in arts has been aimed at attracting new audiences via modified programming and added services (DiMaggio, 1986a; Peterson, 1986). This becomes especially problematic when the grant provides seed money for a new program but inadequate operating support. A spiraling need for funds is created, which can lead to the seemingly backwards scenario where a grant recipient must reallocate its own internal funds toward fulfillment of the grantor's purposes (Kelly, 1991).

The case studies of Gronbjerg show that high levels of effort are expended by NPOs to monitor evolving foundation priorities and package program proposals in conformance with the criteria. And, because foundation initiatives are not stable over time, income volatility is associated with this source of revenue (Gronbjerg, 1992, 1993). Long-term initiatives and multiyear grants buffer the fluctuations, but the large size and episodic nature of many grants (DiMaggio, 1986c) establishes volatility as a constraint associated with foundation funding.

Government Funding

Dependence on government grants and contracts has been associated with various expressions of goal displacement as well as marked process and structure constraints. Revenue volatility, however, appears less a concern with government funds than with private contributions. A study of 75 NPOs serving the handicapped lists "greater security of income" as one advantage of public funds (Kramer, 1981, p. 165). In Gronbjerg's (1993) studies, government funding is portrayed as the most stable revenue source, especially in social service. Respondents stressed the continuity and predictability of government support; one director referred to a major contract as "money in the bank" (Gronbjerg, 1993, p. 173).

The most pronounced effects of government funding involve changes in internal processes and ultimately in the structures of nonprofit organizations. Overwhelming evidence points to government-driven professionalization, bureaucratization, and loss of administrative autonomy. Conclusions of a broad study of government-funded NPOs are clearly expressed by Nielsen (1979), "as a direct consequence of their financial dependence, Third Sector institutions have become entangled in an increasingly dense web of government rules and regulations and have lost a large degree of control over their own policies, procedures, and programs" (p. 18). Peterson (1986) concurs, describing how government agencies require far more formalized and standardized documentation, evaluation, and accountability than other patrons of the arts. Groups lacking such procedures or emphasizing programming ill-fitted to the standardized criteria find it difficult to access government funds. Gradual adaptation occurs, resulting in government as the primary force driving out the technical experts in arts management in favor of professional arts administrators, many of whom know little about the art forms they are managing.

The process and structure transformations eventually impinge on mission and goals, mainly through changing the character of service delivery. Responsiveness to the needs of clients is subordinated to equitable treatment of the public, effectiveness is superseded by accountability, program and method variety are lost to standardization, and the nonprofit's discretion is tightly constrained by government contract expectations (Lipsky & Smith, 1990). In essence, the nonprofit organization risks losing its unique character as it increasingly mirrors the structure and behavior of a government agency (Ferris, 1993; Kramer, 1989; Salamon, 1987; Tucker, 1981). Overall, it appears that the constraints accompanying government funding display complex interactions that cause direct as well as indirect consequences for nonprofit organizations.

Commercial Activity

Commercial activity is not a new endeavor for nonprofit organizations; examples can be found in the United States dating back to the early 1900s (Salamon1989; Weisbrod 1989). Today, however, nonprofits are becoming increasingly dependent on various forms of commercial activity (Weisbrod 1998). Itnot only represents the largest single source of nonprofit revenue but also the most rapidly growing source (Young, 1998), estimated to account for 55% of revenue growth between 1977 and 1989 (Salamon, 1992). This trend is not universally embraced by nonprofit participants and observers, however, and is accompanied by substantial controversy. Whereas private contributions are considered a rather sacred source of nonprofit support, commercial activity is often viewed as sacrilegious.

The concerns surrounding increasing commercialism center on the potential loss of values distinctive to the nonprofit sector. The essence of charity is to provide needed goods and services to the poor—in other words, to those who cannot pay (Hodgkinson, 1989). Nonprofits also foster the expression of ideas and pursuit of values that lack adequate support from either the government or the marketplace (Hansmann, 1987), as seen in community action or arts organizations. If their pursuits must pass the test of the marketplace, worthy endeavors might be discarded (DiMaggio, 1986a). If a cooperative and benevolent spirit is replaced by a mindset of competition, fundamental attributes of charitable organizations might be in danger (Bush, 1992). In general, the fear is that nonprofits will become so like business firms that the social missions will take a backseat to revenue and profitability goals (Bush, 1992; Kramer, 1985; Weisbrod, 1997, 1998), leading to an identity crisis in the sector, a loss of legitimacy, and eventual elimination of special privileges and protections for nonprofit organizations (Hansmann, 1989; Hodgkinson, 1989; Powell & Owen-Smith, 1998; Salamon, 1989).

Although commercial activity is often considered the "hottest area of nonprofit funding" (Kramer, 1985, p. 388), studies directly examining the effects of commercial activity in non-profit organizations are just emerging in the literature. Results thus far suggest that revenue volatility is moderate, albeit amplified by the potential for failed commercial ventures. Some process and structure adaptations have been observed but there is little evidence of goal displacement, as commercial revenues seem less restricted than other revenue sources. On balance, it appears that commercial revenues enable greater flexibility and autonomy for nonprofit organizations than traditional forms of support.

Research findings related to the volatility of commercial revenues are mixed. Gronbjerg's (1992, 1993) case studies are in themselves inconclusive. However, she explains that funding stability involves not just continuity, but predictability and controllability. The latter two attributes are present to a greater degree with self-generated revenue than with funds from outside sources, especially in larger organizations, so the volatility observed is mitigated by these factors. The financial risk associated with venture failure is also relevant, and again, research findings are mixed but do not suggest high volatility.

Effects of commercial activity on organizational processes appear to be minor yet related to structural modifications that have been observed. Peterson's (1986) study of accountability in cultural organizations finds that ancillary revenue-generating activities such as gift shops and restaurants foster more rational accountability practices along with a cost-benefit mentality. Widespread spillover of these adaptations to activities more central to the mission has not been documented. There is some evidence, however, of increasing numbers of finance and marketing personnel in arts organizations (DiMaggio, 1986b) and a tendency to replace traditional, social problem-focused board members with entrepreneurial, business-oriented individuals in voluntary social agencies (Adams & Perlmutter, 1991) in response to higher levels of earned income.

More pronounced structural changes are evident in the variety of organizational forms that a nonprofit might adopt for conducting business. A recent study tracks the increasing commercialization of life sciences research, and accompany-ing growth in university licensing and patenting. Administrative offices to manage the profit-seeking efforts are also growing in number and scope. Related internal governance mechanisms are likely to expand, as they appear inadequate at present to handle the potential conflicts of interest and academic freedom issues (Powell & Owen-Smith, 1998). More generally, NPOs are increasingly found to use structural forms commonly associated with for-profit firms. This includes the application of business franchise approaches to nonprofit associations (Knoke, 1993; Young, 1989); the use of mergers and consolidations (Eckel & Steinberg, 1993; Tuckman, 1998), strategic alliances (Gray, 1991), or vertical integration (Weisbrod, 1997) to achieve market power; the formation of for-profit subsidiaries and/or joint ventures with for-profit or other nonprofit organizations (Gray, 1991; Gronbjerg, 1993; McGovern, 1989; Tuckman, 1998; Weisbrod, 1988, 1997); and what has been called "the ultimate commercialism," the conversion of nonprofit organizations to for-profit firms (Goddeeris & Weisbrod, 1998, p. 215).

Empirical evidence to date does not establish goal displacement as a common correlate of commercial revenue. To the contrary, studies report the flexibility advantages of these funds, and the resultant ability of NPOs to support existing or new programs and serve more clients (Adams & Perlmutter, 1991; Gronbjerg, 1993; Nielsen, 1984; Young, 1998). In general, nonprofits seem to use the flexibility responsibly.

Diversification of Revenue Strategies

To support their missions in an increasingly challenging resource environment, NPOs seek funding not only from individual and corporate donors, foundations, and government sources, but also via a variety of commercial activities. We have seen how each revenue strategy presents constraints specific to the pressures exerted by major resource providers.

A strategy relying on private contributions is associated with higher revenue volatility compared to the other funding strategies. Goal displacement effects are also greater, evidenced by donor facilitation of broadly acceptable traditional pursuits, and encouraging controversy avoidance and tempered innovation in recipient organizations. Restrictions accompanying gifts from large donors, foundations, and corporations also lead to goal displacement via the creaming phenomenon, and internal resource reallocations to subsidize underfunded donor initiatives. The formalization and professionalization of foundation and corporate giving creates accommodating formalized processes and professionalized administration in nonprofit organizations.

A revenue strategy anchored by government funding exhibits low revenue volatility. The cost of income stability is moderately strong goal displacement effects. Although public funds are broadly accessible and support a wide range of missions, government mandates influence both program features and choice of clientele. The allure of stability also creates new programs and NPOs directly in response to current funding thrusts. Underfunded programs and requirements cause internal resource reallocations that magnify the goal displacement effects. A variation of goal displacement in which internal procedures come to dominate attention and supersede outcome goals emerges from the striking effects of government funding on NPO processes. Government funding involves exacting adherence to minute details, intense monitoring, and prolific reporting. This requires highly formalized and standardized procedures, consuming efforts to achieve compliance, and substantially reduced administrative autonomy. The resulting structure can be described as a professionalized bureaucracy similar to that of government agencies.

Commercial strategies show moderate revenue volatility, directly influenced by organizational size, skill, and industry context. Commercial activities have shown little impact on organizational goals, as they typically are strongly related to and directly supportive of a nonprofit's mission. Commercial revenues are perceived to be the least restrictive and most flexible source of funds, enabling subsidization of existing programs and responsiveness to

emerging client needs and program opportunities. Effects of commercial strategies on processes and structures involve greater use of for-profit business techniques. Organizational processes become more rationalized, with explicit cost-benefit considerations in ancillary income activities. Gradual structural adaptations include expanded roles for business professionals, either as employees or board members. More drastic change is seen in the array of new structural forms now employed by nonprofit organizations, including various subsidiary and joint venture options.

Considered within the context of the revenue profiles above, calls of alarm over commercial strategies seem exaggerated. It is clear that each source of funds, not just commercial activity, is accompanied by side-effects that are often similar across various revenue strategies. Moreover, commercial activity appears to have weaker goal displacement effects compared to traditional strategies. A recurring tendency for negative reaction to change is demonstrated here, as nearly identical calls of alarm followed the shift to government funding throughout the 1960s. Salamon (1987) articulates concerns surrounding government funding as "dangers to agency independence, pursuit of agency purposes, and internal management style that may result from involvement with public programs" (pp. 115–116). Today, Weisbrod (1998) captures similar apprehensions as he wonders how NPOs can maintain their social missions and unique character while increasingly turning to commercial activities and operating like business-oriented firms. Basically, it appears that we do not trust nonprofit organizations to maintain their mission focus and distinctive style when faced with external pressures accompanying resource acquisition.

It is important to acknowledge that all revenue strategies have advantages and disadvantages; the ideal scenario with continuous flows of funds for unencumbered mission pursuit is not and never has been the reality for nonprofit organizations. Rather, a variety of funding sources exist, each associated with particular constraints and different management tasks (Gronbjerg, 1993). A key to organizational viability and integrity is to understand the opportunities and tradeoffs, choose revenue strategies that are consistent with the mission, and conscientiously respond to management challenges presented by each strategy (Gronbjerg, 1991). Basically, an organization must manage rather than be controlled by its resource dependencies, and continually adapt its strategies to the resource environment (Pfeffer & Salancik, 1978).

The increase in commercial activity is an example of adaptation to evolving resource realities. Fiscal pressures caused by the growing number of NPOs and simultaneous restraint in government and donor funding, and aggravated by increasing costs and service demands, have led to pressing needs for new sources of income (Cain & Meritt, 1998; Weisbrod, 1997, 1998; Young, 1998). This occurs at a time when consumers are purchasing more service products such as health care, personal counseling, day care, and fitness activities. The service realm has long been the domain of NPOs; thus, market opportunities are expanding precisely in areas where nonprofits have a substantial presence and highly developed skills (Salamon, 1989). This supports the pre-diction that increasingly creative forms of commercial activity will continue as nonprofit organizations explore the potential of this funding source (Weisbrod, 1997).

Whereas some may view the movement to commercial strategies as one of opportunity, others see it as a necessity. Regardless, the addition of another income stream is evidence of the increasing diversification of revenue strategies in NPOs today. The diversification is consistent with prescriptions for reducing resource dependence and maintaining organizational autonomy (Pfeffer & Salancik, 1978; Thompson, 1967). Rather than relying on a narrow set of resource providers, which nonprofits have experienced as an extremely vulnerable position, organizations buffer themselves with commercial activities where they exercise greater control over the stability and predictability of income. The new strategies bring additional constraints as well as altered dependency relationships. Herein lies the crux of the debate—Are the advantages of increasing revenue diversification worth the disadvantages accompanying com-

mercial strategies? Organizations must weigh the anticipated benefits against the costs of elaborated structure and staff to carry out commercial activity and the potential internal conflict and/or legitimacy loss that may result.

Revenue diversification has generally been viewed positively in nonprofit organizations because of its dependence-reducing properties (Chang & Tuckman, 1991; Gronbjerg, 1993; Kramer, 1981; Powell & Friedkin, 1986). See Table 14.1. But, a greater variety of resource providers typically leads to a corresponding increase in funding criteria, and satisfying the criteria of one provider may preclude satisfying another. Resulting goal conflicts and organizational tensions can be difficult to manage (DiMaggio, 1986b). Maintaining the increasingly complex dependency relationships is also expensive, as each income stream requires considerable management effort for ongoing success (Gronbjerg, 1992, 1993; Powell & Friedkin, 1986). Adding to administrative overhead and goal conflict are evaluation difficulties. Disparate types of resource providers tend to differ in their views of effectiveness, creating a melange of performance indicators and contributing to confusion about the extent of mission accomplishment (Tuckman, 1998). Ultimately, the multiple roles and directions of nonprofit activity can result in "mission vagueness" (Weisbrod, 1998, p. 171) and an unclear charitable purpose. This is likely at the heart of reservations about revenue diversification in general and commercial activity in particular. As it becomes more difficult to distinguish a nonprofit organization from a government unit or a business firm, the rationale for nonprofit status and accompanying privileges may dissipate (Weisbrod, 1997). Thus, revenue diversification can be seen as a double-edged sword: It reduces concentrated resource dependence and preserves organizational autonomy, yet blurs the distinctions between the nonprofit and other sectors, eroding legitimacy in the process (Ferris & Graddy, 1989).

The legitimacy effect of each funding strategy was not included in the revenue profiles generated above due to widely disparate empirical findings. The question is generally approached by examining the effect of increasing government funding or commercial revenue on private contributions. The extent to which other income sources reduce or crowd out contributions can be viewed as an indicator of declining legitimacy.

Conclusions and Suggestions for Future Research

A broad review of the literature confirms that nonprofit organizations engage in a wide variety of peripheral activities to provide the financial support necessary for continued pursuit of their charitable missions. Whether through attracting private contributions, obtaining government grants and contracts, or involvement in commercial activities, nPOs must dedicate substantial resources and attention toward revenue acquisition. Each revenue strategy has its appeal and current niches of opportunity but also carries constraints and pressures that may impinge on the autonomy of the organization. As nonprofits strive to reduce their vulnerability to income uncertainties and the influence of resource providers, they have moved away from concentrated dependence on a single revenue strategy. Revenue diversification brings new concerns and greater complexity. The wider variety of management tasks diverts more resources from mission-oriented efforts, and the growing number of constraints requires a delicate balance of often conflicting demands. Fear of the unknown effects of revenue diversification and increasing commercial activity focuses attention on the darker possibilities while ignoring limitations of the more familiar revenue strategies.

It is important to acknowledge the autonomy maintenance motives for revenue diversification and commercial strategies. Concentrated dependence on private contributions and government funding has constrained the activities of nonprofits through revenue volatility, goal displacement, and changes in process and structure. The addition of commercial strategies and resulting revenue diversification offers opportunities for greater income stability and more control over income deployment. The ultimate goal is continued pursuit of the charitable mission. Many

studies note that NPOs maintain strong commitments to their central purposes in spite of the distractions of resource acquisition. Their behaviors are influenced not only by demands of resource providers, but they are powerfully guided by organizational history, norms, leadership, and culture. Maintaining mission-directed activity in the face of resource constraints has always been a challenge that NPOs have met in resourceful ways. Evolving dependency relationships in response to changing resource environments is yet another example of nonprofit resourcefulness; new means of support are employed so that mission accomplishment can proceed.

Although the shifting trends in revenue strategies may be noble in intent and logical given resource dependence considerations, unanswered questions about the ultimate impacts on individual organizations and on the nonprofit sector as a whole cause lingering concern. Evidence indicating that the new strategies are less constraining than traditional means of support could be an artifact of scant research or merely emerging effects at this time. Continued efforts to assess the long-term influence of commercial activities and revenue diversification on revenue volatility, goal displacement, organizational process, and structure are needed before any definitive conclusions are drawn. Studies addressing the resulting implications for nonprofit social performance will be especially valuable. For example, is access to charitable services affected? What proportion of program expenditures are directed toward paying versus nonpaying clients? What are the attributes of expanding programs compared to those that are contracting? Are the new strategies available only to large, established organizations or detrimental to the small, less formal nonprofits? Are nonprofit organizations better able to meet the needs of charitable clients?

A primary concern is the potential impact of commercial activities on organizational and sector legitimacy, yet this question is only beginning to be examined. Does declining availability of traditional funding lead to increased commercial activity? Or, does greater emphasis on commercial strategies lead to reduced efforts

TABLE 14.1   Revenue Strategy Profiles

	Private Contributions	Government Funding	Commercial Activity
Revenue volatility	High	Low	Moderate
Goal displacement effects	Strong	Moderately strong	Weak
Process effects	Formalization	Formalization, standardization	Rationalization
Structure effects	Professionalized administration	Professionalized bureaucracy	Professionalized busines forms

and outcomes in the traditional arenas? Is competition for funds primarily among a set of nPOs or between nonprofits and for-profits? How does competition impact the cooperative strategies of nonprofit organizations? Reduced public and private support directly in response to commercial revenues or indirectly through negative public opinion about altered behavior patterns would provide evidence that commercial activity leads to an erosion of legitimacy. But could it be that increasing commercial revenues also lead to more private contributions or government funds? If so, self-support activities could be considered a new symbol of legitimacy in a changing resource climate. Study of the interrelationships among various revenue streams and strategies will demand intricate research but is arguably among the most critical issues that beg for answers at this time.

Whether general conclusions about legitimacy effects emerge primarily from carefully conducted investigations or more broadly from public opinion, legal and public policy implications are likely. Existing regulatory mechanisms seem inadequate to address the combined variety of resource streams and structural forms that continue to proliferate. Funds that flow within and between nonprofit and for-profit subsidiaries, joint ventures or other types of partnerships, and via contractual agreements present unanticipated complexities. Studies of alternative organizational forms and associated operating mechanisms are needed to address accountability concerns. Perceived failure of accountability, with or without compromised social performance, is likely to result in a rethinking of the role and value of the nonprofit sector. At stake are all of the operating privileges currently enjoyed by nonprofit organizations.

Objective conclusions about the effects of commercial activity and revenue diversification rest with future research. Meanwhile, the trend toward more widespread use of these strategies appears to be accelerating. The resource acquisition function is becoming more complex and more controversial—just another fact of life for today's nonprofit organization.

References

Adams, C., & Perlmutter, F. (1991). Commercial venturing and the transformation of America's voluntary social welfare agencies. *Nonprofit and Voluntary Sector Quarterly, 20,* 25–38.

Bernstein, S. R. (1991). Contracted services: Issues for the nonprofit agency manager. *Nonprofit and Voluntary Sector Quarterly, 20,* 429–443.

Bielefeld, W. (1992). Funding uncertainty and nonprofit strategies in the 1980s. *Nonprofit Management and Leadership, 2,* 381–401.

Boris, E. T. (1998, July). Myths about the nonprofit sector. In E. T. Boris (Ed.), *Charting civil society,* 1–4. Washington, DC: The Urban Institute.

Boris, E. T., & T. J. Odendahl. (1990). Ethical issues in fund raising and philanthropy. In J. Van Til (Ed.), *Critical issues in American philanthropy,* 188–203. San Francisco: Jossey-Bass.

Brooks, A. C. (1999). Do public subsidies leverage private philanthropy for the arts? *Nonprofit and Voluntary Sector Quarterly, 28,* 32–45.

Buckley, W. (1967). *Sociology and modern systems theory.* Englewood Cliffs, NJ: Prentice Hall.

Bush, R. (1992). Survival of the nonprofit spirit in a for-profit world. *Nonprofit and Voluntary Sector Quarterly, 21,* 391–410.

Cain, L. P., & D. A. Meritt. (1998). The growing commercialism of zoos and aquariums. *Journal of Policy Analysis and Management, 17,* 298–312.

Chang, C. F., & H. P. Tuckman. (1991). A methodology for measuring the financial vulnerability of charitable nonprofit organizations. *Nonprofit and Voluntary Sector Quarterly,* 20, 445–460.

Crimmins, J. C., & M. Keil. (1983). *Enterprise in the nonprofit sector.* Washington, DC: Partners for Livable Places.

DiMaggio, P. J. (1986a). Can culture survive the marketplace? In P. DiMaggio (Ed.), *Nonprofit enterprise and the arts,* 65–93. New York: Oxford University Press.

_____. (1986b). Introduction. In P. DiMaggio (Ed.), *Nonprofit enterprise and the arts,* 3–13. New York: Oxford University Press.

_____. (1986c). Support for the arts from independent foundations. In P. DiMaggio (Ed.), *Nonprofit enterprise and the arts,* 113–139. New York: Oxford University Press.

Eckel, C. C., & R. Steinberg. (1993). Competition, performance, and public policy toward nonprofits. In D. Hammack & D. Young (Eds.), *Nonprofit organizations in a market economy,* 57–81. San Francisco: Jossey-Bass.

Ferris, J. M. (1993). The double-edged sword of social services contracting. *Nonprofit Management and Leadership,* 3,363–376.

Ferris, J. M., & E. Graddy. (1989). Fading distinctions among the nonprofit, government, and forprofit sectors. In V. Hodgkinson & R. Lyman (Eds.), *The future of the nonprofit sector,* 123–139. San Francisco: Jossey-Bass.

Fogal, R. E. (1994). Designing and managing the fundraising program. In R. Herman (Ed.), *The Jossey-Bass handbook of nonprofit leadership and management,* 369–381. San Francisco: Jossey-Bass.

Goddeeris, J. H., & B. A. Weisbrod. (1998). Conversion from nonprofit to for-profit legal status. *Journal of Policy Analysis,* 17, 215–233.

Gray, B. H. (1991). *The profit motive and patient care.* Cambridge, MA: Harvard University Press.

Gronbjerg, K. A. (1991). Managing grants and contracts: The case of four nonprofit social service organizations. *Nonprofit and Voluntary Sector Quarterly,* 20, 5–24.

_____. (1992). Nonprofit human service organizations: Funding strategies and patterns of adaptation. In Y. Hasenfeld (Ed.), *Human Services as Complex Organizations,* 73–97. Newbury Park, CA: Sage.

Gronbjerg, K. A. (1993). *Understanding nonprofit funding.* San Francisco: Jossey-Bass.

Hansmann, H. (1987). Economic theories of nonprofit organization. In W. Powell (Ed.), *The nonprofit sector: A research handbook,* 27–42. New Haven, CT: Yale University Press.

_____. (1989). The two nonprofit sectors. In V. Hodgkinson & W. Lyman (Eds.), *The future of the nonprofit sector,* 91–102. San Francisco: Jossey-Bass.

Hodgkinson, V. A. (1989.). Key challenges facing the nonprofit sector. In V. Hodgkinson & R. Lyman (Eds.), *The future of the nonprofit sector,* 3–19. San Francisco: Jossey-Bass.

Hodgkinson, V. A., & Weitzman, M. S. (1986). *Dimensions of the independent sector: A statistical profile.* Washington, DC: Independent Sector.

_____. (1988). *Dimensions of the independent sector: A statistical profile. An interim update, fall 1988* (2nd ed.). Washington, DC: Independent Sector.

_____. (1996). *Nonprofit almanac 1996–1997: Dimensions of the independent sector.* San Francisco: Jossey-Bass.

Hodgkinson, V. A., M. S. Weitzman, S. M. Noga, & H. A. Gorski. (1993). *A portrait of the independent sector: The activities and finances of charitable organizations.* Washington, DC: Independent Sector.

Katz, D., & R. L. Kahn. (1966). *Social psychology of organizations.* New York: Wiley.

Kelly, K. S. (1991). *Fund raising and public relations.* Mahwah, NJ: Lawrence Erlbaum.

Next Kirk, S. A., & H. Kutchins. (1992). Diagnosis and uncertainty in mental health organizations. In Y. Hasenfeld (Ed.), *Human services as complex organizations,* 163–183. Newbury Park, CA: Sage.

Knoke, D. (1993). Trade associations in the American political economy. In D. Hammack & D. Young (Eds.), *Nonprofit organizations in a market economy,* 138–174. San Francisco: Jossey-Bass.

Kramer, R. M. (1981). *Voluntary agencies in the welfare state.* Berkeley: University of California Press.

_____. (1985). The future of the voluntary sector in a mixed economy. *Journal of Applied Behavioral Science,* 21, 377–391.

_____. (1986). *The future of voluntary organizations in social welfare.* Working paper. Berkeley: University of California.

_____. (1989). From volunteerism to vendorism: An organizational perspective on contracting. In H. Demone, Jr., & M. Gibelman (Eds.), *Services for sale,* 97–111. New Brunswick, NJ: Rutgers University Press.

Langley, M. (1998, March 26). Mr. Rose gives away millions in donations, not a cent of control. *Wall Street Journal,* pp. A1, A10.

Liebschutz, S. F. (1992). Coping by nonprofit organizations during the Reagan years. *Nonprofit Management and Leadership,* 2, 363–380.

Lipsky, M., & S. R. Smith. (1990). Nonprofit organizations, government, and the welfare state. *Political Science Quarterly,* 104, 625–648.

McGovern, J. J. (1989). The use of for-profit subsidiary corporations by nonprofits. In V. Hodgkinson & R. Lyman (Eds.), *The future of the nonprofit sector,* 168–182. San Francisco: Jossey-Bass.

McMurtry, S. L., Netting, F. E., & P. M. Kettner. (1991). How nonprofits adapt to a stringent environment. *Nonprofit Management and Leadership,* 1, 235–252.

Milofsky, C., & S. D. Blades. (1991). Issues of accountability in health charities. *Nonprofit and Voluntary Sector Quarterly,* 20, 371–393.

Nielsen, R. (1984). Piggybacking for business and nonprofits. *Long Range Planning,* 17, 96–102.

Nielsen, W. A. (1979). *The endangered sector.* New York: Columbia University Press.

Odendahl, T. J. (1990). *Charity begins at home.* New York: Basic Books.

Peterson, P. A. (1986). From impresario to arts administrator. In P. DiMaggio (Ed.), *Nonprofit enterprise and the arts,* 161–183. New York: Oxford University Press.

Pfeffer, J., & G. R. Salancik. (1978). *The external control of organizations.* New York: Harper and Row.

Powell, W. W., & R. Friedkin. (1986). Politics and programs: Organizational factors in public television decision making. In P. DiMaggio (Ed.), *Nonprofit enterprise in the arts,* 245–278. New York: Oxford University Press.

Powell, W. W., & J. Owen-Smith. (1998). Universities and the market for intellectual property in the life sciences. *Journal of Policy Analysis and Management,* 17, 253–277.

Reiner, T. A. (1989). Organizational survival in an environment of austerity. *Nonprofit and Voluntary Sector Quarterly,* 18, 211–221.

Rossi, P. H. (1978). Some issues in the evaluation of human services delivery. In R. Saari & Y. Hasenfeld (Eds.), *The management of human services,* 235–261. New York: Columbia University Press.

Salamon, L. M. (1987). Partners in public service. In W. Powell (Ed.), *The nonprofit sector: A research handbook,* 99–117. New Haven, CT: Yale University Press.

———. (1989). The voluntary sector and the future of the welfare state. *Nonprofit and Voluntary Sector Quarterly,* 18, 11–24.

———. (1992). *America's nonprofit sector.* New York: The Foundation Center.

Scott, R. A. (1974). The selection of clients by social welfare agencies. In Y. Hasenfeld & R. English (Eds.), *Human services organizations: A book of readings* (pp. 485–498). Ann Arbor: University of Michigan Press.

Thompson, J. D. (1967). *Organizations in action.* New York: McGraw-Hill.

Tucker, D. J. (1981). Voluntary auspices and the behavior of social service organizations. *Social Service Review,* 55, 603–627.

Tuckman, H. P. (1998). Competition, commercialization, and the evolution of nonprofit organizational structures. *Journal of Policy Analysis and Management,* 17, 175–194.

Useem, M. (1987). Corporate philanthropy. In W. Powell (Ed.), *The nonprofit sector: A research handbook,* 340–359. New Haven, CT: Yale University Press.

Useem, M., & S. Kutner. (1986). Corporate contributions to culture and the arts. In P. DiMaggio (Ed.), *Nonprofit enterprise in the arts,* 93–139. New York: Oxford University Press.

Weisbrod, B. A. (1988). *The nonprofit economy.* Cambridge, MA: Harvard University Press.

———. (1989). The complexities of income generation for nonprofits. In V. Hodgkinson & R. Lyman (Eds.), *The future of the nonprofit sector,* 103–122. San Francisco: Jossey-Bass.

———. (1997). The future of the nonprofit sector: Its entwining with private enterprise and government. *Journal of Policy Analysis and Management,* 16, 541–555.

———. (1998). The nonprofit mission and its financing. *Journal of Policy Analysis and Management,* 17, 165–174.

Ylvisaker, P. N. (1987). Foundations and nonprofit organizations. In W. Powell (Ed.), *The nonprofit sector: A research handbook,* 360–379. New Haven, CT: Yale University Press.

Young, D. R. (1989). Beyond tax exemption. In V. Hodgkinson & R. Lyman (Eds.), *The future of the nonprofit sector,* 183–202. San Francisco: Jossey-Bass.

———. (1998). Commercialism in nonprofit social service associations. *Journal of Policy Analysis and Management,* 17, 278–297.

Young, D. R., N. Bania, & D. Bailey. (1996). Structure and accountability: A study of national nonprofit associations. *Nonprofit Management and Leadership,* 6, 347–365.

CHAPTER 15

Returns on Fundraising Expenditures in the Voluntary Sector

ADRIAN SARGEANT AND JURGEN KÄHLER

One way charities can facilitate donations is to develop an understanding of donor motivations for giving and then act accordingly. Although reasons for giving are manifold, it seems clear that the perceived efficiency of nonprofit organizations is increasingly becoming an issue.

There is a general paucity of information regarding appropriate means by which the efficiency and effectiveness of nonprofit organizations might be assessed (Harr, Godfrey, and Frank, 1991), despite the fact that cost effectiveness is becoming an increasingly important issue for nonprofits to manage (Schmaedick, 1993). Although there are very real difficulties in comparing one charity with another, if potential funders are likely to undertake such comparisons, these should be of at least passing interest to charity managers.

It is the purpose of this study to explore one such basis for comparison between charities, namely the returns that an organization might generate from each specific category of fundraising activity undertaken. Although this is only one of the variables that could contribute to the overall ratio of fundraising expenditure to voluntary income reported by a given organization, it would seem a reasonable point at which to begin an analysis of fundraising performance. This

is particularly true given that no prior research has been conducted in this area.

Data and Methodology

After an initial series of in-depth interviews with fifteen charity fundraising managers, a postal questionnaire was developed and sent to the fundraising departments of the United Kingdom's top five hundred fundraising charities as listed by the Charities Aid Foundation (CAF). In total ninety-seven replies were received, of which nine were incomplete or unusable. The resulting analysis is therefore based on a usable response rate of 17.6 percent.

Results

Charities were asked to indicate the total amount of direct costs (including staff costs but excluding administrative overhead) they had incurred for each of the fundraising activities their organization had engaged in during the past twelve-month period. Similarly, fundraisers were asked to indicate the total revenue they had generated in each of these categories of activity. This made it possible to calculate the typical

TABLE 15.1   Revenue Generated per Pound of Fundraising Expenditure

Activity	Percentage of Sample Utilizing	Mean	Coefficient of Variation*	1st	Median	3rd
				Quartiles		
Direct mail: recruitment	66.7	1.75	1.18	0.68	1.01	2.06
Direct mail: development	66.7	5.60	1.19	2.75	3.41	5.33
Telemarketing	25.0	1.99	2.44	1.25	1.97	2.81
Door-to-door distribution	29.5	0.97	0.47	0.41	0.75	1.09
Direct-response press advertising	35.2	1.72	0.81	0.26	0.83	2.05
Major gift fundraising	57.1	66.28	0.88	9.72	57.46	112.60
Local fundraising	33.4	2.14	0.72	1.47	2.35	3.07
Corporate fundraising	85.7	8.62	0.86	2.87	5.32	10.47
Trust fundraising	66.7	14.88	1.61	4.85	7.65	25.00

*The coefficient of variation is defined as the ratio of the standard deviation and the mean.

returns generated by each fundraising activity. (It should be noted that definitions of each activity were provided to facilitate completion and subsequent comparison.) The data in Table 15.1 report the revenues generated per pound of fundraising expenditure incurred. In interpreting the results it is important to remember that many of the techniques listed are used only for the purpose of donor recruitment and that, as a consequence, initial returns on these activities may be low. It is also important to remember, however, that many of the individuals recruited will give a series of subsequent gifts and that hence, over the full duration of a donor "lifetime," the relationship with these individuals is likely to be profitable.

Direct Mail

Two-thirds of the sample were found to utilize direct mail, either as a tool to recruit new donors or as a vehicle for the development thereof. Charities from across the sector are equally likely to include the use of direct mail in their promotional plans, with fundraisers from one category of cause being no more or less likely to utilize it than fundraisers from another.

Donor Recruitment

The data from the survey confirmed the popular view that this form of donor recruitment activity (attempting to attract new donors to an organization) does not yield a high rate of return, with the typical charity achieving no more than a break-even position at the end of a particular campaign. The median value identified in the research was only £1.01 (consistent with the expectations of Bush, 1991, and Warwick, 1994). The mean was somewhat higher, at £1.75, reflecting the presence of a number of high performing outliers in the data set. It thus seems clear that although most charities would expect to achieve no more than a break-even position, a small but significant number of organizations are able to recruit new donors at a profit. A recent award-winning campaign by the charity seeAbility, for example, was able to recruit each new donor at a profit of £14.00 (Tyler, 1997).

No significant variations in performance could be identified when the size of each charity, as indicated by the total level of voluntary income attracted, was taken as the basis for comparison. Charities that ranked near the top of the top five hundred largest organizations fared no better or worse than those ranked toward the bottom.

However, an important difference was noted in the patterns of return reported by specific categories of cause. Although the response rate did not permit a direct comparison between each of the twenty-six categories of the detailed typology employed by CAF, it was possible to determine that in the case of direct-mail recruitment activity some categories of cause consistently

TABLE 15.2   Direct Mail Recruitment:
Mean Revenue Generated per Pound Spent

Category of Cause	Mean Revenue per Pound Spent
Physically disabled	0.78
International aid	0.79
Mental health	0.89
Children	0.95
Cancer	1.00
Blind	1.07
Deaf	1.33
Animal protection	1.68
Religious: welfare	2.77
Religious: internal aid	3.67

NOTE: F statistic = 4.914; empirical significance level = 0.000.

outperformed the others. In particular, those charities related in some way to religion achieve much higher rates of return than all other categories of cause. Similarly, charities concerned with the provision of care or support for persons with a physical disability consistently perform less well than all other categories of cause. A formal statistical test confirmed that the differences reported in the means from one category to another were statistically significant. The details are reported in Table 15.2.

Although the figures in Table 15.2 could form a useful basis for comparison, it is worth noting that for some categories of cause the distinction between recruitment and development mailings can become a little blurred. Although the good performance of religious charities is to be commended, it is likely that such organizations find it substantially easier to identify prospective donors than many other categories of cause. If the charity appeal is based on Christian, Muslim, or Jewish values for example, modern lifestyle lists make it possible to easily identify the members of each of these faiths, greatly facilitating appropriate targeting. Moreover, the recipients of such mailings, by virtue of their faith, are likely to be considerably more sympathetic to the cause than the recipients of standard cold-mailing appeals. This enhanced capacity for targeting might thus help explain a proportion of the variation in returns reported in Table 15.2.

Donor Development

Donor development mailings were defined as mailings to donors who had given at least one previous gift to the organization. Some fundraisers prefer the label "warm" mailings in the sense that recipients are already "warm" to the cause. For this activity the median return per £1.00 of investment was found to be £3.41.

It is interesting to note that in the case of development mailings the sector effects identified in Table 15.2 are no longer observable. It would therefore seem fair to conclude that the differences in performance for recruitment mailings are likely to be due to differing degrees of public support for a given cause and not to variations in the quality of individual fundraising activity per se.

Telemarketing

The use of telemarketing as a fundraising tool has grown in significance in recent years. Telemarketing is now increasingly used, particularly by the larger charities, as a tool to support a range of fundraising initiatives. Typically, it might be used for recruitment purposes, to solicit additional donations when a link with a donor has been established, or even to convert donors to a more committed (or tax-efficient) form of giving.

It is important to note that the use of telemarketing for pure recruitment activity is not widespread and that although some organizations do use it for recruitment, much of this category of activity probably falls somewhere between "cold" and "warm" forms of charity communication. Membership organizations, for example, will often use telemarketing to upgrade their members to donors.

The mean income per £1.00 of expenditure was found to be £1.99, and as the results in Table 15.1 illustrate, returns would tend to vary between £1.00 and £3.00 per £1.00 of investment made. The use of telemarketing for donor development would clearly attract much higher rates of return, but a high degree of sectorwide diversity in its application made any form of direct comparison impossible.

Door-to-Door Distribution

Door-to-door distribution is defined as the household distribution of solicitation material in a given locality by a third-party carrier, such as the Royal Mail. Respondents were specifically asked to exclude door-to-door distribution activity or collections undertaken solely by volunteers. In our sample 29.5 percent of respondents currently utilize a third-party carrier for door-to-door distribution activity.

As with other forms of donor recruitment, the returns from this activity are relatively modest, with the mean amount of income generated per £1.00 of expenditure being only £0.97 and the median even lower at £0.75. It thus costs most charities more to conduct door-to-door recruitment than they would normally expect to see generated in revenue—at least in the short term.

To understand why this form of fundraising is still an attractive option, one has to look at the lifetime value of the donors so recruited. Given that door-to-door recruitment targets all the households in a given locality and not only those on particular lifestyle lists, it has proved possible for many organizations to solicit donations from individuals who have yet to feel the giving fatigue felt by others in their area. It is also important to note that, as with other forms of recruitment activity, charities will generate much better returns over the duration of their relationship with the donors they are thereby able to recruit. Indeed, since the majority of door-to-door campaigns are now designed to recruit donors directly into committed forms of giving, it remains an important fundraising tool.

Interestingly, there would appear to be significant differences in the level of return reported for door-to-door activity by different categories of charity. As was noted previously in the case of cold direct mail, charities attempting to raise funds for causes that relate to a physical disability will find they attract lower returns than other categories of cause. Other variations in returns were recorded, but the absolute level of respondents in each category makes it difficult to generalize from the results in these cases.

Direct-Response Press Advertising

This category of activity was defined as press advertising specifically designed to solicit an immediate donation from potential new donors. The long-term performance of advertising designed for general awareness building was therefore not considered. The survey revealed that 35.2 percent of respondents were using press advertising for direct-response fundraising purposes. Because the median return for this activity in Table 15.1 is considerably smaller than one pound, it seems clear that the majority of organizations would not expect to break even on this activity in the short term. It is important to note in this case that the mean value reflects the enhanced performance of a small number of organizations, and thus the median is potentially of more value as the basis for any form of comparison. The findings for this category are similar to those for other forms of recruitment activity, although the returns accruing to a typical organization from press advertising would appear to be somewhat lower than those that would be expected from other categories of fundraising.

Major Gift Fundraising

The term *"major gift"* refers to those elements of fundraising that are designed to solicit large onetime or recurring donations from individual donors. Many charities are fortunate enough to have links with one or more particularly wealthy individuals who, when they elect to give to charity, will do so at a level where they can feel their gift will make a substantial contribution. Many of the larger charities thus have a major gift department whose role is to develop relationships with a comparatively small number of very wealthy individuals.

Often these individuals will have been recruited because of a personal contact with a staff member or trustee, but they may also have been recruited by many of the means alluded to above. Once the value of such individuals becomes clear, they will usually be removed from the general database, and a uniquely personalized pattern of communication will be adopted. Although in itself this is comparatively inexpensive, it can make considerable demands on a fundraiser's time. Staff costs hence form the major component of cost in this area.

Nevertheless, as the results in Table 15.1 clearly indicate, it is by far the most profitable form of fundraising activity, despite considerable variations in performance being reported from one organization to another. In part these may be due to the often quite considerable time lags between solicitation and the granting of a gift. Interestingly, in the top five hundred charities no significant size effects could be detected. Charities toward the top of the five hundred will perform no better or worse in this area of fundraising than charities toward the bottom. It also proved impossible to identify any significant category effects in the case of this technique.

Local Fundraising

The term *"local* fundraising" (in the United States *"special events* fundraising") refers to a variety of forms of fundraising activity. Although the returns reported by the charities in the sample were surprisingly uniform, it is important to note that of all the forms of fundraising listed, this category is almost certainly the most diverse in its application. Local fundraising can typically include coffee mornings, raffles, flag days, sponsored events, rummage sales, competitions, household collections, and so on. It is also important to note that considerable diversity would typically be encountered between individual charities in the manner in which such activities are managed. In some cases salaried charity staff are responsible for overseeing local fundraising; in others the process is staffed and managed almost exclusively by volunteers. The figures reported in Table 15.2 should therefore be used only as a guide to facilitate comparison and no more. Clearly, however, if the returns generated by a particular organization fall well below those given here, management would be

well advised to ascertain the reasons for the shortfall.

Corporate Fundraising

The proportion of the sample engaged in corporate fundraising activity was 85.7 percent. It is important to bear in mind that only monetary donations were considered in the analysis and not such forms of support as donated goods, services, or staff. It was perhaps to be expected that a wide variation in performance would be reported by charities engaged in this activity, but the quartile data revealed that for 25 percent of the charities in the sample, surprisingly low rates of return were being generated. In an attempt to explain this, size and category effects were once again investigated. Although no significant category effects were identified, there appeared to be a relationship between the size of a charity and the rates of return it could attract from corporate fundraising. This almost certainly reflects the desire of many large corporate sponsors to associate themselves with a top charity.

Trust Fundraising

A significant proportion of U.K. charities can be defined as grant-making trusts (comparable to U.S. foundations), which exist to support particular categories of cause by indirect means only. Such organizations often have little or no direct contact with the recipient groups their missions dictate are worthy of support. These organizations will instead elect to support other charities whose work they believe will have the most beneficial impact on members of their target group. Thus a considerable amount of effort is expended on soliciting funding from the grant-making organizations that, on the face of it, have an appropriate fit with the aims and objectives of a particular fundraising charity. Because grant-making trusts vary in size, the size of their average gift will also exhibit substantial variation—a fact reflected in the patterns of returns that organizations would typically receive from this form of fundraising activity. In this case the mean revenue generated per £1.00 of fundraising expenditure was found to be £14.88, substantially higher than the median of £7.65. The quartile figures clearly reveal, as one would expect, a wide variation in responses. Although size and category effects were once again investigated, no significant variation was encountered in either case.

Conclusions

The United Kingdom's top five hundred charities currently engage in a variety of fundraising techniques. Direct mail remains a popular option, and the returns on both recruitment and development activity in this area compare favorably with those generated by other media. Median returns from pure recruitment activity were found to vary between £0.75 and £1.01, confirming that many organizations take a loss on this category of activity. However, when one considers that mail follow-ups to donors recruited by other means achieve very respectable rates of return, the rationale for continuing recruitment is clear. As might be expected, major gift, trust, and corporate fundraising each generate high returns, with major gift significantly outperforming other categories of fundraising.

Interestingly, in most cases, there would appear to be no relationship between the returns that a charity is able to generate from each activity and its size as measured by the level of voluntary income it is able to attract. The only exception to this general rule was found to be corporate fundraising, where a strong relationship was found to exist between these two variables. In all other respects smaller charities would appear to perform as well as their larger counterparts, although clearly these findings are only applicable to the CAF top five hundred. Further research will be necessary to determine the returns that other much smaller organizations are able to generate from these activities.

It is also important to note that there are comparatively few instances where category effects can be identified within the data set. Only

in the cases of direct-mail recruitment and door-to-door distribution did it prove possible to detect significant variations in performance. Interestingly, in both these cases charities concerned in some way with physical disabilities reported significantly lower rates of return than all other categories of cause. It seems certain, given that these differences disappear when one examines development activities, that these results reflect differing degrees of public attraction to each category of cause rather than any variation in the quality of fundraising per se.

It does seem clear, however, that substantial variations in the effectiveness of fundraising activity do exist within the sector as a whole. Those organizations experiencing returns at or below the lower quartile figures identified in this research should perhaps consider the reasons for this poor performance because donors undertaking broad comparisons may perceive the organization concerned as inefficient and thus less worthy of support. Of course such performance could be entirely justified, but charities need to be increasingly sensitive to how their performance will be perceived by donors. Where explanations of seemingly poor performance are forthcoming, the charity concerned may be well advised to educate donors about the reasons underlying this performance, or even to suggest more appropriate bases for comparison. Where such explanations are not forthcoming, however, further research and corrective action may well be warranted.

Of course many charities are achieving excellent rates of return on their fundraising investment, and it is important to recognize that in the case of many of those activities investigated, the expected returns are much higher than (particularly) the giving public might believe. Many donors suspect that charities spend as much as 50 percent of their revenue on fundraising costs (Doble, 1990). A significant opportunity may therefore exist for particularly efficient organizations to publicize their relative efficiency as a means of building a strong competitive position in the market. Indeed, the sector as a whole could have much to gain by collectively publicizing the excellent levels of fundraising efficiency achieved.

References

Bush, B. "What Fundraisers Should Know About the Law." In D. F. Burlingame and L. J. Hulse (eds.), *Taking Fund-Raising Seriously: Advancing the Profession and Practice of Raising Money.* San Francisco: Jossey-Bass, 1991.

Charity Commission. *Report of the Charity Commission for England and Wales.* London: HMSO, 1997.

Cutlip, S. M. *Fund-Raising in the United States: Its Role in America's Philanthropy.* New Brunswick, N.J.: Transaction, 1990. (Originally published 1965.)

Doble, J. "Public Opinion About Charitable Solicitation and the Law." In *Proceedings of New York University School of Law's Conference on Charitable Solicitation: Is There a Problem?* New York: New York University, 1990.

Glaser, J. S. *The United Way Scandal: An Insider's Account of What Went Wrong and Why.* New York: Wiley, 1994.

Greenlee, J. S., and Gordon, T. P. "The Impact of Professional Solicitors on Fund-Raising in Charitable Organizations." *Nonprofit and Voluntary Sector Quarterly,* 1998, 27 (3), 277–299.

Harr, D. J., Godfrey, J. T., and Frank, R. H. *Common Costs and Fund-Raising Appeals: A Guide to Joint Cost Allocation in Not-for-Profit Organizations.* Landover, Md.: Nonprofit Mailers Federation; Frank & Company, 1991.

Harvey, J. W., and McCrohan, K. F. "Fund-Raising Costs—Societal Implications for Philanthropies and Their Supporters." *Business and Society,* 1988, 27 (Spring), 15–22.

Hind, A. *The Governance and Management of Charities.* London: Voluntary Sector Press, 1995.

Khanna, J., Posnett, J., and Sandler, T. "Charity Donations in the UK: New Evidence Based on Panel Data." *Journal of Public Economics,* 1995, 56, 257–272.

Lindahl, W. E. *Strategic Planning for Fund-Raising.* San Francisco: Jossey-Bass, 1992.

Ormstedt, D. E. "Government Regulation of Fund-Raising: A Struggle for Efficacy." In J. M. Greenfield (ed.), *Financial Practices for Effective Fund-Raising.* New Directions for Philanthropic Fundraising, no. 3. San Francisco: Jossey-Bass, 1994.

Pharoah, C. (ed.). *Dimensions of the Voluntary Sector.* West Malling, U.K.: Charities Aid Foundation, 1997.

Posnett, J., and Sandler, T. "Demand for Charity Donations in Private Nonprofit Markets: The Case of the U.K." *Journal of Public Economics,* 1989, 40, 187–200.

Rose-Ackerman, S. "Charitable Giving and Excessive Fund-Raising." *Quarterly Journal of Economics,* 1982, 97, 193–212.

Sargeant, A., and Kähler, J. *Benchmarking Charity Costs.* London: Charities Aid Foundation, 1998.

Schmaedick, G. L. *Cost Effectiveness in the Nonprofit Sector.* London: Quorum Books, 1993.

Schmittlein, D. C., and Peterson, R. A. "Customer Base Analysis: An Industrial Purchase Process Application." *Marketing Science,* 1994, 13 (Winter), 41–67.

Steinberg, R. "Should Donors Care About Fund-Raising?" In S. Rose-Ackerman (ed.), *The Economics of Nonprofit Institutions: Studies in Structure and Policy.* New York: Oxford University Press, 1986.

_____. "Economic Perspectives on Regulation of Charitable Solicitation." *Case Western Reserve Law Review,* 1988–1989, 39, 775–797.

_____. "The Economics of Fund-Raising." In D. F. Burlingame and L. J. Hulse (eds.), *Taking Fund-Raising Seriously: Advancing the Profession and Practice of Raising Money.* San Francisco: Jossey-Bass, 1991.

Tyler, F. "The 1997 DMA/Royal Mail Direct Marketing Awards." Marketing supplement. *Marketing,* Dec. 1997.

Warwick, M. *Raising Money by Mail: Strategies for Growth and Financial Stability.* Berkeley, Calif.: Strathmoor Press, 1994.

Weisbrod, B. A., and Dominguez, N. D. "Demand for Collective Goods in Private Nonprofit Markets: Can Fund-Raising Expenditures Help Overcome Free-Rider Behavior?" *Journal of Public Economics,* 1986, 30, 83–95.

Young, D. R., and Steinberg, R. *Economics for Nonprofit Managers.* New York: Foundation Center, 1995.

CHAPTER 16

Foundations

ELIZABETH T. BORIS

Nonprofit, nongovernmental organizations that promote charitable giving and other public purposes usually by giving grants of money to nonprofit organizations, qualified individuals, and other entities. Under United States law, philanthropic foundations must serve the public by being organized and operated exclusively for religious, charitable, scientific, testing for public safety, literary, or educational purposes. In addition to providing grants, foundations may provide services, make loans, conduct research, hold conferences, publish reports, and undertake other related activities.

Foundations are formed by individuals, families, and business corporations, which usually donate money, property, or other financial assets. These assets form an endowment or principal fund from which interest is derived and used to support expenses and grant making. Some foundations are not endowed, but receive periodic gifts from their donors.

Public Versus Private Foundations

There are two major types of philanthropic foundations: private foundations (independent, company-sponsored, and operating foundations) and public foundations (community foundations, women's funds, and others). The term "*foundation*," however, is often used by organizations that are not philanthropic grantors, and private foundations may use a variety of terms to describe themselves. In addition to "foundations," they are called "funds" (the Rockefeller Brothers Fund), "corporations" (the Carnegie Corporation of New York), "trusts," (the Lucille P. Markey Charitable Trust), and "endowments," (the Lilly Endowment).

Foundations may be organized in perpetuity or only for a specified time period. When a foundation is terminated, all of its assets must be used for charitable purposes.

In 1992 there were 35,765 foundations, according to the Foundation Center, a nonprofit organization that compiles and publishes information about foundations. The foundation field is highly concentrated. The largest foundations, those with U.S. $50 million or more, are responsible for 66.2 percent of assets and 48 percent of grants. Most foundations are small and do not employ staff. Only about 9,600 have assets of one million dollars or more.

Foundations held assets of approximately $177 billion and made grants of more than $10 billion in 1992. Though significant in impact, this grant making is a modest 8 percent of total charitable giving, estimated to be $124 billion in 1992 by the AAFRC Trust for Philanthropy, an organization that compiles annual estimates of philanthropic giving. Foundations also provide only a small proportion of overall revenues received by nonprofit organizations in the United States, which was estimated at $408 billion in 1989 by the Independent Sector, a national non-profit membership organization.

Private Foundations

Private foundations are created by individual or family donors (or by their representatives, if created by a will after death) or by business corporations. Donors select the boards of directors (or trustees), which determine how the foundations' money will be donated or used for charitable purposes. Private foundations provide donors with a maximum of control over the selection of charitable recipients but a more limited charitable income tax deduction than is available for gifts to public charities. Individuals may deduct from their taxable income cash gifts of up to 30 percent of income. All private foundations are regulated by the "private foundation" rules of the U.S. tax code. These rules are designed to ensure that foundations use their resources only for public benefit.

Public Foundations

Public foundations include community foundations, which are "public charities," the charitable designation that applies to most nonprofit organizations under U.S. law. Public charities are required to have broad public participation both in donations and in governance, and therefore provide less individual control of the assets and grants than private foundations. Public foundations are subject to the less-stringent regulations and more-favorable tax deductibility levels that govern public charities in the United States. For income tax purposes, donors may deduct the value of cash gifts up to 50 percent of their adjusted income.

Public charities are required to demonstrate their public support by raising a certain specified percentage of their revenues each year from the general public, a requirement called the public support test. No one donor may provide a majority of financial support.

Characteristics of Philanthropic Foundations

Private and public foundations in the United States have the following characteristics:

- They are governed by boards of directors or trustees which are responsible for their financial integrity and the fulfillment of their charitable missions.
- They make grants or operate programs or institutions that promote charitable purposes.
- They may employ a staff or use volunteers or consultants to conduct their charitable work.
- They receive gifts of money, property, or financial securities that are deductible from the donors' income tax up to certain limits specified by law (if the donor is alive) or gifts that are deductible from estate taxes if the gift is given through a bequest at the donor's death.
- Financial assets (for those that have endowments) are invested in financial securities (stocks, bonds, etc.), and the interest and dividends earned (and sometimes additional gifts from their donors) provide the money to make grants or operate programs to benefit society. Unless prohibited by their by-laws or trust instruments, foundations may also make grants from the principal fund.
- They are independent of government.
- They do not distribute a profit (nonprofit status).
- They are classified as tax exempt organizations under United States law (501 [c] [3] organizations) and therefore are not subject to taxes on their revenues (except that private foundations must pay an excise tax of one or two percent on their investment income).

Private Foundations

There are three types of private foundations, distinguishable by the source of their assets and the type of work they do.

Independent Foundations

Independent foundations are created by gifts from an individual, a family, or a group of individuals to provide funding for charitable activities, primarily by making grants. Many prominent American entrepreneurs and their families created foundations: the Ford Foundation, William and Flora Hewlett Foundation, Rockefeller Foundation, David and Lucile Packard Foundation, Charles Stewart Mott Foundation, W. K. Kellogg Foundation, and many others.

Foundations may be operated by the donors or their families, by staff hired for that purpose, or by banks or other entities designated by the donors to act in their behalf. Policy and grant decisions are made by the board of directors or trustees, which usually includes the donors and their families (if they are alive), trusted associates, and other civic, business, and academic leaders who can contribute to the work of the foundations. Many independent foundations, like the Ford Foundation, no longer have family members involved in the foundation. The board of directors is legally responsible for overseeing the finances and operations of the foundation; it also elects new directors.

When an independent foundation is primarily governed and operated by the donor and family members, it is often called a "family foundation." Donors and family members form the board of directors and often operate the foundation without employing a staff. In some family foundations, the family lawyer, trusted friends, and business associates may also be asked to serve on the board. (The Meadows Foundation in Texas is an example of a family foundation that includes family members as staff and board members, although it also employs nonfamily members as staff.)

Recently, some independent foundations were formed as a result of the sale of nonprofit hospitals (or similar charitable entities) to for-profit businesses. Several such sales resulted in the creation of new foundations with hundreds of millions of dollars in assets. Although the foundations are legally independent from the resulting for-profit companies, the foundations usually focus on health or issues related to the original charitable purpose of the former nonprofit organization.

Operating Foundations

Private foundations may also be organized as operating foundations to conduct research or provide a direct service; for example, they may operate an art museum or a home for the aged. The interest generated by the endowment pays for staffing and administering the program or organization. Operating foundations must use at least 85 percent of their investment income to operate programs. They are permitted to make grants, but only up to 15 percent of their income. (The Kettering Foundation of Ohio is a well-known operating foundation that publishes papers and organizes public issues forums throughout the United States. The Getty Trust operates the Getty Museum in California.)

Community Foundations

Community foundations are classified as public charities and are formed by a group of individuals to benefit their community or region. An endowment is created from the gifts of many donors, which are pooled, and the interest is used to make grants to nonprofit organizations, individuals, and governments to enhance the quality of life, primarily in their geographical area. Community foundations may have separate funds that are donated by different persons or families or businesses. A donor may name the fund and indicate the types of grants that the fund should make. The community foundation board oversees the foundation, and its staff conducts the grant-making program.

Boards of directors of community foundations (also called trustees or distribution committees) are selected to represent the community. Some members are chosen by certain designated public officials (for example, a judge or civic leader).

Other Public Foundations

There are several other types of public foundations that receive tax-deductible contributions from individual donors and use the money or the interest generated to make grants for specific types of activities. In the 1980s, groups of women in many cities created women's foundations to raise money and make grants to help meet women's and girls' needs that they felt were being neglected by both philanthropy and governments. There are now more than 60 women's foundations in the United States that raise money to benefit women and girls in their communities. Donors usually contribute to public foundations on a yearly basis, although some, like the Ms. Foundation for Women, have raised an endowment. There are women's funds in Chicago, New York, Colorado, San Francisco, and many other areas.

Members of minority groups have created public foundations to raise money and make grants to meet the needs of their groups. The Seventh Generation Fund was created in 1977 to benefit American Indian tribes in the United States and Canada. Public foundations are at present a small part of United States philanthropy, but their numbers are increasing rapidly.

Many public foundations make grants to promote social change. Often called alternative funds, they employ nonhierarchical decision-making structures and invite community members or grantees to participate on the grant making boards or distribution committees. (The Haymarket People's Fund in Boston is a well-known alternative fund.)

Government Foundations

The National Endowment for the Humanities, the National Endowment for the Arts, the National Science Foundation, and the National Endowment for Democracy are examples of foundations established by the U.S. government. Government-initiated foundations are usually supported by public money. They have independent boards of directors, but their programs often become part of the political debate during the budgeting process. In western European countries, government-supported foundations are often larger and more prominent than privately funded ones.

History of Philanthropic Foundations

Private foundations were popularized shortly after the turn of the twentieth century when Mar-

garet Olivia Sage (1907), Andrew Carnegie (1911), and John D. Rockefeller (1913), formed their foundations. These new organizations were created as corporations, like the businesses then responsible for generating the private fortunes that would be turned to charitable uses. Unlike the traditional charitable trusts handed down in common law from Elizabethan times, the new corporations were flexible and could more easily change with the times. They were governed by self-perpetuating boards of directors that had the power to make program and investment decisions and the legal responsibility for financial oversight.

At about the same time, Frederick H. Goff developed the concept of a community trust in Cleveland, Ohio. The community trust was designed to avoid the "dead hand" of the donor whose charitable purposes became outmoded after his or her death. By creating a charitable fund in a community trust, a donor permitted a distribution committee representative of the community to ensure that his or her gift always fulfilled a relevant charitable purpose. The idea caught on, and in 1914 the Cleveland Community Trust was formed. Numerous community trusts, later called community foundations, were formed in the following years.

Although the foundation as an institution was an innovation, it evolved from long-standing traditions of secular and religious giving as well as popular reform movements. Andrew Carnegie's *Gospel of Wealth* [1889] (1990) provides the classic rationale for the proper stewardship of wealth. He called upon men of wealth to regard surplus revenues as trust funds that they are duty bound to administer for the benefit of the community.

Philanthropic foundations flourished during the 1920s, when immense fortunes were made and there was unbridled optimism in the ability of reason and science to solve society's problems. Foundations were to be instruments of scientific charity, controlled by those of superior achievement and designed to support efforts to get at the root causes of poverty, hunger, and disease. Education and research were the favored methods.

The early foundations were formed before the adoption of a national income tax, although foundations were among the charitable organizations exempted from paying income taxes in the Revenue Act of 1913. By 1917 Congress enacted a charitable tax deduction for donors, and in 1919 deductions were permitted for charitable gifts made from estates after the death of the donor.

Despite the tax incentives, the number of foundations grew slowly, until the 1940s, when high rates of taxation (marginal rates up to 90%) and postwar prosperity combined to encourage the creation of a large number of new private foundations. This trend accelerated in the 1950s, slowed somewhat in the 1960s, and declined in the 1970s following the enactment of the Tax Reform Act of 1969, which contained many regulatory provisions that affected foundations. In the mid-1980s the creation of new large foundations reached an all-time high, following the revision of some of the most restrictive provisions of the 1969 law and the creation of huge personal fortunes.

Achievements

In less than a century, philanthropic foundations have produced a long list of achievements. Major foundations that view their assets as social risk capital have financed break-throughs in scientific research, the arts, and the humanities, and have built and sustained major nonprofit institutions both in the United States and in other countries. The majority of foundations, with modest resources and ambitions, have quietly contributed to local colleges, hospitals, and service organizations, providing needed resources and helping to improve the quality of life in their communities.

Foundations supported the research that led to the new grains that produced the Green Revolution in Asia; helped to create public television and its best-known show, *Sesame Street;* funded the Flexner Report that caused major reforms in medical education; funded the experiments that led to white lines on the right side of all of U.S. roads, championed population research before it was politically possible for the government to do so, and much more.

Criticisms

From the beginning foundations received mixed reactions. Even though some welcomed the dedication of surplus wealth to philanthropic purposes, many feared that the concentration of resources in foundations would subvert the public agenda and place too much power in the hands of those who already controlled business and politics. Foundations are faulted for their lack of public accountability, for their elitism, for their arrogance, and for their potential to benefit those who form and run them, rather than the public purposes they are ostensibly designed to serve. Periodic scandals reinforce these fears, although the growth of government, business, and the nonprofit sector over the course of the century has limited the negative impacts that early critics feared.

American culture celebrates individual initiative and daring that leads to financial success, but part of the negative reaction to foundations is a distrust of the donor's motives. In a study reported by John Edie (1987) in *America's Wealthy and the Future of Foundations,* donors' reasons for creating foundations were found to vary significantly. Some had a deeply felt religious background or a tradition of family social responsibility and concern for the poor, and others had political or ideological beliefs they wished to advance. Some donors desired to create a memorial to themselves or their families. Other donors felt a commitment to a community or pressure from their peers to be philanthropic. Relatively few formed foundations because of tax incentives, although the existence of tax incentives often influenced the size of the contribution to the foundation.

Recently, foundations were faulted for being both too political and too timid. Critics of the left challenge foundations for supporting the status quo and neglecting the needs of the poor, of girls and women, of racial and ethnic minorities, and of the disabled. Critics from the right accuse foundations of encouraging the growth of government programs and undermining the free enterprise system. The failure of many foundations to communicate fully with the public about their work inhibits informed assessments of their impacts. Only a minority of foundations issue annual reports or publications that describe their programs.

Government Regulation

The Internal Revenue Service oversees the activities of philanthropic foundations and other nonprofit organizations because the national laws governing foundations are in the tax code. The 1969 Tax Reform Act and its subsequent revisions provide the national regulatory framework for U.S. foundations. Foundations must pay fines for violating the law, and a foundation may lose its status as a tax-exempt entity for a serious offense.

Foundations may not control a business, provide monetary benefits to any donors or directors (except for reasonable compensation for services provided), make risky investments with their endowment funds, or accumulate assets without paying a reasonable amount for charitable activities. Private (nonoperating) foundations must make grants and operate programs that, with administrative expenses, amount to at least 5 percent of their assets each year.

Foundations may not try to influence the legislative process directly, except in their own defense, and they may not influence elections, except by providing independent research and analysis to inform the political debate.

At the state level, the attorney general or charities officer reviews a foundation's state information forms (if they are required) and oversees compliance with state charitable regulations. At the federal level, a foundation is required by law to complete a detailed disclosure form (Form 990-PF) every year. These documents include information on a foundation's revenues, expenses, investments, loans, salaries, gifts received, income-producing activities, and other financial and program information. Private foundations are also required to list all of the grants they make each year and to provide information about how to apply for a grant. These information forms (Form 990-PF for private, corporate, and operating foundations, and Form

990 for community foundations) are public documents. Foundations must make these forms available to the public. The Foundation Center (1994a) facilitates access to the disclosure forms by making them available in library collections around the country.

Foundation Governance

Foundations are governed by boards of directors or by trustees (in foundations that are set up as charitable trusts). Directors and trustees are responsible for the proper management of the foundation's assets and for implementing its grant making and other program goals. The foundation's goals may be spelled out in great detail by the donor, or, as in most large U.S. foundations, the goals may be quite general-to improve the lives of people-which leaves to the discretion of the board the definition and implementation of the foundation's program.

Private foundation boards are self-perpetuating. New members are identified and elected by the existing board. In addition to donors and family members, boards usually include business, professional, educational and community leaders. The majority of foundation board members are white males; approximately 29 percent of board members are women, and 4 percent are members of racial or ethnic minority groups.

Foundation governance may vary from complete donor control to almost complete staff control. There are four main types of foundation governance that capture the continuum: donor, administrator, director, and presidential. These models are somewhat related to the size and longevity of the foundations. Smaller foundations are more likely to be informally run by the donor and family. Larger ones are usually more professionalized, older, and more likely to be run by staffs than by the families that founded them.

The donor model is prevalent in many family foundations in which the donor and family members operate the foundation without a staff and make all of the decisions themselves. The process is informal and the donor's wishes are paramount.

In the administrator model, the foundation employs an administrative staff person who processes the paperwork, but the policy and program decisions are initiated and decided by the board members. In the director model, the foundation employs an executive director and relies on that person to process the requests and provide information and recommendations for the foundation's policy and grant decisions.

The presidential model gives wide discretion to the foundation's chief executive officer (CEO). This model is usually found in the few large foundations that make hundreds of grants and give away many millions of dollars each year. In these foundations, the board of directors employs an experienced national leader to whom it delegates operating and grant-making authority. The board sets fiscal and program priorities and monitors the foundation's finances and programs. It may also make decisions on very large grants.

Corporate Governance

In corporate foundations, the boards of directors usually comprise the chief executive officer of the corporation and other high-level managers. Infrequently, directors from outside the company may be asked to serve on the corporate foundation board. The decisionmaking process varies by company. In some companies all grant recommendations are brought before the board for final decisions, but in other companies staffs have greater discretion and can make many small grants on their own authority. With the trend toward decentralization in U.S. business, corporations are increasingly delegating grant-making authority to local managers.

Grant Making

Foundations make grants primarily to qualified public charities, although they may make grants to almost any type of organization or individual, as long as the purpose of the grant is "charitable" and the grantor monitors the use of the funds. Grants can be made to nonprofit organizations,

individuals, corporations, and governments, both nationally and internationally. The majority of foundation grants are made to nonprofit organizations, often colleges and universities, that qualify as tax-exempt charitable organizations under section 501(c)(3) of the U.S. tax code.

Grant-making patterns do not change greatly from year to year. The Foundation Center reports that in 1993, 24 percent of foundation grant dollars supported educational projects; 18 percent funded health-related projects; 15 percent were for human services; 15 percent for arts and humanities; 11 percent for public or society benefit; 5 percent for the environment and animals; 4 percent for science and technology; 4 percent for international affairs; 3 percent for social science; and 2 percent for religion.

In addition to making grants, foundations may undertake a wide range of activities. They often bring people together in conferences or informally to discuss new research, ideas, or problems. They help other organizations do their jobs better by providing them with management assistance or training. Some provide space for service-providing organizations, and others conduct or publish research. Foundations may also make loans and invest in projects that have a charitable purpose.

Staffing

Most foundations in the United States do not employ staffs. They have limited assets and are operated by the donor(s) or by the board of directors. Some unstaffed foundations employ consultants or other part-time staffs for specific tasks, such as accounting, audits, and legal matters. Corporate foundations are often administered by employees of the sponsoring company.

In the largest 2,500 foundations, program, administrative, and clerical staffs are employed to operate foundations, under the guidance of boards of directors. Fewer than 13,000 men and women work for philanthropic foundations. The staff of a typical foundation may include an executive director who heads the foundation, a program officer who investigates grant requests, and a secretary who does the clerical work. A few very large foundations, like the Ford, Kellogg, and Rockefeller foundations, have a large number of employees and a complex organizational structure.

Foundations Worldwide

Philanthropic trusts and religious funds are traditionally found in many cultures. Recently, increasing numbers of foundation-like institutions of all recognized types are being created throughout the world. Regulations, sources of support, and grant-making patterns vary, but in most cases, foundations are playing important roles in building and maintaining civil societies. As in the United States, foundations often take the name of the individual donor or family. Prominent international foundations include: Soros, Tatas, Calouste Gulbenkian, Aga Khan, Eugenio Mendoza, Bernard van Leer, Sassakawa, and Nuffield foundations. Organizations like community foundations are also evident in many countries and are becoming more common. These include the Asian Community Trust, the Foundation de France, the Puerto Rico Community Foundation, and many others. Company-sponsored foundations are also increasing in number; for example, the Toyota Foundation, Suntory Foundation, and the Prasetya Mulya Foundation.

Government-initiated or -supported foundations are prominent in many countries. The Volkswagen Foundation in Germany, the Japan Foundation, and the Bank of Sweden Tercentenary Foundation are examples. These types of foundations fulfill charitable or educational purposes and may be permitted to receive donations.

The European Foundation Center was formed in the 1980s to provide services and advocate on behalf of the growing number of European foundations. That organization now compiles a directory of European foundations. Similar country-specific directories also exist in Germany, the United Kingdom, and elsewhere.

Foundations are proliferating around the world as wealth is created and societal needs become more pressing. Sources of foundation funding vary, but the basic goals are the same: to use private resources and ingenuity to serve the public and to support alternative solutions to pressing social problems.

References

Boris, Elizabeth, 1989. "Working in Foundations." In Richard Magat, ed., *Philanthropic Giving: Studies in Varieties and Goals.* New York: Oxford University Press.

———, 1992. *Philanthropic Foundations in the United States: An Introduction.* Washington, DC: Council on Foundations.

Carnegie, Andrew, [1889] 1990. "The Gospel of Wealth." In David L. Geis, J. Steven Ott, and Jay M. Shafritz, eds., *The Nonprofit Organization: Essential Readings.* Pacific Grove, CA: Brooks-Cole.

Commission on Foundations and Private Philanthropy, 1970. *Foundations, Private Giving and Public Policy.* Chicago: University of Chicago Press.

Commission on Private Philanthropy and Public Needs, Department of the Treasury, 1975. *Giving in America.* Washington, DC: GPO.

———, 1977. Department of the Treasury, *Research Papers.* Washington, DC: GPO.

Council on Foundations, 1993. *Foundation Management Report.* Washington, DC: Council on Foundations.

Cuninggim, Merrimon. 1972. *Private Money and Public Service: The Role of Foundations in American Society.* New York: McGraw-Hill.

Edie, John, A., 1987. "Congress and Foundations: Historical Summary." In Teresa Odendahl, ed., *America's Wealthy and the Future of Foundations.* New York: Foundation Center.

Foundation Center, 1994a. *The Foundation Directory.* New York: Foundation Center.

———, 1994b. *The Foundation Grants Index.* New York: Foundation Center.

Freeman, D., and the Council on Foundations, 1991. *The Handbook of Private Foundations.* New York: Foundation Center.

Hall, Peter Dobkin, 1989. "The Community Foundation in America." In Richard Magat, ed., *Philanthropic Giving: Studies in Varieties and Goals.* New York: Oxford University Press.

Heimann, Fritz. F., ed., 1973. *The Future of Foundations.* Englewood Cliffs, NJ: Prentice-Hall.

Kaplan, Anne, ed., 1994. *Giving USA 1994: The Annual Report on Philanthropy for the Year 1993.* New York: American Association of Fund-Raising Counsel.

Karl, Barry D., and Stanley N. Katz, 1981. "The American Private Philanthropic Foundation and the Public Sphere, 1890–1930." *Minerva,* vol. 19: 236–70.

_____, 1987. "Foundations and Ruling Class Elites." *Daedalus* 116 (Winter): 1–40.

Lagemann, Ellen Condliffe, 1989. *The Politics of Knowledge: The Carnegie Corporation, Philanthropy, and Public Policy.* Middletown, CT: Wesleyan University Press.

Nielsen, Waldemar A., 1972., *The Big Foundations.* New York: Columbia University Press.

_____, 1985. *The Golden Donors: A New Anatomy of the Great Foundations.* New York: Dutton.

Odendahl, Teresa, ed., 1987. *America's Wealthy and the Future of Foundations.* New York: Foundation Center.

_____, 1990. *Charity Begins at Home: Generosity and Self-Interest Among the Philanthropic Elite.* New York: Basic Books.

Odendahl, Teresa J., and Elizabeth Boris, 1983. "The Grantmaking Process." *Foundation News* 24 (September–October).

Odendahl, Teresa J., Elizabeth Boris, and Arlene K. Daniels, 1985. *Working in Foundations: Career Patterns of Women and Men.* New York: Foundation Center.

Renz, Loren, and Steven Lawrence, 1994. *Foundation Giving: Yearbook of Facts and Figures on Private, Corporate, and Community Foundations.* New York: Foundation Center.

Salamon, Lester, 1991. *Foundation Investment and Payout Performance: An Update.* Washington, DC: Council on Foundations.

U.S. Congress, 1965. *Treasury Department Report on Private Foundations.* 89th Cong. 1st sess., 2 February.

PART 6

ENTREPRENEURSHIP AND COMMERCIALISM

Organizations in the nonprofit sector have always been positioned delicately between the business sector's profit motive and the government sector's drive to meet social needs. The existence, roles, functions, and revenues of nonprofit organizations are affected by changes in the other two sectors, and changes in the other two sectors became dramatic as we entered the new millennium.

At a time when government funding appears to be on a long-term decline, many nonprofits rely on it more than in the past. The media and politicians in Washington, D.C., and in statehouses are clamoring for governments to be downsized and for the devolution of government services and fiscal responsibility to state, county, and municipal governments.[1] The amount of U.S. government money flowing into the human services, the arts, and environmental protection has declined steadily and sometimes dramatically.[2] States, counties, and municipalities have not been eager to replace these declining federal funds when tax and deficit reductions continue to command high public support.[3] As I mentioned in Part 5, the timing of this downsizing and devolution "movement" coincided with a decades-long period of stagnant—and by some measures declining—individual and corporate donations to nonprofit organizations.[4]

Thus, for about twenty years, nonprofits have needed new sources of revenues. They have needed to become more entrepreneurial in pursuing businesses and business-like ventures, and they have had to manage their resources and programs efficiently. For nonprofit organizations to make these types of changes, they had to show more professionalism in their management and more representatives of businesses had to sit on their boards. As a result, many nonprofits have become aggressively commercial and compete for business directly with for-profit firms.[5] These successes, however, created new problems and challenges.[6] Thus, nonprofit organizations were surprisingly successful at becoming more entrepreneurial during the 1980s and 1990s.

Commercialization: Blurring the Line Between Businesses and Nonprofits

Nonprofit organizations in many subsectors have ventured into a variety of commercial markets.[7] Figures and percentages differ with different definitions and sources of information; but in 1992, charitable nonprofits overall raised an estimated 54 percent of their income from dues, fees, and other charges for services and products from commercial-type activities.[8] Nonprofits in the health care subsector have been competing directly and aggressively with for-profit businesses since the 1970s.[9] Many nonprofit hospitals and clinics own for-profit subsidiaries that provide corporate wellness programs, manage condominium physicians' offices, and operate private health clubs.[10] Nonprofits in the mental health, developmental disabilities, and other fields that serve mostly low-income populations regularly buy, manage, and sell companies that operate apartment houses, pet stores, laundries, and other historically low-wage service businesses. "Major museums, such as Chicago's Art Institute, Shedd Aquarium, and Field Museum of Natural History . . . have begun holding after-hours cocktail parties that compete with local taverns. . . . Revenue is produced through admission fees and drink sales."[11] Many of these commercial ventures have proven enormously successful.

Commercial-type ventures can provide multiple benefits for the clients who receive services from nonprofit organizations and for the financial health of nonprofits as well. They often create employment opportunities and make hard-to-find services available to clients. They also generate revenues that can be "plowed back" into more or better services, thereby benefiting clients and advancing a nonprofit organization's mission. It is easy to understand why commercial activities by nonprofit organizations have caused loud cries of "unfair competition," particularly from small businesses.[12]

Several other developments also have contributed to the commercialization of the nonprofit sector. First, for-profit businesses have been "invading turf" that historically "belonged" to the nonprofit sector.[13] For-profit chains have replaced nonprofits as the primary providers of hospital care in the United States. In 1996, aerospace giants Lockheed-Martin and Andersen Consulting "were each preparing to bid for the management of $563 million in welfare operations in Texas."[14] Private emergency medical services (EMS) companies have all but driven nonprofit ambulance squads out of urban and suburban markets, and have made major inroads in many rural areas. Businesses also have aggressively entered the mental health and substance abuse fields, day-care centers, trade and technical schools, and youth and adult corrections. Nonprofits and for-profits thus are competing with each other in fields that used to be each other's "turf"; to compete successfully, nonprofits have had to become more business-like.

Second, the professionalism of nonprofit organization managers has increased dramatically since 1985. Master's degree programs (and concentrations) in non-profit organization management, students, and graduates have proliferated at a dizzying pace during the past twenty years.[15] Many nonprofit organizations recruit business executives who, in a few subsectors, are receiving "Fortune 500" wages.[16]

Third, more business executives and fewer government and nonprofit organization managers sit on boards of trustees than twenty-five years ago. Overall, boards of trustees have become more business-oriented.[17]

Finally, mutually beneficial venture partnerships between businesses and non-profits became commonplace in the 1990s. Planned giving programs, cause-related marketing ventures, and business uses of higher education research facilities and faculty (rather than investing in their own) are a few examples of the array of the relationships.

When nonprofits enter commercial ventures, they must carefully observe principles to avoid (or limit) Unrelated Business Income Taxes (UBIT) and to preserve tax-exempt status with the IRS and state taxing authorities (see Part 2). The stakes, though, are higher than worries about UBIT. "The greatest peril is not that nonprofits may ultimately be driven out of the social service marketplace. Rather, the danger is that in their struggle to become more viable competitors in the short term, nonprofit organizations will be forced to compromise the very assets that made them so vital to society in the first place."[18]

Lester Salamon[19] asserts that the nonprofit sector is facing four categories of challenges "of crisis proportions." Each of these challenges by itself represents a serious danger to the sector's ability to survive in its current form. Salamon's four categories of challenges/crises are: fiscal, economic, effectiveness, and legitimacy, and the crisis of legitimacy is the most problematic. The single greatest force behind this crisis is the sector's inability to find or to define its role in between the government and business sectors. Citizens and elected officials alike are questioning whether the "commercialized" nonprofit sector should continue to receive favorable tax treatment and preferred contracting status with government. "Is the common interest best served when nonprofits aim to compete on for-profit terms?"[20] In the United States, we still have a mental image of a nonprofit as a community-based organization that organizes volunteers to administer to people who are in need—not as a multistate conglomerate with a director who earns a six-digit salary.[21] Unless the nonprofit sector is able to (re)define its role in the minds and perceptions of citizens and elected officials, the crisis of legitimacy eventually may disable it. According to one scholar:

> Because their government partners have changed the rules of the game so dramatically, nonprofits may be retreating from their mission in order to gain market share. Thus, nonprofits can win and lose simultaneously. Can nonprofits win contracts and still be responsive to their clients and communities? Unlike their for-profit counterparts, nonprofits may conclude that winning isn't everything.[22]

Readings Reprinted in Part Six

Dennis Young defines *"Nonprofit Entrepreneurship"* as "a proactive style of management through which leaders of nonprofit organizations seek to implement change through new organizational and programmatic initiatives."[23] Young points to three indicators of the importance of entrepreneurship to nonprofit organizations: (1) the nonprofit sector is growing rapidly, which signals the presence of considerable entrepreneurial activity; (2) many nonprofits have been in existence for only a short period of time, a trend that "reflects the classic mode of nonprofit entrepreneurship—individuals or groups motivated to address a social, health, environmental, or other issue, unsatisfied with existing services and aware of potential resources to support their interests, forming their own organizations"; and (3) many nonprofits were established for the specific purpose of introducing change. Entrepreneurship thus has been a factor in "the sector's ability to transform concern over social issues . . . into new operating programs and services."

Young explores the motivations for entrepreneurship in the nonprofit sector and the requirements—the conditions and skills—needed for successful entrepreneurship; he concludes with Peter Drucker's quotation: "Entrepreneurship and innovation . . . must be consciously striven for. They can be learned, but it requires effort. Entrepreneurial businesses treat entrepreneurship as a duty. They are disciplined about it. . . . They work at it. . . . They practice it."[24]

Alan Andreasen urges nonprofit organizations to seek new sources of revenue in this uncertain environment and, more specifically, to develop mutually beneficial ties with for-profit corporations. In *"Profits for Nonprofits: Find a Corporate Partner,"*[25]

Andreasen describes cause-related marketing alliances between businesses and nonprofits and offers practical advice about how to increase the probability that they will succeed for both parties. He describes the several such successful alliances with American Express that have benefited numerous arts organizations, the renovation of Ellis Island and the Statue of Liberty, and a "Share Our Strength" drive against hunger. Since American Express's early successful cause-related marketing ventures, "the number of alliances between nonprofit and for-profit organizations has skyrocketed. Avon, American Airlines, Ocean Spray, Polaroid, Ramada International Hotels & Resorts, Arm & Hammer, Wal-Mart Stores, and many other corporations have joined forces with national nonprofit institutions, such as the American Red Cross, the YMCA, the American Heart Association, and the Nature Conservancy, as well as local agencies tackling problems in their communities."

Andreasen cautions that there are risks involved with cause-related marketing partnerships, even if they are successful in raising funds for the nonprofits; alliances can drain resources that are needed for other endeavors, reduce donations (because of the public perception that additional funds are not needed), decrease organizational flexibility, damage the nonprofit's reputation through "tainted partners" or the use of unsavory marketing tactics, and "even success presents dangers. One is that the nonprofit will have more funds and more requests for the use of those funds than it can handle [administratively]." Andreasen offers strategic tips to nonprofits that will improve their chances of success in such alliances. Most important for success is early, clear communication between the parties: "They must be explicit about their goals and expectations."

"Commercialism and the Road Ahead," by Burton Weisbrod,[26] is a multifaceted answer to the question, "Should anyone care . . . whether the nonprofit sector becomes increasingly commercial?" His response is a resounding "yes, many people should care: taxpayers, who are affected by the subsidies [paid] to nonprofits; consumers of these organizations' services; governmental policymakers, as stewards for the public interest; owners of private firms, which are affected by nonprofits' activities; and nonprofit managers and directors, who are responsible for their organizations."

Nonprofits choose to engage in certain types of fund-raising to take advantage of their strengths but also to avoid problems with the Internal Revenue Service. They are fluid in responding to changes in their environments. Their need for revenues and their desire to adhere to their social purposes and missions, however, cause dilemmas. The nonprofit revenue trends of the 1990s have required nonprofits to be entrepreneurial—to engage in commercial ventures that do not always fit them well.

Various commercial revenue sources differentially affect the ability of nonprofits to attain their goals, and also have important effects on private businesses and governmental tax revenues. More knowledge is needed in these areas, however.

Notes

1. J. Steven Ott and Lisa A. Dicke, "HRM in an Era of Downsizing, Devolution, Diffusion, and Empowerment and Accountability??" in A. Farazmand, ed., *Strategic Public Personnel Administration/HRM: Building Human Capital for the 21st Century.* (Praeger/Greenwood Press, forthcoming).

2. Lester M. Salamon, "The Current Crises," in L. Salamon, *Holding the Center: America's Nonprofit Sector at a Crossroads* (New York: Nathan Cummings Foundation, 1997); also see Virginia A. Hodgkinson and Murray S. Weitzman, *Nonprofit Almanac, 1996–1997: Dimensions of the Independent Sector.* (San Francisco: Jossey-Bass, 1996).

3. Heather R. McLeod, "The Devolution Revolution—Are Nonprofits Ready?" *WhoCares* (fall 1995):36–42.

4. Alan R. Andreasen, "Profits for Nonprofits: Find a Corporate Partner." *Harvard Business Review* (November–December 1996): 47–59; and David Van Biema, "Can Charity Fill the Gap? Groups That Help the Poor Are Bracing for a Double Hardship; Surging Need and Federal Budget Cuts," *Time,* December 4, 1995, 44–53.

5. Salamon, "The Current Crisis," 11–47.

6. Burton A. Weisbrod, ed., *To Profit or Not to Profit: The Commercial Transformation of the Nonprofit Sector* (Cambridge: Cambridge University Press, 1998).

7. Burton A. Weisbrod, "The Future of the Nonprofit Sector: Its Entwining with Private Enterprise and Government." *Journal of Policy Analysis and Management* 16, no. 4(1997): 541–555.

8. Hodgkinson and Weitzman, *Nonprofit Almanac.*

9. Since about 1995, though, the nonprofit hospitals have been "losing" in the competition.

10. Montague Brown, "Commentary: The Commercialization of America's Voluntary Health Care System" *Health Care Management Review* 21, no. 3 (1996):13–18; also see Malik Hasan, "Let's End the Nonprofit Charade." *New England Journal of Medicine* 334, no. 16 (April 18, 1996):1055–1058.

11. Burton A. Weisbrod, "Commercialism and the Road Ahead," in B. A. Weisbrod, *To Profit or Not to Profit: The Commercial Transformation of the Nonprofit Sector* (Cambridge: Cambridge University Press 1998), 288.

12. U. S. Small Business Administration, *Unfair Competition by Nonprofit Organizations with Small Business: An Issue for the 1980s,* 3d ed. (Washington, DC: U. S. Government Printing Office, June 1984); also, James T. Bennett, and Thomas J. DiLorenzo, *Unfair Competition: The Profits of Nonprofits* (Lanham, MD: Hamilton Press, 1989).

13. William P. Ryan, "The New Landscape for Nonprofits," *Harvard Business Review* (January–February 1999):127–136.

14. Ibid., 127.

15. Naomi B. Wish and Roseanne M. Mirabella, "Educational Impact on Graduate Nonprofit Degree Programs: Perspectives of Multiple Stake Holders." *Nonprofit Management & Leadership* 9, no. 3 (spring 1999): 329–340.

16. For example, *Time's* October 2, 1995, cover story exclaimed: "Tax Exempt! Many non-profits look and act like normal companies—running businesses, making money. So why aren't they paying Uncle Sam?"

17. Melissa Middleton Stone, "Competing Contexts: The Evolution of a Nonprofit Organization's Governance System in Multiple Environments," *Administration and Society* 28, no. 1 (May 1996): 61–89.

18. Ryan, "The New Landscape for Nonprofits," 128.

19. Salamon, "The Current Crisis," 11–47. Also see Patrick J. McCormack. "Nonprofits at the Brink: Lean Budgets, Growing Needs, and the Fate of Nonprofits, *Northwest Report* 20 (April 1996).

20. Ryan, "The New Landscape for Nonprofits," 128.

21. Edward T. Pound, Gary Cohen, and Penny Loeb, "Tax Exempt! Many Nonprofits Look and Act Like Normal Companies—Running Businesses, Making Money. So Why Aren't They Paying Uncle Sam?" *U.S. News & World Report,* October 2, 1995, 36–39, 42–46, 51.

22. Ryan, "The New Landscape for Nonprofits," 136.

23. Young, Dennis R. "Nonprofit Entrepreneurship," in Jay M. Shafritz ed., *International Encyclopedia of Public Policy and Administration* (Boulder: Westview Press,1998), 1506–1509.

24. Peter F. Drucker, *Innovation and Entrepreneurship* (New York: Harper and Row, 1985), 150.

25. Andreasen, "Profits for Nonprofits," 47–59.

26. Weisbrod, "Commercialism and the Road Ahead," 287–305.

CHAPTER 17

Nonprofit Entrepreneurship

DENNIS R. YOUNG

A proactive style of management through which leaders of nonprofit organizations seek to implement change through new organizational and programmatic initiatives. The term "*entrepreneurship*" is commonly associated with the establishment of new ventures in the business sector. However, as a generic concept, entrepreneurship is equally applicable to the nonprofit sector and, in fact, is an intrinsic aspect of successful management and leadership of public organizations.

Entrepreneurship and Innovation

The classic definition of entrepreneurship was given by Joseph Schumpeter (1949), who called it the implementation of "new combinations of the means of production." Schumpeter, who studied economic development, identified five types of entrepreneurial activity, including the introduction of a new economic good or service, the introduction of a new method of production, the opening of a new market, the conquest of a new source of raw materials, and the reorganization of an industry such as the creation or breaking up of a monopoly. The thrust of Schumpeter's definition is the "implementation

of change." Thus, the establishment of a new organization, the making of profits, or the taking of risks per se—all characteristics commonly associated with entrepreneurship—are not its essence. Peter Drucker's (1985) words echo the emphasis on implementation of change as the defining characteristic: "Innovation is the specific tool of entrepreneurs, the means by which they exploit change as an opportunity for a different business or a different service" (p. 19). Firstenberg (1986) adds, however, that risk taking is intrinsic to bringing about change through entrepreneurship: "I label certain organizations 'entrepreneurial' because, in order to reap the benefits that flow from innovative change, they are willing to accept the uncertainty inherent in new endeavors and the possibility of disappointing results" (pp. 211–212).

Evidence of Nonprofit Entrepreneurship

Drucker (1985) cites developments in the nonprofit sector as prime examples of entrepreneurship, including the creation of the modern university in the late nineteenth century, the establishment of new private and metropolitan universities after World War II, the establishment of the modern hospital and the community hospital in the late eighteenth century, the development of specialized health clinics in the early twentieth century, and new program developments in a number of specific organizations in the social services, religion, health care, and professional societies. Dennis Young (1985) documents several different forms that nonprofit entrepreneurial ventures can take, including the establishment of new organizations designed to implement new service concepts, new organizations parented by existing organizations—through mergers or spin-offs, and new program initiatives undertaken within the framework of existing organizations. Overall, numerous examples and case studies of nonprofit entrepreneurship are documented in the literature (Young 1983, 1985, 1990, 1991; Drucker 1985).

Other signs also point to the importance of entrepreneurship as an intrinsic force in the nonprofit sector. First, the nonprofit sector is a fast-growing segment of the overall economy in the United States. In terms of income and employment, the sector's growth has paralleled and often exceeded the growth of government and business over the past two decades (Hodgkinson et al. 1992). Such aggregate growth, while underpinned by the commitment of new public and private resources, suggests the presence of considerable entrepreneurial effort to transform these resources into operating programs.

Second, 57 percent of existing charitable nonprofits came into existence only within the last 20 years (Hodgkinson et al. 1993), and the number of new public charities has increased at a rate of 6.5 percent between 1965 and 1990 (Bowen et al. 1994). These statistics reflect the classic mode of nonprofit entrepreneurship—individuals or groups motivated to address a social, health, environmental, or other issue, unsatisfied with existing services and aware of potential resources to support their interests, forming their own organizations. The fact that the nonprofit sector exhibits a steady entry of new organizations and is populated largely by young, small organizations bears witness to its entrepreneurial character. Although older, larger organizations also nurture entrepreneurial activity, smaller, younger organizations are its principal venue.

Third, many nonprofit organizations are established explicitly to bring about change. Indeed, social welfare advocacy organizations are designated with their own tax code [501(c)4] precisely to enable this function. More broadly, the missions of many foundations and charitable nonprofits are framed in terms of finding solutions to social, health, or environmental problems, supporting new means of expression in the arts or implementing new concepts of service delivery. Although its entrepreneurial character may not be the basic explanation for the nonprofit sector's dynamism, it appears to be a necessary element in the sector's ability to transform concern over social issues and the availability of governmental and private resources into new operating programs and services.

Motivation for Nonprofit Entrepreneurship

In the classical business context, the lure of profits and potential wealth is often assumed to be the primary motivating force behind entrepreneurship. This raises the question, what takes the place of profits in motivating entrepreneurship in the nonprofit sector? The answer to this question can be presented in three steps: (1) Profit is not the sole motivator for entrepreneurship, even in the business sector; (2) profit does sometimes play a role in nonprofit entrepreneurship and (3) other motivators are more important than profit or wealth in motivating nonprofit entrepreneurship.

Motivation for entrepreneurship in the business sector was studied by David McClelland (1973), who found that business entrepreneurs were "achievement oriented" and driven primarily by the need for accomplishment. McClelland also identified the needs for power and affiliation as sources of entrepreneurial motivation, especially in other sectors than business.

In the nonprofit sector, several scholars have studied entrepreneurial motivations. Estelle James (1987) cited promotion of one's own religious values as a key source of nonprofit entrepreneurship; thus, people form educational, social service, and health organizations in order to create environments that allow them to transmit their religious values to others or to maintain those values within their own group. Alternatively, Henry Hansmann (1980) identifies the quest for income and the desire to lead institutions of high quality as dual sources of nonprofit entrepreneurial motivation in nonprofits, especially those in education, health care, or social services, where professionals play an important role. Studying a range of nonprofit, governmental, and business ventures in the social service, Young (1983) identified a spectrum of entrepreneurial motivations including craftmanship and pride of creative accomplishment, acclaim of professional peers, belief in a cause, search for personal identity, need for autonomy and independence, desire to preserve a cherished organization, need for power or control, and desire for personal wealth. In this schema, motivations are correlated with sector, whereby income seeking is more heavily associated with entrepreneurship in the business sector, power seeking more heavily found in the public sector, and other motivations tending to cluster in the nonprofit sector.

Although the seeking of personal wealth is apparently a minor factor in motivating nonprofit-sector entrepreneurship, the role of profits generated by the entrepreneurial activities of nonprofit organizations is nonetheless potentially important. In particular, the undertaking of commercial ventures with the intent of generating financial surpluses has become an increasingly common nonprofit-sector phenomenon (Crimmins and Keil 1983; Skloot 1987; Starkweather 1993). Indeed, such activity has stirred up a storm of controversy in the small business sector over the issue of "unfair competition" (Wellford and Gallagher 1988; Bennett and DiLorenzo 1989). The growth of commercial ventures in the nonprofit sector has paralleled the more general usage of fees to finance nonprofit-sector services. Fee income, consisting of conventional service fees as well as other commercial income, accounted for over half the growth of the nonprofit sector between 1977 and 1989 (Salamon 1992).

The rationale for the undertaking of commercial ventures by nonprofit organizations is twofold: Some activities, such as university sporting events or sales of art reproductions by museums, may contribute directly to the mission and work of the organization. For example, sporting events are presumably a part of a well-rounded physical education program whereas art reproductions help educate people about great works of art. However, other nonprofit commercial activities are not directly related to mission but generate profits that can be allocated to support mission-related services. Profits from such "unrelated business income" are subject to federal unrelated business income tax (UBIT), which is similar to a corporate profits tax. Studies suggest that most nonprofit commercial ventures are related to mission (Skloot 1988). Moreover, relatively little UBIT is actually paid, although such collections and the level of unrelated nonprofit commercial activity are increasing (Schiff and Weisbrod 1991).

Because wealth seeking does not appear to be the primary force, the motivation for nonprofit entrepreneurship is a key question in the development of theory to explain why nonprofits are found to contribute to important parts of the economy. Most economic theory of the nonprofit sector focuses on "demand," attempting to explain why people want and will pay for the services of nonprofit organizations. However, demand-side theory leaves open the question of how such demand is translated into the actual supply of services. In the business sector, it is assumed by standard economic theory that supply will manifest itself in the form of new firms or expansion of existing firms, implicitly driven by profit-seeking entrepreneurs. As noted, for the nonprofit sector, theorists such as James (1987), Hansmann (1980), and Young (1983) have proposed a variety of entrepreneurial motivations to explain the manifestation of supply. Alternatively, Avner Ben-Ner and Theresa Van Hoomissen (1993) postulate that coalitions of stakeholders (consumers, donors, sponsors) assume much of the entrepreneurial initiative in nonprofit organizations, motivated by the desire to closely control the quality and character of services they consider important.

Requirements for Success

Aside from the significance of entrepreneurship as an element in nonprofit theory, understanding the conditions and skills of entrepreneurship is important to successful management of nonprofit organizations. Drucker (1985) identified four conditions or organizational "policies" for successful entrepreneurship in what he called "public-service institutions": (1) a clear definition of mission, (2) a realistic statement of goals, (3) willingness to question the validity of objectives that are not achieved after repeated attempts, and (4) constant search for innovative opportunities.

Paul Firstenberg's (1986) list focuses more specifically on the style of an organization's management. His ten characteristics are (1) coherent aims and values, (2) focus on comparative advantage, (3) intuitive decisionmaking, (4) an adaptive (internal) environment, (5) excellence of execution, (6) staying power, (7) marshalling exceptional talent, (8) finesse with diverse constituencies, (9) having a sense of where the action is, and (10) active-positive leadership.

Young's (1985, 1991) analysis focuses more specifically on the skills and knowledge of the entrepreneurial leader, in the context of an existing organization or in the process of building a new one. These capabilities are (1) developing a sense of mission, (2) problem-solving ability, (3) applying creativity and ingenuity, (4) identifying opportunities and good timing, (5) analyzing risks, (6) consensus and team building, (7) mobilizing resources, and (8) persistence. There is a clear nexus between Drucker's, Firstenberg's, and Young's requirements in the areas of mission focus and proactive searching for opportunities, although Drucker's principles more clearly emphasize the role of organizational culture and policy in creating the context for entrepreneurial management, Firstenberg's focus is on the management style, and Young's focus more heavily on the capacities of entrepreneurs themselves. All three sets of requirements raise the issue of whether entrepreneurial management is a subject that can be taught or whether it relies essentially on the innate talents of individuals. Young's emphasis on creativity, a good sense of timing, problem solving, and persistence and Firstenberg's stress on intuition and talent suggest that much depends on individual capacities. Drucker (1985), however, argues that "entrepreneurship and innovation can be achieved by any business. But they must be consciously striven for. They can be learned, but it requires effort. Entrepreneurial businesses treat entrepreneurship as a duty. They are disciplined about it. . . . They work at it. . . . They practice it" (p. 150).

Bibliography

Ben-Ner, Avner, and Theresa Van Hoomissen, 1993. "Nonprofit Organizations in the Mixed Economy: A Demand and Supply Analysis." In Avner Ben-Ner and Benedetto Gui, eds. *The Nonprofit Sector in the Mixed Economy.* Ann Arbor: University of Michigan Press.

Bennett, James T., and Thomas J. DiLorenzo, 1989. *Unfair Competition.* Lanham, MD: Hamilton Press.

Bowen, William G., Thomas I. Nygren, Sarah E. Turner, and Elizabeth Duffy, 1994. *The Charitable Nonprofits.* San Francisco: Jossey-Bass.

Crimmins, James C., and Mary Keil, 1983. *Enterprise in the Nonprofit Sector.* Washington, DC: Partners for Liveable Places.

Drucker, Peter F., 1985. *Innovation and Entrepreneurship.* New York: Harper and Row.

Firstenberg, Paul B., 1986. *Managing for Profit in the Nonprofit World.* New York: Foundation Center.

Hansmann, Henry B., 1980. "The Role of Nonprofit Enterprise." *Yale Law Journal,* vol. 89: 835–898.

Hodgkinson, Virginia A., Murray S. Weitzman, Stephen M. Noga, and Heather Gorski, 1993. *A Portrait of the Independent Sector.* Washington, DC: Independent Sector.

Hodgkinson, Virginia A., Murray S. Weitzman, Christopher M. Toppe, and Stephen M. Noga, 1992. *Nonprofit Almanac: 1992–1993.* San Francisco: Jossey-Bass.

James, Estelle, 1983. "How Nonprofits Grow." *Journal of Policy Analysis and Management,* vol. 2: 350–375.

_____, 1987. "The Nonprofit Sector in Comparative Perspective." In Walter W. Powell, ed., *The*

Nonprofit Sector: A Research Handbook. New Haven, CT: Yale University Press, 397–415.

McClelland, David C., 1973. "The Two Faces of Power." Chapter 19 in David C. McClelland and Robert S. Steele, eds., *Human Motivation.* Morris, NJ: General Learning Press.

Salamon, Lester M., 1992. *America's Nonprofit Sector.* New York: Foundation Center.

Schiff, Jerald, and Burton A. Weisbrod, 1991. "Competition between For-Profit and Non-Profit Organizations in Commercial Activities." *Annals of Public and Cooperative Economics,* vol. 62.

Schumpeter, Joseph, 1949. *The Theory of Economic Development.* Cambridge, MA: Harvard University Press.

Skloot, Edward, 1987. "Enterprise and Commerce in Nonprofit Organizations." In Walter W. Powell, ed., *The Nonprofit Sector: A Research Handbook.* New Haven, CT: Yale University Press, 380–396.

_____, 1988. *The Nonprofit Entrepreneur.* New York: Foundation Center.

Starkweather, David B., 1993. "Profit Making by Nonprofit Hospitals." In David C. Hammack and Dennis R. Young, eds., *Nonprofit Organizations in a Market Economy.* San Francisco: Jossey-Bass, 105–137.

Wellford, W. Harrison, and Janne G. Gallagher, 1988. *Unfair Competition?* Washington, DC: National Assembly.

Young, Dennis R., 1983. *If Not for Profit, for What?* Lexington, MA: D. C. Heath.

_____, 1985. *Casebook of Management for Nonprofit Organizations.* New York: Haworth Press.

_____, 1990. "Champions of Change: Entrepreneurs in Social Work." In Harold H. Weissman, ed., *Serious Play.* Silver Spring, MD: National Association of Social Workers, 126–135.

_____, 1991. "Providing Entrepreneurial Leadership." In Richard L. Edwards and John A. Yankey, *Skills for Effective Human Service Management.* Silver Spring, MD: NASW Press, 62–75.

► CHAPTER 18

Profits for Nonprofits

Find a Corporate Partner

A L A N   R .   A N D R E A S E N

At a time when society is depending more and more on the nonprofit sector to provide a social safety net, nonprofit organizations themselves have been facing tough times. Although total private giving to charitable organizations, including corporate giving, rose in 1995, the long-term trend has not been encouraging. Total private giving in constant dollars grew at a snail's pace from 1990 to 1994. Corporate giving in constant dollars fell dramatically over the same period. And planned welfare reform will reduce government spending for social services. In this uncertain environment, nonprofits must seek new sources of revenue.

The for-profit world is the most obvious and most promising place to look. In fact, I believe that in order to survive, nonprofit organizations must develop explicit ties with for-profit corporations. Instead of hoping to become the lucky beneficiaries of a company's independent cause-related marketing campaign, such as Benetton's ads promoting AIDS awareness or Ticketmaster's programs to combat violence, nonprofits must enter into cause-related marketing alliances with corporations. Such partnerships, of course, are not risk free. Nonprofits that ally with corporations may find themselves in unproductive short-term relationships and may

end up associated with superficial campaigns and overpriced and inferior products and services. And, as the story of the child welfare foundation makes clear, a nonprofit may even find itself linked to a company whose business practices are completely antithetical to the nonprofit's mission.

The risks, however, should not deter nonprofits from pursuing cause-related marketing alliances. Many of the risks can be avoided if nonprofits think of themselves not as charities but as true partners in the marketing effort. From the corporation's standpoint, cause-related marketing is not philanthropy. In fact, funding for cause-related marketing programs usually comes out of a company's marketing budget, not its corporate giving or community relations budget. Savvy nonprofit managers will approach cause-related marketing alliances with the same bottom-line mentality. They will assess their organizations' strengths and weaknesses and understand exactly how their organizations can add value to for-profit partners. They will investigate many companies and identify those that stand to gain the most from an alliance. And they will take an active role in shaping a partnership and monitoring its progress at every stage.

How Alliances Work

The tremendous potential of affiliations between nonprofit and for-profit organizations was first recognized by American Express in 1982 when Jerry Welsh, then chief executive officer of worldwide marketing, had an idea for a campaign. The company would donate 5 cents to several arts organizations in San Francisco every time someone used an American Express card in the area and $2 every time someone in the area became a member. The campaign was brief but surprisingly successful. In just three months, American Express contributed $108,000 to the arts organizations and saw a considerable increase in transactions with the card. The company also found that its relationships with participating merchants improved and that more local merchants decided to accept the card.

American Express deemed the campaign so successful that the company decided to try a similar program on a nationwide basis. In 1983, American Express promised to donate 1 cent for every transaction with the card anywhere in the United States, and $1 for each new card issued during the last quarter of the year, to the foundation overseeing the renovation of Ellis Island and the Statue of Liberty. That program, too, was a great success. Use of the card increased 28% compared with the same period the previous year, and the company was able to donate $1.7 million to the renovation project.

Since American Express's pioneering ventures, the number of alliances between nonprofit and for-profit organizations has skyrocketed. Avon, American Airlines, Ocean Spray, Polaroid, Ramada International Hotels & Resorts, Arm & Hammer, Wal-Mart Stores, and many other corporations have joined forces with national nonprofit institutions, such as the American Red Cross, the YMCA, the American Heart Association, and the Nature Conservancy, as well as local agencies tackling problems in their communities. It is unusual to go into a supermarket, fast-food restaurant, or drugstore without encountering posters and other promotional materials for a social program cosponsored by one or more private-sector organizations.

When a corporation and a nonprofit organization enter into a cause-related marketing alliance, the corporation agrees to undertake a series of actions that will benefit both the nonprofit and the company. The three principal kinds of alliance are transaction-based promotions, joint issue promotions, and licensing.

Transaction-based promotions are probably the most common form of cause-related marketing alliance. In such an alliance, a corporation donates a specific amount of cash, food, or equipment in direct proportion to sales revenue—often up to some limit—to one or more nonprofits. American Express's Charge Against Hunger is an excellent example of this type of alliance. The program began in 1993, when the company was looking for ways to motivate cardholders to use their American Express cards and merchants to accept the card. Natalia Cherney Roca, senior director of national marketing, recalls that the employees responsible for developing a new marketing program kept coming back to the successful partnership that American Express had formed with the hunger-relief organization Share Our Strength in 1988. At that time, American Express had agreed to sponsor Taste of the Nation, the largest annual food- and wine-tasting event in the United States, the proceeds of which go to SOS. Hunger relief seemed like the perfect cause for American Express to support because a large proportion of the company's credit-card business comes from use of the card in restaurants and hotels.

As a result of the success of Taste of the Nation and the increasing strength of the relationship between American Express and SOS, American Express decided to elevate its hunger-relief efforts with the annual Charge Against Hunger program. Every time someone uses an American Express card between November 1 and December 31, the company donates 3 cents to SOS, up to a total of $5 million per year. American Express's contributions are augmented considerably by other partners that have "joined the charge." For example, in 1994, Kmart agreed to donate 10 cents every time an American Express card was used in its stores from November 27 through the end of the year, yielding an additional $250,000. Other promotions during the second year of the program by the Melville Corporation, Madison Square Garden, Restaurants Unlimited, and the National Football League raised more money.

The program has been a great success for both partners. Over the past three years, American Express and other partners have contributed more than $16 million to SOS. American Express has found that as a result of the program, transactions with the card have increased and more merchants now accept the card. Furthermore, cardholders have expressed strong support for the Charge Against Hunger and greater satisfaction with American Express, and thousands of the company's employees have volunteered their time to fight hunger.

Joint issue promotions are a second form of cause-related marketing alliance. In such a partnership, a corporation and one or more nonprofits agree to tackle a social problem through tactics such as distributing products and promotional materials, and advertising. Money may or may not pass between the corporation and the nonprofit.

A dramatic example of a joint issue promotion is Hand in Hand, an ongoing program to promote breast health that was launched in 1992 by *Glamour* magazine and Hanes Hosiery, and is cosponsored by the National Cancer Institute, the American College of Obstetricians and Gynecologists, and the American Health Foundation. The program aims to reach women between the ages of 18 and 39 through articles in *Glamour,* in-store promotions sponsored by Hanes, and the production of a wide range of free educational materials in cooperation with the nonprofit partners, including inserts that eventually will appear in 120 million pairs of hosiery. The sponsors hope that their target audience will not only learn about breast health but also urge their mothers, aunts, and grandmothers—women at much greater risk for breast cancer—to have regular breast exams. A study on four college campuses found that the Hand in Hand materials increased the target population's understanding of and attention to breast health. The program will undoubtedly help *Glamour* and Hanes position themselves as

organizations closely attuned to the interests of their target audience.

A third kind of cause-related marketing alliance is the licensing of the names and logos of nonprofits to corporations in return for a fee or percentage of revenues. Licensing predates the emergence of cause-related marketing in the 1980s. Colleges and universities, for example, have licensed their names and logos for years. Other nonprofits are now adopting the tactic. In April 1996, the American Association of Retired Persons announced that it would begin licensing its name to health maintenance organizations across the United States.

Some nonprofit organizations have been criticized for their licensing arrangements. Consider, for example, the Arthritis Foundation, which decided in 1994 to allow McNeil Consumer Products, a division of Johnson & Johnson, to market a line of four pain relievers called Arthritis Foundation Pain Relievers. In return, the foundation would receive a minimum of $1 million per year from McNeil to finance research. Some organizations, including consumers' groups, have argued that the arrangement compromises the foundation's ability to give unbiased advice, a charge similar to that made recently against the American Cancer Society, which has a licensing agreement with SmithKline Beecham for its NicoDerm CQ nicotine patch. Roy Scott, the Arthritis Foundation's group vice president for public relations, acknowledges that the arrangement benefits McNeil Consumer Products, but he says that the pain relievers also help arthritis sufferers by enabling the foundation to communicate to people whom the organization might not otherwise reach.

The benefits for McNeil in the highly competitive pain-reliever market are not yet clear, but initial results have shown that many more people are aware of the Arthritis Foundation as a result of the sale and promotion of the pain relievers.

The Risks to Nonprofits

Even if a cause-related marketing alliance yields only minimal returns, what is lost? How bad can the risks be? The answer is that nonprofit organizations may be putting themselves at great risk when they join forces with a corporation, even when the alliance is a great success. Managers of nonprofits must be aware of the risks in order to adopt a strategy for avoiding them.

Wasted Resources

Building a cause-related marketing alliance requires a lot of time and effort. What if the venture fails? A corporation can chalk it up to the cost of doing business. A nonprofit organization, however, which probably has a small staff and limited resources, may find that it has seriously compromised other activities, such as fundraising, educating people about issues, and building alliances with other corporations and nonprofits.

Reduced Donations

Cause-related ventures can generate new revenues for nonprofits. But does that mean that total revenues will increase? Not if the organization's traditional donors decide to cut back. People who used to give money to a nonprofit may decide not to if they believe that they have given enough by, for instance, using a credit card issued by a company involved in a transaction-based promotion. Individuals and foundations may reduce their donations if they think that the nonprofit doesn't need their help anymore or if they are turned off by the nonprofit's ties to the for-profit world. And corporations that used to support a nonprofit may take their philanthropy elsewhere if they come to believe that the organization and the issue it promotes have been co-opted by the nonprofit's corporate partner.

But this downside is not inevitable. Studies by American Express suggest that cause-related ventures sometimes can raise the public's awareness of a nonprofit and actually lead to increased donations.

Loss of Organizational Flexibility

A corporation that enters into an alliance with a nonprofit organization may impose restrictions on the nonprofit. If the restrictions help ensure the expected payoff to the corporation and prevent the nonprofit from engaging in actions that could harm the corporation, they make perfect sense. Nonprofits that enter into a partnership with American Express, for instance, presumably cannot strike a deal with Visa. But suppose one of American Express's nonprofit partners wanted Neiman Marcus to donate $10 for every coat sold in February, after the Charge Against Hunger program had ended. What if American Express accepted the arrangement only if the coat were purchased using an American Express card? A responsible corporate partner like American Express is unlikely to make such demands, but if it does, nonprofits must weigh the benefits of the alliance against possible restrictions on their own fund-raising abilities.

Tainted Partners

Many corporations enter into relationships with nonprofits because they want to bask in the glow of their esteemed partners. When Philip Morris spent $60 million in 1991 to sponsor an exhibit for the 200th anniversary of the Bill of Rights put on by a federal agency, the National Archives, the company was obviously trying to fight off its negative image and lay the foundation for its smokers' rights campaign. The motives behind the donation were transparent, and it is unlikely that the National Archives has suffered by joining forces with a corporation whose marketing strategies many people consider evil.

In some cases, however, a partnership with a tainted for-profit corporation may prevent a nonprofit from carrying out its mission. The child welfare organization described at the beginning of this article, which joined forces with a corporation employing child labor, will most likely have great difficulty collecting funds for its programs in the future. The nonprofit probably could have avoided the fiasco by conducting a thorough examination of the clothing manufacturer. But no amount of research enables a nonprofit to foresee every possible disaster.

Antithetical Marketing

A corporate marketer may use tactics that conflict with a nonprofit's image and strategy. In 1994, for example, the American Heart Association entered into an alliance with the makers of several products, including Quaker Oat Squares and Healthy Choice pasta sauce, to distribute a brochure explaining the Food and Drug Administration's new food labels. Almost two-thirds of the brochure was devoted to coupons for the sponsoring products, and many saw the venture as a tawdry gimmick.

Overwhelming Success

A failed alliance can certainly damage a non-profit organization, but even success presents dangers. One is that the nonprofit will have more funds and more requests for the use of those funds that it can handle. That was one of the concerns that American Express had about its relationship with Share Our Strength. The infusion of money from the Charge Against Hunger program more than tripled SOS's budget. Anticipating that SOS might be overwhelmed as it tried to allocate and monitor the new funds, American Express provided a separate endowment and helped SOS build the necessary administrative systems.

Structural Atrophy

Another potential consequence of a successful cause-related marketing alliance is that the nonprofit will come to rely excessively on corporate funding. What happens if the corporation announces that it will spend its marketing budget in a different way next year and has not helped the nonprofit establish a strong base for fundraising? In many cases, the nonprofit will have devoted most of its energy and resources to supporting the alliance instead of exploring other potential corporate partners and increasing traditional donations. It may have let its marketing muscles atrophy instead of learning how to sustain the marketing program without corporate support. Finally, it may have relied on its partner to manage contacts with other corporate partners and may have difficulty keeping them on board if the primary sponsor decides to step out.

Becoming a Strategist

Some successful cause-related marketing partnerships are the result of chance encounters at

social events. And some fruitful partnerships are developed because a corporate executive or board member has a personal interest in a particular problem or organization. Most alliances that are based on serendipity, however, dissolve before too long.

Nonprofit managers who want partners from the for-profit world must go out and find those partners instead of waiting for corporations to find them. They must develop a strategy that is active rather than reactive. They must become as proficient at marketing their organizations as corporations are at marketing their products and services. In effect, they must become effective strategists.

If nonprofit managers have done their homework, they will understand all the ways in which nonprofits add value to corporate partners, they will have assessed their organizations' strengths and weaknesses, they will have scoped out corporations who might be a good fit, and they will be able to demonstrate to a potential corporate "customer" how the relationship will complement the corporation's long-term strategy.

What Kinds of Value Can a Nonprofit Add?

From a corporate marketer's point of view, a nonprofit organization's most valuable asset is its image. Many companies seeking cause-related marketing alliances hope that a nonprofit's image will define, enhance, or even repair their own.

Consider a study carried out in the fall of 1995 by Roper Starch Worldwide for Cone Communications, a marketing and public relations firm in Boston, Massachusetts. According to interviews with 70 executives at companies engaged in cause-related marketing, the companies used the marketing technique primarily to improve their relationships with customers and enhance their reputations. It seems that the corporate marketers were right to believe that consumers respond to the halo effect. In a survey of nearly 2,000 men and women aged 18 and over conducted by Roper Starch for Cone Communications in August 1993, 31% said that when price and quality are equal, a company's business practices influence their purchases. Fifty-four percent said that they would pay a premium for a product that supports a cause they care about, and 71% said that cause-related marketing is a good way to solve social problems. In particular, companies trying to differentiate themselves in highly competitive markets or attempting to launch a new product or service can gain a great deal from allying themselves with social causes.

A nonprofit can offer a corporation more than its image, however. When a corporation allies itself with a nonprofit, the corporation often saves on advertising and promotional costs because the alliance usually brings free publicity and many public-relations opportunities. The corporation also gains access to the nonprofit's clientele, staff, trustees, and donors, all of whom are potential customers. Such access makes nonprofits with large memberships especially attractive to many companies.

What Are Our Organization's Strengths and Weaknesses?

A nonprofit cannot market itself successfully unless it understands exactly what it can and cannot offer a corporate partner. Managers of nonprofit organizations must ask themselves the following questions:

1:   *What is our image?* A nonprofit organization with a spotless reputation will be a valuable partner for a corporation with credibility problems. Nonprofits that have been touched by scandal or controversy will have a difficult time developing partnerships until they get their own houses in order.
2:   *Do we have strong brand recognition?* Corporations that want to be recognized more widely by the public will be most interested in forming partnerships with well-known charities like the Salvation Army and the Muscular Dystrophy Association. A nonprofit that is the darling of the media makes an attractive partner. When television reporters flock to the Special Olympics, for instance, many companies would love their CEOs to be present and their logos prominently displayed.
3:   *Is our cause especially attractive to certain companies and industries?* Every local charity can

argue that it seeks to make its community a better place to live and work; thus every corporation located there is a potential partner. The best cause-related marketing alliances, however, emerge when partners have complementary goals and interests. For example, the March of Dimes Birth Defects Foundation wanted more pregnant women to be aware of their need for folic acid, a B vitamin that can help prevent birth defects of the spine and brain. Kellogg wanted to increase sales of Product 19, a breakfast cereal rich in folic acid. The March of Dimes agreed to the use of its name on Product 19 packages in association with a message about folic acid. In return, Kellogg donated $100,000 to the March of Dimes.

4:   *Is our target audience particularly appealing to some corporations?* A company is likely to give serious consideration to a partnership with a nonprofit organization whose target audience represents a large group of potential customers. A nonprofit that focuses on childhood diseases, for instance, will find natural allies in toy companies or manufacturers of children's clothing.
5:   *Do we promote a cause that the public considers especially urgent?* Urgent causes generally produce higher payoffs for a corporation than causes on the public's back burner. In a recent document on cause-related marketing, advisers to the American Cancer Society urged corporations seeking cause-related marketing partnerships to ask, "How many people are touched by the cause for which the charity stands, and how strongly are they affected by it?" Some "hot" causes, however, are too hot. For example, many major corporations have shied away from AIDS-related promotions—despite the issue's currency—because they fear that customers would be turned off.
6:   *Do we have clout with certain groups of people?* Some nonprofit organizations can help corporations gain access to people who influence consumers' purchases. Nonprofit organizations devoted to medical issues, for instance, are highly regarded by health professionals. Such organizations are valuable partners for pharmaceutical companies, who depend on health professionals to prescribe their drugs but often have trouble gaining access to those crucial intermediaries.
7:   *Are we local, national, or international?* It is extremely valuable for the parties in a cause-re-

lated marketing alliance to have similar organizational structures and objectives. Large nonprofits that work on many issues both nationally and locally do best by seeking corporations that can simultaneously conduct national campaigns and work at the local level through divisional offices or franchisees. The National Easter Seal Society, for example, has a national headquarters and many independent local affiliates. The organization has built partnerships with companies that have the same national-local characteristic, such as Safeway, Amway, and Century 21 Real Estate, and thus has been able to raise funds nationally and encourage initiatives by local businesses. Easter Seal raised its level of support from corporations from $3 million in 1980 to $13 million in 1989.

In contrast, strictly local organizations should probably avoid a corporation whose focus is national or international. A local women's shelter is best paired with a locally owned retailer or service company.

8: *Do we have a charismatic or well-known leader?* Such a leader can guarantee instant media coverage of the alliance and its programs. He or she can also inspire the corporation's employees to participate in the venture. A major asset that Share Our Strength brings to its partnership with American Express is its charismatic leader, Bill Shore, who appears in Charge Against Hunger ads and at events designed to increase support for the program among American Express's employees.

9: *Is our organization experienced and stable?* Corporations seeking long-term alliances will look for a nonprofit that has a long track record, sound finances, a sizable staff, and, preferably, experience as a marketing partner. Nonprofits without those credentials may have to settle for short-term alliances.

Who Are Our Potential Partners?

Once a nonprofit has assessed its strengths and weaknesses and has determined what it can bring to a cause-related marketing alliance, it should assemble an array of potential partners and begin a systematic investigation of each one. No stone should be left unturned. In addition to reviewing annual reports and speeches by cor-

porate leaders, nonprofit managers must talk to as many people as they can. Board members and community leaders often can recommend possible cause-related marketing partners and provide information about them. Those people might even know a company's CEO and other senior executives and thus may have insight into a potentially unfriendly corporate culture or a company's plans to downsize or decrease its support for social programs.

Of course, the most important characteristic to look for in a partner is the extent to which a cause-related marketing program would complement the corporation's goals and eventually increase its bottom line. Other features to look for include the following:

1: The corporation clearly recognizes the potential value of a cause-related marketing campaign, which makes marketing the idea of the partnership to the corporation relatively easy.

2: The promotion will be a logical—even essential—component of the company's long-term marketing strategy. Partnerships that do not fit a company's strategy and are peripheral to its core interests will ultimately seem superficial to both parties—and perhaps to the public.

3: The company does not engage in any business practices that are antithetical to the nonprofit's mission. Think again of the child welfare foundation that unwittingly associated itself with a company that did not support the welfare of children. Nonprofits must learn as much as they can about a potential partner's ethical standards, how strictly the company adheres to those standards, and whether the company extends its ethics to suppliers and to business partners.

4: The company's senior executives are enthusiastic about the partnership and will champion it. If the CEO and other senior managers don't think that the program fits the company's strategy, the alliance is unlikely to last.

5: The company will devote enough funds and people to the alliance.

6: The corporation indicates that it is willing to stick with the initial cause-related marketing campaign for a considerable period.

7: The corporation indicates a willingness to continue the partnership beyond the initial campaign.

8: The corporation appears eager to involve its employees as well as its suppliers, dealers, and franchisees in the cause-related marketing program. The more ways in which the corporation is connected to the program, the more likely the corporation is to benefit from the partnership and want to continue it.

9: The corporation appears unlikely to place undue restrictions on the nonprofit's activities or otherwise interfere with its operations.

Making the Partnership Work

No matter how thoroughly a nonprofit researches potential corporate partners, and no matter how well it markets itself, a cause-related marketing alliance can fail unless both parties start by communicating clearly. In order to negotiate a mutually beneficial alliance, they must be explicit about their goals and expectations. They should spell out—preferably in a contract—the objectives of the project and how they will be measured, whether the corporation will be the nonprofit's only partner or the only partner from a particular industry, and the resources that each party will commit and the areas for which each will be responsible.

As the project gets under way—perhaps on a test basis in one community or in a one-month trial—the partners should meet routinely to track its progress, and they should look at the program's results as honestly as possible. Most of the executives interviewed by Roper Starch for Cone Communications in 1995 said that their companies did not measure cause-related programs primarily in terms of direct sales. Instead, the companies tracked improvements in their image and increases in customer loyalty and in the satisfaction of employees and customers. Some effects of cause-related marketing programs, such as the long-term consequences for a company's image, are difficult to measure. And there is always the danger that either party will want to put a positive spin on soft data. A partnership will have the best chance of enduring if both sides are candid about their measures. Candor builds trust and increases the likelihood that midcourse corrections will be made in a flagging venture.

Both partners must also communicate openly and honestly with the public. Many good programs can be sabotaged if the public believes that a company is using a nonprofit's positive image to disguise an inferior product, that the nonprofit is being manipulated by the corporation, or that the nonprofit will not actually receive funds from the program. For example, if there is a cap on corporate contributions in a transaction-based promotion, that should be clear from the start. If corporate contributions are unrelated to consumers' actions, the public must be told.

Nonprofit alliances can be difficult to manage. But when they work, they can have great payoffs for both partners—as well as for the public. While a corporation is boosting its image and a nonprofit is securing crucial funds, both parties are also focusing attention on social problems that might otherwise be neglected. Cause-related marketing is about marketing, but it is also about finding new ways to improve people's lives.

CHAPTER 19

Commercialism and the Road Ahead

BURTON A. WEISBROD

Introduction

Should anyone care, whether the nonprofit sector becomes increasingly commercial? The answer is yes, many people should care: taxpayers, who are affected by the subsidies to nonprofits; consumers of these organizations' services; governmental policymakers, as stewards for the public interest; owners of private firms, which are affected by nonprofits' activities; and nonprofit managers and directors, who are responsible for their organizations. We have surveyed the landscape of the nonprofit sector, examining why revenue-generating sources are changing, what forms they are taking, and what the consequences are of their use.

What Has Been Learned About Nonprofits' Commercialism?

Overview

The causes and consequences of commercialization are not abstract issues. Nonprofit organizations' commercial activities are bringing revolutionary changes in traditional behavior, and in the process they are blurring the distinction between nonprofits and private firms. New examples appear almost daily. A recent account involves major museums, such as Chicago's Art Institute, Shedd Aquarium, and Field Museum of Natural History: They have begun holding after-hours cocktail parties, "competing with establishments on the other end of the cultural spectrum: bars" and giving rise to their characterization as "meat markets" (Caro 1997). Revenue is produced through admission fees and drink sales, but the question of whether such activities undermine the museums' cultural-preservation and educational missions remains.

In the hospital industry, a quite recent instance of aggressive marketing of profit-making activities is the decision by the largest nonprofit hospital in Nashville, Tennessee, "to build and operate a $15 million, 18-acre office and training-field complex that it will rent to the Houston Oilers [professional football team]," which moved to Tennessee in the fall of 1997. The hospital's chairman proudly reported that "Baptist Hospital will be on national TV. . . . When a player is hurt, a golf cart will rush onto the field with Baptist's name all over it." The CEO unabashedly spotlighted the market-oriented philosophy: "We are the pioneers of a nonprofit hospital competing with investor-owned hospitals" (Langley 1997).

Commercialism by nonprofits offers real advantages, despite the problems it poses. I have found evidence of significant scientific advances resulting from cooperation between universities and private-sector firms. We have also found evidence, in the higher-education, hospital, and museum industries, that increased commercialism in the form of unrelated business activity is efficient in the sense that it imposes little marginal cost, given the resources already available for production of mission-related activities; thus, it would appear to be inefficient to discourage, let alone prohibit, use of those resources even for business activities that are unrelated to tax-exempt missions.

Earlier chapters have documented not only the many fascinating new forms of profit-oriented activities in various industries, but also the complexity of determining whether use of those finance mechanisms, which mimic private enterprise, is consistent with social missions. Our analytic framework implies that nonprofits select particular revenue-generating activities deliberately, reflecting such variables as their ability to take the labor and capital used for their central, mission-related activities and use them to produce other, ancillary outputs. Choices also reflect the flexibility of the IRS in deciding which activities will be taxed as being unrelated. Thus, forms of money-raising activities can be expected to evolve over time, in response to changes in technology or in IRS administrative practices, in addition to further cutbacks, should they occur, in government support.

Nonprofits can be expected to increase efforts to push outward the margins of the kinds of revenue-producing mechanism they use, continually probing IRS regulatory restrictions. These restrictions have a number of dimensions, including

1. whether an activity will be subject to taxation as an unrelated business,
2. what accounting methods nonprofits may use to calculate their taxable income—including the rules on how nonprofits are permitted to allocate joint costs so as to minimize their tax liability[1]—and
3. which activities are regarded as inconsistent with the nonprofit's mission and, hence, as

justification for withdrawal of tax-exempt status.

With nonprofits' commercialization bringing both revenue needed to finance their unprofitable, collective-goods mission and behavior that may be inconsistent with that mission, difficult choices result. The dilemma is real. Although our analyses generally reflect concerns about the balance between the drive for revenue and adherence to social goals, the precise nature of sacrifices that nonprofits make to raise revenue is seldom clear-cut. Increased commercialization is not ideal. The more important question, though, is whether its many forms, encompassing user fees and various ancillary outputs, are preferable to the alternatives. Those could include greater dependence on government—through grants, tax subsidies, or tax encouragement of private donations—or diminished output of collective goods.

Mission: Its Vagueness and Its Effects on Nonprofits

If it were entirely clear that certain commercial activities were in conflict with nonprofits' pursuit of their tax-exempt missions, the IRS would be revoking tax-exempt status far more often. What is more commonly observed, however, is ambiguity as to the effects—ambiguity that reflects the typically broad scope of mission. Thus, we have found that in light of such mission vagueness, it is understandable that nonprofits typically claim there is no conflict—that commercial sales activities are not simply generating money but are simultaneously advancing organization mission. The Girl Scouts, for example, hold that sale of cookies is not merely a commercial activity to raise money, but an exercise through which young girls gain experience that helps build their character and impart business skills. What, then, are the limits to the goods and services that might be sold in pursuit of that mission, or of AARP's mission of promoting the interests of older Americans (age 50 and over) through advocacy, supportive services, and the provision of information and research?

The contrast with a profit-making firm is stark. The relative simplicity of gauging a firm's profitability stands in sharp contrast to the complex, multidimensional social goals that, whether attained or not, often characterize nonprofits. The complexity is not a weakness of nonprofits but rather a source of considerable difficulty in identifying and measuring their success or failure, and, thus, in making them "accountable."

Mission vagueness is fundamentally important in predicting and evaluating nonprofit-organization behavior: It makes the operational definition of an "unrelated" business activity inherently problematic; it explains why nonprofits can undertake an ever-widening array of revenue-enhancing activities that the organization can argue are related to mission and that the IRS finds difficult to term "unrelated" and, hence, taxable.

Mission vagueness permits managers and trustees to alter behavior in response to changing financial constraints while—at least arguably—continuing pursuit of the same goals. Means and ends are easily confused when goals are vague, and the wider the scope of mission, the greater is the challenge to organization leadership, prospective donors, and regulators to determine whether a profitable commercial activity is mission related.

Narrowness of mission focus is not inherently desirable, nor is wide scope inherently undesirable. Breadth permits latitude for organizations to adjust to changing external conditions, and such flexibility is necessary for efficient use of resources. Drawing a distinction, however, between vagueness of mission and flexibility of resource use is both difficult and important for two reasons: to predict nonprofits' responses to exogenous changes in regulatory, financial, and technological constraints, and to assess the accomplishments of nonprofits in achieving their goals.

Broad mission scope poses a severe regulatory challenge: to determine when the "border" is being crossed between a true mission-focused activity and a mere money-raiser. This is explicit in the admission of the hospital CEO, cited above: "No question," he reportedly admitted; in the selection of revenue-generating activities, "we push the envelope" (Langley 1997).

A question [worth asking] is whether such aggressive commercialism is causing nonprofits to sacrifice subtle elements of their social, collective-good, mission—for which the subsidies and tax exemptions are given—in the interest of generating revenue. In the case of university-industry research collaboration, universities have agreed to delay or even avoid publication of research findings in order to protect proprietary secrecy, actions that conflict with their traditional objective of full dissemination of knowledge. We have seen repeatedly how broad goals make it difficult to determine whether a commercial activity that garners revenue brings any adverse side effect with regard to mission. Without that determination, the true extent of nonprofits' contributions cannot be identified.

Nonprofits' Pursuit of Mission: Effects on Private Firms

To assess the overall contribution of nonprofits it is not enough to focus on those organizations. In addition to the impact of their commercial activities on their own revenues and on achievement of their organization goals, there are effects of those activities on other sectors of the economy—private enterprise, for one. We have seen that nonprofits are expanding into activities that compete with private firms. This may or may not be socially efficient, but it is clearly adverse to the firms. Such competition varies greatly among industries: Food pantries and homeless shelters use technologies that offer few opportunities for commercial expansion, but museums can open retail shops, and public television stations can air announcements for commercial firms. In the hospital industry, where the competition for patients who pay is especially keen, the legitimacy of subsidies to nonprofits is increasingly being questioned in light of evidence that their provision of medical care to the indigent closely resembles that of for-profit hospitals. In the mapmaking industry, the nonprofit National Geographic Society has been charged with having an unfair advantage in its nascent cartographic competition with the for-profit firm Hammond Maps (Hays 1997).

We have also found evidence, for various industries, that nonprofits' tax advantages, although ostensibly given to support mission-related activities, really extend beyond them to unrelated activities. Thus, most of nonprofits' taxable activities actually go untaxed, as nonprofits are typically successful in allocating enough joint costs to the taxable activities to eliminate reported profit. Thus, even when nonprofits expand into commercial activities that are clearly unrelated to their missions, they generally have cost advantages over private-enterprise competitors.

Nonprofits' commercialism is not inevitably detrimental to private enterprise. Sometimes the effects are favorable, involving not competition but collaboration. For example, universities are increasingly engaging in scientific research in cooperation with for-profit biotechnology, chemical, and pharmaceutical firms. Clearly, both the universities and the firms expect to benefit from joint ventures or other collaborations. In such cases, the issue is not any adverse effect of nonprofits' commercialism on their private partners, but of effects elsewhere in the economy.

Nonprofits' Pursuit of Mission: Effects of Commercialism on Governmental Tax Revenues

One cause of social concern is that the gains to nonprofits and private firms may be at the expense of third parties: For example, government tax receipts may fall because nonprofits find ways to sell their tax advantages to private firms. One instance of such "tax arbitrage" across sectors occurred in higher education when, a nonprofit college sold all its buildings to a private firm and then leased them back, thereby "selling" their depreciation. Such an allowable expense has no value to a nonprofit organization, which pays no tax on its profit, but depreciation is a valuable deduction to a private firm that can use it to reduce taxable profit.

Such a sale of nonprofits' tax advantages is not necessarily socially undesirable, for it is a source of revenue for nonprofits. However, unrelated business income is also a source of revenue, and yet Congress has seen fit to tax it. The issue is what the limits should be on how nonprofits may use their resources, including tax advantages, to expand income. Currently, there is a more general public policy against transactions that have no justification other than to reduce taxation—which explains why the IRS disallows them, even when nonprofits are involved.

Nonprofit Organization Goals and Outputs

How problematic any form of commercialism is cannot be determined without assessing the organization's "outputs," its success in achieving its social goals. Because this is so difficult, it is common for the IRS to examine procedural evidence rather than the harder-to-measure outputs. It may explore, for example, whether charitable assets are being used for private or "noncharitable" purposes; but this input-oriented indicator, while useful, tells little about what the organization is accomplishing overall. Similarly, it may attempt to distinguish pursuit of social mission from officers' pursuit of personal gain, but this too is difficult. Clearly, there are potential conflicts, but they are hard to observe and do not directly reflect outputs. Charges of overcommercialization, such as those made by critics of Nashville's Baptist Hospital—"When marketing and personal glory dwarf charity care [in a nonprofit hospital], the mission has changed," and "A nonprofit hospital shouldn't cross the line to spend millions of dollars for blatant advertising and promotion" (Langley 1997)—cannot be assessed until there is better understanding of nonprofits' outputs. Until operational measures of nonprofits' outputs in various industries are developed and standardized, the debate will continue over how to operationalize such allegedly negative influences as the pursuit of "personal glory" and "blatant advertising" on a nonprofit's outputs.

The bold pursuit of profit has brought to the surface of the debate not only tax-related questions but, more broadly, the consistency of commercialism with a nonprofit's social, collective-good goals. Our earlier evidence that missions are often stated in extremely broad terms implies that debate will continue to grow over whether a particular nonprofit's commercialism has gone "too far." The IRS, with very limited resources for enforcement, can be expected to rely heavily on organization self-reports, with each nonprofit deciding how far it can go in terming its activities related, and only occasional IRS disputation.

However, whether commercialization is, on balance, enhancing or impeding achievement of nonprofits' social goals involves much more fundamental matters than the size of the IRS budget for enforcement. The vagueness of many mission statements implies an inevitably large element of judgment to define which specific activities are or are not "substantially related" to the mission.

Revenue and Cost Constraints

Revenues limit what any organization, nonprofit or other, may do, and the nature of those limitations is not simple if revenue sources are interdependent and responsive to the organization's decisions. We have seen that nonprofits may be concerned, for example, about the effects of their decisions to increase revenue from one source or another—user fees or ancillary activities—on their revenue from yet another source—contributions, gifts, and grants (CGG). Such increased self-help could lead either to decreased or increased CGG, depending on whether prospective donors favor or oppose those efforts. Because of such revenue interdependencies, a nonprofit would not necessarily maximize its total revenue by trying to maximize revenue from each individual source; an increase in revenue from one source could diminish revenue from another source even more.

There are still other fiscal interdependencies and associated constraints. Decisions to produce more of certain salable outputs can affect both revenues and also costs. Thus a nonprofit might be enabled to expand its mission-related outputs not only by increasing revenue but also by decreasing costs, and increased production of some ancillary activity could reduce production costs for the organization's mission-related outputs.

Resource interdependencies can take other, complex forms. Increased commercial activity intended to generate revenue to expand production of mission-related collective goods and services can affect the types of manager employed, the types of director selected, and thereby the organization's decisions on how it pursues its mission. This can be seen in the nonprofit National Geographic Society's restructuring and greatly expanded emphasis on commercially profitable activity. In order to increase revenue for its expeditions and educational activities, it is producing full-length feature films, developing commercial cable television partnerships with NBC, and producing, in the fall of 1997, the first National Geographic Road Atlas. To do this it is bringing in new management, not from other nonprofits but from private business. The effects on the quality of research scholarship for the magazine articles are uncertain, but there is already evidence of pressure to diminish the time allotted for field research (Hays 1997). Whether the trade-off is socially efficient cannot presently be resolved, but the balance clearly is changing.

All these interdependencies among revenue sources, costs, and organization behavior add a significant dimension to understanding nonprofits' financial constraints. It has long been understood by economists and argued by nonprofits' leadership hasthat private donations are affected by changes in the individual income-tax law, such as reduction in marginal tax rates or increases in requirements for itemizing deductions for charitable giving (Clotfelter 1990). What has scarcely been noted, however, is that those effects can be expected to trigger additional forces, especially commercial activity, so that the final effects on nonprofits' revenue may be quite different. Our evidence is that there is great variability among industries in their offsetting of losses in contributions, gifts, and grants by increasing commercial activity from "program services", and this suggests that nonprofit-organization behavior is more complex than has been commonly recognized. At this point, however, little is known about the causes of this behavioral heterogeneity across industries. Opportunities to expand commercial markets profitably may differ greatly, as may organizational willingness to adopt or increase user fees or enter new ancillary markets.

Potential Conflict Between Revenue Source and Goal Attainment

Both forms of commercialism, user fees and ancillary activities, have the potential to generate revenue, and both involve private goods, which can be withheld from any consumer. The key difference is that those persons served by ancillary goods are of no special concern to the nonprofit's mission, whereas user fees are charges made to consumers who constitute at least a portion of the organization's target population. We have highlighted the potential conflict between pursuing revenue via user fees and achieving a nonprofit's mission when that mission is to reach some specific population, such as the poor or all school-children. It is certainly feasible to impose charges on patients at a research hospital, where care is related to the clinical research activities, or on undergraduate students, who constitute an undergraduate college's target population, or on museum visitors, whose education is at least one element of the nonprofit's mission. However, barring perfect price discrimination, we have shown the danger that user fees will price out of the market at least some members of the target population. We have seen how increasing revenue through user fees, as through the institution of admission fees at museums and zoos, troubles nonprofits because of the negative effect on attendance and, hence, on their education mission. In this way too, efforts to relax resource constraints can have adverse side effects on the achievement of organization goals. We have emphasized, moreover, that the organization's view of which activities are and are not central to its objectives may differ from the distinction made by the IRS, under the tax law, between related (untaxed) and unrelated (taxed) activities.

Were it not for the links between goals and the revenue-related activities used to attain them, a nonprofit would act as a profit maximizer in those product markets where they seek simply to raise revenue. Nonprofits may not wish to maximize profits in such markets because they view the activities themselves as inconsistent with the mission; in at least some industries, such as zoos and public television, it seems clear that admission fees and sale of broadcast airtime are intentionally restricted because of a sense that generating more revenue from those sources would be inconsistent with mission. At the same time, however, it remains very difficult to distinguish such goal incompatibility from the effects of revenue interdependencies in which some form of commercial activity is disliked by prospective donors, causing them to decrease contributions. In such situations a nonprofit that did seek to maximize profit in commercial markets, in order to subsidize its collective-goods outputs, would not act to maximize profit in each specific market where it can charge prices. The organization, recognizing negative marginal effects across markets, would balance the effect of increasing profit from one commercial activity against the loss in maximum attainable profit from other sources.

Tax-related Constraints: Joint-Cost Allocations Between Taxed and Untaxed Activities

It appears that when nonprofits do report engaging in activities that are unrelated to their tax-exempt mission—and most do not, although the ranks are growing rapidly—they generally allocate so much cost to the taxed activities as to eliminate all tax liability. This is true despite our evidence that costs are heavily "joint." In this way, the actual incremental cost of the unrelated business activity is essentially zero.

From an examination of the relationship between a nonprofit's taxed and untaxed activities it is a short step to recognizing the effects of nonprofit commercial activity on private firms. Although the specific effects on private enterprise of the nonprofit sector's commercial expansion have not been a major focus of this volume, our examination of cost allocations between nonprofits' taxed (unrelated) and untaxed (related and excluded) activities has shed some light on them. As a result of the joint-cost allocations, unrelated business (UB) activities, which presumably have no justification except to generate profit for cross-subsidizing the mission, are reported to be negative by some two-thirds of nonprofits that file Form 990-T returns reflecting taxable activity. Moreover, these "losses" are so great that they exceed the modest profit reported by the others, so that aggregate nonprofit-sector profit from all organizations reporting UB activity is negative! It is striking to note that while nonprofits are reporting increased total UB activity over time, they are also reporting increased losses.

These findings appear to be the result of accounting cost allocations, not genuine unprofitability. In contrast with data reported on Form 990-T returns showing that costs of UB activity increase more than revenues, we found, in aggregate data and in the hospital and higher-education industries, that actual costs do not increase at all; by this reckoning, UB activities are extremely profitable. Thus, the generally negative profits reported by most UBIT filers make clear that a great deal of UB activity carries no tax liability. Cost allocations between nonprofits' untaxed and taxed activities are not merely technical issues; they have broad consequences on resource-allocation neutrality across ownership sectors.

Implications for Research

The search for generalizations as to nonprofits' behavior remains a challenge. So, too, is the identification of differential patterns of behavior across industries. The following five dimensions, involving elements of nonprofit-organization goals and fiscal constraints, deserve increased research attention. Whether the interest is in predicting nonprofits' behavior or in developing wise public policy, it is important to increase understanding of the following:

Nonprofit-Organization Objective Functions.

1. The breadth and multiplicity of goals of individual nonprofit organizations, and the differences among industries in the trade-offs being made among goals;

2. the importance to various nonprofits of not simply providing certain goods or services but of reaching particular target populations; and
3. the degree of willingness to engage in production and distribution of ancillary goods in order to raise funds for subsidizing production of their mission-related goods, as well as the willingness to charge user fees and to adopt commercial approaches to expand donations.

Budgetary Constraints.

4. The opportunities—technological and market—available to various nonprofits to enter private-goods markets and compete successfully with private firms and other nonprofits, or to benefit from joint ventures with private firms; and
5. the interdependencies among nonprofits' various revenue sources and among costs of producing various mission-related and ancillary outputs.

The revenue constraints limiting what a nonprofit can do are not fully predictable. As a result, nonprofits' decisions on how much to pursue each of a variety of revenue sources may reflect not only the expected revenue from each alternative but the differing uncertainty as well. A particular source of revenue may appear to be quite uncertain yet turn out to be quite stable or otherwise predictable; alternatively, a source that seems highly predictable may turn out not to be. Study is needed, therefore, of uncertainty, both as anticipated and as realized. The general questions regarding uncertainty are as follows:

1. Do nonprofits perceive various revenue sources as differentially reliable?
2. Have some sources actually proven to be more dependable than others?
3. How do nonprofits respond to differences in predictability of revenue from alternative sources?

Commercialism: The Road Ahead

For decades the nonprofit sector has been small enough, and its methods of raising revenue innocuous enough, to be largely out of sight. Suc-cess has changed this; with growth has come vis-ibility. The increased public awareness of non-profits reflects growth in their numbers, in their share of the gross domestic product, and in their use of commercial revenue-raising instruments traditionally identified with private enterprise. In light of nonprofits' receipt of public subsidies, demands for restricting their activities and for holding them more accountable for demonstrat-ing their social contribution and its value are increasingly evident. Attacks on their tax exemp-tions, a widening array of penalties ("intermedi-ate sanctions") now available to the IRS for various regulatory violations, and decreases in government funding, or shortfalls relative to "need," all demonstrate growing public concern.

Because nonprofits often see their role as per-forming many elements of the unfinished job of governments, they tend to see their missions as forcing them to become more creative and imaginative in generating revenue. Competition for resources, however, drives all organiza-tions—nonprofit, for-profit, and governmen-tal—to search for new markets, and markets new to one type of organization are likely to be already occupied by one or more others. When nonprofits seek opportunities to raise revenue by producing goods or services they can sell profitably, they enter the domain of the private, for-profit firm. There, the drive for profit de-mands attention to costs and revenues and, hence, to avoidance of activities that, however desirable they may be from a societal perspec-tive, do not generate profit. What happens when nonprofits' pursuit of revenue drives them to act like private firms?

The answer is not simple. There are dangers of goal displacement, as the social mission slips from sight in the drive for revenue. Aggressive marketing and merchandising produce almost inevitable conflict, sometimes forcing organiza-

tions to choose between "capitalist appetites and . . . integrity" (Farhi 1997, 13). Peering ahead, it is likely that:

> missions of nonprofits engaged in commercial ac-tivities will grow more ambiguous through time. New demands on senior management to pay at-tention not only to nonprofit but also to for-profit goals, the adoption of new structures such as joint ventures that create mixed missions and messages for participating entities, and the tendency of se-nior management to look at activities from the perspective of their contribution to revenues may create an environment in which nonprofits must work especially hard to keep their charitable mis-sion in daily focus. Increased responsibility will likely fall on the Boards of Directors of commer-cial nonprofits to insure that a dilution of charita-ble mission does not occur. . . . (Howard P. Tuck-man, personal communication, 1997)

Whether the future finance bases and commer-cial activities of the nonprofit sector as a whole, and of specific industries within it, will be exten-sions of historical paths is not predetermined. Much depends on nonprofits' success in finding new sources of revenue. Barring unlikely changes in government grants or tax-law encouragement of private donations (of money and labor), in-creased user fees and, especially, expanded com-mercial activities are the most promising revenue sources. If nonprofit-organization commercialism continues to increase in magnitude and in scope, nonprofits will become even more entwined with private enterprise and less distinct from it.

Note

1. The issues are actually more complex. A non-profit would wish not merely to minimize taxation, but to maximize aggregate revenue net of both taxes and any disutility from engaging in non-mission-re-lated activities.

PART 7

MANAGING UNDER GOVERNMENT CONTRACTS

Since the 1970s, government has been the largest and steadiest source of revenue for many nonprofit organizations, particularly but certainly not exclusively in the human services: "While the federal government finances most government human services programs, and state and local governments do most of the administration, it is nonprofit organizations that actually deliver the preponderance of services."[1] The percent of total income that nonprofits receive from government varies by organizational purpose and program function, from a high of 42 percent in the social and legal services and 36 percent in health services, to a low of 17 percent in education and 11 percent in the arts.[2] Government agencies in the United States contract extensively for services for persons with mental illness, disabilities (including developmental disabilities), chemical dependencies, youth (including gangs), the elderly, homebound individuals, unstable families, persons who need employment training, and victims of abuse (including legal services).

The reasons for the emergence of the nonprofit sector as the preferred deliverer of many public services are numerous and varied.[3] The benefits government agencies seek through contracting out services to nonprofit organizations include lower costs, more flexibility, less need for permanent government staff, and greater responsivness to clients' needs. The decades-long growth in government reliance on nonprofits for the delivery of health and human services, however, also has benefited from a pervasive antigovernment bias,[4] including a widely shared public perception that government is incompetent and "cannot be trusted to do much of anything right."[5]

Political conservatives have been "champions" of contracting out as a key strategy for restructuring welfare, downsizing government, encouraging multiple suppliers of social services, and increasing government's reliance on the nonprofit sector—especially in the delivery of services to low-income populations. Interestingly, "this right-wing support is virtually indistinguishable [in its effects] from support from the left, which also advocates a larger role for the voluntary sector, and which has long argued the importance of pluralism, self-help, and mutual help in social service provision."[6]

Governmental Administrative Requirements

During the Great Society era of the 1970s, the U.S. government embarked on a quest to strengthen the administrative practices of state governments. The "feds" imposed numerous administrative requirements on state governments as conditions for receiving categorical grants, including upgraded personnel systems and practices, budgeting procedures, and financial reporting standards.[7] Although these requirements probably accomplished their stated purpose—improved administration of grants—in truth the requirements were only part of a larger agenda in Washington: to bring the administration of state governments more closely in line with the process and substance of U.S. government policies and practices. Units of government at all levels have used the same approach and tactics with nonprofit organizations for the last two decades. Eligibility for contracts and contract awards often has been conditioned upon the adoption by nonprofits of government-like systems, policies, procedures, practices, and reporting.

Effects of Government Requirements on Nonprofit Organizations

The substance of governmental requirements has varied, but most are intended to protect the rights of employees, clients, and unserved individuals, and to improve the management of records and fiscal resources. Many nonprofit executives and students of nonprofit organizations have been concerned, however, about the effects that long-term reliance on government contracts may have on the governance, leadership, management, and character of the nonprofit sector. The three greatest concerns are[8]

1. The longer and more extensively that a nonprofit relies on government contracts, the more it will tend to look, think, feel, and act like a small (or not-so-small) government agency.[9] "Involvement with government programs tends to produce an undesirable degree of bureaucratization and professionalization

in the recipient agency. . . . Government agencies therefore often involve more red tape, cumbersome application requirements, and regulatory control than is common with other forms of financial support."[10]

2. Government contracts will cause "mission creep." Over time, a nonprofit organization will tend to engage in activities for clients that government will fund—instead of activities that it believes its clients need most, or that it does best.

3. Nonprofits that rely on government contracts will lose some of their independence. Smith and Lipsky[11] argue that government requirements and resource dependence do indeed reduce independence. Ferris[12] counters that government funding does not necessarily decrease the ability of contracted nonprofits to remain true to their missions or to their community roots. Government contracts provide badly needed resources and thus also can increase the freedom of a contracted nonprofit to act on its mission. Smith and Lipsky and others[13] counter that government's influence on the administration of a contracted nonprofit far exceeds the percent of income received from government. Kramer cautions that the effects of resource dependence can be powerful and pervasive: "The source of resources determines the type of and standards for success and failure, the character of decision making, accountability, and the external relations of an organization."[14] On balance, it appears that resource dependence and government requirements indeed may well reduce the independence of nonprofit organizations.[15] "One of the necessary shifts in intersectoral theory . . . is the abandonment of the notion of the third sector as independent."[16]

Nonprofits and Government Agencies Are Becoming Less Dissimilar

Several other factors and trends have contributed to the blurring of differences between government agencies and contracted nonprofit sectors. Employees at all organizational levels reportedly are moving between organizations in the two sectors. Today's government contract managers may be the nonprofit service deliverers of tomorrow, and vice versa.[17] If so, the historic differences in perspectives and values between employees in the two sectors may vanish.[18]

The nature of contracting relationships also has been changing. The methods that government agencies use to administer and monitor contracts with nonprofit organizations have been evolving away from traditional arms-length, legalistic relationships.[19] Contract relationships appear to be developing into more collaborative, problem-solving types of partnerships. There are advantages and potential disadvantages to this change. Inevitably, close working partnerships lead to shared perceptions, values, expectations, and standards.[20] Thus, interdependence among organizations in the two sectors is growing in many ways. The dependence is *not* solely of nonprofits on government,[21] which represents potentially both "good news" and "bad news"—for nonprofits, government agencies, and their clients.

Readings Reprinted in Part Seven

The four readings reprinted in this part address a variety of issues and problems that most nonprofit managers and board members face when their nonprofit organizations contract with government agencies to provide services.

Nigel Gann analyzes the needs for change as home health services and day programs for persons with disabilities in Great Britain moved from local government service provision to contracts with nonprofit organizations, in *"Towards a Contract Culture."*[22] Changes are needed in the relationships between nonprofit organizations and contracting municipal government social services agencies. Legislation in 1990 required British municipal government social services departments to stop being the sole providers of care and to become instead enablers and guarantors for the provision of social services by nonprofit organizations. Before 1991, "relationships with other providers were largely a peripheral concern to SSDs [social services departments]," many nonprofit social service providers were not prepared administratively for the new contract culture, and public social services employees and nonprofit trustees and executives were less than enthusiastic about the change. "Many officers (and councillors) felt that the new régime was directly opposed to their own ideology of service provision."

Municipal officials had to wrestle with the design of contacts and accountability procedures, and the problems of introducing changes in the roles of government and government employees. Nonprofit boards and executives worried about the loss of "individuality, freedom from the bureaucratic structures endemic in local government," and the need to become aware of their legal responsibilities and to develop and employ management systems. Many nonprofit social services nonprofits did not have clear mission statements, systems of training for staff and volunteers, job descriptions and personnel policies, systematic financial controls, or methods for monitoring or evaluating their services to clients.

Gann identifies several intersectoral coordination issues that must be resolved before a system of contracted services can be effective, including the nature and composition of contracts, development plans, standards of quality, assurance of quality, performance indicators, and a business plan. He also identifies political causes of tension between municipal officials and nonprofit executives and trustees, and steps that the contracting government agency needs to take to ensure that it meets its responsibility to manage the system.

In 1993, Steven Smith and Michael Lipsky wrote the pioneering book about the effects of government contracting on nonprofit organizations, *Nonprofits for Hire: The Welfare State in the Age of Contracting.* Their chapter, *"Dilemmas of Management in Nonprofit Organizations,"*[23] is reprinted here. Smith and Lipsky note that although nonprofits are inclined to seek out opportunities for growth and budgetary stability, they also tend to be influenced by "a strong sense of purpose and commitment. Thus nonprofit organizations are torn between organizational maintenance and pursuit of their purposive objectives." Smith and Lipsky identify three causes of this dilemma:

1. Some government agencies are notoriously poor at meeting their own deadlines for awarding contracts and payment schedules, both of which can cause serious cash flow problems for nonprofit organizations. Reimbursements may be delayed deliberately to help a government meet a temporary cash flow squeeze of its own. "Unfortunately, many contractors do not have the resources to ride out periods of reimbursement withholding. Moreover, they are not allowed to build up reserves." It is not unusual for nonprofits that are having cash flow problems to take actions that get them into trouble. "Real trouble arises when nonprofit managers begin to overlook their debts or to pay expenses for one account from funds allocated for another. Paying salaries of people on one project from another project's allocation is one expedient to which the nonprofit manager may resort. Failing to pay required taxes is another."
2. The "dance of contract renewal" tests a nonprofit's commitment to its mission and goal. At contract renewal time, government agencies are likely to seek concessions in, for example, cost or price of services, service level, and quantity of services. Government's "desire to secure additional increments of service, instead of, say, improving the quality of the ongoing services, also leads to systematic efforts to hold the line on contract costs." Contract renewals thus create problems for management: "From the point of view of government, this is all legitimate. . . . But what to government is flexibility is to the nonprofit sector an important source of instability."
3. In this era of declining government funding for services that are mostly provided by nonprofits, many organizations will be inclined to give priority to activities that are likely to be funded. "Today a critical source of goal succession in voluntary organizations is the preferences and behavior of government. . . . Goal displacement of otherwise autonomous organizations is attributable to the choices made by governments about what will or will not be funded."

Susan Bernstein's chapter, *"The Game of Contracted Services,"*[24] provides rich and instructive insights about how "game playing" allows nonprofit executives to keep from succumbing to the "craziness" of managing contracted government social services. Executives cannot take government requirements too seriously, or they could not survive. Bernstein uses the words of nonprofit executives to communicate the absurdity of conflicts between contract requirements and the realities of delivering social services. Her informants describe the mental approach needed to maintain a sense of perspective during the "games," the process of coping with conflicts between contract requirements and reality, managing an agency when a funding agency fails to meet its contractual requirements (including making timely payments to the nonprofit), and living with skepticism about the validity of evaluation processes and measures.

Three explanations emerge as to why nonprofit administrators remain involved "despite all the craziness": (1) the enjoyment of playing the game—the "experience of flow when playing chess is similar to what administrators say about managing contracted services"; (2) the drive to accomplish a goal that "can be an overriding sense of mission and purpose about the work"; and (3) the satisfaction of mastering complex rules or solving complex puzzles. "Despite all the craziness and complexity, many managers express enjoyment when they describe their work. Research indicates this feeling of pleasure, under trying circumstances, is not at all contradictory."

"Implications of Welfare Reform: Do Nonprofit Survival Strategies Threaten Civil Society?"[25] by Jennifer Alexander, Renee Nank, and Camilla Stivers reports on a research project that examines the effect of welfare reform on community-based nonprofits in a large Ohio county. Their findings are consistent with many of the concerns articulated by Gann, Smith and Lipsky, and Bernstein (above). The capacity of smaller nonprofits to adopt the business-oriented approaches required to meet the expectations of government contracts is profoundly limited, and the implications of these findings are disturbing—for the nonprofits, their clients, and for society as we know it in the United States.

Nonprofit organizations have been integral elements in our civil society for centuries. They have served as "schools of citizenship by enabling citizens to discuss matters of mutual concern, gather information, hear others express their views, and debate policies. In this more politically charged civil society, citizens learn citizenship. . . . Community-based nonprofits . . . make democracy workable." Welfare reform and the "new public management" thus are threatening to change the character of institutions that are essential for a civil society.

Three themes emerge from their research: bifurcation of the sector as nonprofit organizations take on a business orientation; increased dependence of nonprofits on local and state government agencies and a resulting decrease in autonomy; and loss of public service character. "Nonprofits of all types indicated that adaptation to the current changes in funding was changing the nature of their services; it had substantially diminished their capacity to be political," and it was causing them to be reluctant to "act as advocates for client needs or particular services." Indeed, "dependence on government funding reduces the autonomy of nonprofit decision making, causing them to shape development in terms of government demands rather than on the basis of their own consensus about community needs." We are losing something important as our nonprofit organizations turn into "little service delivery businesses." Community-based nonprofits are essential because they "facilitate access to public conversation and, therefore, offer hope for strengthening the political dimensions of civil society."

Notes

1. Lester M. Salamon, *Partners in Public Service: Government-Nonprofit Relations in the Modern Welfare State* (Baltimore: Johns Hopkins University Press, 1995), 79.

2. Julian Wolpert, "How Federal Cutbacks Affect the Charitable Sector," in Lynn A Staeheli, Janet E. Kodras, and Colin Flint, eds., *State Devolution in America: Implications for a Diverse Society* (Thousand Oaks, CA: Sage, 1997), 100.

3. Graeme A. Hodge, *Privatization: An International Review of Performance* (Boulder: Westview Press, 2000); and Steven R. Smith, "Transforming Public Services: Contracting for Social and Health Services in the U.S.," *Public Administration* 74 (spring 1996):113–127.

4. J. Steven Ott and Lisa A. Dicke, "Important but Largely Unanswered Questions About Accountability in Contracted Public Human Services," *International Journal of Organization Theory & Behavior* 3, Nos. 3 and 4 (summer 2000), 283–317.

5. J. Steven Ott and Jay M. Shafritz, "The Perception of Organizational Incompetence," in Arie Halachmi and Geert Bouckaert, eds., *The Enduring Challenges in Public Management* (San Francisco: Jossey-Bass, 1995), 27–46; and J. Steven Ott and Jay M. Shafritz, "Toward a Definition of Organizational Incompetence: A Neglected Variable in Organization Theory," *Public Administration Review* 54 (July/August 1994): 370–377.

6. Josephine Rekart, *Public Funds, Private Provision: The Role of the Voluntary Sector*, p. xii (Vancouver, BC: UBC Press, 1993).

7. See, for example, Chapters 4 and 5 in Phillip J. Cooper, et al., *Public Administration for the Twenty-First Century* (Ft. Worth, Texas: Harcourt Brace, 1998); and Chapter 4 in Jay M. Shafritz and E. W. Russell, *Introducing Public Administration*, 2d ed. (New York: Longman, 2000).

8. Salamon, *Partners in Public Service*, 103–109.

9. Steven R. Smith and Michael Lipsky, *Nonprofits for Hire* (Cambridge: Harvard University Press, 1993).

10. Salamon, *Partners in Public Service*, 107.

11. Smith and Lipsky, *Nonprofits for Hire*.

12. James M. Ferris, "The Double-Edged Sword of Social Service Contracting," *Nonprofit Management & Leadership* 3, no. 4 (summer, 1993): 363–376.

13. See Melissa Middleton Stone, "Competing Contexts: The Evolution of a Nonprofit Organization's Governance System in Multiple Environments," *Administration & Society* 28, no. 1, (May 1996): 61–89.

14. Ralph M. Kramer, "Voluntary Agencies and the Contract Culture," *Social Service Review* 68, no. 1 (March 1994): 33–60.

15. Lisa A. Dicke and J. Steven Ott, "Public Agency Accountability in Human Services Contracting," *Public Productivity & Management Review* 22, no. 4 (June 1999): 502–516.

16. Judith R. Saidel, "Dimensions of Interdependence: The State and Voluntary-Sector Relationship," *Nonprofit and Voluntary Sector Quarterly* 18, no. 4 (winter 1989): 336.

17. J. Steven Ott and Lisa A. Dicke, "HRM in an Era of Downsizing, Devolution, Diffusion, and Empowerment . . . and Accountability?" in A. Farazmand, ed., *Strategic Public Personnel Administration/HRM: Building Human Capital for the 21st Century* (Praeger/Greenwood Press, forthcoming).

18. Steven R. Smith and Michael Lipsky, *Nonprofits for Hire* (Cambridge: Harvard University Press, 1993).

19. Ruth H. DeHoog, "Competition, Negotiation, or Cooperation: Three Models for Service Contracting," *Administration & Society* 22, no. 33 (November 1990): 317–340; and Lester M. Salmon, "Partners in Public Service: The Scope and Theory of Government-Nonprofit Rela-

tions," in Walter W. Powell, ed., *The Nonprofit Sector: A Research Handbook* (New Haven: Yale University Press, 1987) 99–117.

20. Dicke, Lisa, "Accountability in Human Services Contracting: Stewardship Theory and the Internal Perspective (Unpublished doctoral dissertation, Department of Political Science, University of Utah, Salt Lake City, 2000).

21. Judith R. Saidel, "Devolution and the Politics of Interdependence: Management and Policy Trade-Offs in Government-Nonprofit Contracting" (paper presented at the American Society for Public Administration, Seattle, Washington, May 9–12, 1998).

22. Nigel Gann, "Toward a Contract Culture," in N. Gann, *Managing Change in Voluntary Organizations: A Guide to Practice* (Buckingham, UK: Open University Press, 1996), 7–21.

23. Steven R. Smith and Michael Lipsky, "Dilemmas of Management in Nonprofit Organizations," in S. R. Smith and M. Lipsky, *Nonprofits for Hire* (Cambridge: Harvard University Press, 1993), 147–167.

24. Susan R. Bernstein, "The Game of Contracted Services," in S. R. Bernstein, *Managing Contracted Services in the Nonprofit Agency* (Philadelphia: Temple University Press, 1991), 21–39.

25. Jennifer Alexander, Renee Nank, and Camilla Stivers, "Implications of Welfare Reform: Do Nonprofit Survival Strategies Threaten Civil Society?" *Nonprofit and Voluntary Sector Quarterly* 28, no. 4 (December 1999): 452–475.

CHAPTER 20

Toward a Contract Culture

Nigel Gann

The Contract Culture

Of all the changes that voluntary organizations are experiencing, the one which impinges most upon managers is the advance of 'the contract culture'. In summarizing the extensive consultation, investigation and legislation leading to the NHS and Community Care Act 1990, Wistow et al. (1994) write: 'It would . . . be misleading to understate the "cultural" revolution which this legislation implies for traditional ways of working'.

This period of very rapid transformation followed a lengthy period of time during which exhortations to [public sector] social services departments to move towards a policy of care in the community were substantially forestalled by, among other things, the arrangements which allowed for the payment of benefits to those in institutionalized residential care, but not in their own homes.

The recommended reforms would also allow the emphasis to shift to enable people, wherever possible, to live in their own homes, to allow people to make choices about the nature of the care they receive, and to establish forums where the consumer's voice could be heard. Between the publication of the Government White Paper *Caring for People* (HMSO 1989), which led to the enactment of the NHS and Community Care Bill in 1990, and the full implementation of the Act in 1993, SSDs [social/services departments] were obliged to shift from effectively being the sole providers of care to partners in the provision of care. It was the new character of SSDs—as enablers and as guarantors for provision made by other agencies—that dictated the need for contracts, as opposed to grant aid, to form the basis of the relationship between them and voluntary sector providers.

As Wistow et al. (1994) illustrate, until 1991 the independent sector was a marginal factor in the local authority financing of provision. Relationships with other providers were largely a peripheral concern to SSDs. In contrast, the transfer of funds from central to local government to cover the cost of the new responsibilities was subject to the condition that 85 per cent of all funding was to be spent in the independent sector.

The Voluntary Sector and Local Government

Meanwhile, the voluntary sector had been experiencing considerable hardship itself. Although voluntary sector funding was only a small part of social services expenditure, it was seen as the most expendable. Voluntary organizations were more likely to provide day as opposed to residential care, and were more likely to specialize in campaigning, advocacy and in ethnic minority provision—areas which, while seen as worthy, might nevertheless be the most 'expendable'.

Contract funding introduced a new element into the equation for the voluntary sector. First, although contracts have always existed, they became 'the fastest growing component of statutory sector support for non-statutory bodies' (Wistow et al. 1994: 82). A principal drawback here was the lack of experience of the lead officers of SSDs, whose role was to implement the new arrangements. A host of new expectations were thrust upon them, with a very tight timetable for implementation. Not only were there practical difficulties. Many officers (and councillors) felt that the new regime was directly opposed to their own ideology of service provision.

From Grants to Contracts

Contract funding allowed a number of concerns about the operation of the voluntary sector to be aired. Local authorities could hardly be expected to enter into legal relationships with any organization, let alone those that were being run amateurishly, or just plain incompetently. Whereas the earlier relationship was just about tenable— 'We give you (the ratepayer's) money to spend for yourselves, with a few safeguards, because we must not seem to be patronizing'—there was now a clear need to ensure that trustees and management committees were educated to run their own show effectively and efficiently. Far-sighted local authorities saw this as an opportunity to empower organizations and their management committees or boards of trustees. This was predicated on the belief that voluntary management committees have both a right and a duty to be actively involved in developing the policies and procedures by which a voluntary organization operates. For many, this was a new idea. Many groups understood the committee's role as being largely supportive in nature, enabling the paid manager or coordinator to run

the service. This may result in an efficient and effective service, but it allows very little opportunity to develop a strategic approach to a sector where the ability to react to current trends, whether demographic or legislative, is essential. Some management committees did not even go so far as this, tending to hold a very loose rein, if any rein at all. Others veered towards the alternative end of the spectrum, employing staff with very little scope for autonomous action, while being largely ineffective themselves. Thus, where the voluntary sector is poorly organized, with little collective strength, the individual groups too may not be geared up for action or growth or development.

There was a wide variation in voluntary organizations' state of preparedness for the contract culture. The contracting system assumes that an organization has a distinct, autonomous identity, independent in terms of planning and decision-making, though interdependent in terms of funding and cooperation. Indeed, many would claim that the strength of the voluntary sector, and its ability to make appropriate provision, is founded in its individuality, its freedom from the bureaucratic structures endemic in local government. The voluntary sector is presumed to have many characteristics in common with the private sector—it is responsive to need, reactive and quick to respond to market forces. However, this is only true of some voluntary organizations. Others, for example, do not work to a budget of any sort, and their only financial record-keeping is against the application for grant aid for the year. Many management committees are not aware of their legal responsibilities; do not have a clear statement of aim; have no arrangements for user participation in management; no system for training of staff or volunteers; no up-to-date job descriptions or terms and conditions of employment; no system of staff supervision or appraisal; no systematic financial controls; are deficient in meeting the legislative requirements upon employers to have written policies and procedures in such areas as health and safety; and have no system for monitoring or evaluating the service they provide.

The change from grant aid to contracts requires significant shifts in an organization's cul-

TABLE 20.1   Stages of Development of Voluntary Organizations

	Stage of Development		
Area of Operation	*Immature*	*Adolescent*	*Mature*
Management committee	Subordinate to its national headquarters or to a dominant individual	Aware of legal responsibilities and generally participating in decisions	Individual functions shared out; a full partnership with staff
Funding	Dependent on one source; probably initiated by the source	Some fund-raising and variation of sources	A variety of sources, probably including contracts
Service	A single service with no development plans	Some development of service and some development ideas	Strategic plans in place, costed and with action plans
Quality of Service	Static	Some development of ideas	Quality of service a key notion
Staffing	Staff dependent on management committee, or dominant	Some interchange of ideas, and some partnership	Management committee and staff in partnership, with each given appropriate responsibilities
Employment	Loose informal arrangements	Some terms and conditions and job description/ some review	Job descriptions regularly reviewed and negotiated; appraisal systems; long-term employment conditions
Financial controls	Dependent on one member of management committee or of staff	A partnership, with some financial planning	Financial controls appropriately distributed, with regular reporting
Development	Static user profile	Some attempts at growth and/or diversification	Detailed plans for development of the user profile

ture. In considering the wide variation in effectiveness of voluntary organizations, Table 20.1 suggests eight areas of operation and three levels of development. The contract culture requires participating organizations to have at least reached the adolescent stage of development.

Considerations in Changing from Grant Aid to Contract Funding

The nature and composition of the contract must be understood by management committees. A 'block contract' is most akin to a grant, in that it specifies the quantity and quality of the inputs (or facilities to which the council will have access for its clients) rather than the outputs. It enables annual guaranteed purchase of access to the facility, while allowing the purchaser to specify an estimated size of client base. Facilities such as this are characterized by a loose relationship between the number of clients and the cost of the facility. A typical example is the day centre. A specified amount of money may provide places for, say, five clients more or less than anticipated, without incurring extra costs or saving money, since labour and premises costs will remain the same. However, an increase or decrease beyond a certain number, depending on the size of the premises and the care worker to client ratio, may cross 'critical break points' in costing where, for example, the acceptance of one more client has cost implications that are quite out of proportion. Clearly, block contracts provide considerable security to voluntary organizations, guaranteeing an income which is to some extent independent of take up rates. They also allow some freedom of movement, in that spare capacity can be offered to referrals from elsewhere, and other sources of funding can be used to increase capacity. Another example of services suited to this type of contract is phone-in or drop-in advice services, where demand is unpredictable, but can be monitored to ensure value for money and to allow renegotiation of contract terms in future years. Through such a system, the department meets its legal requirements, where users have been assessed as needing a number of day care places in a week, and the organization is guaranteed its income.

A 'cost and volume contract' specifies a volume of service and a total cost. This also offers some security to groups offering more client-dependent activities. Standard care packages and visiting services are suited to this type of contract. It allows the purchaser to buy, in advance, an agreed number of care units (say, client visits by the hour). The cost of such a service can be costed accurately because, although there may be some variation according to the distances travelled by visitors, and the time of day visits take place, there is the potential to calculate an average cost per hourly visit. There is a more or less direct relationship between the cost of providing the service and the number of care units delivered. This is equally applicable to complex care packages and those providing intensive support. Again, it is assumed that payments will be made in advance, and the purchaser needs to calculate how many units are likely to be needed and are affordable. Calculation of a unit cost is critical with this type of contract.

With 'price by case contracts', a price is quoted for each type of case or unit of provision bought on an individual basis. This is clearly the least satisfactory type of contract for providers, because it is unpredictable, with payment most likely to follow the service (sometimes after a considerable interval of time). It is closest to the marketplace demand and supply model. Although it is therefore theoretically a model that is most suited to the needs of the purchaser, it does require clear lines of communication and information within the purchasing agency, as far as the available budget and the authority of the purchasing officer are concerned. More impor-

tantly, it is more expensive in the longer term because it means that, in addition to the actual service cost, organizations have to include in the price the cost of maintaining service availability when it is not actually needed (i.e. keeping workers available, maintaining a central contact, etc.). The interdependence of purchaser and supplier beyond a simplistic market model is, of course, already recognized in the private sector, where large production industries may step in to keep their smaller suppliers afloat. However, while less than satisfactory as the sole basis for a purchaser-provider relationship, price by case contracts can be a useful adjunct to a block contracted service, allowing flexibility to the purchaser to increase demand through what is often called 'spot purchasing'. There are two instances when it is an efficient method of buying care: spot purchasing of a service offered over and above a service purchased through a cost and volume contract (e.g. an organization offering standard care packages might offer an intensive service on a price by case basis, costed at an hourly rate), and spot purchasing used to supplement a block contract or a cost and volume contract, when the number of units included in the original contract is about to be surpassed within the contract period.

While the initial feeling of many potential purchasers was that price by case contracts offered them the best deal, it was soon realized that it was as much their function to ensure that a range of providers continued to survive, as it was to buy the best available deal. The consensus now is that block contracts on an annually reviewed basis offer the best prospects for a secure but competitive service.

Once an organization understands the nature of contracts, it is important to emphasize that the composition of a contract is as much the responsibility of the provider as it is of the purchaser. It is vital to the viability of the service that contracts should be couched in accessible language and not in the jargon of legal departments. One model is for organizations to produce a draft document outlining the nature and costs of the service they provide, which can be used as a basis for a legal contract drawn up by the SSD.

Development plans are seen as an essential requirement by potential purchasers. No purchaser, whether social services department, health authority or private customer, can afford to enter into what should be a stable and long-term relationship with an organization that has no vision of the future, nor any long-term financial viability. For the organization, a development plan should comprise a statement of aims (sometimes created out of a mission statement), an outline organizational audit, a set of targets or objectives, a statement of costs (with outline financial planning), an action plan and a strategy for monitoring and evaluation.

It is usually necessary to identify the separate costs of the core structure and the delivery of services. In single-service groups, this enables a distinction between the organization itself—its management, administration, support, training, central premises costs, campaigning and so on (the 'community' aspects of its work)—and its service delivery costs (contact staff, transport, specialist premises and other expenses). In multi-service groups, it enables differentiation between the core organization and the variety of projects and services offered. One reason for identifying this split is founded in the funder's commitment to supporting and maintaining the voluntary sector beyond the mere purchase of services. Whether or not an authority chooses to purchase its services for its own clients, it is argued, the voluntary organization deserves to exist—and to make some call upon public funds—in order to deliver either to its own clients or to clients paid for by other agencies. Any other arrangement assumes a synonymity of funder and referrer which does not always exist.

In theory, the combination of core grant and contract funding offers both local authority funders and voluntary organizations the best of both worlds. The grant encourages innovativeness, experimentation, campaigning and a degree of independence, while the contract demands the highest level of service delivery. From the authoritative base established by providing services, a voluntary organization can best develop new and improved services, while continuing to lobby for greater resources.

Quality standards need to be agreed. In one borough, organizations agreed to accept fourteen areas within which they would develop their own statements of quality. Seven of these standards related to the management of the organization:

- training of staff, volunteers and management committee;
- user participation in management;
- terms and conditions of employment for staff;
- job descriptions, regularly reviewed;
- equal opportunities employment;
- financial controls operating within the organization;
- systems for staff supervision, including appraisal.

The other seven standards related to service delivery:

- a procedure for client assessment (it was agreed that this should match, although not necessarily be identical to, the assessment procedure used by the SSD);
- written procedures in, for example, health and safety, user complaints, disclosure of abuse;
- equal opportunities policies and procedures in access for, and treatment of, users;
- an agreed list of services provided in addition to the core function (for a day centre, this might include visits from health services, shopping services, etc.);
- building conditions and facilities;
- reporting, monitoring, evaluation and the collection of statistics;
- networking with other organizations.

Quality assurance assumes, at the least, the following characteristics (which are not always evident in the voluntary sector):

- people are trusted to work as professionals;
- there is a strong emphasis on teamwork;
- there is a weak emphasis on hierarchy;
- goals are clear;
- communications are good;
- everyone has high expectations of themselves and others;
- the organization is 'fit for purpose'.

Organizations are encouraged to consider appropriate performance indicators. While some emphasis is placed by funding departments upon the significance of unit costs, these are not, at the last, critical. Nevertheless, unit costs, the cost of overheads against outputs, occupancy rates and response times, all offer useful indicators of success. Quality standards themselves, of course, offer an agreed set of targets against which performance can be measured.

Finally, a business plan is essential. The term *'business plan'* is used, as opposed to development or strategic plan, in order to emphasize that the prime aim of the document is to identify the financial basis upon which the organization is to operate in the near future. Within such a plan, the organization's vision of potential developments is critical, but a detailed strategic plan can follow the business plan rather than precede it, which is perhaps more usual. Organizational business plans might comprise:

- an organizational audit, achieved by means of a simple SWOT (strengths, weaknesses, opportunities, threats) chart;
- a statement of organizational aims, in the form of a mission statement;
- a set of targets or objectives, including perpetuation of the current service and some development plans;
- a statement of current and likely future costs, with an element of financial planning;
- an action plan for implementation in the current year;
- plans for monitoring and evaluation of the service.

Consideration should also be given to the respective roles of the staff and the management committee in the organization, and a strategy for developing and defining these roles.

Political Structures

There is always likely to be tension between council officers and members in the allocation of funds to the voluntary sector. Council officers are likely to have a monitoring role, with direct access to decision-making structures either formally, through reporting to committees, or informally, through regular contact with other officers and members. They can, and do, contribute towards the formulation of a corporate perception of voluntary organizations. In such perceptions, certain characteristics are likely to be significant:

Professionalism

Officers and members are impressed by the way in which an organization presents itself. Where possible, this means that a voluntary organization should display characteristics similar to those which officers and members see themselves displaying—a detached business-like approach to service delivery and organizational matters. For officers, this is interpreted as giving primary responsibility to senior paid staff in decision-making and, to a significant extent, policy-making. For members, however, this means conducting the management of the organization in a detached and businesslike manner. Both of these characteristics might be seen by the voluntary sector as inappropriate to their own ways of working.

Traditionalism

Some councils still see themselves as the major direct providers of services. There are expectations that the voluntary sector should either (or perhaps both) continue to see itself as peripheral to service provision, or look upon the council departments as the primary role-model in the style and quality of service delivery. Many voluntary organizations, taught over the years to regard themselves as amateurish and dispensable, are content to accept both these perceptions. Others, who are attempting to be innovative, find a clash of cultures with officers and members accustomed to comparatively traditional services.

The Work Ethic

While local authorities are under pressure to 'delayer', to flatten out management structures, to ensure efficiencies at all levels, the voluntary sector is seen by some officers—and perhaps by some members—as a protected area. One of the traditional characteristics of the voluntary sector is that employees choose to work for it. They are freed from many of the mind-bending rules, codes and expectations of local government, and have much greater control over the way they do their jobs. They may therefore legitimately be paid less, but can expect to enjoy their work, gaining all sorts of intrinsic rewards. Local authority work, on the other hand, may be seen as boring, dominated by systems and bureaucracy, but safe. With the safety gone, some officers (who themselves may initially have come from the voluntary sector) may see the advantages accruing to the voluntary organization employees.

Factionalism

In some councils, the prevailing views—often shared by officers and members—about the ways in which organizations ought to be managed, often contrast with cultural traditions displayed by voluntary groups. At best, this is factionalism—the favouring of one group over another for legitimate as well as unacceptable reasons. At worst, it can result in an unintentional racism. For instance, all grant-aided groups might be required to subscribe to the equal opportunities policy of a council; however, the cultural pressures which lead, for example, some Black and Asian organizations to be even more male-dominated than their white counterparts, could be regarded as anti-equality by politically conscious officers or members. Alongside a proper concern that minority and disadvantaged groups should be accorded fair and equal treatment, there may be a tendency to discount the cultural reasons for apparently discriminatory behaviour, or sometimes to condemn what are just different ways of going about business, by those groups.

Representativeness

Understandably, elected members present themselves as the voice of the people, legitimized by the ballot box. Similarly, management committee members in the voluntary sector will see themselves as having a unique insight into the expectations and aspirations of the user. This allows them to formulate policy, which it is the function and duty of the paid staff to implement. Just how closely in contact with the grass roots local politicians are is a matter for debate. Arrangements for election or appointment to management committees vary between organizations. Whatever these may be, it is likely to be true that the paid staff of both councils and of voluntary organizations will have more frequent and meaningful contact with clients and users than will the users' supposed chosen representatives, just as a shop assistant has greater contact with customers than do the members of the store's board. There will be legitimate and ongoing debate between officers and members, and between staff and trustees, about who can more accurately represent the needs of users. But inevitably, each group will tend to see itself as having the only true perspective.

One of the key questions to be asked in terms of a voluntary organization's ability to secure and retain the financial and other support of the major funder is the extent to which it will conform to the funder's expectations. The change of culture to contracting can have some side-effects on relationships between the voluntary sector and the council. Whatever else, the critical importance to a voluntary organization of a mutually robust relationship with the funder cannot be overstated.

Actions Needed When Changing to a Contract Culture: A Case Study

Sandwell Borough Council adopted some enlightened strategies in order to ensure that the providing base remained in place and had the capacity to grow. Both key elected members and officers were committed to a vital voluntary sector. In the autumn of 1993, the two key committees involved in funding the voluntary sector—the Social Services Strategy Committee, and the Community Development and Urban Policy Strategy Committee—formed a joint sub-committee to oversee the implementation of contract arrangements with twenty-two organizations concerned in the delivery of community care. This sub-committee received a number of recommendations:

1. There should be two distinct methods of funding for voluntary organizations in community care: grant aid from the Community Development Committee for the infrastructure costs of organizations, and contracting for the purchase of specific services by Social Services Committees.

2. Block contracts should be used to purchase access to facilities; cost and volume contracts should be used to purchase standard care packages and visiting services, where individual units can be identified; and price by case contracts should be used only for the spot purchase of services over and above existing contracts.

3. A book-keeping service should be offered to voluntary organizations taking up contracts, to enable them to overcome one of the major administrative problems they are likely to face. Ideally, this service should be offered by one of the voluntary organizations (Sandwell Citizens Advice Bureau was one of the organizations well placed to offer this service at a reasonable charge).

4. The training of management committees and paid staff within the voluntary sector should be urgently addressed.

5. Transport issues should be clarified. There was currently a very mixed provision of transport, which in particular affected day centre services. The transport used included the SSD's own direct labour transport with no charges attached for some of their clients; Sandwell Community Transport—one of the twenty-two organizations—at a basic cost to some; a group's own adapted minibus; and some private arrangements for yet other clients. A separate research consultancy was recommended to iron out these anomalies.

6. The issue of how many existing clients were to be paid for by social services should be clarified before contracts were formulated. One of the stipulations regarding the change in funding arrangements was that there should be no consequent increase in costs to the council in real terms. It was therefore important to establish what proportion of existing clients would be paid for by the SSD, and what spare capacity would remain to be sold to other potential purchasers should they emerge, or to be given away by the organization to its own clients. This would allow the SSD to meet its legal obligations by providing care in accordance with statutory assessments. Remaining places or units purchased by the SSD but not allocated to assessed clients might then be allocated by the organization on behalf of the SSD, provided assessment arrangements matched those of the SSD.

7. There should be a clear and accessible system by which purchasers could gain information about the range of care available. In the absence of such a system, organizations would stand or fall by patronage. Such a system should include, but might well go beyond, the compilation of a list of approved providers.

8. The role and intentions of the health authority should be clarified. Sandwell Health Authority had been standing back from negotiations regarding the purchase of care, supporting only one provider. How likely they were to buy from other organizations was unknown.

9. Where support to voluntary organizations was provided in kind, this should be translated into cash terms at the earliest opportunity. This arose most commonly where, in the process of 'downsizing', the SSD seconded staff on permanent contracts to the voluntary sector in lieu of funding. While this system worked for some organizations and individual workers, this was only by chance. It was an important statement to make that organizations should be free to appoint and manage their own staff. In some instances, seconded staff worked alongside employed staff with less favourable terms and conditions; in others, where disputes occurred, seconded staff had appealed to their SSD managers rather than to the management of the organization. Such tensions came about only out of the administrative convenience of the council, and it was agreed that they would be phased out over a short period of time.

10. All organizations receiving funding, whether by grant or contract, whether from Community Development or social services, should have freedom of virement within and across budget heads.

11. Both funding committees should aim to develop the contract culture with all voluntary groups in the longer term.

The change to the contract culture has more far-reaching implications for the voluntary sector than at any other time in its history. It follows that the change has to be managed. In all council areas, but especially where voluntary sector organization is weak, it is the local authority that has the responsibility for managing the transition. Not only must the SSD, in order to protect all its services, support the voluntary sector, but it must also define and meet its own needs. The Policy Studies Institute identified the needs of purchasers as follows:

1. Choice of low-cost high quality providers to ensure competition at the contract stage.
2. Ongoing choice of low-cost high quality providers to (i) ensure flexibility over time to meet new needs and (ii) avoid monopoly suppliers and provide continuing competition. In addition, purchasers need to avoid 'cosy' or dependent relationships, based on perceived moral obligations and liabilities, between purchasers and suppliers.
3. The ability to ensure value-for-money, drive 'hard bargains' and contain costs within predetermined budgets.
4. To have trust in the ability and reliability of suppliers.
5. To exercise control over who is served and how.
6. To maintain standards and accountability via easily applied, common procedures.
7. To keep transaction costs low and, more generally, to achieve managerial and administrative efficiency throughout the contracting process from initial selection to ongoing maintenance of standards (Leat 1993: 43).

It is self-evident that these conditions will not arise spontaneously. Their provision is being managed by a number of local authorities. In others, however, a short-sighted approach has been adopted. Many local councils have seen themselves as bystanders, allowing the voluntary and private sectors to fight it out amongst themselves, awaiting the opportunity—it has to be presumed—to pick out and work with the survivors. What the service needs is not so much competition as variety. Its absence will be to the disadvantage of the purchaser, as much as to the detriment of the providing sector and, ultimately, to the concept of client choice and quality of service.

References

Leat, D. (1993). *The Development of Community Care by the Independent Sector.* London: Policy Studies Institute.

Sandwell Metropolitan Borough Council. (1994). *Investing in Community.* Metropolitan Borough of Sandwell.

Wistow, G. et al. (1994). *Social Care in a Mixed Economy.* Buckingham: Open University Press.

CHAPTER 21

Dilemmas of Management in Nonprofit Organizations

STEVEN RATHGEB SMITH AND MICHAEL LIPSKY

The boards of two nonprofit organizations gather for their monthly meetings. One meets in an airy, sunlit, tastefully furnished, high-ceiling room with potted plants and framed woven wallhangings. The other meets in a cramped basement recreation area where a pingpong table has been shoved to one side and posters of sports heroes look down to inspire achievement among admiring youth. Both boards, different as they appear, are likely to share two permanent items on their agendas.

One is how to handle the all-too-familiar cash flow crisis. Receipts from government agencies are in arrears while bills are mounting. Questions come from around the table.

A second item common to both boards is a familiar conversation about renewing or possibly seeking further contracts.

A cash flow squeeze may have a specific cause. The state or city is in a fiscal crisis and has difficulty paying its bills. New government personnel have frozen payments until they can sort things out. Personnel cutbacks in the finance division of the state agency have delayed payments. The government's computers are down. The wrong paperwork was submitted.

The organizations' attitudes toward demands to change program priorities may vary. They might be perceived as challenges or misfortunes that arise because of a fiscal crisis, intense new government priorities, or other specific developments in the policy world. Or the organization may well share with government officials a view of the needs of the region and thus accept the legitimacy of new priorities even when those priorities require it to expand its program base. And it needs the money if it is to retain central office staff and other key personnel, and maintain core functions.

Nonprofit agencies that contract with governments tend to experience these problems regularly. At least, every nonprofit agency should expect to encounter them if it becomes involved in contracting. These are not issues that arise out of poor management in the public or voluntary sector, although poor management may sometimes be found. What at the level of individual organization appears to be bad luck, parlous times, or inept management is in large part rather a matter of coping with chronic problems of the contracting regime. It is perhaps significant that the only periods in which these problems do not arise are periods of rapid growth in contracting, when government officials are eager to initiate programs and identify agencies willing to accept service contracts.

To be sure, nonprofit agencies do not experience contracting dilemmas to the same degree.

The frequency and severity of the problems are likely to be greater the more an organization depends upon contracting for its income, and the less diverse is its resource base. Some organizations will have minimized contracting problems because of an unusual relationship with a government sponsor. For example, in the case of long-term residential placements, government agencies that rely on nonprofit organizations for continuous services may have long-established relations with their service providers. Other agencies may have powerful advocates within the legislative or executive branch or in the commissioner's office.

Understanding the Nonprofit Organization

How do our boards of trustees and executive directors get themselves into situations in which they continually live on the edge of financial crisis and programmatic compromise? A useful point of departure in the analysis of organizations generally is to think of them as oriented toward maintaining themselves and, where possible, making themselves stronger. Organizations therefore tend to seek out opportunities for growth and budgetary stability while seeking to be indifferent to possible inconsistencies such opportunities present to their missions. This organizational perspective would predict that nonprofits will accept a newly offered contract in order to grow, and agree to conditions imposed on them by government in order to increase their program capacity.[1]

However, although the assertion that nonprofit organizations seek to secure their interests is a useful guide, other motives drive them as well. In particular, voluntary agencies are typically influenced by a strong sense of purpose and commitment. Thus nonprofit organizations are torn between organizational maintenance and pursuit of their purposive objectives.[2] If nonprofit organizations were not purposive at least to some degree, then government demands that they change their program or client profiles would hardly pose any problems for them. The tension is acute in more zealous and recently

founded organizations, whose original social commitments are still intact. But they are evident as well throughout the full range of nonprofit organizations, from the struggling shelter to the affluent family service organization.

In considering whether to accept initial contracts, officers of nonprofit organizations are mindful that raising money the traditional way, through sources other than contracting, is no easy task. Going again and again to the same donors and putting together raffles, auctions, and annual drives can be exhausting and hard to sustain year after year. Also, many of the newer community-based organizations are controversial and undercapitalized; thus they are unattractive to established donors such as foundations and the United Way. Private alternatives to charity such as fees from clients and insurance agencies are limited sources of revenue.

While government contracts entail some risks at the beginning of the contracting relationship, they represent a welcome infusion of substantial funds, with certainty of ultimate delivery, and a release from the grinding annual problems of raising money. Leaders of the organization may also believe that they can continue to raise funds from traditional sources while adding on a government contract component.

A few additional comments are in order to modify this crudely schematic outline. First, we do not want to suggest that nonprofit agencies were the hallmarks of fiscal stability before the development of government funding. Nonprofit agencies typically had to cope with uncertainties associated with unexpected demands on staff, financial miscues, and the difficulty of generating adequate fees and charitable contributions. But these problems tended to have less serious implications for fiscal stability and agency autonomy for three reasons. Nonprofit agencies were smaller, thus possible financial losses tended to be less serious. Because of the "blockiness" of government contracts, a contract loss can have more profound implications for agency operations than simply the inability of the agency to generate sufficient fee income or receive its entire requested United Way allocation. Furthermore, sources of private revenues for nonprofit service agencies such as the United Way, local foundations, and individuals were usually very reluctant to try to intervene directly in agency operations.

Second, we do not mean to suggest that every nonprofit agency is willing to bid for a contract simply because funds are available. The organization will consider whether the contract will interfere with existing programs, whether the agency has the capacity to fulfill a contract, and even whether it can develop a competitive proposal in time for the submission date. Nonetheless, a nonprofit will find it difficult to turn down an opportunity to expand in established program areas, particularly if it has some reason to think it might land the contract. Its commitments in the area, and the potential for expanding services to its target population, present too great a set of incentives to be passed up easily.

As suggested above, some nonprofits are clearly more vulnerable to the instability resulting from contracting than others. Most vulnerable perhaps are the new community organizations that live hand-to-mouth while initiating new services to new groups, and which have only recently received government funds. These groups may be nursed along by public agencies up to a point, especially when their policy specialities are in great demand. But they become vulnerable when the salience of their services or clients begins to fade from public view,[3] or when governments encounter a fiscal crisis.

At times, the ability of nonprofits to mobilize political resources neutralizes their vulnerability to the erratic and unreliable nature of contracting. For example, programs for children with severe physical handicaps whose parents have effective lobbying organizations may be able to withstand pressures to change or accept contracts for less money. In contrast, respite care for welfare parents of homebound infants and children is a service whose clients are not able to mobilize effective political support.

Cash Flow

If we think of a contract as an agreement between two parties free to enter into such an arrangement, we might think that the test of the

contract is the extent to which each side produces what it said it would produce. In social services, this means that the voluntary agency must produce the service it promised, in exchange for money. Conceptions of contracting of this sort underlie the concern of many critics that government agencies are not able to hold contractors accountable.[4]

Much less is said about the other side of the equation: the extent to which government undermines contracts and contractors by failing to fulfill its part of the bargain to make payments in a timely fashion.[5] For if reimbursement is delayed long enough to add significantly to the cost of providing services, government effectively rewrites the terms of the contract unilaterally. Moreover, if these delays weaken the financial condition of the agency, the agency may be forced to take government clients previously not covered by the initial contract understanding. This shift in agency policy is further encouraged by the agency's bank and creditors who want a demonstration of financial soundness.

Keeping in mind that we are generalizing over a vast range of organizations and relationships, we offer a few ideas about why nonprofit organizations are chronically confronted with cash flow problems, and how they distort themselves and sometimes get into trouble in their attempts to cope with the consequences.

Nonprofit agencies sometimes enter into contracts below levels of funding that would allow them to provide service of appropriate quality. This remarkable development occurs for a combination of reasons. The agency executive may misjudge the organization's ability to cut expenses or generate client contacts. She may incorrectly believe that she will be able to renegotiate the contract once it is secured. And the executive may yield to the pressure of public officials because she believes that the agency can build a long-term relationship with government for which the present contract is only the first installment. In any case, the opportunity to diversify may have gains that balance the initial uncertainty over the ratio of costs and revenue.

Some payment schemes place providers at a disadvantage. Payment on the basis of monthly or nightly censuses, for example, place contractors at a disadvantage because they are paid on the basis of the clients they actually serve, while their costs are not variable but fixed. This payment method works to the benefit of both parties if intake is reliable. The state only pays for what it gets, and the contracting agency has an incentive to maintain the numbers it serves.

But what happens when, through no fault of the contracting organization, the census fall off? It could fall off because the service it provides is not required evenly across time. For example, the need for shelters for the homeless declines in the summer. An organization providing shelter may have overestimated the numbers that would be seeking shelter as the calendar moved into spring. Or another shelter may have opened which temporarily draws clients away from the first.

More troubling from the point of view of nonprofit providers is the problem of depending for referrals on other agencies. Many providers, as in the case of referrals within the criminal and juvenile corrections systems, are entirely dependent on referrals from other agencies to make up their clientele. Some state agencies will only contract with agencies that agree to restrict their referrals to the state agency funding the contract. But personnel difficulties or policy disputes within the agencies may leave contractors with unfilled beds for weeks or months at a time. Through no fault of the organization, they will be paid less during such a period.

All would be well if the contractor had mostly marginal costs and could simply spend less money during a low census period. For example, it could buy less food or reduce the subcontracted psychiatric hours it buys if it temporarily had fewer clients. But almost all costs are not of this type. The organization still needs the same number of custodial staff people and must heat its buildings to the same temperature. So the organization must carry on with essentially the same costs but lower revenues.

Both parties may be aware of the risks associated with client flows, but both will proceed on the more optimistic assumptions that client flows will remain stable. Government will do this to maximize service availability; the nonprofit organization will do this to maximize in-

come and avoid what its director expects will be a losing argument in light of the pressing and unfunded public needs of which it is aware.

Costs may increase unexpectedly during the terms of the contract. This is a hazard of all contractors, from the private as well as the voluntary sectors. It is noteworthy here only to the extent that nonprofit contractors may be reluctant to insist that the contract build in expected yearly increases into the terms of the contract; and in a multiyear period government may seek to change the terms of the contract by "level-funding" future years, despite previous expectations that it will provide for cost-of-living and inflation increases. Government can do this while private parties cannot, because while contracts may be for two or more years, government can plausibly seek to renegotiate terms after the first year, claiming that it does not have the money. Nonprofit contractors then find themselves in the position where they must accept receiving less money or risk overturning the entire arrangement. Government officials also realize that nonprofit staff are committed to addressing a certain problem or helping a specific disadvantaged group; thus they are unlikely to protest their frustration with government by closing their programs.

These concerns represent defects that are built in from the start of the contracting arrangement. Others follow not from the structure of the contract but from the process of obtaining payment.

Reimbursement may be delayed, sometimes seriously.[6] The most severe form this problem takes is when government deliberately exploits its systems for providing regular contract payments or for reimbursing contractors upon the submission of vouchers to withhold payments in order to solve governmental fiscal problems. Questioning by the government agency of the claims of contractors about services provided or costs incurred also results in holding up reimbursements.

Unfortunately, many contractors do not have the resources to ride out periods of reimbursement withholding. Moreover, they are not allowed to build up reserves;[7] as nonprofit organizations they are not in a position to do so; funds established to bear them through rough times might appear to be undistributed and inappropriate "profits." Public agencies may take amiss an organization's financial claims if reserve balances are too high. Moreover, as service-providing organizations they have internally generated reasons to abhor reserves when there are underserved clients who could be assisted.

Further compounding the problem is the difficulty nonprofits experience in gaining lines of credit. Banks are often reluctant to lend to nonprofit agencies because they are undercapitalized, with government contracts as their only significant asset. Since these contracts can be cut or even terminated, banks will not regard them as secure assets. Consequently, the bank often requires an extensive track record from a nonprofit before it will provide a line of credit. Additionally, banks tend to dislike such lines of credit because even though they earn market rate interest from them, the handholding and work entailed in dealing with nonprofits sometimes makes the loan line unprofitable on balance. For these reasons, the bank may grant only part of a line of credit request, leaving the nonprofit still vulnerable to major delays in payment.

In self-defense, nonprofit organizations develop coping devices to try to sustain themselves over the rough times of high standard costs and reduced revenue flows. While the nonprofit is experiencing cash flow problems, its own creditors must be managed. Nonprofit organizations are run by people who are artists at avoiding paying the nonessential bill.

One set of rules for governance developed by nonprofits is creating payment priorities. Staff salaries usually have first claims on limited cash resources. Employees of nonprofit organizations—daycare workers, counselors, custodial attendants, cooks, for examples—tend to be lowly paid and even more lowly paid than their counterparts in other sectors. The organization will put their needs first partly because they are among lower income workers, but mostly because it is often so difficult to recruit staff to some of these unrewarding, entry-level positions in human services. Still, directors of some of the more zealous nonprofit agencies have been known to seek temporary pay holidays if the entire agency is up against the wall.

Some creditors are treated as absolute, while others are regarded as more forgiving and flexible. The landlord and telephone company may be treated as requiring timely payments, while others may have to be satisfied with partial payments and sustain regular backlogs of debt. When the agency comes under fiscal stress, creditors will be strung along, put off as long as possible, and receive a downpayment on the mounting debt when absolutely necessary. Up to certain limits, nonprofits often treat bank loans as flexible debts, foregoing repayment on the principal of the loan while maintaining interest payments. Like business lenders, some purveyors and banks may be owed so much that they continue to support the nonprofit organization for fear that if the organization collapses they will never receive what they are owed.

Real trouble arises when nonprofit managers begin to overlook their debts or to pay expenses for one account from funds allocated for another. Paying salaries for people on one project from another project's allocation is one expedient to which the nonprofit manager may resort.

Failing to pay required taxes is another. In the 1980s Massachusetts Fair Share, a citizen action organization, was fatally tarnished with charges of mismanagement. Among other things, it had failed to pay its employees' social security taxes. In 1988, the New York Urban League also came under charges of fiscal mismanagement and failing to pay its social security taxes.[8] Many other nonprofits have also got into trouble over social security taxes in recent years.[9]

Is it coincidental that important, and in their way quite distinguished, nonprofit organizations have come to neglect this particular obligation? On the contrary, the incidents reflect the systemic problems of the nonprofit agency. Faced with revenue shortfalls and ongoing, continuing obligations, buoyed by the hopes of their directors that saving devices would materialize, reluctant to cut back on activities when the message was that the needs the organizations were addressing were great, managers may have understandably given in to immediate financial pressures by neglecting regular tax payments in the hope that they would be able to make them up in the near future.

The troubles outlined above are not the product of mismanagement by poorly trained executives of nonprofit agencies, although this is the usual charge. Undoubtedly there are ways in which the voluntary sector could be more sophisticated in administration, but the problem is more systemic. Nonprofits are virtually expected to cope with erratic revenues, underfunding, and slashes to established budgets. One might say that through contracting, nonprofit agencies are enlisted into an alliance with government to manage the failures of the public sector to deal with clients reliably and consistently.

It would be abhorrent if a pensioner receiving, say, five hundred dollars per month in a given year received three checks one month late, one check that bounced and was cleared only after several tearful telephone negotiations, and two checks late in the year that were each short fifty dollars because the government was strapped for funds. Yet this is the situation of the nonprofit organizations expected to serve the pensioner population with home care aides, meals-on-wheels, daycare and transportation services.

The Dance of Contract Renewal

Some buyers may go into a market once, seeking the best value for money, never needing or intending to return. Others may be required to go back into a market again and again. They may go back because the number of suppliers may be limited. The costs of going elsewhere, to the next town, say, may be too high. The buyer may have a stake in keeping a reliable supply coming to market. Like a country purchasing arms or a homeowner intent on preserving the neighborhood hardware store, the long-term interest of the purchaser may constrain his wandering off in search of bargains.

This is the case with government nurturing of contractors in many service areas. Suppliers of some services are limited, and government must have suppliers if it is to maintain reliable contractors. Ironically, while government has a stake in maintaining reliable suppliers, it regularly undermines voluntary agencies through a dance of contract renewal which leaves the organizations in flux and uncertainty.

Contracting parties are perhaps most autonomous when a first contract is arranged. The voluntary organization has not yet come to depend upon public funds, and government has not yet come to depend upon the voluntary organization to supply services. While the lure of government contracts may be attractive to some organizations (and of questionable value to others), the signing of the first contract is not particularly destabilizing. Once the match is consummated, however, subsequent interactions frequently cause debilitating uncertainties and require managerial acrobatics on the part of nonprofit officers to minimize the often high costs of doing business with the state.[10]

It may be possible for some organizations to maintain stable and mutually supportive relationships with government, particularly when governments fully accept their dependence on the voluntary organizations—for example, in the case of health centers and correction agencies. Moreover, governments increasingly recognize their growing dependence on nonprofit agencies and the severe instabilities they often impose on these organizations. Nonetheless, normal relations in contract renewals are characterized by difficulties that the nonprofit partner is expected to bear.

These difficulties exist despite a generally high rate of contract renewal. For example, an agency for the developmentally disabled received a contract for residential group care in 1980. The agency still had the contract in 1991. But this seeming stability masks the profound uncertainties and difficulties the agency experienced in the course of contract negotiation and award as well as the differences in the substantive content of the contract over the 11-year period.

Voluntary agencies that contract with government seek stability in programming for several reasons. They are expected to provide government with reliable service "supplies." As conscientious service organizations, they desire stability in their programming. And they need to offer stable programs in order to present themselves to the public and their own constituencies as reliable. But like the problem of maintaining ade-

quate cash flow, the vicissitudes of contract renewal are destabilizing for systemic reasons that
are built into the logic of government actions in
the contracting regime.

We recognize that there are exceptions to the
dynamics of contract renewal we sketch below,
and times when the dynamics are more evident
than others. Some service areas (say, child abuse
investigations) are more vital to government
than others (say, English-as-a-second-language
for new immigrants), which may be currently
fashionable but not part of core governmental
functions. Nonetheless, we will proceed to describe the archetypical case, as a way of illumi-
nating an important dimension of the contracting regime which is not captured by statistics or
general discussions of how nonprofit organizations may be changing over time.

Nonprofit organizations cannot rely on government to maintain funding levels or provide
increases consistent with reasonable expectations for cost of living and price index inflation.

At the same time that government agencies
are motivated to spread resources over a broader
client base, legislatures in their role as keepers of
the public purse maintain a tight grip on the
budgets of line agencies such as the Department
of Mental Health or Social Services. On occasion, the politics of a jurisdiction will yield
place-holding salary adjustments or other increments in recognition of inflation or increased
costs. Or a particular service area may become
recognized as requiring shoring up and receive a
budgetary allocation disproportionate to those
of other service areas. But otherwise, the process
of funding ongoing contracts results in squeez-
ing current providers, because government
agencies do not have enough money to meet all
pressing demands, or they wish to expand programming in some areas by nibbling at the budgets of current providers in others.[11]

Nonprofit organizations cannot rely on government to sustain its priorities over time. New
constituencies arise to compete for funds within
the compass of ongoing agency budgets. New
ideas are developed which appear to offer innovative ways to serve old constituencies. The new
ideas may be untested, but their novelty has the
appeal of permitting government agencies to

represent themselves as having innovative approaches to service.

From the point of view of government, this is
all legitimate. It is a hallmark of the contracting
regime—and to government a prime attraction
of contracting—that over time government
can have maximum flexibility to move funds
around. But what to government is flexibility is
to the nonprofit sector an important source of
instability.

With the knowledge that government will
seek new approaches to old problems and policies for new constituents, nonprofit agencies will
strive, if possible, to turn their program profiles
toward the apparent preferences of government.
There are undoubtedly many reasons for this.
One is the straightforward belief that governmental preferences are correct for the target
population. In some instances, the agency or
groups of agencies may have participated in discussions with government in which the new priorities were hammered out.

A second is that a contract for services is likely
to represent a large part of an organization's
budget. Its loss would affect not just the program in question but the organization's core
functions as well. And, nonprofit agencies often
find it difficult to tap alternative sources of
funds such as fees or private charity.

A third is the desire to diversify so as to maintain fiscal health. Executives of nonprofit organizations widely believe that the only way to maintain the core functions of their agencies is to
increase the number of contracts they hold. New
contracts will pay current costs at a time when
cost-of-living increases may be difficult to obtain under existing contracts. Thus agency directors can try to stay even with current expenditures. In addition, contracting with several
public agencies provides partial insurance
against coming into disfavor with any single
agency, or the collapse of a single agency's contracting capacity.

Many contracts, especially in today's strained
budgetary climate, allocate insufficient money
for administrative expenses. Consequently, a
nonprofit executive may seek a new contract in
the hope that the additional increment for administrative expenses may be enough to hire the

bookkeeper, the assistant director, or the new program coordinator. In the worst-case scenario, an agency will obtain a new but substantially underfunded contract (because government knows that the agency dearly wants the deal), and the agency loses money from the day it assumes the contract. The agency is then in an even more vulnerable position vis-à-vis government.

A particularly desperate part of the dance comes when contract renewal bids have been made, and the process of deciding the awards is in process, but for one reason or another the government agency is unable to make a timely decision. As the period covering the current contract winds down, months may go by without a decision.

Our agency director now must do some fancy footwork. As she waits for assurances that the agency's contract will be renewed, she risks losing staff, particularly the better and more experienced workers whose skills are in demand elsewhere. The program may be severely eroded as staff members become unwilling to continue to take the risk that the program will not be renewed. Whether or not individuals are themselves looking for new jobs, staff morale suffers, with implications for program and clients.

Aside from waiting and offering hollow reassurances, our director can take some actions, although they may have a degree of desperation attached to them. She may begin to juggle personnel among contracts in order to keep important staff and maintain organizational continuity. This strategy may be most plausible in service agencies that have relatively coherent programs so that such substitution makes a degree of sense. Although disruptive to programs and demoralizing to staff because it confirms that the organization is in trouble, this remains an effective albeit difficult step the director can take.

A parallel course of action is to seek other funding and move the organization in directions tangential to its stated mission. In doing so, our director hopes to salvage something of the agency's objectives on a sounder footing.[12] This approach may be pursued at the moment contracts come up for renewal; more likely it will be followed in anticipation of losing contracts as the director comes to see that a program area is being abandoned, or that it has become an unreliable source of support. Thus the organization may go from experimenting with alternative sentencing arrangements for troubled youth, to serving youths already in custody who have severe psychological needs. The organization is still serving youth in trouble with the law, but, with no funds available from government, it has abandoned its original agenda to provide alternatives to jail for first offenders.

This shift is facilitated by the professionalization of management following the receipt of government funds. Professional managers tend to be less committed to the founding mission of an organization and thus are more likely to advocate a change of direction in agency purposes in the interests of organizational preservation.

Important cues on proper performance in the contract dance are given by the contract award decision. After months of time and energy the nonprofit agency has devoted to keeping or obtaining a particular contract, government may decide to award the contract to another agency. Sometimes this decision is purely political—the other agency may have better, more influential political connections. Other awards will be decided on substantive grounds. For example, a developmental disabilities agency lost a contract because government officials decided, on the basis of new treatment theories, that the behavioral approach of the agency was an outdated treatment method. Thus government awarded the contract to a second agency, which was more willing to adapt to new government treatment priorities. Subsequently, the first agency sharply reduced its behavioral focus in the hope of scoring points with government for future contract award decisions.

The Question of Goal Succession

Diversification of revenue sources clearly is desirable for nonprofit service organizations. Alternative sources of income, such as endowment or fees for services, buffer organizations from total reliance on contracts. If contracts are the main source of income, however, the greater the number of contracts, and the more diverse the sources of contracting, the more likely is the organization to withstand the difficulties of any particular contract renewal experience. Yet the current austere fiscal climate for government social programs is such that even agencies with a relatively low government funding (25 percent for example) may feel that they need to "dance" with government officials for their contract because of the difficulty of raising outside revenue. When an agency loses a contract, even if it is for a small portion of its budget, it not only loses money for direct service to clients but money for overhead expenses such as utilities and the director's salary.

Faced with fickle governmental policymaking that maximizes policy flexibility at the expense of support for ongoing organizations, nonprofits themselves will develop devices to cope with uncertainty. They will seek alternative means of support, as suggested above. They will organize politically so they can lobby government collectively to reform the contracting process.[13] And they will look for ways to diversify their operations so that the effects of fickleness in any single issue area may be contained by the variety of other activities. Thus there may be some truth to the charge that nonprofit service organizations are opportunistic—that, to overstate the case, they are willing to bid on anything that moves. But it is an opportunism that arises in part from the position in which they find themselves in the contracting regime.

It is not a far reach from this conclusion to recognize that today a critical source of goal succession in voluntary organizations is the preferences and behavior of government. If in general the goals are determined by the structure of opportunities available to an organization as it seeks to maintain itself, in the era of contracting goal displacement of otherwise autonomous organizations is attributable to the choices made by governments about what will or will not be funded.

Noticeably, the classic cases in the sociology of goal succession are nonprofit organizations. The question might well be raised whether nonprof-

its are will-o'-the wisps which can easily be turned from one activity to another.

It should be remembered that when a nonprofit organization is considering a government contract, it is not entirely in charge of its environment. It is weighing its future in recognition of the increased resources it would have to have to pursue its work, and also in view of the likelihood that funds for programs it would like to pursue may not be available. The nonprofit organization is not in charge of the policy climate either, although it seeks to contribute to it. And it is in a bargaining position with government agencies that can assist or decline to assist the organization's work. In this, nonprofits dependent on government funding are not particularly different from the "classic" organizations that have been described as going through goal succession, because these organizations also had to be concerned about their sources of support. Thus nonprofit organizations under contracting offer a specific case of one of the primary reasons organizations are said to change their goals: to meet the demands of other organizations with which they have implicit negotiations.[14]

We should also bear in mind that organizations and social policy environments change over time; indeed, change sometimes is quite rapid. Views on the proper disposition and care of juvenile offenders, for example, have embraced large reform schools, probation and court diversion, small-scale, home-like settings, "tough" army-like regimens, and other developments, suggesting how quickly fashions can change in one policy field. Methadone maintenance programs were heralded as an innovation in the 1960s and 1970s but have been overtaken by the crack problem. Government, too, changes over time. Why should voluntary agencies be rigid in programming approaches while the rest of the world is innovating? It seems reasonable to suggest that nonprofit agencies should be changing, not the other way around.

Directors of nonprofit organizations do not casually or cynically drive their organizations to change goals, but are often fully aware of the possible costs that contracting may involve for their agencies. They anticipate the possibility that they will be forced to compromise service values, and they accept contracts only after agonizing consideration. Some nonprofits reject government contracts so as to avoid the anticipated loss of autonomy.

Ultimately, whether it is regrettable that an organization changes its goals cannot be stated in the general case. In any particular instance, some partisans of an organization's orientation may regret a change, but other supporters will welcome or tolerate a choice that favors the maintenance of the organization over an insecure future.

Unfortunately, many agencies do not make a switch easily or well because of certain aspects of the "dance of contract management." Government officials usually want agencies to take on new responsibilities for a minimum of additional funds. Government often achieves this goal because nonprofit agencies are unable to develop alternatives to government referrals and support. Thus an emergency shelter may have started as a respite place for troubled youth. Faced with escalating demands for placement of severely disturbed young people, government officials manage to change the service of the agency without giving it additional funds needed by its new client population. The result may be a deterioration in the quality of the agency's service.

It is in this sense that the arguments of the methadone clinic that resists or refuses to accept crack addicts may be more than simply nonprofit parochialism. The clinic may contend that it does not have the expertise to treat crack addicts, and that in any case government is not going to provide enough funds to deliver adequate service. To accept the proposed contract for crack addicts might lead to a decline in all of the agency's programs. In a sense, underlying this dilemma is the difficult question: what are the public obligations of nonprofit agencies? Should nonprofit agencies address pressing public problems such as AIDS or crack even if government does not provide sufficient resources?[15]

Finally, we should recognize the possibility that government contracting may actually facilitate nonprofit organizations' founding purposes. Some might say that the inner-city settlement house which follows its ethnic group of origin to the suburbs instead of staying within the city to serve new immigrant groups has changed goals. In the past, some settlement houses did move to the suburbs because that is where their sources of support were. But today they might stay put even if their original constituency moves out, because government contracting may allow them to pursue their mission to new inner-city migrants.

Notes

1. Nonprofit service agencies also would tend to accept offered contracts to cross-subsidize favored programs that are financially precarious, stabilize funding of core capacity (such as rent and administrators' salaries), and seek stability by diversifying their resource base. Some of these considerations are discussed in Estelle James, "How Nonprofits Grow: A Model," *Journal of Policy Analysis and Management*, 2, 3 (1983): 350–366.

2. For further discussion of purposive incentives see Wilson, *Political Organizations,* chap. 3. See also Thomas Wolf, *The Nonprofit Organization: An Operating Manual* (Englewood Cliffs, N.J.: Prentice-Hall, 1984); J. David Seay and Bruce C. Vladeck, eds., *In Sickness and in Health* (New York: McGraw-Hill, 1988).

3. Nonprofit agencies funded by government, especially the upstart agencies, are thus susceptible to the "issue-attention cycle" of government. For example, rape crisis centers, programs for elderly crime victims, and battered women shelters benefited by the interest of policymakers in their issues during the 1970s but suffered cutbacks when government priorities shifted to other issues. See Smith and Freinkel, *Adjusting the Balance,* chap. 7. Also see Anthony Downs, "Up and Down with Ecology—The 'Issue-Attention Cycle,'" *The Public Interest,* 28 (Summer 1972): 38–50.

4. On this general problem of accountability see D. C. Hague, W. J. M. Mackenzie, and A. Barker, eds., *Public Policy and Private Interests* (London: Macmillan Press, 1975); Smith and Hague, eds., *The Dilemma of Accountability in Modern Government.* Also see John D. Donahue, *The Privatization Decision: Public Ends, Private Means* (New York: Basic Books, 1989).

5. The fiscal instability within nonprofit contract agencies created by payment delays is described in an excellent case study: see Melissa Middleton Stone, "POS Reform in Massachusetts," Boston University School of Management, 1991.

6. Stone, "POS Reform," pp. 15–16, 20.

7. Peter Nessen, former director of the Massachusetts Office of Purchased Services and later Massachusetts Secretary of Administration and Finance, argues that nonprofit organizations are expected to be run like businesses, except they are not allowed to do more than just barely survive. Thus, unlike businesses, they cannot build up treasuries in good times to protect them against bad times. He suggests that this is one of the key reasons that so many nonprofits fail.

8. Kathleen Teltsch, "New York's Urban League, Riddled by Debt, Searches for Aid," *New York Times,* March 27, 1988, p. 37.

9. Until the early 1980s, nonprofit agencies were exempt from paying social security taxes. New federal legislation required nonprofit agencies and their employees to pay these taxes. However, contracts rarely were renegotiated to reflect the imposition of these new costs; consequently agencies and their employees were forced to absorb them.

10. See also Bernstein, "Contracted Services as a Game"; Gronbjerg, "Nonprofit Management."

11. Another reason for the inability of government contracts to keep up with inflation may be its lack of information about funding levels. The contracting regime, because of its fragmentation, masks the true costs of service and the actual costs borne by individual agencies. Thus government officials have broad discretion to set rates. See Anthony Downs, "Why the Government Budget Is Too Small in a Democracy," *World Politics,* 12, 4 (July 1960): 541–563.

12. A minor discomfort may result if the organization wrongly anticipates that contracts will not be renewed and has to take on more work than it expected. As this discussion suggests, this is a problem with which most nonprofit agencies are glad to be confronted.

13. A major part of the platform of the MCHSP is reform of the contracting process.

14. See James D. Thompson and William J. McEwen, "Organizational Goals and the Environment," *American Sociological Review,* 23 (1958): 23–31, reprinted in Amitai Etzioni, ed., *Complex Organizations* (New York: Holt, Rinehart and Winston, 1962), pp. 177–190. See also William E. Berg and Roosevelt Wright, "Program Funding as an Organizational Dilemma: Goal Displacement in Social Work Programs," *Administration in Social Work,* 4, 4 (Winter 1980): 29–39.

15. It is this public role of nonprofit agencies which has received substantial attention in the debate about the current role of nonprofit hospitals in serving the poor. See GAO, *Nonprofit Hospitals: Better Standards Needed for Tax Exemption* (Washington, D.C.: GAO, 1990); Seay and Vladeck, eds., *In Sickness and in Health.*

► **CHAPTER 22**

The Game of Contracted Services

SUSAN R. BERNSTEIN

M anagers from different agencies, positions, and backgrounds present remarkably similar verbal portraits of
their work. In the language, magnitude, and passion of their reactions to managing contracted services, they make "game playing" the appropriate
metaphor for articulating their experience.[1] This
metaphor was not part of the conceptualization or
conduct of the research; however, most managers
make specific reference to game playing, and all
use the language of games in their descriptions of
what they do and why. Managers find contracted
services "crazy"; the game metaphor keeps them
from succumbing to "craziness."

The paradoxical nature of contracted services
makes the metaphor compelling. Managers talk
of being very serious about what they do, but of
not taking contract compliance too seriously.
Many are managers in NPAs [nonprofit agen-
cies] in which over 90 percent of the funding is
from GFOs [government funding organiza-
tions], yet the NPA mission is the most crucial
factor in their decision making. Repeatedly,
managers describe situations in which aspects of
the management of contracted services conflict
with reality. In accepting these paradoxes, managers perceive their task as a game. This perception enables them to understand, get control of,
and keep in perspective contracted services.

One manager, in describing the qualities her
NPA should seek if she had to be replaced, uses

the game metaphor to stress the importance of
understanding the GFO system.

> I think you have to be the kind of person who's
> interested in how the system works. If you can
> understand how all the pieces fit together, it's
> not quite so onerous. I've always approached it
> from the point that if you can understand why
> you have to fill out the form and what it gener-
> ates and how it fits into the whole larger system,
> filling out the form doesn't become quite so bad.
> It has a meaning. It's not just an exercise in fill-
> ing out a form. You have to have that interest be-
> cause we're a small program, but we fit in some-
> where. When we object to certain things, and
> [GFO] say, "But if we have this piece of informa-
> tion, then that can happen," then giving them
> that piece of information isn't quite so tough. I
> think that, to me, that's the game of it.

Another manager describes the system as
"overwhelming" but also "fun" and explains, "If
you start to take it so, so seriously, you would
just be really nuts." She describes her feelings
about her job in language that could be used to
explain the exhilaration that comes from getting
control of any difficult game of skill.

> It's always a new dilemma every day. Just to fig-
> ure out how to send those UCRs [uniform case
> records] down [to the GFO] without [the

GFO's] losing them—that's a problem that's fun to solve.

There's something about being a part of the [GFO] system that's a challenge. To know that it doesn't make sense for [the GFO] not to fund a [particular program]. It just doesn't make sense. So that, in a way, I know that I'm writing something that they have to fund. It's fun to start figuring out how it works.

It gives you a sense of real mastery when you've learned how and where and what system to address one's needs to. A real sense of mastery. It's like when you drive a stick-shift car—I found that fun, while it was scary as anything in the beginning. So, now it's fun because we have a track record of having gotten funded two proposals—learning the numbers, being able to give the jargon back, to be able to communicate in their language, with their figures, but not take it so, so seriously at this end.[2]

For another manager, the game metaphor is a way of keeping the paradoxical, crazy quality of managing contracted services in perspective.

I guess it's always been part of my personality and the way that I am that you can only take these things just so seriously. It's like—when you fill out the UCRs—there are some people who are really very, very serious about this, and you have to do it all precisely and you have to include absolutely everything in this and it has to be correct and you have to use this as a tool. My feeling is you fill it out as best as you can, you hit the points that you have to, but don't put all of your time and your effort into a form. Put your time and your effort into a client and into service delivery.

So that's what I mean when I say it's a game. Not that I'm saying don't take it seriously and don't do it as best as you can, but don't obsess about it, because you'll get crazy.

Playing the Game

A manager who has directed a foundation-funded NPA program for many years explains why she seeks a GFO contract and what it is like when she gets it.

We were always having to put so much energy into looking for funding that the reality was that the service piece always suffered for about three months a year. Then it suffered because we were always anxious whether we'd have jobs. Then, everyone [foundation funders] kept telling us, "Get into the system. Get into the system. Get into the system." We finally just said, "Okay."

We were all new, green at this whole system. The first week we had gone to [GFO] training, and they started rattling off these numbers and we thought, "Oh God, we're intelligent people. How are we ever going to figure this out?" It seemed so overwhelming. So we [NPA managers] started this group, to commiserate and support each other and to learn from each other in the beginning days because no one knew how these programs were going to fit in with [NPA] systems.

Coping with conflicts with reality is a consuming task for managers.

We're very active. We always comment to the city on everything. We're notorious for sending them letters about everything, going to meetings, complaining, and giving them unsolicited advice.

Reality—the truth, the fact, the way things are—is, of course, as managers perceive it. That their perception is correct is often verified by the GFO's yielding "to reality."

Contract requirements may conflict with the purpose of the service. A manager's frustration with a youth services contract is that the way it is written and monitored does not "take into consideration you're dealing with kids."

So you [the GFO] come and you don't see a hundred on the playground. I mean be real. Be real. That's on a piece of paper. We're talking about kids. These are human beings and there are a hundred other things they could be involved in—so understand that.

While some monitors do "understand that," others "are very sticky" about "holding" NPAs to whatever the contract says.

Another manager expresses her fury with a GFO requirement, eventually abandoned, that a contracted dropout prevention program be restricted to the academic year.

> They [GFO] said you're funded for ten months. I said, "What are we supposed to do with the staff?" They said, "Let them go and rehire." I said, "Oh—and that's why you have dropouts." That was a battle.

The manager of a different dropout prevention program explains what he does when the GFO does not fund the "whole list of things that we had to do" contractually and the NPA is incapable of providing them without funding. In a program for seventh graders, the GFO includes career/vocational counseling in the list of required services.

> How much of that are we going to do? In reality, we're not going to do that. We're going to help the kids fill out Summer Youth Employment job applications, and maybe we'll help the kids get some jobs, but as a whole, we're not in a position to do that.

An executive director describes the "incredible" loan contract the GFO expects her NPA to sign for the renovation of a residence for the homeless. The contract conflicts with the purpose of the service in its stipulation that for twenty years neither the building use be changed nor the loan prepaid.

> Our attorneys and our board of directors took issue with that and it took us a long time to come to the point of negotiating with them [GFO] that after ten years, we could pay the remainder of the loan and have the only restriction on the building be that it would provide housing and supportive services to the homeless or people of low income.

Contract requirements often conflict with the capability of GFOs to uphold their contractual obligations. For example, the seemingly simple task of delivering mandated reports on children in foster care to the correct GFO unit can re-

quire herculean effort because the GFO does not have accurate records on which units have which cases.

> We've got a UCR that came back telling us that the unit that it's been in has been dissolved six months. They [GFO] cannot find the [child's] case record. They do not know what unit is now covering the case.

The burden is now on this manager to track down the correct GFO unit. This involves making multiple calls to various GFO offices and, eventually, to the computer-systems people.

> "Look, this is our problem—we can't locate where this case is, if it's anywhere. Can you find out anything?" They'll call back and say, "Well, the case record's been lost," or "Yeah, the worker is over on such and such, but they haven't done anything with the case and, therefore, nothing has come up under their number."

The manager explains the GFO worker may not have "done anything" because there is no indication that there is an immediate problem and the case record is in a "stack of 170."

Another manager explains the absurdity of a new level of service standard established by the GFO for homemaker services.

> One of their [GFO's] initial plans was that they would require each of our case coordinators to be responsible for thirty-five families receiving homemaker services, on the premise that each family had a [GFO] social worker. It's true they have, on paper, [GFO] workers, and in the best of all possible worlds, if [the GFO] were able to function better, the [GFO] worker could realistically take care of the family's needs. But in the real world, [the GFO] can't take care of these cases and can't address the crises as quickly as they need to be addressed.

Asked how she accounts for the GFO's eventually reducing the required level of service, which her NPA "argued in a big way about," she replies, "Reality must have impinged on them."

The contracting process itself often conflicts with reality. Given that her NPA's contracts are consistently renewed, a manager bemoans the absurdity of the annual cycle.

> In my mind, there should be—you meet program objectives, the funding stream is there, it's a very simple renewal process, and you renegotiate your budget. To do this every year, the cost of this, for them and for us—it's crazy. But, no one's talking about it.

Another manager describes the "real catch-22" of making a case for additional funding when contract requirements virtually guarantee that all current funds are not spent. Underutilization of services, leading to accruals, is a result of staffing realities.

> For instance, I have a worker closing a case who's going on a month's vacation starting Monday. Now, he's going to take my utilization down, but I'm not going to assign a new case to him now when he's going to be gone for a whole month. They [GFO] don't want to hear from that. Workers who are brand new—they expect you're going to hand them twelve cases as they walk through the door, and I won't do that.
> If you have had a worker with an extended illness and maybe you have fallen in the number of contacts, we may still be covering the case because the case aide is in there, but they only count the case planner's contacts.

One manager expresses her exasperation at the impossibility of the NPA's planning for additional services because of the GFO's approach to planning.

> I said to the guy at the city, "Why are you contracting with somebody else? Why don't you give us a chance to expand?" He said, "Well, we gave you the chance to expand. We would call you up and offer you a case." I said, "Yeah, but calling me up and saying, 'Can you take a case tomorrow or can you take two cases the next day?'—that's not a plan to expand. We need something like, 'Your program size is going to be twenty-five or fifty or seventy-five or one hun-

dred cases bigger.' We'll hire the workers and the homemakers, and we'll pick up the cases. We can't just accrete them a day here or a day there."

To varying degrees, NPAs depend on timely, equitable payment from GFOs to provide the contracted service. GFO rules and procedures for payment often conflict with the reality of an NPA's dependence on this payment. A "major irritant" for one manager is the reimbursement contract.

> I have to have the private money available to pay for things, and then I get reimbursed, which puts me in this crazy position of having all this money budgeted, but if I don't have the cash to spend it, then I can't get the money back. So I may have four thousand dollars in supplies. If I don't have any cash on hand, I can't go out and buy supplies.

GFO reimbursement is typically two months after his NPA has submitted receipts. Since salary is the priority, any other expenditures are delayed.

> And what happened last year was, finally at the end, they gave us money, the last two weeks of the year. We spent something like forty thousand dollars in two weeks' time so that we could get it spent by June 30, which is obviously not the best way.

One manager decries the complexity of GFO hurdles that need to be overcome to obtain authorization for payment for renovations to contracted service offices, despite the reality that the program has existed for over a decade and will, in all likelihood, continue.

> They [GFO] are so concerned about anybody they contract with ripping them off—it's like fighting your way through a thorn hedge or something to get through all the rules and regulations.

This fight, involving her NPA's attorney, is a "major headache," which is "highly nerve-wracking."

After getting a GFO to agree that the purchase date for a $279 item is acceptable, another manager's exasperation, when the expenditure is rejected for being over $100, is palpable. He talks to his monitor, who is authorized to issue waivers.

"You know I'm not taking the $279 and putting it in my pocket. I'm not just buying balloons with it. I bought an SRA [educational] kit. The kids use it. It's useful. It's going to have a long lifetime, and you know I'm getting a contract next year. It's not going to be abused."

I was furious by this time. I was practically in tears. She said, "Can't you pay for this out of some other category?" I said, "I don't have the money. I don't have any other money." She could tell [I was at the end of my rope]. She said, "Well, this time I'll approve it, but don't let this happen again."

Even when the GFO has authorized payment, the process of getting a check is an enormous problem for some managers. A GFO's computerized system to keep track of which foster children are in whose care is used to determine GFO funds owed NPAs. However, according to the compliance coordinator in a large agency, this system is "so inaccurate" that it is "a tremendous pain" to prepare her NPA's monthly bill to the GFO.

For every single difference [in whom the GFO says we are serving and whom we are actually serving], we have to make out a form. It's absolutely horrendous. The whole billing system now is very time consuming and very frustrating.

The executive director of a small agency feels that GFOs do not grasp the significance of timely payment. Asked to hold a check so the director can pick it up, the GFO agrees, but then mails it. When the check is lost in the mail, the GFO will not reissue it for three weeks. The implications are serious.

Right now, I haven't collected my paycheck for this month. Luckily, my tax return came. We borrowed money from [a loan fund]. You

scramble the best you can. What we're going to do in the long term is the board has committed themselves to coming up with a cash reserve fund of $50,000 or more to try to help with this problem. We try to get foundations—you know somebody's going to pay you a grant, maybe you can get them to give it to you a month early. You scramble. You hold off on paying anything you don't have to pay. And have a lot of anxiety attacks, let me assure you.

Given the conflicts with reality in the other dimensions of contracting, it follows that conflicts exist in the evaluation process as well. An executive director expresses her skepticism about the validity of the GFO's primary criteria for assessing preventive services.

The first two years, our program was a success. I get very dubious about these statistics—it was a success because none of the children in the families we worked with were removed from the home. This past year, in two families, the children had to be removed.

She attributes the lack of "success" to the increase in drugs and to overcrowded housing, factors that the GFO does not consider in its evaluation of outcome.

The same executive director points out that unrealistic criteria for the accomplishment of interim objectives also conflict with clients' reality. The GFO neither recognizes nor reimburses advocacy. For example, every month for four years, her NPA advocates for housing for a particular family but the first time this effort counts is the month the family moves.

Another manager expresses a conviction that a GFO's evaluation system has no relationship to the reality of client needs, the program delivered, or fiduciary responsibility.

The [GFO] has such a mindset, they're so schizoid about accountability. On the one hand, the system is totally devoid of accountability. Devoid. On the other hand, they think they've got all these structures that provide accountability, and they thought this was a way to assure accountability.

It doesn't assure accountability. Yes, somebody can give the [GFO director] a memo saying the programs are doing X, Y, and Z, but it doesn't mean that they are. And ultimately it doesn't mean that the kids are getting what they need.

After summarizing the problems resulting from performance-based contracting, a manager explains, in the most poignant way, why she feels the demands of playing the game conflict with the ability to affect these problems.

Why I don't think it's being dealt with is because I think you've got social workers—and I use myself as an example—who are drowning, who are trying to go after every penny we can find in terms of services for people, trying to get workers to work to greater productivity, and we're running in place and we're using all our energy spinning our wheels. Because government contracts are where the money is. If that's what the government's demanding, that's what we do. If they want us to stand on our heads, we stand on our heads. I almost believe we don't have the energy, and maybe we don't feel we have the power.

Dynamics

What are the forces motivating or inducing managers to act, or not act, as they do?[3] What keeps them so involved despite all the craziness? Enjoyment has been conceptualized as "the holistic sensation that people feel when they act with total involvement—as flow."[4] A description of the experience of flow when playing chess is strikingly similar to what administrators say about managing contracted services.

Flow in chess, as in other activities, depends on a very delicate balance between being in control and being overwhelmed. It is this tension that forces the player to attend to the game, with the resulting high pitch of concentration and involvement.[5]

The drive to accomplish a goal emerges repeatedly. The goal can be an overriding sense of mission and purpose about the work or an in-

termediate objective toward achievement of that goal. Goals are often multiple; typically, they conflict. Analyzing the way managers choose to act is crucial in understanding the significance of this drive: "Effective managers have a vision for the business that makes sense of unrelated problems and actions."[6]

In describing the relationship of NPAs to GFOs as cordially adversarial, a manager stresses her NPA's mission and the perception of that mission by GFOs.

I think, as an agency, people know that we are extremely serious about what we do, that we are determined to do it well, and we are also determined to do it as much as we can in conformance to the way in which we want to deliver [services], so that we will argue, and we will go to the mat, and we will mobilize, and whatever.

Many managers find navigation of the playing field extraordinarily complex. An executive director says, "It's a puzzle; if you like puzzles then you're okay." In the beginning, she says she was "really in the dark" about the contracting process for special legislative grants.

You go through so many different senseless steps, and I think once you go through it the first time and they know who you are and things have gone through without any incident, then things come fairly quickly—even though we have not yet received [the monies for the first contract year], and I have right here and am just finishing, the application for the second round.

Managers who have worked in GFOs feel that experience makes it easier to navigate the GFOs. One manager who does not have GFO experience but thinks it would have been valuable, explains, "It is a help to know how their mind, how the bureaucratic mind, works."

Surviving the competition is complex in the management of contracted services. An NPA's competitors can be GFOs, other NPAs, or, increasingly, for-profit organizations. While managers express great fervor about their battles with GFOs, their objective is most often to endure in what they understand to be an ongoing, unending struggle. Competition with other NPAs is usually just alluded to by managers. A great deal of cooperative effort among NPAs is directed toward GFOs; however, they are competing for the same GFO resources.

An executive director explains that while a GFO funds some NPAs in full for programs, his and others are required to match a portion of the contract amount. However, he says, "The reality of it is basically that you try to hold on to what you've got." As the result of a demographic evaluation of need, the GFO cuts funding for programs in his community, and his NPA is "slashed" $40,000. He is concerned that the remaining funding is in jeopardy because the GFO's director has changed since the last contracts were issued: "I don't know what's going to happen. I just hold my breath."

The GFO can be formidable competition. An executive director describes what happens when NPAs try to change the planned implementation of a home-care program for the elderly

> The city [GFO] kept saying in the meetings they did have: "This is the way it is." And the whole city [NPAs] was up in arms over this. No matter how much we talked, it didn't work. The city [GFO] just went ahead like a juggernaut.

When a manager hears the GFO is going to contract with additional NPAs for homemaking services, she suspects an issue of competition.

> I may be imagining this, but my suspicion is they [GFO] are going to contract with vendors at a lower rate, and the only way anybody can do this at a lower rate is to sacrifice the quality. We have two MSWs and two BAs, and we try to offer the homemakers a decent wage, as decent as we can make it, and try to treat the homemakers fairly and do a good job on the training and provide the support. Some of that's going to have to go with a lower rate.

Mastering the rules is extraordinarily complex; this is not a game with one rule book. Rules are clear and unclear, explicit and implicit, enforced and not enforced. They are ever changing. What is acceptable one year may not be the next. What is acceptable to one monitor may not be to another.

To be able to affect the terms of his contract, an executive director describes the necessity of learning "how things work" in the state legislature.

> There's a legislative committee of [the NPA coalition]. You stay on top of bills that are being introduced and so forth and you just see how the game is played because you're there. So when we develop strategy then that's part of the information that flows into our leadership: This is what they want to see, this is how it should be presented.

Another manager explains what happens when the GFO changes a rule without informing NPAs and then penalizes them for violating it.

> It caused a bit of a disturbance because [NPA coalition] also does a lot of the contract negotiations for the agencies, and their people hadn't spotted it either. Nobody was really aware of it. So all of a sudden you had a whole group of agencies that were quite upset that someone had pulled the wool over their eyes and slipped something through.
>
> They [GFO and NPA coalition] came to terms verbally on how if something was changed, how it would be indicated. But they never made a commitment in writing that all changes must be in bold, with the old in italics and the replacement in bold. Nothing like that, anything that's formal. They came to a verbal agreement, basically, that changes should be identifiable. Nobody wanted to be pinned down.

For managers, strategies for dealing with GFOs are a necessity. Most express the need for having a philosophical perspective on affecting GFOs. One manager explains, in describing her efforts to get changes in a contract.

> Going in [to the GFO] you can't really expect very much of a response. And, whatever response you want, you have to create.

In a similar vein, another manager says:

I don't think they [GFO] like or dislike me per se, but there's a mutual respect. I may not agree with the priorities that are selected down at their end because I would have different priorities, but then I realize that I need to work with them. It's something I cannot control, but I will attempt to influence them.

Many managers talk of the need for positioning the NPA to affect the GFO.

Actually our program assessment statistics have improved on a yearly basis, and I just think it's a game. I think it's a question on a lot of levels of what kind of systems can you put in place.

All managers believe an NPA coalition strategy is essential. According to one manager:

It keeps you tuned into what's happening, and it also means you don't have to fight your battles alone all the time. When city contract time comes around and there're all these issues about how the contract is written, we worry all the time. We don't all have to go singly and try to tackle [the GFO], and we all have our say. And, [NPA coalition] has more and more meetings, just because issues have become so much more complicated.

The challenge of managing contracted services is constant for some managers. For one, who feels she has mastered management of her program, the challenge is being involved in contracting issues affecting all NPAs funded by her GFO. She explains how and why she makes the time to be involved in this way.

I really like this. I get very fed up with the routine; I've done this for a long time. It's getting pretty boring, but I've been lucky being on these [NPA coalition] committees, and I really have found that's a whole new challenge and new learning in terms of trying to work out procedures. There're a few of us who've been tapped by [NPA coalition] as being people who are willing to make the time, and I am. I'd rather go out and do that and sit at night and read progress notes than sitting here in the office all day. I seem to so far be able to manage both.

After a successful NPA coalition fight with a GFO, her attitude and that of many of her colleagues changed.

All of these things have made us very aware and much more willing to not just sit and do what's handed to you, but be an active participant. Obviously, it has some limitations, but I really find it a learning experience. Somehow, that great big, thick, boilerplate contract doesn't look quite so long.

Despite all the craziness and complexity, many managers express enjoyment when they describe their work. Research indicates this feeling of pleasure, under trying circumstances, is not at all contradictory: "Apparently, something that is enjoyable to do gives a feeling of creative discovery, a challenge overcome, a difficulty resolved."[7] One manager, who feels that doing her job is "an art," explains how she deals with GFOs.

I'm conniving if I want something, like if I go into contract negotiations. I have told the city [GFO] on a number of occasions: "We won't take the contract unless you give us what we want." And sometimes it works and sometimes not. We walk out. It's just like seductiveness. It's a chess game, and I can do that. So we do a little acting-out behavior, but that's what I like about it. That's fun.

Notes

1. While social work administration has apparently never been conceptualized as a game, politics, business, and even living itself, particularly in the United States, have. See Hedrick Smith, *The Power Game: How Washington Works* (New York: Random House, 1988), for a recent book using the game metaphor for politics. For applications of the game metaphor in business, see Ardis Burst and Leonard A. Schlesinger, *The Management Game* (New York: Viking, 1987); Betty Lehan Harragan, *Games Mother Never Taught You: Corporate Gamesmanship for Women* (New York: Warner Books, 1977); Rosabeth Moss Kanter, *When Giants Learn to Dance: Mastering the Challenges of Strategy, Management, and Careers in the 1990s* (New York: Simon and Schuster, 1989), pp. 18–22; Robert

Keidel, *Game Plans: Sports Strategies for Business* (New York: E. P. Dutton, 1985); Robert Keidel, *Game Plans: Designs for Working and Winning Together* (New York: John Wiley and Sons, 1988); and Michael Maccoby, *The Gamesman: The New Corporate Leaders* (New York: Simon and Schuster, 1976). "All life is a game of power" is the thesis of Michael Korda, *Power! How to Get It, How to Use It* (New York: Random House, 1975), p. 3. For a comprehensive application of the game concept to organizations, see Michael Crozier and Erhard Friedberg, *Actors and Systems: The Politics of Collective Action* (Chicago: University of Chicago Press, 1980), pp. 45–63.

2. The "mastery" and sense of control the manager feels in playing the game of contracted services parallels Smith's analysis of politics in *The Power Game:* "Some like to say that the power game is an unpredictable casino of chance and improvisation. But most of the time politics is about as casual and offhand as the well-practiced triple flips of an Olympic high diver" (p. xvii).

3. The benefits of answering this question are analogous to those of conceptualizing politics as a game: "Sometimes it explains why some good people don't play the game better, why they don't win." Ibid., p. xvii.

4. Mihaly Csikszentmihalyi, *Beyond Boredom and Anxiety: The Experience of Play in Work and Games* (San Francisco: Jossey-Bass, 1975), p. 36. See also Mihaly Csikszentmihalyi, *Flow: The Psychology of Optimal Experience* (New York: Harper and Row, 1990); and Mihaly Csikszentmihalyi and Isabella S. Csikszentmihalyi, eds., *Optimal Experience: Psychological Studies of Flow in Consciousness* (Cambridge: Cambridge University Press, 1988).

5. Csikszentmihalyi, *Beyond Boredom and Anxiety,* p. 64.

6. Morgan W. McCall, Jr., and Robert E. Kaplan, *Whatever It Takes: Decision Makers at Work* (Englewood Cliffs, N.J.: Prentice-Hall, 1985), p. 82.

7. Csikszentmihalyi, *Beyond Boredom and Anxiety,* p. 181.

CHAPTER 23

Implications of Welfare Reform

Do Nonprofit Survival Strategies Threaten Civil Society?

JENNIFER ALEXANDER, RENEE NANK,
AND CAMILLA STIVERS

Nonprofit organizations play a pivotal role in ongoing efforts to devolve federal government programs and transfer public responsibilities to the local level. In the era of welfare reform, the capacity of social service organizations to serve as the public safety net in the manner implied by devolution proponents has come under question. Partnership between governments and the nonprofit sector has undergone significant stress as it is transformed by welfare and related policy initiatives; the long-term effects of these changes on both partners are still imperfectly understood (Salamon, 1995; Smith, 1995).

Devolution refers to the collective efforts to shift responsibility for federal programs down to the state and local level. The driving force behind these changes is the idea that social programs run by the federal government have been ineffective, unwieldy, and excessively expensive (Gold, 1996). Concomitant with efforts to downsize government has been the global push to incorporate new public management techniques in public and nonprofit organizations. Devolution is a piece of this larger reform movement. The new public management has been characterized by the following two assumptions: (a) free-market competition is a valuable strategy for improving organizational performance; and (b) private sector practices and technologies are superior, and management is a generic practice that can be imported into all organizational forms to their betterment (Kaboolian, 1998). For nonprofits, devolution and the new public management have been manifest in contractual expectations of funders and the need to compete with for-profit entities.

This article reports on a multiphase research project focused on the impact of welfare reform on social service nonprofits in Cuyahoga County, Ohio.[1] The question that we raise is whether the marketization of nonprofits threatens not only their ability to promote and express values and aims particular to their communities but also, in a larger sense, their function as schools or laboratories of democratic citizenship. In this discussion about how to build capacity among nonprofits, which frequently means how to make them more businesslike and efficient, the loss of the public spiritedness and the public goods that have traditionally marked their activities is in danger of going unnoticed.

The Threat to Civil Society

Although persons with disparate views value the existence of what Alexis de Tocqueville (1945) called *associations* at the community level, they have different ends in mind. Conservatives tend to look to associations to stabilize society by fostering civic virtue and to protect against government expansiveness. Pluralists value clubs and nonprofits for their ability to divert activism away from the political process, keeping participation relatively low and preventing too much democracy. Thus, a good many people who want to strengthen civil society regard it as an important means of maintaining order and mediating citizens needs and demands so that they do not heat up the political process unduly.

Civil society—the space occupied by associations—is thus not simply a way of mediating between private citizens and the state. It is also "a space of social experimentation for the development of new forms of life, new types of solidarity, and social relations of cooperation and work" (Cohen & Arato, 1992, p. 38). Here, civil society becomes a school of citizenship by enabling citizens to discuss matters of mutual concern, gather information, hear others express their views, and debate policies. Although these exchanges happen in various units, such as particular associations, there is a larger public sphere that is constituted by them and, in turn, generates politically relevant public opinion (Cohen, 1998, p. 14).

In this more politically charged civil society, citizens learn citizenship partly through public-spirited activity and partly through bringing their experiences to bear on the consideration of public questions in open debate. Associations—in this argument, community-based nonprofits—provide the institutionalized base for this activity and debate. They make democracy workable by creating arenas of manageable size and scope for public life; thus, they serve as tangible refutation of the longstanding argument that participatory democracy does not work because the modern state is too big and the issues too complex. Community-based nonprofits set boundaries within which the public

meaningfulness of action can be grasped (Stivers, 1990).

In this version, civil society combines private and public dimensions. It is less a bulwark against the expansiveness of government than a practical site for the achievement of public aims. Because it makes room for individual and small-scale creativity and experimentation, it enables a public-spirited dynamism that government has difficulty matching. Because it makes possible individual self-development, as well as collaborative action that has public meaning, it blends public and private dimensions in a way that neither government nor purely private activity permits. As such, civil society needs to be understood as distinctive and clearly demarcated from both the government and the for-profit economic sphere.

Survival Strategies of Social Service Organizations Under Welfare Reform

Nonprofits are central to devolution in several respects. Considered a largely voluntary, low-cost alternative to big government, nonprofits are seen as the embodiment of active citizenship. In fact, political conservatives have predicted that social service organizations will step in to provide the necessary social services for lower income citizens as the federal government retreats. Unfortunately, this vision may be an optimistic assessment compared to what research on the voluntary sector would predict.

Nonprofit social service organizations are caught in an environment that challenges the values and methods that have characterized the sector to date. They are experiencing pressures from government and funders to emulate the private sector, both in structure and practice. There is increased attention to accountability and outcome measures in an effort to bring about organizational efficiency and effectiveness. Nonprofits are now competing with for-profit organizations for contracts and clients in their traditional domains. The funding environment is tight, as government has decreased funding and corporate donations have lagged behind inflation since 1989. In short, the current environmental changes have reconfigured the rules for organizational survival.

Survey Results

[Nonprofit 501(c)(3) organizations that provide services to youth and children in Cuyahoga County, Ohio] were classified into one of four categories based on a core set of characteristics, which included funding sources, staff, mission, organizational age, and size. These types included the traditional/established organizations, community-based organizations, faith-based organizations, and semipublic organizations.

Themes from Focus Groups and Survey Data

Transcripts of the focus groups were analyzed using a combination of ethnographic and content analysis. Three themes relevant to this research are discussed below (for further detail, see Alexander, 1999).

Bifurcation of the Sector as Nonprofits Take on a Business Orientation

One of the overriding impacts of the demand for new public management techniques on nonprofit service organizations is the bifurcation of the sector. Particular types of nonprofits are better positioned to professionalize themselves, although all of them seemed aware that it was a necessary adaptation. Long-established, traditional organizations such as the Young Men's Christian Association, Red Cross, and Salvation Army are strained by the requirements to adopt a management orientation, but their organizational structures and processes have already attained a level of maturation and specialization necessary to make such a shift.[2] They indicated that they were challenged but adjusting.

In contrast, a diverse array of community-based and faith-based organizations, including neighborhood centers and settlement houses,

were in a different circumstance. Many of these organizations lack the service capacity, economies of scale, revenue flows, and trained staff necessary to adjust to the new demands.[3] Community-based and faith-based nonprofits were responding to the current environmental shifts by cutting programs, rationing services, and charging fees when possible. In focus groups, organizational representatives indicated that the current shift to market-directed and business-directed management was resulting in more and more organizational resources being directed to administration and management and less to service delivery. They were spending more organizational: resources on administration grant writing, fund-raising, and documenting the need for their services, and less on service delivery than in the past.

Organizations with a strong charitable mission indicated that they were finding it increasingly difficult to serve indigent clients because they often lacked the service capacity, fiscal resources, and staff necessary to meet demand. Even services that are reimbursed through government programs are difficult to sustain because the costs of serving clients frequently exceed reimbursements. Medicaid was one of the examples offered by participants as problematic because the paperwork was extensive.

The choice of whom an organization can afford to serve can present a conflict in mission that is nearly unresolvable. This dilemma was particularly trying for community-based and faith-based organizations that comprised a substantial portion of the safety net in the area of emergency and crisis services. For example, one director of a faith-based organization that now offers job training indicated that the city funding agency will be using performance measurement to distribute future Community Development Block Grant funds for job training. The city wants government dollars expended more efficiently, and they are interested in funding agencies that demonstrate a higher probability of success in the program. This particular faith-based organization appears ineffective based on current measures because their job-training participants are predominantly disabled people who seek part-time employment to supplement their low incomes rather than full-time jobs with benefits. Focus group representatives indicated that the conflict between fulfilling the organizational mission and meeting funding requirements was sometimes too disparate to bridge.

Increased Dependence on Local and State Government Agencies

Since the late 1970s, state and local funding, as a percentage of total social service public funding, has been on the rise. However, welfare reform and the progressive devolution of federal programs appear to have intensified linkages between social service nonprofits and local government. Although there are references in scholarly literature to the growing interdependence between governments and nonprofits (Nevin-Gattle, 1996; O'Toole, 1997), nonprofits of all categories clearly indicated in focus group discussions that they regarded themselves in an increasingly dependent position vis-à-vis the county and state.

The multiple dependencies that are developing between nonprofits and local government agencies have allowed county and state governments more opportunities to shape services. Nonprofit agencies with a history of county contracts repeatedly indicated that they saw their agencies' long-term survival closely linked to meeting county needs.

The agencies most profoundly affected by shifts in policy and county demand were large agencies with a history of government contracts and, therefore, with an established dependence on county funding. These agencies were struggling with the uncertainty as to how to prepare for their agencies' futures as local government had not yet articulated a clear direction. As agency heads contemplated various policy options that the county might pursue, they questioned how to best prepare themselves for the pending changes and even whether they could afford to do so.

Loss of Public Service Character

Nonprofits of all types indicated that adaptation to the current changes in funding was changing the nature of their services; it had substantially diminished their capacity to be political. Nonprofits have historically generated a variety of public goods. They have provided the institutional base where citizens could come together and discuss their problems, thereby engaging in an active form of citizenship. Nonprofits have advocated for their client communities, giving voice to their needs in policy dialogues; they have provided community education through outreach program; and they have served the indigent. Organizational representatives of all types indicated in focus groups and in survey results that these various public goods of research, teaching, advocacy, citizenship, and serving the poor are progressively falling away as nonprofits push to adopt more market-oriented practices, and to meet individual client demand rather than community need.

This trend toward the depoliticization of nonprofits is attributable not only to marketization but also to devolution, which occurs as a progressive bumping down of responsibility and risk as each level of government seeks to minimize costs until the last provider in the continuum absorbs the difference.

One of the greatest indications of how nonprofits are losing the capacity to act as advocates for client needs or particular services was the reluctance of nonprofits with strong county linkages to speak frankly about the impact of county policies on clients or client services. Although agency representatives would occasionally convey misgivings in private, they believed that agency relationships with the county were too important to jeopardize. Nonprofits represented by county boards believed that they were better positioned to advocate on behalf of their services or clients. This dynamic suggests that as linkages between nonprofits and local government become closer, nonprofits may maintain some ability to advocate for client communities through umbrella organizations such as boards, federations, and coalitions.

Summary of Findings

Given the changing nature of the public-nonprofit partnership, the study found that these particular nonprofits are under pressure to alter their traditional character. This was most clearly evident in a bifurcation of the sector as the larger, more established nonprofits were expanding and continuing along a trajectory of business-oriented practices. The current environment also favors multiservice organizations that can offer revenue-generating programs to offset unreimbursed costs in other service areas. Organizations that are younger and have a strong commitment to serving the indigent and unreimbursed clientele, which are often community-based and faith-based organizations, are finding their survival more threatened. These organizations depend on federal funding to continue serving unsubsidized populations, and their capacity to compete with larger, multiservice organizations is limited.

Organizations of all types found their public service character threatened by the marketization of the sector, specifically, public services that nonprofits have provided in the areas of research, education, advocacy, and serving the indigent. In keeping with the private sector model, the current environment encourages nonprofits to provide reimbursable services of individual benefit, such as substance abuse programs funded by Medicaid. It financially discourages an organization from educating community groups about substance abuse.

For nonprofits to continue providing quality services, relationships between nonprofits and local governments need to become interdependent in practice. As nonprofits will need to become more fiscally and programmatically accountable, state and local governments would do well to acknowledge the knowledge base that nonprofit professionals have developed in particular service areas. Organizations in the study repeatedly noted that, at some point, it is not possible to do more with less. The quality of care is jeopardized. State and local governments will need to find a way to support quality services and fiscal accountability in the human service sector—and work in partnership with them to serve citizen needs.

Beyond the continuation of service provision, however, lies the deeper question of the extent to which the nonprofits in our study will be able to continue to serve as sites where community people, through their involvement as staff and board members, can join together in active civic work. Many of the comments made by nonprofit representatives suggest that the public-spiritedness of community nonprofits is threatened by increasing pressure to become more businesslike and professional. The shift from service delivery to increasing emphasis on management concerns such as need documentation, fund-raising, and outcome measurement makes the less tangible civic dimensions of nonprofit organizational life increasingly tenuous. Civic mindedness and participation are not efficient, and pressure to do more with less—or less with less—inevitably forces priorities to be set in terms of the bottom line rather than in terms of building social capital. Similarly, a business orientation encroaches on the public service orientation of nonprofits, pushing smaller organizations to forswear advocacy that threatens the flow of government dollars, and forcing them to compromise their own sense of the public interest—serving the most needy—in favor of looking effective on outcome assessments. Dependence on government funding reduces the autonomy of nonprofit decision making, causing them to shape development in terms of government demands rather than on the basis of their own consensus about community needs. In addition, pressure to professionalize puts a premium on technical expertise, which regards the lived experience of community residents as unscientific and anecdotal, and the time spent on participatory deliberation as a waste of time because the professional answer to problems is already clear. Finally, the interorganizational networks that are a vital aspect of a democratic civil society are threatened by the competition set in motion by the survival-of-the-fittest devolution dynamic.

Conclusion

Tocqueville's (1945) classic work argued that associations of citizens served as schools of democratic politics by teaching citizens, through experience, to care about the public interest and to make judicious public decisions. In the present concern over how to build capacity among non-profits, which usually means how to make them more businesslike and efficient so that public responsibilities can be transferred to them, the loss of the public thinking that has traditionally marked their activities is in danger of going unnoticed. If this were to happen, Hannah Arendt's (1958) fear could be realized. The focus on diagnosing and meeting survival needs, what Arendt calls "the social," might obliterate "the political," the realm in which professional and technical expertise, outcome measurement, and the bottom line take a backseat to public-spirited dialogue and debate. Our research suggests that there is more at stake in the transformation of the nonprofit sector than may be immediately apparent in the current policy debate, let alone the rush on the part of governments to divest themselves of public responsibilities regardless of the impact on civil society.

The opportunity for people to debate issues is lost in the face of bureaucratic rules that produce "normal behavior" and "exclude spontaneous action or outstanding achievement" (Arendt, 1953, p. 40). When talk in public is only about survival, the differences between us disappear, and with them, the political world itself. Survival necessity wins out over political freedom. So far, Arendt's argument simply underscores the idea that turning nonprofit organizations into little service delivery businesses dissipates their political potential.

Yet, because Hannah Arendt believed so strongly in the distinctiveness and open potential of every human being, she held out hope that, even in the face of the triumph of the social, "islands of freedom" would continue to pop up (Villa, 1996, p. 270). The birth of each person represents a new beginning, someone who "came out of nowhere in either time or space" (Arendt, 1963, p. 206), someone whose deeds cannot be "accounted for by a reliable chain of cause and effect" (quoted in Villa, 1996, p. 118).

Hannah Arendt (1963) once observed that, after the fundamental fact of their material deprivation, the predicament of the poor is that "their lives are without consequence . . . they remain excluded from the light of the public realm where excellence can shine; they stand in dark-

ness wherever they go" (p. 69). By creating situations in which community residents come into contact with public officials, Family to Family offers the possibility that ordinary people can move into the light of the public. In this regard, one of the best things about the program is not just that it facilitates access to services but that it facilitates access to public conversation and, therefore, offers hope for strengthening the political dimensions of civil society. Rather than settle for rule by nobody, should we not pay closer attention to nourishing those out of the ordinary circumstances in which practices of freedom, even if fleetingly, may appear?

Notes

1. Cuyahoga County, Ohio, includes the city of Cleveland, and it is the 13th largest county in the United States. In 1990, it included 13 percent of the population of the state and 25 percent of the total welfare rolls for the state. In 1995, it had an estimated population of 1,386,803, with an average of 20 percent living in poverty.

2. The organizational profile of traditional/established organizations includes having an average age of 70 years, an average budget of $5 million, and an average of 255 employees.

3. The organizational profile of community-based organizations revealed an average age of 31 years, an average budget slightly less than $500,000, and an average of 12 full-time staff.

References

Alexander, J. (1999). The impact for devolution on nonprofits: A multi-phase study of social service organizations. *Nonprofit Management and Leadership, 10*(1).

Arendt, H. (1958). *The human condition.* Chicago: University of Chicago Press.

_____. (1963). *On revolution.* Harmondsworth, UK: Penguin Books.

Cohen, J. L. (1998). American civil society talk. [Special issue]. *Philosophy and Public Policy, 18,* 14–20.

Cohen, J. L., & Arato, A. (1992). *Civil society and political theory.* Cambridge, MA: MIT Press.

de Tocqueville, A. (1945). *Democracy in America* (Vol. 2). New York: Vintage Books.

Gold, S. D. (1996, March 5). *The potential impacts of devolution on state government programs and finances: Hearings before House Budget Committee* (testimony of S. D. Gold). Washington, DC: Urban Institute.

Gronbjerg, K. A., Kimmich, M. H., & Salamon, L. M. (1995). *The Chicago nonprofit sector in a time of government retrenchment*. The Urban Institute Nonprofit Sector Project. Washington, DC: Urban Institute.

Kaboolian, L. (1998). The new public management: Challenging the boundaries of the management vs. administration debate. *Public Administration Review*, 58, 189–193.

Liebschutz, S. F. (1992). Coping by nonprofit organizations during the Reagan years. *Nonprofit Management and Leadership*, 2, 363–380.

McMurtry, S. L., Netting, F., Kettner, E., & Kettner, P. M. (1991). How nonprofits adapt to a stringent environment. *Nonprofit Management and Leadership*, 1, 235–252.

Nevin-Gattle, K. (1996). Predicting the philanthropic response of corporations: Lessons from history. *Business Horizons*, 39, 15–22.

O'Connell, B. (1996). A major transfer of government responsibility to voluntary organizations? Proceed with caution. *Public Administration Review*, 56, 222–225.

O'Toole, L. J., Jr. (1997). Treating networks seriously: Practical and research-based agendas in public administration. *Public Administration Review*, 57, 45–52.

Salamon, L. M. (1994). The nonprofit sector and the evolution of the American welfare state. In R. D. Herman and Associates (Eds.), *The Jossey-Bass handbook of nonprofit leadership and management* (p. 84). San Francisco: Jossey-Bass.

_____. (1995). *Partners in public service: Government-nonprofit relations in the modern welfare state*. Baltimore: The Johns Hopkins University Press.

_____. (1997). *Holding the center: America's nonprofit sector at a crossroads*. Report to the Nathan Cummings Foundation.

Selznick, P. (1949). *TVA and the grass roots*. Berkeley: University of California Press.

Smith, D. (1995). Some challenges in nonprofit and voluntary action research. *Nonprofit and Voluntary Sector Quarterly*, 24, 99–101.

Smith, S. R., & Lipsky, M. (1993). *Nonprofits for hire: The welfare state in the age of contracting*. Cambridge, MA: Harvard University Press.

Stivers, C. (1990). The public agency as polis: Active citizenship in the administrative state. *Administration and Society*, 22, 86–105.

Villa, D. R. (1996). *Arendt and Heindegger: The fate of the political*. Princeton, NJ: Princeton University Press.

Zimmerman, U. (1996). Exploring the nonprofit motive (or: What's in it for You?). *Public Administration Review*, 54, 398–401.

PART 8

BUDGETS, FINANCIAL REPORTS, AND MANAGEMENT CONTROL

Budgeting, accounting, financial reporting, and management control are the most essential tools for responsible governance, accountability, planning, and management in nonprofit organizations.

Budgets and Budgeting

Budgeting "is a process which matches resources and needs in an organized and repetitive way so those collective choices about what an entity needs to do are properly resourced. . . . A *budget* is an itemized estimate of expected income and operating expenses . . . over a set period of time."[1]

Budgets breathe life into mission statements and goals. Mission statements may speak globally and inclusively about a wide variety of problems and opportunities that are of concern to the organization, but a budget divides an organization's finite resources among its competing needs and wants. Budgets thus reduce an array of noble intentions and high ideals into the ability to act on a select set of problems or opportunities. In this sense, budgeting is an energizing function as well as a definitive governance activity.[2] It is the "tool" for a board's use in managing the numerous competing visions, requests, and—often—demands of client groups, patrons, donors, staff, trustees, government agencies, and an assortment of community groups. Executives and boards give energy to their preferred policies and programs by allocating funds to them. A given program or initiative may be the beneficiary of increased funding; others may have their funds eliminated or decreased.

A budget also is an organization's short-term financial plan that identifies planned expenditures and expected revenues. It requires such decisions as whether the organization should borrow or draw-down savings to finance a program expansion, or whether it should eliminate another program that is proving less effective than hoped. In a balanced budget, revenues and expenditures are equal. A budget deficit identifies the need to borrow, draw-down funds from savings, or increase fund-raising. A budget surplus allows funds to be budgeted for new activities, to be set aside for future uses, or to reduce a former year's deficit.

Budgets as Financial Operating Reports and Management Control

After a budget has been adopted by the board of trustees, it continues to serve two vitally important purposes: (1) as a governance and accountability tool for the board and the executive director; and (2), as a management tool that provides an executive director and the management staff with discretion—the freedom to run the organization with some flexibility.

Budgets Are a Governance and Accountability Tool

Budgets are the basis—the foundation—for an organization's financial operating reports, reports that almost always contain (at least) two columns of numbers: budgeted income and expenditures, and actual income and expenditures. (See, for example, Table 27.1 in "Financial Statements and Fiscal Procedures," by Thomas Wolf, reprinted in this part.) When an executive director and the trustees know the shortages and surpluses (the over and under gaps) between budgeted and actual income and expenditures, they can exert management control over operations.

A financial operating report serves as a mechanism of control in much the same way as a thermostat attached to an air conditioning unit. The board of trustees sets the temperature it desires on the thermostat (the amount it budgets for a given category of expenditures). When the thermometer (financial expenditure report) measures that the actual room temperature (actual expenditures) has risen above the desired temperature (budgeted expenditures), it sends a message to the air conditioning unit (the board of trustees or the executive director) to initiate corrective action. The air conditioning unit is activated (the purchase order system, for example, will not permit the manager to purchase more supplies or fill a position vacancy).

Most boards of trustees spend considerable time reviewing and stewing over financial operating reports because financial accountability is a fundamental governance function. All too often, though, trustees spend too much time on the details of budgets and operating reports. The executive director and staff need "space" to make day-to-day management decisions without trustees second-guessing their moves.[3]

Budgets Are a Source of Management Flexibility

Program managers should not need to obtain board approval to make routine expenditures. This degree of micromanaging would be inefficient, create a terrible working environment for staff, waste a lot of the trustees' time—and probably cause everyone to resign! Budgets and financial operating reports thus also serve an essential management function—these documents give managers the freedom they need to act within preset parameters: budgets at the start of the year, financial operating reports as the year progresses. They establish the limits of a manager's discretion to spend certain amounts of money for different categories of expenditures—without requiring them to obtain approvals. Budgets thus allow staff to act freely and responsibly—because they know the limits. This management freedom also allows the board of trustees to turn its attention to more important governance issues—budgets and financial reports also free the trustees to govern.[4]

Accounting, Financial Reports, Management Control, and Accountability

Accounting is the process of recording financial information that is presented in various financial reports. Financial reports inform management and the board of the organization's financial status and the need for corrective actions. Without financial reports, the trustees and management cannot govern with accountability. Accounting, financial reports, and corrective actions thus comprise a system that is essential for the health of a nonprofit organization. Despite their importance, however, "financial analysis and managerial control remain among the most difficult areas for managers and directors [trustees] of nonprofit organizations to conquer."[5] Few individuals are recruited or agree to serve on boards because of their skills or experience with finances. Particularly in smaller nonprofits, few trustees are educated or experienced in financial analysis or management controls. Many trustees would rather leave responsibility for budgets and finances to others, preferring instead to devote their time and energy to the organization's programs, clients, fund-raising, or public relations. "Attaining a balance between sober financial management and the creation of enlightening services is far from easy."[6]

As we emphasized in Part 1, however, trustees are legally and ethically accountable and responsible for an organization's actions and assets. They cannot avoid these responsibilities without risking individual and collective liability. Thus, trustees and executive directors do not have a choice. They must learn at least the basics of accounting, budgeting, financial reporting, and management control procedures and systems. These are the primary instruments of responsible governance and accountability.

Readings Reprinted in Part Eight

Regina Herzlinger and Denise Nitterhouse explain the importance and the difficulties of maintaining management control and accountability in nonprofit organizations in *"A View from the Top."*[7] "Most individuals who volunteer and work for nonprofits do so because they care. They are the caretakers of the national conscience . . . people of extraordinary courage and altruism, who risk their lives in raging fires and festering slums for the greater good of humanity. They uphold the highest values of civilization: knowledge, beauty, charity, and freedom." The primary challenge for nonprofit organization trustees and executive directors is to "balance the passionate advocacy of their professional employees with signals of organizational effectiveness divined from an ambiguous external environment." Trustees are responsible for participating in the measurement of managerial effectiveness through financial analysis, and when effectiveness "is found wanting," for improving it through management control.

Herzlinger and Nitterhouse use Frances Hesselbein's turn-around of the Girl Scouts of the USA as an example of "the dazzling organizational results that can be achieved through financial analysis and managerial control." After taking office in 1976, Hesselbein initiated four organizational analyses: (1) the match between financial resources and goals, (2) intergenerational equity, (3) the match between sources and uses of resources, and (4) sustainability of financial resources that identified core long-term problems. She then "undertook a program to correct the problems by building on the base of the organization's considerable strengths."

Jerry McCaffery defines *"Budgeting"*[8] as "a process which matches resources and needs in an organized and repetitive way so those collective choices about what an entity needs to do are properly resourced. Most definitions emphasize that a budget is an itemized estimate of expected income and operating expenses . . . over a set time period. Budgeting is the process of arriving at such a plan." A budget is a plan, and "the budget process is a planning process. It is about what should happen in the future."

McCaffery explains the difference between capital and operating budgets: "The capital budget is usually used for investment type functions, including buying . . . lands and constructing buildings . . . whose consumption will span generations." In contrast, "it is the operating budget that allows for daily activities . . . in and around that building." The budget represents "a prediction about the future, consequently budgets become links between financial resources, human behavior, and policy accomplishments. . . . In this sense, a budget represents a series of goals with price tags attached."[9]

Formal management control has four principal phases: strategic planning, budget preparation, operating and measurement, and reporting and evaluation. For a management control system to be effective, it must satisfy several criteria. It should be a total system; have goal congruence; have a financial framework; have a rhythm; and be integrated.

Part 7 concludes with Thomas Wolf's primer on accounting, fund accounting, financial statements (balance sheets and income statements), Financial Accounting Standards Board (FASB) requirements, financial and management controls, and reporting requirements, *"Financial Statements and Fiscal Procedures."*[10] Wolf explains: "Because nonprofit organizations enjoy numerous financially lucrative privileges and benefits . . . , they must be able to demonstrate that their fiscal houses are in order. Board members are ultimately responsible for these organizations and must be able to read financial statements and be aware of reporting requirements and fiscal systems." "Financial Statements and Fiscal Procedures" provides a "down-to-earth" introduction to financial reports and controls. It was written expressly for board members who want to know how to be fiscally responsible and accountable trustees.

Notes

1. Jerry L. McCaffery, "Budgeting," in Jay M. Shafritz, ed., *International Encyclopedia of Public Policy and Administration* (Boulder: Westview Press, 1998), 294 (reprinted in this part).

2. See Part 1, "Governance of Nonprofit Organizations."

3. Including Robert N. Anthony and David W. Young, "The Management Control Function," in R. N. Anthony and David W. Young, *Management Control in Nonprofit Organizations,* 6th ed. (New York: Irwin/McGraw-Hill, 1999), 3–22 (reprinted in this part).

4. Ibid.

5. Herzlinger, Regina E., and Denise Nitterhouse, "A View from the Top," in R. E. Herzlinger and D. Nitterhouse, *Financial Accounting and Managerial Control for Nonprofit Organizations* (Cincinnati: South-Western, 1994), 8 (reprinted in this part).

6. Ibid., 2.

7. Ibid., 1–10.

8. Jerry L. McCaffery, "Budgeting," in Jay M. Shafritz, ed., *International Encyclopedia of Public Policy and Administration* (Boulder: Westview Press, 1998), 294. This essay was written

originally about government budgeting processes, but it has been edited here to include information only about aspects of budgeting that are directly applicable in the nonprofit sector.

9. In this quotation, McCaffery cites Aaron Wildavsky, *The Politics of the Budgetary Process* (Boston: Little, Brown, 1964) (a revised edition was published in 1984).

10. Thomas Wolf, "Financial Statements and Fiscal Procedures," in T. Wolf, *Managing a Nonprofit Organization in the Twenty-First Century* (New York: Fireside/Simon & Schuster, 1999), 209–231.

CHAPTER 24

A View from the Top

REGINA E. HERZLINGER AND DENISE NITTERHOUSE

Nonprofit organizations fulfill the noblest PURPOSESof our society. They educate us, nourish our souls with music and art, feed our poor, and protect the helpless among us. They are the caretakers of the national conscience, pushing and prodding our system of government to uphold the tenets of democracy. They employ people of extraordinary courage and altruism, who risk their lives in raging fires and festering slums for the greater good of humanity. They uphold the highest values of civilization: knowledge, beauty, charity, and freedom.

What Is a Nonprofit Organization?

Nonprofit organizations comprise a very diverse set. Under our nonprofit umbrella, we include any organization that is exempted from payment of taxes and whose primary purpose is to benefit society. Our definition thus includes federal, state, and local government, hospitals, museums, associations, foundations, cultural institutions, national service organizations, religious groups, community-based welfare, and similar organizations.

Others provide different definitions. Some define them as "*nonbusinesses*," arguing that nonprofit organizations are unlike businesses because they do not exist to earn a profit. This negative definition of a positive organization is not ours. While we concur that nonprofit organizations do not exist to earn a profit, they should be defined positively, by their immense contributions to a civilized way of life, rather than negatively, by the absence of a profit-seeking motive.

Others seek to define them legally. The benefits nonprofit organizations provide are so highly valued by our culture that they are exempted from paying income and other taxes, and complex legal strictures have been created to define precisely the types of organizations that qualify for these valuable tax exemptions. But we reject these legalisms as adequate definitions for nonprofit organizations. Their judicial basis deflates the essentially spiritual concept of these organizations with the pinpricks of its legal details.

Defining the nature of nonprofit organizations is no mere academic quibble—it is fundamental to their success. An organization defined by legal or financial requirements cannot serve as the keeper of civilization's heart, mind, and soul. And that is ultimately the purpose of non-profit organizations—our great colleges and universities, museums, symphonies, charities, governments, and public interest groups.

The Role of Management in Nonprofit Organizations

Our definition of purpose imposes extraordinary demands on the managers of nonprofit organizations. Maintaining financial and organizational stability or growth is not sufficient for successful exercise of their responsibilities, as it would be in a business. In nonprofit organizations, their foremost mandate is a spiritual one. Attaining a balance between sober financial management and the creation of enlightening services is far from easy. The difficulty is amplified by two characteristics of these organizations. First, they are staffed by dedicated, articulate service providers, who rarely value prudent financial management. Few educators, curators, physicians, musicians, social workers, mayors, or public-interest lawyers will ever concede that their activities are adequately funded or that managerial review of their work is appropriate. For example, after Professor Herzlinger's presentation of her analysis of the managerial strengths and weaknesses of the Costa Rican health care system, one listener responded: "That's all very well and good. But, why are we discussing management? Is not our largest and foremost obligation to provide health care services to the poor?" To him, as to many other professionals, management concerns must always take a back seat.

Second, nonprofit organizations lack the signals of success or failure generated for businesses by the working of the marketplace. When General Motors' sales are down, the market provides it with a clear signal: we prefer other cars to yours. But when patrons fail to throng an avant-garde museum exhibition, the signal is not nearly so clear. After all, it is the museum's purpose to shape and guide our artistic taste and, in its initial phase, cultural leadership is almost inevitably unpopular. Another important market message also is absent in nonprofit organizations. When General Motors' financial performance is weak, its stock takes a pounding. In

this way, the millions of people involved in the stock market send the company a clear message of their assessment of its management. But no stock exchange exists for nonprofit organizations. They lack the unambiguous evaluation of managerial success or failure it provides.

Managers of nonprofit organizations must balance the passionate advocacy of their professional employees with signals of organizational effectiveness devined from an ambiguous external environment. Although it is not our purpose here to help managers best fulfill the service mandates of their nonprofit organizations, we hope to help nonprofit managers and their boards with the latter skill—we can help them to measure their managerial effectiveness and, if it is found wanting, to improve it. We label this measurement process financial analysis and the process of improvement as managerial control.

Financial Analysis and Managerial Control

Frances Hesselbein exemplifies the dazzling organizational results that can be achieved through financial analysis and managerial control. When Mrs. Hesselbein was appointed the national executive director of the Girl Scouts of the USA (GSUSA) in 1976, she found a somewhat dispirited organization. Some of the members feared that the days of its former glory were long gone. Both adult and girl memberships were waning and revenues were dropping. When she resigned in 1990, the GSUSA was completely turned around: membership at an all-time high, positive staff morale, and stable finances.

Achieving this reversal of fortunes was akin to turning a battleship around in a lake. For one thing, GSUSA is a massive organization, with 3.2 million girl members and 751,000 adult volunteers. For another, it is an affiliation of local councils, each directed by an autonomous board of directors, rather than an hierarchical organization. While Mrs. Hesselbein could inspire, prod, and cajole local councils, she could not hire or fire their officers, determine their salaries, or in any other way directly supervise their work. Last, GSUSA was rich in history—some would say mired in it. The organization had a strong sense of its heritage, one it was reluctant to change.

An Example of Financial Analysis

When she took office, Mrs. Hesselbein evaluated the organization's status. She found many positives as well as negatives. On the positive side were the dedicated volunteers, board members, and career employees (each council employs staff members). Then too, many young girls increasingly required GSUSA's services—the friendship of other girls, the familiarity with nature, and the mastery of the outdoors that are the hallmarks of the scouting experience. Selling the famous Girl Scout cookies could also be an important part of their development: making a sale, delivering the cookies, and collecting the money increased young girls' sense of competence and self-confidence. And the organization was virtually debt free.

But there were negatives as well. Girl and adult membership was decreasing. Those who could most benefit from the services, the inner-city girls who were far removed from the Girl Scouts' camping properties, were not sufficiently represented. There seemed to be far too many camps—some were barely used and others were in bad physical shape. And Mrs. Hesselbein was concerned about the magnitude of the revenues generated by the cookie sale. They were accounting for an increasingly larger fraction of total revenues. Were means and ends being inverted? Were cookies sold for the revenues they generated rather than for their role in the Scouts' development? Many councils were surprised by their year-end financial results. If they were negative—and bad news was becoming more frequent—the staff understandably became depressed. Morale was plummeting.

Let us restate Mrs. Hesselbein's analysis in financial terms. She performed four fundamental analyses:

1. *Match between financial resources and goals.* This analysis evaluates whether the organizations's financial resources are being generated and used in a manner consistent with its mission.

2. *Intergenerational equity.* This analysis assesses whether the present generation is using no more and no less than its fair share of organizational resources (the amount it contributed).
3. *Match between sources and uses of resources.* This analysis examines whether assets are matched with appropriate sources of funds.
4. *Sustainability of financial resources.* This analysis assesses the stability of revenues, expenses, assets, and liabilities.

The terms of financial analyses might seem far removed from GSUSA and nonprofit organizations. We will illustrate their relevance below, fitting Mrs. Hesselbein's observations to them.

1: *Match between financial resources and goals.* When Mrs. Hesselbein observed the possibility of "too many camps," she was questioning whether the quantity of Girl Scouts resources invested in camping activities was appropriately matched with the importance of camping as a goal. Almost all of the assets of some councils and nearly 60 percent of their expenses were used for camping; but only about 20 percent of their girl members attended the camps. Her concern about the fraction of revenues generated by the sale of cookies focused on yet another potential mismatch between goals and financial resources: the possible subversion of the goal of developing girls' character for the achievement of financial resources. Finally, the absence of liabilities was a mixed blessing. Perhaps the councils with substantial real estate were unwittingly tying up resources that could otherwise produce services. A loan secured by some of the council's substantial property holdings, or their sale, would free up this money for use in service delivery, particularly to poorer girls.
2: *Intergenerational Equity.* Another appropriate match is between revenues and expenses. Revenues should generally exceed expenses by a reasonable margin, even in a nonprofit organization. With this "profit margin," the organization can maintain its physical plant and provide a cushion against adverse financial events. But if revenues are less than expenses, the organization consumes past resources to provide current services. Organizations with a continual pattern of losses cannot survive. They deplete the past and rob the future to finance the present. Mrs. Hesselbein's concern with "losses" reflected a deeper concern with GSUSA's ability to perpetuate itself.

3: *Match between sources and uses of resources.*
Capital sources and uses should have similar
lifetimes. When we buy a house, a long-lived
asset, we usually finance it with a long-lived
loan. Expensive long-lived assets generally cannot be purchased over a short period of time.
Similarly, long-lived expenses should be
matched with revenue sources that are likely to
last for a similar period. For example, the costs
of maintaining a building should be financed
with a long-term source of revenue, such as the
income earned from invested capital. But in the
Girl Scout councils, the cost of the camps, a
long-term expense, was paid primarily from
short-term cookie sale revenues.

4: *Sustainability of financial resources.* Revenues
earned from only one or two sources are riskier
than revenues earned from many sources because the loss of these few sources has much
more serious impact on the organization. Mrs.
Hesselbein's concern about the large fraction of
revenues generated by the sale of cookies and
her recommendation for development of other
sources of money proved prescient. Her wisdom was borne out a few years later when reports of glass shards found in the cookies
caused sales to plummet. (The reports were
false.) The councils that heeded her advice and
diversified their revenue sources were much
less affected by the decline in cookie sales.

Just as dispersion of sources is a hallmark of
sustainable revenues, flexibility and controllability are desired characteristics of expenses. Fixed
costs—for example, those of a tenured faculty or
long-term employees—are virtually impossible

to change even if demand declines. They thus
impose a heavy burden on an organization. Provision of a camping program entails considerable fixed costs in staff and facilities.

Assets should be as dispersed and stable as
revenues. Excessive concentration of resources
in any one asset increases the organization's vulnerability to changes in the usefulness, cost, or
market value of that asset. Organizations whose
assets are invested primarily in a computer risk
its obsolescence. Girl Scout councils whose assets were invested primarily in camps experienced the unhappy consequences of the sizeable
decline in their use.

Ratio Analysis

Financial ratio analysis formalizes and quantifies
the financial data used in these four analyses.
The most frequent financial ratios and their relationship to each of the four analyses are described in Table 24.1.

Like Mrs. Hesselbein, we should use accounting information to evaluate the financial health
of the organization. Is it in excellent health?
Does it have a cold? The flu? Or is it time to put
out the RIP sign? The diagnostic dimensions of
liquidity, solvency, asset management, return on
invested capital, profitability, and revenue and
expense composition presented in Table 24.1 are
like medical diagnostics such as temperature,
blood pressure, cholesterol count, heart rate, and
reflexes. Each is designed to detect a certain type

TABLE 24.1   Financial Ratios Used in Financial Analysis

Ratio	*Role in Financial Analysis*
Asset turnover	Matches assets and goals. Slow turnover assets require considerable investment and reduce flexibility.
Profitability and return on invested capital	Analyzes intergenerational equity and the match between sources and uses of money. Neither excessive profits nor losses are desirable.
Liquidity and solvency	Matches sources and uses of financial resources. Is the organization flirting with bankruptcy in the short-term? In the long-term?
Percentage of revenues, by source	Analyzes quality of revenues and relation to mission. Is the organization excessively dependent on a few revenue sources? Are revenue sources consistent with the organization's mission?
Percentage of expenses, by type	Analyzes quality of expenses and relation to mission. A large percentage of fixed expenses decreases the organization's flexibility. Are expenses consistent with the organization's mission?

of symptom; a collection of symptoms, in turn, reflects the underlying state of health and suggests an appropriate treatment plan.

An Example of Managerial Control

Having noted these problems and opportunities, Mrs. Hesselbein undertook a program to correct the problems by building on the base of the organization's considerable strengths. Her purpose also was to instill greater confidence in council employees and to celebrate their contributions to American society. "I want you to see yourselves life-size," she would say at annual conventions.

Her methods for accomplishing these goals were many, but primary among them was a "corporate management" process. Councils were urged to use the techniques of business—indeed, to think of themselves as businesses, for managerial purposes. The process was depicted in a series of manuals on each of the following topics: Planning, Budgeting, Pricing, Reporting, and Control.

The corporate management process was wildly successful. Not only did overall membership soar, but minority membership also increased from 5 percent in 1979 to 15 percent in 1989. Financial resources became more consistent with the Girl Scout mission and of higher quality. And staff morale levels zoomed. The corporate management process gave them dignity and strength. They were no longer surprised by year-end financial results. Instead, they planned the results and, because they were superlative managers, they caused their plans to materialize.

None of this was easy. Ten years and enormous effort were required. But the turnaround was accomplished. And financial analysis and management were key to its success.

The Current Status of Financial Accounting and Managerial Control in Nonprofit Organizations

Despite their importance, financial analysis and managerial control remain among the most dif-

ficult areas for managers and directors of nonprofit organizations to conquer. The inherently difficult basic subjects are shrouded in a mysterious veil of technical jargon, guarded by the high priests of the accounting world. Moreover, these subjects are relatively foreign to nonprofit cultures based in "people skills" and "social concerns." There is simply no good way to acquire and polish such financial analysis and management skills in most nonprofit organizations. Historically, there has been little support or reward for doing so: no well-developed body of knowledge, no set of curricula, and no pool of trained personnel from which to draw. Finally, the accounting and management information systems required of nonprofit organizations are much more complex than those required of business organizations of comparable size. Although the requirement that nonprofits be accountable to their many constituencies is entirely appropriate, it is onerous because nonprofits have so many more constituencies than profit-oriented organizations. They must track not only financial resource generation and consumption but also outputs that cannot be measured in financial terms, and may be very difficult to measure in any quantifiable terms.[1]

Nevertheless, effective accounting and managerial control practices are at least as important to nonprofits as to for-profit organizations. Several educational institutions have already closed their doors and a number of hospitals are following suit. And the financial scandals of nonprofit organizations that abuse the public trust are all too frequent. Among the latest of these is the tragic misuse of funds in the United Way, a multi-billion dollar U.S. charity.

Role of Accounting

We all speak a common language to communicate. Although accounting has been called the language of business, it is really the language of management. The accounting language helps to frame the way we view our organizations and the things on which we focus.

Speaking the language of accounting is complicated by the existence of accounting practices in different nonprofit organizations that are more diverse than the substantive organizational and mission-related differences would lead one to predict. Different types of organizations may follow different accounting rules, and similar types of events may be accounted for differently within the same organization. The absence of uniform accounting standards enabled the development of a variety of practices, each with its proponents and detractors.

The rigid structure of double-entry bookkeeping mechanics may mask the essentially interpretive nature of accounting. Accounting rules and procedures consist of social conventions rather than physical-science principles; they are negotiated and invented more than they are discovered. Many otherwise savvy managers are astonished at the difficulty and the lack of guidance in recognizing certain types of accounting events. There is seldom a single, hard and fast, right answer; there are often many ways of viewing, and thus of accounting for, a given event. And even when accounting rules are clear, it may still be appropriate to develop supplementary information based on different accounting procedures for certain tasks.

Notes

1. See Regina E. Herzlinger, "Managing the Finances of Nonprofit Organizations," *California Management Review* (Spring 1979) and "Why Data Systems in Nonprofit Organizations Fail," *Harvard Business Review* (January 1977) for further discussion.

CHAPTER 25

Budgeting

JERRY L. MCCAFFERY

A process which matches resources and needs in an organized and repetitive way so those collective choices about what an entity needs to do are properly resourced. Most definitions emphasize that a budget is an itemized estimate of expected income and operating expenses for a given unit of government over a set time period. Budgeting is the process of arriving at such a plan. Once a fiscal year has started, the budget becomes a plan for disbursing resources to attain goals.

At its heart, the budget process is a planning process. It is about what should happen in the future. For agencies, this planning process might involve estimates of how many audits or accounts will be done in the next year; for welfare advocates, it might involve estimates of what it will take to provide a decent standard of living to the poor; although numbers give the budget document the aura of precision, it is still a plan; this is seen most clearly in budget execution when agencies struggle to execute the budgets they have prepared in an environment that is usually changed slightly from the one in which the budget was developed. Budget systems usually provide some capacity to modify the enacted budget during budget execution.

Budgets come in different types. Many, but not all, jurisdictions have a separate capital and operating budget. The capital budget is usually used for investment type functions, including buying lands and constructing buildings whose consumption will span generations. Thus, these projects are usually paid for by issuing bonds whose principal provides the money for the capital budget projects. These bonds normally will be paid back over a time period that approximates the consumption of the asset—usually set at 30 years.

The operating budget funds the annual operational needs of the jurisdiction. If the capital budget allows for the construction of an office building, it is the operating budget that allows for daily activities in and around that building. This includes hiring of personnel of different type and rank, equipping them with computers and office supplies, and providing them with telephones and heat and light and desks and chairs and all the apparatus of modern offices.

Operating budgets are produced and presented in various forms. The most basic type of operating budget form is the object of expenditure budget. This type of budget identifies, sometimes in excruciating detail, the items that will be purchased with budget funds. These objects of expenditure usually include personnel, supporting expenses, and minor capital outlay amounts for desks and office machines and the like. Personnel are usually listed by position type and position grade and perhaps by seniority, with a certain percentage added on to represent the cost of fringe benefits like vacation, sick leave, health, life and disability insurance, and retirement plan costs. Consumable items range from computer parts to telephone installations to pencils. A budget of this type is called a line-item budget because each item is presented on a separate line in the budget document. The line includes the name of the item, the budgeted amount for the current year, and a requested amount for the next year. Many also include what was spent on that item the previous year. Most line-item budgets have some brief explanations of the reason for the change from the amount in the budgeted year to the amount requested. Revenue sources may be broken into equally excruciating detail.

Building budgets with this level of detail for large and complex [organizations] quickly approaches information overload and reviewers have to struggle to avoid being trapped questioning inconsequential details about office supplies while major policy concerns are not fully addressed. Aaron Wildavsky's classic portrayal of the budgetary process (1964) suggested that the overwhelming complexity of the budget drove an incremental approach, where programs were reviewed a piece at a time, with different parts being reviewed in different places and reviewers relying on participant feedback to tell them if they had cut too much from one program or another. The complexity of the budget process dictated that some people must trust others in this process because they can only check up on them a small part of the time and because no one can be an expert in everything. Wildavsky saw man's inherent intellectual limits making an incremental approach a necessity. This view assumed constant making and remaking of the budget, with a heavy concentration of review on what is changed in the current year from the previous year. The picture of an incremental process with specific roles for budget participants dominated how people saw the budget process in the United States in the last third of the twentieth century.

Irrespective of the accuracy of this portrayal, much of the history of budget reform for the last 50 years involves finding ways to present budget information to decision-makers in a more meaningful way so that better decisions can be made about how to allocate scarce resources. These reforms have included performance budgeting, program budgeting, zero-based budgeting, planning-programming-budgeting and various systems focused on target or mission-based budgeting. Some reforms have focused on the budget process itself in the belief that better staff or a more timely process would provide a better budget process.

Ultimately, budgeting always involves a rationing process. Allen Schick (1990) has argued that claiming and rationing are at the center of the budget process.

Aaron Wildavsky (1964) has argued that the purposes of budgets are as varied as the purposes of men (pp. 1–3). The words and figures in the budget represent a prediction about the future, consequently budgets become links between financial resources, human behavior, and policy accomplishment. In this sense, a budget represents a series of goals with price tags attached.

Budget History

The word *"budget"* appears to be derived from the Middle English "bouget," or "wallet," which derives from Old French "bougette," meaning leather bag. This bag or purse was where the funds of the king were kept (Burkhead, 1956 p. 2.) In England, "budget" first meant the leather bag in which the government's plans for taxing and spending were carried to Parliament by the chancellor of the exchequer subsequent to the fourteenth century; eventually "budget" came to mean the plans themselves. This is perhaps the origination of the term *"public purse."*

References

"As Inflation Burns, Brazil Fiddles," 1994. *World Press Review,* vol. 41, no. 4 (April), 20.
Budget in Brief, December 1994. London: Ministry of Treasury.

Burkhead, Jesse, 1956. *Government Budgeting.* New York: John Wiley and Sons.

A Citizen's Guide to the Federal Budget. Fiscal Year 1996. 1995. Washington, DC: U.S. Government Printing Office, 1995.

"The 'Enlightened' Welfare-Seeker's Guide to Europe." *The Economist,* vol. 330, no. 7854 (March 12, 1994).

Lee, Robert D., and Ronald W. Johnson, 1989. *Public Systems,* 4th ed. Rockville, MD: Aspen.

McCaffery, Jerry, 1987. "The Development of Public Budgeting in the United States." In Ralph Clark Chandler, ed., *A Centennial History of the Ameri-can Administrative State.* New York: Macmillan, 345–379.

Rubin, Irene, 1993. "Who Invented Budgeting in the United States?" *Public Administration Review,* vol. 53, no. 5 (September/October), 438–444.

Schick, Allen, 1990. *The Capacity to Budget.* Washington, DC: Urban Institute.

Wildavsky, Aaron, 1964; rev. ed. 1984. *The Politics of the Budgetary Process.* Boston: Little, Brown.

_____, 1975. *Budgeting: A Comparative Theory of Budgetary Processes.* Boston: Little, Brown.

_____, 1988; rev. ed., 1992. *The New Politics of the Budgetary Process.* Glenview, IL: Scott, Foresman.

CHAPTER 26

Financial Statements and Fiscal Procedures

THOMAS WOLF

Nonprofit organizations do not enjoy the luxury afforded to individuals who can conduct their financial affairs in a relatively casual and lax manner and get away with it. Individuals can forget to enter a check that they have written, or assume the bank is correct when monthly bank statements arrive and simply skip doing a reconciliation. Nonprofits must maintain records carefully and should have these records reviewed periodically by an independent outside examiner who can certify that the organization is operating legally and according to generally accepted accounting procedures. Because nonprofit organizations enjoy numerous financially lucrative privileges and benefits, they must be able to demonstrate that their fiscal houses are in order. Board members are ultimately fiscally responsible for these organizations and must be able to read financial statements and be aware of reporting requirements and fiscal systems. It generally falls to staff people to implement these systems.

Accounting

Accounting is the term used for financial record keeping. There are two common accounting methods. The first, *cash basis accounting*, has the advantage of being simple and straightforward; the second, *accrual-based accounting*, is more complex but gives a more complete view of the organization's fiscal health.

Cash basis accounting. Most people are familiar with cash basis accounting because they do it when they maintain financial records for their checking and savings accounts. Financial transactions are recorded only when cash changes hands. When a person receives money and deposits it in the bank, the deposit is recorded as income and is added to the bank account balance. When cash is withdrawn from the bank (or when a check is written which is the equivalent of a withdrawal), the transaction is recorded as an expense and the amount is subtracted from the bank account balance. The cash basis accounting system is quite straightforward if all a person needs to know is how much money is in the account. However, what it does not reveal is the financial health of the person maintaining the account, because it tells nothing about what that individual owes and how much is owed to him or her.

Accrual-based accounting. For many individuals, credit cards have forced a kind of informal accrual-based accounting into their personal systems of financial record keeping. This system takes into account not only their actual payments and deposits but also what they owe and what is owed to them. Although few of us do formal accrual-based accounting, a lot of us do something very much like it when we estimate whether or not we will have enough cash to pay the mortgage or rent during the next month. If we see a nice article of clothing and try to figure out whether we can afford it by thinking about our outstanding bills and yet-to-be-received paychecks, we are engaged in informal accrual-based accounting.

Accrual-based accounting recognizes expenses not only when money changes hands but also when expenses are incurred and income is committed. If the Compton Community Center purchases office supplies for $125, an accrual-based system recognizes the $125 as a financial obligation from the moment the purchase order is written, and the amount is deducted from the organization's net worth at that time. Similarly, if the Compton Community Center receives an official notification from a funding agency of a $5,000 grant, the $5,000 is added to the net worth figure for the organization as soon as the letter is received. In the case of the $125 owed for supplies, the amount is reflected in the financial statements as a *payable* until the check is actually written. In the case of the $5,000 grant, the amount is entered on the books as a *receivable* until a check is actually deposited.

In the case just cited, if the Compton Community Center has $3,000 in the bank on the day that it charges $125 worth of office supplies and receives the grant letter for $5,000, a cash basis accounting system ignores these transactions and only indicates the organization's bank balance of $3,000. An accrual-based accounting system, on the other hand, adds the $5,000 grant receivable and subtracts the $125 payable showing a net figure of $7,875, which is a truer picture of the organization's net worth (see Table 26.1).

Choosing Methods

Cash basis accounting is much simpler than the accrual method and provides many people in the organization with enough financial information most of the time. It keeps accurate track of

TABLE 26.1 Cash Versus Accrual

	Cash	Accrual
Beginning cash in bank	$3,000	$ 3,000
Purchased supplies (payable)	0	– 125
Grant commitment (receivable)	0	$+5,000
Ending cash in bank	$3,000	
Net worth		$ 7,875

SOURCE: Compiled by the author.

income and outflow, and it tells people whether there is sufficient cash in the bank to pay the bills. Occasionally, however, the information from an accrual-based system is also necessary.

Fund Accounting

A small organization may have a simple budget for its entire operation—a kind of composite statement of the predicted expense and income for the entire organization. As organizations grow more complex, however, they may need to develop several subdivisions of this type of budget in order to gain an accurate analysis of the operation.

Fund accounting is a method that allows organizations to track their financial resources according to various categories or "funds." Each fund becomes its own accounting entity, with its own categories of revenue and expense, its own assets, and its own liabilities. Some funds that are commonly established include:

- *Operating or unrestricted current fund.* Any monies received, expended, held, or owed by the organization without conditions as to their use
- *Restricted current fund.* Any monies received, expended, held, or owed by the organization with conditions placed either on when they may be used or for what purpose they may be used
- *Plant fund.* Any monies received, expended, held, or owed by the organization in conjunction with land, buildings, and major equipment as well as the value of such items held by the organization
- *Endowment fund.* Any monies received, expended, held, or owed by the organization in conjunction with an endowment

- *Cash reserve fund.* Any monies received, expended, held, or owed by the organization in conjunction with a cash reserve

The total of activity in all funds becomes the total activity of the organization.[1]

Table 26.2 shows a financial statement using fund accounting. The first column summarizes the income and expenses associated with general activities. The second column summarizes income and expenses associated with two contributions restricted for use in connection with a program for gifted and talented children. The third column summarizes income and expense associated with improvements to the school building, and the fourth column represents the sum of the first three.

Financial Statements

Just as accounting systems are standardized, so are financial statements. When trustees and others want to assess the organization's financial health, they will look at two financial statements, the balance sheet and the income statement.

The balance sheet and the income statement serve the same function in the financial area as the vital signs chart and the medical history do in the health area. The balance sheet, like the vital signs chart, is similar to a freeze frame, a snapshot of the organization's financial condition as of a particular date (often the last day of the final month of the fiscal year). It summarizes the organization's vital financial signs—the value of what it owns, what it owes, what is owed to it, and how much is left over. The income statement, by way of contrast, is like the medical history. It summarizes financial activity over a period of time (often a month or a year). Unlike the balance sheet, which tells only where the organization's finances stand as of a particular moment in time, the income statement helps the financial diagnostician determine whether the manner in which the organization arrived at that state was "healthy." Armed with the income statement, more formally referred to as the Statement of Revenue and Expenditures or Statement of Activities, it is possible to deter-

TABLE 26.2   Multiple Funds of the Compton School

	Unrestricted Current	*Restricted Current*	*Plant Fund*	*Total*
Income				
Tuition	$41,222			$ 41,222
Book store sales	10,173			10,173
Foundation grant	5,496	$50,000		55,496
Business scholarship	5,000			5,000
Individuals	15,621	1,000	8,000	24,621
Total	$77,512	$51,000	8,000	$136,512
Expenses				
Salaries	$47,500	$24,500		$ 72,000
Benefits	7,122	3,621		10,743
Honoraria	2,500	16,586		19,086
Supplies and materials	5,287			5,287
Equipment rental	3,401			3,401
Promotion	6,526			6,526
Utilities/heating	3,212			3,212
Repairs/maintenance			9,997	9,997
Contingency/reserve	711		2,900	3,611
Total	$76,259	$44,707	2,897	$133,863

SOURCE: Compiled by the author.

mine whether the organization had a surplus, a deficit, made any unusually large expenditures, or had any revenue windfalls.

FASB Reporting Requirements

In the mid 1990s, the Financial Accounting Standards Board (FASB) issued new guidelines and language into nonprofit accounting.

These FASB standards must be used by all organizations in their annual audited statements (see section on audited statements presented later in this chapter). However, most organizations do not use these standards for their regular internal financial reports because the FASB changes do not facilitate strategic financial planning. This section on financial statements will focus primarily on the basic financial statements most organizations use for internal reporting. When these statements vary from those required by FASB, a reference will be made to this variation.

The Balance Sheet

The balance sheet (see Table 26.3) is so called because each half adds up to the same total number. One half of the balance sheet (shown at the top of the statement) lists all of the organization's assets (that is, everything that the organization owns). The other half (shown on the bottom of the statement) lists both the organization's liabilities (everything that it owes) and its net assets (formerly known as fund balance). Thus the *balance* in a balance sheet is between assets on the one hand and liabilities and net assets on the other. Put in mathematical form:

Assets = Liabilities + Net Assets

Understanding this formula, we can easily see how the net assets are calculated. If we know how much we own and how much we owe, the net assets are simply the difference between the two numbers:

Net Assets = Assets – Liabilities

TABLE 26.3   Balance Sheet (Statement of Financial Condition) as of June 30

ASSETS	
Current Assets	
Cash	$ 2,173
Accounts receivable	8,324
Prepaid expenses	8,423
Total Current Assets	$18,920
Noncurrent Assets	
Fixed Assets (land, building)	$305,362
Grants receivable	7,885
Total Noncurrent Assets	313,247
TOTAL ASSETS	$332,167
LIABILITIES AND NET ASSETS	
Liabilities	
Current Liabilities	
Accounts payable	$18,142
Deferred revenue	5,247
Total Current Liabilities	$23,389
Noncurrent Liabilities	
Notes payable	$ 18,010
Mortgage	154,840
Total Noncurrent Liabilities	$172,850
Net Assets	
Unrestricted	$115,391
Temporarily restricted	7,885
Permanently restricted	7,431
Net income/(loss) YTD	5,221
Total Net Assets	$135,928
TOTAL LIABILITIES AND NET ASSETS	$332,167

SOURCE: Compiled by the author.

In a profit-making corporation, the net assets are referred to as profit or owner's equity. In a nonprofit organization where there are no owners and no profits, the net assets show the organization's financial net worth when all of its financial obligations are subtracted from all of its cash and noncash assets. The net assets also provide a link to the income statement, because the organization's financial net worth is obviously affected by the net income (or loss), the so-called bottom line from the income statement.[2]

Let us look more closely at a balance sheet to find out what it is really telling us. First, look at the Assets section of the statement in Table 26.3.

Assets are what the organization owns: cash in the bank, land, buildings, a collection of paintings, and equipment (such as computers and copiers). In addition, because balance sheets are commonly prepared on an accrual basis, all the money owed to the organization is counted as an asset. These are called the receivables and might include things like grants on which the letter of commitment but not the check has been received or items sold and invoiced but for which the organization has not received payment.[3] There is also a line for prepaid expenses, which include such things as expenses paid for an event that is actually occurring in the next fiscal year or a final month's rent on off-site storage space.

Note that these assets are divided between current assets and noncurrent assets. Current assets are those that are cash or are expected to become cash within the next year; noncurrent assets are those that are not as liquid (including contributions or grants pledged to be paid two or more years into the future).

Moving to the other half of the balance sheet, there is a listing of all of the organization's liabilities (what it owes). On the first line under Liabilities are all of the unpaid bills (the accounts payable). Next is the revenue collected for activities that will not occur until the next fiscal year (deferred revenue).[4] Finally there are the longer term obligations such as outstanding loans (the notes payable and mortgage).[5] As with the assets, these liabilities are classified as current (due within one year) and noncurrent (due in more than one year).

All of the liability categories are then totaled and the sum is subtracted from total assets. The resulting difference produces the net assets.

What does all of this information tell us? Beginning with the net assets, we know the organization's net worth. In the case of the organization whose balance sheet is shown in Table 26.3, the net worth is $135,928. Often a large net asset line connotes a healthy organization. But not always, and this is precisely the reason why the other numbers on the balance sheet are so important. In Table 26.3, for example, the organization shows fairly sizable net assets. But on closer examination, we see that the reason for this is because it owns land and a building. Its cash position is relatively poor. It has only $2,173 in the bank and $8,324 in receivables. It owes $18,142 (exclusive of the mortgage and a loan). In one sense, the organization could be called healthy. If it sold its land and building it could pay its debts and have plenty of money left over. On the other hand, if it hangs on to the property, it will have to raise cash to pay its debts. Generally speaking, an organization that has insufficient cash and/or receivables to pay near-term debts is not considered financially healthy.

The balance sheet is an excellent tool for prospective trustees, funders, regulators, and others to decide whether the organization is a good financial risk. Prospective trustees will want to check whether the organization is saddled with debt because this will provide a clue about whether they will spend a lot of time on the board scrambling for funds; potential funders will want to see whether an organization has large accumulated deficits because this often means that it will be so preoccupied with debt that it will be unable to focus on its programs and other activities; from the regulator's perspective, debt-ridden organizations are often tempted to draw on restricted funds to cover operating needs. Indeed, it is not uncommon for government auditors to check on whether restricted public funds have been properly used in financially troubled organizations.

The balance sheet can be most important to trustees and employees of an organization as a diagnostic tool if there is an understanding of how to use it. Unfortunately, many people are mystified by all the numbers. They are content to study the income statement, which is more familiar to them and easier to understand. The assumption is that it contains all the information they really need to know. But this is not the case, as we have just seen. An organization may have a surplus on the income statement (and/or a significant total of net assets) and be in serious financial trouble. Only the balance sheet will reveal this.

The Income Statement

If the balance sheet tells us what we need to know about an organization's financial health at a particular moment in time, why is another financial statement necessary? The reason is simply that we not only need to know what the organization's health is today but must view the progress of that health over time. Two organizations may have identical balance sheets but one may be improving its financial condition and the other's financial health may be rapidly deteriorating. The income statement (Table 26.4) shows these financial trends over time and gives the historical perspective, which the balance sheet ignores.

Historical perspective is not the only value of an income statement. It also gives an idea of an organization's income sources and its expenditures. Revenues and expenditures are subdivided into categories that reveal such things as how much of the organization's income is earned, how dependent the organization is on certain kinds of grants, how much is spent on personnel, or how much it costs to provide program materials.

Unlike a balance sheet, in which a large number of the line item categories are predictable and similar from one organization to another and from one industry to another, the various revenue and expenditure categories on the income statement vary greatly (they usually closely parallel an organization's budgetary chart of accounts). The bottom line, Net income/(loss) year to date, shows whether the organization had a surplus or deficit for the year (or whatever time period is reported on); it is calculated by subtracting total expenditures from total revenues and is carried over to the balance sheet (Table 26.3).[6]

FASB changes also had an impact on income statements. FASB required that income statements be referred to as "Statements of Activities." They also required that all expenses be

TABLE 26.4 Income Statement (Statement of Activities) from July 1 to December 30

Revenue	Current Month			Year to Date		
Earned income	Actual	Budget	% of Budget	Actual	Annual Budget	% of Budget
Tuition	$ 2,111	$ 2,000	106%	$ 48,201	$110,500	44%
Interest	404	450	90%	2,955	5,000	59%
Other earned	2,450	1,800	136%	11,222	21,500	52%
Total Earned Income	$ 4,965	$ 4,250	117%	$ 62,378	$137,000	46%
Contributed Income						
Membership	$ 525	$ 1,000	53%	$ 14,225	$ 25,000	57%
Individual donations	4,230	5,000	85%	5,225	18,000	29%
Corporate gifts	2,000	1,250	160%	9,753	15,000	65%
Government grants	0	0	0%	12,655	20,000	63%
Total Contributed Income	6,755	7,250	93%	41,858	78,000	54%
Total revenue	$11,720	$11,500	102%	$104,236	$215,000	48%
Expenses						
Salaries and benefits	$ 9,374	$10,750	87%	$ 56,244	$129,000	44%
Professional fees/contractual	2,500	1,200	208%	15,400	15,000	03%
Office supplies/telephone	333	500	67%	2,987	6,000	50%
Travel and subsistence	400	0	400%	5,531	7,500	74%
Printing and promotion	723	1,000	72%	2,423	10,000	24%
Educational materials	3,655	2,500	146%	4,091	18,500	22%
Utilities and insurance	562	425	132%	2,755	5,000	55%
Mortgage interest	295	295	100%	1,750	3,500	50%
Grounds maintenance	245	500	49%	4,000	10,000	40%
Other	1,150	875	131%	3,834	10,500	37%
Total expenses	$19,237	$18,045	107%	$ 99,015	$215,000	46%
Net income (loss) YTD	($7,517)	($6,545)	115%	5,221	0	

SOURCE: Compiled by the author.

reported in the three functional categories of program, management, and fund raising.

The income statement presented in Table 26.4 shows activity in the operating fund of this organization. For most organizations, the operating fund incorporates the majority of financial activities and is most carefully analyzed and reviewed. The statement not only shows activity for the month that was most recently completed but also shows all activity thus far this year *and compares both to a monthly and annual budget.* The annual budget is the budget approved by the board prior to the start of the fiscal year; the monthly budget uses the monthly allocation of revenue and expenses from the cash flow projections described in the previous chapter.

What can we tell about this organization from looking at this statement? To begin with, the organization is half way through its fiscal year (the statement covers the period from July 1 through December 30). This means that one would expect that roughly 50 percent of the budget has been met. This organization is doing well—48 percent of its revenues have been collected, and 46 percent of its expenditures have been made. However, there are some potential areas of concern. For example, individual donations are well below what was projected for the year. If we knew that the annual appeal to individuals was scheduled for February, this would be expected. However, if the annual appeal happened in October, there would be cause for some concern.

Similarly, there are some potential problem areas with expenses. Professional fees are over budget already—and there is still half the year ahead! On the other hand, a number of expense categories are at less than half of what was budgeted, which indicates careful planning. A trustee of this organization might be concerned, however, that only 22 percent of projected expenditures for educational materials had been made. Does this reflect a planned delay, or are programmatic materials not receiving the attention they should?

Clearly, there is much information to be gained from examining the financial statements of an organization. The intimidating columns of figures can actually be quite revealing if the reader has a sense of where the most important information lies. Responsible board members will take the time to familiarize themselves with at least the highlights of each statement in an effort to be as informed as possible about the organization they are overseeing. A narrative report accompanying the statements can draw attention to the more significant numbers.

Controls

One of the major responsibilities of board members is to establish fiscal policies that protect the organization from either intentional or unintentional misuse of funds. They must decide how money will be handled internally to ensure that it will be safely received, recorded, deposited, and expended in a manner that seems appropriate. The policies that board members set in this area are called controls and there are guidelines that they can follow. Any responsible accountant can advise them on what are generally accepted and appropriate procedures. For example, many fiscal controls are based on the notion that two people are far less likely to make a mistake, either intentionally or unintentionally, than one. So one kind of financial control is to be sure that two people are involved in transactions involving the receipt of cash, the preparation of financial statements, the expenditure of funds, and other financial matters. Other controls are discussed below.

Budget Monitoring and Amending Procedures

To establish a reliable procedure, the board generally requires that two people should be involved in processing all payments. One person who is familiar with the budget, the organization's operation, and the appropriateness of specific expenditures should be responsible for approving payments. That person is often the director of the organization or his or her designate. Another person should actually write the checks and monitor the expenditures for the trustees. If the limits established by the budget, or the limits beyond the budget set by the board, are adhered to, a check can be written. If payments that exceed these limits are requested, the matter must be referred to the treasurer, the finance committee, or the full board for approval or for an amended budget.

Other Controls on Check Writing

It is generally not recommended that the person who writes checks have the power to issue a check to himself or herself without at least a countersignature on the check. While banks probably will not monitor this, the policy can be recorded in the minutes of a board meeting and a person can be held in violation of a fiscal policy if the rule is not followed. One control that banks often may be willing to monitor is that of requiring two signatures on all checks over a certain amount ($5,000, for example). To further monitor expenditures, use of checks made out to "cash" should be forbidden or severely restricted.

Controls on Incoming Monies

Again, in this area, the assumption is that two people are less likely to err than one. Where incoming monies are involved, the person who opens the mail should record all incoming checks and cash and keep a list. Checks and cash should then be forwarded to the fiscal officer who prepares the deposit slip and keeps a record. Periodically, someone other than these two people (authorized by the board treasurer or the executive director) should check to see that the two sets of records agree. In addition, all incoming money, whether cash or check, should be deposited promptly in the organization's bank account before it is used to pay a bill.

Bonding

Bonding is a form of insurance that protects an organization from financial losses stemming from either intentional or unintentional irregularities in the handling of money. Generally, those people who handle money and sign checks are listed in the bonding document. Like any form of insurance, a limit is placed on the amount an organization can collect in the case

of a loss. Some funding sources require evidence of bonding before they will contribute dollars to a nonprofit organization. Whether or not they do, it should be a comfort both to funders and trustees to know that such insurance against loss is in place.

Reporting Requirements

Nonprofit corporations may not have to file income tax forms, but there are other forms that must be filed each year for an organization to maintain its nonprofit status. Although generally the forms are prepared by staff or by the independent auditor who reviews the books each year, it is important for board members to be aware of the reports that must be filed in order to ascertain that it is done in a timely manner. Because requirements vary from state to state, board members should check their own state regulations to determine what specific state forms should be filed. The following is a general overview of federal forms required:

1: *Annual return.* Most nonprofit organizations must file an annual information return with the IRS called Form 990. This form provides information on the ongoing activities of the organization in support of its tax-exempt status and includes statements regarding all income and expenditures for the year. The returns are due on the fifteenth day of the fifth month following the fiscal year end. Failure to file can result in civil and criminal penalties.

2: *Unrelated business income tax.* In recent years, nonprofit organizations have come under increasing scrutiny as more inventive and atypical methods of raising money have been implemented. Tax must be paid on "unrelated" business income, which is income produced by regular activities that are not substantially related to the exempt purpose of the organization (excluding income from passive investments such as money market interest, stock dividends, etc.). This income (if it exceeds $1,000) must be reported on Form 990-T, which is due with Form 990. As it is sometimes complicated to determine whether or not income is considered unrelated, it is best to consult with the independent outside examiner who prepares the Form 990 or conducts the annual audit as to whether or not this form is required.

3: *Employment taxes.* All organizations with employees are required to withhold income taxes, social security, and Medicare from salaries and to pay and report amounts withheld to the IRS. Nonprofit organizations other than 501(c)(3) organizations must also pay federal unemployment taxes (FUTA) on salaries paid. Details on payment of withholding and FUTA are available from the IRS through the publication *Circular E—Employer's Tax Guide.*

4: *Other information returns.* Form 1099-MISC must be used to report on an annual basis any nonemployee compensation paid in amounts exceeding $600. Form 8282, Donee Information Report, must be filed with the IRS if a donee organization sells, exchanges, or otherwise disposes of gifts of property other than money or publicly traded securities within two years of the gift. This form is not required if the gift was valued at less than $500.

Audited Statements, Reviews, and Compilations

Many nonprofit organizations are required to provide an annual audited statement of their financial activities to their state, a funder, or others. This audit provides a formal statement in a standardized format about an organization's financial status, activities, and history (an audited statement generally compares the current year's activities with those of the previous year). Whether or not this statement is required varies from organization to organization and state to state. However, generally organizations with budgets of $100,000 or more must have audited statements prepared.

An audited statement is prepared by an independent certified public accountant (CPA) who prepares a formal report that includes a Statement of Position (balance sheet), Statement of Activities (income statement), and Statement of Cash Flows (a report on how the organization's cash position changed during the year). These reports must comply with all the FASB requirements. An audit also includes notes that provide details on various items presented in the various reports. It may also include a Statement of Changes in Net Assets, Supplemental Schedules (details on various revenue or expense breakouts), and a Statement of Functional Expenses (allocation of line item expenses into program, administration, and fund-raising categories). The audit also includes an opening letter from the CPA as to the reliability of the reports. These letters most often state that the reports are considered reliable by the CPA and that they reflect generally accepted accounting principles. However, sometimes the CPA will also issue a separate comments and recommendations report that makes suggestions about improvements to the existing financial systems.

Because the audit can be such an important document for an organization, selection of the appropriate CPA is an important process. If possible, a CPA should be selected who is familiar with the operations of nonprofit organizations in the organization's field, whether it be human services, the arts, education, or some other area.

Evaluation of proposed cost is another important step. Because one often gets only what one pays for, a pro bono audit may mean a lower priority for project completion, less qualified personnel assigned to perform the work, and potentially a report that is of lesser quality. Once a CPA has been selected, it is important to sign a letter of agreement that specifies the services to be performed and the cost.

There are two lower cost options for organizations not required to provide audited statements. The first of these is a review, which is a more limited examination of financial statements by a CPA. A review provides limited assurances that the financial statements are accurate. A compilation, also prepared by a CPA, presents an organization's financial information in standard financial reporting formats, but makes no statement about accuracy and involves no review of supporting documents. A compilation is the least expensive option.

This chapter has explained accounting procedures, financial statements, and financial controls and has reviewed reporting requirements that nonprofits need to meet to maintain their special tax status. Too many nonprofit organizations have failed because of lack of attention to these areas. Staff members may have been lax in the maintenance of financial records or trustees may not have bothered to analyze the financial statements or put controls in place. Although the plethora of procedures and reports described in this chapter may seem overwhelming, no nonprofit organization can afford to be casual about its financial affairs if it wants to protect its nonprofit status and ensure its continued survival. No board member can afford to be casual about these matters either, if he or she is to meet the responsibilities of public trust, which are part of the conditions of trusteeship.

Notes

1. Many organizations do both fund accounting and departmental or program accounting. A fund may include a number of projects or departments. A project or a department may span funds as well, for example, when a particular program is supported by both unrestricted and restricted funding.

2. Usually the net assets or equity figure portion is adjusted only at year end; it does not change during the year and the changes in the total net assets are reflective of the net income (or loss) from the income statement. Again, for a profit-making corporation, this equity could be the owners' original investment, which is augmented or reduced by any profit or loss that the corporation makes.

3. Note that one of the requirements of FASB was that organizations must recognize pledged contributions as revenue at the time of the pledge, no matter when the pledge is to be paid. Most organizations do not do this until the time of the audited statement, since people feel that recording pledged contributions as revenue any earlier overstates revenue and creates a false sense of well-being on the part of those review-

ing the financial statements. To the extent that this recording is done, the line item on the balance sheet reporting uncollected pledges is generally called *Contributions Receivable*.

4. One of the results of the FASB changes is that funds previously classified as deferred revenue (for example, a restricted grant received in advance of the project it is funding) may now be classified as temporarily restricted net assets. However, some revenues will still be classified as deferred.

5. The balance sheet allows someone to calculate the equity of property owned by the organization. The value of the property is shown under Assets and the outstanding debt on the property is shown under Liabilities. The amount of equity in the property is the difference between these two figures. Thus in figure 7.3, the equity is calculated as $305,362 minus $154,840, or $150,522. Interest payments do not appear on the balance sheet but are shown on the income statement.

6. On year-end audited statements, there is generally a section at the bottom of the Statement of Activities (income statement) that indicates the increase (decrease) in net assets, which is actually simply a different name for net income (loss). This line is followed by the following reconciliation:

Increase (decrease) in net assets	5,221 (same as net income)
Net assets at beginning of year	130,707 (from prior year's balance sheet)
Net assets at end of year	135,928 (sum of the above)

This net assets figure must also be broken out among unrestricted, temporarily restricted, and permanently restricted net assets, which is done with a Statement of Changes in Net Assets report. Alternatively, the income statement may be presented with three columns, one for each of the net asset categories.

PART 9

MANAGING
VOLUNTEERS*

Volunteers represent one of the most decidedly distinctive aspects of nonprofit organizations.[1] It is almost impossible to discuss the nonprofit sector without mentioning volunteers and, indeed, in recent years it has been relatively common to hear the nonprofit sector called the "voluntary sector." Because volunteers and nonprofits go hand-in-glove, naturally, many of us mentally connect voluntarism with the nonprofit sector even though many citizens also volunteer with government libraries, fire departments, emergency medical services systems, schools, veterans hospitals, and numerous other public agencies and programs.[2]

Volunteer and Voluntarism

Voluntarism: "Actions undertaken freely by individuals, groups, or organizations that are not compelled by biological need or social convention, mandated or coerced by government, or directed principally at financial or economic gain, regarded as beneficial by participants or the larger society."[3]

As such, voluntarism is a component or dimension of the larger concept, *philanthropy:*

> Voluntary giving, voluntary serving, and voluntary association to achieve some vision of the public good; includes charity, patronage, and civil society. . . . The usual inclusive contemporary definition of philanthropy is "values, organizations, and practices that entail voluntary action to achieve some vision or the public good" or the "private" production of "public goods."[4]

---

*This chapter was written with Peter M. Nelson.

Cnaan, Handy, and Wadsworth[5] rightfully argue that *voluntarism* and *volunteer* are "rich concepts" that cannot be explained adequately in a single-sentence definition. They observe that definitions of *volunteer* vary on four key dimensions: the voluntary nature of the act; the nature of the reward; the context or auspices under which the volunteer activity is performed; and who benefits. Cnaan, Handy, and Wadsworth found that each of these four dimensions has "steps" that differentiate between volunteers and nonvolunteers.

> For example, in the dimension of free choice, we identified three key categories: (1) free will (the ability to voluntarily choose), (2) relatively uncoerced, and (3) obligation to volunteer. Whereas all definitions would accept category 1 (free will) as relevant in defining a volunteer, pure definitions would not accept category 2 (relatively coerced), and only the broadest definition would define court-ordered volunteers or students in a required service program as volunteers.[6]

Why People Volunteer

Various motives cause people to give such tangible assets as their money, shares of stock and acreage, and nontangible resources, including their time, energy, reputations, endorsements, and access to people with power and influence. Why do some people give more time to some causes and organizations than to others, or to volunteer more time than others do? To what extent is giving driven (or influenced) by sympathy, empathy, a sense of justice, to alleviate guilt, or by rational calculation of personal utility? Is altruism—or egoism—a characteristic of human nature that emanates from genetic structure?[7] Is giving an inherited personality trait—a "drive"? Or is altruism learned from others around us, developmentally over years? How and why do peoples' giving and volunteering patterns differ at various life stages?

Questions such as these indicate why scholars have been interested in the nature of volunteers and the phenomenon of voluntarism. Answers to questions such as these would help us understand the distinctiveness and the complexities of the nonprofit sector and of nonprofit organizations. The answers also are vitally important to the trustees and managers of the thousands of nonprofit organizations that rely on volunteers to staff their programs, serve on their boards, and stuff their envelopes.

Whether volunteering involves serving on a board of trustees, providing direct services, or helping with support activities, successful nonprofit organizations are able to appeal successfully to the motivational needs of volunteers and to use their talents in ways that meet the needs of the organization and also satisfy the individuals. One way of understanding motivational needs is through the ideas of David McClelland,[8] who posited that three motives determine human activity: the need for achievement, the need for power, and the need for affiliation. Simply stated, the need for achievement is a drive to "doing something better." The need for affiliation refers primarily to the need people have for interacting one with another. The need for power is commonly used to refer to the need to influence the actions and beliefs of others. Different individuals have varying degrees of need in these three areas. Some individuals may be high in their need for achievement, but relatively low in their needs for power and affiliation. Others may be high in the need for power, but low in the other areas; still others are high in their need for affiliation, but relatively low in their need for power and achievement. Recognizing this difference in motives can assist an executive director in developing recruiting approaches and also in shaping volunteers' tasks. For example, a volunteer with a high motivation for achievement will generally do better in a job/task with definable boundaries, measurable outcomes, and feedback on progress.

Abraham Maslow articulated an alternative perspective on motivation[9] that also is useful for understanding the motivations of volunteers. In Maslow's needs-hierarchy model, an individual can move on to meet higher-level needs only after lower-level needs have been satisfied. Thus, an individual who is struggling to meet the basic physiological needs of food, clothing, and shelter cannot be "motivated" by higher-level, more abstract needs. Maslow believed that most people in our society move among the need levels of safety and security, affiliation, and self-esteem.

Most good managers in nonprofit organizations would not need to read McClelland and Maslow's theories. They already know that people behave in ways that allow them to satisfy their needs. When their needs are being met, they can be valuable contributors; when needs are not being met, they usually leave.[10]

Usually a director of volunteers, or the executive director in smaller nonprofits, is responsible for matching the needs of volunteers with the organization's needs to get work done. Although this may appear to be a straightforward exercise of inserting "round pegs in round holes and square pegs in square holes," people often do not truly understand why they volunteered or know what they want from their volunteer experience—except that they "want to help." Although most volunteers affiliate with organizations whose values and goals match well with their own, agreement with an organization's purposes rarely causes an individual to volunteer time and resources for a particular nonprofit.[11] It takes more than enthusiasm for—or sympathy with—a nonprofit's goals to motivate individuals to donate their time and effort. A volunteer coordinator must remain alert to the goodness of the alignment between volunteers' needs and their assignments, and assignments that are not "fits" should be changed quickly.

Identifying the needs of volunteers from observable behaviors can be a tricky undertaking. People can meet the same needs in different ways and use similar behaviors to meet different needs. Different individuals with many varying needs will join the same organization.

Example: A nonprofit organization has a single purpose—to preserve and restore a historical building. One of the volunteers who is seeking to satisfy a need for influence[12] may serve the organization best if her responsibilities allow her to work directly with potential major donors or legislators. A second volunteer who has a high need for achievement (accomplishment) may work better alone on a task with tangible results, such as a field study of the neighborhood or a preliminary cost analysis. The needs of a third volunteer who joins the association primarily to make new friends may be met best as a member of a small working group that will remain intact for months or years.

All volunteers have different needs, and the needs of individuals do not remain constant over time. Needs change as people pass through various stages of their lives. If an organization hopes to recruit and retain a productive and reliable bank of volunteers, it must help them meet their needs—and this is a time-consuming task. Thus, most larger nonprofits employ directors of volunteers to plan, organize, recruit, place, train, and manage the activities of volunteers.

Recruiting and Retaining Volunteers

Nonprofit organizations need to identify what they need and expect from volunteers before they start to recruit. Volunteers consume a lot of staff time and require considerable effort and patience. Thus, nonprofits that are considering using volunteers first need to think through how the organizational needs can be matched effectively with the needs of volunteers. What tasks require what skills? Should only paid staff perform some tasks, or should volunteers be used wherever needs arise? Is it permissible for volunteers to supervise staff? Many nonprofit organizations conduct periodic organizational needs analyses to answer these types of questions. An organizational needs analysis can help forecast future recruiting needs and identify underused stakeholder groups that could be "mined" for volunteers.

What types of skills and abilities does a nonprofit need in its volunteers? Does a given nonprofit organization need individuals with high energy and physical stamina, for example, to deliver meals to shut-ins or to help people with disabilities in and out of vans and wheel chairs? If so, recruiting elderly citizens or individuals with disabilities may not be helpful. Most organizations, however, have a variety of tasks to be performed, and good fits usually can be found between volunteers and tasks. For example, a local hospice program may recruit only registered nurses to supplement staff in providing skilled nursing care for the terminally ill, because existing laws specify that only physicians and RNs can provide specific types of care. This hospice program probably also needs volunteers to manage paperwork, answer telephones, schedule visits, and interact with the media and the community. It may also need volunteers to provide respite care for families, a service that could be provided by volunteers with a variety of skills and abilities. By differentiating the types of skills needed to provide different types of services, the volunteer base can be broadened to accommodate a wide variety of volunteer interests and abilities.

Differentiating among the many types of tasks an organization needs to have done not only makes it easier to match individual volunteers with job needs, it can also help identify possibilities for existing volunteers to develop new skills and abilities. A nonprofit organization that provides services to victims of violent crimes and their families, for example, might enlist a volunteer to help with clerical tasks such as filing, answering telephones, and helping people complete a bewildering array of forms. After a while, this volunteer might become interested in serving as a court advocate who helps victims and families find their way through the legal process and to access victims' reparation funds. Someday, this experienced and confident volunteer could begin to help train other volunteers to become court advocates. The process of developing volunteer skills, as in this example, requires an organization to 1) know what tasks it needs to have performed that require what skills, 2) know what individual volunteers want to do and 3) have a responsive development process in place that allows volunteers to grow through job enrichment and enlargement.

Recognizing Volunteers

As with employees, volunteers need to know that their time and effort make a difference. Successful volunteer organizations plan and budget ways to recognize volunteers and their contributions. Some organizations have an annual recognition dinner and celebration. Other nonprofits present certificates, plaques, or items with engraved organization logos as evidence that they acknowledge and appreciate the services of their volunteers. Many nonprofit organizations track the number of hours of all the volunteers and proudly announce to the media and the community how much time and energy its volunteers gave to "the cause."

Well-run organizations know, however, that sooner or later all volunteers will move on. Wise directors of volunteers conduct exit interviews to help them identify changes that would improve the experience for future volunteers. Exit interviews identify what worked well, what didn't work, and why volunteers leave an organization. Information collected in exit interviews can help the director of volunteers and the executive director detect trends and identify general opportunities and problems. Exit interviews also can identify problems that could adversely affect the organization if left unremedied.

Risk Management: Reducing the Risk of Liability

The use of volunteers involves an inevitable potential of legal liability for individuals and organizations. Thus, nonprofit organizations that use volunteers need to have a variety of safeguards in place to protect against injury and legal action, including policies and procedures, a variety of training programs, individual performance plans, and arrangements to help volunteers in the event they are injured or sued while providing services on behalf of the nonprofit.

Although state and federal courts have held that volunteers do not have contractual or property interests in their positions (if their "contract" allows for termination), the relationship between the volunteer and the organization should be clear from the outset. This relationship should be described carefully in performance plans that describe the duties that individual volunteers will perform, performance expectations, and the limits of their authority. For example, will a volunteer regularly handle funds for the organization? If so, there is a fiduciary responsibility between the volunteer and the organization, and expectations must be put in writing regarding the accounting for funds and limits on the volunteer's authority to act. There should be clear, documented, workable procedures for handling funds. Should the volunteer be bonded? Similar policy questions should be asked and answered for any task before volunteers are assigned to it.

Are effective procedures in place for screening potential volunteers? If a nonprofit organization provides direct services to vulnerable recipient groups, such as children, abused spouses or the aging, does it have criteria for screening out potentially dangerous volunteers? Does a nonprofit that serves children aggressively seek information to identify individuals who have been previously convicted of crimes against children? Are its procedures "reasonably successful"—and able to withstand legal challenge? Failure of the organization to protect vulnerable recipient populations can result in charges of negligent recruiting or negligent hiring.[13]

Organizations and individuals also risk liability when volunteers perform services that are not within the scope of the volunteer's training or performance expectations. For example, a volunteer hospice respite worker who assists clients with injections or other medical care procedures that the volunteer is not trained or certified to provide has put herself and the hospice at risk. Although this volunteer may have had the purest of motives, allegations of negligent supervision could be upheld against the agency. The volunteer's supervisor knew—or should have known—about the actions and stopped them.[14]

Volunteers may be assigned to tasks if they can reasonably be expected to perform them acceptably with adequate training. For example, volunteers who have received specialized training in crisis intervention, listening techniques, and referral procedures staff many suicide and prevention hotlines. Although the stakes are high, volunteers who successfully complete such training may provide valuable services—but only within the limits of their training. If no qualified person is available to provide assistance, however, could—or should—unqualified volunteers refuse to offer help that is beyond their training in crisis circumstances—legally and morally? If demand for a nonprofit's services outgrows its staffing and funding, and people in need are being denied services, would it be reasonable to provide a few new volunteers with quick-and-dirty temporary training and allow them to provide services only until the staffing crisis abates? If a tragedy occurs in either of these cases, would the courts find that the organization had been negligent in training its volunteers? These are the types of questions that executive directors and boards need to consider when adopting and managing a volunteer program.

Before allowing volunteers to provide services, a nonprofit organization should train its volunteers to perform their tasks at a level that a reasonable person would expect of anyone else who provides similar services for the organization. Nonprofits also should train volunteers in its organizational policies and procedures, including *at least* harassment prevention, workplace violence prevention, protecting the confidentiality of service recipients, safety procedures, grievance rights and procedures, and the duties and responsibilities of volunteers.

Even if an organization has training programs, adequate policies and procedures, and a performance management process for volunteers, it still must consider other areas of protection for volunteers: helping volunteers who are injured while providing services for the organization or who are sued because of actions or events that occurred while they were providing services.

A nonprofit should carry liability insurance to protect volunteers and the organization in the event of injury or sickness directly related to the provision of services. For example, volunteers in a local needle exchange program are at risk of "a stick" from a dirty syringe. Who should pay for the HIV and hepatitis prevention treatment? Who should provide counseling for the volunteers whose lives will change dramatically? Who should pay to treat a volunteer driver who injures her back while assisting elderly patients in and out of an assisted living center's van? If a volunteer is sued while providing services, who will pay for the legal defense of the volunteer, the volunteer director, the executive director, and members of the board of trustees?

Indemnification for volunteers in some form is essential in this litigation-happy environment of the twenty-first century. Often, legal action taken against a volunteer's actions is only a first step. The plaintiff may have little or no desire to take any or all of the volunteer's assets, but establishing the legal culpability of the volunteer is a first step toward also establishing the nonprofit organization's responsibility and culpability. This is the doctrine of deep pockets.

Legal liability is an unavoidable part of the volunteer environment in the United States today. The old adage is painfully true: "There are only two types of volunteers (and employees)—those who have been sued and those who are going to be sued." Nonprofit organizations are at least partially responsible for the actions of their volunteers. An attorney who is well versed in tort liability law can be an invaluable resource for an executive director and a board of trustees.

The Future of Volunteers and Voluntarism

The importance of volunteers for nonprofits should continue to rise over the upcoming decades for several reasons.

1: Our population will live more and more productive years after retirement. Volunteering provides retirees with opportunities to use their skills and feel useful while making a difference.
2: Many educational institutions now offer volunteer opportunities as a way for students to learn to live more fulfilling lives. These universities offer community service, service learning, internships and outreach programs; some are requiring participation for graduation.
3: A few government programs, such as AmeriCorps, are providing a new variety of paid volunteers that may be available to nonprofit organizations. AmeriCorps pays stipends and grants to qualified individuals that enable them to provide services through nonprofit organizations while also helping them to finance their college education.
4: Perhaps the most important reason, though, is that the nonprofit sector will require more services, skills, and energy of volunteers in the upcoming years because we are in a long-term era of declining government funding for human services and the arts, increasing service populations and needs, and expanded service mandates.[15] If nonprofit organizations do not provide services for many vulnerable populations, it is questionable whether other organizations will. Thus, more volunteers will be needed than perhaps at any other time in our nation's history.

To meet the rising needs for their services, nonprofit organizations need to strengthen their ability to manage volunteers well, recruit and retain volunteers, match volunteer needs with organizational needs, develop training programs, and reduce the liability risks.

Readings Reprinted in Part Nine

In *"Voluntarism,"* Jeffrey Brudney[16] examines the conceptual underpinnings of voluntarism, the importance of voluntarism for the delivery of many services, and how voluntarism fits between the market and state. Brudney defines and explains the nature, magnitude, and motivations for voluntarism. Voluntarism consists of "actions undertaken freely by individuals, groups, or organizations that are not compelled by biological need or social convention, mandated or coerced by government, or directed principally at financial or economic gain, regarded as beneficial by participants or the larger society." People volunteer informally, "as helping a friend move," and more formally through the hundreds of thousands of 501(c)(3) charitable organizations across the United States that are engaged in religious, scientific, literary, and educational activities.[17] Brudney advises against underestimating the size and importance of the voluntary, nonprofit sector. "American nonprofit organizations employ more civilians than the federal and all state governments combined, and the yearly budget of the sector exceeds the budgets of all but seven nations in the world." Survey information collected in 1993 led to an estimate that "47.7 percent of Americans volunteered an average of 4.2 hours per week."

Although one might suspect that the "cause" or "mission" of an organization would be the single strongest factor leading persons to volunteer, instead it is to have been recruited well. Other factors that are correlated with volunteering include financial contributions, level of formal education, and "higher socioeconomic status and participation in other forms of social activity."

"Volunteers at Work," by Jone Pearce, is a chapter from her groundbreaking 1993 book, *The Organizational Behavior of Unpaid Workers.*[18] As the title of the book indicates, Pearce focuses on the behavior of individuals and groups after they have decided to volunteer with specific organizations. Her "exploration begins by suggesting that the central theme to understanding volunteers' organizational behavior is uncertainty. . . . The uncertainty experienced by organizational volunteers is inherently more extensive and more central to their experiences than is the case for employees." Organizational expectations of volunteers seldom are clear, and staff reactions to their presence vary. "The problems of volunteers' limited time, uncertain motives, and a high degree of individual independence can result in debilitating levels of uncertainty for organizational volunteers."

Volunteering with organizations provides opportunities and freedoms that employment does not. "Guiding constraints" that exist for employees, particularly in business and government, "simply do not apply." We tend to assume that differences between the behaviors of volunteers and staff are related to this freedom that volunteers have—to the freedom generated by lack of concern about employment status or financial remuneration for their work. Pearce suggests, however, that to do so would be to overlook "a valuable opportunity to study the advantages and disadvantages of harnessing nonmonetary controls for organizational reward systems. . . . Thus, an understanding of volunteer organizational behavior can serve as a mirror that provides a reflection on and, it is hoped, a contribution to general theories of organizational behavior."

Jeffrey Brudney turns this chapter's readings specifically to the practice of *"Volunteer Administration,"*[19] the "profession concerned with the study and practice of integrating volunteers effectively and ethically into an organization to enhance performance and results." The integration of volunteers into the workplace "does not happen by accident or without considerable planning and preparation on the part of the sponsoring organization. . . . The field of volunteer administration is dedicated to the effective, ethical involvement of volunteers for the benefit of host organizations, their clientele, and the volunteers themselves." Brudney lists and describes the essential components of effective volunteer administration in some detail. The components include: establishing the rationale for volunteer involvement; involving paid staff in volunteer program design; integrating the volunteer program into the organization; creating positions of program leadership; preparing job descriptions for volunteer positions; recruiting volunteers; managing volunteers; and evaluating and recognizing the volunteer effort.

Ivan Scheier's essay, *"Building Staff/Volunteer Relations: Setting the Stage,"*[20] emphasizes the importance of preventing the development of tensions between staff and volunteers. "The co-existence of volunteers and staff in human service agencies is, with a few shining exceptions, like a marriage that hasn't settled down yet, after twenty-five years!" In the process of trying to retain volunteers, the work and achievements of the paid staff go unnoticed or underappreciated. Often, there is an underlying tension between staff and volunteers because two groups of people are trying to meet a variety of needs in many of the same ways. The tension may be aggravated by the attitude that the volunteers have all the answers. Scheier explores myths regarding volunteers and proposes a diagnostic approach to assist in the integration of volunteers and staff. "Look for subtler signs from staff. It's not so much active sabotage as passive resistance." Scheier's "Teamwork Checklist" for staff and volunteers (included in the reading) could be used as a diagnostic instrument. Overall response patterns and answers to individual questions can provide the focus for team-building, for other organizational improvement activities, and for developing volunteer program policies.

Notes

1. See "Giving Theories of the Nonprofit Sector," Part 9 in J. Steven Ott, ed., *The Nature of the Nonprofit Sector* (Boulder: Westview Press, 2001).

2. Jeffrey L. Brudney, *Fostering Volunteer Programs in the Public Sector* (San Francisco: Jossey-Bass, 1990).

3. Jeffrey L. Brudney, "Voluntarism," in J. M. Shafritz, ed., *International Encyclopedia of Public Policy and Administration* (Boulder: Westview Press, 1998), 2343.

4. Warren F. Ilchman, "Philanthropy," in J. M. Shafritz, ed., *International Encyclopedia of Public Policy and Administration* (Boulder: Westview, Press, 1998), 1654.

5. Ram A. Cnaan, Femida Handy, and Margaret Wadsworth, "Defining Who Is a Volunteer: Conceptual and Empirical Considerations," *Nonprofit and Voluntary Sector Quarterly* 25, no. 3 (September 1996): 364–383.

6. Ibid., 370.

7. Alan Wolfe, "What is Altruism?" in Walter W. Powell and Elisabeth S. Clemens, eds., *Private Action and the Public Good* (New Haven: Yale University Press, 1998), 36–45.

8. David C McClelland, *Human Motivation* (New York: Cambridge University Press, 1987).

9. Abraham Maslow, *Motivation and Personality* (New York: Harper & Row, 1954).

10. J. Steven Ott, "Perspectives on Organizational Governance: Some Effects on Government-Nonprofit Relations," *Southeastern Political Review* 21, no. 1 (winter 1993): 3–21.

11. Jone L. Pearce, *Volunteers: The Organizational Behavior of Unpaid Workers* (New York: Routledge, 1993).

12. Using McClelland's needs classifications of "power/influence," "achievement," and "affiliation."

13. Negligent recruiting, hiring, retention or supervision occurs when the organization knows its responsibility but fails to act to meet that responsibility. A variety of Circuit Court of Appeals and Supreme Court cases have upheld the responsibility of an organization for adhering to proper practices in these areas. See *Hartsell v. Duplex Products, Inc.* (4th Circuit, 1997), *SCI v Hartford Fire Ins.* (11th Circuit, 1998), *Burlington Industries, Inc. v. Ellerth*, 524 U. S. 742, 754 (1998), *Faragher v. Boca Raton*, 524 U. S. 775, 804, n. 4 (1998).

14. The concept of "knew or should have known" has origins in both tort and common law. Under common law, the concept *of respondeat superior* (let the master answer) held that the master was responsible for the actions of the apprentice because "he knew or should have known." (Black's Law Dictionary). Refer to such court cases as *United States v. Shearer,* 473 U.S. 52 (1985), *Sheridan v. United States,* 487 U.S. 392 (1988), *Brooks v. United States,* 337 U.S. 49 (1949), *Panella v. United States*, 216 F.2d 622 (CA2 1954), *Meritor Savings Bank v. Vinson,* 477 U.S. 57 (1986).

15. See Part 10, "The Blending and Blurring of the Three Sectors: Nonprofit, Government, and Business," and Part 11, "Challenges Facing the Nonprofit Sector," in J. Steven Ott, ed., *The Nature of the Nonprofit Sector* (Boulder: Westview Press, 2001).

16. Brudney, "Voluntarism," 2343–2349.

17. Many people also serve as volunteers in government organizations, including, for example, fire departments, schools, emergency medical services units, and libraries.

18. Jone L. Pearce, "Volunteers at Work," in J. L. Pearce, *Volunteers: The Organizational Behavior of Unpaid Workers* (London: Routledge, 1993), 3–14

19. Jeffrey L. Brudney, "Volunteer Administration," in Jay. M. Shafritz, ed., *International Encyclopedia of Public Policy and Administration* (Boulder: Westview Press, 1998), 2365–2372.

20. Ivan H. Scheier, "Setting the Stage," in I. H. Scheier, *Building Staff/Volunteer Relations* (Philadelphia: Energize, 1993), 3–11.

► CHAPTER 27

Voluntarism

JEFFREY L. BRUDNEY

Actions undertaken freely by individuals, groups, or organizations that are not compelled by biological need or social convention, mandated or coerced by government, or directed principally at financial or economic gain, regarded as beneficial by participants or the larger society.

As suggested by the complexity of this definition, the study of voluntarism is not for those who insist on precise terms, crisp distinctions, and tidy categories. Most research on the subject concentrates on either the organizational aspects of voluntarism, such as the origin, history, role, and management of not-for-profit institutions, or the voluntary behavior of individuals, particularly the motivations that lead people to donate their time and/or money to preferred causes, and the implications of such gifts for the giver and the recipient. The definition of voluntarism offered here embraces—and attempts to unify—both principal foci.

On the one hand, voluntarism encompasses behavior as micro and seemingly insignificant (from a societal point of view) as helping a friend move, leading a church choir, contributing time to a homeless shelter, or attending a meeting of an arts club or self-help group. It includes many thousands of informal groups and grassroots associations that may meet only spo-

radically, have no paid personnel, rarely accumulate a respectable treasury, and struggle merely to survive, let alone pursue objectives.

On the other hand, voluntarism is concerned with the founding, operation, governance, and impacts of many of America's preeminent educational, medical, and cultural institutions, which qualify as nonprofit organizations. Voluntarism is responsible for launching and sustaining vanguard social and political movements whose effects continue to reverberate in important areas, for example, civil rights, women's rights (and the women's suffrage movement that preceded it), consumer protection, environmental preservation, mental health, public health, progressive governmental reform, assistance for the needy, and numerous others (O'Neill 1989, pp. 9–122).

Voluntarism: Between Market and State

Voluntarism can be understood as individual, group, or organizational behavior located in that sizable chasm between the marketplace and economic enterprise on the one hand (business, commerce, profitmaking, and the like) and government and the state on the other (authority, law, compulsion, and so forth), outside of the family or household. Although huge in scope and importance, this sphere is typically characterized as a "residual" category, supplementing ("following") the two predominant sectors of society: the private (the market and economic gain) and the public (government and the force of law) (Wuthnow 1991, pp. 5–8; Van Til 1988, pp. ix–x, 5–6). The sector comprises a wide variety of institutions, such as charities, research institutes, religious organizations, private colleges and universities, cooperatives, associations, foundations, hospitals, day care centers, youth organizations, advocacy groups, neighborhood organizations, and many more yet the proportion of income generated by each of these sources has remained remarkably consistent (Hodgkinson et al. 1992, pp. 136–137, 150–151).

Magnitude of the Voluntary, Nonprofit Sector

In a similar way, the title "third" may give a misleading impression of insignificant size and status of the voluntary, nonprofit sector. To the contrary, according to O'Neill (1989, pp. 1–2), American nonprofit organizations employ more civilians than the federal and all state governments combined, and the yearly budget of the sector exceeds the budgets of all but seven nations in the world. The scale of nonprofit activity in this domain is almost as large as government activity as a whole, more than twice as large as the state and local government role alone, and 20 percent larger than the federal role alone.

As impressive as these statistics may be, David Horton Smith (1994b) argues persuasively that they still likely underestimate the extent of voluntarism in the United States. Because standards for official reporting by nonprofit organizations are based on revenue criteria and other formal measures, the figures reported here describe the wealthiest and largest entities, but may overlook at least 70 percent, if not more, of the voluntary sector (p. 12). Smith's analysis of what he terms "the rest of the nonprofit sector"—the huge number of locally based, volunteer-run, member-benefit, largely informal, grassroots associa-

tions not tapped by these statistics—suggests an even more robust presence. By his estimates, it contains 7.5 million associations, 124 million members, 98 million active members, 264 million memberships (members can belong to several groups simultaneously), and 28 billion hours of association activity per year.

Voluntarism and Individuals: Donating Money and Time

About three-fourths of American households make charitable contributions. Giving money and volunteering time are closely interrelated: People who make charitable contributions are much more likely to volunteer, and the incidence of volunteering increases dramatically with the percentage of income given (Hodgkinson and Weitzman 1994, pp. 27–30).

The study of volunteering behavior has stimulated considerable interest. Beginning in 1981, the INDEPENDENT SECTOR organization has commissioned a series of national surveys on volunteering in the United States, conducted at two-year intervals since 1985. Over this period, the percentage of Americans stating that they have spent time "working in some way to help others for no monetary pay . . . over the past twelve months" has hovered at around half the population. According to the results of the most recent survey at the time of this writing, in 1993, 47.7 percent of Americans volunteered an average of 4.2 hours per week. Projected to the population, these statistics indicate that nearly 90 million people (89.2 million) volunteer, the equivalent of about 9 million full-time employees (8,839,200). If the fortunate organizations that are the recipients of this labor had to pay for it, the price tag would have been a staggering US$182.3 billion (Hodgkinson and Weitzman 1994, p. 23).

Converted to a full-time equivalent basis, of all volunteer time contributed in 1989, 69 percent went to the nonprofit sector, which also accounted for a like percentage of all volunteer work assignments (66 percent). As Jeffrey Brudney (1990) has shown, U.S. governments are markedly dependent on volunteer labor as well, in service domains such as fire and public safety, culture and the arts, health and emergency medical, education and recreation, food and homelessness. In 1989, about one-quarter of all contributed time (26 percent) and 28 percent of volunteer work assignments went to government. For-profit firms are responsible for the remainder (about 6 percent of both volunteer time and assignments). Although the number of full-time equivalent volunteers as a proportion of total employment is negligible in the for-profit sector (far less than 1 percent), volunteers constitute 40.4 percent of total employment in the U.S. nonprofit sector and 10.2 percent in government (Hodgkinson et al. 1992, pp. 7, 18–19, 29).

Two recent studies, the doctoral dissertation of Gabriel Berger (1991) and a review article by Smith (1994a), attempt to synthesize the results of the voluminous research on the determinants of volunteering. Based on a 1990 national survey of giving and volunteering behavior in the United States, Berger (1991) concluded that the strongest factor leading one to volunteer is to have been the target of recruitment efforts, a finding corroborated in many other surveys (e.g., Hodgkinson and Weitzman 1994). He also found that making philanthropic contributions is closely associated with volunteering to organizations (see earlier). The level of formal education received is the individual characteristic with the strongest impact on volunteering. Smith (1994a) concurred with these findings and identified other variables important volunteering, such as higher socioeconomic status and participation in other forms of social activity. Smith's research also illustrates the complexity of volunteer behavior: A complete explanation must take into account the context or environment of the individual (e.g., size of community), the individual's social background (e.g., gender), personality (e.g., sense of efficacy), attitudes (e.g., liking volunteer work), situation (e.g., receiving services from the organization), and social participation (e.g., neighborhood interaction). While Smith's (1994a, p. 256) review shows that "we know a lot about why people participate in volunteer programs and voluntary associations," because studies have not been able to incorpo-

rate such an imposing range of variables, our understanding of volunteering behavior must be limited.

Conclusion: Toward Cross-National Comparison

Aside from findings from survey research strongly suggesting that rates and amounts of charitable giving and volunteering in the United States surpass those of other nations (Hodgkinson et al. 1992, pp. 50–52, 81–87), little firm knowledge seems to exist cross-nationally.

References

Berger, Gabriel, 1991. "Factors Explaining Volunteering for Organizations in General, and Social Welfare Organizations in Particular." Doctoral dissertation, Heller School of Social Welfare, Brandeis University.

Brudney, Jeffrey L., 1990. *Fostering Volunteer Programs in the Public Sector: Planning, Initiating, and Managing Voluntary Activities.* San Francisco, CA: Jossey-Bass.

Brudney, Jeffrey L., and Teresa K. Durden, 1993. "Twenty Years of the *Journal of Voluntary Action Research/Nonprofit and Voluntary Sector Quarterly:* An Assessment of Past Trends and future Directions." *Nonprofit and Voluntary Sector Quarterly,* vol. 22 (Fall) 207–218.

Cnaan, Ram A., and Peter D. Hall, 1994. "Book Reviews: *Government and the Third Sector: Emerging Relationships in Welfare States* and *The Nonprofit Sector in the Global Community: Voice from Many Nations." Nonprofit and Voluntary Sector Quarterly,* vol. 23 (Spring): 79–85.

Hodgkinson, Virginia A., and Murray S. Weitzman, 1994. *Giving and Volunteering in the United States: Findings from a National Survey, 1994 Edition.* Washington, D.C.: INDEPENDENT SECTOR.

Hodgkinson, Virginia A., Murray S. Weitzman, Christopher M. Toppe, and Stephen M. Noga, 1992. *Nonprofit Almanac, 1992–1993: Dimensions of the Independent Sector.* San Francisco, CA: Jossey-Bass.

Lohmann, Roger A., 1995. "Commons: Can This Be the Name of 'Thirdness'?" *Nonprofit and Voluntary Sector Quarterly,* vol. 24 (Spring): 25–29.

O'Neill, Michael, 1989. *The Third America: The Emergence of the Nonprofit Sector in the United States.* San Francisco, CA: Jossey-Bass.

Salamon, Lester M., 1992. *America's Nonprofit Sector: A Primer:* New York: Foundation Center.

Salamon, Lester M., and Helmut K. Anheier, 1992. "In Search of the Non-Profit Sector. I: The Question of Definitions." *Voluntas,* vol. 3 (August): 125–151.

Seibel, Wolfgang, and Helmut K. Anheier, 1990. "Sociological and Political Science Approaches to the Third Sector." In Helmut K. Anheier and Wolfgang Seibel, eds. *The Third Sector: Comparative Studies of Nonprofit Organizations.* Berlin, Germany: Walter de Gruyter.

Smith, David Horton, 1994a. "Determinants of Voluntary Association Participation and Volunteering: A Literature Review." *Nonprofit and Voluntary Sector Quarterly,* vol. 23 (Fall): 243–263.

_____, 1994b. "The Rest of the Nonprofit Sector: The Nature and Magnitude of Grassroots Associations in America." Paper presented at the Annual Meeting of the Association for Research on Nonprofit Organizations and Voluntary Action, Berkeley, CA, October 20–22.

Van Til, Jon, 1988. *Mapping the Third Sector: Voluntarism in a Changing Social Economy.* New York: Foundation Center.

Wuthnow, Robert, ed. 1991. *Between States and Markets: The Voluntary Sector in Comparative Perspective.* Princeton, NJ: Princeton University Press.

► CHAPTER 28

Volunteers at Work

JONE L. PEARCE

It's hard to say exactly why, they [volunteers] probably decide they are doing it for a good reason so they assume a positive attitude about it. If you are paid you probably don't question it, you just assume you are doing it for a living. Volunteers don't know why they are working; they don't know the answer. I guess they assume they do it because they want to do good. These assumptions lead to different ways of doing things. Not that paid people aren't cheerful; it's just that it's not needed.

(Volunteer in a non-sectarian food distribution program)

I see myself as a volunteer and do not feel that my work is judged in accordance with employee standards. As a volunteer, I tend to hand in my work when "my own free will" dictates that I should do so. If I felt that I were an employee of this organization then I would perform to the best of my ability. I believe that any organization, whether it is based on volunteer relationships or employee relationships, should be arranged in a manner whereby the volunteers felt their positions were as credible as working for an employee-based organization. . . . As a volunteer I accomplish assignments at my own free will, or I don't. It doesn't seem to matter to anyone whether the assignments are completed or not. The attitude is "do what you want" or "you're just a volunteer." I like to believe I am

more than a volunteer, but it is hard to convince myself otherwise. As a volunteer I feel as though I am "one of the millions" instead of an individual. If this organization wants to keep this staff it needs more rules, regulations, procedures, and incentives. Nothing can exist with "your own free will" as an objective or standard. It's not logical or ethical or rational.

(Volunteer reporter, college newspaper, written by respondent in space provided for open-ended comments, questionnaire)

We know very little about how and why individuals volunteer to work in organizations, and we know even less about how their efforts are organized and directed once they are at work. As these quotations suggest, this uncertainty is experienced by the participants as well as outside observers. We have all heard stories about (or have experienced) the acute frustrations of volunteering to help on a worthy project but finding either disorganization, frayed nerves, or situations in which good people somehow seem to exploit and insult one another. Yet there are millions of volunteer-staffed organizations which quietly and effectively provide invaluable services and promote significant societal change. Why such wide variation in organizational behavior?

This exploration begins by suggesting that a central theme to understanding volunteers' organizational behavior is uncertainty. This uncertainty is reflected in the efforts of the above volunteers to understand their own roles in their organizations, and their responses suggest the variety of understandings and potential frustration that this uncertainty elicits.

The study of uncertainty and of the related concept of ambiguity has long been prominent in organizational behavior; research in role ambiguity and task uncertainty continue to hold a prominent place in its theories (Dess and Beard 1984). Yet the uncertainty experienced by organizational volunteers is inherently more extensive and more central to their experiences than is the case for employees. Volunteers simply face less crystallized expectations about their behavior, purposes, and affective reactions than do paid workers. This stems from the uncertain role of voluntary organizational work in society and from the conflicting or vague purposes of many of these organizations.

The uncertainty individual volunteers face originates, in part, with the societal role of volunteers' organizations. Their organizations vary widely—including self-help groups, political parties, large social welfare institutions, advocacy associations, youth clubs, and so forth. These organized bodies have always fascinated social philosophers and students of social institutions, since they seem to hold great symbolic power to represent freedom from coercion, whether it be from the constraints of family and tradition, the state, or the economic pressures of employment. The "free" character of volunteer-staffed organizations seems to invite social theorists to see them as reflections of the true nature of a society. Thus, volunteers' associations have been praised and condemned, held as examples of virtually every moral or ideological position. Tocqueville's (1968, 1835–40) observation that voluntary associations represent a fundamental characteristic of Americans is one of the earliest and most widely known. This view of associations as representatives of societal character persists (as is reflected, for example, in McPherson and Smith-Lovin 1986).

Thus, volunteer organizational effort is not as constrained as paid work. Volunteers are free to adopt objectives and to organize themselves in any way that suits the participants. Yet, while this

may be ideologically attractive, it poses serious practical problems for the participants. Guiding constraints from other settings, such as "efficiency" for business or "voters' preferences" in governmental organizations, simply do not apply. If volunteers are going to work in an integrated and organized fashion to achieve their goals, they need to find procedures by which they can insure that sufficient and appropriate individual behavior is harnessed. This work reports how this is accomplished in a particular set of organizations.

In addition to the question of the integration of volunteers' actions into organized behavior, we also know very little about volunteers' experience of work life. We do not know why they are attracted to such work or their reactions to their organizations once they have joined. The work life of employees has drawn extensive attention, yet research and theory concerning the psychological and social experiences of volunteers in organizations have been modest and fragmented. Social theorists have assumed that experiences as a volunteer have powerful effects on the volunteers and their larger society, but exactly how this influence occurs is rarely addressed.

Furthermore, a thoughtful study of organizational volunteers raises questions that are central to theories concerning organizational behavior of employees. Volunteers, as organizational members, differ from employees in several fundamental respects, and, as will be detailed below, the traditional focus on employees as representatives of all organizational workers has occasionally resulted in misleading interpretations. In brief, in organizational behavior, employees' status as "organizational workers" and "wage/salary earners" has been confounded. It will be suggested that many features of the organizational behavior of employees and their work which we have assumed to be universal are influenced in important ways by their status as "employees." For example, volunteers provide a valuable opportunity to study the advantages and disadvantages of harnessing nonmonetary controls for organizational reward systems. A thoughtful examination of the organizational behavior of volunteers can help extend our understanding of

such concepts as organizational design, the role
of individual motives and attitudes, the exercise
of interpersonal influence, and the role of pay in
organizational behavior. Thus, an understanding
of volunteer organizational behavior can serve as
a mirror that provides a reflection on and, it is
hoped, a contribution to general theories of organization behavior.

A clearer understanding of the organizational
behavior of volunteers is also important because
volunteer workers are a force in their own right.
Virtually all of the readers of this book and most
of the people they know have worked as organizational volunteers at some time in their lives.

Certainly, all members of society benefit from
the unpaid labor of many volunteers. A clearer
understanding of how volunteers can more successfully organize themselves in the face of uncertainty has both practical and theoretical import.

Theoretical Overview

The fundamental difference between volunteers
and employees is that volunteers receive no financial remuneration for their organizational
work. This is a simple difference and may initially seem to be relatively small, given the very
significant differences in the roles of members
within a single organization and the great variety of tasks and environments facing organizations. Further, many in the human relations tradition have argued that money really is not a
very significant force affecting workers' actions
in organizations. For example, Herzberg, Mausner, and Snyderman (1959) argued that pay was
a mere "hygiene" and not a "motivator" of work
performance. Yet, it will be suggested here that
this difference in mode of compensation appears to have quite profound effects on how the
work is structured for these different kinds of
workers, on their own and others' expectations
concerning their actions in the workplace, and
even on how they are expected to think and feel
about their organization and its work. This absence of pay for organizational work seems to
remove a psychologically important rationale
and, therefore, creates uncomfortable disso-
nance for participants and observers. The disso-
nance is resolved through explanations that do

not depend on money, but the indeterminacy
and ideological character of these explanations
do not fully resolve the uncertainty. The reasons
for these pronounced defining features of pay
are interesting. The theoretical arguments are
introduced by a brief outline of some of the psychological, social, and structural effects of working without wages.

The uncertainty volunteers face can be
framed by drawing on Barker's (Barker 1968;
Barker and Gump 1964) concept of "behavior
setting." Such settings are "time-place-thing" mi-
lieus with their own attendant social meanings.
Barker and his colleagues hold that behavior settings "coerce" behavior, that is, they provide
more uniformity and predictability in a set of
individuals than do the differing characteristics
of the individuals. This work is an attempt to
discover and to articulate the particular situational demands upon organizational volunteers
and to reflect, indirectly, on the distinct demands upon employees. The features of organizational volunteers' settings that seem to be
most important are introduced below.

The Meaning of Volunteer Work

Volunteers are seen as occupying a fundamentally uncertain societal position. In contrast to
volunteers, employees have very visible incentives, and so society tends to believe that it
knows what they are. (That employees cannot,
in practice, be reduced to simple "economic individuals" is virtually the defining characteristic
of organizational behavior as a field.) However,
organizational volunteering is inherently contradictory in nature. It is "work"—working
within a formal structure to provide a service to
others—and it is a "leisure activity"—something
done whenever convenient because it is person-
ally rewarding. The problems caused by facile
assumptions about the motives of employees
have been well documented, but the difficulties
for volunteers are in many respects more basic.

The problems of volunteers' limited time, uncertain motives, and a high degree of individual
independence can result in debilitating levels of
uncertainty for organizational volunteers. Volunteers need to adopt a shared "definition of the situation" before they can take action. Within a sin-

gle organization different members may hold conflicting definitions of volunteer work—some that it is something to do when in the mood, others that it is work that must be conducted in a "businesslike" manner—and the ease of exit means that differences of opinion about these assumptions can lead to organizational dissolution.

This lack of clear definition extends to the mixed messages volunteers receive about the value of their work. On the one hand, their efforts are degraded by expressions such as "you get what you pay for," and "if society really wanted it done, it would pay for it." Yet volunteers are also virtuous, self-sacrificial contributors—"givers" not "takers." Without the concrete crutch of "working for a living," volunteers are suspect: they are too autonomous and, therefore, cannot be made reliable; they have no visible "payoff" and, so, are not predictable; they must have hidden, "selfish" reasons for working and, so, are hypocrites. Under these circumstances, it is not surprising that practitioner writings concerned with volunteers take on such normative and crusading tones. This inherent feature of volunteer work sets the context in which volunteer organizational behavior takes place.

Volunteers' Jobs

Volunteer work tends to be structured differently than the work of employees. Research evidence presented here suggests that the jobs and relations between jobs are different than the jobs of employees working on the same organizational tasks. For example, volunteer work is usually done part-time, often just a few hours a month. It is a spare-time "leisure activity." Without paying these workers, the organization usually cannot expect more than a few hours per week or month from them. Therefore, work must be broken up into small part-time pieces. This leads to different interaction patterns among workers and to a need for additional coordination positions. Further, volunteers simply do not spend as much time at their work and with their co-workers as most employees do. This leads to a social network structure in which a central person or people (the "core membership") interact(s) with all other individuals (the

"periphery"), who interact only with the core members. This division between core and periphery is not based directly on formal organizational authority as are the divisions in bureaucratic organizations, but on personal characteristics, such as level of commitment to the organization. In contrast, linkages among full-time employees tend to be much more extensive (they know more people) and stronger (they know them well).

In addition, volunteers, since they are unpaid, are all "paid" equally and relatively cheaply, and so there is little economic reason to differentiate among them. For many volunteer-staffed organizations, this results, for example, in a less compelling need to keep clear records of who is a worker, a client, or occasional helper, since there is no risk of mistakenly paying a nonworker. Thus, there is little need to make the fine status distinctions characteristic of many employee-staffed organizations. Despite the attractiveness of these egalitarian workplace structures, they occasionally contributed to uncertainty in organizational responsibility in several sampled organizations. This can lead to the "chaotic" character of many organizations that are staffed and run by volunteers.

Unpaid Labor

Volunteers have no direct monetary reason for joining or staying with the organization. This creates unique pressures both for volunteers and for organizations that rely on volunteer labor. As noted above, volunteer motives are uncertain; they do not have the clear and compelling "reason" for working that employees can always claim. Why, then, do they work? This central uncertainty of volunteer motivation has led to the largest body of academic research on volunteers, and it has spawned a lively debate among those concerned with the motivation of volunteers. For example, what is the role of altruism in volunteering? Is altruism simply a socially acceptable explanation for a process that often is not subject to careful rational calculation?

Additional insight into volunteer motivation can be gleaned from the fact that substantial numbers of volunteers are recruited through personal contacts, and volunteers are significantly more likely than employees to report that friendly co-workers are important in their decisions to remain with their organizations. That is, social contacts seem to be more important for volunteers than for employees, or at least important in different ways.

The fact of volunteers' unpaid labor also leads to a different pattern of affective reactions to the workplace. There is also substantial uncertainty about the meaning of one of the most consistently supported empirical findings: that volunteers have significantly more positive workplace attitudes than do employees. Further, there is evidence that volunteers may not engage in an elaborate rational analysis of their options before joining, but "try on" the work and decide later whether or not they want to stay. Thus, volunteering appears to be a less behaviorally committing act than taking a paid job. This tentativeness about the act of volunteering leads to multiple interpretations about volunteers' more positive attitudes. The first interpretation is that, since volunteers receive little extrinsic gain, they must have joined because of their positive feelings about the work itself, the organization, its mission, or the other people involved. Alternatively, volunteers could experience insufficient justification for their work and, therefore, attribute positive attitudes or a high degree of intrinsic motivation to themselves to justify their actions. The role of attributions in employees' attitudes is attracting increasing interest, and volunteers provide a unique opportunity for analyses of the attributional processes in attitude formation.

Workplace Independence

This lack of concrete committing mechanisms for volunteer workers has wider implications than simple uncertainty about volunteer motivation and attitudes. It creates an additional difficulty for those who are responsible for directing and coordinating their work: volunteers are not as dependent on their organizations as are many employees. Therefore, they are free to work in a much more independent and even idiosyncratic manner. Since there are very few "carrots" and virtually no meaningful "sticks,"

the control of volunteers' actions is quite uncertain. Yet volunteer workers do perform reliably for many organizations, and they do submit to influence; volunteer workers are very rarely "out of control."

Many have speculated about how such control can be maintained, suggesting that selective recruitment, symbolic rewards, manipulation of social influence, and the ability of organizational leaders to make the values of the organization salient to members predominate. These ideas have all been offered by sociological theorists of voluntary organizations, and so these arguments rarely are accompanied by analyses of the actual social influence at the interpersonal level. Further, available data on interpersonal influence among volunteers suggests that the process is more complex. For example, results reported here suggest that volunteers have significantly more potential influence in their organizations than do comparable employees, but that most volunteers seek to avoid the actual exercise of influence. Therefore, evidence from this study suggests that volunteers are brought into the system of organizational behavior through combinations of formal bureaucratic requirements and direct interpersonal influences.

References

Barker, Roger G. (1968). *Ecological Psychology.* Stanford, CA: Stanford University Press.

Barker, Roger G., and Paul V. Gump (1964). *Big School, Small School.* Stanford, CA: Stanford University Press.

Dess, G.G., and D.W. Beard (1984). "Dimensions of Organizational Task Environments." *Administrative Science Quarterly,* 20, 613–29.

Herzberg, F., B. Mausner, and B.B. Snyderman (1959). *The Motivation to Work.* New York: Wiley.

McPherson, J.M., and Lynn Smith-Lovin (1986). "Sex Segregation." *American Sociological Review,* 51 (1), 61–79.

Tocqueville, Alexis. (1968). *Democracy in America.* New York: Washington Square Press (first published in 1835–40).

CHAPTER 29

Volunteer Administration

JEFFREY L. BRUDNEY

The profession concerned with the study and practice of integrating volunteers effectively and ethically into an organization to enhance performance and results.

Each day, countless volunteers stream into the offices of a huge number of organizations. They settle into their places and begin to perform jobs that contribute substantially not only to the internal operations of the agency but also the delivery of goods and services to clients and constituents. Although these citizens are not compensated monetarily, their donations of time and talents can dramatically affect the efficiency and effectiveness of the organization, as well as the capability to attend to needy clientele.

Such a smooth integration of volunteers into the workplace does not happen by accident or without considerable planning and preparation on the part of the sponsoring organization. As societies have grown increasingly dependent on volunteer labor to meet popular demands for goods and services, especially those provided by government and nonprofit organizations, a profession has emerged concerned with introducing unpaid citizens and sustaining their constructive participation. The field of volunteer administration is dedicated to the effective, ethical involvement of volunteers for the benefit of host organizations, their clientele, and the volunteers themselves.

Volunteer Administration as a Profession

Research studies, reaction, and commentary, have gradually culminated in a well-accepted approach for structuring and managing volunteer programs to achieve service quality and effectiveness. Although just as in the study of private management, not all authorities concur on every particular, sufficient agreement has been attained to present requisites for a successful, organization-based volunteer effort. These components are elaborated in the following section.

Headquartered in Boulder, Colorado, the Association for Volunteer Administration (AVA) is the leading professional association in the field. AVA conducts a variety of professional development activities: The association holds an annual international conference on volunteer administration as well as numerous regional meetings, publishes a quarterly journal (*Journal of Volunteer Administration*) and newsletter (*Update*), establishes and promulgates standards of ethical conduct as well as areas of competency for practitioners in the field, and awards a performance-based "Certificate in Volunteer Administration" (CVA).

An AVA committee found that 56 institutions of higher education in the United States and

Canada offer coursework in volunteer administration; 88 percent of the schools offer 18 or
more hours of classroom instruction on the
topic (Stringer 1993).

Findings from a major survey of AVA members
further substantiate the trend toward greater professionalization (Brudney, Love and Yu,
1993–1994) completed by two-thirds of the membership, the mail survey showed that most of these
officials have high levels of formal education: Over
one-half have graduated college and another one-
quarter have earned a master's degree or more.
They profess great interest in continuing education in volunteer administration, especially advanced training; 65 percent had attended a training program in the previous year. Most hold
full-time positions in volunteer administration
and devote well over half their scheduled hours to
this responsibility. They tend to believe that a college degree is necessary to perform their job effectively and report that they find at least some time
during the week to keep up with research in the
field. A solid majority claimed volunteer administration as their primary occupation and stated
their intention to remain in the field.

Essential Components of
Volunteer Administration

Volunteer administrators go by a variety of titles, including volunteer coordinator and director of volunteer services. In many organizations,
officials in departments of personnel or human
resources who also deal with paid employees are
responsible for the volunteers. Regardless of job
title, the volunteer administrator attends to the
design, implementation, management, and evaluation of the volunteer program. These programs are intended to facilitate and coordinate
the work of volunteers and paid staff members
toward the attainment of agency goals. The essential components of volunteer administration
are as follows (Brudney 1994):

1. establishing the rationale for volunteer involvement;
2. involving paid staff in volunteer program design;

3. integrating the volunteer program into the organization;
4. creating positions of program leadership;
5. preparing job descriptions for volunteer positions;
6. recruiting volunteers;
7. managing volunteers;
8. evaluating and recognizing the volunteer effort.

Establishing the Rationale for
Volunteer Involvement

The first step in creating a volunteer program is
to determine the purposes underlying citizen
participation. Although well-intentioned, pre-
mature efforts to enlist volunteers to "help" often turn out to be damaging instead: They raise
apprehensions of paid staff members, who may
question the need for volunteers, and frustrate
volunteers, who may wonder precisely what jobs
they are needed to perform and why. This scenario must be avoided.

The foundation for a successful volunteer
program rests on a deliberate consideration by
the agency of the rationale for citizen involvement and the development of explicit policy and
procedures to guide this effort. Especially in
times of fiscal stringency, top organizational officials may seize on economic motivations, such
as "cost savings," as the principal reason for introducing volunteers. However, since a volunteer
program requires expenditures of its own (for
example, for recruitment, orientation, training,
reimbursement, promotion, materials, and so
forth), the goal is misleading. A more accurate
description of the economic benefits of a volunteer program is "cost effectiveness." A well-de-
signed program that supplements or complements the work of paid staff with that of citizens
can help an agency to hold costs down in achieving a given level of service or to increase the services provided for a fixed level of expenditure
(Brudney 1990; Karn 1983, 1982–1983).

A significant strength of a volunteer program
is the variety of additional purposes that it
might serve for an organization. For example,
agency leadership may enlist volunteers to inter-

ject a more vibrant dimension of commitment and caring into its relationships with clients. Or, the goal may be to learn more about the community, nurture closer ties to the citizenry, and renew public awareness and support. Volunteers may be needed to reach clients inaccessible through normal organizational channels, that is, to engage in "outreach." They may be called upon to provide professional skills, such as computer programming, legal counsel, or accounting expertise, not readily available to an agency. The purpose may be to staff an experimental program otherwise doomed to fiscal austerity. Organizations often seek volunteers to assist with fund-raising (Hodgkinson, Weitzman, Toppe, and Noga 1992, p. 46). Enhancing responsiveness to client groups may offer yet another rationale.

Prior to recruiting volunteers, organizational leaders should decide on the appropriate goals for citizen involvement. An explicit statement of goals is useful for several reasons. First it begins to define the types of volunteer positions that will be needed and the number of individuals required to fill them. Second, it aids in delineating concrete objectives against which the program might be evaluated, once in operation. Finally, a statement of the philosophy underlying volunteer participation and the specific ends sought can help to alleviate possible anxiety on the part of paid staff members—especially if they are included in planning and development of the volunteer program.

Involving Paid Staff in Volunteer Program Design

Although the support of top organizational officials is crucial to the establishment and vitality of a volunteer program (for example, Ellis 1986; Scheier 1981), paid staff and volunteers, if they are already known to the agency or can be identified, should also be involved in defining its mission, philosophy, and procedures. Involvement adds to the knowledge base for crafting policy and inculcates a sense of ownership and commitment instrumental to gaining acceptance for innovation. Because the incorporation

of volunteers into an agency can impose dramatic changes in work life, the participation of paid staff is especially important. The sharing of needs, perspectives, and information among agency leadership, employees, and prospective volunteers that ensues is crucial to determining how the volunteer program might be most effectively designed, organized, and managed to further attainment of agency goals.

Planning meetings and discussions should yield policies and procedures governing the involvement of volunteers. Agency guidelines for the program should address the central aspects of volunteer participation, including attendance and absenteeism, performance review, benefits, grievance procedures, reimbursement for expenses, confidentiality requirements, probationary acceptance period, suspension and termination, and record keeping. Steve McCurley and Rick Lynch (1989, p. 22) advised that in all areas these policies should be as comparable as possible to the respective guidelines for paid employees.

Explicit policies for the volunteer program demonstrate that the agency takes citizen participation seriously and values that contribution of volunteers. By setting the standards as high for volunteers as for paid staff, as agency builds trust and credibility, increased respect and requests for volunteers from employees, a healthy work environment, and, perhaps most important, high quality services (for example, McCurley and Lynch 1989; Wilson 1984). The guidelines should be published in a manual distributed to all volunteers and paid staff members expected to work with them. A volunteer manual greatly facilitates managing for consistent results and handling problem situations, should they arise.

Although volunteers may not be known to the agency at the time of program formation and, thus, not involved in initial discussions concerning planning and design, once this effort is launched and in operation, they should definitely have input into major decisions affecting the program. Just as for paid employees, citizen volunteers are more likely to invest in and commit to organizational policies, and provide useful information for this purpose, if they enjoy ready access to the decisionmaking process.

Integrating the Volunteer Program into the Organization

In order to sustain citizen involvement, an organization must integrate the volunteer program into its structure and operations. A small nonprofit agency may accommodate one or several volunteers with few if any structural modifications, but larger organizations should consider alternative structural arrangements for integrating volunteers. In order of increasing comprehensiveness, these arrangements consist of ad hoc volunteer efforts, volunteer recruitment by an outside organization with the agency otherwise responsible for management (the "contract" model), decentralization of the program to operating departments, and a centralized approach.

Ad Hoc Volunteerism

Volunteer involvement may arise spontaneously to meet exigencies confronting an organization, especially on a short-term basis. Normally, citizens motivated to share their background, training, skills, and energy with organizations that could benefit by them are the catalyst. The responsiveness and alacrity with which an ad hoc volunteer effort can be mobilized are inspiring. Frequently, crisis and emergency situations provoke a spectacular response, arousing vast numbers of citizens to action in a remarkably short time.

Such spontaneous help can infuse vitality (and labor) into an agency and alert officials to the possibilities of volunteerism. Despite this advantage, only selected parts or members of the organization may be aware of an ad hoc citizen effort and, thus, be able to avail themselves of it. In addition, because energy levels and zeal wane as emergencies are tamed or fade from the limelight of publicity, the ad hoc model is quite vulnerable to the passage of time. A volunteer program requires not only an ongoing, rather than a sporadic, commitment from citizens, but also an organizational structure to sustain their contributions and make them accessible throughout the organization.

The Contract Model

A second option sometimes open to agencies is to rely on the expertise and reputation of an established organization, such as a volunteer center or clearing house, to assist in the recruitment of volunteers but to retain all other managerial responsibilities internally. Since recruitment is the most fundamental program function, professional assistance can be highly beneficial, particularly for an agency just starting a volunteer program. Some business firms seeking to develop volunteer programs in the community for their employees have extended this model: They contract with volunteer centers not only for recruitment but also other program functions, for example, placement and evaluation of volunteers (Haran, Kenney, and Vermilion 1993).

Decentralized Program

A volunteer program can be decentralized to individual departments in an organization. The primary advantage of this approach is the flexibility to tailor programs to the needs of specific organizational units and to introduce volunteers where support for them is greatest. Unfortunately, duplication of effort across several departments, difficulties in locating sufficient expertise in volunteer management to operate multiple programs, problems in coordination across programs, and higher overall costs pose significant liabilities. Nevertheless, under the right circumstances, the decentralized approach can work admirably, for example, in starting a pilot or experimental volunteer program that might eventually be expanded to the rest of the organization. Alternatively, a lack of tasks appropriate for volunteers in some parts of the agency or, perhaps, strong opposition from various quarters may confine voluntary assistance to selected departments.

Centralized Program

The final structural arrangement is a centralized volunteer program serving the entire agency. With this approach, a single office or department is responsible for management and coordination of the program; volunteers are deployed and supervised in departments throughout the organization. The volunteer office provides guidelines, technical assistance, recruitment, screening, training, placement, and all other administration. The advantages of centralization for averting duplication of effort, assigning volunteers so as to meet their needs as well as those of the organization, and producing efficient and effective voluntary services are considerable. Yet, the approach demands broad support across the organization, especially at the top, to overcome any objections that may be raised or limitation in resources. When such backing is not forthcoming, the other structural arrangements can serve an agency quite well.

Creating Positions of Program Leadership

Regardless of the structural arrangement by which the volunteer program is integrated into the agency, the program requires a recognized leader. Just as any other manager, the volunteer coordinator (or administrator) should be a paid position. This designation sends a powerful message to other managers and employees regarding the significance and value organizational leadership places on the volunteer component. For the same reason, the position should be located as close as feasible to the apex of the agency's formal hierarchy. The volunteer administrator should enjoy prerogatives and responsibilities commensurate with positions at the same hierarchical level, including participation in relevant decision-and policymaking and access to superiors.

The volunteer coordinator has many key duties. The position bears accountability for the volunteer program, presents a focal point for contact with the program for those inside as well as outside the organization, and rewards the officeholder in relation to the success of the volunteers. As chief advocate of the program, the coordinator endeavors to express the volunteer perspective, allay any apprehensions of employees, and facilitate collaboration between paid and unpaid personnel. The incumbent repre-

sents the volunteers before the organization, promotes their interests, and builds and maintains the program.

The volunteer coordinator is responsible for recruitment and publicity, a critical function requiring active outreach in the community and highly flexible working hours. The incumbent communicates with department and organizational officials to ascertain their requirements for voluntary assistance, this task is not a one-time exercise, but an ongoing responsibility that changes with the needs and demands of the various units. The coordinator interviews and screens all applicants for volunteer positions, maintains appropriate records, places volunteers in job assignments, assists employees with supervision, and monitors, evaluates, and recognizes volunteer performance. This official must hammer the bewildering array of backgrounds, preferences, and time availabilities brought by volunteers into a workable schedule for the agency. The coordinator is responsible for orientation and training of the volunteers; since employees are often unfamiliar with the approach, the coordinator must arrange for training for them as well. Given these demands, as a volunteer program increases in size, the coordinator should plan to delegate some of these duties to volunteers and/or paid staff members.

Preparing Job Descriptions for Volunteer Positions

The essential building block of a successful volunteer program is the job description. In allocating job tasks to volunteers, the overriding consideration is that work assignments reflect the unique capabilities that citizens and employees might bring toward the realization of organizational goals.

As described above, the process of sharing the work-place begins at the program planning stage, when top agency officials and employees (and, if possible, volunteers) meet to work out explicit understandings regarding the rationale for the participation of volunteers, the nature of the jobs they are to perform, and appropriate policies and procedures governing involvement.

These meetings should result in agreements concerning the types of jobs to be assigned to volunteers and those to be retained by paid staff. In conjunction with planning meetings, organizations might also conduct a survey of employees or personal interviews with them to help prepare for volunteer involvement. At a minimum, the survey should ascertain those aspects of the job that employees most enjoy performing, those that they dislike, and those for which they lack sufficient time or expertise. Organizations have enjoyed success delegating to volunteers job tasks with the following characteristics (Ellis 1986, pp. 89–90):

1. tasks performed periodically, such as once a week, rather than on a daily or inflexible basis;
2. tasks that do not require the specialized training or expertise of paid personnel;
3. tasks that might be done more effectively by someone with special training in that skill;
4. tasks for which employees feel uncomfortable or unprepared;
5. tasks for which agency does not possess in-house expertise.

This process should culminate in a set of job descriptions for volunteers based on extant organizational needs and citizen talents and backgrounds. The objective is to achieve an effective deployment of paid and unpaid personnel. As changing organizational conditions warrant, and/or recruitment efforts flag, the job descriptions should be updated. To prevent conflict, organizational policy must firmly state that neither volunteers nor employees will occupy the positions reserved for the other.

Because volunteers will need the same information as paid staff to determine whether a position is of interest, the respective job descriptions should be analogous. Specifications for volunteer positions should include job title and purpose, responsibilities and activities, qualifications and time commitment, reporting relationships and supervision, and benefits and obligations. The volunteer coordinator uses the job descriptions as a basis to recruit potential volunteers, screen them for relevant competencies and interests, conduct an interview with applicants, and place them in suitable positions with the in-

tent of matching citizen needs with those of the organization.

Recruiting Volunteers

Although job descriptions for volunteer positions greatly facilitate the recruitment process, attracting citizens for service roles may well pose the most significant challenge to organizations attempting the approach. Surveys of volunteer coordinators bear out this conclusion (Brudney 1990; Duncombe 1985). In some service domains, potential volunteers have proven sufficiently scarce or resistant to calls for assistance that it can actually prove cost-effective to hire paid personnel instead (Brudney and Duncombe 1992).

Given the centrality of recruitment to a thriving volunteer program, voluminous literature has addressed the problem and suggested potent strategies to surmount it (for example, Brudney 1995; Ellis 1994). As astute volunteer coordinators have learned, depending upon organizational needs, these techniques can be used selectively or in combination.

Job design strategies focus on meeting volunteers' needs and motivations through the content and variety of the work they are asked to perform, as well as offering greater responsibility for those volunteers who seek it. Human capital strategies place interested volunteers in positions to acquire contacts, training, and references that will increase their market value for paid employment. Ceremonial strategies present volunteers the opportunity to work with important policymaking bodies (commissions, boards, and other institutions), meet elected officials, and receive public recognition for service. Organizational change and development strategies concentrate on building an organizational culture receptive to volunteer involvement. Flexibility strategies attempt to adapt the agency to volunteer involvement, for example, by establishing volunteer jobs that can be performed outside the agency or tasks and assignments that are conducive to group-based volunteering (for example, by the family, religious congregation, or work unit or organization). Facilitation strategies increase the pool of volunteers by such practices as allowing citizen participation during nontraditional working hours and reimbursing all out-of-pocket expenses of volunteers (for example, child care). Outreach strategies also aim to enlarge the pool by publicizing the volunteer program at the workplace, school, church, synagogue, neighborhood group, civic and other associations, and so forth.

Managing Volunteers

Managing volunteers is, perhaps, the most delicate aspect of the volunteer administrator's job. Volunteers are much less dependent on the organization than are paid employees: They can almost always leave the organization and find comparable opportunities for (donating) their labor with far less effort and inconvenience than can an employee who must have remuneration. As a result, managers do not have as much control over volunteer workers.

These differences in control help to explain some oftnoted characteristics of volunteers in the workplace. Volunteers can afford to be more selective in accepting job assignments. They may insist on substantial flexibility in work hours. They may not be as faithful in observance of agency rules and regulations, particularly those they deem burdensome or "red tape." Part of the reason may stem from the fact that nearly all who volunteer do so on a part-time basis and, thus, can be expected to have less information about organizational policy and procedures. Social interaction is part of the fun and spark of volunteering, and participants may place high value on this feature of the experience.

Given the relative autonomy of volunteers, a traditional approach to management and supervision can be expected to elicit antagonism and turnover rather than productivity and compliance. Standard organizational inducements for paid employees, such as pay, promotion, and perquisites, are not operative for volunteers. Similarly, conventional organizational sanctions are likely to prove abortive (for example, referring a problem to hierarchical superiors for resolution or disciplinary action, or threatening to do so.)

By contrast, effective management of volunteers rests on applying different techniques and

incentives than commonly used for paid employees to motivate and direct work behaviors toward agency goals. Managerial investment in building trust, cooperation, teamwork, challenge, growth, achievement, values, excitement, commitment, and empowerment are much more practical strategies for this purpose than are the conventional methods. Interestingly, as contemporary management theorists have noted, the best-run commercial enterprises use these same techniques for paid personnel to yield impressive benefits and profits (Daft 1995).

To achieve success, a volunteer program must do more than promote changes in managerial style, however. It must also institute to facilitate volunteer supervision. An effective program channels talents and energies productively through such mechanisms as guidelines for volunteer involvement, formal job descriptions for volunteer positions, and interviews and careful placement of applicants. These measures help to define what volunteer service means to the agency and to citizens and to coordinate the needs and motives of both parties. Probably no factor aids more in supervising volunteers (and paid staff) than placing them in positions where they can put their strongest motivations and best skills to work.

Evaluating and Recognizing the Volunteer Effort

Organizations that rely on the assistance of volunteers may be reluctant to appear to question through evaluation the worth or impact of well-intentioned helping efforts. Nevertheless, for individual volunteers, the employees expected to work with them, and for the volunteer operation as a whole, evaluation and recognition activities are essential program functions.

Evaluation and Recognition of Volunteers

Volunteers have cogent reasons to view personnel assessment in a favorable light. A powerful motivation for volunteering is to achieve worthwhile and visible results; evaluation of performance can guide volunteers toward improvement on this dimension. No citizen contributes time to have the labor wasted in misdirected activity or to repeat easily remedied mistakes and misjudgments. Moreover, for many who contribute their time, volunteering offers an opportunity to acquire or hone desirable job skills and/or to build an attractive résumé for paid employment. To deny constructive feedback to those who give their time for organizational purposes, and who could benefit from this knowledge and hope to do so, is a disservice to the volunteer.

Normally, the volunteer coordinator will prepare the evaluation of performance; the evaluation should be conducted at regular intervals. To complement this agency-based perspective, volunteers might evaluate their own accomplishments and experience. The self-assessment should tap volunteer satisfaction with important facets of the agency work assignment, including job duties, schedule, support, training, supervision, opportunities for personal growth, and so on. Whatever the format, the goal of the evaluation is to ascertain the degree to which the needs and expectations of the volunteer and the agency have been met so that job assignments can be continued, amended, or redefined as necessary.

Agency officials might recognize and show their appreciation to volunteers through a great variety of activities: award or social events (luncheons, banquets, ceremonies), media attention (newsletters, newspapers), certificates (for tenure or special achievement), expansion of opportunities (for learning, training, management), and personal expressions of gratitude from employees or clients. A heart-felt "thank you" can be all the acknowledgment many volunteers want or need. Others require more formal recognition. The volunteer coordinator should make letters of recommendation available to all volunteers who request them. Recognition is a highly variable activity that, optimally, should be tailored to the wants and needs of individual volunteers.

Evaluation and Recognition of Employees

In general, volunteer-based services require the participation of not only citizens but also paid

staff. If organizational leaders want volunteers and employees to work as partners in service delivery, program functions of evaluation and recognition should apply to both members of the team. Although frequently neglected in job analysis, employees expected to work with volunteers should have pertinent responsibilities written into their job descriptions and be held accountable for performance. Just as demonstrated talent in this dimension should be encouraged and rewarded, an employee's resistance to volunteers, or poor work record with them, should not go overlooked and, implicitly, condoned in the review. As necessary, the organization should support training activities for paid staff to develop competencies in volunteer administration.

Recognition activities for employees should follow evaluation. Like volunteers, paid staff value recognition, especially when awards ceremonies, social events, media coverage, agency publications, and the like bring their efforts and accomplishments with volunteers to the attention of organizational leadership. By taking seriously the evaluation and recognition of paid staff with regard to their collaboration with volunteers, agency officials provide incentives for an effective partnership.

Evaluation and Recognition of the Volunteer Program

The primary goals of a volunteer program are to improve agency operations, exert a positive effect on the environment, and better the circumstances of agency clients. Periodically, agencies that mobilize volunteers should undergo evaluation of the impact or progress registered by this component.

The volunteer coordinator should consider several valuable types of program evaluation. The most common is a compilation of the number of volunteers who have assisted the organization, the hours they have contributed, and the amount of client contacts or visits they have made. Many agencies go a step further by calculating the "equivalent dollar value" of the services donated by volunteers, based on the market price the organization would otherwise have to pay to employed personnel to accomplish the same tasks (for example, Karn 1983, 1982–1983).

A second type of evaluation of the volunteer program is an impact analysis. With this method, the volunteer coordinator assesses the outcomes of the program against its stated goals or mission. The analysis should review the aggregate performance and effects of the volunteers in assisting clients, addressing community problems, expediting agency operations, and meeting other objectives. Often, monetary costs are weighed against program results, as in a "cost-effectiveness" or "cost-benefit" analysis.

A third type of assessment is a process evaluation. This approach attempts to determine that procedures to meet essential program functions, such as recruitment, training, and orientation, are in place and operating effectively. Additionally, the evaluation should attempt to gauge the satisfaction of volunteers and paid staff members with the program, as well as their perceptions concerning its impact on clients and the external environment. By detecting, diagnosing, and ameliorating operational problems, a process evaluation can further the objectives of the volunteer program.

Conclusion

Volunteer administration is a profession. In the past two decades, scholars and practitioners in this field have developed and refined useful techniques for the design, implementation, management, and evaluation of volunteer programs. If volunteers are to make the kind of contribution that societies increasingly ask of them to help address pressing problems in the human and social services, effective volunteer administration holds the key.

References

Brudney, Jeffrey L., 1990. *Fostering Volunteer Programs in the Public Sector: Planning, Initiating, and Managing Voluntary Activities.* San Francisco, CA: Jossey-Bass.

_____, 1994. "Designing and Managing Volunteer Programs." In Robert D. Herman, ed., *The Jossey-Bass Handbook of Nonprofit Leadership and Management.* San Francisco, CA: Jossey-Bass.

_____, 1995. "The Involvement of Volunteers in the Delivery of Services: Myth and Management." In Steven W. Hays and Richard C. Kearney, eds., *Public Personnel Administration: Problems and Prospects,* 3d ed. Englewood Cliffs, NJ: Prentice-Hall.

Brudney, Jeffrey L., and William D. Duncombe, 1992. "An Economic Evaluation of Paid, Volunteer, and Mixed Staffing Options for Public Services." *Public Administration Review,* vol. 52 (September–October): 474–481.

Brudney, Jeffrey L., Teresa G. Love, and Chilik Yu, 1993–1994. "The Association for Volunteer Administration and Professionalization of the Field: Suggestions from a Survey of the Membership." *Journal of Volunteer Administration,* vol. 12 (Fall–Winter): 1–22.

Daft, Richard L., 1995. *Organization Theory and Design,* 5th ed. Minneapolis/St. Paul, MN: West Publishing.

Duncombe, Sidney, 1985. "Volunteers in City Government: Advantages, Disadvantages, and Uses." *National Civic Review,* vol. 74, no. 9: 356–364.

Ellis, Susan J., 1986. *From the Top down: The Executive Role in Volunteer Program Success.* Philadelphia, PA: Energize.

_____, 1994. *The Volunteer Recruitment Book.* Philadelphia, PA: Energize.

Fisher, James C., and Kathleen M. Cole, 1993. *Leadership and Management of Volunteer Programs: A Guide for Volunteer Administrators.* San Francisco, CA: Jossey-Bass.

Haran, Lena, Sarah Kenney, and Martin Vermilion, 1993. "Contract Volunteer Services: A Model for Successful Partnership." *Leadership* (January-March) 28–30.

Hodgkinson, Virginia A., Murray S. Weitzman, Chrisropher M. Toppe, and Steven M. Noga, 1992. *Nonprofit Almanac, 1992–1993: Dimensions of the Independent Sector.* San Francisco, CA: Jossey-Bass.

Karn, G. Neil, 1982–1983. "Money Talks: A Guide to Establishing the True Dollar Value of Volunteer Time, Part I." *Journal of Volunteer Administration,* vol. 1 (Winter): 1–17.

_____, 1983. "Money Talks: A Guide to Establishing the True Dollar Value of Volunteer Time, Part II." *Journal of Volunteer Administration,* vol. 1 (Spring): 1–19.

McCurley, Steve, and Rick Lynch, 1989. *Essential Volunteer Management.* Downers Grove, IL: VM Systems and Heritage Arts.

Naylor, Harriet H., 1973. *Volunteers Today—Finding, Training, and Working with Them.* Dryden, NY: Dryden.

_____, 1985. "Beyond Managing Volunteers." *Journal of Voluntary Action Research,* vol. 14, nos. 2, 3: 25–30.

Scheier, Ivan H., 1981. "Positive Staff Attitude can Ease Volunteer Recruiting Pinch." *Hospitals,* vol. 55, no. 3: 61–63.

Stenzel, Alfred, and Helen N. Feeney, 1976. *Volunteer Training and Development: A Manual,* rev. ed. New York: Seabury.

Stringer, Gretchen E., 1993. "Report from the AVA Subcommittee on Volunteer Administration in Higher Education." *Journal of Volunteer Administration.* vol. 11, no. 3: 5–12.

Wilson, M., 1976. *The Effective Management of Volunteer Programs.* Boulder, CO: Johnson.

_____, 1984. "The New Frontier: Volunteer Management Training." *Training and Development Journal,* vol. 38, no. 7: 50–52.

► CHAPTER 30

Building Staff/Volunteer Relations
Setting the Stage

IVAN H. SCHEIER

A Rough-and-Ready History

In the beginning there were volunteers. Every human service occupation or profession has volunteers in its ancestry. The first social workers were volunteers; the first teachers; the first nurses and other health care workers. Firefighters were originally volunteers, and still today, about 80 percent of the fire departments in the U.S. are volunteer. Early clergy weren't paid and many still aren't today (or anyway, not much). There's an old Judaic tradition that the Rabbi never accepts money for his services from the Congregation; he supports his family by taking other jobs.

In the beginning, police officers were volunteers, and much of law enforcement is still done on that basis. Elected officials were at first unpaid and that still occurs in some cases today, especially in smaller communities. The entire concept of probation, employing thousands today, originated in 1841. John Augustus, the world's first probation officer was a volunteer. Early child care workers were unpaid; they were called "parents."

And on and on. In the beginning there were only volunteers and they pioneered all the paid positions in human services today.[1]

Sometime quite early in this century, the pendulum began to swing away from all-volunteer human services toward paid personnel to replace volunteers. The irony is that while many worry today about volunteers replacing staff, historically the process has always been precisely the reverse: staff replacing volunteers.

The pendulum which had swung first from all-volunteer to nearly all paid staff, finally edged back again to somewhere in the middle—significant numbers of both volunteers and staff in the human service delivery system. It's been oscillating there ever since the 1960's, give or take a decade, depending on which service area you're talking about. This oscillation is all too often uneasy, adversarial in tone, when it could be mutually supportive. Thus, we need to get back to the kind of meaningful volunteer job assignment which permits this year's volunteer job to be next year's new paid position. Then volunteers can go on to pioneer other positions.

There are certain fundamental lessons this history can teach us:

- It's difficult or impossible to do the job with just volunteers.
- It's equally difficult or impossible to do the job just with paid staff.

Therefore, we're going to have to find the right mixture of staff and volunteers, and make it work. Nobody is telling you it will be easy. The co-existence of volunteers and staff in human service agencies is, with a few shining exceptions, like a marriage that hasn't settled down yet, after 25 years! But, for sure, the honeymoon is over.

Time now for realism, rather than romance.

What Doesn't Work (Usually)

Without meaning to tease, it's probably useful to get out of the way a few things that *don't* work, and never have. It seems silly to waste time trying them over and over. Maybe that's a trifle overstated. These three approaches have hardly ever worked in the last thirty years: inspirational intimidation; psychologizing the situation; and rubbing on a little training. A fourth loser is separatism.

Inspirational Intimidation

We admire our wonderful volunteers so much. It pains us when others greet righteous enthusiasm with indifference or disdain. We're prone to overreact with over-sell. What comes out then—as well as at most every annual volunteer recognition event—is anecdotes suggesting that all volunteers are either "Miracle Workers" or "Brilliant Amateurs" or "Achievers of Incredible Results as if By Magic."

We mean well, but see how such statements can come across to skeptical staff:

Miracle Worker—Sounds like a rescue operation. Nobody likes to be seen as needing to be rescued.

Brilliant Amateurs—I once heard this prideful announcement by a volunteer: "The theories said this kid could never learn to read. But I didn't know about all the theories, and I never studied any textbooks on it. SO, I just went ahead and taught him to read." Scattered applause I didn't join. I wanted both hands free to strangle the guy. Because what came across was that all staff's struggle and expense of getting professional training and experience wasn't worth

a thing. Why can't we upgrade volunteers without downgrading all that staff stands for?

Get Incredible Results as If By Magic—Magic shows are great to watch—from a distance. But I'm not sure I'd want to work up close to a magician—my job might disappear!

These kinds of implications are almost always unintentional, but no less insulting to staff, for that reason. They also ultimately do a disservice to volunteers by setting up unrealistic expectations for their performance—a "set-up" in more than one sense.

If you must miracle-ize volunteers, at least tell a few counterpart stories about exemplary staff (there almost always are such stories if you look for them). Better yet, regale with anecdotes about the great achievements of staff-volunteer teams. Praise the partnership. Best of all, prevent inspirational intimidation of staff by emphasizing that volunteers, by and large, are just decent folks who want to help out. Helpful human beings are much more satisfying as co-workers than saintly wizards.

Psychologizing the Situation

One of the hardest things to do is respect staff skeptics, realizing and believing that, though we regret their "resistance" to volunteers, they may still be fine people and good, caring staff. That's not only the ethical position to take; it's often a fully truthful one and frequently effective as well. People see you as someone they can talk to and negotiate with, rather than as an implacable fanatic on the subject of volunteers.

On the other hand, it is terribly tempting to ascribe a staff person's skepticism to basic defects in character or problems in mental health. The insinuations are almost always unintentional, but they are there.

Please watch, for example, the use of clinically-connected terms and phrases such as staff are "*threatened by,*" "*anxious about,*" or "*paranoid*" about volunteers. Unfortunately that kind of concept can easily insinuate itself in otherwise productive dialogue.

There are several problems with psychologizing the staff-volunteer relational issue. First, such statements are very often untrue, unfair and misleading. Even where grains of truth may exist, performing psychoanalysis or the like on all affected staff (or volunteers) is impractically expensive and time-consuming! Also, psychodynamic finger-pointing at staff naturally provokes a retaliatory finger pointed right back at you. Thus, it may well account for the equally absurd legend of the neurotic volunteer.

Let's Just Rub on a Little Training

If there's a problem at the agency, a favorite quick fix is to hire a trainer, have a workshop, and move right on to something else.

Similarly, some seem to believe that mandatory staff training in the use of volunteers will make resistance magically disappear. I doubt it, as a rule.

A case in point: I used to volunteer with juvenile delinquent boys who were school dropouts or kick-outs. At first I suffered from the prevailing prejudice that these boys actually weren't too smart. Then it came time for them to take the written test for becoming licensed automobile drivers. One and all blew that test out of the water, with scores ranging from 90 percent on up (far better than I did with my finely honed test-taking skills fresh from graduate school). Why? These boys desperately *wanted* to drive a car (with a slight preference that it be done on a legal basis). Therefore, they readily absorbed the necessary material. Unfortunately, no teacher had ever been able to get through to them that things like English and math were nearly as important as driving a car.

The case is parallel for "training out" staff resistance to volunteers and "training in" support for same. You can sit staff down in a classroom and give them great information on how to involve and supervise volunteers, but if they don't see any gripping reason for learning the material, they won't even hear it. Certainly, training staff in how to work with volunteers can be a useful auxiliary tactic if, at the same time, other approaches described in this book are building staff motivation to learn the material.

And while we're at it, orientation of volunteers is at least equally important for assuring

good staff-volunteer relations. Strongly recommended here is a deliberate, well-planned session on "the care and feeding of staff." From the very beginning, be sure volunteers understand that a primary part of their job is to make staff's job easier by providing relevant sympathy and support. Let staff themselves handle some of the sessions on this, sharing, for example, insights on why they're sometimes grouchy (it isn't because they hate volunteers) or maybe don't always answer telephone calls promptly (it isn't because they think volunteers are unimportant; it's because the ceiling just fell down). Whether directly involved in this staff-sensitizing training or not, staff will probably appreciate your making efforts to orient volunteers in this way.

Too few volunteer programs make such an effort at representing the staff perspective as a significant, self-conscious part of volunteer orientation and training. A spot poll suggests maybe one in thirty programs do. This may be just another consequence of a secret assumption that staff resistance to volunteers is *their* problem. *They* must change *their* ways; we needn't change ours. Yet, the best way to get a smile is to give one and not expect staff to produce them out of thin air. And, generally, the best way to earn support is to offer it. We volunteer people need to think about that.

Diagnosis as a Basis for Action

How do you know when you have a problem in staff-volunteer relations?

On the one hand, don't go looking for trouble where none exists. On the other hand, don't wait to be hit on the head with a two-by-four before reacting.

Look for subtler signs from staff. It's not so much active sabotage as passive resistance; it's not so much what staff does as what they don't do. Don't expect snarls, but worry at the absence of smiles. Staff may not overtly "bad mouth" volunteers but they may fail to show up at volunteer recognition events. Visible hassling of volunteers is a far less likely sign than sheer absence of staff requests for volunteers in meaningful work.

Finally, it's not so much that staff hate volunteers as that they have other more important priorities. Hating volunteers today is something like hating motherhood, God, and the right to boo the home team. You don't directly challenge such conventionally sacred values; you just ignore or trivialize them by putting your time elsewhere.

On the volunteer side, signs of a staff-volunteer problem are relatively more straightforward: volunteers start dropping out all over the place.

Organizational Receptivity to Volunteers

In addition to significant signals from staff and from volunteers, there is a third basis for deciding where you stand on staff-volunteer relations: organizational climate and receptivity.

At the end of this chapter is a "Teamwork Checklist" designed to help you diagnose your own organizational situation carefully, identify and capitalize on strengths, raise awareness on issues and challenges, and launch positive planning to do something about current problem areas. The questions themselves may help respondents discover the scope and depth of issues related to volunteers.

Before using the checklist, consider changing some of the more abstract terms to more concrete, relevant ones. Thus, "the overall organization or agency" in Checklist Statement #1 might be changed to the name of your agency or organization. "Top management" in Statement #2 might be similarly specified for your agency, and so on for other statements. You should also feel free to add or delete statements, according to their relevance for your organization.

Select several different people to fill out the checklist, independently of each other. Representation should include the person most directly responsible for the volunteer program (one hopes this is a professional volunteer coordinator or director), a volunteer or two, one line staff person who works with volunteers, and one who does not. Wherever anonymity can encourage candor, it should be offered as an option.

Ideally the checklist will also be completed by at least one middle management and one top management person. In any case, management should be involved in discussion of results and receive a report on outcomes. Remember here that some of the statements probably represent areas management has never really thought about in connection with the volunteer program. The whole process can be educational.

Using Checklist Results

Once the checklist has been administered, convene a group to compare and discuss results. The group should include all those who completed the checklist, plus others selected on a need-to-know basis.

Now compare responses statement by statement among those who complete the checklist. You may want first of all to discuss and clarify your understanding of what each statement means.

Then, consider first the case where solid consensus exists among strengths (high scores) in your staff-volunteer situation. These factors can be pretty much left alone for now, though a review of "what are we doing right here?" could be helpful in preserving the happy state of affairs. Complacency is certainly not recommended.

Otherwise, planning for improvement of staff-volunteer relations should focus on those statements which consensus rated as low, insofar as they indicate factors on which: we agree positive change is desirable; and such change is reasonably within the capability of planners. Thus, if discussants concur that the agency does not have an effective policy statement on volunteers (checklist statement #2), and further agree that such a policy is needed, they can recommend or actually launch development of appropriate agency guidelines.

Indeed, *virtually every checklist statement is a nucleus around which a volunteer program policy statement can be developed*. The only exceptions are checklist statements #1 and possibly #11 as well. A policy on volunteers is high priority for agencies seriously interested in cultivating volunteer support. This policy should be clear, realistic, specific, in writing and widely disseminated throughout the agency. As implemented, it will prevent all the damage ambiguity can do to a volunteer program, and also deter willful misunderstanding of the organization's commitment to volunteer involvement. There should be wide agency participation in formulation of the volunteer program policy.

Lack of consensus on a checklist statement is valuable when it triggers clarifying and productive discussion. Thus, if management thinks that goals for increased numbers of volunteers are realistic (#8), while the volunteer coordinator and line staff feel these goals are too high, we have something about which we need to communicate better. More realistic numerical targets could well result from clarification, information exchange, and negotiation.

Here and throughout the checklist, one is struck by the extent to which top management must be involved in key decisions affecting the volunteer program. Indeed, top management is often the only place where such decisions can finally be made. How different this is from the token theory of top management involvement: show up once a year at the volunteer recognition event; symbolically put your arm around volunteers; breathe a sigh of relief; and opt out of the process until next year at the same time.

Certain of the individual statement ratings can be especially revealing of the overall situation. Thus, statement #1 is a stopper. Consensus on a low score suggests that somehow volunteers are expected to rescue a seriously ailing organization. It usually doesn't work that way. In fact, quite the reverse: a deeply troubled agency will almost certainly destroy its own volunteer program or never allow the program to develop properly in the first place, before that volunteer program ever "rescues" the organization.

It is generally accepted that checklist statement #1 is the top priority and foundation for both volunteer program and staff. Past checklist users have also commented that if checklist factors #1, #2, and #3 are in place, everything else will follow. To this, I would add: until factor #1 is in place, other factors are unlikely to follow, or mean much if they do follow.

I suggest you re-administer the checklist every three to six months to gauge progress, spot new problems early, and re-stimulate the problem-solving process.

Note

1. For a complete history of the impact volunteers have had on American society, see *By the People: A History of Americans as Volunteers,* revised edition, by Susan J. Ellis and Katherine H. Noyes (San Francisco: Jossey Bass, 1990). The book is also available from ENERGIZE, Inc.

FIGURE 30.1 Teamwork Checklist

1. Our overall organization or agency is stable, healthy, and free of serious conflict and basic survival anxiety. _____

2. The top management of this organization has developed and effectively communicated a policy on volunteers which is clear, specific, well-informed, positive, and has teeth in it. _____

3. Roles of staff and volunteers are clearly defined both generically and in terms of specific tasks. _____

4. Volunteers are clearly perceived by everyone as either a direct or indirect support for staff and the organization as a whole. Volunteers are not seen as a means of replacing staff. _____

5. Most volunteer job descriptions are directly based on staff needs for assistance in their work. Information about these needs is provided by staff themselves as specific things which are inefficient or unnecessary for paid staff to do or as additional things they can accomplish with volunteer help. _____

(continues)

FIGURE 30.1   Teamwork Checklist *(continued)*

6. We have a wide variety of volunteer jobs and roles from which staff may select those with which they are most comforatble. Staff members actively participate in developing this wide range of volunteer job designs. _____

7. Staff have solid ownership of the vounteer program via their participation in planning, recruiting, screening, job design, orientation and training, supervision, and evaluation of volunteers. (Volunteers can be fired and staff know it.) This staff participation involves both policy-setting and whatever program implementation staff have time for. _____

8. The targets for increased number of volunteers are realistic. We do not play the numbers game here with our volunteer program. _____

9. A significant well-planned part of orientation and training for volunteers emphasizes sensitivity and sympathy to staff problems and the primary importance of being supportive to staff. _____

10. Wherever possible (and this means frequently), volunteers are recognized and rewarded in conjunction with their staff supervisors or associates. That is, the recognition goes to a staff-volunteer team or partnership. _____

11. Volunteers regularly choose and publicly commend staff people they consider outstanding; for example, "the staff person of the month." _____

12. Our organization consistently implements a system of concrete, specific rewards for staff who work effectively with volunteers. The need for mobilizing community volunteer support to achieve organizational or job goals is built into every staff job description. _____

13. A staff person's performance with volunteers is regularly evaluated and seriously considered in decisions concerning that person's status and promotion in the organization. _____

14. Individual staff receptivity to volunteers is carefully assessed. With rare exceptions, volunteers are first assigned to more receptive staff who are also knowledgeable about working with volunteers. _____

15. Experience working with volunteers, openness to delegating meaningful duties to them, and creative belief in their potential are criteria actively used in recruiting and selecting new staff at all levels in the organization. _____

16. We regularly conduct both pre- and in-service orientation and training programs for staff on how to work effectively with volunteers. This training is carefully planned, and sufficient time is allowed for it. _____

17. A well-qualified person has been designated to coordinate/direct the volunteer program and act as a bridge linking staff and volunteers. This person is allowed enough time to do the job properly. _____

18. The above-described volunteer coordinator position is at management level. The coordinator has ample opportunity to participate in organizational decisionmaking, particularly as it might affect the volunteer program. _____

19. The volunteer program office is conveniently located and easily accessible to staff and volunteers. _____

20. We have effective grievance mechanisms for handling staff/volunteer problems. These mechanisms are available to volunteers and staff. _____

Total sum   [   ]

PART 10

ACCOUNTABILITY AND EVALUATION

Accountability means *answerability* for one's actions or behavior.[1] The more difficult questions for nonprofit organizations are: accountable to whom and accountable for what? Within any organization, the primary accountability is up to the organization's higher levels of management, the executive director, and the board of trustees. This, however, is only a limited view of accountability in and around nonprofit organizations and for the people who work and volunteer in them. A nonprofit organization and its volunteers, staff, executives, and members of the board are accountable to all individuals, groups, and organizations to which they are answerable—at least for some things and to some extent. Thus, a performing arts nonprofit is accountable to its many types of paying and nonpaying audiences; the rising and established performers; high schools and universities that provide interns; individual, family, corporate, and nonprofit donors and sponsors; government grant-making agencies; and the "community" including community influentials, elected officials, and the print and electronic media. Accountability indeed is *answerability* to individuals and groups who have stakes in the organization and its activities.

Accountable for What?

People who own stock in corporations regularly scrutinize the fine print in the stock market reports, because stockholders want to know how their corporate investments are doing. For a business, trends in its stock price, profits, earning ratios, market penetration, and dividends serve as measures of organizational performance—its efficiency and effectiveness. Thus, a business can satisfy most of its accountability requirements by regularly publishing data about these performance measures for its shareholders, government regulators, and the general public.

In nonprofit organizations, efficiency—the quantity of resources consumed in the production of services or outputs to the public or its members—also is a clear and useful measure of performance. Demonstrating accountability for efficiency does not raise unique problems for most nonprofits. Accountability for effectiveness, however, is a different story; it is far more complex for reasons that cannot be resolved easily.

Effectiveness As Seen Through Whose Eyes?

First, effectiveness seldom, if ever, means the same thing to all stakeholders.[2] Effectiveness is not "a thing." It is instead a subjective phenomenon that is construed differently by different constituencies. Effectiveness is defined from the divergent perspectives of many beholders. Each of the many constituencies of an organization shares some goals with others but also has its own specific and sometimes changing goals, priorities—and thus also criteria of organizational effectiveness.[3] Because each constituency brings its own interests and expectations into its relationship with a nonprofit organization, some priorities are almost always in competition with others for scarce organizational resources and attention. Thus, nonprofit organizations are webs of fluid interactions, constantly changing interests, and forever shifting balances of power among coalitions of constituencies.

> For example, nonprofit organizations that house and provide services to troubled youths, adults on parole, and individuals who have been in mental hospitals provide a not-uncommon example. These "halfway house" programs help individuals re-integrate into society, but in doing so often cause neighbors to believe that they and their children have been placed at risk ("not in my backyard"). What is effectiveness for these types of programs? What measure(s) should be used?
>
> How effective is a symphony orchestra that fills its halls for performances but performs only well-known works by long-established composers? If this orchestra were to offer some performances by up-and-coming local composers that only half-fill the hall, would this programming change increase or decrease its effectiveness? Or, if it were to decrease the frequency of its symphony hall performances and initiate instructional activities and performances in elementary and secondary schools across the state? Different stakeholders would have different opinions.

Nonprofit organizations sometimes face difficult decisions about which of several competing constituencies' interests will have priority. When this occurs, the interests of some stakeholders must be set aside either temporarily or permanently. They may decide to "fight" or to withdraw their support from the organization, either of which may weaken it.[4]

Difficulties Measuring Effectiveness

Second, many of the services that nonprofit organizations provide can be difficult to measure.[5] For example, how can and should the effectiveness be measured of programs that strive to improve the quality of life for persons with life-long disabilities or chronic mental illness—including changes in beliefs, attitudes, and behaviors that are co-produced by the service providers and the recipients of services?[6] The mission of most nonprofit organizations is to change the lives of individuals in some way—make lives better somehow or prevent deterioration of the current quality of life. Collecting information to evaluate effectiveness of programs sometimes requires intrusion into sensitive personal areas.[7] Consider the privacy problems involved, for example, in collecting data to evaluate the effectiveness of a program that is trying to prevent teenage pregnancies. Few of us would accept pregnancy rates—the ultimate outcome measure—as an adequate single measure of effectiveness. We also would want to know at least something about sensitive private behaviors, including frequency and patterns of sexual activity; prevention methods used and not used; STD prevalence; and abortions performed. Even if we were able to collect this information, would we know whether or not the information was accurate and could we convince others of its accuracy?

Evaluation measurements are less difficult when the important processes, outputs, and/or outcomes can be quantified or observed objectively; for example, it is not difficult to measure how many pregnant women attend prenatal classes; how many contact hours there are between service providers and patients with Alzheimer's disease; or how many people are removed from the welfare roles during a given year. All too frequently, however, the variables that can be measured are not particularly important. Does anyone truly care how many pregnant mothers attend classes if they do not change their unhealthy lifestyles, or if the individuals who are removed from the welfare roles have nowhere to live except on the streets and are not eligible for health care services?

Usually it is not especially difficult to measure the quantity of inputs, activities, and outputs for a nonprofit's services; but it is often difficult to measure the quality of activities, outputs, and either the quantity or quality of outcomes. It is yet more difficult and much more expensive to measure and establish cause-effect relationships between activities and outcomes, especially co-produced services where activities only influence outcomes.[8] When changes in behavior or lifestyle are the desired outcome (for example, programs to improve the outcome of pregnancies or to treat individuals with chemical dependencies), the timeliness of measurements often poses additional serious problems. Outcomes can take years or even decades to establish.[9]

The limited abilities of the populations served by many nonprofits introduce yet another difficulty when measuring program effectiveness. For example, many nonprofit programs use some aspects of quality of life or changes in the quality of life as indicators of program effectiveness. Evaluators attempt to measure quality of life through surveys administered to recipients of services, people who know them, or the public. Surveying for quality of life has many difficulties and limitations in and of itself; with recipients of services who have severe cognitive, emotional, or communication disabilities, these difficulties are compounded. How should quality of life be determined for people with severe disabilities? Answers to this question require difficult value judgments, not technical solutions. Are the judgments of family members or professionals acceptable as proxy measures? Should we accept the judgment of professionals who provide services to the clients, or only professionals who represent supposedly neutral-objective funding agencies or groups that advocate for the clients and their families? Can family members always be trusted to make decisions that are in the best interests of their relatives/clients? These questions are far from hypothetical: They reflect some of the difficult realities of being accountable for effectiveness in nonprofit organizations.

Accountable for What?

Accountability has at least five often-competing dimensions: hierarchical, legal, professional, political, and moral or ethical.[10] The evaluation methods that are used most commonly today are best able to achieve and verify hierarchical, legal, and political accountability and least able to achieve and verify ethical or moral accountability—the dimension of accountability that most directly associated with quality of services. Accountability thus means far more than compliance with contractual, legal, or financial reporting requirements.[11] It also includes responsibility for moral, professional, and ethical dimensions of service, which means that they need to be answerable for the quality of their services as well as for the quantity of services.

Accountability problems of this nature and complexity are not limited to nonprofit organizations. They cross sector boundaries:

> Far too much attention has been paid to traditional or compliance accountability and process accountability, and far too little to . . . managerial accountability (which focuses on the judicious use of public resources), program accountability (which is

concerned with the outcomes or results of government operations), and social accountability (which attempts to determine the societal impacts of government programs).[12]

Readings Reprinted in Part Ten

Kevin Kearns' chapter, *"Accountability Concepts and Controversies,"*[13] traces the origins of the current "epidemic of accountability fever in the private nonprofit sector" back to the English common law doctrine of charitable trusts, but argues that "it was not until the twentieth century that the legal and regulatory environment of nonprofit organizations began to grow in complexity and sophistication." In recent decades, the "epidemic of accountability fever" has been fostered by highly publicized scandals, congressional inquiries, weak traditions of nonprofit scholarship, and the absence of a "consistent professional ethos." Managers in nonprofit organizations often "bring the valuable attributes of passion and idealism to their work, but they may have very narrow perspectives on their accountability either in the legal sense or in the broader sense of preserving the public trust." Kearns asserts that in the current environment of constant change, "customer service and responsive entrepreneurship" are becoming the bases of accountability for government agencies and nonprofit organizations.

Susan Paddock's essay, *"Evaluation,"*[14] provides a useful introduction to program evaluation and examines the purposes for program evaluation and its relation to program planning and design. Paddock also discusses the utilization of evaluation findings and notes how political, measurement, and usefulness problems may emerge. She advises that evaluators can increase the usefulness of their work by communicating clearly and by carefully limiting the use of technical terms and complex statistical analyses. Paddock argues that the current environment of financial constraints and rapid social/political changes increases the importance of program evaluation.

"Multiple Constituencies and the Social Construction of Nonprofit Organization Effectiveness," by Robert Herman and David Renz,[15] reports on their study of nonprofit organization effectiveness in Kansas City and the surrounding area. They investigated the divergent views that stakeholder groups had about the effectiveness of specific nonprofit organizations. They also attempted to determine whether subjective ratings of board effectiveness or any of several objective measures were correlated with these subjective ratings of organizational effectiveness. They conclude that different stakeholder groups do indeed use different indicators of organizational effectiveness. Thus, "assertions such as '(management practice X) leads to or is associated with higher or increased nonprofit organization effectiveness' must be qualified by adding and providing evidence for 'according to (whom).' The idea that there is a

single objective organizational effectiveness independent of the judgments of various stakeholders is no longer tenable or useful." A subjective assessment of board effectiveness, however, "is the most important determinant of organizational effectiveness for all . . . types of stakeholders."

Notes

1. Kevin P. Kearns, *Managing for Accountability: Preserving the Public Trust in Public and Nonprofit Organizations* (San Francisco: Jossey-Bass, 1996), 11.

2. For more information about the "multiple constituency theory" approach to organizations and their effectiveness, see Robert D. Herman and David O. Renz, "Multiple Constituencies and the Social Construction of Nonprofit Organization Effectiveness," *Nonprofit and Voluntary Sector Quarterly* 26, no. 2 (June 1997):185–206 (reprinted in this part); Thomas Connolly, E. J. Conlon, and S. J. Deutsch, "Organizational Effectiveness: A Multiple-constituency Approach," *Academy of Management Review* 5 (1980): 211–217; and Robert E. Quinn and John Rohrbaugh, "A Competing Values Approach to Organizational Effectiveness," *Public Productivity & Management Review* 2 (1981): 122–140.

3. See, for example, Herman and Renz, "Multiple Constituencies," 185–206; and Jay M. Shafritz and J. Steven Ott, "Multiple Constituencies/Market Organization Theory," in J. M. Shafritz and J. S. Ott, eds., *Classics of Organization Theory,* 3d ed. (Belmont, CA: Wadsworth, 1992), 343–349.

4. J. Steven Ott, "Organization Theories," in J. S. Ott, ed., *The Nature of the Nonprofit Sector* (Boulder: Westview Press, 2001); and J. Steven Ott, "Perspectives on Organizational Governance: Some Effects on Government-Nonprofit Relations," *Southeastern Political Review* 21, no. 1 (winter 1993): 3–21.

5. J. Steven Ott and Lisa A. Dicke, "Important but Largely Unanswered Questions About Accountability in Contracted Public Human Services," *International Journal of Organization Theory & Behavior* 3, nos. 3 and 4 (summer 2000), 283–317.

6. Bruce B. Clary, "Coproduction," in J. M. Shafritz, ed., *International Encyclopedia of Public Policy and Administration* (Boulder: Westview Press, 1998), 531–536.

7. J. Steven Ott and Lisa A. Dicke, "Challenges Facing Public Sector HRM in an Era of Downsizing, Devolution, Diffusion and Empowerment . . . and Accountability??" in Ali Farazmand, ed., *Strategic Public Personnel Administration/HRM: Building Human Capital for the 21st Century* (Westport, CT: Greenwood Press, forthcoming).

8. Edward A. Suchman, *Evaluative Research: Principles and Practice in Public Service and Social Action Programs* (New York: Russell Sage Foundation, 1967).

9. Except through indirect and/or proxy measures, which introduce additional measurement difficulties. See Emil J. Posavac and Raymond G. Carey, "Program Evaluation: An Overview," in E. J. Posavac and R. G. Carey, *Program Evaluation: Methods and Case Studies,* 5th ed. (Upper Saddle River, NJ: Prentice-Hall, 1997), 1–21.

10. See Lisa A. Dicke and J. Steven Ott, "Public Agency Accountability in Human Services Contracting," *Public Productivity & Management Review* 22, no. 4 (June 1999): 502–516; Barbara S. Romzek and Melvin J. Dubnick, "Issues of Accountability in Flexible Personnel Systems," in P. W. Ingraham and B. S. Romzek, eds., *New Paradigms for Government* (San Francisco: Jossey-Bass, 1994), 263–294; and J. G. Jabbra and O. P. Dwivedi, eds., *Public Service Accountability* (West Hartford, CT: Kumarian Press, 1988).

11. Lester M. Salamon, *Partners in Public Service: Government-Nonprofit Relations in the Modern Welfare State* (Baltimore: Johns Hopkins University Press, 1995).

12. Gene E. Caiden, "The Problem of Ensuring the Public Accountability of Public Officials," in J. G. Jabbra and O. P. Dwivedi, eds., *Public Service Accountability* (West Hartford, CT: Kumarian Press, 1988), 23–24.

13. Kevin P. Kearns, "Accountability Concepts and Controversies," in K. P. Kearns, *Managing for Accountability: Preserving the Public Trust in Public and Nonprofit Organizations* (San Francisco: Jossey-Bass, 1996), 15–27.

14. Susan C. Paddock, "Evaluation," in J. M. Shafritz, ed., *International Encyclopedia of Public Policy and Administration* (Boulder: Westview Press, 1998), 818–823.

15. Herman and Renz, "Multiple Constituencies," 185–206.

► **CHAPTER 31**

Accountability Concepts and Controversies

KEVIN P. KEARNS

At a recent faculty meeting, one of my colleagues quipped that the life of a graduate student consists of long periods of dreadful boredom punctuated by brief moments of sheer terror. This humorous (and remarkably accurate) observation also describes the history of the nonprofit sector in terms of public scrutiny and government oversight.

Popular interest in the private nonprofit sector has been cyclical, if not sporadic. Years and even decades of relative disinterest or benign neglect of the nonprofit sector have been interrupted by periods of intense public scrutiny and criticism, typically following a highly publicized incident like the New Era scandal that thrust the nonprofit sector into the public eye.

A notable recent controversy involved the national office of the United Way of America and its former president, William Aramony. In 1992, national attention focused on Aramony's $460,000 compensation package and his appropriation of United Way funds for travel and living expenses, and on the appearance of inadequate oversight by the board of trustees (Glaser, 1993). In April 1995, Aramony was convicted of multiple felony counts including fraud, money laundering, and filing false tax returns.

The United Way incident, the Covenant House scandal (Sennot, 1992), and the case of

television evangelist Jim Bakker all contained three things that people find irresistibly titillating—money, power, and sex. They were prime targets for extensive coverage on television and in newspapers and tabloids around the country.

Also, there are many scholarly works that have challenged the underlying rationale of tax exemptions for certain types of nonprofit organizations such as hospitals (for example, Herzlinger and Krasker, 1987).

Simmering Controversies in a Laissez-Faire Environment

Dramatic controversies—and the books that follow them—might explain, in part, the current epidemic of accountability fever in the private nonprofit sector. But it would be a mistake to conclude that widespread public concern about nonprofit accountability is a recent or merely temporary phenomenon. In fact, a kind of simmering controversy over the appropriate role of the nonprofit sector and how it should be regulated has existed for more than two hundred years—ever since the emergence of charitable organizations in the United States (for example, see Hall, 1987a, 1987b; Bremner, 1994).

The broad legal parameters governing modern nonprofit organizations can be found as early as the sixteenth century, in the portions of English common law related to charitable trusts. The general stipulations were that the trust should be organized solely to carry out its charitable purposes, that the assets of the trust should be kept productive, and that trustees were prohibited from making improper investments or engaging in self-dealing for personal gain (Fremont-Smith, 1989, p. 76). Today we see these broad principles embodied in the ever-growing, and increasingly sophisticated, register of federal and state laws governing nonprofit organizations.

But the current legal and regulatory framework took many years to evolve. The formal concept of a private charitable corporation was not even firmly established under federal law until the mid 1800s (Hall, 1987a, pp. 4–8), and it was not until the twentieth century that the legal and regulatory environment of nonprofit organizations began to grow in complexity and sophistication. Even today, accountability in the nonprofit sector has been defined almost entirely in terms of fiduciary responsibility, with the IRS as the primary national enforcement mechanism. Thus, the federal tax laws have been the primary mechanism for regulating the nonprofit sector at the national level (Fremont-Smith, 1989; Scrivner, 1990).

There continues to be wide variation among the fifty states regarding their efforts to hold nonprofit organizations accountable to the public trust (Simon, 1987). While most states require some form of registration and annual reporting, many do not have rigorous enforcement or oversight mechanisms.

Periodic Inquisitions

From time to time, there have been national reviews and investigations regarding accountability in the nonprofit sector. In recent years, the strongest advocate for tighter controls at the national level has been Representative J.J. Pickle of Texas. As former Chair of the Oversight Subcommittee of the House Ways and Means Committee, Pickle convened public hearings on several occasions to explore alleged abuses in the nonprofit sector. In 1987, his subcommittee heard testimony from small businesses alleging that exemptions from the federal income tax give certain nonprofit organizations (especially those engaged in commercial activities) an unfair competitive advantage in the commercial marketplace. In 1993–1994, the subcommittee undertook a much larger agenda including proposed limits on executive compensation, limiting the proliferation of nonprofit organizations, improving public access to reports filed annually with the IRS, and giving the IRS authority to issue graduated sanctions (short of revoking tax exemptions) to curb abuses. The subcommittee made recommendations on only some of these issues, primarily those involving public access to information and IRS enforcement powers. It is clear that the subcommittee's broader agenda was driven, at least in part, by media coverage of alleged abuses by certain organizations and several of the recent books that are highly critical of the nonprofit sector.

More recently, Congress has considered legislation to severely constrain the advocacy activities of nonprofit organizations, especially those that receive grants or contracts from the federal government. And incidents like the New Era scandal will no doubt provide additional ammunition to those who insist on much greater governmental oversight of nonprofit activities.

Weak Traditions of Scholarship

In comparison with the government sector, the literature on accountability in the private nonprofit sector is neither substantial nor sophisticated. True, there are many specialized textbooks on financial accountability in nonprofit organizations (Olenick and Olenick, 1991) and written materials dealing with the growing array of legal and regulatory mandates with which nonprofit organizations must comply in order to preserve their tax-exempt status (Bookman, 1992; Hopkins, 1992, 1993). But most general texts on nonprofit management and governance contain only brief and relatively narrow sections on the broader ideals of serving the public interest and preserving the public trust, and I know of no books dealing exclusively with this topic. Curiously, some of the most innovative insights on accountability in nonprofit organizations (for example, understanding and responding to the expectations of multiple constituencies) are embedded in the emerging literature on nonprofit marketing (Kotler, 1982; Espy, 1993).

No Consistent Professional Ethos

Another way to understand how accountability is interpreted in the nonprofit sector is to examine the academic credentials needed to enter the world of nonprofit management. In comparison with government, these credentials are extraordinarily diverse. Therefore, they offer no common reference point or professional ethos on the notion of accountability. Private human service agencies are staffed largely by people trained in social work or clinical specialties. Cultural organizations often are managed by artists or historians. Nonprofit health care organizations sometimes are led by doctors or public health professionals. Educational and research institutions are managed by people representing a plethora of academic disciplines, sometimes with predictable results! Finally, many small nonprofits are founded and subsequently managed by people who have no formal training whatsoever. They bring the valuable attributes of passion and idealism to their work, but they may have very narrow perspectives on their accountability either in the legal sense or in the broader sense of preserving the public trust.

Trustees and others who donate their services to nonprofit organizations bring an even more diverse set of credentials. While many are professionals from the world of business or government, some are simply concerned citizens who represent the special interests of particular client or advocacy groups. Some observers have suggested that even the professionals leave their business sense and their understanding of accountability behind when they assume volunteer positions on nonprofit governing boards (Chait

and Taylor, 1989; Dayton, 1987; Herzlinger, 1994).

A small number of universities now offer specialized programs of study in nonprofit management. But these programs tend to focus on building generic skills such as fundraising, financial management, and working with boards of trustees. Most of them do not contain specific courses on the broader context of accountability or social responsibility in nonprofit management. Moreover, the emergence of these specialized programs of study is a recent phenomenon, and they have not yet matured to the point of having a shared perspective on the notion of accountability or consistency in their pedagogical strategies for conveying this notion to students.

Thus, in summary, the general notion of accountability has not been as pervasive in the nonprofit sector as it has been in government. This is not to say that nonprofit professionals and volunteers are unaware of or insensitive to their obligation to preserve the public trust. Rather, the people who work and volunteer in the nonprofit sector, unlike their counterparts in government, do not have a shared value system or even a common vocabulary with which to engage in a sectorwide, intellectually coherent dialogue on the notion of accountability. In the absence of a shared value system, many nonprofit professionals and volunteers are first exposed to the principles and instruments of accountability after they begin their service. Unfortunately for some, their first exposure comes as a result of a particular controversy or accountability crisis in their organization.

Public Perceptions of Government and Nonprofit Organizations

In the United States, the nonprofit sector emerged and subsequently evolved in an environment characterized by ambiguous legal frameworks, regional idiosyncrasies, and ad hoc accommodation between government and charities. This stands in sharp contrast with our government institutions, which were founded upon relatively explicit and widely endorsed principles of accountability. In effect, the nonprofit sector has been allowed to evolve and grow according to a free-market philosophy, not unlike the competitive environment in which business organizations exist (see, for example, Steinberg, 1987). Thus the notion of accountability in the nonprofit sector has, until recently, been largely defined by the market rather than by any overarching regulatory framework.

Public Perceptions of Nonprofit Organizations

For a variety of reasons, nonprofit organizations are a mystery to the general public. First, the nonprofit sector is vast in size and diversity. The Internal Revenue Code contains nearly thirty categories of tax-exempt organizations, ranging from the familiar (religious, charitable, and educational organizations) to the arcane (cemetery companies). Few people understand how deeply their lives are affected by the nonprofit organizations they encounter on a daily basis. Perhaps they think the nonprofit sector is dominated by charities to serve the poor. They forget that the nonprofit sector includes the Girl Scouts, the Boy Scouts, the YMCA, many hospitals and universities, industrial development corporations, public television and radio stations, and even the National Football League.

Second, the revenues of nonprofit organizations (typically some mixture of philanthropic donations, fees for service, and contracts and grants) are complicated and not terribly interesting to the average person. Few citizens fully understand how their tax dollars subsidize, either directly or indirectly, the activities of nonprofit organizations. Even fewer understand that nonprofits are legally permitted to generate profits, form subsidiary corporations, and engage in other commercial activities. And fewer still have even a cursory understanding of the type of fiscal pressures that are forcing more and more nonprofit organizations to diversify their revenues through entrepreneurial strategies like commercial enterprises, subsidiary corporations, and more aggressive investment strategies.

Third, the governance structures of nonprofit organizations more closely resemble those found in business than those in government. Trustees of nonprofit organizations rarely are in the public spotlight. They do not run for election, their meetings are not necessarily open to the public, and few citizens understand how they obtain their positions of public trust.

In sum, most average citizens do not feel the same kind of ownership of the nonprofit sector that they feel toward government agencies. On a day-to-day basis, the nonprofit sector is relatively invisible to the general public. This is both a blessing and a curse for the people who work and volunteer in nonprofits. On the one hand, the relative invisibility of these organizations can insulate them from the distraction and drain of dealing with public inquiries. On the other hand, widespread misunderstanding of the nonprofit sector can lead to pseudocontroversies in which nonprofits are forced to defend actions that are entirely legal and appropriate.

Some New Notions of Accountability

The discussion thus far has demonstrated that there are important differences in the accountability environments of government and the nonprofit sector. In both sectors, however, accountability can be a moving target that can frustrate even the most committed professionals and volunteers.

Customer Service

Managing for greater accountability is made more challenging by recent thinking in management theory that suggests that public serving organizations need to be "reinvented" (Osborne and Gaebler, 1992) or "reengineered" (Hammer and Champy, 1993) to better serve the needs of customers. Customer service has emerged as a dominant theme in business management, and this theme is rapidly spreading to government and nonprofit organizations as well.

The publication in 1992 of *Reinventing Government* by Osborne and Gaebler sent shock waves through bureaucratic and political circles. The book became a best-seller, provided some of the political rhetoric of the 1992 Presidential campaign, and was an intellectual blueprint for Vice President Al Gore's *From Red Tape to Results* (1993), which recommended actions to improve the effectiveness and efficiency of the federal government.

States and localities also are being held to higher standards of accountability, reflecting the general principles of customer service and quality management (National Commission on State and Local Public Service, 1993). Consider, for example, the following exchange of viewpoints reported recently in the *Pittsburgh Post-Gazette*. In a news story on logistical problems encountered in a new public housing project, the executive director of the City's Urban Redevelopment Authority (URA) was quoted as saying that minor glitches were inevitable in any new project, "Just like when you buy a new car and take it back for servicing" (Rotstein, 1994). Not long ago, such an excuse might have passed without notice. In this case, however, the explanation of the URA director prompted a stinging letter to the editor from a private citizen, obviously well-versed in the vocabulary of Total Quality Management (TQM). The citizen wrote: "[The URA's explanation] is exactly the type of thinking that should be obsolete in the 1990s—expecting things to be wrong (even when new) and then having to fix them. . . . The URA should do things right the first time, and demand the same from its suppliers. To tolerate shoddy quality is the mentality that allowed the Japanese to kick us in the global market place. . . . Bureaucrats . . . should learn what private industry is now realizing—getting it right the first time is better for everyone in the long run" (Goldberg, 1994).

The nonprofit sector also is under growing pressure do a better job of identifying and meeting customer needs (Kearns, Krasman, and Meyer, 1994). The United Way, for example, has responded to growing demands for consumer choice by allowing donors to designate annual gifts to specific agencies or classes of agencies rather than giving the United Way unlimited discretion in its allocations. Beyond this, the local campaigns of United Way affiliates are themselves facing more intense competition from other fundraising federations that are challeng-

ing the quasi-monopoly that the United Way has enjoyed. On the granting side, foundations are demanding greater accountability from the nonprofits they support by requiring more sophisticated methods of outcome measurement, more advanced management systems, stricter compliance with a growing array of reporting requirements, and greater commitment to diversity and quality in governance structures (for example, O'Connell, 1988).

Increased Public Awareness of the Nonprofit Sector

Finally, there are two other forces emerging especially in the nonprofit sector that are likely to have lasting impact on how accountability is defined and assessed. First, the debate on accountability in the nonprofit sector has emerged from the chambers of legislatures and the courts and entered the living rooms of citizens across the country. Issues of compliance with complicated tax laws and regulations will, of course, continue. But increasingly these controversies are spilling over into broader discussions of lucrative compensation packages for nonprofit executives, the proliferation of nonprofit organizations, excessive commercialism in the nonprofit sector, and fraudulent or misleading fundraising practices. One does not need to be a lawyer or a tax accountant to participate in dialogue on these issues (for example, Nielsen, 1992).

The second broad trend has to do with historic distinctions between the public and nonprofit sectors, which are becoming increasingly blurred. Prior to the War on Poverty in the 1960s, government relied very little on the nonprofit sector as a partner in human service delivery. Today, the situation is far different. On average, nonprofit organizations receive 31 percent of their annual revenues from government grants, contracts, and reimbursements (Salamon, 1992, p. 27). Consequently, their spending on social welfare programs (excluding education, pensions, and veterans' benefits) is slightly higher than that of the federal government and far exceeds the spending of state and local governments combined (Salamon, 1992, p. 37). In the 1980s, the role of nonprofits in delivering public services increased as the Reagan and Bush administrations sought to divest and privatize many domestic government programs. Similarly, the Republican Congress elected to office in 1994 turned quickly to the nonprofit sector as a potential safety valve for anticipated reductions in domestic spending on social programs.

This evolving partnership between government and the nonprofit sector will have implications for the accountability of both sectors. At a minimum, professionals in each sector will need to know far more about the accountability environments in which the other operates. Nonprofits, therefore, can learn a great deal from government officials about fishbowl life. Also, the public sector can provide valuable lessons to nonprofits in the development of stricter internal management controls and more rigorous governance policies.

Conversely, governments have much to learn from nonprofit organizations about the role of accountability in a competitive, market-driven environment. Nonprofits tend to have more experience than governments in developing entrepreneurial responses to public problems, in monitoring customer needs and satisfaction, and in assessing the impacts and outcomes of their services.

Summary

The basic challenge is the same for both government and nonprofit organizations: to manage resources, internal processes, and services in ways that serve the public interest and preserve the public trust. The history and traditions of the two sectors (and, consequently, their respective views of accountability) are different. But these parallel streams are beginning to converge in a new accountability environment that is more dynamic and complex than at any time in history. It is an environment in which emerging themes of customer service and responsive entrepreneurship are beginning to compete with the more traditional reporting mechanisms for ensuring accountability. It is an environment in which historical distinctions between the public and nonprofit sectors are beginning to disap-

pear. It is an environment of intense public scrutiny that has spilled over from the public sector to the nonprofit sector. It is an environment of constant change.

References

Bookman, M. *Protecting Your Organization's Tax Exempt Status: A Guide for Nonprofit Managers.* San Francisco: Jossey-Bass, 1992.

Bremner, R. H. *Giving: Charity and Philanthropy in History.* New Brunswick, N.J.: Transaction Press, 1994.

Chait, R. P., and Taylor, B. E. "Charting the Territory of Nonprofit Boards." *Harvard Business Review,* Jan./Feb. 1989, 67(1), 44–54.

Dayton, K. N. *Governance is Governance,* Occasional Paper Series, Washington, D.C.: Independent Sector, 1987.

Fremont-Smith, M. R. "Trends in Accountability and Regulation of Nonprofits." In V. A. Hodgkinson, R. W. Lyman, and Associates (eds.), *The Future of the Nonprofit Sector: Challenges, Changes, and Policy Considerations.* San Francisco: Jossey-Bass, 1989.

Glaser, J. *The United Way Scandal: An Insider's Account of What Went Wrong and Why.* New York: Wiley, 1993.

Goldberg, D. "Letter to the Editor." *Pittsburgh Post-Gazette,* Apr. 14, 1994, p. B–2.

Gore, A. *From Red Tape to Results: Creating a Government That Works Better and Costs Less.* Washington, D.C.: National Performance Review, 1993.

Hall, P. D. "A Historical Overview of the Private Nonprofit Sector." In W. W. Powell (ed.), *The Nonprofit Sector: A Research Handbook.* New Haven, Conn.: Yale University Press, 1987a.

Hall, P. D. "Abandoning the Rhetoric of Independence: Reflections on the Nonprofit Sector in the Post-Liberal Era." In S. A. Ostrander, S. Langston, and J. Van Til (eds.), *Shifting the Debate: Public/Private Sector Relations in the Modern Welfare State.* New Brunswick, N.J.: Transaction Books, 1987b.

Hammer, M., and Champy, J. *Reengineering the Corporation: A Manifesto for Business Revolution.* New York: HarperCollins, 1993.

Herzlinger, R. E. "Effective Oversight: A Guide for Nonprofit Directors." *Harvard Business Review,* July/Aug. 1994, 72(4), 52–59.

Herzlinger, R. E., and Krasker, W. S. "Who Profits from Nonprofits?" *Harvard Business Review,* Jan./Feb. 1987, 65(1), 93–106.

Hopkins, B. *The Law of Tax Exempt Organizations.* New York: Wiley, 1992.

Hopkins, B. *A Legal Guide to Starting and Managing a Nonprofit Organization.* New York: Wiley, 1993.

Kearns, K. P., Krasman, R. J., and Meyer, W. J. "Why Nonprofit Organizations Are Ripe for Total Quality Management." *Nonprofit Management and Leadership,* 1994, 4(4), 447–460.

Kotler, P. *Marketing for Nonprofit Organizations.* (2nd ed.) Englewood Cliffs, N.J.: Prentice-Hall, 1982.

National Commission on State and Local Public Service. *Hard Truths/Tough Choices: An Agenda for State and Local Reform.* (Winter Commission Report.) Albany, N.Y.: Nelson A. Rockefeller Institute of Government, 1993.

Nielsen, W. A. "Reporters, Not Trustees, Make the Best Watchdogs." *Chronicle of Philanthropy,* Mar. 24, 1992, 4(11), 41–42.

O'Connell, B. *Evaluating Results.* Occasional Papers in Nonprofit Management, no. 9. Washington, D.C.: Independent Sector, 1988.

Olenick, A., and Olenick, P. *A Nonprofit Organization Operating Manual.* New York: Foundation Center, 1991.

Osborne, D., and Gaebler, T. *Reinventing Government.* Reading, Mass.: Addison-Wesley, 1992.

Rotstein, G. "Domestic Disillusionment: Crawford Square's New Tenants Report Series of Problems." *Pittsburgh Post-Gazette,* Mar. 10, 1994, p. B–5.

Salamon, L. *America's Nonprofit Sector: A Primer.* New York: Foundation Center, 1992.

Scrivner, G. "100 Years of Tax Policy Changes Affecting Charitable Organizations." In D. L Gies, J. S. Ott, and J. M. Shafritz (eds.), *The Nonprofit Organization: Essential Readings.* Pacific Grove, Calif.: Brooks/Cole, 1990.

Sennot, C. *Broken Covenant.* New York: Simon & Schuster, 1992.

Simon, J. G. "The Tax Treatment of Nonprofit Organizations: A Review of Federal and State Policies." In W. W. Powell (ed.), *The Nonprofit Sector: A Research Handbook.* New Haven, Conn.: Yale University Press, 1987.

Steinberg, R. "Nonprofit Organizations and the Market." In W. W. Powell (ed.), *The Nonprofit Sector: A Research Handbook.* New Haven, Conn.: Yale University Press, 1987.

► CHAPTER 32

Evaluation

Susan C. Paddock

Evaluation determines the value or effectiveness of an activity for the purpose of decisionmaking.

The valuing or judging of people, processes, and things is a pervasive daily human activity. As such, most evaluation is informal. Formal evaluation makes the explicit judging process an integral part of program management. Evaluation determines value by weighing costs, both tangible and intangible, against benefits. It determines effectiveness by assessing whether a service or program has met identified needs or objectives, or has made a difference. In this process, evaluation provides information that aids decisionmakers in determining whether to continue, modify, or terminate a funded activity or which of several alternatives to support. Good evaluation improves the quality of those decisions.

In formal evaluation we make explicit (1) the object of our review, (2) the criteria with which value will be assigned and a judgment based, and (3) the behavior or outcomes necessary if the object of the evaluation is to be judged as having met standards or expectation. An evaluation that is not explicit about these three issues will generate fear or frustration among those affected by the evaluation and will mitigate its effect.

History of the Development of Program Evaluation

Formal evaluation is not new. We find formal evaluation as far back as 2000 B.C.E., when Chinese officials conducted civil service exams (DuBois 1970). Within Western tradition we find evaluation in a number of places, most notably in 1870 during the Age of Reform in England. There, the evaluation of educational achievement led to a call for what today we might term incentive pay or pay for performance (Madaus et al. 1983).

In the United States, the formal evaluation of organizations and their programs and services began in schools. In 1897–1898 Joseph Rice conducted a comparative study of the spelling performance of 33,000 students in a large city school system (DuBois 1970). Originally, formal evaluation in education was closely associated with the measurement tradition of psychology. Robert Thorndike, sometimes called the father of the educational testing movement, was an important influence in encouraging the application of measurement technology to the determination of human abilities (Thorndike and Hagen 1969). His prestige led to the introduction of standardized testing in the 1920s as a means to assess students. Evaluation approaches were next applied to pedagogy, in an effort to improve teaching (Smith and Tyler 1942). The evaluation practices developed for schools were applied to work relief and public housing programs of President F. D. Roosevelt's New Deal.

Evaluation gained in importance and visibility after World War II. In education, the Cold War threat of Soviet preeminence and the concern that American schools were second-class caused evaluators to increase their scrutiny of educational practices and outcomes. This work led to the development of a language, a research process, and a theoretical basis for the evaluation discipline (Cronbach and Suppes 1969; Scriven 1958). By the end of the 1960s the focus of educational evaluation included policy and political questions, especially related to equal education (Coleman et al. 1966; Jencks 1972).

Evaluation in public administration initially focused on programs of the federal government. There were two schools of development. One school focused on the management and allocation of resources for national defense programs. The Program Evaluation Review Technique (PERT), for example, was developed to correlate different contractor management systems in the development of complex weapon systems (Cook 1966). Planning, Programming, and Budgeting System (PPBS) also was developed primarily as a means of applying economic analysis to management systems (Wildavsky 1966). Systems analysis techniques were intended to improve decisionmaking about the development and implementation of military operations (Miser and Quade 1985). These were primarily planning or front-end analysis evaluation approaches.

The other school of public administration evaluation was linked to earlier efforts in education and focused on outputs or outcomes. Evaluation efforts with a foundation in experimental design, for example, were used to judge the relative merits of federally funded agricultural programs and products. The social welfare programs of the Great Society, which accounted for rapidly increasing federal expenditures, were accompanied by an increase in attention paid to evaluation (Rossi et al. 1979).

In the 1970s the U.S. Office of Management and Budget (OMB) created an Evaluation and Program Implementation Division, a reflection of the growing importance of evaluation. State governments also began to pay attention to evaluation in the mid–1970s, although there it was called productivity measurement rather than program evaluation, and often was linked to sunset legislation. The two schools of evaluation in public administration began to coalesce. Awareness and use of program evaluation grew with the publication of *The Handbook of Evaluation Research* (1975) and the initiation in 1977 of the journal *Evaluation Quarterly*.

In the past decade, evaluations of governmental programs have changed their focus from being dominated by the evaluation of achievement of great objectives, typical of the Great Society and War on Poverty programs, to using multifaceted approaches (Rossi and Freeman 1993). Evaluation continues to be an important part of most federally funded programs. As a result, the federal government plays a central role in the development of evaluation approaches, methodologies, and techniques.

Evaluation Purposes

Evaluation is a process to judge success, assure accountability, and determine more effective resource allocation. It does not simply measure; it also judges, or assigns value. It seeks to assess social utility. It is concerned with both program process and program product. Evaluation serves a variety of purposes. These purposes, and the name of the approach most frequently associated with each purpose, are (1) to inform planning decisions, particularly in the development of policy (front-end analysis); (2) to answer policy execution questions and determine if a full-scale evaluation of the program is useful and feasible (evaluability assessment); (3) to track program progress and identify actual or emerging problems (program and problem monitoring); (4) to determine whether a program has accomplished its goals or met its objectives (impact analysis or product evaluation); (5) to determine if a program has been implemented as planned, regardless of outcomes (process analysis or process evaluation); (6) to measure the effectiveness or efficiency of units or practices (management analysis or context evaluation); (7) to determine if there are unintended consequences from program implementation (goal-free analysis); (8) to assess the degree of public or stakeholder satisfaction with the program (service analysis); and (9) to compare various programs or approaches to determine which might be the best to implement in a new setting (policy analysis). In addition, a branch of evaluation research examines whether evaluation findings are used, or compares evaluation findings (utilization analysis, evaluation synthesis, or meta-evaluation). Program evaluation should result in a good explanation or generalization about why change did or did not take place.

Evaluation differs from the related practices of research and auditing. Research is a test of a theory and represents a more disinterested study, but results are intended to be generalizable to the greater population. Auditing is an attempt to measure the extent to which the procedures of a program are consistent with those intended in original legislation and to identify deficiencies or discrepancies.

Relation to Program Planning and Implementation

To be effective, program evaluation must be integral to the program cycle, from the initial needs assessment to the final formal evaluation stage. Failing to plan for program evaluation from the beginning of a program usually means the data or data sources necessary for making a judgment may not be available. An evaluation conducted under these circumstances can only answer questions for which data are available, which may not be the most important or most interesting questions.

Evaluation can occur in any phase of a program. During needs assessment evaluators ask, "What needs attention? What is the program trying to accomplish?" During planning, evaluators assess the outcomes to be achieved and the courses of action to be taken. During development, evaluators examine the extent to which program execution is taking place as planned.

This is formative evaluation and can suggest changes to assure goal achievement or program improvement. Finally, during program delivery, evaluators judge the overall effectiveness of the project or program and recommend future courses of action. This is summative evaluation, which describes a program as a finished work.

Determination of Evaluation Feasibility

The temptation for most evaluators is to spend most of their time planning the design and technical elements of the study. However, it is at least as important to spend time thinking about the purpose of the evaluation and how its findings will be used, and to plan the evaluation with that in mind. Before undertaking any evaluation, three questions about the study's feasibility should be asked. First, can the results of the evaluation influence decisions about the program? If there are strong, preconceived ideas on the part of policymakers about the program, the effect of the evaluation will be limited or nonexistent. In addition, the evaluation schedule must be such as to assure that the study can be completed in time to inform decisions. Second, can the evaluation be carried out? There must be sufficient resources available to support the evaluation, and the program must be stable enough so that it can be studied. Finally, is the program consequential enough to merit evaluation? Programs most eligible for evaluation are those that require significant resources, those that are operating in a marginal or improvable manner, or those that are candidates for expansion or replication. A negative response to any of these questions will bring into question the likelihood that the study will be completed or that its results will be useful.

Audience and Constraints

It is important to identify the evaluation's audience. Evaluators should ask; Who needs the information to be provided by the study? What kind of information do they require? When will they need it? How will they use it? The early identification and involvement of potential users of evaluation results is critical to the study's success (Chelimsky 1985; Weiss 1982).

After having identified purpose, feasibility, and audience, the evaluator must determine what decisions must be informed by the evaluation and what constraints exist. Constraints exist when there are insufficient materials and equipment, personnel, or funds, or when the political climate is adverse. Because evaluation takes place in a political environment, it is subject to political constraints and pressures. Understanding this political environment is important for the person who must manage the evaluation effort.

Approach or Design

The evaluator must determine the evaluation approach or design. At least twelve kinds of evaluation approaches or models have been identified, many of which can be used at any stage in a program's development or to inform any of the evaluation purposes identified earlier. These approaches are: (1) objectives-based or goal-oriented, in which the evaluation assesses the discrepancy between planned and achieved objectives (Smith and Tyler 1942); (2) consumer-oriented, or goal-free evaluation, which discovers what the program is by what it does, not by what is purports to do (Scriven 1972); (3) testing, or the comparison of performance against norms or preestablished criteria (Thorndike and Hagen 1969); (4) evaluation research, or the identification of causal relationships between variables (Campbell and Stanley 1966); (5) cost assessment or cost-benefit analysis, or the assessment of the costs and benefits of proposed or actual policies (Coleman et al. 1966; Jencks 1972); (6) accreditation or certification, or the determination if programs or people meet established standards; (7) management information systems, which provide information needed to fund, direct, and control programs, but which are not related to program outcomes directly; (8) accountability or performance contracting, which provides information to funding

agencies on the extent to which program objectives have been met; (9) client-centered evaluation, which attempts to understand activities from the users' perspectives (Stake 1970; Guba and Lincoln 1989); (10) decision-oriented evaluation, used to provide information specifically to assist legislators or administrators in making or defending decisions (Stufflebeam et al. 1971); (11) adversary evaluation, which provides policymakers with opposing views in a kind of "judicial" framework (Wolf and Arnstein 1975); and (12) just-in-time evaluations, which are geared for smaller, more responsive evaluations of isolated elements of programs.

Although the tools, techniques, and methodologies used by each of these approaches may be the same, the perspective assumed by the evaluator influences the focus of the study, and thus the kind of information provided to decisionmakers.

Decisions about the procedures or methods to be used for gathering data are critical to a study's success. Data collection will be affected by costs associated with various methods, as well as by the availability and accessibility of records, documents, and informed sources, and the willingness of clients, program staff, or other stakeholders to provide accurate, reliable, and honest information. It is tempting to evaluate that which is easy to measure or for which data can be easily obtained. Evaluators should resist that temptation, since the most significant or interesting information may not be quantifiable or easy to access or report.

Data can be obtained from questionnaires (multiple-choice, checklist, ratings, rankings, or open-ended questions), surveys, tests, interviews, observations, performance records, data banks; or organizational documents (ordinances, laws, resolutions, and other public documents). Data should be both quantitative and qualitative (subjective). Information sources include legislators, citizen groups, individuals, program personnel, other executives in government, program clients, and evaluations by other governmental agencies. Multiple measures of the evaluation objects should be obtained whenever possible. Criteria must be valid, reliable, timely, and credible.

Data Analysis and Reporting

Analysis of data begins with the determination that data collected are useful. Data must be relevant, timely, accurate, and understandable. The evaluator, in analyzing data, also must be aware of the effects of attrition, the Hawthorne effect, evaluator bias, or any changes in organizational facilities, personnel, policies, or funding that may have affected the program or the analysis of program data.

The final role for the evaluator is the reporting of findings. The evaluator must decide how and to whom the evidence will be presented. The evaluation report should present information in a way that is useful to policymakers and aids in their decisionmaking. It should be structured so as to inform future decisions. Effective evaluation reports are free of jargon, focus directly and specifically on decisions or problems, provide the basis for setting priorities, and involve program administrators in the recommendations process.

Utilization of Evaluation Findings

Recently, critics have argued that the requirements of Total Quality Management (TQM) or of the "new public management" described by Osborne and Gaebler (1993) are antithetical to program evaluation (Behn 1991). These approaches require public managers to move decisionmaking to the lowest level possible, to eliminate unnecessary rules and regulations, and to innovate quickly. By contrast, traditional program evaluation requires time and a more-hierarchical decisionmaking process. "New" program evaluation must, therefore, be "just-in-time," providing smaller packages of evaluation findings for use in assessing innovations. TQM practices, such as statistical process control and the Plan-Do-Check-Act cycle, can be integrated into traditional evaluation practices.

Rapid change increases the requirement to demonstrate that an agency's program is accomplishing something (Behn 1991). Small-scale, timely evaluation can help others understand innovations and, if appropriate, replicate them (Levin and Sanger 1994). Formative evaluations, or evaluations that are process-oriented, that answer the questions of primary stakeholders, and that include qualitative methods that allow a "holistic assessment of relevant phenomena" (Thomas 1995), will be more useful to public managers and policymakers. The application of technological tools such as automated information systems, telephone surveys, and computer-assisted analysis and reporting can increase the possibility of evaluation being timely and useful to public managers. Benchmarking, or the establishing of standards or "best practices," leads not only to evaluation of current programs but also to goal-setting for program improvement.

The problems with evaluations fall into three categories: political, measurement, and usefulness. Political problems result from the tension between those being evaluated and the evaluators, especially when there is a probability of program termination or reduction. In public management, political problems also emerge when the priorities of a legislative of funding body are different from those of the agency. Measurement problems occur because many governmental programs or services are difficult to measure, and evaluators must develop measures for selected objectives. Stakeholders in the evaluation process may not agree as to the appropriateness or accuracy of those measurements. The usefulness of evaluations is compromised if the study is ad hoc or ex post facto rather than an integral and inherent part of the program from its inception. Then, necessary data may be incomplete or absent.

Usefulness is also limited when evaluators issue reports filled with technical terms and complex statistical analyses that confuse and mislead. Evaluation reports that are simple and easy to understand, however, may miss important, more complex elements of the program. Practitioners of the "new" evaluation must be more involved in the program planning and development process, building alliances with public managers so that these problems are avoided or minimized and evaluation findings have an impact on how social services are delivered.

The usefulness, and therefore the utilization of program evaluation, can be improved in a number of ways: (1) Be clear about premises underlying a program and conduct the evaluation in such a way that those premises are addressed; (2) identify objectives and evaluation criteria that are people-oriented; (3) explicitly consider potential unintended consequences of programs, especially negative effects; (4) specify processes inherent in the program that the evaluation ought to investigate; (5) identify potential users of evaluation results early in the process; (6) analyze alternative approaches within the program; (7) consider more than one objective and multiple evaluation criteria; (8) do not reject evaluation criteria because they are difficult to measure; (9) err on the side of too many objectives or criteria, rather than two few; (10) specify client groups on which the analysis should attempt to estimate program impacts; (11) always include dollar costs as one criterion; (12) involve administrators and program practitioners at every step of the evaluation, from planning to the writing of the draft report; (13) involve potential users of the evaluation where possible; (14) complete the evaluation on time and release the results as soon as possible; and (15) use effective teaching and marketing approaches in presenting and disseminating findings. (Chelimsky 1985; Hatry 1987; Weiss 1982).

Evaluation is always a political process, since it involves identifying objectives, selecting measurement criteria, accessing a variety of information sources, analyzing data within a specified environment, and reporting those data in ways that are understandable and useful. The impact of politics on evaluation in the public management setting is even more profound. Evaluations can be used as a political tactic; evaluators who are aware of implicit or explicit politics can minimize this practice. Alternatively, evaluation can be used as a guide in shaping policy or program changes.

The very act of conducting an evaluation may be important, if it encourages members of the organization to examine their work and the structure that supports it (Weiss 1977). Evaluation may help agency administrators and staff, as well as legislators and other important parties, to review program goals and renew their commitment to program outcomes. This review may lead to behavioral and policy changes at a number of levels, regardless of the findings of the evaluation study. Thus effective evaluation may be even more important in today's environment of frequent and rapid changes and increasing fiscal constraints in assuring the success of public management programs and services.

References

Behn, Robert D., 1991. *Leadership Counts: Lessons for Public Managers from the Massachusetts Welfare, Training and Employment Program.* Cambridge: Harvard University Press.

Campbell, David T., and Julian C. Stanley, 1966. *Experimental and Quasi-experimental Designs for Research.* Chicago: Rand-McNally.

Chelimsky, Eleanor, (ed.), 1985. *Program Evaluation: Patterns and Directions.* Washington, DC: American Society for Public Administration.

Coleman, James S., et al., 1966. *Equality of Educational Opportunity.* Washington, DC: U.S. Government Printing Office (GPO).

Cook, Desmond L., 1966. *Program Evaluation and Review Technique.* Washington, DC: GPO.

Cronbach, Lee J., and P. Suppes, 1969. *Research for Tomorrow's Schools: Disciplined Inquiry for Education.* New York: Macmillan.

DuBois, P. H., 1970. *A History of Psychological Testing.* Boston: Allyn and Bacon.

Guba, Egon C., and Yvonne Lincoln, 1989. *Fourth Generation Evaluation.* Newbury Park, CA: Sage Publications.

Hatry, Harry, 1987. *Program Analysis for State and Local Government.* Washington, DC: Urban Institute.

Jencks, Christopher, 1972. *Inequality. A Reassessment of the Effect of Family and Schooling in America.* New York: Basic Books.

Levin, Martin A., and Mary Bryna Sanger, 1994. *Making Government Work: How Entrepreneurial Executives Turn Bright Ideas into Real Results.* San Francisco: Jossey-Bass.

Madaus, George F., Michael Scriven, and Daniel Stufflebeam, 1983. *Evaluation Models: Viewpoints on Educational and Human Services Evaluation.* Boston: Kluwer-Nijhoff.

Miser, Hugh J., and Edward S. Quade, eds., 1985. *Handbook of Systems Analysis.* New York: North-Holland.

Osborne, David, and Ted Gaebler, 1993. *Reinventing Government: How the Entrepreneurial Spirit Is Transforming the Pubic Sector.* New York: Penguin.

Rossi, Peter H., Howard E. Freeman, and Sonia R. Wright, 1979. *Evaluation: A Systematic Approach.* Beverly Hills, CA: Sage Publications.

Rossi, Peter H., and Howard E. Freeman, 1993. *Evaluation: A Systematic Approach.* 5th ed. Newbury Park, CA: Sage Publications.

Scriven, Michael, 1958. "Definitions, Explanations, and Theories." In H. Fiegl, M. Scriven, and G. Maxwell, eds., *Minnesota Studies in the Philosophy of Science,* Vol. 2. Minneapolis: University of Minnesota Press.

_____, 1972. "Prose and Cons About Goal-Free Evaluation." *Evaluation Comment* 3:4.

Smith, E. R., and Ralph W. Tyler, 1942. *Appraising and Recording Student Progress.* New York: Harper & Row.

Stake, Robert E., 1970. "Objectives, Priorities, and Other Judgment Data." *Review of Educational Research* 40: 181–212.

Stufflebeam, Daniel L., et al., 1971. *Educational Evaluation and Decision Making.* Itaska, IL: F. E. Peacock.

Thomas, John Clayton, 1995. "Adapting Program Evaluation to New Realities: The Challenge of the New Public Management." Paper presented at Trinity Symposium, San Antonio, Texas, July 23.

Thorndike, Robert L., and E. Hagen, 1969. *Measurement and Evaluation in Psychology and Education.* New York: Wiley and Sons.

Weiss, Carol H. 1977. "Research for policy's sake: The enlightenment function of social research." *Policy Analysis* 3: 532–545.

_____, 1982. "Measuring the use of evaluation." *Evaluation Studies Review Annual* 7: 129–145.

Wildavsky, Aaron, 1966. "The political economy of efficiency: Cost-benefit analysis, systems analysis and program budgeting." *Public Administration Review* (December) 293–302.

Wolf, R. L., and G. Arnstein, 1975. "Trial by jury: A new evaluation method." *Phi Delta Kappan,* 57:3 185–190.

CHAPTER 33

Multiple Constituencies and the Social Construction of Nonprofit Organization Effectiveness

ROBERT D. HERMAN AND DAVID O. RENZ

I s a nonprofit charitable organization (NPO) that is attracting funding and adding clients rapidly more effective than one that is not? Is an NPO with low expenditures on fund-raising more effective than one with moderate fundraising costs? No doubt many would respond that NPO effectiveness is more complicated and contingent than these questions imply. Others might respond that what is really important about NPO effectiveness is the extent to which an organization's mission is being achieved, even though in many instances it is technically difficult (at best) to assess the extent of mission accomplishment. Further, comparing the extent of mission accomplishment across different types of NPOs is impossible.[1]

For example, how could the mission accomplishment of an organization established to reduce (and ultimately eliminate) child abuse be assessed with any certainty? How could the mission achievements of women's shelters and at-risk youth development organizations be fairly or objectively compared?

In spite of the difficulties, funders such as foundations, corporations and federated bodies, individual donors and volunteers, government officials who contract with nonprofit service providers, and board and staff members of NPOs do make and act on assessments of NPO effectiveness. On what bases do such varied stakeholders assess effectiveness? Are stakeholder assessments based on similar criteria? Are stakeholder assessments consistent? Are stakeholder assessments related to what some define as objective indicators of NPO effectiveness?

These sorts of questions and issues are fundamental to the work of nonprofit charitable organizations, especially in an era of enhanced demands for accountability and of increased emphasis on outcomes evaluation. They are the sorts of questions that animated the research to be reported here.

We began this research with the hopes (but not the hypotheses) that various stakeholders would express very similar judgments about effectiveness and that judgments of organizational effectiveness would be clearly and positively correlated with judgments of board effectiveness and with certain management practices. Such results would both substantiate that effectiveness is a meaningful and measurable concept for nonprofit organizations and that achieving higher effectiveness is related (if not caused) by use of various management practices. Though the results are not of this sort, we maintain that organizational effectiveness is a meaningful concept for nonprofit organizations. Decisions are made, or at least justified, on the basis of beliefs about effectiveness. As we will more fully argue later, individual nonprofit organizations cannot ignore effectiveness judgments by various stakeholders. It is possible and important for any NPO to carry out actions that will be judged as improving effectiveness. Whereas effectiveness is clearly meaningful and important for individual NPOs, our results suggest that making general claims about NPO effectiveness (what it is and what causes it) is much more difficult. Nonetheless, researchers and theorists can neither ignore effectiveness nor assume that there is a simple, objective effectiveness that can be applied to all nonprofit charities.

Theoretical Perspectives on Organizational Effectiveness

We believe two contemporary approaches to organizational effectiveness are especially relevant to research on nonprofit charitable organizations. The multiple constituency model recognizes that organizations have (or comprise) multiple stakeholders or constituents who are likely to differ in the criteria they use to evaluate the effectiveness of an organization (see Kanter & Brinkerhoff, 1981, for an early statement of the model; Zammuto, 1984, for a review of differences within the multiple constituency model; Tsui, 1990, for an empirical study; and D'Aunno, 1992, for a discussion of multiple constituency models in relation to human service organizations). In contrast with the competing values model, a goal-based model suggesting that organizations, as such, have multiple and conflicting effectiveness criteria (Quinn & Rohrbaugh, 1983), the multiple constituency model holds that differing sets of stakeholders have (probably) different goals. Students of and participants in NPOs have often observed that such organizations are characterized by the large and varied number of constituencies that have expectations of them.

The other approach that informs this research, social constructionism, is not a specific model of organizational effectiveness. Rather, social constructionism is a more general ontological perspective that considers reality or some parts of reality to be created by the beliefs, knowledge, and actions of people. This reality is not a thing independent of people, though people may also believe that what they have created exists independently.

Our research is based on (rather than being an attempt to test) both the social constructionist perspective and the multiple constituency model. We assume that nonprofit charitable organization effectiveness is not a real property (in the way that the number of employees is a real property) of an organization but a set of judgments by various stakeholders. Our research also incorporates an attempt to identify what groups of practitioners (chief executives of nonprofit charities, representatives of funder organizations, and technical assistance providers) consider objective effectiveness criteria. We do not assert that these types of practitioners (as contrasted with board members, frontline staff members or volunteers, for example) somehow better know objective reality. Rather, we believe these practitioners are likely to make judgments about their own and other nonprofit organizations' effectiveness and that we can discover what criteria they think they use to make such judgments (details of our procedures follow in the next section). We use these practitioner-defined criteria to determine if and how they are related to judgments of effectiveness by different types of stakeholders. With this study, we intend to provide initial answers to the following questions.

- What objective criteria do practitioner-experts agree are meaningful indicators of nonprofit charitable organizational effectiveness?
- Do different stakeholders report similar judgments of the effectiveness of specific NPOs?
- Is board effectiveness related to both objective organizational effectiveness and organizational effectiveness judgments?
- Are the objective indicators of NPO effectiveness correlated with stakeholder judgments of effectiveness?
- Are there differences among different stakeholders in the relation between objective effectiveness and judgments of effectiveness?

- What organizational characteristics are correlated with the objective indicators of or stakeholder judgments of NPO effectiveness?

Measuring Board Effectiveness Judgments

The normative literature on the management of nonprofit organizations assigns the board of directors a fundamental role in the governance and leadership of such organizations, arguing that board effectiveness is a condition for organizational effectiveness (for example, Carver, 1990; Chait, Holland, & Taylor, 1991).

We believe that board effectiveness should be considered a social construction. To collect stakeholder judgments of board effectiveness, we adapted the 11 items in *Self-Assessment for Nonprofit Governing Boards* (Slesinger, 1991). We used this instrument because it has been widely used with boards and is considered meaningful by board members. It also covers, in our judgment, what many informed people regard as the fundamental responsibilities of boards. The items in this instrument ask respondents to evaluate how well (with a 1 to 5 scale where 1 represents the highest score) a board fulfills the following tasks or responsibilities: mission definition and review, the board role in CEO selection and review and the working relationship between the board and the CEO, program selection consistent with the mission and program monitoring, the board's role in giving and soliciting contributions, the board's role in financial management, strategic planning by the board, new board member selection and training, the working relationship between the board and staff, the board's role in marketing and public relations, the conduct of board and committee meetings, and the board's role in risk management.

Measuring Organizational Effectiveness Judgments

Because no instrument for collecting stakeholder judgments of nonprofit organizational effectiveness previously existed, we developed one. The final version of the instrument contains nine items asking for judgments (with a 1 to 5 scale

where 1 is the highest score) about an organization's performance in relation to financial management, fundraising, program delivery, public relations, community collaboration, working with volunteers, human resources management, government relations (referring to managing contracts, meeting licensing and regulatory requirements, and lobbying government officials), and board governance. This instrument was sent to the same types of stakeholders but to different individuals than the board effectiveness instrument: the president and a nonofficer board member of each organization's board, two senior management staff members of each organization, and two funders of each organization. We received returns from 162 people, including 35 board presidents, 28 board members, 60 staff members, and 39 funders (again, several funders rated several organizations).

Other Organizational Characteristics

We expected that other organizational characteristics would affect or be related to either judgments of board effectiveness, judgments of organizational effectiveness, or objective indicators of organizational effectiveness. Thus data on several organizational characteristics were collected either during interviews with chief executives or from examination of various documents, including the three most recent IRS Forms 990. We expected that judgments of organizational effectiveness and objective indicators of organizational effectiveness would be related: positively to organizational age (that is, older organizations would be more effective); positively to total revenues (size); positively to financial surplus; positively to pursuing a strategy of seeking new sources of revenues (see Bielefeld, 1992, for discussion of this and other strategies); positively to pursuing a strategy of enhancing legitimacy; and negatively to pursuing a strategy of retrenchment; and positively to the (chief executive's) perceived certainty of future growth in revenues.

We also expected that board prestige would affect or be related to judgments of board effectiveness and organizational effectiveness (Galaskiewicz, 1985, shows that differences in the pres-

TABLE 33.1   Sample Organization Characteristics

	H&W (n = 46)	*DD* (n = 18)
Organizational age (mean)	40 (approximately)	27 (approximately)
Total revenues in 1992 (mean)	$1,640,000	$1,250,000
Surplus in 1992 (mean)	$29,000	$19,000
Board size (mean)	21	15
Number of FTE service/administrative volunteers (mean)	8 (43 report using volunteers)	5 (10 report using volunteers)

tige of nonprofit boards are widely known). We measured board prestige by asking three long-time participants in the area's charitable sector to rate the prestige of the members of each board in our sample. They were presented with listings of the names and, when available, the employers of board members but not with the names of the nonprofit organizations being rated.

Sample Organizations

We selected our sample from two populations of nonprofit organizations—health and welfare charities that receive some funding from the local United Way and charities that provide services to customers with developmental disabilities. See Table 33.1

United Way H&W charities were included because they are a very prominent part of the publicly supported charity portion of the local nonprofit community and there are a large enough number to ensure an adequate sample for analysis. Though quite diverse in terms of programs and clients, H&W organizations are fairly similar in other ways, such as relative size and complexity, sources of voluntary financial support and sources of potential board members. DD services organizations were included because they are fairly similar in size and complexity to H&W organizations, but likely to differ in terms of funding dependencies (receiving greater proportions of their revenues from government agencies).

Results

What objective criteria do practitioner-experts agree are meaningful indicators of nonprofit orga-

nizational effectiveness? Our effort to identify the objective organizational effectiveness criteria used by practitioner-experts led to a set of correct procedures. That nonprofit managers identify "doing things right" as indicators of effectiveness reinforces the view that nonprofit charities are not (and perhaps cannot be) comparatively assessed on bottomline outcome measures.

Do different stakeholders report similar judgments of the effectiveness of specific nonprofit organizations? Because the social constructionist perspective considers effectiveness a judgment reached by various stakeholders and not a real, independent property of organizations, it is possible for different individuals to report quite varied judgments about the same organization. The correlations of each stakeholder group's judgments in relation to the other groups show rather low agreement (or no agreement, in one case); staff member judgments correlate with funder judgments at .27 and with board member judgments at .06, and board member judgments correlate with funder judgments at .28.

For the same reason—frequent high variability in judgments—we compute and analyze not only an overall board effectiveness score for each organization but also board effectiveness judgment scores for chief executives, board officers, and funders for each organization. These correlations show relatively low agreement among the three groups; funder judgments of board effectiveness correlate with board officer judgments at .42 and with chief executive judgments at .25; and board officer judgments correlate with chief executive judgments at .28.

These correlations among the disaggregated stakeholder groups for judgments about both organizational and board effectiveness show substantial differences in effectiveness judgments. As the multiple constituency approach suggests, these differences imply that there is not a single organizational or board effectiveness "out there" that stakeholders perceive similarly but that each group creates effectiveness on the basis of criteria and impressions mostly relevant to it. Given the differences in stakeholder judgments of both organizational and board effectiveness, we will emphasize analyses of judgments of separate stakeholder groups rather than analyses of overall averages.

Is board effectiveness related to both objective organizational effectiveness and organizational effectiveness judgments? One of the most fundamental assertions of the normative literature on the governance and management of NPOs is that the performance of boards strongly influences the effectiveness of NPOs.

In our data, the correlation between the aggregated average of all stakeholders' judgments of board effectiveness and the aggregated average of all stakeholders' judgments of organizational effectiveness (where these are different individuals) is .64 ($n = 59$, one-tailed $p < .000$). This strong correlation supports the normative assertion, but it may derive from the stakeholders who provided each kind of judgment basing their rating of either board or organizational effectiveness on the prestige of an organization's board. Controlling for board prestige, the partial correlation between the aggregated averages of judgments of board and organizational effectiveness is .62. This suggests that the relation is not spuriously due to board prestige and that organizations that have (socially constructed) effective boards are also very likely to be (socially constructed) effective organizations.

We believe this pattern of consistent correlations among different stakeholder judgments of board and organizational effectiveness offers strong support for the view that NPOs that have (socially constructed) effective boards are also (socially constructed) effective organizations. Clearly, funders and board members rely on some information or impressions about or related to a nonprofit organization's board (other than its prestige) in forming judgments of that

organization's effectiveness. (Senior management staff member judgments correlate only once with judgments by other stakeholder groups, suggesting that they are a distinct constituency and are likely not to evaluate board or organizational effectiveness in the same way as the chief executive.)

Are the objective indicators of nonprofit organization effectiveness correlated with stakeholder judgments of effectiveness? As described earlier, the objective indicators, as defined by practitioner-experts, are matters of correct procedure. Thus this question becomes, Are organizations that use more of the correct procedures also judged to be more effective? The global correlation between the index of objective effectiveness and the overall average of judgments of organizational effectiveness is .09. Doing things right does not seem to affect external stakeholders' judgments of organizational effectiveness, at least when considering all three types of stakeholders together.

Are there differences among different stakeholders in the relation between objective organizational effectiveness and judgments of effectiveness? We interpret [our] results as supporting the view that those stakeholders with more in-depth knowledge of an organization (that is, board members and senior management staff members) are more likely to base effectiveness judgments on substantive outcomes in relation to their own expectations, whereas outsiders (funders), lacking that in-depth knowledge, are more likely to rely on evidence that an organization does things right.

What organizational characteristics are correlated with the objective indicators of or the stakeholder judgments of nonprofit organization effectiveness? The analyses reported to this point suggest that organizations that do things right are not also universally judged to be effective. What are the characteristics of organizations that do things right and of those that are judged effective? Several characteristics are related to the index of objective effectiveness.

The causal connection between these characteristics and objective (procedural) effectiveness is not obvious. It may be that using correct procedures helps organizations become larger, more affluent, and more actively managed organizations. Alternatively, larger, more affluent, and more actively managed organizations may be more able and willing to use the correct procedures.

Analyses suggest that the three kinds of stakeholders use some of the same as well as different bases to reach judgments of organizational effectiveness. Board effectiveness (as measured by the judgments of other individuals) is fairly strongly correlated with the organizational effectiveness judgments of all three stakeholder types.

The organizational effectiveness judgments of all three types of stakeholders are also related, though more modestly, to their organization's total revenues.

Only funders seem to use indicators of correct procedure in reaching judgments of organizational effectiveness; the correlation between funder organizational effectiveness and the index of objective organizational effectiveness is $-.28$ ($p < .05$). Only board members' judgments are related to not using retrenchment strategies ($r = .23, p < .05$). That is, board members judge their organizations as more effective the fewer retrenchment strategies that have been used, suggesting that those organizations facing less troublesome financial situations are seen as more effective by board members.

Conclusions and Implications

Because NPO effectiveness is a complex issue, this study has necessarily used multiple methods of data collection and collected data on many variables—leading to many and complex results.

We draw the following principal conclusions from this study.

1: Practitioner-experts do not rely on bottom-line outcomes as meaningful indicators of objective organizational effectiveness, preferring instead evidence of following correct procedure or doing things right. The practitioner-experts involved in our effort to identify indicators of objective effectiveness were mostly chief executives, along with a few foundation and government agency officials. Other types of organizational stakeholders, excepting funders, do not seem to think of adhering to correct procedures as evidence of organizational effectiveness. Neither board members nor senior management staff members apparently rely on the extent of an organization's use of correct procedures in forming judgments of organizational effectiveness. This implies that evidence of following correct procedures is also a limited, though incomplete, indicator of organizational effectiveness.

2: All stakeholders seem to use some socially constructed evidence of board effectiveness in forming judgments of organizational effectiveness. Board effectiveness is the most important determinant of organizational effectiveness for all three types of stakeholders. Board effectiveness judgments are unrelated to board prestige ratings, but on what bases and how this socially constructed board effectiveness is created needs much additional study.

3: At the most general level, we believe the results of this research imply that assertions such as "(management practice X) leads to or is associated with higher or increased nonprofit organization effectiveness" must be qualified by adding and providing evidence for "according to (whom)." The idea that there is a single objective organizational effectiveness independent of the judgments of various stakeholders is no longer tenable or useful. The conception that there is multiple effectiveness obviously means that investigating the relation of organizational characteristics and management practices to effectiveness becomes more complex, yet there are advantages to such investigations. For example, we see an advantage in avoiding the uncritical assumption that the most recent widely advocated management practices will necessarily lead to improved effectiveness (such as that adopting the practice of creating vision statements will improve effectiveness).

Another advantage is that research based on multiple stakeholder judgments of effectiveness will provide much more convincing evidence of the extent of the relation between various practices or characteristics and judgments of effectiveness. We may not be able to make bold and sweeping claims that X or Y is the key to improving effectiveness, but we will be able to make justified claims.

In discussions with practicing nonprofit managers, including chief executives and other senior managers, about the results and their practical implications, we have found that some feel the results and their implications are unsurprising whereas some others feel that the results and their implications are worrisome.

We have suggested to these managers that the basic implication of our results is that they recognize that different constituencies are judging their organizations' effectiveness in different ways and that they (the managers) should find out what criteria are important to the different constituencies and provide favorable information on how their organizations are doing on those criteria. In effect, we are recommending tailoring the effectiveness message to each audience. Some managers tell us this is not something they have not thought of or already done. The more cynical have stated that all good managers are "spin doctors."

Others have said that they know that different things are important to different groups but that there must be a true objective assessment for their and others' organizations. They have worried that the idea that there is not an independently real effectiveness will lead (or has led) to efforts to slant (or worse fabricate) data about various possible effectiveness criteria. We appreciate such concerns. However, we hold that recognizing that how and on what bases different constituencies reach effectiveness judgments varies and that differentially emphasizing information of interest to differing constituencies is not tantamount to advocating lying. Managers can (and many do) present information that is as accurate as possible while still presenting it in ways that make a good case for their organization.

Tassie, Murray, and Cutt (in press), in a recent qualitative study of how two governmental funders and one federated nonprofit funder evaluated the effectiveness of two nonprofit service providers, demonstrate that all three funding bodies used both formal and nonformal evaluation processes and that the nonformal were often regarded as more important and more accurate than the formal procedures. They also suggest that the three funders differed in the bases on which they nonformally judged the two agencies and that the managers of the two agencies presented their agencies and their performance in different ways to the differing funders. This suggests that these managers recognized that perceptions regarding effectiveness differed by different stakeholders.

Given the evidence that board members and funders evaluate NPO effectiveness differently and, especially, that funders' judgments are related to correct procedure, we recommend that managers attempt to get the best possible reading on the criteria that are important to each group and then communicate any differences to the board. However, it should be recognized that the two groups are likely to vary to at least some extent on criteria. Further, participants may be unwilling or even unable to communicate what they use as criteria and evidence important to assessing their criteria.

It will be important for the board to explicitly decide how it will evaluate the effectiveness of the organization and how its evaluation of the organization's effectiveness will affect its appraisal of the CEO's performance. The board also should work to understand these alternative perspectives on effectiveness, determine which are important to the organization (whether for performance, political, or other reasons), and incorporate these criteria into its assessments. We recommend that the board and CEO do more than merely identify stakeholders' criteria for effectiveness, however. Effective NPO leaders will engage in an ongoing dialogue about these criteria with key stakeholders to actively influence expectations and perceptions. Such dialogue can enhance the development of shared understanding about expectations for NPO performance and what constitutes effectiveness for a given community and organization. That said, we recognize that boards and CEOs are also likely to find advantages in maintaining some looseness in the effectiveness evaluation process.

Note

1. In a recent study of Columbus, Ohio, nonprofit charitable organizations, Sheehan (1996) found that

only 14 percent of the responding organizations supplied outcome measures when asked to explain how they determined mission accomplishment. Mission accomplishment was more often assessed in terms of inputs and processes. In responses to a follow-up questionnaire sent to the organizations that had outcome measures, Sheehan found in fewer than half did any other respondent (for example, board chairperson, board member, or staff member) provide an outcome measure identical to that supplied earlier by the chief executive. Sheehan's study suggests that mission accomplishment is not often used to assess NPO effectiveness. Our study suggests why not.

References

Bielefeld, W. 1992. Funding uncertainty and nonprofit strategies in the 1980s. *Nonprofit Management & Leadership* 4: 381–401.

Bradshaw, P., V. Murray, & J. Wolpin. 1992. Do nonprofit boards make a difference? An exploration of the relationships among board structure, process and effectiveness. *Nonprofit and Voluntary Sector Quarterly* 21: 227–249.

Cameron, K. S. 1986. Effectiveness as paradox: Consensus and conflict conceptions of organizational effectiveness. *Management Science* 32: 539–553.

Campbell, J. P. 1977. On the nature of organization effectiveness. In P. S. Goodman & J. M. Pennings, eds., *New perspectives on organizational effectiveness,* pp. 13–55. San Francisco: Jossey-Bass.

Carver, J. 1990. *Boards that make a difference: A new design for leadership in nonprofit and public organizations.* San Francisco: Jossey-Bass.

Chait, R. P., T. P. Holland, & B. E. Taylor. 1991. *The effective board of trustees.* New York: Macmillan.

Cohen, M. D., J. G. March, & J. P. Olsen. 1972. A garbage can model of organizational choice. *Administrative Science Quarterly* 17: 1–25.

D'Aunno, T. 1992. The effectiveness of human service organizations: A comparison of models. In Y. Hasenfeld, ed., *Human services as complex organizations,* pp. 341–361. Newbury Park, CA: Sage.

DiMaggio, P. J., & W. W. Powell. 1983. The iron cage revisited: Institutional isomorphism and collective rationality in organizational fields. *American Sociological Review* 48: 147–160.

Dinius, S. H., & R. B. Rogow. 1988. Application of the Delphimethod in identifying characteristics big eight firms seek in entry-level accountants. *Journal of Accounting Education* 6: 83–101.

Elmore, R. F. 1978. Organizational models of social program implementation. *Public Policy* 26: 185–228.

Galaskiewicz, J. 1985. *The social organization of an urban grants economy: A study of business philanthropy and nonprofit organizations.* Orlando, FL: Academic Press.

Galaskiewicz, J., & R. S. Burt. 1991. Interorganization contagion in corporate philanthropy. *Administrative Science Quarterly* 36: 88–105.

Garde, V. D., & R. R. Patel. 1985. Technological forecasting for power generation. *Long Range Planning* (August): 73–79.

Green, J. C., & D. W. Griesinger. 1996. Board performance and organizational effectiveness in nonprofit social service organizations. *Nonprofit Management and Leadership* 6: 381–402.

Helmer, O., & N. Rescher. 1969. On the epistemology of the inexact sciences. *Management Science* (June): 146–157.

Herman, R. D., & R. D. Heimovics. 1993. *The social construction of nonprofit organization effectiveness: An interim research report.* Paper presented at the annual meeting of the Association for Research on Nonprofit Organizations and Voluntary Action, October, Toronto.

———. 1994. A cross-national study of a method for researching non-profit organizational effectiveness. *Voluntas* 5: 86–100.

Herman, R. D., D. O. Renz, & R. D. Heimovics. Board practices and board effectiveness in local nonprofit organizations. *Nonprofit Management and Leadership.* In Press.

Kanter, R. M., & D. Brinkerhoff. 1981. Organizational performance: Recent developments in measurement. In R. H. Turner & J. F. Short, Jr., eds., *Annual review of sociology,* pp. 321–349. Palo Alto, CA: Annual Review.

Meyer, J. W., & B. Rowan. 1977. Institutionalized organizations: Formal structure as myth and ceremony. *American Journal of Sociology* 83: 340–363.

Mohr, L. B. 1982. *Explaining organizational behavior.* San Francisco: Jossey-Bass.

Murray, V., & B. Tassie. 1994. Evaluating the effectiveness of nonprofit organizations. In R. D. Herman, ed., *The Jossey-Bass handbook of nonprofit leadership and management.* San Francisco: Jossey-Bass.

Murray, V., B. Tassie, & J. Cutt. 1995. The negotiation of funder-fundee evaluation processes: A case study of failed action research. *Abstracts of Proceedings of the 1996 Association for Research on Nonprofit Organizations and Voluntary Action Annual Conference* (November): 257–262.

Nonprofit Management Group. 1991. *Enhancing the quality of public reporting by nonprofit organiza-*

tions. New York: Baruch College/City University of New York, Department of Public Administration.

Pfeffer, J. 1982. *Organizations and organization theory.* Boston: Pittman.

Quinn, R. E., & J. Rohrbaugh. 1981. A competing values approach to organizational effectiveness. *Public Productivity Review* 2: 122–140.

———. 1983. A spatial model of effectiveness criteria: Towards a competing values approach to organizational effectiveness. *Management Science* 29: 363–377.

Rohrbaugh, J. 1981. Operationalizing the competing values approach: Measuring performance in the employment service. *Public Productivity Review* 2: 141–159.

———. 1983. The competing values approach: Innovation and effectiveness in the job service. In R. H. Hall & R. E. Quinn, eds., *Organizational theory and public policy,* pp. 265–298. Beverly Hills, CA: Sage.

Scott, W. R. 1995. *Institutions and organizations.* Thousand Oaks, CA: Sage.

Sheehan, R. M., Jr. 1996. Mission accomplishment as philanthropic organization effectiveness: Key findings from the excellence in philanthropy project. *Nonprofit and Voluntary Sector Quarterly* 25:110–123.

Slesinger. L. H. 1991. *Self-assessment for nonprofit governing boards.* Washington, DC: National Center for Nonprofit Boards.

Tassie, B., V. Murray, & J. Cutt. Evaluating social service agencies: Fuzzy pictures of organizational effectiveness. *Voluntas.* In press.

Tsui, A. S. 1990. A multiple-constituency model of effectiveness: An empirical examination at the human resource subunit level. *Administrative Science Quarterly* 35:458–483.

Zammuto, R. F. 1984. A comparison of multiple constituency models of organizational effectiveness. *Academy of Management Review,* 9, 606–616.

PART 11

NONPROFIT ORGANIZATIONS INTERNATIONALLY

During the past three decades, nonprofit organizations in the United States have expanded their international presence and importance. U.S. nonprofits and counterpart organizations in Europe, Asia, and Australia have been reaching out aggressively across national boundaries to find new sources of funding and to operate programs and provide services in new territories.

It is not possible to know with precision how many nonprofit organizations are engaged in international activities or what their operating budgets are.[1] Estimates about their magnitude are usually extrapolated from reports of government agencies or international organizations, such as the United Nations, the World Bank, and the Organization of Economic Cooperation and Development (OECD). Dichter,[2] for example, uses reports produced by governments of developed nations and organizations such as the World Bank and USAID: "NGOs [nongovernmental organizations] themselves, have accounted for between $60 billion and $65 billion in aid to developing countries annually for about the past decade. . . . An OECD estimate for 1994 is that $5.7 billion in aid to developing countries passes through NGOs."[3]

U.S.-based international nonprofit organizations and their operating budgets are few in comparison with other nonprofit subsectors, such as health, the human services, and education. Over the past thirty years, however, the growth has been rapid.[4]

Structures of International Nonprofit Organizations

As one would expect, the structures of international nonprofit organizations vary widely from large nonprofits with highly centralized controls to loose confederations of small, essentially free-standing nonprofits. A recent conference on globalization sponsored by the University of Washington created a five-category typology of structures that is based on the degree of centralized control over a nonprofit organization's mission and performance:[5]

- separate independent organizations;
- independent organizations with weak umbrella coordination;
- confederations;
- federations; and
- unitary, corporate organizations.

Conference participants noted that "globalization puts immense pressure on many organizations to move toward more coordinated rather than purely decentralized or unitary models."[6]

The Growth of Nonprofits Internationally

During the 1970s and 1980s, the U.S. government (and several other governments) decided to use nonprofit organizations as their "nonpolitical" hands and arms for delivering foreign aid, development assistance, and humanitarian relief. "As the Cold War continued, the U.S. government and private citizens alike shared an interest in keeping newly emerging nations from opting for alliances with the Soviet Union. Accordingly, the creation of private institutions to alleviate poverty and stimulate popular participation in the civic life of these societies became a major objective of U.S. foreign policy."[7] The major impetus behind the expansion of nonprofit organizations' international activities during this period, therefore, was increased government financing—not private philanthropy.

Definitions

There is a notable lack of agreement about the meanings of many terms related to international nonprofit organizations. A few important definitions on which there is general agreement include:

- *Globalization.* "The internationalization of major financial markets, technology, and of important sectors of manufacturing and services. . . . The world economy [is] . . . dominated by uncontrollable global market forces and has as its principal actors and major agents of change truly transnational corporations which owe allegiance to no nation state and locate wherever on the globe market advantage dictates."[8]

"Globalization refers to the emergence and spread of a supraterritorial dimension of social relations. In institutional terms, the process has unfolded through the proliferation and growth of so-called 'transnational corporations,' popular associations, and regulatory agencies (sometimes called global companies, global civil societies, and global regimes respectively)."[9]

- *NGO* (or *nongovernmental organization*). As defined originally by United Nations ECOSOC resolution 288[X], Article 71, 1950, a *nongovernmental organization* is "any international organization which is not established by intergovernmental agreement shall be considered as a nongovernmental organization."[10]

  A more current definition is "a group brought together by common aims and with a basic organizational structure; it does not rely upon governments for its formation or for most of the resources of its continued existence, and it is not profitmaking in its aim."[11]

- *Intermediary NPO* (*nonprofit organization*). "Indigenous nonprofit organizations in developing countries at the national and regional levels [that] act as intermediaries in channeling . . . international assistance to the poor in their own societies. . . . These intermediary NPOs sometimes carry out projects but more frequently act as brokers between local groups at the grassroots level who have formed their own smaller NPOs."[12]

  In contrast with voluntary membership nonprofits (see below), "intermediate organizations are neither membership based nor are they fully voluntary. They have part-time or full-time staff, seek funding, and deliver programs and services to people, communities and/or to voluntary membership organizations themselves."[13]

- *Voluntary Membership NGO.* "Voluntary membership organizations include grassroots organizations where members come from the same community, and organizations where the members come from different communities but are linked by a professional, religious, or other affiliation. The common characteristic of voluntary membership organizations is that they work for the members' own interests."[14]

The Roles of Nonprofits Under Different Governments

In the nineteenth and early twentieth century, the primary task of most governments was to protect citizens against internal disorder or external attacks.

Other aspects of public life could be left to the family or to organized groups not directly under governmental control. . . . As governments increased their involvement in building the foundations of an international society with rules and norms for activities such as trade and commerce, travel and transport, health services and even warfare, so the potential arose for international nongovernmental organizations (INGOs). These bodies represented nongovernmental organizations working across frontiers to particular ends.[15]

As the twentieth century came to a close, two types of organizations had moved to the forefront of international nonprofit activities: "humanitarian relief and private-development assistance organizations, and interest associations."[16] The role that IN-GOs—or, as they are more commonly known today, *nongovernmental organizations* or simply *NGOs*—play in various nations around the world depends mostly on particular governments' views of the state and international relations.

> A view of the state based on, for example, the U.S. Constitution might see it as a servant of the people and their needs. Insofar as these needs can be achieved by other means—by use of the market or by voluntary associations—then the state has less to do and private enterprise and civil society [and NGOs] are to the fore. . . . [In contrast,] a government that believes it has the monopoly of wisdom—as well as power—has little time for nongovernmental organizations.[17]

In nondemocratic societies, governments may attempt "to control not only political and economic activities but also that in the social, religious, and family sphere. Such governments have thus been opposed to the existence of independent nongovernmental organizations."[18] A government may suppress nonprofit organizations coercively or more subtly. For example, government sets the subsidies it will pay for services provided by nonprofits, the services it will contract out into the nonprofit sector, and the regulations it will use to encourage or discourage the health—and the existence—of organizations in the nonprofit sector. "In the extreme, the state can proscribe NPOs, nationalize them, or prohibit consumers from using their services. . . . Thus, although the nonprofit sector flourishes at the will of the government, its existence also limits the power of the state, in democratic societies."[19]

Readings Reprinted in Part Eleven

"Internationalization of the Nonprofit Sector," by Helmut Anheier and Kusuma Cunningham,[20] traces the rise of nongovernmental organizations (NGOs), particularly humanitarian relief, private-development assistance organizations, and interest associations, through the decade when the League of Nations was established and the 1945 Founding Conference of the United Nations in San Francisco. From 1950 through the 1970s, they note, "most of the recently independent countries of Africa and Asia shared the distrust socialist régimes had for NGOs." In the 1980s and 1990s, NGOs emerged "to become an accepted and increasingly integrated part of an international policy network. . . . NGOs are basic ingredients of an emerging international society of organizations."

Anheier and Cunningham analyze the roles that NGOs have played in development in third world nations, U.S. developmental assistance policy, and international philanthropy. They report on a study of USAID-funded NGOS that identified an array of management problems across a wide range of projects in numerous countries: "insufficient institutional planning, weaknesses in fundraising, suboptimal financial planning, poor human resource management, inefficient headquarters-field office relations, lack of project evaluation, bad information management and lack of data processing facilities, administrative difficulties, and inefficiencies in project implementation."

Thomas Dichter describes the characteristics and attributes of nongovernmental organizations (NGOs), including its rapid growth, its newly found legitimacy, and national and regional differences among NGOs in *"Globalization and Its Effects on NGOs: Efflorescence or a Blurring of Roles and Relevance?"*[21] In this comprehensive overview, Dichter also offers definitions; presents estimates of the size and scope of international NGOs and their activities; explains differences among NGOs in different regions of the world; and "discusses some of the tensions, tradeoffs, trends, and strategies posed by globalization as the political economy in which NGOs operate has changed." NGOs risk seeing the positive promise of NGO globalization outweighed by the dangers of commercialization and "commodification" of their work.

Dichter is concerned that "many NGOs, largely because of competitive pressures around money, have taken on aspects of the current commercial zeitgeist, beginning to act as if they were corporations engaged in the world of commerce." A return to the roots of altruistic activism may prove to be the best strategy in response to today's complex challenges.

In *"Nonprofit Organizations in International Development: Agents of Empowerment or Preservers of Stability?"*[22] Brian Smith examines the contrasting roles of transnational nonprofit organizations that help to support the status quo in nations and of those that advocate for change. "Some . . . NPOs are staffed by persons who articulate strong criticisms of home-country foreign policies. . . . Abroad, those staffing intermediary NPOs often criticize their government's policies toward the poor. . . . One might expect, given these differences, that cooperation between governments and NPOs might break down at the sending and receiving ends of the international NPO network and that private donors in the north would soon stop supporting organizations that threatened some of their economic interests." Smith contends that the system continues to function because there are enough overlapping interests among the partners "despite some diverging objectives each espouses." Most governments of lesser-developed nations tolerate NPOS because they mostly emphasize socioeconomic projects rather than activities aimed at increasing political participation among the poor. "Some of the more innovative and extensive [nonprofit organization] activities have been in areas of basic health and family planning, credit and management training for small businesses, small-scale agriculture and water development that is linked with environmental preservation, and production and consumer cooperatives." Thus, "most governments in developing countries, regardless of their political ideology, find NPOs at the intermediary and local levels useful. . . . NPOs in developing countries are not a serious threat to established economic and political elites."

Whether or not the activities of international NPOs have "empowered" populations in developing countries has been fiercely debated in recent years. Smith concludes: "There clearly have been some forms of empowerment of the poor as a result of [NPO] activities. . . . Grassroots NPOs of all types have been particularly helpful to women in their efforts to advance their social power. . . . Women collectively have begun to erode some of the stereotypes in their respective countries, stereotypes that assume male leadership is essential for the implementation of effective development."

Notes

1. Comparisons among different estimates about the size and magnitude of the nonprofit sector's international presence should be made only with considerable caution. There is not widespread agreement on terms, and whereas some estimates include some international nonprofit organizations, others do not. Sources of data should be noted carefully.

2. Thomas W. Dichter, "Globalization and Its Effects on NGOs: Efflorescence or a Blurring of Roles and Relevance?" *Nonprofit and Voluntary Sector Quarterly* 28, no. 4 (1999), supplement:38–58.

3. Ibid., p. 40. On this point, Dichter cites D. Hulme and M. Edwards, *Beyond the Magic Bullet* (West Hartford, CT: Kumarian, 1996).

4. See the three readings that are reprinted in Part 11 for a variety of reports on the growth of this subsector.

5. Marc Lindenberg and J. Patrick Dobel, "The Challenges of Globalization for Northern International Relief and Development NGOs," *Nonprofit and Voluntary Sector Quarterly* 28, no. 4 (1999), supplement:13.

6. Ibid., p. 14.

7. Brian H. Smith, "Nonprofit Organizations in International Development: Agents of Empowerment or Preservers of Stability?" in Walter W. Powell and Elisabeth S. Clemens, eds., *Private Action and the Public Good* (New Haven: Yale University Press, 1998), reprinted in this part.

8. P. Hirst and G. Thompson, *Globalization in Question* (Cambridge, MA: Polity, 1996), 194.

9. J. A. Scholte, "Beyond the Buzzword: Toward a Critical Theory of Globalization," in E. Kofman and G. Young, eds., *Globalization: Theory and Practice* (London: Pinter, 1996), 43–46.

10. United Nations ECOSOC resolution 288[X], Article 71, 1950.

11. Clive Archer, "Nongovernmental Organization," in Jay. M. Shafritz, ed., *International Encyclopedia of Public Policy and Administration* (Boulder: Westview Press, 1998), 1504.

12. Smith, "Nonprofit Organizations in International Development," 217.

13. Dichter, "Globalization and Its Effects on NGOs," 39.

14. Ibid., 38.

15. Archer, "Nongovernmental Organization," 1504.

16. Helmut K. Anheier and Kusuma Cunningham, "Internationalization of the Nonprofit Sector," in Robert D. Herman, ed., *The Jossey-Bass Handbook of Nonprofit Leadership and Management* (San Francisco: Jossey-Bass, 1994), 102, reprinted in this part.

17. Archer, "Nongovernmental Organization," 1505.

18. Ibid., 1505.

19. Estelle James, "Introduction," in E. James, ed., *The Nonprofit Sector in International Perspective: Studies in Comparative Culture and Policy.* New York: Oxford University Press, 1989), 9.

20. Anheier and Cunningham, "Internationalization of the Nonprofit Sector," 100–116.

21. Dichter, "Globalization and Its Effects on NGOs," 38–58.

22. Smith, "Nonprofit Organizations in International Development," 217–227.

► **CHAPTER 34**

Internationalization of the Nonprofit Sector

HELMUT K. ANHEIER
KUSUMA CUNNINGHAM

The internationalization of the nonprofit sector is certainly not a recent phenomenon. For centuries, "operating across borders" has been deeply imprinted in the objectives of many religious (nonprofit) organizations, and, indeed, institutions linked to the Catholic Church, Islam, or Judaism precede the emergence of both the modern nation state and the modern business firm. Religious institutions present some of the earliest examples of nonprofit organizations working in different political, economic, and cultural systems. Monastic orders, missionary societies, or Islamic schools and universities are cases in point. Today, the increased internationalization of the nonprofit sector is, however, rarely discussed in reference to its religious roots (see Smith, 1990); rather than this, the internationalization of modern nonprofit sectors is a process that began in the nineteenth century, that has achieved much momentum since 1945, and that will most likely lead to significant growth rates in the future. What is new, therefore, is not internationalization itself; it is its size, scope, and form.

While the overall proportion of international nonprofit organizations may be small, the area has nonetheless shown some of the highest growth rates in the sector.

The *Yearbook of International Organizations* (Union of International Associations, 1992) shows a global increase in international organizations between 1977 and 1992 of about 122 percent. In the United States, a growth rate of 92 percent during the same period indicates the significant expansion of nongovernmental organizations (NGOs) internationally. The total increase in Canadian international organizations amounted to 96 percent also, and in Japan to 99 percent. Increases in Europe were on average somewhat higher (107 percent), and the bulk of relative growth occurred in the developing world: in Africa, 164 percent, and 142 percent in Asia.

The Rise of NGOs

Two types of nonprofit organizations are at the center of the sector's internationalization: humanitarian relief and private-development assistance organizations, and interest associations. Though somewhat imprecisely, these very different types of organizations are summarily referred to as nongovernmental organizations, or NGOs.

NGOs played an important role in the formation of the modern world of international relations. Not only did NGOs participate alongside governments in the first international human rights conferences, they also helped bring about a system of international contracts and agreements that paved the way for the establishment of the League of Nations. While the league did not officially recognize NGOs as parties to treaties, a modus operandi developed that allowed representatives to participate, speak, and introduce resolutions in plenary sessions and meetings. This form of informal participation proved increasingly difficult as the international climate deteriorated in the 1930s. As relations among governments worsened, the role of NGOs became politicized and controversial.

This mixed record was one important reason why the Founding Conference of the United Nations in San Francisco in 1945 decided to establish a formal consultative status for NGOs. We should also take into account that 42 U.S. NGOs participated in an official advisory role to the U.N. conference, and that an additional 240 U.S. NGOs enjoyed "observer status."

The role of NGOs in the U.N. system has changed significantly since the founding period of the 1950s. Until the 1970s most of the recently independent countries of Africa and Asia shared the distrust socialist regimes had for NGOs. However, to the extent to which the Third World was able to organize its own interests relatively independent of either the U.S. or Soviet spheres of influence, attitudes toward NGOs became more positive. This development coincided with the first major economic crises since World War II and the beginning of a disillusionment with the role of the state in the process of development. Ironically, distrust previously aimed at NGOs was now redirected toward the state; and particular interests represented by NGOs were now seen as more universalistic and impartial than some Third World governments themselves. This changed perspective about NGOs was prevalent in the Third World as well as in North America and Europe, and it paved the way for their popularity in the 1980s and 1990s (see below).

NGOs maintain consultative status with specialized U.N. organizations, and not with the U.N. in general. About 130 NGOs are linked with the World Health Organization, such as the League of Red Cross Societies. Similar committees exist for the U.N. High Commission for Refugees, the Drug Control Program, the United Nations Educational, Scientific, and Cultural Organization (UNESCO), and the U.N. Development Program. Several hundred NGOs are tied into the U.N. news and information system. Together with governmental and intergovernmental representatives, NGOs are part of a global interorganizational network, in which policies are discussed and formulated.

Many important social and political issues were first brought to the attention of the U.N. and other international bodies through the lobbying activities of NGOs, and much less so through the regular political channels of member states. Examples are fundamental equity issues of social and economic development, concerns for democracy, participation, human rights, and the environment. The 1992 United Nations Conference on Environment and Development ("Earth Summit") in Rio de Janeiro, Brazil, witnessed not only the historically largest gathering of heads of states (118) but also the highest participation of NGOs in an international, intergovernmental conference.

The Earth Summit in Rio de Janeiro underlined a general tendency in international policy arenas: the rise of NGOs to become an accepted and increasingly integrated part of an international policy network. In this way, NGOs replicate at the international level the development of complex national policy networks—among government agencies, corporate representatives, and nonprofit organizations—to formulate and implement domestic policies (Laumann and Knoke, 1987). NGOs are basic ingredients of an emerging international society of organizations.

NGOs and Development

Industrialized countries' interest in providing aid through NGOs to the developing world can be largely explained by the poor performance of many Third World governments in bringing about equitable and sustainable development. NGOs are seen as an alternative to state-led and state-dominated development. The planned development efforts after colonialism had not had the intended effects among the world's poorer countries. Many of the countries are still in the grips of poverty and in a continued state of dependence on foreign assistance. Some African countries depend to over 50 percent of their GDP on international financial assistance in one form or another. Many developing countries are victims of excessive corruption and other forms of distributional inefficiencies, thereby causing a severe obstacle to developmental efforts through planned governmental intervention.

At the same time there is a strong emphasis on human resources development, or "human capital formation." The realization that investment in capital-intensive technology has not resulted in "trickle down" development has added to the growing consensus among planners that it is time to take seriously the "basic needs approach" to development (Toye, 1987). International agencies such as the World Bank and OECD see a potential in NGOs to help negate the harmful effects of macroeconomic policies on poor and disadvantaged groups by promoting local reforms and institution building (World Bank, 1989; OECD, 1988b, 1990). Simultaneously many Western governments see the activities of NGOs as a contribution to civil society, thereby strengthening democratic traditions in Third World countries.

U.S. Development Assistance and NGOs

Although the pattern of relief and development assistance financing between NGOs and the U.S. government emerged during the immediate post-World War II era, the biggest push came in the 1970s. At that time, the U.S. Congress promoted the "new directions" approach in development assistance as part of revamping the politicized and negative image of U.S. activities abroad. Congress tried to promote a humanitarian image of its foreign aid programs and espoused a basic human needs approach to development activities. In doing so, Congress

emphasized that NGOs were ideal conduits for delivering these kinds of services. Thus the 1973 "new directions" legislation was a very important step that led to the growth of the NGOs involved in developmental efforts.

In the 1960s, total development assistance funds channelled through NGOs amounted to $282.2 million. In the 1970s, it increased to $643.5 million, and to $1.09 billion in the 1980s. Currently, the U.S. AID funds to NGOs cover a wide range of activities: agriculture, rural development, nutrition, population planning, health, child services, education and human resources, economic support, disaster relief, and technical assistance.

According to Congressional legislation, in order to be eligible for government development assistance, NGOs must register with U.S. AID, and they are required to come up with 20 percent of financial support from non-U.S. government sources. U.S. AID grants and contracts fund direct service delivery as well as technical assistance and training. Non-U.S. government funding comes from several sources, such as international organizations and multilateral institutions, individual donations, private fundraising, and endowments, as well as revenue from sales of goods and services.

Overall, NGOs received less than 30 percent of their revenue from government. There are, however, significant variations in the extent of government support, and larger NGOs such as Catholic Relief Service, World Vision, and CARE receive between 60 percent and 80 percent of revenues from the public sector. The pattern of NGO financing seems characteristic for the general pattern of third party government in the United States, by which government delegates public tasks to private nonprofit organizations (Salamon, 1987). Over the years, U.S. government funding for NGOs has increased considerably.

Largely in response to the alleged failure of public-sector programs in many developing countries to bring about sustained development, the international aid community has developed a favorable attitude toward NGOs and refers to their flexibility and ability to reach the grassroots as well as to their low-cost, participatory management style. However, whether NGOs are in fact able to meet such high expectations is increasingly doubtful. Judith Tendler's study (1982) of NGOs operating in Latin American countries concludes that NGOs do not necessarily reach the poorest segments of the population, nor are they successful in ensuring sustainable projects. Moreover, increased government funding has many in the development field concerned about the nature and direction of NGO goals and direction. They fear that NGOs are being co-opted to comply with the government's agenda for development, and that NGOs may lose some of their creativity and initiative.

From the perspective of the host country governments, there is a certain ambiguity to the entry and proliferation of international NGOs funded by donor countries. On the one hand, NGOs seem to relieve some of the host government's burden in performing service delivery functions and promoting development. But on the other hand, as Bratton (1989) has noted, they tend to react negatively if NGOs become an alternative mechanism to reallocate development assistance away from governments. In such situations, autocratic governments may fear that they are no longer in control of the developmental agenda.

International Philanthropy

The activities of foundations such as the Ford Foundation and the Rockefeller Foundation in Africa, Latin America, and Asia are among the earliest examples of international philanthropy by the United States. Such activities peaked during the independence period of the 1960s, when U.S. foundations established and helped create universities and research institutions in the newly independent countries. Legal changes in the United States and changing economic conditions, in particular the relative devaluation of the U.S. dollar, make it impossible now for foundations to engage in large-scale development activities. Instead, U.S. foundations like Ford see their role in facilitating and initiating, rather than implementing institution building in the Third World.

Foundation Giving

According to the survey reported by the Foundation Center on Giving (Renz, 1991), the 100 largest foundations give a total of about $2.4 billion, out of which about 4.4 percent, or $109 million, goes toward international activities. Of the total number of grants made in this category, 812, or about 3.5 percent, are to international activities. And among the 372 other foundations with a total of about $789 million, $17 million, or 2.2 percent of the funds, are given to international activities. Out of the total number of grants made, about 548 are international grants, amounting to only 2.3 percent of the total. International activities are defined as constituting the following categories: peace, security, and arms control; exchange programs; development and relief services; research; policy and management; and "other." In Canada, the Foundation Directory (McClintock, 1991) lists close to sixty foundations that are focusing on international activities.

Individual Giving

At the end of the 1980s, data on individual giving noted an increase in the area of international affairs, especially in the area of peace, security, and arms control (Renz, 1991). And according to the *Annual Report on Philanthropy* (Weber, 1991), giving to organizations involved in international affairs, including projects on international peace and security, amounted to an estimated $2.23 billion, an increase of nearly 30 percent compared to the previous year, which was estimated at $1.71 billion.

One of the most important reasons for this surge in individual giving to international causes is the end of the cold war, which has led to revelations of new needs and opportunities for private philanthropy in Eastern Europe. Not surprisingly churches and religious groups have been major players in the field. In 1990, the American Catholic Church, for example, launched a multimillion-dollar campaign over the next three years to assist churches in the former communist bloc countries. Many other churches have launched their own campaigns and are putting considerable effort into this endeavor.

Management of NGOs

Research on nonprofit management has long emphasized the complex environment in which nonprofit organizations operate (Herman and Heimovics, 1991). Nonprofit organizations have to reconcile the demand of multiple constituencies, such as board members, clients, and donors (Powell and Friedkin, 1987). This complex management task is made even more precarious for nonprofit organizations operating internationally and in different social, cultural, and political settings. For international advocacy organizations, Young (1992) argues that they are successful if they adopt organizational structures and strategies that accommodate the problems associated with international operations. These are cultural diversity, geographical distance in operations, economic barriers, and political fragmentation. Young finds that decentralized and federated structures appear more successful over time than both centralized organizations and hierarchical federations in meeting the challenges of international environments.

Of course, organizations vary to the extent to which they are able, willing, or formed to find a match between organizational structure and environment. U.S. AID sponsored a study of AID-funded NGOs and their operations, both in the United States and in the developing world (Biddle, 1984). The study was able to identify several management problems that seemed characteristic across a wide range of projects and countries: insufficient institutional planning, weaknesses in fundraising, suboptimal financial planning, poor human resource management, inefficient headquarters-field office relations, lack of project evaluation, bad information management and lack of data processing facilities, administrative difficulties, and inefficiencies in project implementation. We will briefly discuss some of them.

Lack of Institutional Planning

Nearly 75 percent of the respondents mentioned that some aspect of planning was a problem.

Many NGO members complained that because NGOs do not have long-term planning, they deal with challenges on an ad hoc basis and "move from one crisis to the other." The need to secure funding opportunities means that NGOs frequently opt for working in the area where there is funding available rather than where there is demand for their services. This results in a serious lack of a "strategic focus" to their programs. They are unable to set clear goals and priorities in terms of funds and activities needed to meet the demand for their services.

Some of the main reasons cited to explain difficulty and resistance to institutional planning was that planning establishes rigid frameworks that prevent adaptation and flexibility—which are seen as characteristics of NGOs. Institutional planning is more complicated to implement when dealing with diversified international operations. The program staff are geographically separated from the planning staff; the political context may be full of uncertainties; government policies may be ambiguous, and local as well as international funding uncertain.

The Management of Fund Raising

Nearly 49 percent of the respondents mentioned that obtaining a secure financial base had become increasingly difficult—not only because of scarcer resources and increased competition but also because NGOs are moving away from direct relief and rehabilitation to working toward institutional development and policy reform. This has created problems for fundraising. It is not always easy to justify complex development goals to a potential constituency of donors. Some NGOs fear losing their funding base unless they make direct emotional appeals to the public (see also Smith, 1990).

Besides this, NGOs may not be able to obtain strong support and help toward fundraising from their boards; many staff felt that boards interfere too frequently in daily operational matters. Twenty-two percent of the respondents felt that relations with the board in matters of fundraising were not always smooth sailing. Another problem was that NGOs are generally reluctant to use professional fundraising experts.

They fear that professionals would not have the same values as those within the NGO community. Recently, however, there has been a growing trend toward hiring professional fund raisers.

Financial Planning

Most NGOs face considerable problems in the field of financial planning. Nearly 34 percent of the respondents alluded to budgeting as a problem in allocating funds to competing priorities. Not only the delays and uncertainties of obtaining available funds in an international financial environment contribute to this problem but also the complexity of different sources and types of funds, which, combined with donor preferences and restrictions, has created a complicated financial system. Few NGOs have the capacity to track the variables at work in a financial system that would allow them to predict financial outcomes with a degree of certainty. As a result, NGOs seek stable funding from a few sources, and few follow a strategy by which they try to optimize return across several funding arenas under conditions of uncertainty.

Management of Human Resources

Human resources involves a whole range of problems, such as recruitment, salary, training, and technical and managerial skills. However, this situation has currently improved; as the NGOs have matured and gained in stature, they have become highly professional and are able to recruit well-trained and educated staff. Yet finding experienced people willing and able to work overseas at often noncompetitive wages remains a problem. As a consequence, managerial and technical competence at the field level may be lacking. Still, for many organizations, due to budgetary pressures, there is a tendency to hire junior staff and rely on "hands on" training to substitute for experience. Budgetary pressures also reduce the ability of NGOs to finance programs suited to their special needs.

Headquarters/Field Staff Relations

At least 26 percent of the respondents felt that management difficulties flowed from the geo-graphical separation of operations. Communication becomes difficult and lack of information creates managerial distrust and need for action; as a result many NGOs have developed centralized management styles. But the growing influence of semiautonomous indigenous and local organizations in the field has brought additional problems of coordination and responsibility. Frequently, however, managers at headquarters are faced with the problems of weak local accounting systems, inexperienced staff, high turnover, and low job security at the field level.

Project Evaluation and Information Management

Many NGOs recognize that one of their weaknesses is the lack of proper evaluation of their projects. This is only partially due to budgetary or staff constraints, which make it difficult to devote time and resources for evaluation. In other cases, these difficulties serve as a protective shield to maintain the myth of the cost-effective, responsive, and participatory NGOs.

Administrative Difficulties

Government procedures and regulations in grant management tend to be complex. Many NGOs wish for technical assistance and help in the interpretation of AID rules and regulations. Changes in federal policies with regard to procurement or financial management policy may create uncertainties for NGOs. However large, well-established NGOs are better equipped to cope with this problem than small, newly established ones.

Professionalization

Although managers may be well versed in project design and evaluation, when it comes to project implementation at the field level, managers frequently find that there is a greater need for training in day-to-day project management, contracting, procurement, listening skills, and training. The rapid growth of the NGO community over the last two decades has also brought about some dramatic changes in all aspects of the NGO operations, including the management culture of the NGOs.

Increased growth has brought along with it increased professionalization. The managers of NGOs may no longer see themselves as primarily guided by idealistic notions. They see themselves as development professionals. Those entering the profession are no longer generalists, but well-trained specialists. Increased professionalization brings with it, however, a greater potential for bureaucratization and a certain rigidity—a loss of flexibility.

As NGOs move into more complex areas of development such as promoting institutional development and policy reform, they are also beginning to borrow terminologies and techniques from the corporate culture, such as "strategic management," "risk taking," "marketing a product," and "participatory management." The traditional ideology of NGOs, as exemplified in Dichter (1987), stresses group processes and popular participation: team building, problem solving, facilitation skills, active listening skills, conflict resolution, and coalition building skills.

The term *"participatory management"* has become increasingly popular among the development community. Although it is a simple sounding term and makes sense intuitively, there is much debate as to what it means and how it can best be effectively practiced. Even though the notion of participatory development has its roots in socialist thinking of the nineteenth century, it entered current management debates via the theology of liberation in Latin America and the secular NGO community in OECD countries. It is now given considerable importance and attention by development experts as well as multilateral institutions such as the World Bank, which in 1992 hosted a three-day workshop on participatory management. Development experts are also learning to build on indigenous traditions, which often include elements of cooperation and mutual self-help, in addressing the public goods problem in communities within developing countries.

Future Trends

In recent years NGOs have become major actors in an emerging international society of or-

ganizations. Three trends are part of this ongoing development: the emergence of local NGOs in developing countries, the increased prominence of Japanese foundations, and the European Association Statute that will make it possible for nonprofit organizations to operate as pan-European associations (6 and Kuti, 1992).

Developmental NGOs have changed somewhat over the last decade as these organizations have matured and are asked to be more accountable. At the same time, NGOs are faced with competition for financial resources, not only because of the number of such organizations seeking funding but also because of growth in an unexpected area, namely southern NGOs, which is to say, nongovernmental organizations based in the developing countries. The southern NGOs have grown so rapidly that it is conceivable that they pose some challenges to the northern NGOs (Fisher, 1993).

As Dichter (1989) points out, the trend among the southern and northern NGOs is toward a "shift in responsibilities." In the future, donor agencies may bypass established "northern" NGOs and deal directly with those in the south. Not many solutions exist to this possible dilemma, except that U.S. NGOs could maintain their comparative advantages in terms of research, education, institution building, and environmental protection, and their traditional forte—emergency and disaster relief.

Global interconnectedness and a highly competitive international economic environment will bring new opportunities and new challenges to the NGO community. NGOs, with their years of experience in developing countries, may be useful in initiating commercial activity in those areas. For example, NGOs are now intermediaries between the U.S. government and the local populations of some developing countries. In the future, NGOs may also act as intermediaries between private business interests and potential markets in developing countries. Another related factor to the globalization of the economy is the increasing numbers and scope of corporate philanthropic activities. The notion of a "good corporate citizen," which Japanese corporations are currently being asked to abide by

(Koike, 1992), may become one of the yardsticks for measuring the success or failure of global corporations.

References

Agency for International Development. *Implementation of "New Directions" in Development Assistance: Report to the Committee on International Relations on Implementation of Legislative Reforms in the Foreign Assistance Act of 1973.* Washington, DC: AID, 1975.

_____. *Voluntary Foreign Aid Programs: Report of American Voluntary Agencies Engaged in Overseas Relief and Development Registered with the Agency for International Development.* Washington, DC: AID, 1992.

_____. Advisory Committee on Voluntary Foreign Aid, 1990 Report. *Responding to Change: Private Voluntarism and International Development.* Washington, DC: AID, 1990.

_____. Office of Private and Voluntary Cooperation, Bureau for Food for Peace and Voluntary Assistance. *The AID-NGO Partnership: Sharing Goals and Resources in the Work of Development.* Washington, DC: AID, 1987.

Amenomori, T. "Defining the Nonprofit Sector: Japan." Working papers of the Johns Hopkins Comparative Nonprofit Sector Project, no 15. Baltimore: Johns Hopkins University Press, 1993.

Arnove, R. F., ed. *Philanthropy and Cultural Imperialism: The Foundations at Home and Abroad.* Boston, MA: G. K. Hall, 1980.

Biddle, S. C. "The Management Needs of Private Voluntary Organizations." In *A Report Prepared for the Office of Private and Voluntary Cooperation, AID.* Washington, D.C.: Agency for International Development, 1984.

Bratton, M. "The Politics of Government-NGO Relations in Africa." *World Development* 17(4), 569–587.

Dichter, T. W. "The Contexts and Cultures in Which NGOs Manage." *AID Technical Paper.* Washington, D.C.: Agency for International Development, 1987.

_____. *Issues Critical to a Shift in Responsibilities Between U.S. PVOs and Southern NGOs: Paper presented to the Advisory Committee on Voluntary Foreign Aid.* Washington, DC: AID, 1989.

Fisher, J. *The Road to Rio: Sustainable Development and the Nongovernmental Movement in the Third World.* Westport, CT: Praeger, 1993.

Herman, R. D., and R. D. Heimovics. *Executive Leadership in Nonprofit Organizations: New Strategies for Shaping Executive-Board Dynamics.* San Francisco: Jossey-Bass, 1991.

Hodgkinson, V., M. Weitzman, C. M. Toppe, and S. M. Noga. *Nonprofit Almanac 1992–93: Dimensions of the Independent Sector.* San Francisco: Jossey-Bass, 1992.

Inside Japanese Support. Rockville, MD: TAFT Publications, 1992.

Koike, I. "Japanese Giving at the Grassroots." *Foundation News* (January/February 1992):41–43.

Laumann, E. O., and D. Knoke. *The Organizational State: Social Choice in National Policy Domains.* Madison, WI: University of Wisconsin Press, 1987.

London, N. *Japanese Corporate Philanthropy.* New York: Oxford University Press, 1991.

McClintock, N., ed. *Canadian Directory to Foundations.* Toronto: Canadian Center for Philanthropy, 1991.

Organization for Economic Cooperation and Development. *Directory of Nongovernmental Organizations in OECD Member Countries.* Paris: OECD, 1981.

_____. *Development Cooperation 1988 Report.* Paris: OECD, 1988a.

_____. *Voluntary Aid for Development: The Role of Nongovernmental Organizations.* Paris: OECD, 1988b.

_____. *Development Cooperation 1989 Report.* Paris: OECD, 1989.

_____. *Development Cooperation 1990 Report.* Paris: OECD, 1990.

_____. *Directory of Nongovernmental Organizations in OECD Member Countries.* Paris: OECD, 1991.

Powell, W., and R. Friedkin. "Organizational Change in Nonprofit Organizations." In W. Powell, ed, *The Nonprofit Sector: A Research Handbook.* New Haven: Yale University Press, 1987.

Renz, L. *Foundation Giving: Yearbook of Facts and Figures on Private, Corporate and Community Foundations, 1991 Edition.* New York: Foundation Center, 1991.

Roy, D. "Japanese Philanthropy in the U.S.: The 1990s and Beyond." Speech given by the president of the Hitachi Foundation at NOVA University, Fort Lauderdale, Florida, 1992.

Salamon, L. M. "Partners in Public Service: The Scope and Theory of Government-Nonprofit Relations." In W. Powell, ed., *The Nonprofit Sector: A Research Handbook.* New Haven: Yale University Press, 1987.

6, P., and Kuti, E. "Into the European Community: Impacts of Future Membership on Hungary's

Nonprofit Sector." Paper presented at the Arnova Conference, Yale University, New Haven, Connecticut, October 1992.

Smith, B. *More than Altruism: The Politics of Private Foreign Aid.* Princeton: Princeton University Press, 1990.

Tendler, J. *Turning Private Voluntary Organizations into Developmental Agencies: Questions for Evaluation.* AID Program Evaluation Discussion Paper 12. Washington, DC: AID, 1982.

Toye, J. "Development Theory and the Issues for the Future." In L. Emmerij, ed., *Development Policies and the Crisis of the 1980s.* Paris: Organization for Economic Cooperation and Development, 1987.

Union of International Associations. *Yearbook of International Organizations, 1992–93.* Munich: K. G. Saur Verlag GmbH, 1992.

Weber, N., ed. *Giving USA: The Annual Report on Philanthropy for the Year 1990.* New York: Joanne Hayes, 1991.

World Bank. *The World Bank Development Report.* Oxford: Oxford University Press, 1989.

Yamamoto, T., and T. Amenomori. *Japanese Private Philanthropy in an Inter-dependent World: The JCIE Papers.* New York: Japan Center for International Exchange, 1989.

Young, D. "Organizing Principles for International Advocacy Associations." *Voluntas* 3, no. 1 (1992): 1–28.

CHAPTER 35

Globalization and Its Effects on NGOs

Efflorescence or a Blurring of Roles and Relevance?

Thomas W. Dichter

The term *NGO* is close to a half-century old. It was first used in legalistic fashion by the United Nations in 1950: "Any international organization which is not established by intergovernmental agreement shall be considered as a non-governmental organization" (ECOSOC resolution 288[X], Article 71). The term's age is appropriate in that it reflects nearly the entire history of the formal international development assistance endeavor, between the periphery and the center of which NGOs have threaded their way.

Definitions

There is no single widely used definition or typology on NGOs; one must choose from among the many that have evolved as NGOs themselves have. But because the concern of this volume is international NGOs, one useful distinction is that between voluntary membership organizations and intermediate organizations.

- Voluntary membership organizations include grassroots organizations where members come from the same community (e.g., a registered village women's group in Kenya), and organizations where the members come from different communities but are linked by a professional, religious, or other affiliation. The common characteristic of voluntary membership organizations is that they work for the members' own interests.

- Intermediate organizations are neither membership based nor are they fully voluntary. They have part-time or full-time staff, seek funding, and deliver programs and services to people, communities, and/or to voluntary membership organizations themselves. Internationally, there are two basic types of intermediate organizations: (a) charitable welfare and relief organizations, and (b) development organizations (although even this distinction has become blurred, as will be noted below).

Though many would now include voluntary membership organizations in the broad term *NGOs,* this article is concerned primarily with internationally oriented intermediate organizations (the term *NGO* will be used as a shorthand for this). Incidentally, these are the organizations still most often generally thought of by the public when the term *NGOs* is used. The Co operative for Assistance and Relief Everywhere (CARE), Save the Children, Amnesty International, Oxfam, Christian Children's Fund, Plan International (formerly Foster Parents Plan), World Learning (formerly the Experiment in International Living), Catholic Relief Services, ActionAid, Christian Aid, Earthwatch, and World Vision are examples of these NGOs. They were all founded to work internationally.

The oldest of these NGOs generally began as relief and welfare organizations and evolved into development organizations concerned with poverty alleviation, primary health care, the environment, education, legal rights for women, human rights, and so forth. Nowadays almost all NGOs in international development seek positive change—they exist to improve the lot of people, whether their focus is poor or unjustly treated people, the state of health of the earth, or the fostering of democracy. Even those NGOs specializing in disaster relief are no longer content with Band-Aid kinds of assistance. Across the board, NGOs now seek lasting effects of their work, and it is this trait that makes most of them developmental.

Numbers and Sizes

Partly because the terminology around NGOs continues to change, there are no reliable statistics about how many intermediate NGOs currently exist. We do know that the Organization for Economic Cooperation and Development (OECD) in the late 1980s listed about 4,000 NGOs among its advanced economy members.[1] But the growth of NGOs of the intermediate type has been in the developing countries, and there we have only speculation. It is safe to say, however, that the combined total of NGOs in the advanced economies and the developing countries is at least in the tens of thousands.

The largest number of internationally oriented NGOs among the OECD nations come from the United States. In 1996 there were 417 U.S. NGOs registered with USAID as organizations engaged in overseas relief and development. The total support of these organizations

was $7.2 billion, of which $4.8 billion (66.7 percent) was private support, the rest coming from public monies (directly or indirectly). The number of U.S. NGOs engaged in partnership with government has increased steadily since the 1980s. Of the total of $7.2 billion, $4.2 billion went to overseas programs and the rest to domestic programs (USAID, 1997).

Of these organizations, 237 (57 percent) had overseas program expenditures under $2 million, 155 organizations (37 percent) had overseas expenditures between $2 million and $40 million, and 25 (6 percent) had overseas program budgets over $40 million. The top 25 alone accounted for $2.5 billion of overseas expenditures, or 60 percent of the total for overseas programs of all 417 agencies.

With few exceptions, NGOs did not really exist outside the advanced economy countries until 25 years ago. But as globalization has spread certain values and ideas about development, the growth in numbers of indigenous NGOs has been dramatic and the job of development and relief has begun to be taken on by them.[2] In partial response to this phenomenon, many advanced economy NGOs have been changing their role—in addition to direct interventions in development and relief, they now have also become providers of technical assistance and often funding to indigenous NGOs. They have become much more global than ever, in response to the rise of the indigenous NGOs as well as a number of other forces and factors that will be discussed below.

National and Regional Differences

In this newly global world of NGOs there are country-specific differences in governing legal regimes that determine how NGOs and other nonprofits can be registered, what they can do, and how they can be financed. There are differences in terms of their colonial history and their philanthropic traditions, as well as cultural meanings attached to ideas like civic responsibility, social action, and voluntarism that influence local roles played by NGOs.

In Latin America, for example, the Catholic church has played a direct and indirect role in the work of many NGOs, both those with an explicit political reform agenda and those that work directly on economic or social development (many agricultural cooperatives were founded with the help of priests).

In much of sub-Saharan Africa until recently, what we in the advanced economies have come to accept as a tripartite division of society's institutions (corporate sector, public sector, and third or independent sector) hardly existed. Until recently, the public sector in most of postindependent Africa has overwhelmingly dominated. Consequently, NGOs are a relatively new phenomenon in Africa.

All these differences notwithstanding, hardly any NGO in international development is immune to the challenges posed by globalization.

Globalization of What?

Ten years ago were we to have asked what common characteristics NGOs share, three things could have been said with some assurance: They are self-governing, they are characterized by some degree of voluntary involvement, and central to their organizational culture are "values and ideologies" (Brown & Covey, 1986). But at the end of the 1990s even these assertions do not hold up well. Globalization has been a mixed blessing for NGOs. As they have evolved into a worldwide movement, their influence has grown. This has brought them new opportunities and raised expectations placed on them. As they struggle to meet these, the special characteristics they had in common are eroding.

Influence

The influence of advanced economy NGOs has spread globally. The growth of developing country NGOs is in part a response to that influence as well as a response to the globalization of the idea of democracy. In the past 10 years the relationship between governments and NGOs has also become globalized, certainly in the sense that now almost every government incorporates NGOs into their public rhetoric (if not their planning) in much the same way—they are seen increasingly as partners, as implementers of programs or deliverers of services.

As NGOs have grown in numbers and strength, and especially as they have tried to become more developmental, their voice has begun to be heard by governments and multilateral policy makers (e.g., the Food and Agricultural Organization [FAO], UNICEF, the International Fund for Agriculture and Development [IFAD], the International Labor Organization [ILO], and the World Bank).

For some time, major foundations like Ford, Rockefeller, Carnegie, and others have been leaders in setting the policy agenda domestically as well as internationally. There is also little question that NGOs which implement the kinds of programs that a foundation like Ford might fund have been at the forefront of several movements that, once considered marginal, are now part of modern day development discourse. In the realms of people's participation, the role and importance of women in development, the environmental movement, and the carryover of the notion of sustainability from the physical to the financial and social organizational realm, NGOs have led with prominent voices. There is little doubt that significant elements of U.S. foreign policy (e.g., positions on human rights, the rights of and involvement of women, child labor, and the environment) have been influenced by NGOs.

Watershed conferences in the past 20 years have either been instigated by, dominated by, or heavily influenced by NGOs. The Alma Ata conference on Primary Health Care in 1978 is an example. It was NGOs at that conference who put the importance of breast feeding on the international health agenda, which in turn led to a decline in the use of infant formula feeding in the developing countries, thus eliminating a major source of disease among infants (because dry formula was frequently mixed with contaminated water). The 1992 Rio conference on Environment and Development was influenced strongly by NGOs, and the term *sustainable development* became part of the policy lexicon. At the 1995 Beijing Conference on Women, the

NGOs, meeting separately, got far more news coverage than the official conference itself.

NGOs have had technological influence in almost every sector. They have pioneered techniques in diverse fields such as child nutrition, special needs in the classroom, bilingual education, the introduction of energy efficient cookstoves, agricultural processing, irrigation, improvements in water and sanitation systems, micro-hydro electric systems, and so on (Conroy & Litvinoff, 1988). There are by now countless examples of NGOs influencing national and global policies on health, the environment, and social development. They have influenced policy in forestry. They have shown governments the value of native crops and thus influenced national trade policy. They have shown government-subsidized credit programs the developmental importance of nonsubsidized interest rates. Through the microcredit movement, NGOs have begun to convince commercial banks that poor people without collateral can repay small loans.

As NGOs have gained influence and prominence in the development industry, the bar of achievement has been raised. The record of lasting change turns out to be thin. And for the first time, there are a number of voices who ask whether international NGOs can really make a substantive difference at all in the lives of the poor.

There are perhaps three aspects of globalization that create a set of Hobson's choices for many NGOs: (a) Expectations about NGOs on the part of governments and multilateral agencies have risen and are increasingly universally shared. The very relationship between NGOs and government has itself become blurred and a darker, negatively productive, side of the relationship has emerged as worrisome. (b) The roles of many advanced economy NGOs, especially American, vis-à-vis developing country NGOs and other governments, are increasingly blurred; for example, once grant recipients, they now also provide grants. (c) Finally, the political economy, and particularly the funding marketplace in which NGOs live, has become less secure and thus more openly competitive. As a partial result of this, the values base of NGO culture has changed and become blurred. Indeed, it is argued here that the most important blurring now occurring among NGOs is that between the culture of the for-profit and the nonprofit world. Each of these three aspects will be dealt with in turn.

Expectations

NGOs' relatively new legitimacy and reputation (roughly in the past 20 years) has been based on a contrast with both the private and the public sector in terms of the will, talent, and capacity to accomplish social good. Countless papers emphasize the assumed comparative advantages of NGOs: They are innovative, nimble, and flexible; adjust quickly to change and to local differences; and operate close to those they wish to benefit (because they are able to listen and interested in listening). Their services (when they provide them) are lower in cost and more cost-effective, their staffs and leaders are highly motivated and altruistic, and their independence of commercial and governmental interests puts them in position to put pressure for change on those interests.[3] Because of these presumed (and largely unquestioned) traits, expectations about NGOs have grown significantly in the past 20 years, especially on the part of government and in direct proportion to the spread of thought and discussion about a smaller, more sustainable role of the state.

But ironically, as the expectations of the state have pulled closer in to realism, expectations of NGOs have pushed in the opposite direction, often beyond the real capacity of NGOs to meet these expectations effectively. Whereas many NGOs write highly ambitious mission statements, quite a few worry privately that they promise more than they can deliver. Many NGOs are on one hand proud to be recognized—to have arrived—but at the same time are confused about their identity and function. The pressures to meet new expectations are a growing burden, especially for the most prominent of the international NGOs, and especially among the majority—those who exist to alleviate poverty.

The ambivalence and internal tension within these NGOs about what they can/should take on, and how they can/should pay for it, is also matched by continued, though often below the surface, ambivalence on the part of government. For in fact many in government(s) continue to harbor private doubts about NGOs.

A brief historical overview is necessary to understand why.

International NGOs are relatively new actors in civil society. It is really only after World War II that we see a gradual, and then rapid, rise in the founding of advanced economy NGOs devoted to social action in other countries, motivated perhaps in equal parts by a secular ethic of progress; a belief in ensuring that in an interdependent world not just the rich move forward; and a feeling (emanating from Judeo-Christian ethics) of paying something back for our good fortune or, more simply, that helping others is the right thing to do. American NGOs in the first postwar decades very much had a sense of a calling. Their operations were also characterized by a degree of amateurism. They raised much of their money privately from small contributors, and were generally content to believe (rather than prove) that what they did really helped others. As such, it is important to recall that many of the large American NGOs began at the periphery of the foreign aid establishment and remained generally unsung, unquestioned, and free to do good works as they saw fit. Their ambitions were, compared to today, relatively modest. Many did not explicitly seek to create development initially, so much as simply to alleviate distress.

Most NGOs were not taken very seriously by most government agencies and all but totally ignored by multilateral agencies like the World Bank and the United Nations agencies. At worst they were seen as bumbling do-gooders motivated by heart more than mind. At best—when they were taken seriously—they still could not entirely avoid a reputation as utopian, antagonistic to government, and potentially obstructionist. In the 1960s and later, when the human rights and environmental NGOs began to be founded, the same negative view not only persisted but was strongly reinforced. NGOs and

government did not feel particularly comfortable with each other.

These mutual discomforts take on different weight, depending on which country one looks at. For example, generally today in developing countries the newer the local NGO phenomenon is, the more wary government is of them.[4] Also generally speaking, the character of the governing regime will influence the extent to which NGOs can act freely.

In the later 1960s, 1970s, and early 1980s concerns about poverty and inequality, injustice and rights, the degradation of the environment, and the need to conserve resources became part of the development agenda, concerns which were propelled onto the establishment agenda in part by NGOs. Impatience with trickle-down effects grew, a sense that the poor cannot wait. Growth was not good enough—it had to be growth with equity. Trickle down was seen as a patronizing view of human development. There was the beginning of a major focus on basic needs and community level development, and a rediscovery of agriculture as a source of livelihood. NGOs were particularly active in promoting the idea that growth that did not benefit the poor was exploitative.

In the later 1980s and 1990s, a series of reality checks occurred, exacerbated by the mid-1980s' famines in Africa, the debt crisis in many developing countries, growing evidence of corruption and cronyism in developing country governments, and the financial crisis in Asia. There was growing awareness, especially in Africa, that decades of development assistance, much of it embodying the new emphases of the 1970s and 1980s, had had little lasting effect. There was much more awareness of the dangers of dependency creation through giving things away, expressed in the axiom "teach a man to fish instead of giving him a fish." Recognition grew of the limits of centrally (state) managed social and developmental engineering. There was more open discussion of corruption and of the policy environment in which development interventions take place. There was budding recognition that development without people having a stake in its outcomes is not sustainable. The very notions of sustainability, self sufficiency, and participa tion become wide-spread. Again, NGOs were active in moving forward the dialogue on these issues. And not surprisingly, given the nature of the issues, NGOs arose throughout this period as perhaps the one universal hope for solving both the problems of development generally and of inequitable development specifically. NGOs came to be seen, by donors and governments, not only as service providers in lieu of government, but as the primary mechanism for harnessing social and human capital for social good.[5]

NGOs could play these new roles, for the first time defined as complements to government's roles, because of those natural advantages cited earlier: (a) their commitment, (b) their experience at the grassroots, (c) their organizational form (being unencumbered by heavy bureaucracy made direct action much more plausible), and (d) their relatively low cost.

In developing countries, particularly those with nondemocratic regimes, there developed two sides to government's view of NGO capacity to play a role in development. The first view was positive—the NGO as agent, capable of identifying local target groups for what (little) government programs may have to offer, acting as intermediaries between communities and formal institutions. The second view was negative—the NGO as an incipient threat to government, capable of, indeed often set out to do, consciousness raising and quite good at creating participation at grassroots levels. To a fragile government, they thus represent countervailing power.

In Latin America and Southeast Asia, NGOs have been involved in agrarian reform, often opposing government or other establishment interests. NGOs have prevented governments from razing slums, often able to get services like electricity and water into illegal slums. In times of civil unrest and war, NGOs are often the only organizations that all sides are willing to allow unencumbered passage (Bosnia, Zaire, Somalia).

But the NGO record of aggregate achievement remains in doubt, in part because so much of what they do cannot be measured and also because it is still a relatively short span of time during which NGOs have been at the center of the world of development. Yet expectations

about NGOs have reached the point where some of their more tireless champions are in danger of placing the NGO promise beyond its own reach. These hopes vary from seeing NGOs as a major force in a new global order (Korten, 1990); as the genetic material for the eventual democratization of the former soviet bloc countries; and much more prosaically, but equally grand, as the likely future practitioners of virtually all social action programs and permanent mediating structures enabling those with little or no power to participate in the larger society (Hyden, 1983).

On the other hand, there are those who are pro NGO but less inclined to cheerlead. They worry about NGOs losing their heart as they grow, worry about them becoming an industry, and fear the professionalization of NGOs. Some exhort NGOs to resist fad and fashion, and form coalitions instead of competing with each other. In this way, they will be a more serious force for good (Smillie, 1990). Still others wish NGOs were indeed big enough to fill the new boots being cobbled for them, noting that for all their good work at the local level, NGOs are really small-potato operators. Sheldon Annis, for example, has pointed out that small scale and local can also mean insignificant, and innovative can also mean temporary and unsustainable (Annis, 1987).

So, the first significant blurring in this new world is a blurring of clarity between government and NGOs, and sometimes among NGOs, about who should do what. As NGOs began to try to be partners with government, and government began to take seriously their capacities, neither actor could remain what it was. At the same time, behind this blurring, underlying distrusts and remnants of the differences in the two cultures (NGOs' and governments') persist, adding tension to the shift—tension that is not always constructive.

As the expectations about NGOs rise and are translated into a funding relationship between government and many NGOs, a feedback loop phenomenon seems to be occurring. Ironically, today those in both advanced economy and developing country governments who remained ambivalent about NGOs are being reinforced in their concerns. The successful few NGOs have pumped up expectations of the many, in turn opening the way for new NGOs to be formed. A large number of these have entered the picture for less than honest reasons and the NGO field is now strewn with somewhat suspicious newcomers. And so ambivalence has returned, symbolized again by new acronyms in the lexicon: GONGOS, government organized NGOs; GRINGOs, government run, inspired, or initiated NGOs; QUANGOS, quasi-NGOs; BONGOS, business organized NGOs organized as tax dodges or to create a benevolent image for a company (Constantino-David, 1992); BRINGOS, briefcase NGOs, which exist on paper only; BENGOS, bent or crooked NGOs; and COMENGOS, NGOs which disappear and then resurface elsewhere or later.

As for some of the more venerable and often larger NGOs, those from whom much was expected and that often have delivered on those promises, they are becoming more cautious, more bureaucratized, and less nimble and bold, mirroring the very traits of the governments they disdained. They find themselves, ironically, like floundering multiproduct multinational corporations, hiring consultants to help them find themselves again, to remind them what business they are in, and to find acceptable ways to downsize and become leaner.[6]

In those countries where the NGO phenomenon has truly exploded—often the poorest countries and those most donor dependent—it is not surprising that much donor money (official development assistance from advanced economy countries) has gone to NGOs and these have become large equivalents of the largest U.S. and European NGOs. In South Asia alone, there are a number of NGOs that have become larger than most advanced economy NGOs. In Bangladesh, for example, there is the Bangladesh Rural Advancement Committee (BRAC), Proshika and Grameen Bank; in India, the Self-Employed Women's Association (SEWA) and Myrada; in Pakistan, the Aga Khan Rural Support Programme (AKRSP) and the Orangi Pilot Project (OPP); and in Sri Lanka, Sarvodaya. The field keeps evolving, and as expectations have led to bringing NGOs closer into relationship with government, the idea of complementarity has gone further than anyone could originally have expected. In Bangladesh, one national NGO, BRAC, has taken on the job of running 30,000 primary schools on behalf of government, which has tacitly said is not up to the task. It is thus not just a complement to government, but a parallel structure. Whether this state of affairs will give way to destructive competition remains to be seen.

Finally, there is some danger that the positive and dynamic tension which has only recently begun to characterize NGO government relations (where NGOs have been able to get government structures to be more sensitive to issues of concern) could revert to a less positive state (Hanley, 1989).

The Blurring of the Political Economy in Which NGOs Exist

The Taking on of For-Profit, Commercial Values

Perhaps the most important (and the most subtle) blurring taking place is that between the cultures of the NGOs and the for-profit sector. There are factual/economic reasons for this, as well as ideological ones. Some of the forces at work are outlined here.

Sources of Money

The most dramatic change on the official development assistance front in the last 50 years has occurred in just the last 5 years or so: the shift in dominance from official to private capital flows. This has occurred between 1989 and now, with the trend truly identifiable from 1992 on.

Foreign direct investment by private capital has become the main fuel for development funding in the developing world, far surpassing official development flows (largely concessional loans and grants) and bank loans. Read large, it is capitalism—the for-profit sector—that is driving development in an area where heretofore the public and the nonprofit sector (NGOs), relatively recently allied with governments, had been in the driver's seat.

Finally, we see a strong tendency of advanced economy governments to pull back on their bilateral support of developing countries. Net disbursements of official development assistance (ODA) by the OECD countries to all lesser developed countries (LDCs) (OECD's term for developing countries, which do not include the former east bloc countries), peaked at $43.3 billion in 1991. In 1992 they were $43.1 billion; in 1993, $39.3 billion; and there was a small move up in 1994 to $42.18; but clearly for the first time in history, bilateral development assistance is heading downward in terms of real dollars (OECD, 1996).

From the 1970s on, official money was a major funding source for northern NGOs as well as for large southern ones. In the early 1970s a very small percentage (as little as 1.5 percent) of NGOs' support came from official donors, whereas by the mid–1990s this source had grown to provide 30 percent of NGOs' total income (Hulme & Edwards, 1996). But the present proportion seems to have stablilized.

Looking at NGOs in the development field as a global group, in 1989, for example, for every dollar NGOs had to spend on development assistance, $.35 came from governments. And private philanthropic sources (nongovernmental), the traditional mainstay for many large U.S. NGOs (e.g., CARE, Plan International, Catholic Relief Services, World Vision, Save the Children, Christian Children's Fund) as well as for many smaller NGOs in the $1 million to $10 million annual budget category, are not keeping up with past trends. The mass public may continue to send $10 to $100 contributions to such organizations, but by and large there is donor fatigue in most northern countries when it comes to NGOs. It is also important to note that donor fatigue in a realm that has never attracted truly mass public philanthropy is ominous. In the United States, for example, less than 5 percent of individual giving goes to international work or to foreign organizations. And even within this narrow band, donor fatigue is tied to the average giver's sense that his or her full dollar is not directly reaching the poor child in Africa or being effectively used to save the rain forest in Brazil. The average giver may harbor inchoate doubts about the overall value of her charity.

It is in this global financial context that the changes taking place among NGOs must be viewed. Quite simply, the funding pie is shrinking just as the growth of NGOs around the world continues to expand. For the developing country NGOs this has dire implications. They cannot yet count on corporate or foundation contributions locally, and certainly not on individual contributions (though in large diversified countries like India, this is changing as the middle class grows). They must depend on some flow-through from internationally oriented foundations like Ford and others and from bilaterals and large international NGOs, who are themselves squeezed.

There is a chicken and egg phenomenon here as well. Whereas many developing country NGOs came into being to address genuine needs and were thus demand driven, the fact is that many also came into being because they were aware that foundations, northern NGOs, and bilateral funders were looking for local partners. As for the advanced economy NGOs, their expectations were changed also by the rise in governments' expectations of them. As their ambitions followed, so did their funding strategies. Expansion and growth (fueled by the new public source of funds) began to become an imperative similar to that in the for-profit corporate sector (grow or die). Yet some 20 years later, the larger political economy of development is undergoing a sea change that is bound to cause serious problems for NGOs. One thing is clear—competition for funding has risen. One could argue, as is done in the corporate world, that competition breeds more effective organizations. But in the development world, where there is no clearly measurable product, the need for funding (which is not the same as money that comes from sales of products) can lead an NGO inadvertently to let image dominate substance and fundraising dominate program.

The Commercial Zeitgeist

Indeed, many NGOs, largely because of competitive pressures around money, have taken on aspects of the current commercial zeitgeist, beginning to act as if they were corporations engaged in the world of commerce. Management and corporate financial strategies have been translated or adopted in whole cloth fashion by NGOs.

Transfer Fundaising

Smillie (1996), for example, talks about growing similarities between transnational NGOs (CARE, SCF, Plan, Oxfam, World Vision, etc.) and transnational corporations. He notices an adaptation into the NGO world of the phenomenon of transfer pricing (in other words, taking advantage of being global), and talks about transfer programming and transfer emergencies, whereby an NGO demonstrates to donors that it is on the ground in many places and so well positioned to be on the ground elsewhere if needed.

Not surprisingly, there are also transfer fundraising—transnational agencies can take advantage of better matching grant formulae by opening offices where the ratios are good, investing in fund-raising at a lower cost, and requesting a match to the funds raised from a donor. An example is PLAN International, which in 1991 raised $28 million in the United States but $58 million in the Netherlands. World Vision raised less than $1 per head in the United States in 1991, but $1.50 in Australia and $1.78 in Canada (Smillie, 1996). Thus, new markets are aggressively tackled.

The Rhetoric of Commerce

Many NGOs have spent money and time on retreats where they have examined their souls as well as their operational culture, with the tacit goal of becoming more competitive. Competition for funding is one of the main sources of the pressures producing these changes. And it brings in its train the same kinds of new values that competition in the for-profit sector brings: (a) efficiency (among NGOs this means professionalization), (b) customer satisfaction (among NGOs this means accountability and better stewardship of public and private funds), and (c) product differentiation (among NGOs this means specialization). But although the rhetoric of the reinvented corporation is taken on, the issue of actual performance remains the dilemma for NGOs it always was. In the end poverty alleviation is not a product, and this fact remains the fundamental flaw in these seemingly benign cultural transfers.

Brown and Korten's (1989) analysis of sector differences between the commercial, the government, and the voluntary sectors offers useful insight into the kind of cultural shift that is occurring among many NGOs engaged in development (see Table 35.1).

In almost every respect, the defining characteristics of NGOs have drifted toward the left-hand side of the chart: the commercial sector. To survive, today's NGO has been forced to be more corporation-like and less church-like. Its primary concern, though rhetorically still to actualize social visions, is also to cater to a marketplace (of ideas, funders, backers, supporters). Therefore, internally the idea of product and service and customer satisfaction has taken hold. The "Implicit Organization," to use Brown and Korten's (1989) term, of today's NGOs is clearly more market than clan/consensus, and shared

TABLE 35.1 Analysis of Sector Differences

	Commercial	Government	Voluntary
Primary concern	Produce goods and services	Preserve social order	Actualize social visions
Implicit organization	Markets	Hierarchies	Clan/consensus
Coordination mechanisms	Negotiated exchange	Authority and coercion	Shared values
Enforcement mechanisms	Contracts and reciprocity	Supervision and rules	Moral obligation and professional ethics
Prototype	Corporation	Army	Church

SOURCE: Brown and Korten (1989).

values as the primary coordination mechanism have less clout now than negotiated exchange. Most important, the role of moral obligation and professional ethics as enforcement mechanisms has eroded. This is in keeping with the kinds of people who now staff many NGOs. To the extent they come from the same pool of young professionals for whom personal (career) motivations are a key, there is a sense of reciprocity inherent in their taking a job with an NGO. For more and more employees of NGOs (and this is the case in developing countries as well), an NGO job is a step in a career, often leading to the private or public sector.

In the advanced economies, as we reach the stage where more and more people are knowledge workers, one could argue that as the number of educated people grows, more jobs beyond the primary, secondary, and tertiary kinds of occupations need to be created, new kinds of jobs that did not exist before. Some of these are bound to be created in the third sector. And the stake in protecting, preserving, and professionalizing these new jobs and functions increases. Thus, one of the things that has largely gone out of the NGO world is the voluntary character of staff. U.S.-based NGOs (and some prominent developing country ones) now seek to hire MBAs and others with postgraduate professional degrees, especially in management. A further irony ensues: Those few (usually older) organizations that are still staffed by retired professionals who contribute their time to the cause are the organizations that are increasingly out of the loop—organizations that are seen by the new professionals as irrelevant and ineffective and indeed nondevelopmental. It is telling that such voluntary staff are seen in the end as mere do-gooders, a term that has become one of denigration among those whose business it is to do good.

Conclusion

As a consequence of the subtle cultural shift to private sector commercial values, large numbers of NGOs now exist in what one might call a global marketplace of altruism. Altruism is not only now an industry, in a sense it has itself become commoditized just as other cultural and social phenomena have (perhaps an inevitable effect of late capitalism). And the altruism marketplace is increasingly crowded. Competition among NGOs for attention, voice, prominence, roles, even grassroots venues for their work (without stepping on each other's toes in the field), as well as government contracts, has become intense. More and more, NGOs take the pulse of their organizational health by checking with their fund-raisers first. The key question for many has become not "Are we doing a good job?" but "Are we continuing to grow our donor base?" Money has become a driving force, whereas once it was merely assumed as a fairly readily available means to an end.

In the messy day-to-day real world, NGOs' relatively new influence and credibility may backfire. First, because of the legitimacy given to them (based on an untested view of their effectiveness in solving societal problems), the NGO world in many developing countries increasingly attracts a number of free riders attracted to the prospect of getting donor funds. Interestingly, the free rider problem is occurring now in the developing world, the very place where we in the north were hoping NGOs would represent the best of the new civil society values.

A recent and prominent article in India notes the rising tendency of "racketeers masquerading as voluntary organizations" to "siphon off funds." It notes the existence of a blacklist of corrupt NGOs totaling over 3,500 organizations. The real problem is that no one, not even in Parliament, knows how many NGOs there are, how much funding they get, how many are genuine and how many bogus. . . . The reason for the growing number of cases of fraud is the sheer amount of money that's available. (*India Today,* 1997, p. 58)

And when local NGOs receive foreign funding, it comes with the aura of luxury. The dynamic that ensues can be complex. It is not uncommon in developing countries to see local government officials cadge rides in NGO jeeps (funded by foreign governments or foundations) to see the very projects that their own government agencies are involved with. At the same time, their incipient jealousy is compounded:

Not only are they envious that NGO workers have jeeps or motorcycles and reasonable per diems for stays away from home, but they begin to see their own ineffectiveness negatively mirrored in the NGO worker whose enthusiasm for his work is in stark contrast to the demoralization of the long-time government civil servant. Thus, some government officials will denigrate the accomplishments of local NGOs, and finally intimidate and harass them (Tandon, 1987).

A further potential for backfire exists in the fact that internationally, the official development assistance funding pie is shrinking. One result is that funds from some donors are shifting to needier regions and/or sectors and are often earmarked for NGOs. Thus, there are new incentives for NGOs to enter (and crowd) similar marketplaces.[7] When this occurs, because the measures of success for NGOs are different than those in the commercial world, there is no easy basis for the market to sort out good from bad. Finally, to continue the syndrome, the new competitive demands in a crowded marketplace increase the tendency to declare success before it is or really can be demonstrated. Thus, many genuine NGOs who have worked innovatively, and as a result are on the road to success in promoting social good, risk becoming convinced themselves by image messages meant for outsiders. Hype works in selling widgets. In the long run it cannot work in selling social good.

Globalization is a two-edged sword. The positive promise of NGO globalization is far outweighed by the dangers of the commoditization of their work. Moreover, the power of the for-profit private sector is beginning to have its effects both on what NGOs can do and on the market of funds for NGOs. The right niche for NGOs may well turn out to be what it was more or less at the time when they were first recognized for their special skills. Their capacity to do good by working for change quietly, locally, and modestly may well be their last best hope.

Notes

1. Led by the International Monetary Fund's (IMF's) recent classification, the use of the three terms *developing countries* (of which the IMF lists 127), *countries in transition* (28 former communist countries), and *advanced economies* (also numbering 28) is replacing the widespread use of the terms *First* and *Third World*.

2. This is not to say that advanced economy NGOs have not expanded. InterAction (1987), a U.S. association of NGOs in the development assistance field, has shown a 47 increase in membership in the last 10 years, from 106 member NGOs in 1987 to 156 at the end of 1997.

3. See, for example, Fowler and Biekart (1996).

4. In some countries (e.g., India, Kenya), an official visitor from outside is free to make contact with an NGO directly. In others (e.g., Morocco) it is considered improper for such an official to talk to an NGO without first talking to and informing the government.

5. There are a number of different cuts at the phasing of the development industry since the 1950s, each with slightly different emphases. For example, see Griffin (1988) and Arndt (1987). The above interpretation is the author's own.

6. The author has had personal experience with two prominent international NGOs, both with annual budgets over $75 million and thousands of employees, which have undergone such exercises.

7. For example, since the microcredit summit conference in Washington in early 1997, new microcredit NGOs have begun to spring up (many without capacity to undertake such work), sensing that official money will shift toward this sector. The World Bank, now decentralizing its lending in India, for example, is planning major investments in NGOs and is already facing the dilemma of discriminating between charlatans and real performers.

References

Annis, S. 1987. Can small-scale development be large scale policy? *World Development* 15 (fall):129–134.

Arndt, II. W. 1987. *Economic development: The history of an idea.* Chicago: University of Chicago Press.

Brown, D. L., & Covey, J. G. 1986. *Organizational development in social change organizations: Some implications for practice.* Boston: Institute for Development Research.

Brown, D. L., & Korten, D. C. 1989. *The role of voluntary organizations in development.* Concept paper prepared for the World Bank, March 9.

Clark, J. 1991. *Democratizing development: The role of voluntary organizations.* Hartford, CT: Kumarian Press.

Conroy, C., & M. Litvinoff. 1988. *The greening of aid.* London: Earthscan.

Constantino-David, K. 1992. The Philippine experience in scaling-up. In M. Edwards & D. Hulme, eds., *Making a difference,* pp. 137–138. London: Earthscan.

Fowler, A., & K. Biekart, K. 1996. Do private agencies really make a difference? In D. Sogge, K. Biekart, & J. Saxby, (Eds.), *Compassion and calculation: The business of private foreign aid* (p. 132). London: Pluto Press.

Griffin, K. (1988, March 25–28). *Thinking about development: The longer view.* Paper presented at the SID 19th World Conference, New Delhi, India.

Hanley, E. (1989). *NGOs and government: Maintaining the dynamic tension.* Unpublished manuscript, University of Edinburgh, Department of Social Anthropology, Scotland.

Hulme, D., & Edwards, M. (1996). *Beyond the magic bullet.* West Hartford, CT: Kumarian.

_____. (1997). *NGOs, states and donors: Too close for comfort?* London: Macmillan.

Hyden, G. (1983). *No shortcuts to progress: African development management in perspective.* Berkeley: University of California Press.

India Today. (1997, November 17). p. 58.

InterAction. (1987). *Member profiles.* Washington, DC: Author.

International Council of Voluntary Agencies (ICVA). (1998). *The reality of aid 1997–1998.* Geneva, Switzerland: Author.

International Monetary Fund (IMF). (1997, May). *World economic outlook.* Washington, DC: Author.

Korten, D. C. (1990). *Getting to the 21st century.* Hartford, CT: Kumarian Press.

Organization for Economic Cooperation and Development (OECD). (1996). *Geographical distribution of financial flows to AID recipients 1990–1994.* Paris: Author.

Smillie, I. (1990). *Government, the third sector and the third world.* Unpublished manuscript.

_____. (1996). Interlude: The rise of the transnational agency. In D. Sogge, K. Biekart, & J. Saxby (Eds.), *Compassion and calculation: The business of private foreign aid.* London: Pluto Press.

Sogge, D. (1996). Settings and choices. In D. Sogge, K. Biekart, & J. Saxby (Eds.), *Compassion and calculation: The business of private foreign aid* (p. 16). London: Pluto Press.

Tandon, R. (1987). *The state and voluntary agencies in India.* New Delhi: Society for Participatory Research in Asia.

_____. (1991). *NGO-government relations: A source of life or a kiss of death?* New Delhi: Society for Participatory Research in Asia.

United States Agency for International Development (USAID). (1988). *Report of American voluntary agencies engaged in overseas relief and development registered with the Agency for International Development 1986–1987.* Washington, DC: Author, Bureau for Food for Peace and Voluntary Assistance.

_____. (1997). *Report of American voluntary agencies engaged in overseas relief and development registered with the Agency for International Development 1997.* Washington, DC: Author, Bureau for Food for Peace and Voluntary Assistance.

► CHAPTER 36

Nonprofit Organizations in International Development

Agents of Empowerment or Preservers of Stability?

BRIAN H. SMITH

In the past two decades nonprofit organizations (NPOS) have significantly expanded their involvement in international development.

Funds for NPO development work originate primarily from two sources: individual private donations and grants from the foreign assistance ministries of North Atlantic governments. Over the past two decades not only has the total amount from these two sources dramatically increased (as indicated above), but the proportion contributed by each has changed significantly.

The major factor in the expansion of NPOS' international commitments since the 1970s has been increases in public, not private, aid.

Indigenous nonprofit organizations in developing countries at the national and regional levels act as intermediaries in channeling this international assistance to the poor in their own societies. They have also grown in number significantly over the past two decades. It is estimated that there are now at least 30,000 to 35,000 intermediary nonprofit development organizations at the national and regional levels in Asia, Africa, and Latin America.

There is a clear hierarchy in the transnational nonprofit aid network: NPOS in the North At-

lantic countries raise private and public funds for development projects overseas. National and regional NPOS in developing countries receive these funds from abroad and disperse them on a project-by-project basis. Finally, local NPOS in these same societies run the actual projects at the grassroots level among the poor.

The indigenous NPOS in developing countries—national, regional, and local—have been able to function under different types of governmental regimes. Democracies and authoritarian governments alike have allowed them to support projects in their territories even though NPO foreign assistance is not dispersed through their own public agencies.

Intentions of Donors vs. Character of the Projects

In spite of [the] convergence of factors that stimulated the growth of NPOS both north and south of the equator in the 1970s and 1980s, questions arise as to why governments, private donors, and NPO would continue to collaborate even though they had differing interests. Some northern NPOS are staffed by persons who articulate strong criticisms of home-country foreign policies, and who advocate changes that will cost private citizens in increased taxes or higher prices for imported goods. Abroad, those staffing intermediary NPOS often criticize their government's policies toward the poor. Some are former activists in political movements that openly opposed governments, and others support projects that assist those suffering from some of the worst effects of government repression.

One might expect, given these differences, that cooperation between governments and NPOS might break down at both the sending and receiving ends of the international NPO network and that private donors in the north would soon stop supporting organizations that threatened some of their economic interests. What keeps the system functioning, however, are a sufficient number of overlapping interests among all the partners, despite some diverging objectives each espouses. Moreover, the actual projects among the grassroots poor abroad do not threaten either developing country governments or the interests of North Atlantic public and private donors.

Citizens in North Atlantic countries tend to give the most to NPOS during times of well-publicized disasters like famines, earthquakes, migration of refugees in civil wars, and so forth, and the large North Atlantic NPOS still act as major conduits of relief aid to the victims of such disasters when they occur. In spite of the shift to long-term development as the first objective of many North Atlantic NPOS since the 1960s, many still operate as short-term relief agencies—even the Canadian and European NPOS that do not receive substantial food aid from their respective governments. This continued humanitarian focus maintains strong credibility for all NPOS among private donors at home. It also gives them added legitimacy with governments of different ideologies, all of whom need immediate relief assistance whenever natural or human-made crises occur.

Although some North Atlantic NPOS, especially in Canada and Europe, engage in education and lobbying campaigns at home that challenge some of the interests of their governments

and private citizens alike, their influence in effecting policy changes in these areas has been minimal (Smith 1990, 215). Their dissent is thus tolerated even by parliaments dominated by right of center coalitions. Such criticisms actually find some support among leftist parties in parliaments. Whether they wield executive power or not, leftists often favor liberalization of trade, aid, and immigration policies but are not in a position to implement them owing to a lack of public support.

The airing of criticisms by NPOS thus is accepted as part of the political debate in countries with a much wider ideological spectrum than the United States. Citizens in Europe do not view the call for significant political changes as beyond the legitimate purview of NPOS. French NPOS, for example, have been significant lobbyists in domestic welfare reform over the past decade.[1]

More so than American NPOS, Canadian and European ones tend to favor political change as a major goal of the projects they sponsor abroad.

Notwithstanding [a] sharp difference of objectives among North Atlantic NPOS, the kind of development projects they sponsor abroad do not differ significantly. These tend to cluster around skill- and resource-enhancement programs that generate new income and social opportunities among the poor rather than challenge dominant elites to surrender some of their existing privileges or power.

Although intermediary NPOS in developing countries are frequently staffed by persons critical of their governments for not adequately addressing the needs of the poor, they do not normally espouse as part of their goals a redistribution of wealth or political power. Under authoritarian regimes in Latin America in the 1970s and early 1980s some NPOS carried out legal assistance to victims of oppression or offered economic assistance to those ostracized for political reasons, but they did not engage in popular mobilization to thwart government policies or to stimulate open political opposition (Smith 1990, 267–69; Smith 1980).

In some democratic countries, NPOS sometimes take more openly critical stances toward government policy. For example, AWARE, an NPO in the state of Andhra Pradesh in India, has orchestrated a series of public demonstrations by grassroots groups it assists to pressure the local government to implement land reform legislation promulgated by the central government but largely ignored thereafter. It has also encouraged members of local groups to run for election to the local parliament, and forty of the two hundred seats are now held by AWARE local groups. NPOS in neighboring Bangladesh have urged the same strategy for landless groups they have been assisting (Clark 1990, 98–99).

NPOS rarely seek, however, to replace political parties or to act primarily as partisan political groups themselves. Some rather tend to use political structures that are responsive to public pressures as conduits for furthering their causes within the rules of the system (Clark 1990, 99).[2]

In democratic regimes throughout Asia, Africa, and Latin America, however, most NPOS focus on supporting economic projects that have some impact on enhancing skills or resources rather than aiming at political participation of the poor (Smith 1990; Fisher 1993; Clark 1990). These national and regional NPOS work closely with self-help organizations (grassroots NPOS) formed by the poor themselves to gain some well-defined improvement in their lives.

Some of the more innovative and extensive activities have been in areas of basic health and family planning, credit and management training for small businesses, small-scale agriculture and water development that is linked with environmental preservation, and production and consumer cooperatives. All of these have included both technical assistance and financial help from intermediary NPOS, but individuals and groups at the local level manage the projects themselves through their local NPOS. These have also been some of the areas in which techniques have been replicated through dissemination of information by intermediary and northern NPOS, and sometimes governments have adapted these into their own public service programs (Fisher 1993, 119–28, 202–03; Clark 1990, 86, 110–11; Smith 1990, 241–47).

The poorest of the poor (the landless, the sick, the elderly, the handicapped) usually do not directly benefit from all of these grassroots associations because many grassroots NPOS—especially those that are cooperatives or credit unions—require a minimum of resources and skills to participate. Many local projects tend to miss the poorest 5 to 10 percent in their regions. The reach of grassroots NPOS, however, clearly extends beyond that of most government agencies, which do not go below the bottom 20 percent of the poor in service delivery. Moreover, even the poorest groups benefit from the activities of those grassroots NPOS that are multiservice organizations and include as part of their mission nutrition and health assistance to all in need (Carroll 1992, 67–69; UNDP 1993, 96).

Thus, most governments in developing countries, regardless of their political ideology, find NPOS at the intermediary and local levels useful. Although public officials normally do not have access to NPO funds, NPOS leverage new international resources for their societies not available to the governments themselves. Sometimes local development projects such as those sponsored by private agencies act as surrogates for social services formerly provided by the governments facing shrinking resources; or they pioneer in delivering new cost-efficient services later to be adapted by public institutions. By acting as important gap-fillers and troubleshooters, NPOS shore up social stability, head off potential unrest, and sometimes pave the way for governments to learn better techniques of reaching isolated regions or marginalized groups. Even authoritarian governments have tolerated NPO activities so long as they operate within the boundaries of relief assistance or economic development—which the vast majority do.

Are the Poor Empowered?

In spite of the above caveats and limitations on the political power of NPOS in developing countries, there clearly have been some forms of empowerment of the poor as a result of their activities.

Grassroots NPOS of all types have been particularly helpful to women in their efforts to advance their social power throughout developing countries. Health and family planning NPOS have not only given women more security and choice, but they have often been run by women themselves, thus enhancing their own self-esteem and their stature in their respective communities. Revolving credit funds have given rise to many new small businesses run by women in regions where such projects have been created. Buying and selling of cooperatives have enabled women to supplement their family incomes through more effective linkages to markets for the labor-intensive goods they produce. Through all of these new roles women collectively have begun to erode some of the stereotypes in their respective countries, stereotypes that assume that male leadership is essential for the implementation of effective development (Clark 1990, 101; UNDP 1993, 96–97).

Linking all of these dimensions of social empowerment are the new organizations operated by the poor themselves.[3] Although not financially autonomous, thus far they have operated with some autonomy from governments and political and economic elites in their societies. This has given the participants increased control over their immediate environment and a sense of group awareness that they can do things for themselves. Moreover, their benefactors—that is, intermediary NPOS, international NPOS, foreign private donors, and foreign governments—have allowed them a range of freedom to define their own objectives so long as they stay within broad parameters of economic development. If these grassroots NPOS can maintain their relative autonomy and continue to set their own economic goals, the social empowerment of their members is likely to grow.

L. David Brown, building on the work of Robert Putnam, identifies the greatest contribution of NPOS as expanding the "social capital" of the poor—structural arrangements of voluntary cooperation that nurture attitudes of trust, self-confidence, tolerance, and hope for a better future (Brown 1998). These new collective experiences and the gradual attitudinal changes they foster do not translate into an immediate increase of political power for the poor—more voice in governments, more parties responsive to their interests, more effective laws protecting their rights, and so on. But the expansion of so-

cial capital is laying the groundwork for a different type of future society in which the poor will have enhanced capacities to articulate, pursue, and realize some important interests on their own. Eventually, if such capital continues to accrue it cannot help but have a positive impact on political systems. Growing numbers of the poor are coming to believe that they have a stake in society and that they can make institutions work in their favor and for the good of others—one basis for healthy democratic politics.[4]

Currently, NPOS in developing countries are not a serious threat to established economic and political elites. As indicated above, they serve some important interests of governments in developing countries, and their existence makes it possible for other actors in the transnational NPO network to achieve some of their objectives. In the north and south alike, therefore, NPOS enable groups in both public and private spheres to achieve a variety of objectives that would not be as easily realized if the transnational NPO network were not in place.

Challenges for the Future

Despite overlapping interests in the transnational NPO network, there are some emerging trends that may create serious problems for its future stability. Governmental pressures on northern NPOS to professionalize and specialize, the increasing competence of southern NPOS vis-á-vis their northern NPO funders, the shrinking state in developing countries searching for private contractors for public services, and the latent political potential of grassroots NPOS in poor countries—all of these factors are creating challenges for the transnational NPO network in the future.

Increasing Ties Between Intermediary NPOs and Home Governments

As the reputation of intermediary NPOS grows, there is an effort by governments to incorporate them into public social service systems as they privatize their economies and cut back on state expenditures. This trend has existed for some time in parts of Africa and now is expanding rapidly in Latin America.

Newly constituted Latin American democratic governments, some of whose policymakers worked for intermediate NPOS during previous military regimes, are setting up special funds for private service programs (Carroll 1992, 177–78). There are popular expectations that a return to democracy will better the economic situation of the poor, who suffered both political repression and economic austerity under previous military regimes. Newly elected civilians, however, are also under continuing pressures from international lending institutions (to whom large debts still are owed) to continue privatizing their economies. They need to find ways to increase social services for the poor but do not have adequate resources or delivery mechanisms to do so.

The World Bank, the Inter-American Bank, and AID are all providing these countries with additional loans and grants to help meet these service needs. Because NPO administrative costs in Latin America are still lower than those of the state—a situation that does not hold in North Atlantic countries—and because NPOS can leverage additional foreign money on their own through the transnational NPO network, Latin American governments are seeking them out as new partners to meet public needs.[5]

If such funds grow and NPOS take increasing advantage of them, it could help them expand and scale up considerably their service delivery capabilities to meet the ever-growing demands of the poor. Moreover, moving into a closer association with the public sector might result in governments adopting innovative NPO techniques in their own service agencies (see Brown, in this volume). Some of the recent literature on NPOS in developing countries, in fact, has been urging that they extend their reach, seek to have their projects replicated on a wider scale, and search for more effective ways to impact on public policy making (Fisher 1993, 209; Clark 1990, 78–79; UNDP 1993, 98; Carroll 1992, 179–80).

Developing country governments, however, will likely place more stringent conditions on their contracts with intermediate NPOS than do current international NPOS on their grants. If this occurs, the danger of being co-opted to serve government interests will grow, and NPOS' ability to serve as independent advocates for the poor will decline (Smith 1993, 341). In fact, such co-optation is already happening to those NPOS in advanced capitalist societies that, as government contractors, are suffering the effects of the welfare state crisis (Hyde 1993).

If such controls emerge in developing countries, the credibility of intermediary NPOS in the eyes of grassroots NPOS and the poor whom they now serve could be significantly diminished. They could become parastatal organizations, thus losing their capacity for innovation and flexibility. More research is needed on how local government funding is affecting the autonomy and performance of those intermediary NPOS because the implications of such arrangements have yet to be explored in developing countries.

The Growing Political Potential of Grassroots NPOs

Just as there is a tendency for intermediary NPOS to establish federations, networks among grassroots NPOS are now emerging. Some are regional organizations (cooperatives), some informal economic networks (bartering systems), and other, more heterogeneous groupings combining grassroots NPOS and social movements seeking redress of grievances for their members (for example, peasant unions, tribal organizations, environmental groups) (Fisher 1993, 57–74). As a result of such coordination, the political potential of grassroots NPOS (as discussed earlier) may be increasingly realized in the years ahead. Strategies deployed in India and Bangladesh, where some NPOS are encouraging participants to run for local office, may evolve into trends in other contexts as NPOS become more coordinated.

This scenario is fraught with both positive and negative implications. On the one hand, if grassroots NPOS establish closer bonds with one another at the regional and national levels in their societies and also forge closer links with popular protest movements, they might be able to create new political organizations (or reform existing ones) that are truly representative of the interests of the poor. These, in turn, may then be able to shift some political power away from landed, industrial, and commercial elites in these societies. This would please many European and Canadian NPOS.

On the other hand, greater involvement in politics could divert the energies of grassroots NPOS away from some of the solid economic and social accomplishments they have achieved thus far and embroil them in debilitating partisan battles. Governments could begin to resent those who link closely with social protest movements and remove their nonprofit status. Others might gradually take on the characteristics of parties, which they currently criticize, if they eventually decide to compete in the electoral arena—exaggerated campaign promises that outrun performance in office, leaders who become enamored of power and lose their interest in caring for the needs of their clientele, compromises with other parties that sacrifice principle for expediency.

In sum, the world of politics could have more of an impact on NPOS than vice versa, and, if so, they would lose some of their comparative advantage in development. Ironically, the closer NPOS come to assisting the poor toward political empowerment, the more jeopardized is their viability. Whether grassroots NPOS can join forces with other social movements of the poor to exert more coherent pressure on governments for equitable public policies while avoiding the debilitating effects of partisan politics remains to be seen.

The choices open to NPOS in the north and south as they face all of these new challenges will not be easy. Managing new opportunities will require adjustments in their interrelationships and in their linkages with public and private donors if the transnational NPO system is to continue to operate as an important instrument for global equity.

Notes

1. A sizable proportion of the population in Europe views development problems abroad as requiring political, not merely economic, solutions. This segment is not upset by NPOS that call for major changes in power relations between rich and poor nations and inside poor nations. A random survey of more than 9,700 persons in ten West European countries in 1983 indicated that 60.6 percent believed that rich countries (including their own) exploited poor countries, and 83.3 percent felt that within developing countries a rich minority exploits the rest of the population—in contrast to only 6 percent of Americans, who viewed the poor in such societies as victims of unjust systems (Rabier, Riffault, and Inglehart 1985, 81, 84, 92, 93, 96; Contee 1987, 49; Laudicina 1973, 11).

2. I found this to be the case in Colombia, where I studied a variety of intermediary NPOs (thirty-six in all) in 1984. Although the activities of some of their staff included political tactics (e.g., petitioning local government agencies to adopt land reform already required by law), the NPOs to which they belonged did not become competitors of political parties in their respective regions (Smith 1990, 255–56).

3. John Friedmann (1990) has defined the social power that is accruing to various low-income groups through grassroots NPO projects as greater control over their "life space," their economic resources, social networks, and autonomous organizations.

4. Daniel Levine makes a similar argument based on behavioral and attitudinal changes he observed among those participating in new local communities sponsored by the Catholic Church in Latin America, many of which function as grassroots NPOS. These organizations foster attitudes of respect and cooperation among their members in carrying out needed social services and act as training grounds for potential new community leaders among the poor (Levine 1992, 319–20, 340–44).

5. The governments of Colombia, Peru, Bolivia, Chile, Guatemala, Honduras, and Mexico all now have social investment funds; these pay private agencies to deliver needed social services to the poor. The funds range in amounts from $20 to $60 million (Colombia, Bolivia, Chile, Guatemala), to $100 million to $200 million (Peru and Honduras), to $2 billion (Mexico). Telephone interview and correspondence with Dr. Charles A. Reilly, Thematic Studies Officer, Office of Learning and Dissemination, Inter-American Foundation, Alexandria, VA, October 1993.

References

Advisory Council on Voluntary Foreign Aid (ACVFA). 1990. *Responding to Change: Private Voluntarism* and *International Development*. Washington, D.C.: U.S. Agency for International Development (US-AID).

_____. 1993 *International Development and Private Voluntarism: A Maturing Partnership*. Washington, D.C.: USAID.

Adelman, Irma, and Cynthia Taft Morris. 1973. *Economic Growth and Social Equity in Developing Countries*. Stanford: Stanford University Press.

Bratton, Michael. 1989. "The Politics of Government-NGO Relations in Africa." *World Development* 17:569–87.

Brown, L. David. 1998. "Creating Social Capital: Nongovernmental Development Organizations and Intersectoral Problem Solving." In *Private Action and the Public Good*, eds. Walter W. Powell and Elisabeth S. Clemens. New Haven, CT: Yale University Press.

Carroll, Thomas F. 1992. *Intermediary NGOS: The Supporting Link in Grassroots Development*. West Hartford, Conn.: Kumarian Press.

Clark, John. 1990. *Democratizing Development: The Role of Voluntary Organizations*. West Hartford, Conn.: Kumarian Press.

Contee, Christine E. 1987. *What Americans Think: Views on Development and U.S.-Third World Relations*. Washington, D.C.: Interaction and the Overseas Development Council (ODC).

Curti, Merle. 1963. *American Philanthropy Abroad: A History*. New Brunswick: Rutgers University Press.

Durning, Alan B. 1989. "Action at the Grassroots: Fighting Poverty and Environmental Decline." Worldwatch Paper No. 88. Washington, D.C.: Worldwatch Institute.

Fisher, Julie. 1993. *The Road from Rio: Sustainable Development and the Nongovernmental Movement in the Third World*. Westport, Conn.: Praeger.

Fleet, Michael, and Brian H. Smith. 1997. *The Catholic Church and Democracy in Chile and Peru*. Notre Dame, Ind.: University of Notre Dame Press.

Friedmann, John. 1990. "Empowerment: The Politics of an Alternative Development." Graduate School of Architecture and Urban Planning, University of California at Los Angeles. Mimeographed.

Garilao, Ernesto D. 1987. "Indigenous NGOS as Strategic Institutions: Managing the Relationship with Government and Resource Agencies." *World Development* 15:113–20.

George, Susan. 1990. *A Fate Worse than Debt: The World Financial Crisis and the Poor*. Rev. ed. New York: Grove Weidenfeld.

Goulet, Denis, and Michael Hudson. 1971. *The Myth of Aid: The Hidden Agenda of Development Re-ports*. New York: International Documentation (IDOC) North America.

Hyde, Cheryl. 1993. "Class Stratification in the Nonprofit Sector." Paper presented at the conference Private Action and the Public Good, Indiana University Center on Philanthropy, Indianapolis, November 4–6, 1993.

Korten, David C. 1987. "Third Generation NGO Strategies: A Key to People-Centered Development." *World Development* 15:145–59.

Landim, Leilah. 1987. "Non-Governmental Organizations in Latin America." *World Development* 15:29–38.

Laudicina, Paul A. 1973. *World Poverty and Development: A Survey of American Public Opinion*. Washington, D.C.: Overseas Development Council (ODC).

Levine, Daniel H. 1992. *Popular Voices in Latin American Catholicism*. Princeton: Princeton University Press.

Organization for Economic Cooperation and Development (OECD). 1981. *Collaboration between Official Development Cooperation Agencies and Nongovernmental Organizations*. Paris: OECD.

_____. 1988. *Voluntary Aid for Development: The Role of Nongovernmental Organizations*. Paris: OECD.

_____. 1989. *Directory of Nongovernmental Organizations in OECD Member Countries Active in Development Cooperation*. 2 volumes. Paris: OECD.

_____. 1996. *Directory of Nongovernmental Organizations Active in Sustainable Development, Part I: Europe*. Paris: OECD.

Paddock, William, and Elizabeth Paddock. 1973. *We Don't Know How: An Independent Audit of What They Call Success in Foreign Assistance*. Ames: Iowa State University Press.

Putnam, Robert D. 1993. *Making Democracy Work: Civic Traditions in Modern Italy*. Princeton: Princeton University Press.

Rabier, Jacques-René, Hélène Riffault, and Ronald Inglehart. 1985. *Euro-Barometer 20: Aid to Developing Nations, October 1983*. Ann Arbor: Inter-University Consortium for Political and Social Research, University of Michigan.

Ringland, Arthur C. 1954. "The Organization of Voluntary Foreign Aid, 1939–1953." *Department of State Bulletin* 30:383–93.

Smilie, Ian. 1993. "Changing Partners: Northern NGOS, Northern Governments." Paris: OECD Development Center. Mimeographed.

_____. 1995. *The Alms Bazaar: Altruism under Fire—Nonprofit Organizations and International*

Development. Ottawa: International Development Research Centre.

Smith, Brian H. 1980. "Churches and Human Rights in Latin America: Recent Trends in the Subcontinent." In *Churches and Politics in Latin America,* ed. Daniel H. Levine. Beverly Hills: Sage Publications.

———. 1990. *More than Altruism: The Politics of Private Foreign Aid.* Princeton: Princeton University Press.

———. 1993. "Nongovernmental Organizations in International Development: Trends and Future Research Priorities." *Voluntas* 4:326–44.

Stremlau, Carolyn. 1987. "NGO Coordinating Bodies in Africa, Asia, and Latin America." *World Development* 15:213–25.

Teltsch, Kathleen. 1993. "Despite Slump, Giving to Charities Rose 6.4% in '92." *New York Times,* May 26, A8.

United Nations Development Program (UNDP). 1993. *Human Development Report 1993.* New York: Oxford University Press.

United States Agency for International Development (USAID). 1992. *Voluntary Foreign Aid Programs 1992.* Washington, D.C.: Bureau for Food and Humanitarian Assistance, Office of Private and Voluntary Cooperation, USAID.

U.S. Congress. 1973. *Mutual Development and Cooperation Act of 1973: Hearings before the Committee on Foreign Affairs.* 93d Congress, 1st session. Washington, D.C.: Government Printing Office.